THE COMPLETE DICTIONARY OF GUOSA LANGUAGE 3RD REVISED EDITION

A West African (ECOWAS) indigenous zonal Lingua-franca evolution for Peace, Unity, Identity, Political Stability, Tourism, Arts, Culture and Science

BY

ALEX EKHAGUOSA IGBINEWEKA

A Publication of: Guosa Educational, Scientific & Cultural Institute, Inc., and Guosa Publication Services, (2023)

P.O. Box 22121, Oakland CA 94623

Tèlìwáya (Telephone): +15108609619
Ímél guosa.language@gmail.com

Inquiries and Book Orders should be addressed to:

Great Writers Media

Great Writers Media
Email: info@greatwritersmedia.com
Phone: 877-600-5469

ISBN: 979-8-89175-043-2 (sc)
ISBN: 979-8-89175-044-9 (ebk)

ACKNOWLEDGEMENT

To God be the honor and glory
Special thanks to
My family, and special friends including but not limited to
Laurie Schrager
Mr. Kamoudeen Ani, APSP, Inc
Brad Buckman and Beth Wurzburg
Linda and Stephanie Brown
Janice Brickley & Art Abelson
Delvin Washington & Lan Hodges
Chuck,Carol Russell
Sarah & Luc Barthelet
Tom Rubin
Erika Anderson & Dan Summer
Margaret & Bruce Wetter, etc
WMLB Patrol Area
WrennStreet
MelvinStreet
BywoodStreet
Leimert Blvd
WMLB Board, Subscribers,
Residents and Neighborhood Associations, Oakmore, etc. Oakland CA
who rose to their feet for me when I was attacked and seriously injured by
three armed robbers while on duty on Wednesday, February 22, 2023
Other Gúosà language motivational friends are Brad Buckman & Beth Wurzburg, Dr.
Veronica Ùfóegbùnè, Father Ray Ògbèmúrè and, Mr. Emmanuel Ògúnléye respectively.

Gúosà: shèndó
Thank
You

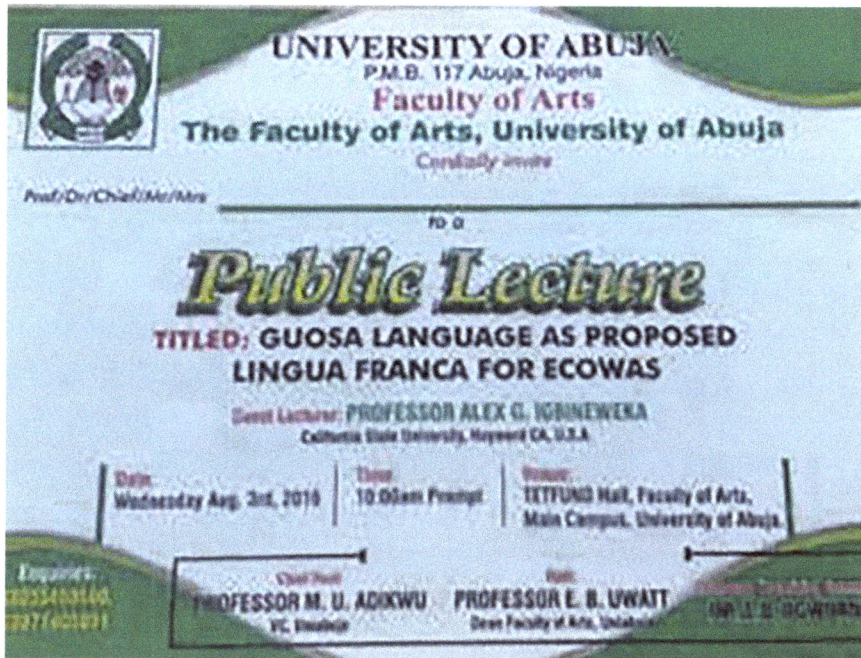

UNIVERSITY OF ABUJA
P.M.B. 117 Abuja, Nigeria
Faculty of Arts
The Faculty of Arts, University of Abuja
Cordially invite

Prof/Dr/Chief/Mr/Mrs _____

to a

Public Lecture

TITLED: GUOSA LANGUAGE AS PROPOSED LINGUA FRANCA FOR ECOWAS

Guest Lecturer: PROFESSOR ALEX G. IGBINEWEKA
California State University, Hayward CA, U.S.A.

Date:	Time:	Venue:
Wednesday Aug. 3rd, 2016	10.00am Prompt	TETFUND Hall, Faculty of Arts, Main Campus, University of Abuja

PROFESSOR M. U. ADIKWU
VC, Uniabuja

PROFESSOR E. B. UWATT
Dean Faculty of Arts, Uniabuja

Language is an art of spoken, written, manual, mechanical, signed, symbols and other effective methods by which human beings, animals, plants expressed themselves individually and or collectively. Whereas the use of spoken, written, artificial or professional languages sets man apart from all other creatures of God.

Òtòheén (Professor) Alex G. Ìgbìnéwéká

Gúosa Language Evolutionist, Creator

CONTENTS

WHAT LANGUAGE IS CALLED GUOSA?

Guosa is an indigenous zonal lingua-franca evolution for the West Africans, by the West Africans, and from the West Africans (ECOWAS) – a linguistic democracy for peace, unity, identity, political stability, tourism, arts, culture, and science. If you are Igbo or Twi speaking and I say to you, 'Bia nbi', you already know that 'bia'or "bra" means 'come'. It will not take you much time to figure out that 'nbi' is a Yoruba language word meaning 'here', and that the whole sentence means, 'Come here' i.e. Igbo, Twi and Yoruba linguistic words interlacing evolution.

In the Guosa language, "bia" (verb) is the key word for "come" whereas "bra" is the "alternate". If I say, 'Bia k'awa je abinchi', 'k'awa' is a Yoruba word, meaning 'let us'. 'Abinchi' is Hausa word for 'food'. Therefore, 'bia k'awa je abinchi" simply meant: "come and let us eat food" in Igbo/Yoruba/Hausa/Kanuri/Fulani/Twi etc language evolution. This is the centerpiece of ECOWAS unity brought about in Guosa inspirational linguistic science. So, no matter where you are coming from in West Africa, there are words in the language you speak in Guosa that will not only encourage you to learn the language, but also help you to understand other West African languages and dialects.

Nations Building Timeline

Oto. "Prof." Alex Guosa Igbineweka
Guosa Language Evolutionist, Creator
A West African (ECOWAS) indigenous zonal lingua-franca for Peace,
Unity, Identity, Political Stability, Tourism, Arts, Culture and Science

Sir Frederick Lord Lugard (Frederick John Dealtry Lugard)
Baron Lugard of Abinger. Amalgamator and first Governor-
General, Federal Republic of Nigeria, 1914-1919

BOOKS OF REFERENCE:

Before writing this Guosa Language dictionary I read some linguistics books including but not limited to the list below, for which I am very grateful to the authors and publishers:

Books	Authors, Or Editors	Year Of Publication
A Dictionary of the Yoruba Language	University Press Limited; and Oxford University Press	1968
Teach Yourself Guosa Language Book I	Alex G. Igbineweka	1981
The Dictionary of Guosa Language Vocabularies Vol. I	Alex G. Igbineweka	1987
The Dictionary of Hausa Language	R.C. Abraham	
The Dictionary of Modern Yoruba Language	R.C. Abraham	
Igbo-English Dictionary	Kay Williamson and others	
The Dictionary of R.N. Agheyisi Edo Language		
English-Hausa Illustrated Dictionary	Neil Skinner	
Oxford Advanced Learner's Dictionary	A.S. Hornby	

ALEX EKHAGUOSA IGBINEWEKA

J.F. Wallwork

of Current English

Languages and
Linguistics Alex
Ekhaguosa Igbineweka
The Complete Dictionary
(Alex G. Igbineweka)
of Guosa Language,
2nd Revised Edition

2019

Names Of Persons, Places And Things In Reference

S/N	NAMES	REFERENCES
1.	African shrine	shrine
2.	A.I.D.S.	syndrom
3.	Akogun, Tunde	army
4.	Anglican Church	Anglican
5.	Anglo-India	Sir (sahib)
6.	Arab	Sheikh
7.	Aro Hospital	Mental
8.	Bosah	Bursar
9.	Celestial Church	Celestial
10.	Co-Operative Bank	Co-operative
11.	Corner Rest Hotel	Corner
12.	Durbar Hotel	Durbar
13.	Ebenezer Obe	Pomp
14.	Etemah	Cadge
15.	Faminu, Kenneth	Hour
16.	First Bank	First
17.	Gbongbon	Beat
18.	Greek	Nectar
19.	Gulf oil	Gulf
20.	Guobadia, Anofi (Chief)	Name
21.	Hebrew	Shalom
22.	Haile Selasie	Emperor
23.	Irish	Airish
24.	Itotowa, Michael	Suppose
25.	Jews	Shekel
26.	Joromi	Transmigration

27.	Kabu-kabu	Taxi
28.	Kessin-Sheen	Sheen
30	Kilimanjaro	Mountain
31.	Liberty Stadium	Liberty
32.	Margret Thatcher	Thatch
33.	Mentholatum	Mentol
34.	Metusellah	Longevity
35.	Ministry of External Affairs	External, internal
36.	Murtala Muhammed	Airport
37.	NASCO	Waifer
39.	Nigerian Tourists Board	Tour
40.	N.N.S. Gurara	Wreck
42.	Nigerian Police Force	Force
43.	NTA Channel 10	Channel
44.	NTA Studio	Studio
45.	Ogboni	Mafia
46.	Okosun, Sunny	Songi, songa
47.	Oliver Twist	More
48.	Omo Soap	packet
49.	Covid19	
50.	Chief A.Y. Eke	

Ìfìnèrí:

Introduction:

IN 1914, THE NORTHERN AND SOUTHERN PROTECTORATES of a colony, administrative boundaries set up by the British colonialists, were dismantled and the colonies merged by Sir F. Lord Lugard. The merger became the first political turning point and a milestone development. It brought about the birth through the amalgamation of a unit geo-entity and nation called Nigeria. Consequently, Nigeria did not evolve through any known ethnographic origins. The amalgamation was cosmetic and that can be seen as such because there were no elements of homogeneity in the peoples that occupied the vast landmass.

And then, in 1960, a new Nation State earned her right to self-determination and government. Nigeria, now a sovereign entity followed in the wake of the traditions willed to her by her colonialists. She readily embraced the English Language as her tentative Linguafranca. This was not done in isolation as the country took due cognizance of the fact that Nigeria is a land of contrasts.

From present day projections, about 224 million people populate Nigeria, as evidenced by figures from the current National Population Census. Out of this astonishing number, it is believed that one out of every four Africans or one out of every six black persons in the world is a Nigerian by birth or otherwise. In the same vein also, there are at least 98,000 communities with a heterogeneous populace who speaks about 400 different languages in this same country.

These data raise questions which border on the basis for cohesion, comprehension, and unity in such diversity. It is an anthropological fact that Language plays a unifying role in the beginning, development, beliefs, and customs of any group of people. Language is a means by which words or expressions find meaning and is put into use. Basically, it is used as a means of giving out information, thoughts, skills, ideas, reasoning and ensure receipt of same from varied sources without losing track of the desired objective.

Language can wear several meanings and its message, mode, receptacle, or feedback loop can influence action, behaviors, norms, mores, values and other extra preceptory roles of human beings in society.

As a direct result of the diverse cultural and ethnic peculiarities of Nigeria and other West African countries, the development of a common indigenous language has been at a very sluggish pace. Our adopted lingua-franca of English, Spanish, French, Portuguese etc are imported impostors in the true sense of indigenous lingua-franca usage. This reasoning explains why it has become difficult to formulate decisively, an educational and socio-political, economic as well as culturally integrated policy than can form the foundation for a purposeful agrarian, industrial and even technological revolution.

It is in the light of the ethnocentric peculiarities of Nigeria and her West African neighbor countries, coupled with the wide marginal differences in terms of their people, their customs and value system; their resources, environment, divergent cultures, and religions, that the Guosa Language was evolved as a medium of common indigenous socially interwoven language and as a unifying mold towards building a virile and formidable society.

The Guosa

There are about 500 different ethnic languages and fractionalized tongues in Nigeria, and about twice this number in other West African countries. The Guosa language now contains at least 150 ECOWAS languages. Whereas it began with just a pair in the mid-sixties when I conceived and evolved the language, as a teenager living with my uncle who was the immediate past Oba "King" of the Great Benin Kingdom. The Guosa language is made up of carefully detailed units of the different ethnic languages and cultures, so that in the future years, Nigeria and indeed the West African regional countries will be able to take their positions in the communities of lingua franca nations of the world, such as the East Africa, the North Africa, Europe, America, Asia and so on. You will find below a vibrant list of languages presently supporting the conception of the Guosa language.

As you will observe an abbreviated timeline in Nigeria consisting of a series of unfolding national achievements as follows:

1914 brings about with it, the unification of Nigeria by the gathering of the various ethnic groups (which have their own cultures languages). The coming of 1960 heralds the realization of Nigerian National Independence. An event of such magnificent proportion, that independence alone certainly and naturally led to the inspirational genesis of the Guosa Language; in 1965. A revisit of the 1914 coming together as a united Nigerian nation; as well as a re- unification of languages and tongues which hitherto had been disunited and scattered even from the historical "Tower of Babel".

Should the adoption of the Guosa Language be accomplished and cemented into the multi-ethnic and cultural fabric known as the country of Nigeria and other West African countries, it will progressively and purposefully move the populace towards regional and national consciousness, a sense of identity and homogeneity.

Below are some of the current lists of languages single-handedly evolved into the Guosa Language:

Some of the current language listings into the Guosa language:

Below are some evolutions of languages and dialects into the Guosa language. There are rules and criteria for the inclusion of more West African (ECOWAS) languages and dialects as soon as I received grants and research assistance.

Languages	Languages	Languages
Aduge	Ibibio-dialects	Dirim
Fulani dialects	Ogba	Ikwerre
Kono	Bada	Ora
Agbo	Idoma	Dukanchi
Fulfulde	Ogba-dialects	Ilue
Kukuruku	Bagirmi	Oron
Ajawa	Igala	Ebira
Fulfulde dialects	Ogbia	Isoko
Kwale	Bali	Oron-dialects
Akaan	Igbo	Edo
Fungwa	Ogbogolo	Itsekiri
Lenyima	Bana	Oruma
Akan	Igbo-dialects	Edo-dialects
Gade	Ogori	Izon
Mabas	Bassa	Ososo
Ake	Igbo (Guosa)	Efai
Gamo-Ningi	Ogori-dialects	Jagba
Nembe	Banyum	Sabon-gari
Akpa	Ika-Igbo	Efik
Gbede	Okodia	Kagoro
Ngizim	Begere	Sabongida-Ora
Alago	Ikale	Efik-dialects
Ayetoro-Gbede	Okpameri	Kaje
Gwari	Bendel-Igbo	Samba-leko
Nkem-Nkum	Ijaw	Kalabari
Aniocha	Okpe	Shagawu
Hausa	Berom	Egon
Nkoro	Okpe	Kalabari dialects
Anioma	Iko	Siri
Hausa dialects	Okrika	Egun
Nupe	Bete	Kamo

Arabic
Hausa-(Guosa)
Nupe dialects
Arum
Ibibio
Obulom
Arum
Engenni
Kataf
Twi-Ghana
Enuani
Kolokuma
Urhobo
Epie
Kolokuma dialects
Wolof–Gambia/Senegal
Eruwa Esan

Ikpeshi
Okrika-dialects

Sobe
Ekpeye
Kanuri
Temene–S/Leone
Emai-Ora
Kanuri dialects
Tiv

ELAMBA ASUSU GUOSA: GUOSA LANGUAGE NUMERALS:

Gousa

1. – daya
2. – eji
3. – eta
4. – inan
5. – isen
6. – isii
7. – asaa
8. – asato
9. – esse
10. – goma
11. – godaya
12. – goeji
13. – goeta
14. – goinang
15. – goisen
16. – goisii
17. – goasaa
18. – goasato
19. – goesse
20. – ji
21. – jidaya
22. – jieji
23. – jieta
24. – ji'nang
25. – jisen

Gousa

56. – senisii
57. – senasaa
58. – senasato
59 – senesse
60 – sii
61. – siidaya
62. – siieji
63. – siieta
64. – sii'nang
65. – sii'sen
66. – sii'sii
67. – siiasaa
68. – siiasato
69. – siiesse
70. – saa
71. – saadaya
72. – saaeji
73. – saaeta
74. – saainang
75. – saaisen
76. – saaisii
77. – saa'saa
78. – saa'sato
79. – saaesse
80. – sat

26. – jisii
27. – jiasaa
28. – jiasato
29. – jiesse
30. – ta
31. – tadaya
32. – taeji
33. – taeta
34. – tainang
35. – taisen
36. – taisii
37. – ta'saa
38. – ta'sato
39. – taesse
40. – na
41. – nadaya
42. – naeji
43. – naeta
44. – nainang
45. – naisen
46. – naisii
47. – na'saa
48. – na'sato
49. – na'sato
50. – sen
51. – sendaya
52. – seneji
53. – seneta
54. – seninang

81. – satdaya
82. – sateji
83. – sateta
84. – satinang
85. – satisen
86. – satisii
87. – satasaa
88. – satasato
89. – satesse
90. – sse
91. – ssedaya
92. – sseeji
93. – sseeta
94. – sseinang
95. – sseisen
96. – sseisii
97. – sseasaaa
98. – sseasatp
99. – sse'sse
100. – daya gogo
200 – eji gogo
300 – eta gpgp
400 – inang gogo
500 – isen gogo
600 – isii gogo
700. – asaa gogo
800. – asato gogo
900. – sse'sse
1000. – igiodo

KALANDA GUOSA
GUOSA CALENDA

Guosa	English	Evolution
Árdún	Year	From Igbo, Yoruba, Itsekiri: aro + odun
Ùkì	Month	Edos (Edo group of languages)
Úzòlá, Yùlá	Week	Edos/Wolofs
Àrín-úzòlá, àrín-yùlá	Mid-week	
'rín-úzòlá, 'rín-yùlá	Mid-week	
Ìgúmá-úzòlá, iguma-yùlá	Weekend, month end	

UKI ARDUN
MONTHS OF THE YEAR

Guosa	English	Evolution	Definition
Ùkìdáyá	January	Edos/Hausas	Hausa and Edo related languages
Ùkìejì	February	Edos/Yorubas	Edo and Yoruba related languge
Ùkìètá	March	Edos/Yorubas	Yoruba and Edo related languages
Ùkì'nàng (Ùkìnàng)	April	Edos/Efiks/Ibibios	Edo, Efik, Ibibio related languages.
Ùkì'sén (Ùkìsén)	May	Edos	Edo and Edo related languages
Ùkì'síì (Ùkì'síì)	June	Edos/Igbos	Igbo and Edo related languages
Ùkìàsâ	July	Edos/Igbos	Edo and Igbo related languages
Ùkìàsáto	August	Edos/Igbos	Igbo and Edo related languages
Ùkìèssé	September	Edos/Izons	Izon and Edo related languages
Ùkìgómà	October	Edos/Hausas	Hausa and Edo related languages
Ùkìgódáyá	November	Edos/Hausas	Hausa and Edo related languages
Ùkìgóèjì	December	Edos/Hausas	Edo, Hausa,and Yoruba related languages

Note: Edos: (Edo and related languages).
Hausas: (Hausa and related languages) etc.

TONAL PATTERNS

Tones: ` low tone ´ high tone v low to high ^ high to low; midtone unmarked NOTE: due to lack of research equipment I have been unable to reflect the above tonal marking on each of the Guosa language alphabets and vowels. Hopefully in the next edition of the Guosa language dictionary.

Alphabetization:
A B D E E F G I H J K L M N O O P R S T U V W Y Z

Graphic Alphabetization:
Aa Bb Dd Ee Ee Ff Gg Ii Hh Jj Kk Ll Mm Nn Oo Oo Pp Rr Ss Tt Uu Vv Ww Yy Zz

Ìlòwé Africa Huest (Guosa-West African) peculiar syllable consonants)
c: (ch) as in àbíncí: [food]
gb: as in gbóntì: [hear/listen]
Present continuous: ng, as in mo ng shìengá: [I am going] kp: as in íkpikpi: bacteria

GUOSA LANGUAGE EVOLUTION:

I N THE GUOSA LANGUAGE, VISIBLE AND CONCRETE objects are of Hausa, and or other northern Nigerian languages vocabularies origin; example:

Guosa   **English**

Kwàndó   basket
Kázá   hen
Ból   ball
Líttáfí   book
Fénsà   pencil

Invisible or abstract things are of Igbo, Yoruba or other southern Nigeria language origin. Their evolution from either Igbo and or Yoruba depends mainly on the alphabetical sequences. For instance, let us take the word "come" in English which meant: bìa (in Igbo language); and a corresponding wá (in Yoruba language) respectively. To decide which word should come in first or which word should evolve into the Guosa, you go on alphabetical sequence. In the above words from Igbo and yoruba languages, you will see that bìa comes before wá alphabetically.

Therefore, a sentence like please, give me water (English) is thus evolved and translated as: bíko, fún mi ní rúwá (in the Guosa Language) because water is rúwá; and fún mi ní refers to give me.

Verb Patterns:

Guosa	English
ò chètó ájì 'wá shìengá lá gídá	our class Monitor has gone home
ó shìhé lá_kófà?	Have you opened the door?
báasì, mó shìhé lá_kófà	yes, I have opened the door.

Present continuous/Progressive:

mó ng wùam	I am eating food
abókí mí ng sámbà	my friend is dancing
àwá ng mùkó èdè Gúosà nǐa	we are learning/studying Guosa now
kázá mí ng mùbí kwái	my hen is laying eggs.

Past Progressive:

árdún gómà fífèjá, mó húsí nà Béljíum…ten years ago, I was living/lived in Belgium Kádíri bìawá hún mí làyén Kadiri came to see me yesterday.

mó yámá lá mótà zúum-zúum I have bought a motor-car. Èyí wù wàsíkà Engineer Wàkómbo This is Engineer Wakombo's letter.

Òtògí Amos Dlìbùgùnáya wù òkólí rámá: Doctor Amos Dlìbùgùnáya is a good teacher.

mótà mí mèjé la	my motor has broken down
mà	know
ìmà	knowing, knowingly
mî mà	I do not know
mó mà	I know/I knew
mó mà/mo ma la	I have known
ó mà la /o ma	you have known/you knew

Verb Tense

Present		Past		Past
Guosa	English	Guosa	English	Guosa
jìndé	arise	tí jìndé	arose	jìndé lá
kùndé	awake	tí kùndé	awoke	kùndé

fòjí	brake	tí fòjí	broke	lá fòjí lá
rèbí	begin	tí rèbí	began	rèbí lá
kèdí	bind	tí kèdí	bound	kèdí lá

Some Verbs related sentences:

Guosa:	English:
kùndé sá ìzuan.	awake from slumber
mó kùndé la	I am awake/I am awaken
ó kùndé lá mí	he/she awaken me
ó kùndé la	he/she is awoke

Singular and Plurals:

Ìsígéné (Singular)	Ifé 'ji (Plural)
rédíyo kílikíli (transistor radio)	è rédíyo kílikíli (transistor radios)
tèlìwáya (telephone)	è tèlìwáya (telephones)
tèlìhóto (telivision)	è tèlihóto (telivisions)
tèlìyáh (telifax/fax)	è tèlìyáh (faxes)
kònkítí (computer)	è kònkítí (computers)
míjì (man)	è míjì (men)
máchè (woman)	è máchè (women)
dántàkélé (little child)	è dántàkélé (little children)
ómóntàkélé (little child)	é móntàkélé (little children) mótà
zóóm-zóóm (motor car)	è mótà zóóm-zóóm (motor cars)

Prepozi..............(Preposition)

Prèpòzi	Preposition
nà	on, in, at
nàsí	with, along, together
sá	from
sí	to
sínà	into
àtì	and
sá	from

AVAB …. ADVERB

Adverb is represented by a prefix of the first two letters commencing the verb, e.g. English: "stagger" v. Guosa: "yeji"v. Guosa: yeyeji, (adverb) English: staggerly

MORPHEME:

Guosa: o:mo:n:ta:ke:le: (omontakele) ….little child e:mo:n:ta:ke:le: (little children)

Words Evolution:

úzòlá	week
árdún	year
ùkì	month
wátà	moon
báwó màkà úzòlá fífèjá	how about/was last week?
ìtùnchè	revision, re-thinking
ìrùshé	work
tùnchè	revise, re-think
ìrùshè títùnchè	revision work
tùnchè ìrùshé	revise the work
ìkózí	lesson
ò kózí	teacher, lesson organizer or person
ò kózí 'wá	our teacher
kà 'wá tùnché ìkózí fífèjá	let us revise the past lesson
síoko	wish
ìbísí	success
ìbísí	successful
mó síokò ìbísí fún yín	I wish you success
mó síokò ìdùnsó ìyíbó màtá yín	I wish you a happy marriage
ìwédé	wedding
ìlùbàsé	anniversary
ìlùbàse ìwédé	wedding anniversary
gùeré	play
ìgùeré	playing
ò gùer	player
è gùeré	players
è gùeré ng gùeré ból	the players are playing ball
fílì	field
fílì ból káfà	a foot ball field
dùchén/du	stop
dù árímkpó	stop noise

Conversational Drill:

báwó	how
kà ó dì	is it
báwó k' ó dì?	How is it?
dádá/rámá	good/fine/well
ó dì dádá/rámá	it is good, or fine, or well/o.k.
bìa/bìawa	come
mbí	here
mbíbà/mbiafu	there
bìa mbí	come here
ba mbíbà/mbiafu	come there/be there
mò ng bìawá	I am coming
míi bìawá	I am not coming
jé/wùam	eat/eat/consume
àbínchí	food
kà	let
kà 'wá	let us
bì kà 'wá wùam	come and let us eat/consume
bìa kà 'wá jé àbínchí	come and let us eat food
shèndó	thank you
khà	very much
shèndó khà	thank you very much
o gwùebí	a hungry person (neutral gender)
ò gwùebí míjì	a hungery person (male/masculine gender)
gwìnú	anger, angry, annoy
ò gwùebí wù ògwìnú	an hungery person is an angry person
mèní?	what?
mèní ó chè í wùam?	what would you like to eat?

Note: the word "meni?" i.e. (what?) is an evolution from Hausa, Igbo and Yoruba as follows: Hausa: menini? ….meaning 'what'?

Igbo: gini? (or) o gini? …meaning 'what?'; and, Yoruba: kini? also meaning 'what'

In the Guosa language evolution the word 'what' is 'meni', evolved from the Hausa, Igbo and the Yoruba, Edoid (Edo-north-AkokoEdo) languages. These languages have so many other dialectical groups using and sharing the word 'what' or 'meni' vocabulary, carrying along with them their respective cultural and traditional value systems. Therefore 'what' or 'meni' in the Guosa language transcends beyond the linguistic entities of the Hausa, Igbo and the Yoruba languages. This is one of the numerous linguistic tentacles of the Guosa language to be found in the Guosa language.

Another Guosa language word of tremendous interest is "mouth" (English) and "ónu" (órnúh) in Guosa, with the morpheme: ó:nu. This word is evolution of the Igbo, Edo/Edoid, Igala, Yoruba languages, and various dialectical group of words. In Igbo, it is 'ónu'. Yoruba: 'énu' and Edoid groups: 'ùnú respectively. Each of the words ended with similar or same consonants and vowels "n" and "u" respectively. In the Guosa language evolution, the word 'mouth' is 'ónu', (ó:nu); from Igbo, Yoruba, Edo/Edoid and Igala languages/dialects.

Íkpèrè	Adjectives	
Oka	**word**	**positional**
rámá/dáadá	good	positive
rámá jù	better	comparative
rámá jù khà	best	Superlative
rámá jù khàkáa	super-superlative: A1, Excellent, extreme-extreme, first class etc.	

Numerical And Positional Adjectives:

1st nke dáyá	11th nke gótìdáyá	21st nke jìtìdáyá
2nd nke 'jì	12th nke gótìejì	22nd nke jìtìejì 3rd
nke ètá	13th nke gótìetá	23rd nke jìtìetá 4th
nke ìnàng	14th nke gótìnang	24th nke jìtìnàng
5th nke ìsén	15th nke gótìsén	25th nke jìtìsén 6th
nke ìsîî	16th nke gótìsíí	26th nke jìtìsîî 7th
nke asáà	17th nke gótìsáa	27th nke jìtìsáà 8th
nke asáto	18th nke gótìsáto	28th nke jìtìsáto
9th nke 'ssé	19th nke gótìssé	29th nke jìtìssé
10th nke góma	20th nke jì	30th nke tá, etc. etc.
NAO..	**NOUN**	
mákáràntá	school	
kásúwá	market	
súlé	farm	
o mákáràntá	a scholar/student	
ò kásúwá	a trader	

29

ò súlé	farmer
rùshé	work, (verb transitif)
ìrùshé	work
o rùshé	worker
Guosa: Pronao:	**English Pronoun:**
Pronao wu oka ti an ng luwen' iyefe Nao, n' ifinere:	*A pronoun is a word used instead of a Noun, for example:*
mi,	me
yin	yin
nke mi	mine
nke yin	yours
mi wan	myself
yin wan	yourself
eyin wan	yourselves
awa wan	ourselves
na owen wa	by ourselves
na owen yin	by yourselves
fa	them/they
*na owenfa	by themselves
*fawan	themselves
*nkefa	theirs
o	he, she
ya	it
*nkeya	its, its own
*na	b

Note: the above under-lined words ought to have been written separately e.g: (owen fa; fa wan; nke fa; nke ya; na owen ya) in ordinary Igbo language from where they evolved into the Guosa but it is thus written in Guosa language as a clear indication that the words, though of Igbo origin, have been Guosalized, in other words, (Igbo Guosalized words)	

Sentence construction:

mèni wu èyí?	What is this?
èyí wù túkúnyá	this is a pot
wù èyí túkúnyá?	is this a pot?
báasì, ó wù túkúnyá	yes, it is a pot
mèní wù èyí?	What is this?
èyí wù kújèrá	this is a chair
ùa ló wèn né kújèrá?	Who has the chair?
Mámbézè ló wèn né kújèrá	the King has the chair.
mèní wù ngbà?	What is the time?
ngbà wù ágógó ìnàng	the time is four o'clock
ó wù ágógó ìnàng?	Is it four o'clock?
Báasi, ó wù ágógó ìnàng	yes, it is four o'clock.
kèwó?	when?
kèwó kà yíen wù?	when was that?
yíen wù ágógó èjì	that was two o'clock
mèní sò 'kà nà ágógó èjì?	What happened at two o'clock?
two o'clock? mèní sò 'kà éh	nothing happened.

Conversational:

ùaní?	Who?
ùaní wù yíen?	Who is that
ó wù míwàn	its me, or, I am the one
ùaní ó wù?	who are you?
ó wù mí, dán yín	I am the one, your child
nùré mbí, mèní wù áfà yín?	Come nearer, what is your name?
Áfà mí wù Ìhùféàbàsì	my name is Godslove
Ìhùféàbàsì sá mbó?	Gods love from where?
Sá gàrí Máfárá	from Mafara city
èkú à bía, dán mí, jòndú nà	
Kújèrá yíen…	welcome my child, sit on that chair
shèndó, ùbá mí	thank you, my father.
Okangba……………………	*Present Tense*
guma	finish
guma la	finished (note the word "la" meaning past, finished) come
biawa	has come, come and gone
biawa la	

Elementary Guosa Language

Tones: ` low tone ´ high tone v low to high ^ high to low; midtone unmarked

Guosa	English	Sources of evolution
èkú sáfé	good morning	Y/H (Yoruba + Hausa
èkú ráná	good afternoon	)
èkú yámmá	good evening	"
k' ódí láchi	until tomorrow/good night	"
bìá/bìawá	come	Y/Igbo languages
èkú à bìá (not) èkú à bìawá)	welcome	I/Y
èkú à bìá sí Àméríka	welcome to America	Y/I
shèndó	thank you	Y/I
khà	very much	Y/I
shèndó khà	thank you very much	I/Afrika
Àbàsì	God	Y/I/A
ó wà	there is	Efik/Ibibio
àbókí	friend(s)	Y/E/Ib.
mbí	here	H
àbókí, bìá mbí	friend, come here	Y(Guosalized)
mákáràntá	school	H/Y(G)
émón mákáràntá	school children/pupils	H
ìhùfé	love	Urhobo/Edo/Yoruba
mó hùfé é	I love you	etc./H

33

mó hùfé Naijeria	I love Nigeria	I/Y
mó hùfé Amerika	I love America	Y/I
mó hùfé Abasi	I love God	Y/I
màtá	wife	"
mí	me/mine/my	Y/I/E/Ib.
mó hùfé màtá mí	I love my wife	H
mó hùfé màigídá mí	I love my husband	Y
ómón/dán	child	Y/I/H
ónéné	bird	"
kélé	little	Y/E/Ur./Itsekiri, etc.
ónéné kélé	a little bird	Ogori
ìjóngò	bottle	Y/I
bàíyo	goodbye	Og/Y/I/Ebira/Izon

Prof. Alex G. Igbineweka
Guosa Language Train-the-Trainers Class
University of Abuja, Faculty of Arts Abuja, Nigeria Wednesday March 20, 2019

English to Guosa words list
English to Guosa Comparative Words List

ENGLISH	GUOSA
0001 skin of human	jìkí, h
0002 body, corps	gáwá, h
0003 head	kái, shùgàbá, kásírí, kéisí. h/i/y
0004 forehead	whídò kásírí, whídò kéisí (not whídò shùgàbá)
0005 face	fuska, h
0006 eye	ídò, h
0007 eyebrow	gira, h
0008 eyelid	fata-ido
0009 eylash	gashin-ido
0010 pupil of eye	bak'ido, h
0011 nose	hánchì, h
0012 bridge	kátákó, gádà, h/gen
0013 ear	kùnné, h
0014 cheek	kúnchì, h
0015 mouth	bàkí, ónu, h/y/i/edoid
0016 lip, lips	lébé, bìkí, h
0017 tongue	hàrshé, h
0018 tooth	hákòrí, h
0019 molar	kwànkwása hákòrí, h
0020 palate	bákí nkè cíkì (bákín cíkì), h/i
0021 jaw	mùkàmúkì, h
0022 chin	hábá, cín-dúrì, h
0023 neck	wúyà, wúyánsa, h
0024 nape	zùbá-wúyà
0025 throat	wúyà, makogwaro
0026 voice box	ìkpà-wúyà, ìkpà-vòisí, tiv/h/fr
0027 hair	mágàjí nkè jìkí, mágàjí n jìkí, h/i
0028 beard	bái
0029 hair (body hairs)	mágàjí nkè jìkí, mágàjí n jìkí, h/i
0030 tuft	zánkò, tùntú, h
1.1.2. Trunk	gòrá, h
0031 shoulder	karfada, kartata, h
0032 shoulder blade	allo nke karfada, (allon kafarda) h/i
0033 chest	kirji, bàbá ìkpà, h/tiv
0034 breast	nono, kirji, bòbí

English to Guosa Comparative Words List

ENGLISH	GUOSA
0035 side of body	àkúe, y/gen.
0036 waist	kugu, bìdín, h/y
0037 navel	chibiya, h
0038 umbilical cord	igiyar cibi, h
0039 abdomen	ciki-waje, h
0040 stomach	ciki-waje, h
0041 womb	mahaifa, h
0042 back	baya, zuba, h/gu.
0043 small of back	kadan-daga-baya, h
0044 buttock	gindi, h
0045 anus	dubura, h
0046 penis	búrà, h
0047 testicle	lunsayi, ìkpà-búrà, h/tiv
0048 vagina	farji, bótù, h/i/y
0049 clitoris	bizr, clitoris, Arabic/west African Spanish
0050 labial-lips	kpònmón-bótù, kpònmón-farji, a.k.a.(show-girl)
1.1.3 **Limbs Members**	**1.1.3 Ìtùmbé Gaba**
0051 arm	hánnù, h
0052 armpit	kótó- hánnù, gu./h
0053 upper-arm	hánnù-sama, h
0054 elbow	gwiwar, gwiwar hánnù, h
0055 forearm	hánnù,-whídò, h/y
0056 wrist	wúyá- hánnù, h
0057 hand (main)	kwáno-hánnù, kwánhánù, ùupe/kanuri/h
0058 fist	dúnkù- hánnù, h/g
0059 palm	gingiya, h
0060 finger	yatsa, h
0061 thumb	bugu, h
0062 knucle	ìsóbá, gu.
0063 fingernail	firche, h/gu.
0064 leg	káfà, h/ful/fulf/kanuri/etc
0065 hip	wàtán, h
0066 thigh	chinyar, hatara, h
0067 knee	gwiwar, kunlu, h/y/i
0068 calf, of leg	maraki, h
0069 ankle	ídòfá, h/gu
0070 foot	kada, taki, anamɔn, h/kanuri/ful/twi

English to Guosa Comparative Words List

ENGLISH	GUOSA
0071 heel	karsana, h.
0072 sole	sònshó, (of single)
0073 toe	yatsar kafa, h
1.1.4 **Internal parts**	**Ìkpáká-mènú**
0074 bone	kashi, h.
0075 bone marrow	asusuwa, h.
0076 skeleton	tsiko, jiki mutum, h
0077 skull	konki,h
0078 breastbone	kashi nono, h.
0079 spine, back bone	kashin baya, h
0080 rib	hakarkari, h.
0081 brain	kwakwalwa, kwanya, kyeya, ichegbon, h/i/y
0082 heart	zuchiya, rai, hali,, iyobi, h/i/y, etc
0083 liver	hanta, h
0084 kidney	koda, h
0085 lung	huhu, h
0086 intestines	ana, afizere/Jarawa/jos
0087bladder	mafitsara, ikpa-chiki, h/tiv
0088 gall bladder	dutse mafitsara, h/ful/ful/nupe etc
0089 muscle	tsoka, h
0090 tendon	jijiya, h
0091 breath	mìmì
0092 vein	ijiyar jinni, h
0093 saliva	salimoninta, h
0094 phlegm	xëy. Wolof
0095 nasal	hanci, h.
0096 earwax	kunnen kunne, h
0097 tears	àrìrì, àrígó, i/kwale/bendel-i
0098 blood	jinni, h
0099 bile, gall bile	báilì
0100 semen, sperm	ijijo, h
0101 urine	fitsari, (noun) yùntò (verb), h/y/i
0102 excrement, feces	kashi

English to Guosa Comparative Words List

ENGLISH	GUOSA
FUNCTIONS OF THE BODY	ÌRÙSHÉ JÌKÍ
0103 blink	jìní, y/i
0104 wink	shìshídò, y/h/i
0105 blow nose	gbòsà, lùgbú
0106 breathe.	mìmé, y/i
0107 yawn	mìyán, mían, y/bassa
0108 snore	gòrón, gònó (guosa onomatopoeia)
0109 pant	mìké, y/i
0110 blow (with mouth)	béu, (guosa onomatopoeia)
0111 spit	típí (guosa onomatopoeia)
0112 cough	kòhó, uvw
0113 belch	bakin ciki (baki nke chiki), h/i
0114 hiccough	sùké, (guosa onomatopoeia)
0115 sneeze	grììhh, éh-chìì (guosa onomatopoeia)
0116 groan	béfù, kèbéfù, (guosa onomatopoeia)
0117 palpitate.	gbùlù (guosa onomatopoeia)
0118 grunt	gaun (guosa onomatopoeia)
0119 urinate.	yùntò, i/y
0120 break	fòjí, fékù, i/y
0121 defecate.	yùnká, yùnkáshí, i/h
0122 shiver	rìhrì, grì-grì, (guosa onomatopoeia)
0123 perspire.	gùmí, y/h
0124 bleed	tùe, edo
0125 coagulate.	kìyú, (guosa onomatopoeia)
0126 be.	wùdí, i/edo
0127 faint	chùmí, y/guosa
0128 sleep	sùnlá, y/i
0129 dream	ròzá, ròlá, y/ed
0130 wake (wake-up)	jìndé, i/y
1.2.1. SENSE, SENSES	1.2.1. CHÈGBÓN, Ì CHÈGBÓN
0131 see.	hùnrí, nèrí, i/y
0132 notice	kíèsí, y/gu.
0133 look	nèrí, i/y
0134 hear.	gbóntì, nùgbó, gbòlú, y/i
0135 listen	gbóntì
0136 smell	zízì, (guosa onomatopoeia)
0137 feel	wùchè, chèfé, dìfé
0138 touch	tùkó, mèkón, y/i
0139 taste	léonu, i/y/itsekiri/Edoid
1.2.2. INGESTIN	NKWASƐM, ÌKWÀSEÉM, twi-guosa
0140 eat	Wùam, (guosa onomatopoeia)

English to Guosa Comparative Words List

ENGLISH	GUOSA
0141 bite	jètá, wùtá, y/i
0142 crunch	tègbú, wàrà, y/i/gu.
0143 chew	bèjé, wàrà,y/i/gu.
0144 gnaw.	jéwùm, y/gu.
0145 swallow	kpúrú, gu.onomatopoeia
0146 choke	pian, Bassa
0147 lick	chàmú, g/y/i
0148 suck	nyòn, pío, pìòrò, Bassa/gu.
0149 drink	wònmú, edo/y/itsekiri
BODY MOVEMENT	ÌYÍKPÓ JÌKÍ
0150 sit	jòndú, y/i
0151 sit up.	jòndú núkè
0152 lie down.	bèbú, bèbú núkè
0153 turn around.	yìzzú,yíntŭa, dàzú
0154 walk	rìngá, rìnshìen, rìnjè, shìenèn, y/i
0155 step	sòlé, i/y
0156 stumble	shùdá, mèbè, y/i
0157 limp	tùké, shùké gu.-generic
0158 crawl	rìngákele, rìntúéfí, y/i/ed/ur
0159 run	rósó, gbére, lòféh
0160 swim	fòrú, y/h
0161 jump	fòmá, fòrú, y/h
0162 kick	tìgbá, y/gu.-generic
0163 stamp	kpái, kpàwà, gu.-onomatopoeic
0164 sample	kpŭníshí, y/i
0165 wave	yèjì
0166 indicate.	fìné, fìnèrí, y/i
0167 clap	kwà, onomatopoeic
0168 slap	kpàwài, kpà, gu.-onomatopoeic
1.4 BODY CONDITIONS	ÌKPÓNGBA NKÈ JÌKÍ
1.4.1 Body positions	1.4.1 Ìjùmá jìkí
0169 stand	kùndú, i/y
0170 straddle	yàkàtà, gu.onomatopoeic
0171 lean against	tà, fìyénjì, y/h/i
0172 bend down	kòró kása, yísí, y/h/i
0173 bow (like greeting)	bòlŏ, Edo/Wolof
0174 be.	dì, wù, i
0175 squat	jěkírí, i/y

English to Guosa Comparative Words List

ENGLISH	GUOSA
O176 kneel.	kùndú, y/i
0177 be.	bù, dǐa, i/y
1.4.2 Body conditions	**1.4.2. Ìwàhé nkè jìkí**
0178 be, of human.	bù, dǐa, i/y
0179 be, non-human.	dìwà, i/y
0180 be, satisfy.	dìsọ̀kén, i/edo
0181 be, thirsty.	dì, ìháhá, dì háhá, i/onomatopoeic
0182 be, drunk.	dì wònmú, edo/y
0183 be, tired.	dì rèngú, rèngú, y/i
0184 be, sleepy.	dì sùnlá
0185 rest	símíní, y/edo
0186 be, awake.	kùndé, i/y
.	
1.5. **Irregular condition**	**Ìwàhé frèfrèshìendé (irregular condition)**
0187 winkle	kàtí, y/guosa
0188 pimple	ìfín, h/guosa
0189 hump	rúpù, y/i
1.5.1. Abnormal quality	**1.5.1. Ìmìnìwà frèfrèshìendé**
0190 be, bald.	gòrí, dì gòrí, gòrí-gòrí, y/general
0191 be blind	fídò, òfídò, y/h
0192 be myopic	ìhúnkúrú, nékúrú, inèrí kúrú, i/y
0193 be thin	dì kíntín, kíntín, y/edo
0194 be impotent	dì kúbúlà, kúbúlà, y/h
1.5.2. Handicapped Persons	**Ìdìhán Èmùtúm**
0195 barren woman	máchè èfù
0196 blind person	òfídò, òfídò mùtúm, y/h
0197 deaf	kítíkói, ìkítíkói, ò kítíkói, edo/esan
0198 hunchback	búkó, bassa-liberia
0199 cripple, cripple person	kìmósà, òkìmósà, òkìmó mùtúm
0200 dwarf	wada, h
0201 giant	kato, h
0202 stupid	múgù, mùmú, zùgó, h/generic/edo/kwale, etc
0203 senile person	bùjélé, òbùjélé, senegal/guosa
0204 mad	féwéh, hausa/kanuri/fulfude/senegambia
1.6. **Health and Disease**	**Lafia nasi Ìrùn**
0205 be healthy	dì láfía, láfía, y/h/kanuri/berom/generic
0206 be sick, ill	dí bùjèn, ài-láfía, ai-gbándù, generic

English to Guosa Comparative Words List

ENGLISH	GUOSA
0207 hurt oneself	Gbùjí, i/edo/h/fulani, etc
0208 heal	kùlè, guosa-onoma.
0209 medicine	Mágàní, h/kanuri/fulfulde/berom/nupe etc
0210 get well	nwén láfía, dì láfía
2011 revive	dì sháká, jìndé
1.6.1 Abnormalities	**Àigéntù**
2012 abscess	kúrjì, h
0213 swelling	béu, kùkù, edo/y/i
0214 tumour	kari, h
0215 bruise	kurma, h
0216 burn	tòwú, y/h
0217 goiter	makuko, h
0218 hernia	dadali, h
0219 ulcer	gyambo, muki, h
0220 wound, sore	sògbú, y/i/kwale
0221 pus	yúmá
0222 scar	tábó, kufai, adabali, h
0223 intestinal worm	tána àná, h/afi-zere
1.6.2 Disease	**ìrùn, ìbùjén**
0224 illness, disease	ìrùn, ìbùjén, y/guosa
0225 elephantiasis	ìkòtókò,guosa
0226 ringworm	tána òrùká, tána kawanya, h/guosa
0227 leprosy	lèpúrú, guosa/y/h/edo
0228 malaria, fever	íbà, generic
0229 fever, hot fever	íbàwútá, generic/hausa
0230 pain	ìrìyà, ìfòtá, edo/y/i
0231 give pain or hurt	fún ìfòtá,
0232 throb	lùkú, y(Guosa)
0233 vomit	hùó, Gu.Onoma.
0234 stomachache/stomach upset	ìfòtá chíkì, ìfòtá tùnbí
0235 headache	ìfòtáísí, nsòhálà, y/i/h/Guosa/gen.
0236 diarrhea	pìorò, ípìorò, Gu.Onoma.
0237 scabies	kàzáwá, (ìrùdí ìrùn fata): a type of skin disease
1.6.3 **Life and Death**	**Míndù nàsí Ìkúowún**
0238 life	míndù, y/i
0239 be alive.	dì míndù, wà nà míndù, dìá míndù, edo/y/i
0240 menstrual time/period	ngbà íhùenèn

English to Guosa Comparative Words List

ENGLISH	GUOSA
0241 (be) pregnant	mènú, bìkí
0242 miscarriage	shìmèinú, shìlókwá, y/h/Gu
0243 labour (n), birth pains	ìfòtá mùbí, i/y
0244 bear (child), give birth.	mùbí, múmùbí, i/y
0245 (be) born	mùbí
0246 (be) young	móntàkélé, yárò (young boy) mónkélé, generic
0247 grow up.	húgbó, húgbó núkè (grow up), i/Ed/y
0248 (be) old (not young)	dígbó, i/y
0249 die	kpáí, kìú, kúowún, generic/i/y
0250 death	ìkpáí, ìkìú, ìkúowún, generic/i/y
0251 (be) dead	dì kpáí, dì kìú, dì kúowún, generic/i/y
2. Man's Nonphysical Being	**Nke Mutum**
2.1. Know, Believe, Teach	**Ìmà, Ìnìkón, kòlí,**
0252 think	lòró, y/i
0253 belief, believe.	kpáníko, nìkó, ìnìkón, efik/Guosa

English to Guosa Comparative Words List

ENGLISH	GUOSA
0254 hope	rèkón, réntì, ìrèkón, ìréntì Y/I/Bassa
0255 know	mà
0256 knowledge	ìchègbón
0257 wisdom	ìchègbón, ìmà
0258 (be) wise	dì chègbón
0259 (be) intelligent	dì yézé
0260 (be) stupid	dì múgù; zùgó I/Y
0261 (be) confused	di dàrúgù, dàrúgù
0262 learn	mùkó
0263 teach	kòlí
0264 show	ìfìnérí, fìné; fìhún; hòné; íkùakùa
0265 remember	chèrón ìchèrón, lòrón
0266 forget	gbáfù
2.2 EMOTIONS	ÌTÚKÍ
0267 (be) happy, (be)	wù, dùnsó, gbándù, Y/I
0268 rejoice	yònsó, iyònsó, dùnsó, idùnsó
0269 laugh	kuakua G
0270 smile	kùa-kùa kélé
0271 (be) sad	kónu
0272 cry, weep	kèbé, lìbó; kémkpó, y/I, agbo..
0273 sorrow	rítí, ikónu; ìrìrì; Bendel Igbo/I/Y/Itsek
0274 shame	fèjú
0275 pity	ìréré, ìnùbé
0276 fear	ìrúgù, ìgùeru Y/I
0277 frighten	ìrúgù, ìgùeru Y/I
0278 startle, surprise.	ìyàlíonu; yàlíonu
0279 (be) angry	gwìnú
0280 calm (oneself)	kùlè, Y
0281 (be) proud	tòló, yàngá, Gen: (General)
0282 respect	kùmbé, Y/I/Banyum (Senegal)
0283 honour	fànzí, v., ìfànzí, n. G/I
0284 love	hùfé, v., I/Y/Its
0285 hate	jùhú, jùhór, G
0286 despise	mètá, I/Y

English to Guosa Comparative Words List

ENGLISH	GUOSA
2.3 HUMAN WILL	ÌSHÈKWÀ MUTUM
0287 want, desire (v)	Chè, v. I/Y
0288 decide decider	Chèrí, v. I/Y
0289 choose, pick	mìyón;, y/h/g
0290 hesitate	mèyèjì, I/Y
0291 abstain	kùzú, Agbo/Fr./Ga
0292 allow, permit	gbàkwé, Y/I
0293 forbid	lèwò, Iz/I
0294 prevent	bòghá
0295 plan (n)	ìgbíchè, Y/I
0296 try	tìrí, tìké, G/Y/I
0297 succeed	bísí, v. Y/I
0298 fail	shìgó ìdìofóh, dìofóh, ìfòh, foh I/Y
0299 pretend.	mèbí, mèshèbí, I/Y
2.4 HUMAN CHARACTER	ÌMÌWÀ MÙTÚM
0300 (be) kind	rènú, dí rènú, I/Y
0301 (be) generous	mèaré, I/Y
0302 (be) selfish	tíntín, dì tíntín, Y/I/Edo/Urh
0303 (be) honest	zíokà, dì zíokà, I/Ikwerre
0304 (be) corrupt	wàyó, wùrùwúrú, dì wàyó, dì wùrùwúrú, Gen.
0305 (be) wicked	njìkà; dì njìkà, I/Y (njo+ika)
0306 (be) fierce	gìrì, gbòwú G/Y/H
0307 (be) jealous	yòwú, G/Y
0308 (be) shy	féjú; ìféjuú
0309 (be) courageous	gùdjì; gùdílí h/y.
0310 coward lâche, poltroon	matsorachi, mùmú, h/gen
0311 (be) curious (être) curieux	yàlíchá, I/Y
0312 (be) eager, (be) zealous (être) zélé	yájìchè, winche, dì chè, I/Kwale/Y
0313 (be) lazy (être) paresseux	gbùirùshé, jàfá Y/I
0314 (be) patient (être) patient	isùndí, Y/I/Gu. (suru+ndidi)
0315 (be) impatient (être) impatient	gbùisùndí, àisùndí, ài wèn isùndí, I/Y
0316 (be) restless, (be) unsettled	àisímíní, àisùndó, Edo/I/Y
0317 (be) stubborn (être) têtu	shìgìlé; sòhálà; aigbonti, Y/I/Gen.
0318 reputation réputation	inoki, katazi, I/Agbo/Edo

English to Guosa Comparative Words List

ENGLISH	GUOSA
2.5 DIFFICULTY	ÌSÌLÉ, ÌSHÌLÉ
0319 hardship, distress	sìlé, ìlèshí, ìsìrí, ìsìlé. y/I
0320 (be) difficult	sìlé, lèshí, ìsìrí, ìsìlé. y/I
0321 suffer	jèáfún, Y/Its/I
0322 obstruct	dìhán, ìdìhán, gbùhán. Y/I/H
0323 stumbling block, obstruction obstacle	ò fàtá ìmèbú; gòdò-gódó. I/Y/Gen. dânjà, vb. Ìdánjà, n., French/H/Gen.
0324 danger danger	nsòhálà, wàhélà, wàhélé, I/Y/Gen.
0325 problem, trouble ennui	
3. PERSONS PERSONNES	ÈMÙTÚM
0326 human being, person	mùtúm, món, ómón, H/Its/Y/Ed
0327 self	wénjì, I/H
0328 man	míjì, námíjì, ìmíjì; ìkágbá, H/I/Y
0329 woman femme	máche, H
0330 white man	bàtúrè; o bóchá míjì
3.1 STAGES OF LIFE ÉTAPES DE LA VIE	ÌKPÓBÍ MÍMDÙ
	fètú, fètúsà, Gu. (frm French/English)
0331 fetus	járírì, írì, ómóntàkírí, H/Y/Ed/I/Gen
0332 baby	tagwaye, jìmón, èjìmón, H/Y/I/Gen.
0333 twin	yárò, ómón, món, ómóntàkélé, H/Ed/Au/Is/So/Ur
0334 child	yáríny, budurwa, H/Kan/Nupe/Ful etc
0335 boy	bàbbă, babba, día, H/Kan/Nupe/Ful/Y/Ed/Gen.
0336 girl	takele; yárò; kélé, yárò míjì
0337 adult	budurwa, H/Ful/Nup/Kan etc
0338 young man	o dígbó mùtúm, I/Y/H
0339 virgin	
0340 old person	ÌNÙRÉ JINI
	nure, yiore, inure, iyiore, Etsakor/Afen.
3.2 BLOOD RELATIONS	kaka, ikaka, H/H.Gv
0341 relative (by blood) parent, relation	íyaye tonbi H/i/y
0342 ancestor	ùbá, baba, mahaifi H/Y/Ed/Gen.
0343 grandparent grand-parent	ùwá, mahaifiya, mma, mami
0344 father	m'ùbá, h/y/ed/ur/iso/it/h
0345 mother	mùwá; Gen.H/Nupe/Kan etc
0346 brother (elder/younger)	mùbá bàbá
0347 sister (elder/younger)	mùbá ùwà
0348 father's brother (uncle)	mùwá ùwá
0349 mother's brother (uncle)	
0350 mother's sister (aunt)	

English to Guosa Comparative Words List

ENGLISH	GUOSA
0351 father's sister (aunt)	mùwá bàbaá, mùwá papa, mùwá pappy, H/Gen
0352 cousin	mùwénén, Y/Ed./Urh/Iso/Iselle-Uku/so/is/i/Gen
0353 firstborn	mókòndá, Y/Ed./Urh/Iso/Iselle-Uku/so/is/i/Gen
0354 descendant	kòlògúa, zurchiya, Guo/H/Gen.
0355 son	dánmjì, mónjì; mòngí, Y/Ed./Urh/Iso/Iselle-Uku/Gen
0356 daughter	mónchè, Gen.
0357 grandchild	jìká, mótòmbí, H/Y/Ed/Ur/Is/Sob/Au/I/Gen
0358 nephew	mònwá Gen/H
0359 name	áfà, kònó, (kònó yá – name it), I/G/Gen.
0360 namesake	jìmónfà, H/Y/Ed/Ur/Is/Sob/Au/I/Gen
3.3 MARRIAGE RELATIONS RELATIONS DE MARIAGE	ÌCHÒGÉBÉ, TÌNÙRÉ, NÙRÉ, ÌNÒJÓ. .from Ets/Y/I/Y/H
0361 in-law	siriki, sirika, H
0362 husband	míjì, màigídá, "mègí" H/Gu(Guosa frm Hausa)
0363 wife femme,	màtá; aure, wòríngídá, "wòrí" H/Guosa (frm H)
0364 fellow-wife, co-wife	màtá-múkè, H
0365 father-in-law	Suruki, H
0366 mother-in-law	Suruka, H
0367 brother-in-law	áfuba, Gen/H
0368 sister-in-law	mónwàtá; munwata, H//Isok/Urhobo etc
0369 son-in-law	suruki; siriki
0370 daughter-in-law	mónchè-kùwá, matada., y/ed/sob/is/ur/is/au/h
0371 widow	òkpòmá, Edo/H
0372 widower	òkpòmá, Edo/H
373 orphan	màráy, H
0374 fiancé	saurayi, fians H/G
0375 fiancée	budurwa, fiansi H/G
0376 bastard, illegitimate child	shégè, ómó shégè, y/ed./ets/is/so/ur/H/Gen
0377 tribe, ethnicity	ìyàtú; yàtú Y/I/Gen
0378 clan clan	bílà, dènái, h, g.v.
0379 family	yálì, ìyálì, dangi, H
0380 friend	àbókí, òí, òyì, H/Idoma/I
0381 neighbour	òkúsá, òkúsá, ònùré, H/Etsakor
0382 acquaintance	igòhón, gòhé, ògòhé, Y/I
0383 host	mèlè, òmèlè Y/I
0384 guest, visitor	òkìelé, Y/I
0385 stranger	bako; oshiriche, H/Bassa/I
0386 enemy	ìtíwé, òtíwíé, it'ilo Y/I
0387 traitor	òfielé, G
0388 thief	òráwò bàráwò, ráwò, H/H(G.v)
0389 guide	ìmàhán, ìchèbó, Y/H
0390 messenger	òzìrón, I/Y

English to Guosa Comparative Words List

ENGLISH	GUOSA
0391 crowd	tàrómùùútà, mútàní, èmùtúm h, g.v..
0392 chief, headperson	mónbézè, bàbá, sarki, shugaba, oleze,
0393 elder	lágbádì, lìádí Y/I/H
0394 master	màigídá, màlàmín, ògá, kàtàzìì, íwín,
0395 slave	báwa, báiwa H
3.5 PROFESSIONS	ÌRÙSHÍWÍN, ÌRÙSHÉ, I/Y
0396 farmer	òsúlé, súlé, Tiv
0397 fisherman	màsunchi, òkífíi-míjì H(G.v)
0398 hunter	Jàmbaar, Wolof
0399 blacksmith	dadefo, Akan-Ghana
0400 potter	njaay, Wolof
0401 weaver	mai-saƙa, òwùntú, H/I/Y
0402 butcher (n)	láƒlela, Ewe-Ghana
0403 trader	òlètá, I/Y
0404 (domestic) servant	òzìdá
0405 beggar	òroƙo, ògbìyó, nuiala, H/Y/Its/Ewe
0406 soldier	sójà; íséza; òjăghá, G(from Engl)/Y/I
0407 prostitute	karuwa, (ashawo), òfìkì-fíkì
0408 midwife	rínmàtá, Y/H
0409 medicine man, traditional healer	òmágàní, kúngà, H/Bassa-
0410 fetish priest 0411 sorcerer(male)	Liberia èshùgú, Y/Ed/I/H
0412 witch (female)	òmàyé; hatsabibi; òmàjìkélé
0413 fortune-teller, diviner	òjósó: "evil and magic-power woman òsòlí ìshìendé, òsòlíwhídò
PERSONAL INTERACTION:	NKÉNI KPÀRÚ
4.1 ASSOCIATION OF PERSONS	ÌKÁMFANÌ NKÈ 'MÙTÚM
0414 meet, encounter	hùndé, I/Y
0415 accompany	gàlé, ìgàlé, I/Y
0416 (be) together	jujutu; jutu; nòjó Y/I
0417 assemble, meet together.	nòjó
0418 invite	ìkònójó
0419 (be) alone	sòshó I/Y
0420 abandon	bùkó, hápù,
0421 flee, run away from	rósó, fè,fèpéh, dòmpéh, Y/I/G
0422 drive away.	yànwá péh, yànwá tá, I/Y/Gen.
0423 avoid.	shírí
0424 (be) same	séme, baasì, G/I/Y/G
0425 (be) different	ìfàmbú

English to Guosa Comparative Words List

ENGLISH	GUOSA
0426 resemble.	yìjó, ìyìjó, I/Y
0427 imitate.	mèrá, ìmèrá, I/Y
0428 admire.	chèvú I/Y/lt
0429 befit	yéu
4.2 SPEECH, LANGUAGE PAROLE	ÌSỌ̀LÍ, ÁSÙSÚÚ KPÀRÓ
0430 language	ásùsú, I
0431 word	ókà, I/Ikwerre/Okrika
0432 meaning	jḗwù, ìròndí, I/Y
0433 say.	sòlí, gbāmĕh Y/I/Izon
0434 voice	voisi; lùví G/French/Eng
0435 speak, talk	kwùsó; gbāmĕh
0436 whisper	jèwan; sòlítín, Y/I/Ed/Ur/It. Etc
0437 shout	kémkpó; ìkémkpó, Y/I
0438 chat	yàyá, (ókà yáyàyá), Gen.
0439 mumble	brùmbrúm, G
0440 stutter	brúmbrùm, G
0441 eloquent	ìzùumkpó, n. zùumkpó, v. I/Ik
0442 silent	dánkìtì, tìkpónu, Y/I
4.2.1 Greeting	Ìkìné, kìné, ékìné, I/Y
Salutation	Kìné
0443 greet (v.)	Kònŏ, G
0444 call (someone)	àbáiyo, báiyo, Izon(frEng)
0445 goodbye	
4.2.2 Information and questions	ìkólí nàsí ìjùbí, Y/I
0446 announce	ìkémkpó
announcer	kwìró, ìkémkpó. I/Y
0447 announcement	mèdíye, mèlíye I/Y
0448 news	shèníye
0449 explain.	mèbó, Y/Ed/Gen
0450 advise.	sìró
0451 gossip (v)	jùbí, I/Y
0452 lie, falsehood	gbì, I/Y/Its
0453 ask, request.	jùbí
0454 plead, implore.	fèzá
0455 request (n)	shèndó
0456 answer, reply (v)	
0457 thank.	kwàdé
4.2.3 promise	ìkwèbá,
0458 promise (n)	ìbulinji (ibu.li.n.ji)
0459 oath	bùhí
0460 swear	

English to Guosa Comparative Words List

ENGLISH	GUOSA
4.2.4 Strife, n	Ìjàmbélé, n.
0461 insult (v)	G(fY(S.Ade)
0462 insult (n)	yìhí, Y/I
0463 slander (v)	iyìhí, Y/I
0464 threaten, n	shátá, ókà rúbì
0465 argue.	ìrùngú, n. Y/I/G
0466 argument, dispute	sàrókà
0467 grumble, complain.	ìsàrókà
0468 contradict.	ráhùn, rókà, y, g.v..
0469 accuse, accuser.	chètò, fàmbú, I/Y
0470 deny.	kàsín, kàsínwúya Y/I/H
0471 admit.	kònú
0472 agree.	ìjìyènlé, n. jìyè, Y/I
0473 agreement, accord	kwèbá, I/Y
0474 persuade.	kwèbá, I/Y
0475 praise (n)	yòbí, ìyòbí, Y/I
0476 bless.	yìnbó, ìyìnbó, Y/I
0477 congratulate.	kùzíe, Y/I
0478 boast, brag	èkwúbùkún, Y/French
	shàkàrá, sòhó, Y/General
4.2.5 Discourse	
0479 tell.	rókà
0480 story (tale)	sòlí
0481 proverb	ìlìdà, Ágbó
0482 speech, discourse	ìlùwé, okatun I/Y/Ikw/Ed
0483 account (report) (n)	ókà; ìkwùsó
	chèró,vb. Ìchèró, n. I/Y
4.3 INTERPERSONAL CONTACT	ÌJÌKÓN MÙTÚM/ ÌJÌKÓN ÈMÙTÚM
0484 embrace, hug, v	Fànjìì, Y/H
0485 caress, v	tòntòn, tòntònrí, Guosa(onomatopoeic)
0486 kiss, v	kònú, I/Y/Urhobo/Edo/Esan, etc
0487 copulate, sexual intercourse	ífìòkò, n. ífìòkò, v. Guosa(onomatopoeic
0488 nurse, suckle.	nés, múmáridà, Guosa(frmEng./Arabic
0489 tickle, v	ríjìn, v. Ahoda/H
0490 spank	kwànké, kpànké, Gu.(Onomatopeic)
0491 whip, n	bókò, v. ìbókò, n. Gu.(Generic)-kòbóko
4.4 HELP AND CARE	RÒNHÁN NÀSÍ ÌBÒ
0492 help	rònhán, Y/H
0493 protect, defend.	chèbó, ìchèbó, I/Y
0494 look after.	chèbó, ìchèbó, bíbò I/Y
0495 bring up	mùbìwá, Y/Ed/I

English to Guosa Comparative Words List

ENGLISH	GUOSA
4.5 DOMINION AND CONTROL	JÙKÀ NÀSÍ KÓSÓ
0496 rule over, dominate.	wùfín, ij'ézè, wùfín Y/I
0497 order, command	imàshẹ́, jùbélé
0498 command (n)	ìjùbélé,
0499 duty, obligation	ìrùshẹ́, ìkáyá, káyá H(G.v)
0500 send.	ròngá, rònshìen Y/I
0501 serve	rùshé, I/Y
0502 lead, guide v.	gòsìn, I/Y
0503 follow	sòlé, v. I/Y
0504 obey.	tìsíbá, Y/I
4.6 CONFLICT AND RESOLUTION	bíko, v. I
0505 please	gwìnú, bìlíọnú, I/Y/Ed/Urh/Isoko/Esan
0506 annoy.	wàyó, kòjé , Gen/I/Y
0507 deceive.	jámélé, gòní. Gen
0508 quarrel	jăghá, Y/I
0509 fight	gúnmà: vúbè, poignarder. Y/I/Gen/Fr
0510 stab	gbu, kpàgbú, I/Ed/etc
0511 kill	bòsá, I/Y
0512 revenge	chènúnù
0513 resolve, settle.	kpèyòn
0514 intercede.	kwèbá, lăghá, , i/y.
0515 compromise	gbárùn, I/Y
0516 appease.	
	ÌLÚPÙ NÀSÍ ÌDÀKPÉ
4.7 CRIME AND JUSTICE	ráwò, Nupe/Kanuri/Hausa
0517 steal	jígbà
0518 rape	àlkálì, òdàkpé, H/Ful/Kan/Y/I
0519 judge	ìwùfín, I/Y
0520 law	sèrá
0521 fair/just	dẹ̀bí I/Y/(G.v)
0522 guilty	àijòshè, Y/I
0523 innocent	rìyà, wùòyà
0524 punish.	ìrìyà, ìwùòyà
0525 penalty	
	ÌMÀSHÁKÁ MÙTÚM
5. HUMAN CIVILISATION	ÌHÚSÍ
5.1 SETTLEMENT	Húsí, Agbo
0526 dwell, inhabit.	Zauni, òhúsí
0527 inhabitant, resident0528 bush dweller	òhúsí daji, Agbo/H/Kan/Nupe etc

English to Guosa Comparative Words List

ENGLISH	GUOSA
0529 move	yikpó, Y/Egun
0530 country	kásá, H/Kan/Fulf/Ful
0531 frontier	dajiya; gefe, matuka, iyaki, H/Ful/Kan
0532 town, city	gàrí, H/Kanuri/Ful/Ful
0533 village	kauye, kuje, H/Kan/Ful/Ful/Nupe
0534 camp	Tanti-tanti, sansani, zángó , h/Ful/Ful/Kan
0535 market n.	Kásuwá, H/Ful/Berom/Kan
5.2 CLOTHING	ÈSÁ
5.2.1 Clothing	Ēsá, Ogori/H
0536 article of clothes	ífé èsá, I/Ogori
0537 wear clothes	yìwó èsá, I/Y/Ogori
0538 dress (v)	èsá
0539 undress	nòhó
0540 naked	nòhó

A	A	Gen.
abandon (vt	gbèzú	Ed/Igbo
abandonment, n.	gbèzú	Ed/Igbo
abate, vt.	bùkó, bùkóló	Y
abattoir, n.	dabbobi, gidaigbu,	H/I/Ed.
abbreviate, vt.	bèkúrú	I/Y
abbreviation, n.	bèkúrú	
abdicate, vt, vi	bòesá	Y/I
abdomen, n.	chiki, Ime, imenu tabi menu	H/I/Y
abdominal,	techiki, lime, fimenu	
adj. abet, vt.	ronliaka, ronhaann	Y/H
abeyance, n.	Idachen	Y/I
abhor, vt.	Kohun	..
abhorrence, n.	Ikohun	
abide, vt, vi.	babl, bit gbe, balu	Y/I
(abide by)	balu ns, ba bltlu,	
(abide with)	balu kpe bit gbe	
(abide with me)	bit mi gbe, baru kpe mi	
ability, n.	igbaran	Y(Gu. ton.)
abject, adj.	ainwen	Y/I
ablaze, adj., adv.	gbawu, gbawuta, jowu, jowata	Y/H
Able, adj.	Ie, kanbo, meshee	
(able to)	Ie meshee	
ablution, n.	alwars, ilwars, (iwars)	Y(Gu. ton.)
aboard, adv., prep.	agboko	I/Y
abode,n	Ihusi, ibigbe, ibibl, gida	Y/I/Ha.
abolish, vt	dioto	Y/I
abominable, adj.	fengi, gii	I/Y
abominate, vt	mefeni (mefengi)	
abomination, n.	Ifengi, imefengi	I/Y
Aboriginal/aborigine, adj.	Mokasa	Y/Ed/Ur/It
abortion, n.	Imemeyun	I/Y
abound, vi	Kponso	Y/I
(Abound here and here)	o kponso n'bi ati nbi-atu	Y/I

about, adv., prep.	mani, so, che	I/Y
(about to)	mani si.	
above, adv., prep.	Kaju	I/Y
(a. all)	kaju nine	
abrade, vt	zuwe, nupu	G/Y/I
abrasion, n	Izuwe, inupu	G/Y/I
abreast, adv.	Lebe	Y/I
(keep a.)	nwe lebe, di lebe	
abridge, vt	Meku	I/Y
abroad	ilode	YI/Y
(he went a.)	o shienga ilode	
abrupt adj.	n'oji, n'ojiji	I/Y
abscess, n.	kurji	H
abscond. vi	gbate	
absconder. N	Igbate, nya gbate	
abscence. n.	isingi	
abscent. adj.	singi	
(a. minded)	Sin yobi, singi yobi, sinyobi	
absolute. adj.	Kpata-kpata, gbohan	
absolution, n.	Ikpata, ighohan	
absolve, ¥t.	Fij	
absorb, absorbed, ¥t.	chAmu	
abstain. vi	Kuzu	
(a. from)	Kuzu na	
abstention, n.	Ikuzu ikuzu, awe, aije abinchi	
abstinence. n.	Ikuzu	
abstract. adj. vt.	chonda. chonja	
(a. noun)	chonda nao	
absurd, adj.	Ewo	
absurdity, n.	Yewo	
abundan!:e. n.	Ikpone	
(In a.)	N'ikpone	
abuse. n.	Iloku, ibuihi, ibu li'hi	
abusive, adj.	Loku, buihi,bu li 'hi	

abyss, n.	Abes	
Abut, vt.	abat	
acacia, n.	gawo, gabaruwa. bagaruwa	
academy, n.	Jamkolej,makaranta, kolej, jam'iyya	
accede, vi.	Kweohun, nnohun, nnohunsi	
accelerate, vt.	Toto, te totor	
accelerator, n.	Fene totor, fen totor	
accent, n.	Itenumo, aashe, tebemo	
accept, vt, i.	Kweba	
acceptance, n.	Ikweba	
access, n.	Hanyar: (uzo), yefe, meiye	
accession, n.	iflun, fA, imelye	
accident, n.	Asidenta, asidento, jambe, ijambe	
(by a.)	N'ijambe	
accidental, aclv.	Lai chero swene, na'sidento N'ijambe, fen 'sidento	
acclaim, vt.	Gbakwe, gbawen	
acclamation, n.	Igbah, Igba	
accommodate, vt.	Nnonhan, kweba	
accommodation, n.	yesaukl, sulhu, fnnonhan	
accompany, vt.	Gale, leje, leshien, kpe	
accomplice, n.	Yetamaki, itega, tega	
accomplish, vt.	meton I/Y	
accord, n., vt., vi	bare, yobi daya, iyobi da Y/I ibare, iyobi Y/I	
accordance, n. (in a. with)	na iyobi, n'ba I/Y	
according, conj.	bietu	I/I
according to, conj.	bietu na	
accordingly, adv.	tutuge; bibietu	I/Y
account, n.	ilissafi, labari ka, akauni, ka, chero	H/G
account, VI (on account of) accountable, adj.	akaunt, chero, ka, (na akaunt nke) tabari, di akaunt, kasinwuya	H/I/Y/G H/Y
accountant, n.	Akaunta, nye labari, nye chero	H/l/Y

accumulate, vt, vi.	Ko, kowuam	Y
accumulation, n.	1koj, Ikowuam fene koi, nye ko	Y(G.v)
accumulator, n.	dede, saun, saunsaun	I/Y
accurate, adj.	Mekpe	Y/Gen.
accurse, vt	Ikasinwuya, swezon Kasinwu, kasinwuya	I/Y
Accusation, n.	nye swezon, oswezon, o kasinwuya	Y/I/H/G
accuse, vt.		Y/I/H
accused, n.		
accustomed, vt.	Monji, monji, monji lyashi,	Y/H
ace, n.	isarki, ikaigama, duzu	H(G.v)
ache, n. achieve, vt.	igbun, ifota nweni	Y/I
achievement, n. acid,	Inweni, nwinweni rubat, rubatir, wassid	Y/I
n. acknowledge, vt.	Nwhan, jehan	Y/I
Acknowledgement, n.	Inwehan, ijehan	H(G.v.)
		I/Y/Y/H
		I/Y/Y/H
acquaint (ted), vt.	Goho, gohe mo gohon mo gohe	Y/I
(a. with) acquaintance, n.	igohon, igohe gbahe, dake,	Y/I
Acquiesce, vi. acquire,	fiji basa wuam, wuamere	Y/I
vt. acquit, vt. acre, n.	dilare ikadada, elei yawan eka, fene'ka	Y/H Y/G
acreage, n. acrobat, n.	Igazoka	I/Y
		H/G
		H/G/I
		G
acrobatic, adj.	Di'gazoka, fen'gazoka	I/G
across, adv. (a: the	Biako, jekei	Y/H/I
road) (a. the nation)	Jekei hanyar	I/Y/H
act, n., vt., vi.	Jekei obodo, jekei kasa	
	Meshe, imeshe aiki, lushe	
(an a. of God)	Imeshe abasi	
(a. of parliament)	Imeshe majalisar wakilai	I/Y/H
acting, adj.	Dayi, meshe	Ed/l/Y
action, n.	imeshe, ishemu,	I/Y/Y/I
active, adj.	shemu Yaji	Y/H

(a. part)	Aka'ji	I/Y/H
actor, n.	(aka yaji)	I/Y
(actors, pI. n.)	Nye meshe, o mese	G/U/Y
actress, n.	Emeshe	H/I/Y
actual, adj.	O meshe	I/H/Y
actually, adv.	mache	Y
actuate, vt.	Zioka, gon	Y/I
acute, adj.	Gon-gon	I/Y
(a. shortage)	mume	I/Y
adage, n.	zugon, zun zun buku	Y/Ed.
adam (n)	iwetan, wetan	G
(a. apple)	adamu	I/Y
adapt, vt.	bizama adamu diye	I/Y
add, vt, vi)	tisi	I/Y
addition (n)	itisi	H
Addle, adj.	dakwaye dakwaye	H
(an a. egg)	lambit, eb'igbe,	Ha(G.v.)/
address, n.	isoli ola	I/Y
(House a.)	lamba gida	Ha(G.v.)/I/Y
(Self a.)	la 'wenji (la 'wenji) isoli oka	H(G. v)/l/Y
(speech a.)	chegbon, o	Y(G.v)
adept, adj.	chegbon, yechegbon	I/Y
adequate, adj.	zuto izuto	I/Y
Adequacy, n.	fajimo, gbonti gbonti si,	I/Y
adhere, vi.	fajimo si ifajimo, igbonti	Y/H/I
(a. to)	fefajimo, fe'gbonti	Y/H/I
Adherence, n.	likewa gam	I/H/Y
adherent, n.	k'odi mgba,	H
adhesion, n.	baiyo n'tosi	H
adhesive, adj.	(na itosi)	I/Y/lz.
adieu. adv.	isifa, kama	Y/I
adjacent, ad.	mekusa,	H
adjective, n.	meshekusa meshekusa	I/H/Y
adjoin, vt., vi.	kuara ikuara	I/H/Y
adjoining, adj.	daligana, daligan	G
adjourn vt., vi.	bebe, gbi	G
adjournment, n.	(mo gbi yinwan)	Y/H
Adjudge, vt	tunme	Y/It.
adjure, vt (I a.	itunme	Y/I
you) adjust, vt.	hafsa,	Y/I
adjustment, n.	ajatant,	Y/I
adjutant, n.	ozukata	H/Ed/G.

(Adjutant General)	Ozukata Janar), (Ajatant Janar)

administer, vt., vi.	klfunnt	I/Y
administration, n.	ikefunrii, gwamnati,	I/Y
(a, Department)	kefunni, kefunli	I/Y
administrative, adj.	kefunni, kefunli	I/Y
(a. officer)	hafsa 'kefunni o	H/l/Y
administrator, n.	kefunni, le nyoli,	I/Y.
Admirable, adj.	chevu	I/Y/I/G
admiral, n.	hafsa konga,	H/Y/I/G
admire, vt.	ihessa chevu	I/Y/lt
admission. n.	ijiyenle, jiyenle	Y/I
admittance, n.	n'ijiyenle iyenle	Y/I
admonish. vt.	sola	Y/I
admonition. n.	isola	V/G.v/I
ado. n.	yaisimini, arimkpo	I/Y
adolescent, adj.	mgbodo	Y/I
adopt. vt.	gbali	I/G
adore, vt.	kelelo	I/G I/Y
(i a. theej	mo kelelo yinwan	I/Y
adoration. n	ikelelo	V(G.v)
adom. vt.	Meosho imeosho	I/Y
adornment, n.	ikponi Dia	Y
Adulation, n.	Bula	Y
adult, adj.	ibula imiwagbe	I/Y
adulterate. vt.	e ma fila	H/I/Y
adultertion, n.	'miwagbe	H/I/Y
adultery, n.	miji miwagbe	G/l/Y/H
(thou -shall not	mache miwagbe	
commit a.)	ishien	
Adulterer. n.	whido,	
adulteress, n.	shienwhido,	
advance. n., vti.	shienwhi	
(in a.).	n'ishienwhi	
advantage, n.	enfani, anfa	
advantageous, adj.	n'enfa, n'anfani, di enfa	Y/H(G.v)
		I/Y/H(G.v)
adventure. N.	idayen, idaen ye	Y/I
adventurer. n.	'daen, o dayen	I/Y/I
adverb. N.	ihali, hali ijoota,	H I/Y
adversary, n.	ijota, inota mesi,	I/Y
adverse, adj.	njota yoka njota	I/Y
(a. effect)	Ifekede, fekede	I/Y
advert. N.	fekede, ifeke	I/Y
Advertise. vtI.	Ifekede, ifeke	
advertisement,	imeniye, imeniye	
n. advice. N.		

advise. vtI.	mesheniye le meshenive	I/Y
advisable. adj.	ye o mesheniye,	I/Y
adviser, n.	ye mesheniye	Y/I/Y
advocate. n.	ilauya, lauya,	H/Y/I/G
advocacy, n.	o zeli Ilauya	
adze, n.	gizago	H
aerial. adj. (a. wire)	senma waya	H(G.v)
aerodrome. n.	senma senmadrom	G
aeroplane, n.	senmaflen jinhan,	H(G.v)
afar, adv.	jinzo	Y/H/I I/Y
affair. n.	imani kontu, wuko	Y/I
affect. vt.	kontu, ti wuko iwuko wuko,	It/Y/I/G
affected affection, n.	isinkwa le wuko,	It/Y/I/G
ffectionate. adj.	di wuko n'iwuko	
affectation ate.	isinje ibuji:	Y
n. affidavit. n.	bujl ibadana	Y/H
affinity. n.	tebekimo,	Y
affirm. vti:	tekimo n'iteki,	Y/H/I/Y
affirmative.	n'itekimo	V/H/Y
adj. n.	jeafufu, jeta	Y/I
afflict. vt.	lemon	Y
affix. vt.	yaro, iyero	I/Y
affluence, n. adj.	le me, le meshe,	Y/I
afford, vt.	memeshe	
affray, n.	ijagha, arimkpo	Y/I
affright. vt.	di li ambu,	I/Y
affront. vt.	di rugu na	I/Y/H Y
afloat, adj.	whido,	I/H
afoot. adj.	nawhi lolo nakaf	I/Y/I
aforesaid, adj.	nakosoli nakongba	I/Y/I
aforetime. adv.	rugu,	Y/I
afraid, adj.	ambu mo ng	Y/I
(i am a.)	'rugu en rugu?	G/Gen.
(are you a.?)	ma rugu o	I/Y
(don't be afraid)	bia rugu	
(he/she was a.)	brelu Afrika	
afresh, adv.	zueine, si na,	
Africa after, adv.. adj.	chowa, chele	
(day a tomorrow)	rana zuein lachi	
(one a. the other)	tukon si na nkeji meni k'	
(what is he a.?)	on chowa?	
(he/she came a.)	o biawa zuein	

Afterbirth	n'izuein'bi	
Afternoon, n.	iyamma, zuein yamma, rana	H/I/Y
afterwards. adv. again,	n'izuein	I/Y
adv. (ask him/her a.)	mozo, n'ekeji, n'nkeji biju ya mozo	I/Y (again
(he/she asked me a.)	o biju mi n'ekeji	
(don't say it a.)	ma soli ya mozo	
(don't say that a.)	ma soli yen mozo	
(don't repeat ,it a.)	ma tumozo ma tumozo dikei,	
against. prep.	nakei idigbo, igboye, gboye	
(It is a.) age, n.	meni gboye ya? awa di n'igboye kengba	
(what is hislher a.?)	(his/her a.	
(we' are in a modern a.)		I/H
		I/Y
is....)	igboye ya wu … o wa n'igboye … age. adj	
.his/she was at the a. of)	gboye … o gboye … gboye.	

		H/Id.
(he/she is a.) (a.		H/G
motherlfather) agency,	mama/baba	H/G
n. (postal a.) agenda, n.	iwakili, omaye, ofis kpoz, ofis, ofis	H/ld.
agent, n. aggrandize, n.	waya ajanda, zlki wakili, omaye	Y/I
vt. (don't.a. matters)	igbega, gbega ma gbega nsohala	Y/I
aggravate, vt.	biki	Y/I Y/H/I
(don't a. me)	ma biki minwan, ma biki mi	
agressive, adj	chowa ijagha, cho ijagha	I/Y
aggregate, vt. n.	kojo, ikojo meje .	Y
aggrieve, vt	Wonye kasa	I/Y
Aground, adv. the	ugboko ruwa wonyela kasa	Y/I/H
ship ran aground		
aghast, adj.	diji yaji iyajl	Y/I
agile, adj.	solioka isolioka	Y/H
agility, n. agitate,	shiengala.	Y/H
vti. agitation.	ti shienga,	Y/I/H
n. ago, adv.	ardun inang zuein ngba nshiengala,	Y/I/H
(4 years ago)	ngba nke ti	Y/I zuein
(long time a.)	shienga na ngba ewo?,	
(how long a. ?)	meni ngba?	

agony, n.agree,	ofufu kweba,	I
vito agreeable, adj.	kwede ie ikw6b&. ie kwede	I/Y
agreement, n.	ikweba. ikwede,	H/G.v) I/H/Y
(come to an a.)	rude si 'kwede, bia si igona	I/H/Y
agriculture. n.	ye 'gona, o gona	
agriculturist, n.	na kasa,	
aground, adv., adj.	si kasa ugboko	
(the ship is a.)	ruwa yenle kasa	
ah, inter.	ah whikei	Gen.
ahead, adv	o wa na whikei	Y/I/H
(he is a. of us)	'wa e wa na whikei	
(you are a. of us)	'wa mo wa na	
(i'ma. of you)	whikei yinwan	
aid, vt. ahoy. into	mlsa, ronhan ahoe	G/Y/H Gen.
aide-de-camp, n.	odalen gomna, yetaimaki	
ail, vt.	dunta, tashien	H/Y/
ailing, adj.	idunta, itashien	Y/I
ailment, n.	aison, aijiki	Y/H
aim, vii, n.	chowa, fido, ichowa, ifido	I/Y/H
(the a. is to)	icowa wu, n'chowa wu	
aimless, adj.	lai wen ichowa, aifido, aichowa	
air, n. vii.	feku, the ita, nufe, nufe, soli	Y/I
(in the open a.)	n'ita	
(he came by a.)	o biawa na feh	
(a. your complaint)	soli 'rahun e	
airconditioner, n.	fetu, fetuoyi	I/Y
aircraft, n.	jirsama, fehsonma	H(G.v)
airport, n.	fili jirsama, filifeh	H/Y/I
(M. Muhammed a)	filife nke M. Muhammed	
ajar, adj.	laigwutan, aigwuton	Y/I
akin to, adj. alacrity, n.	baton yaya	Y/I
		Y(G.v.)
alarm, n.	gram-gram, nsohala, asogbu, arimkpo	G
(no cause for a.)	sedi nsohala (kosi nsogbu)	
(raise a.)	ke arimkpo	

alarm-clock, n.	agogo gram-gram, agogo arimkpo	
alas, int.	ah	Gen.
albino, n.	batu-afrika, zabaya	H/G
album, n.	lifinhoto	H(G.v)
(photo a.)	lifinhoto	
alchohol, n.	aikwan, baras, giya, ogogoro, kain-kain	H/Gen.
alcove, n.	sako, alkuki	H
alderman, n.	bamagar	H(G.v)
ale, n.	giya	H
alert, adj., vt.	yaji, sundi	Y/H/I
(be on the a.)	wen yaji, wen sundi, di sundi	
algebra, n	ajlbra, ozotrik	G
alias, n.	jela	G
alibi, n. alien, n.	zai, aibi kolejo	G
		H/Y(G.v)
alienate, vt	me' kolejo	H/I/Y(G.v)
alight, adj., vi	bonka	Y/I/H
alight, adj., vti	jowuta	Y/I
(the lamp is a	fitila njowuta	
align, vti.	jera, mike	H
alike, adj.	joka, kabi	Y/I
(they are a.)	ha kab!	
alive, adj.	di akpor, wa n'akpor, akpor, mindu	I/Ur/Y
(be a. to your responsibility)	jukun si aiki re	
a. and kicking)	di n'akport kamkpe	
all, adj., adv., n.	nchani, ncha, nile, igwukpin	Y/I/Bendel Igbo
allright)	o kamada, o.k., o di rama	
by atl means)	hanyar ku hanyar	H/Y/H/I
not all)	sedi nile	
(not at all) .	ah-ah, bate	Gen/l/Y
all pron.	gwuton, sho-sho, nke	I/Y
(alii know is)	nke mi ma wu	
(I like them a.)	mo che na nile, (mo che ha nile)	

allay, vt.	basa	Y/H
allegation, n.	itekimo	Y/H
allege, vt	tekimo	Y/H
allegiance, n.	itekeba	Y/H
Alliance, n.	yeamila, iyamila I/H	
Allocate, vt.	kekpin I/Y	
allot, alloted, vti, n.	kekpin	
(we were a. 9 bags)	ha kekpin ikpa esse fun 'wa	
allow, allowd, vti	gbakwe Y/I	
(smoking not a. here)	(a-o gbakwe koko/ciga n'ebe a,	
(you are not a.)	a-o gbakwe fun e, a-o gbakwe fun yinwan	
(you're a. to)	a gbakwe fun e, a gbakwe fun yinwan.	
allowance, n.	alawas, ikudi, iyele	H(G.v)Y/I
(mak! A. for)	meshe 'kudi/iyefe fun	
alloy, n.	àlò	Guosa-from.E
ally, vt.	bamboki	Y/I/H
Allusion, n.	itokasi	Tokasi
almanac. n. Almighty, n.	kalanda, pizio, amanak imeagbara, owen agba,	H/G
almost, adv.	bu, ku, fiene, ku wantlntin	
(it is a. six o'clock)	agogo isli ku wantintin	
(I'am almost satisfied)	mo ng fiene soken	
alms, n.	sakada	H
(give alms)	me sakada, nno sakada, fun sakada	
alone, adj., adv.	sosho	
(do it a.) alone, adv.	me n'sosho n'egbe, kpe, nasi	
(all a. the line)	n'egbe lavi, na layi nile	
(along the road)	nasi hanyar	
(come a.)	biawa kpe, bia nasi, biawa nasi	
alongside, adv.	nasiegbe	
aloof, adv.	lokere, n'taketake	
aloud, adv.	Senu	Y/I

(read a.)	ka senu	
(reading a.) alphabet, n.	i ka senu	
	bakake, haruffa, afabit	H/G
alphabetical, adj.	na 'fablt, na haruffa	It/G/H
already, adv.	ti, ia, te	Y/G
I have a. done it), ,	mo ti meshe	
Also, adv. Nasc.	ati, kpe(lu)	Y
altar, n. alter, vti	loho, tebur chochi tabi masallachi	G/Y/H Y/I
	itunme, itunmeshe	
alteration, n.	itunme, itunmeshe	Y/I
alternate, adj.	sonda isonda	Y/H.
alternative, n,	isonda 'wa,	Y/H
(there is a.)	isonda dia	Y
although, conj.	amp igiga	Y/I
Altitude, n.	kpatakata,	Y
altogether, adv	kprakpata samfolo	(G.v)
aluminium, n.	na ngba nile,	H
always, adv.,	na ngba gbogbo	I/Y
am,	mi, miwu,	Y/I
I'm amalgamate,	mo ng mekpo kojo	Y
vti. amass, vi.	zingata, o	Y
amateur, n.	zingata, ozinga	G
.amaze, VI.	yalibe, ya li onu iyalibe,	
amazement, n.	iya li onu jaghache	
amazon, n.	akawu	Y/I/H
amanuensis, n.	adido, aimetara	H/Y
ambiguous, adj.	(lai-) ichowu,	Y/H/I
ambition, n.	chowu ichowu gànú	I/Y/It.
(high a.)	kilisa, takama,	
amble, vi.	shienga, saun-saun	
ambulance, n.	monkejiji, monkejiji, motar asibiti	H/I/Y/H

ambuscade, n.	buba ibibuba	H
ambush, n.	tunme, delaj,	Y/I
ameliorate, vii, n.	idelaj aashe amin	Y/G/Gen.
amen, int.	itunmeshe tunmeshe	Y/I
amenability, n.	itunmeshe	Y/I
amend, vti	ifilo	Y/I
amendment, n.	menure	I/Y
amenity, n.	n'arin, n'ime,	I/Y
amiable, adj.	si'me shihan	Y/H
amid, amidst, prep.	harashi idariji	Y/H
amiss, adj.	n'ime, narin	H
ammunition, n.		Y
amnesty, n. among,		I/Y
amongst, prep.		

amorous, adj. amount, vi kile, di kife yole, di kife   Y/I

(amounted to)   yole si

amphibian, n. adj. jorujoka, ijorujoka, o jorujoka   Y/H

ample, adj.   tobu

amplify, amplifier, vi. n.   ziarimkpo, iziarimkpo   G/Y/I

amputate, vi.be, bepu, beku   I/Y

amulet, n.   daga   H Y/I

amuse, VI. n.   muerin, imuerin, o muerin

anaemia, n.   animaya saminsa   G
.english   guosa

analogy, n.   ijohu, johu   Y/I
analyse, vt, n. analyst, n. johu, ijohu, tuka, ituka ye tuka   Y/I I/Y

anatomy, n.	ifejikl, fejiki	I/H
anatomize, vt.	tukaji	I/Y/H
anatomist. n.	ye fejiki, o tukaji	
ancestor, n.	kaka, ikaka	H/H(G.v)
anchor, n.	ankad, zimkpor	H/G
ancient, adj.	kera	I/H
(ancient times)	mgba kera	
and, conj.	da	G
and so on, and so forth	da shishienen shienga	
anecdote, n.	itonifiene	Y/Ed.
anew, adv. angel, n.	mehuntun	I/Y H/I
	malaika (yelaika) + i	
anger, angered, n.	ibilionu, bilionu, ibi li	Y/I
(he/she was a.)	o bili ya onu	

angle, n.	iyego, kusurwa	G/H
angler, n.	kpeja	Y(G.v)
angery, adj.	bi li onu, bili, bilibe	Y/H(G.v)
(don't be a.)	ma bi li/ma bi li onu oka 'bi li	
anglican, n.	anglika, yangika	G
anguish, n.	ichekon	I/Y
animal, n.	dabba, bias, inama, nama	H/H(G.v)
(wild a.)	nama nke gboro	
(senior a.)	inama 'gba (inama agba)	
animate, adj.	sodi	Y/I
animation,	isodi	Y/I
animosity, n.	ikohunj, ikohunji	Y/I/G
ankle, n.	idofa	H(G.v)
anklet, n.	imudufa, anklit	H(G.v)
anomaly, n.	iseno aisinhanyar	G/Y/I/H
annals, n. annex, n.	iton duniyar chii,	G/I
annihilate, vt.	ichii, yagalaba rnediofo	I/Y
annihilation, n.	imediofo	I/Y
anniversary, n.	yanivase, anivase	G
anno domini (a.d.)	ardun ubanjiji (a.u.)	I/Y/H
announce, vt.	kemkpo, fishien	Y/I
announcement, n.	ikemkpo, ifishien	
annoying, n. adj.	ibi li be, ibili onu	Y/I/H
annual, adj.	n'ardun	I/Y
annually, adv.	n'ardun adun	I/Y
annual, vt.	fure	I/Y
anoint, vt.	torosi	Y(G.v)
annointed, n.	itorosi, ye a torosi	Y/I
anonymous, adj.	ai wen afa, ai wen su, feohon isimoloke	I/Y
anopheles, n.		G
(a. mosquito)	sauro simoloke	H/G
another, pro., adj.	nkeji,	I/Y
anulty, n.	kula	H/Y
(lite a.)	kula mindu	

answer, n.	daza, songi, feza	Y/I/G
(a. sheet)	takada songi	H/G
(a. sheets)	etakada songi	H/G
(a. back) ant, ants, n.	feza kpadabia, fezada gara, egara, tururuwa	H/H(G.v)
(ant-hill)	tudu gara	
antagonist. n.	ye ijagha	I/Y
Antarctic, adj.	semboga	G
antecedent. adj.	whawhido, nawhido	Y/H
antediluvian. adj.	shahara, shishaido	G
antelope. n.	gwanki	H
ante meridian, A.M.	sha sate (s.s.)	Y/H
antennae. n.	dohulo	.H
antenatal, adj.	sha'bi	Y(G.v)
anthem, n.	irinbu mimo, songa, rinbimo	Y/I/G
(S. Okosun sang a national a anthrax, n.	S. Okosun songi songa kasa yabata, abata, yekarau	H/I(G.v)
anti, pret.	soko	G
anti Christ. n.. adj.	kristi	G/Gen.
anticipate. anticipated, vt.	rekun, reche	Y/H/I
anticipation, n.	irekun, ireche	Y/H/I
(he/she a.)	ya reche	
(he/she is anticipating)	ya n' reche	H/I
antidote, n. antimacassar, n.	ikatala, yekari itufafi, kujera	H/I H
antimony, n.	nkiro	
antipathy. n.	aicho, yaichowa	Y/I
antipodes, n.	isukuwah	G
antiquity. n.	isugala	G/I
antilion, n.	isukulu	G
antiseptic. n.	fekashe	I/Y
antitype, n.	isukota	G(H.t)
antithesis, n.	akasi, kishiya, isukota	G/H
antlers, n.	haula	H
anus. n.	dubura	H

anvil. n.	makera	H
anxiety. n.	yaja, ichereji	I/Y/H
anxious, adj.	yajo, di yajo dic chereji	I/Y/H
any. adj., pron.	eni	Y(G.v)
(have you a.?)	e wen eni?	
(is there a. person)	eni mutum? eni 'fe?	Y/H
(anything)	eni mutum, eni ji eni han	Y/I
anybody. n.. pron.	eni yen, eni mutum eni han,	Y/H
any how, adv. anyone,	nihan eni 'be kiakia yaji	Y/H
n., pron. anyway,		Y/H
adv. anywhere, adv.		Y/I
apace, adv.,		Y/I

	Y/H	
apart, adv.	nahann kon, fambu fambu si ezioka kpe Y/H/I	
(a. from the fact that)		
apartheid, n.	yafataid, afataid G	
apartment, n.	indeki Y/H	
ape, n.	gwaggo H	
aperient, n.	ogun zawo I/Y/H	
apex, n.	kokuwa H	
apologetic, adj.	gbl It.	
apology, n.	igbi, gbi-gbi, biyo it.	
apostasy, n.	ilapkeda I/Y	

apostle, 'n.	aposteli	Y/G
apparatus, n.	ikayanki	H(G.v)
apparel, n.	itufa	H
apparent, adj.	honka	VII
(heir a.)	o honka	
appeal, vi.	gbibi, biyo	It/Y/I
(court of a.)	kotu 'biyo	
appear, appears vi.	jihon, jihun, puja	H/Y/I
appearance, n.	ijihon, ijihun, ipuja	H/Y/I
appease, vt.	tunime	Y/I
appeasement, n.	itunime	Y/I
appendicities, n.	afendisatis, afendi ichebinchi	G
appetite, n.		I/Y/H

(he has a big a.)	o wen baba 'chebinchi	
(i have no a.)	mi se wen ichebinchi	
applause, n.	kpahann	Y/H
(give him/her an a)	kpahann fun ya	
apple, n.	apul	G
applicant, n.	o chowa 'iki	I/Y/H
apply, applied, vti	jube	I/Y
application	ijube, ijubele	I/Y
appoint, vt.	kinsi	I/Y
appointment, n.	ikinsi	I/Y
appraise, vt.	diye	V(G.v)
appreciate, vii,	maye	Y(G.v)
appreciation, n.	imaye	Y(G.v)
apprehend, n.	jimu, yela, ijimu	I/Y
apprehensive, adj.	yela	Y/I
apprehension, n.	iyela	Y/I
apprentice, n.	ifrentis, afrentis, yemuka yemuka	G/I/Y
appropriate, adj.	keli yema	Y/I
appropriation, n. (a. of fund)	Ikeli, iyema Iyema kudi	I/Y
(a. noon)	nso rana	
(a. midday)	nso tsa tsakar rana	
(a. evening	nso yamma	
(a. you)	nso e, nso o; nso yinwan	
arouse. pt.	jiwe, ji, jine	Y/I
araign. vt.	baroka, koka	Y/I
arrange. vtl	arrangement. tole	Y/I
n. array. n.	itole. itolele itole, itolele	Y/I
arrears. n.	izuba	Y/I I/H
aside, adv.	akue, na 'kue	I/Y
put aside	Finye si na 'kue, finye si akue	
ask, asked, vti.	Jubi you asked for it o jubi fun ask, and you shall receive jubi, e yihi, jubi, e wenri	I/Y

askew, ascant, adv., adj.	Zarai	G
asleep, adv., adj.	sunla, sunra he/ she is asleep o sunlala, o sunrala I am sleeping Mo ng sunla, mo ng sunra	Y/I
aspect, n.	Iyakah the major aspect iyakah katazi	Y/I
asphalt, n.	asfat, irudi kwalta	G/fr. Eng.
aspire, vtn.	Chekon	I/Y
ass, n.	Jaki	H
assassin, n.	Igbujiji	I/Y/Ed/etc.
assassinate, vt.	Gbujiji	
assassinator, n.	o gbujiji	
assault, n.	Ikogba others	Y/I/Ed/
assail, n.	kogbu	
assailant, n.	o kogbu	
assemble, vti.	kolojo	H/G/Y
assembly, n.	Ikolojo house of assembly gida ikolojo, majalisar wakili	I/y
assent, n	kweba	Y/I
assert, vt.	tonusi, tonumo assertion, n itonusi, itonumo	
assess, assessment, n.	bukeli, ibukeli tax assessment ibukeli haraji	Y/I
assessor, n.	o bukeli	
assignment, n.	iyansi	
assize, n.	ikpado, ikpado 'ka	Y/I/Ikwere
assist, vti.	ronka, ronhann	Y/I/H
assistant, n.	o ronka	
associate, adj.	sukumbu, o sukumbo	
association, n.	isukumbu	
assuage, vt	sasanyaya	H
assume, vt.	cheni	I/Y
assume duties	cheni 'rushe	

assumption, n.	icheni	
Assunder, n.	ìká, igesai	Igbo(Guosa)
assurance, n.	iyobile	Y/I
assure me/give me an a.	yobile mi/fun mi li 'yobile	
assuredly, adv.	yoyobile	
assure, vt.	yobile	
I assure	mo yobile yin	
you asthma	fuka, "irudi irun" "a type of sickness"	H
n. asterisk, n.	Ikiyesi	Y/Edo/I
astray, adj., adv.	Shihan, yapu, yata	Y/H/I
A dog that will go astray	Kera keti o maa shihan Malu shihan	
The cow went astray	malu yapu malu yata	
An astray bullet	Harsashi keti o yapu	
Astonish, vt.	Yalijiki, yapepeh	Y/I/H
I am astonished	Mo yalijiki, mo yanjiki, mo yapepeh	
Astrology, n.	Iskaloji	H/G
Astrologist, n	O skaloji	
Astronaut, n.	Iskanomi H/G	
Astute, adj.	Kwayo, (quick in making cleverly profits)	
Assylum, n	Aro, bike ifeweh Y	
Assylum, n	Isalam G	
Assylee	O salih G	
At, prep.	Nani I/Y	
At the house	Nani gida	
Ate, vt. Pt.	Wuam G/Ikwerre	
Atheism, n.	Itungbo G	
Atheist, n.	O tungbo	
Athlete, n.	O gberenji; o roso	Y/I
Athletic, adj., n.	Roso, rosokiti, O gberenji, o rosokiti	Y/I/Ed
Atlantic, adj.	Tekunu	G/Y
Atlantic ocean	Osha tekunu	
Atlas, n.	Asahe	G

Atmosphere, n.	Ayika	G
Good atmosphere	Ayika rama, ayika dada	
Atom, n.	Atum, zarra	
Atomic, adj.	Nke atum, atuma	
Attach, vti., n.	Fite, ifite	Y/I
Attache, n.	Ifite, o fite	
Attachment, n.	Ifite, ififite	
Attack, n., vti.	Itagbu, itako, tako, ikogbu	
Armed robbery attack	Itako barawo, itako o rawo	
Attain, vti., n.	Weni, iweni	I/Y
Attainment, n.	iweni	
Attempt, vit	Done	Y/I
Attempted coup	Idone zaikpokpo	
Attend, vit.	feza, loga, chenduti, dazi, biawa	I/Y
Attend to me	Feza mi,	
I Attended a university	Mo loga yunifasiti	
In attendance is	Na ifeza wu Mazi Okon	
Mr. Okon	O feza gazh, ochenduti na gida gazh	
Gas attendant		
Meeting attendee	O biawa ikolojo	
Dispensary attendant	O feza disfensa, o chenduti	
Attention, n.	Ifeza, ikiesi	
Pay attention	Kiesi, feza si, gbonti	
Attitude, n.	Imiwa	I/Y
Bad attitude	Imiwa rubi	
Good attitude	Imiwa rama	
Attorney, n.	Ilauya, atone, o rushe oka	
Attorney-general	Atone-janar, o mawa-janar, o lauya- janar	
Attire, n.	Itufa, esa H/Ogori	
Attract vti,	Faji, fane, mine	
Attraction, n.	Ifaji, ifane, imine	
Attrocity, n.	Njika	Y/I
Auction, n.	Gbanjo, ileta	Gen/I/Y

Auctioneer, n.	O gbanjo, o leta	
Auction sales	Ileta gbanjo, gbanjo	
Audacious, adj.	Zuwele	G
Audible, adj.	Di gbigbo, nugbo, gbigbonti	I/Y
Audience, n., vt.		
Audience please!	Inugbo, igbonti Gbonti biko!	
Audit, n	Inelita	I/H
Audit report	Takarda inelita, wasika inelita	
Auditor, n.	O nelita	
Auditor-general	Baba onelita	

b	bi	G
babble. vi. vt.	besoli, me ofofo, mebo	G/I
baboon. n.	bika, gwaggo	H
baby. n	jariri, jinjiri, omontakiri	H/Y/Ed/It/Ur
bachelor. n.	tuzuru	H
back, n	zuba	I/H
(come b.)	bia zuba, (bia-ba)	
(basket ball)	kwando boi, tabi boi kwando	
ballad, n.	baro	I/Y
balloon, n.	blomblo, kumbura	Gen./Ha.
ballot, n.	tabo	Y/H
(b. box), n.	ìkpà tabo	H/I/Y
balm, n.	kunji, kude	Y/H/I
bamboo, n.	gora, gwangwala, tukurwa	H
(b. stick), n.	itache gwangwala	
ban, vt.	taun, fitegba	Y(G.t)
banana, n.	ayaba	H
band, vt.	sòké	Y/I
band, n.	dauri, oja	H/Y
blind man	míjì o fídò	
blind	ò fídò	
blindfold, vt.	fídò	
blindness , n.	ìfídò	
don't argue blindly	má sàrókà fídò	
blink, vit..	jìné	Y/I
bliss, n.	ìlándù	Y/I/H
blister, n.	bororor	H
bloat, vt.	kumbura	
bloated, adj., pt.	Kumbura, kumbura la	
block, n.	bangori, tìkpó, búlókì	H/gen.
road block	ìtìkpó hányar	
cement block	búlókì sùmúntì	
blond, n. adj	fangashi ,	H.
blood, n.	jínní ,	H.

bloom, n.	húgbo	Yoruba/ Edo/Igbo
blossom, n.	ìhúgbo	
blot , n.	bulota; gwale	Gen/H
blotting paper	bulota, takarda búlótà	
blotter , n.	o sháká, búlótà,	
blouse , n.	abokara, jagu	H
blow , vit….to blow or hit on something solid, wall, human,	lùgbú, gbòsàh	
Nigeria's boarder	matuka Naijeriya	
boast , n.	ìshàkàrá, shàkàrá, sòhó	
boat , n.	kwalekwale, abara, moru ,	H.
speed boat	kwalekwale iroso, kwalekwale igbere	
bobbin , n. bodily , adj.	kwarkwaro , *a spindle for holding thread,* nke jiki, jiki-jiki , jijiki	H. I/H.
body , n.	Jiki, gawa, taro, rukuni ,	H.
bog , n.	fadama , soft and wet ground. ,	H.
bogus , adj.	gbólójá : *something sham and a counterfeit.*	
boil , n., adj.	ìgbòwútá, gbígbòwútá	
boil , vti.	guse, gbowuta	I/Y/H
boilder , n.	o guse, iguse	
bold , adj.	gboaya, gburu	Y/G
boldness , n.	ìgboaya, igbru	
bole , n.	gajishiya	
boll , n.	kwanso, gululu: *nut, shell, catridge-case; also*	
boll worm	tsutsar auduga, tsutsar gululu	

bolster , n.	domakei , long under-pillow for hed.	
bolt , n.	buot ,	G.
bomb , n.	igbum, bam, igbuduh ,	G.
bomb blast	ìgbàtá bám	
bond , n.	ìkèdéi, ikedejo	
bondage , n.	ìshònrú ,	I/Y.
bondsman , n.	ò kedejo; o kedi	
bone , n.	kashi,	H.
bonfire , n.	baba wuta; toyi, buyar wuta:, big fire.	
bonus , n.	awui	
bonnet , n.	yuma	
car bonnet	yuma mota zoom-zoom	
book , n.	yittafi, akweda	H/I/H
book case	akwati littafi	
book binder	O kedi littafi	
book , vti.	jube	
booking , n. booking office	ijube; ijublle	
	ofis ijube	
book clerk	akawu ijubele; akawu tikiti	
book – keeping , n.	Ichero littafi; o chero littafi	
bookshop , n.	gisuwa litaffi	
boot , n.	butu; takalmi; Kurfai	
boot-out	kono ja; kono 'ta	
car boot	butu mota zoom-zoom	
booth , n.	buka; rumfa, baba kantin	
telephone booth	buka teliwaya	
boom , vt.	bumu	
booty , n.	ganima: , items captured from enemy	etc..
boot , n.	bata lau , large or big shoe.	
border , vtiu.	dajiya; gefe, matuka, iyaki	
bore , vti.	gara, dalu; yolionu, mubi	

borne , p.p..	mubi beka , to bear, not birth.	
borough , n.	buro: , a type of English town.	
borrow , vt. borrower , n. please, borrow me money:	bolo o bolo biko, bolo mi kudi	
bosom , n.	kaiya	
boss , n.	oga, megisi	
botany , n.	izola Jieji	
both , adj, adv., pron.		
both of you	E yin jieji	
bother , vti.	Yolionu , yol'onu.	
don't bother me bottle , n.	Ma yomil'onu Ijongo, , exceptional case: "buta".	
water – bottle	Ijongo ruwa	
bottom , n.	Gindi, kasa, ikebe	
fat bottom	Isamba	
bottomless , adj.	Lai wen gindi abi kasa	
bough , n.	Reshe,	H/Y.
bought, buy ,vti/pt.	Gora, rata, zura,	
please, buy me soap	Biko, gora mi sabulu	
faminu bought a car	Faminu te gora zoom-zoom	
boulder ,n.	Yoi: ,a large rock of stone.	G
bound, ,n., vt., adj.	Kedi, ikedi, foga	Y/I/H.
bounce ,vit.	Fozoka; fozo,	
boundary ,n.	Yaka, matuka,	H.
boundless ,adj.	Lai wen ikedi abi matuka	
bounteous, bountiful	Nawo, kponso, ikunzi	
bounty ,adj.; adv.	Kunkunzi	
bow ,v.	Bolo,	
i bow	Mo bolo	
bow down your head	Bolo isi	
bow ,n.	Bobo: curved end of a ship.	G
bow-legged	Kafa bobo; o bobo kafa.	

bowels ,n.	Hanji
bower ,n.	Tibaba
bowl ,n.	Tasa, Kwano, Kasko, akushi, H/Gwari godo–
bowstring ,n.	Tsirkiya, H.
box ,n.	Akwati, dambe, H.
box ,vti.	Gbosah , G/Gen.
boxer ,n.	O gbosah
boxing ,n.	Igbosah
boxing day	Rana igbosa
boy ,n.	Yaro, saurayi,
boy friend ,n.	Abokii yaro
boycott ,vt.	Meti,
boyhood ,n.	Ngba yaro, h
bracelet ,n.	Hilalaini, watau,
bracket ,n.	Irondo
brackish ,adj.	Winshiri, i/
brag ,vi.	Shakara , y/gen.
braggart , n.	Ishakara, o shakara,
braid , n.	Amara: "of hairs woven together",
braille , n.	Breil: "system of writing and reading by the blind
brain , n.	Kwakwalwa, kwanya, kyeya, ichegbon , h/i/y.
brake , n.	Ifachiu: "a device for stopping or reducing moving object", y/i.
brake drum	Hobu
bramble , n.	Guntache: "blackberry bush or rough shrub",
brain , n.	Dusa: "the outer covering of grain", h/I/y.
branch , n.	Iyaga, iyahan, y/i/h.
branch , vt.	Yaga, yahan
branch office	Iyaga ofis
tree branch	iyaga itache

brand , n.	Alama,
	h.
this is a new brand	Eyi wu alama huntun
brandish , vt.	Mesi , i/y.
brandy , n.	Barande , f/fe.
brass , n.	Farin, karfe , h.
bravado , n.	Ifari, igboaya , y/i/h.
brave , adj.	Chegbon, wen iybi , i/y.
be brave	Chegbon, di 'yobi, wen iyobi; yobi
bravery , n.	Bravu; yah , g, fe./g.
brawler , n.	O 'rimkpo; o arimkpo , y/I.
bray , n.	Igbekete , y/h/ed.
braze , vt.	He , gu.
brazen , adj.	Hihe, he , i/y.
brazen-face , n.	Ai feju – "shameless" , y/I.
brazier , n.	Janono; kunta: "of portable metal like a basket for holding a charcoal or coal fire" G
breach , n.	Meru: "breaking or neglect of duty or law" , y/i.
breach of contract	Imeru ikwede
bread , n.	Buredi , h/y/gen.
breadth , n.	Ibu , y.
break , vti.	Foji, meje, meru, shaka , i/y/g.
day break	Ishaka rana
bredak/broken glass	Maidubi fifoji: fifoji gilas
till day break	Siti ishaka rana
breakfast , n.	Kalachi, abinchi safe , h/i/y.
breakwater , n. "structure that breaks water force"	O kpakunu:
breast , n.	Nono, kirji, mama, bom-bom; buh-buh , h/g.
breast plate	Faranti nono
breath , n.	Imime, imi, imimi , y/I.
breath in	Mimi si menu
breath of life	Imimi mindu
breadth out	Mimi ' ta
bred, breed , vti.	Webi, bone , i/y.

breech , n.	Gindi-bindiga , h, g.v.
breeches , n.	Shokoto , y/gen.
breeze , n.	Fekuku , y/I.
bretheren , n.	E muba, e mo baba , h/ed/y/ur/isc.
brevity , n.	Ibekuru, bekuru , i/y.
brevity of life	Ibekuru nke mindu
brew , vti.	Sekpon , i/y.
brewery , n.	Gisekpon , h/ti/nu/i/y.
bribe , n.	Ikunde , g.
don't give bribe	Ma non ikunde; , or. ma fun n' ikunde
don't take bribe	Ma yi 'kunde
brick , n.	Tubali; biriki , h/g, fe..
bricklayer , n.	O toka tubali; o toka birikip; , bigila.
bride , n.	Amarya , h.
bride chamber , n.	Iyere amarya , y/i/h.
bridegroom *n.	Ango , h.
bridesmaid , n	Ango budurwa; , omote-ango. , ur/y/ed/it/h.
bridge , n.	Kadarko; katako; gada , h/gen.
under the bridge	N'abe katako; n'abe gada , i/y/h.
bridle , n.	Linzami , h.
brief , adj.	Kuru; sam , y/g.
briefly , adv.	Kuru; sam-sam; n'ikuru
brief visit	Ikende kuru
brigade , n.	Birige , g/fe.
brigade of guards	Gade birige
the old brigade	Birige idugbo
the boys brigade	Birige yaro
brigade commander	O kwamanda birige
rigadier , n.	Birigedi , g, ge..
brigand, n.	O fashi; o tugbe irawo , member of robbers. , i/h.
bright , adj.	Shaka , g/h.
everything is bright	Ife ncha di shaka; ife ncha shaka
bright light	Wuta shaka
the moon is bright	Wata di shaka
brightness , n.	Ishaka , y, g.v..

brim , n.	Kunu; nukun , i/y/h.
brim-full	Jukunu
brimstone , n.	Sulfuri , h.
fire and brimstone	Wuta ati sulfuri
brine , n.	Wakun: "of salt water" , h, g.v..
bring, brought , vt..	Mubia , y/I.
bring out	Mubia 'ta
bring me water	Mubia me ruwa
bring forward	Mubia si 'shido
bring up	Mubia si nuke
brink , n.	Ikiki , i/y/h.
brisk , adj.	Yakia , y, g.v.
brisk business	Irushe yakia
bristle , n.	Gashishi: one of shoret stiff hairs on an animal , e.
britain , n.	Biriteh; biriteteh , g, fe..
british/briton , n.	Biriteh; o biriteteh
brittle , n.	Gaggautsa , h.
broad , adj.	Banyar , h, g.v..
broad minded	Iyobi banyar
in broad day light	N' ibanyar rana
broadcast , vti.	Soliwaya , y/i/gen.
broadcaster , n.	O soliwaya , y/i/gen.
, j. usen is a broadcaster.	j. usen wu o soliwaya broil , vti.
brocade , n.	Brokedi , g.
broke , adj.	Fojie, aiwen, , brokeh. , y/i.
, i'm broke.	Mo ti brokeh/mo brokeh
broken	Di foji, meje
, broken down.	Meje si kasa,
broken pot , n.	Tukunya fifoje , h/y/i.
broken plate , n.	Kwano fifoje, faranti fifoje
broker , n.	O foje, o brokeh
bronchitis , n.	Nokaitis , g.
bronze , n.	Tagulla, oze , h/ed.
brood , n.	'ya'ya , h.

brook , vt.	Bruk , g.
broom , n.	Tsintsiya, bale,
, broom stick.	Itache siya
, a new broom.	Siya huntun
broth , n.	Room , h.
brothel , n.	Huta, giruwa , h, g.v..
brother , n.	M'uba , y/ed/ur/iso/it/h.
half-brother , n.	Afuba , h. "brother by different mother"
, elder brother.	Wa , h.
, younger brother.	Kane , h.
, brother-in-law.	Suruki , h.
brought, bring	Mubia, muyen, munno , y/i/ef/ed.
brow , n.	Sido , i/h.
, eye brow.	Isi'do , i/h.
brown , adj.	Saa , h, gv..
browse , vi.	Janya , y/h.
bruise , n.	Kurma , h.
brunt , n.	Lishi , g.
brush , vti.	Landi , g.
brush , n.	Burosh, magogi, kurmi , h.
brushwood , n.	Kirare, itache burosh , h.
brutal , adj.	N'ika , i/y.
brutality , n.	In'ika , i/y.
brute , n.	Dabba , h.
bubble , n.	Folo-folfo, blom-blom , g.
bubbling , adj.	Di blom-blom, blom-blo , i/g.
buck , vit.	Lafe , y, g.v.
bucket , n.	Bokiti, guga, ankuru , h.
buckle , n.	Bokul , g.
bud , n.	Tohu, dumbaru , h.
budge vti.	Mira , y.
budget , n.	Istimat , h.
annual budget.	Istmat ardun
buffalo	Bauna , h.
, buffalo soldier.	Soja bauna

buffet , n.	Bafit, bafet , g.
bug , n.	Kudi, kwaro , h.
bugle , n.	Bigila , h.
bugler , n.	O bigila, ye bigila , y/h/g/i.
build , vti.	Kogi , y/h.
building , n.	Ikogi, gida, gini , y/h.
bulb , n.	Guda, gulob, gilob , h/y/gen/g.
bulge , n.	Kumbura , h.
bulk , n.	Dushi, girma , h.
bulky , adj.	Di dushi, di girma , i/h.
bull , n.	Bijimi , h.
bull elephant , n.	Toron giwa, giwa bijimi , h.
bull dog , n.	Kare bijimi , h.
bullet , n.	Harsashi , h.
, bullet proof.	Kwat harsashi , h, g.v..
bulletin , n.	Bulatin, kwiro , g/i/y.
bullock , n.	Hurtumi , h.
bullion , n.	Zubi , g.
bulrush-millet , n.	Gero, dauro , h.
bully , n.	Ijimi , y/I, g.v...
bump , vti.	Rupu
bump , n.	Luba
"to blow or hit"	
t. oyatedo bumped into my house	T. Oyatedo rupu si gida mi
bumper , n. "of motor-vehicle"	Bumpa
bun , n. bunch , n. bundle , n.	Ban rudi akara bature , g/h.
	Dinshe, kurshe, nono, taro , h.
	Dami, kai, kaya, kunshi, adila, kaya, bandir
bundle , vti.	Di, didi , y.
bungalow , n. bunion , n. bunk	Bandeki , g/h.t.
, n. bunkder , n. buoy , n.	Kokiya , h.
buoyant , vti, n. burden , n.	Gado wana, bank , h/g.
	Banka , gen.
	Yume , g.
	Shasha, ishasha , g.
	Kaya, ikaya, nsoha, sohala , h, g.v..
bureau , n.	Ofis, buru , h/i/h.

bureaucracy , n.	Iburu , i/h.
burglar , n.	Barawo , h.
burglary , n.	Ifoje gid , y/i/h.
, burglary proof.	Kwat ifoje
burial , .	isinkwuowun , y/i.
bnurnish , vti. burnish	Di towu , h, g.v..
, vti. burnouse , n.	Di towu , h, g.v..
burrow , n. bursar , n.	Gitowu, banuz , h/g.
	Rami, haka , h.
	Bosah , g.
burst , vti.	gbábé, béu Igbo/Yoruba
, he burst into the house.	O gbabe si gid
bury , vt.	Sikwuowun , y/I.
bus , n.	Bos, bas, safa, baba mota , h, g.v..
bush , n.	Daji , h.
, bush man.	Kiji daji
, bush woman.	Mache daji Nama dai
, bush meat.	Makwarwa , h.
, bush fowl.	Alade daj
, bush pig. bushel, n.	Bushal, frisho , g.
bushy, aj. business, n.	Di daji , i/h.
, mind your business.	Irushe, ishobeh
bustard, n.	Konbi sheleki e
	Bugudu, tuji, kadafkara , h.
busle , vit.	Arimkpo, baba arimkpo nsohala, noha
bustler, n. busy, adj. i'm	Ole arimpko, ole nsoha
busy but, conj. butcher,	Ruaiki mo ng ruaiki e Ama, amo , y.
n. butchery , n.	Yanka, azzalumi, hauchi, gbu Igbugbu, igbu , I, g.v.
butler, n. butt, n.	Baa shamaki , h.
	Itache, bindiga, kotar, tunkuya , h.
butter, n.	Man Shanu, bota , h/g.
, shea-butter.	Man kadai , h.
, butter milk.	Nono tsala, nono bota , h/g.
, butter cup. butterfly,	Yifinjali , h, gv.
n. buttock , n.	Yifitashi , h, gv.
	Gindi, ikebe, duwawu , , h/y/ed/ur/is.
button, n.	Botin, maballi, anini, riga, anini , h.

button-hole , n.   Iho anini , y/h.
buy, vti   Gora, Zura, rata , h/I.

Kasa isinkwuowun,
iboji , h/y/I.
Foba , g.
Towu, owu , h, g.v...

buy all. buyer, , n.   , c. nwachukwu came by air.

, by chance. , adj..   Rata nile , y/I.

, by the way. ,   O gora, O rata, O zura Sie,
by and by.

, day by day. , stand   na , h/i/y.
by your word.

by gone, , adj..   Nwachukwu sie feh biawa

, let bygone be   Sie hanyar,
bygone by-pass ,

n. bye ,   ba hanyar Sie sie

n. bye-bye ,   Rana sie rana,

n. bystander , n.   rana ba ran Chiu na oka e/yin

Ka shiensie wuj sie   Shiensie, tishien , y/I.

Isie-koja, isie-ko

Baiyo Baiyo, iz.

Baisanda , g.

caloric,
(Jones Usen seti naira sa Etemah) kule aboki

(c. down my friend) calorie, n.   ikala, kala

kala, fonkala

calumny, n.   meata

I/

calvary , n.   kalfari , g.

came , pt.   bia, bra, biawa, bia ah , i/y/Ga/Twi

came out   bia'ta, biawata, brawata , i/y/Ga/Twi.

camel , n.   rukumi , h.

camera , n.   kamara, akwatin hoto , g/h/gen.

camouflage , n.   ibido

camp , n.   tanti-tanti, sansani, zango, h.

, labour c.   Sansani aiki , h.

, c. bed.   kambet, sauka, kafa tanti , h.

campaign , n.   iyaki, kemkpo , h, g.v./y/i

camphor , n.   kanfo , h, gv..

campus , n.   fili makaranta, fili-kolej, kamfos , h/g.

camwood , n.   majigi , h.

can , n.   kwan, kwankele, gwangwani , h/nu.

can, could   kanbo, ka , g/i/y.

, c. i go?.   kam' shienga?

, i cannot.   mii kanbo

, you cannot.   ŏ kànbò, ee kanbo

, watering can.   ìjóngò gadina, rakiti , ib/h.

canal , n.   aizumkpa hanyar ruwa, atifisa , y/i/h/g.

canal , adj..   Feakpor , i/ur.

cancel, vti   Gbure , i/y/ed..

cancerin   Kinekine, Kensa , g/n.

candid , adj..   Daido , y/h.

, candid camera.   Daido , hoto dido.

candidate , n.   Imonta, kandida , y/ed/it/ur/h/g.

candle , n.   Abela

, c. stick.   Itache abela

candour , n.   Inure, imenure , i/y..

candy , n.	Izibi , g.
cane , n.	Sanda, kwagiri, kara , h.
, sugar cane.	Reke , h/y.
canine , adj..	Rereke , i/h/y.
, canine tooth.	Bika , h.
canker , n.	Imesherugu, irugu , i/y/g.
canker-worm , n.	Tana rugu , h/g.
cannibal , n.	O Jemutum , y/h.
cannon , n.	Igwa , h.
cannot, can	Kanbo , g.
, i cannot.	Mii kanbo
cance , n.	Abara, kwami, jirgi, falange , h.
canon , n.	Lura , g.
canonise, , vt.	Ilura, mi di lura , g/i/y.
canopy , n.	Laima, kanopi, baba laima , h/g/h.
cantankerous , adj..	Konji, konjiki , y/h.
canteen , n.	Kante, daki abinchi
canter , n.	Igane y, g.v.
cantonment , n.	Salangana , g.
canvas , n.	Tamfol, Kamfas , h/g.
cap , n.	Hula, Tagiva, Murfi, Koko , h/y.
, knee cap.	Hula gwiwa, di agba, , g/f/y.
capable , adj..	Wen, agba di agba, , g/f/y.
capacious , adj..	Gboro , xy.
capacitate , vt..	Metisi , , i/g.
capacity , n.	Igbike , y/I.
cape , n.	Bidi, kabido , h.
, cape coast.	Gate bidi , h/h, g.v..
, cape town.	Gari bidi
capital , n.	Hedkwatar, bab, jari warkudi kapitye , h/g.
, capital city.	Jari birni, bab birni
capitalist , n.	Ye kapite, o kapite , i/g/y/g.
capitulate , vt, n.	Jolanke, iolanke , g.
capon , n.	Izaka , g.
capricious , adj.	Di zaka, le zaka , i/y/g.

capricon , n.	Okara , g.
, capricon of cancer.	Okara kinekine te , g.
capsize , vti.	Zhuuh , g.
, the boat has capsized.	Kwalekwale ti zahuuh
capsule , n.	Kasol, keniko , g.
captain , n.	Kaftin, shugaba , eval. , h/agboo.
, army captain. kafito	Kapiteh soja, kapiteh o j'agbha
captivate , vt.	Gbayobi , y/I.
captive , adj, n.	Kamamme , h.
captivity , n.	Ikamamme , h, g.v..
captor , n.	O kamamme , y/h.
capture , vt.	Mugba , y/ed..
car , n.	Mota zoom-zoom motakere , h/y/ed/g.
caravan , n.	Ayari , h.
carbohydrate , n.	Sukaromba , h/g.
carbolic	Kaboliki , g.
, carbolic acid.	Wassid kaboliki
carbon , n.	Gawayi , h.
, carbon paper.	Fefa gawayi
carbuncle , n.	Dususu , h.
carburettor , n.	Kareta, kafreta , ed/g.
carcase , n.	Gawa , h.
card , n.	Kwali, kad , h/g.
post card , n.	Foskad , g.
card board , n.	Kwali , h.
cardinal , n.	Muhimmi , h.
, cardinal numbers.	Lamba muhimmi , h.
care , n.	Shokpa, ijun-ene, bo, shokpa , h/y.
, take care.	Junene ijune , i/h/y.
, baby care.	Ijunene, jariri, ijune omontakili
, car care.	Ijunenmota , y/h.
career , n.	Waiki , y/h.
careful , adj.	Di junen wen junene , i/y/h.
, be careful.	June-june c/n shokpe
careless , adj.	Aijunene , y/h.

cargo , n.	Kaugbo , h/i/y.
, cargo ship.	Kaugbo ugboruwa
caricature , n.	Muzantawa , h.
carnal , adj.	Feji , i/y.
carnival , n.	Inambi inambe , g, h/v..
carnivours , adj.	Inambe o nambe , g, h.v.y.
carol , n.	Sonfeh , g.
carp , n, vt.	Siri , h.
carpenter , n.	Kafinta, masassaki, o sassaki , h/h/y/h.
carpet , n.	Kafet, kafit , h/g.
carriage , n.	Kurusa , h.
, railway carriage.	Wagunun fasinja, kurusa reluwe
carrier , n.	Kariya, ilebura, o kaya , h/ur/y.
carrion , n.	Yakonba , h/ef.
carrot , n.	Karat, karas , h.
carry , vti.	Yibou, gbe
carry out	To ita
carry on	To shien
carrying , n.	Ibugbe
cart , n.	Kendo, kura, amalanke, kokwa
cartilage , n.	Gurunguntisi, girtsi , h.
carter , n.	O kura, ye kura, fe kura , y/h/I.
carton , n.	Katan , h.
cartoon	Zane , h.
cartridge , n.	Kwafsa harsashi, tako , h/g.
carve , vti.	Fin , y.
, carver , n.	O fin , y/I.
case , n.	Oka, nsohala , i/y/ik/gen.
case , n.	Ikpa, akwatin, gida, ngba , ti/h/ed/i/y.
brief case	Ikpa-kele
in any case	N'eni o ka; n'oks di oks
casement , n.	Wundo, akwatin , h/ed.
cash , n.	Kabodais,k tsaba kudi, kasi , g/h/g.
i cashed a cheque	Mo kasi seki, mo gbawe kudi

cash and carry	Kpa to
cashew , n.	Kajiu, fisa, yazawa , g/h.
cashier , n.	Kasia, o kudi , g/ti/h.
cask , n.	Ganga , h.
casket , n.	Kaskit, ikpamutu , g/ti/h.
cassava , n.	Gari, rogo , h/gen.
cast , vti.	Jutu, tu, nese, kaste , y/I.
cast your vote	Jutu loka e
cast iron	Ijutu ayan
castanets , n.	Sambani, kyandi , h.
castaway , n.	Miskin, ai che, idoti, o jutu , h/y/I.
caste , n.	Asali, kabila , h/y.
castle , n.	Asali, kabila , ed.
castigate , vt.	Gbeta , ed.
castle , n.	Bnandehara, bandehar , h, g.v..
cast-off , adj.	Juta , y/I.
castor , n.	Kasta , g.
castor oil	Man kasta , h/g.
castor sugar , n.	Kasta kasta, fari suka
castrate , vt..	Tenda , y , g.v..
casual , adj.	Labapeh , y, g.v..
casual visit	Ikeni labapeh
casual work	Aiki labapeh
casualty , n.	Igbam-gbam
casualty department	Iyaka gbam-gbam, iyahan gbam-gbam
cat , n.	Muzuru, kyanwa, mage, kpasha-kpasha- , h/y.
it rained cats and dogs	O zo kpasha-kpasha
cat-fish , n.	Karaya, tarwada , h.
cataract , n.	Ketara , g.
catalogue	Lihoto , h, g.v..
catapult , n.	Basusa , h.
catarrh , n.	Ichin , g.
catastrophe , n.	Ijagbu, jagbu , y/i/ed.
catch , vti.	Jimu , g.
catechism , n, vt.	Katikizim , g.

90

category , n.	Itugbe, tugbe , y/I.
cater , vi.	Cheto , i/y.
cater for	Cheto fun
caterer	O cheto, ye cheto
catering rest house	Gida icheto ati isimini
caterpillar , n.	Katafila, katagada , h/g.
cathedral , n.	Bachochi , g.
catholic , adj.	Katoli, nke gbogbo akpor , g/i/y/ur.
cattle , n.	Shanu , h.
cattle rearer	O shanu
cauldron , n.	Baba tukunya , g/gen..
cauliflower , n.	Muwa kabeji , yh/ed/ur/iso/h.
caugh , n, vt.	Koho, ikoho , uvw.
cause , n.	Fata, irinshien , y/I.
my cause is just	Irinshien mi di gege
causeless , adj.	Aiwen irinshien, ai fata , y/i.
causeway , n.	Hanyar irinshien
caustic , adj.	Fesambi
caution , n.	Akiesi, notes, isoleji, soleji
caution him/her	Soleji ya
exercise caution	Wen isoleji
cautious , adj.	Soliki , , y/I, g.v..
calvacade , n.	O zoda , g.
cavalier , *n.	O doki, o hayi, ye hayi , y/i/h.
calvary , n.	Diga, kufi , h.
, cave in. , vti.	Yin si menu
cavern , n.	Yinmenu , y/I.
cavity , n.	Kogo , h.
caw , n.	Kukan hankaka , h.
cease , vti.	Dachen, dusi, jimu , y/I.
the rain has ceased	Ruwa ti dachen
cease fire agreement	Ikweba idachen ij'agha
ceiling , n.	Silin , h.
celebratge , vt, adj, n.	Iseliba, iselogbe
the oba is celebrating	Oba ng, seiba

celestial , adj.	Nke sele, selwe, iseleshe , g.
celestial church	Chochi nke selesha,
	h/i/g.
celibate , n.	O zuhudu y/h.
Cell, n	monsu, y/ed/ur/it/ti.
battery cell	Batiri monsu
lock him in the cell	Tikpo ya si monsu
cellar	Monsu izi , y/ed/ur/it/ti/gu.
cement , n.	Sumunti, siminti, laso , h.
cemetery , n.	Hurumi, makabarta , h.
cenotaph , n.	Zonene , g.
censer , n.	Kwanbela , nu/y.
censor , n.	Zove , g.
censure , vt.	Meshitan, meshiwi , i/ed/i/y.
census , n.	Ikami , y/ed/h.
cent , n.	Senti , g/f/e.
, per cent.	Na senti, na oveh
centenary , n.	Sentiri , g.
centennial , adj..	Nke sentiri
centigrade , adj..	Sentigad, zoveleh , g.
centime, , n.	Iyagogo Kudi Fransa, Zovini , y/g/h.
centipede , n.	Shanshani, Kunafula , h/fu.
central , adj..	Barin, Centra , gen/y.
, central nervous system.	Barin Jijiya , gen/h.
, central police station.	Barin Ofis Mondoka, Baran Tasha Mondoka
, central hotel.	Barin Huta
centralize , vti.	Meshe si barin, me di barin
centre , n.	Arin , gen/y.
, centre school.	Babarin makaranta
, examination centre.	Babarin ichondi mbi'chondi
, trade centre.	Babarin itakasuwa
centurion , n.	Balumona , y/I.
centrifugal , adj..	Santiuga , g.

century , n.	Adungogo, idungog
cerebra-spinal meningitis	Manomano dungogo , h, g.v. ceremonial , adj..
ceremony , n.	IgboanduIgbandu, anivaseh, serimona, konogbandu
certain , adj..	Dido , y/h.
, i am certain that.	Mo dido kpe
, it is certain.	O dido
certainly , adv..	Ididdo , y/h.
certainty , n.	Idido
certificate , n.	Tashaida, satifuket , g, h.t.
certify , vit.	Jeneri , y/I.
, i certify that.	Mo jereri kpe
, that is to c. that.	Eyi wu lati jenei kpe
cessation , n.	Idachiu, idachendu , y/g/I.
cesspit , nn.	Salaga, shadda , h/y.
cesspool , n.	Kotogbin , y, g.v.
chafe , vit.	Goga, guga , h.
chaff , n.	Kaikayi, buntu , h.
chain , n.	Sanka, che , h/g.
, saw-chain.	Zarto-chen
, chain mail. , n.	Sulke , h.
chair , n.	Kujera, jera , h, g.v.
, he took the chair.	O jondu si na kujera, o gbawe kujera
chairman , n.	Mijera, mijera, O jera
, chair lady.	Majera
, chair person.	Tumjera chalit, mondeki , g/y/ed/au/ur/is/it/h.
chalet , n.	Chalit
challenge , n.	Ikonoga , g/I.
chamber , n.	Iyefe, ikonojo, chemba , y/I.
, chamber of commerce.	Ikonojo kasuwa, kasuwa chemba chameleon , n.
champagne , n.	Champagene , g.
champion , n.	Zakara , h.
chance , n.	Nakomgba, Iyefe, Iyoge, , ag/fa.

, i met you by chance.	Mo mien e n'iyefe, mo hun e n'yefe chancellor , n.
, vice chancellor.	Era shujami'a era
change, , vti.	Loyi, sengi, chote, yintua, kansilo = reminder or surplus , h.
changer , n.	Fene sengi, o sengi , i/y/h.
, it is changeless.	Lai yintua
channel , n.	Chana; hanya, gudana , h/h/, g.v.
, nta channel 10.	, NTA chana 10.
chant , n.	Krumbu , y/I.
chaos , n.	Irugurugu , y/g.
chap , vti.	Monkrimbu , y/
chapel , n.	Chaple , g.
chaplain , n.	Shafien , g.
chapter , n.	Chafta, babi, suna, daftari , h.
chapters , n.	Echafta, ebabi, esura, edaftari , h/g/v.
char	Taba, fewuta , gen/i/h.
character , n.	Imiwa, kareta, ikarela , i/y.
, character training.	Ikozi miwa
characteristic , adj..	Femiwa, ikareta , i/y/g.
charcoal , n.	Gawayi , g.
charge , vt.	Gbowu, kasinwu, kasi , y/h.
, take charge.	Di kasinwu di kasi, kasi; jubi fun kudi
, charge the battery.	Gbowu batri
, charge him/her.	Kasinwu ya, kasi ya
charge , of money/cost.	Ofis ikasi
, charge office.	Ofis ikasinwu
chariot , n.	Shariat
charity , n.	Ichiwa, ichemi , i/y/h.
charm , n.	Ipiri , g.
, charm man.	Miji 'piri
, charm man	Miji 'piri
, snake charmer.	O piri machiji
chart , n.	Ikuata, kuata , g.
charter , n.	O kuata , y/g.

chase , vti.	Chowa , i/y.
, chase out/away.	Chowa 'ta
chasm , n.	Icheto , i/y.
chassis , n.	Gado, firem, kiasibi , h.
, chassis number.	
chaste , adj..	Shaka , g.
chasten , vt.	Noti, soli si, bionusi , y/I.
chastity , n.	Ishaka , g.
chat , n.	Ikoka , g/ik.
chattel , n.	Kaya , h.
chatter , vi.	Meshe arimkpo, arimkpo , i/y.
, chatter man.	Miji arimkpo
, chatter woman.	Mache arimkpo
chauffeur , n.	Chufa , g.
cheap , adj..	Flesi , i/y.
, c. article. , n.	Ife flesi
cheaply , adv..	Fleflesi , i/y.
cheapen , vt. , vi.	Me di flesi , i/y.
cheat , vit.	Tije , i/y.
, don't cheat.	Ma tije
check , vti.	Dache, wone , h/i/y.
cheekbone , n.	Kasu
cheek , n.	Kunchi
cheeky , adj..	Fido
cheer, cheers , vti.	Dunso, yanyah , y/I.
cheerful , adj..	Di, dunso, di yahyah , g/y/I.
cheerfulness , n.	Idunso, iyanyah , g/y/I.
cheerless, , adj..	Lai yahyah, ai yahyah, ai dunso
cheerio	Cheerio , g.
cheery , adj..	Jikia , h/y.
cheese , n.	Chuku , h.
cheetah , n.	Rabbni , h.
chemical , adj..	Kamika kamikal , i/y/g.
chemist , n.	Kamis, gimagani, kamis , h/g.
chemistry , n.	Ikamisri, igimagani, ikamis , h/g.

cheque , n.	Cheki, takadar kudi , h/f/e.
cherish , vt.	Chefe , i/y.
cherub, cherubim , n.	Kerubu, mala'ika , g/h/y.
, cherubim and seraphim.	Kerubu ati serafin
chest , n.	Kirji, baba akwati, aljihu , gen. V.
, c. of drawers. , n.	Ealjihu tebur
, c. of plate.	Kirji kwano/filanti
, c. bones.	Ekashi kirji
chevalier , n.	Shevala , g.
chew , vti.	Beje , i/y.
, chew it.	Beje ya
, chew the meat.	Beje nama
, chew-stick. , n.	Kpako
chick , n.	Monsako , also: chikite. , y/ed/ur/it/au/is/h.
chicken , n.	Kaji, , sikin. , h/g.
, c. hearted.	Aiwen 'yobi, osorachu , y/i/h.
chicken-pox	Karambau
chide, , vti.	Solisi , Y/g.v.
chief , n.	Monbaeze baba, sarki, shugaba, oleze , gen/h.
, chief of staff.	Baba kata
chief justice.	Baba izoka
chiefly , adv..	Bababa, ezumkpa , gen.h/I.
chieftain , n.	Ibaba, isarki, ishugaba , gen. /h, g.v..
child , n.	Omo, mon, omontakale , y/ed./au/is/so/ur.
childbirth , n0	Ibimu mon , y/ed/au/is/so/ur/I.
childhood , n.	Ngba omo , y/ed/au/is/so/ur/I.
, little child.	Omotakele , y/ed/au/is/so/ur/I.
childish , adj.	Di omontakili, bika omontakili
children , n.	Emontakili, yara, ya'ya , y/ed/au/is/ur/h.
childless , adj.	Laiwen omo,k aiwen omo , y/ed/au/is/isow/ur.
chill, chilly , n.	Itutu , y, g.v..
, i'm feeling chilly0	Mon gn tutu
chillies , n.	Barkono, tsiduhu
chime , n.	Serin , g.
chimney , n.	Chimini, filisin , g.

chimpanzee , n.	Biri, sirokazi , h/g.
chin , n.	Haba , h.
china , n.	Tangaram , h0
chink , n.	Amo , h.
chip, chips , n.	Bagura, bangare, bagure , h.
chirp , vt.	Kebe bika tsuntsu, pain , y/i/h/g.
chisel , n.	Chzo, kurfi, gizago , g/h.
hammer and chisel.	Masaba/hama ati chizo/kurfi
chit , n.	Takarda, wa sikere , h.
chivarlry , n.	Miwarama, igboya , i/y/h.
chiloroform , n.	Lambawan , h.
chocolate , n.	Chokalit , h.
choice , n.	Imayon; , y, g.v./g.
, the choice yours.	May wu nke yin: chois wu nke yin
choir , n.	Tarambu , y/h/I.
, choir master0	Magida tarambu, oga tarambu
choke , ti.	Shaka, kware, kwaru "choked up" , h.
cholera , n.	Kolera, kovra , g.
choleric , adj.	Ikovra , g.
choose	mayon; synonym: choisi , y/h/g/, fe..
chop , vti.	Jeta, jemu, wuam , y/i/ur/iso/gu.
chopper , n.	O jeta, ojemu, owuam, ake
, chop up/off.	Jeta ton, jemu ton, wuam ton
, chop–chop.	Jeta-jeta, jemu-jemu
choral , adj.	Tagburu, fifa , i/h.
chord , n.	Whuaya , g.
, spinal chord.	Whuaya kinien
chorus , n.	Fafa, ifafa , y/g.
chorister , n.	Mutarambu , h/y/I.
christen , vt.	Nnoafa, nn'afa. , ef/I.
christ , n.	Kristi, kraist , gu/gen.
christian , n.	Krista , gen.
christendom , n.	Gbohan Krista, Krista nile
christmas , n.	Kristmas , gen.
christianity , n.	Ikrista , gen/gu.

chronic , adj.	Kiene , g/ur.
, chronic decease.	Arun kiene
chronicle , n.	Kroniko , g.
chuckle , n.	Kioko muteji , g.
chum , n.	Abioki, , h/i/y.
chump , n.	Pium , g.
chunk , n.	Banta , h, g.v..
9a chunk of bread.,	Banta buredi
church , n.	Chochi, gida abasi tabi Chiolu , g/h/ef/y/I.
, the church.	Ne chochi
church warden 9n.	Mondoka chochi
church , n0	Koda, buga, caba, tugunya , h.
cigar , n.	Taba, siga , gen.
cinema	Sinima, sinimani , gen/g.
cinematograph	Fewonene , i/y0
cinnamon , n.	Kirfa , h.
chipher , n.	Seifa , g.
circa , lat.	Seika , g.
circle , n, vti .	Kawanya, yika, iyika, kiri, yikiri, yigha, yintua
, well learned circle.	Iyika imuko
circuit , n.	Seri , g.
circuitous	Di seri , i/g.
circular , adj.	Birikiti, iyigha , y/g/I.
, circular letter.	Wasika iyigha, birikiti
circulation	Iyigha, ibirikiti , i/y.
circulate , vt.	Yigha , i/y.
circumcise , vt.	Kola , y.
circumcision , n.	Ikola
circumlocution , n.	Isokolisa, isinolisi , g.
circumstance , n.	Ngba ifazi, , g/i/y.
circumspect , adj.	Soki , y/h, g.v..
circus , n.	Saikos , g.
circuit	Sakut , g.
circumstantial , adj.	Fazi , g.
cistern , n.	Tankwa , h, g.v..

98

citadel , n.	Sitadeli, rokwesa , g.
citron , n.	Saitron , g.
citizen , n.	Mongeri, mongari, mutum kasa, monkasa
, i am a citizen of nigeria.	Mi wu monkasa Naijiriya citrus , n.
, citrus fruits.	Yaya itache lemo
city , n.	Birni , h.
civet, civet cat , n.	Inyawara, tukun juda , h.
civic, civics , adj.	Fegeri, efegeri , i/h.
, civic duty.	Shobe geri , y/g/h.
civil , adj.	Sifoh finja , y.
, civil servant.	Bara finja; sifoh safante
, civil war.	Ijagha finja
, civil service.	sini finja
civilian , n.	Farula , h, g.v..
civilization , n.	Isivili, imuko, imosha, imoshaka
civilize , vt.	Sivili; muko, mosha, imoshaka , g.
clad	Suweh , g.
claim , vtn.	Yite, yihun, iyite, iyihun
claimant , n.	O yite, o yihun
claiming , n.	O yihun
clamour , n.	Arimkpo , iyihun.
clan , n.	Bila, danai , h, g.v..
clap , vti.	Kwa , i/h/y.
, clap your hands.	Kwaehan e
clapper , n.	O kwahan
clarify , vti.	Mediye , i/y.
clarion , n.	Fere , y.
clarity , n.	Idiye, imediye , i/y.
clash , vti.	Luji , y/h.
clasp , n.	Kama , h.
class , n.	Ktuegbe; aji , h, g.v..
class , of rank.	Tuegbe , i/ed/y.
classify , vt.	Totu: tuegbe , y, g.v..
, i'm not your class.	Mi o wu ituegbe e
clause , n.	Klaus, sofe , g.

claw , n.	Kambori, kumba, sosa, kaifa , h.
clay , n.	Yumbu , h.
clean , adj.	Shaka , y, g.v..
cleanliness , n.	Ishaka , y, g.v..
cleanly , adj.	N'ishaka
clear , adj.	Hone, diye, leta, ropu, yela , y/I.
, clear away from.	Kua sa, roputa
clearing , n.	Ikuaa
clearify , adv.	Didye, mediye, diye, yebi , i/y.
clearly , adv.	Shaka, n'shaka , y/I.
cleave , vti.	Lemonji , y.
clement , adj.	Benu , i/y.
clemency , n.	Ibenu , i/y.
clench , vt.	Dunkule , h.
clergy , n.	Likrista; klaji , h, g.v./g, fe..
, clergy man. , n.	Miji, likrista , h, g.v./g, fe..
clerical , adj.	Kawu , h, g.v..
, clerical officer.	Hafsa kawu
clerk , n.	Akawu, o gatarda , h/y.
, clerk of the house.	Akawu gida
, court clerk.	Akawu kotu
clever , adj.	Ilagbon
, clever boy.	Ilagbon yaro , h/y/I.
, clever girl.	Ilagbon yanrinya , ur/h/y/I.
cliff , n.	Boga , i/h.
client , n.	Biena , g.
climate , n.	Ikuepe , g.
climax , n.	Iguini , i/y.
climb , vti.	Gunyan , y/i.
, climb up.	Gunyan nuke, gunyan sama
, climb the wall.	Gunyan bango
climber , n.	O gunyan , y/I.
climbing , vt, n.	Gunyan, igunyan , y/I.
cling , vi.	Faji , y/h.
clinic	Klinike, asbitin , g/h.

, maternity clinic.	Kilinike asbitin; asbitin mata
clip , n.	Klif, katse, kili, kilifi , h/g, fe..
clique , n.	Ikotum , y/h.
cloak , n.	Boye , h.
, cloak room.	Daki boye , h.
clock , n.	Agogo , gen.
clod , n.	Hoge , h.
clog , n.	Monfai, toshe, imonfa , y/ed/ur/is/so/h.
close , adj.	Tikpo , y/I.
close , n.	, of roads. feru , h, g.v..
close , adj. , near.	Nure auch
clot , n.	Ikio, shogaga , g.
cloth , n.	Esa; , syn: atamfa , ogori/h.
clothes , n.	E'sa; , h/og.
clothing , njh.	E'sa; itamfa , h, g.v..
cloud , n.	Mare , h, g.v..
cloudy , adj.	Di mare , i/h, g.v..
clout , n.	Kisa , y.
clove , n.	Kanumfari , h.
clown , n.	Wawa , h.
club , n.	Ituge, klob, kulki, huta, tuegbe , h/g.
clubs , n.	Dusa, suffa, gbohan, bigbe , h/y/I.
, club house.	Gida klob
, club together.	Bigbe ju
cluck , vi.	Fakpa , g.
clue , n.	Amonhan, imonhan , y/I.
clumsy , adj.	Goru , y/g.
cluster , n.	Idi, didi , y, g.v..
clutch , n.	Monduma 9y/ed/rr/it/is/so/h.
coach , n.	Wagunu , h/g.
, railway coach.	Wagunu reliwe , h.
coach , training.	Iguko , i/y.
coagulate , vit.	Kiun , g.
coal , n.	Kwal, gawayi , h.
coal – tar , n.	Kwalta , h.

coalition , n.	Imekpo, imekono, ijambe , i/y/g.
coarse , adj.	Shakisha 9y, g.v..
coast , n.	Ngate 9g.
, ivory coast. , n.	Ngate haure; aiviri kos
coat , n.	Kwat, gashinba , g/h, g.v..
, coat of may colours.	Kwat o wen elauni
, coat of paint.	Fenti kwat
coax , vti.	Roforofo , y.
cob , n.	Toto, goyo, monsara , h/y/ed/ur/it. etc
, western cob.	Monraya
cobbler , n.	Baduku , h.
cobra , n.	Gamsheka, kumurchi , h.
cobweb , n.	Yana, sakar gizo , h.
cocain , n.	Kokuun , g.
cock , n.	Zakara , akuko. , h/i/ed.
cock-crow	Ikebe zakara , y/i/h.
cockerel , n.	Mon zakara , h/y/ed.ur/it.iso.
cockney , adj, n.	Dunke, idunke
cockpit , n.	Ramkera, h, g.v./g.
cockroach , n.	Kulekule, kyankyaso 9h.
cocoa , n.	Koko , h/gen.
coconut , n.	kube
coco-yam , n.	Koko-doya, koko-ya, koko-yaya , g.
code , n.	Kodi, ikojo, kojo, ilahan , y, g.v..
, code of conduct.	Imiwa ikojo
, code of conduct bureau.	Ofis miwa ikojo
coerce , vt.	Zati , g.
coffee , n.	Fili, kafi , g.
coffer , n.	Kwakudi , h/g.v.
coffin , n.	Ukpadidi , g/h/g.v.
cogent , adj..	Juido , y/h.
coil , vti.	Kajo , y.
, mosquito coil.	Kajo sauro , y/h.
coin , n.	Keredi , h/g.v.
cohabit , vt.	Jumohi, Jubigbe , y/I.

coincidence , vi.	Mede, koyisiden , n. , i/y.
coherence , n.	Imede, ijiemu , y/I.
, verbal c..	Imede fionu , y/I.
cola, kola , n.	Guoro, kola , h/gen..
cold , adj..	Tuoyi , y/I.
, uduak had a cold yesterday.	Uduak wen ituoyi colic , n.
collaborate , vi.	O'labo,m meshekojo, jumeshe , i/y.
collapse , vi.	Wosika , y/h.
cognizance , n.	Ikiesi, imoma , y/I.
collar , n.	Penzi , g.
, white collar job.	Aiki bature, aiki penzi
, dog collar.	Dakare , h/g.v.
, collar-bone.	Penzi-kashi
colleague , n.	Mboke , h/g.v.
collect , vti.	Kodo , i/y.
collect	Kodo , i/y.
collection , n.	Ikodo , i/y.
collector , n.	O kodo , i/y.
collective , adj..	Kr-kole , i/y.
college , n.	Kolej, manji , g/h/y.
collide , vi.	Koluji , y/h/.
collision , n.	Ikoluji , y/h.
colloquial , adj.	Loko , g.
, colloquial english.	Turanchi loko , loko turanchi. , h/g
colon , n.	Yame, iyame , y/g.v. colon , punctuation mark.
colonialist , n.	O kolo , i/g, v.
, colonial master.	Megida okolo
colony , n.	Ikolo
colonize , n.	Medi kolo
colossal , adj..	Tobu , y/I.
colour , n.	Launi , h.
, colour-blind. , n.	Launi makaho
, colour-bar. , n.	Sanda launi
colt , n.	Dukushi , h.
column , n.	Ginshiki , h.

comb , n.	Kom, monsarchi , h/y/ed./it/ur/is, etc..
, cook's comb.	Monsarchi kuko , y/y/i/ed./it/ur/is, etc..
combat , n.	Ija'gha whido-si-whidoIkakopumu
combatant , n.	Ikakpumu
single combat.	O kakpumu
coma , n.	Ikoma , g.
combination , n.	Ikukpo , y/g.v.
combine , n.	Meshekpo, jukpo , i/y, g.v.
combustible , adj..	Chau-chau , g.
come , vi.	Biawa , i/y.
, come in/into.	Biawa si 'me
, come back.	Yintua, dazu
coming	Ibiawa, kenbiawa, biawa, bibiawa
, i'm not coming.	Mii biawa
, i'm coming.	Mo ng biawa
, come here.	Bia mbi
, come back home.	Kpadazu si gida, yintua si gida
, come out.	Biaw' ita, bia ita, jaita
, we came to town.	Awa biawa si gari
, come forward.	Biawa si whido, biawa whido
, come across.	Biawa hun, bia kei
comedian , n.	O marshi, dawashi , y/h.
comedy , n.	Dawashi, marshi, , y/h.
comet *n.	Tawutsiya , h, g.v.
, harley's comet.	Tawutsiya harley
comfort , n.	Idunso, imela, meliji, soleji , y/h.
comfortbale , adj.	Mela, de mela, le mela , y/h/I.
comforter , n.	O mela , y/h.
comic , adj.	Eeh , g.
comma , n.	Dachen , y/I.
command , vti, n.	Meaashe, imeaashe, oka , i/y.
, i command you.	Mo meaashe yin
commandant , n.	Omeaashe, kwamandant , y/i/h.
commander , n.	Kwamanda, o meaashe
commander-in-chief	Baba kwamanda

commandment , n.	Imiwaashe
, commandments of god.	Imiwaashe Abasi
commemorate , vt.	Mecheron , i/y.
commemoration , n.	Imecheron , i/y.
commence , vti.	Rindo , I;/y.
, we shall commence.	Awa ga rindo
commend , vt.	Kiene , y/I.
comment , n.	Isoliye , ik/y.
commentary , n.	Isoliye , h, g.v..
commentator , n.	O soliye , y/h, g.v..
, commentary box.	Akwatin isoliye
commerce , n.	Ikasuwa , h, g.v..
commerciamml , adj. m	Di kasuwa, fe kasuwa, kasuwa , i/h.
, commercial house.	Gida 'kasuwa
commission , n.	Kwamishan, ijara , g/h.
commissioner , n.	Kwamishana, o jara , g/y/h.
, high commissioner.	Kwamishana Ga
commit , n, vt.	Fadon, fila, file, fadon , y/I.
committee , n.	Ikwamiti, ikonokojo , g/h/y, v...
commodity , n.	Ifiniki , i/h.
, scarce commodity.	Ifiniki chiri
commodore , n.	Kwamando, samalo , g.
common , adj.	Dile , i/y.
common , n.	Idile
, the house of commons.	Majalisa walea
, common sence.	Ichegbon lea
, the common people.	Talakawa lea, jama'a lea, jamale
, common prayer. mm	Ikpredu lea
commotion , n.	Iruguru
commonly , adv.	Lelea
commonwealth , n.	Lalea , y/I.
communal , adj.	Fe jama'a , i/h.
, c. labour.	Aiki fejama'a
communicate , vt.	Komunika, leasso, sole , komunica. , i/y.
communication , n.	Komunikashon, ileasso, isole , i/y.

communist , n.	Ikwaminis, okojo , g/y.
community , n.	Ijama'a , h, g.v..
communiqué , n.	Ikemkpo
commute , vt.	Mitin, Jikpo , h/y.
companion , n.	Osole, aboki , i/y/h.
compact , adj.	Lema , y/h.
company , n.	Kamfani, kungi, ikungi , g/h.
comparative , adj.	Fifeka, nke ifeka , y/I.
compare , vti.	Feka
comparison , n.	Ifeka, , y/I.
compass , n.	Kamfas , g.
compassion, compassionate , n, adj.	Meanu, imeanu , i/y.
compationately , adv.	Memeanu , i/y.
compel , vt.	Fashe , y, g.v..
compatible , adj.	Muso , i/y.
compensate , vti.	Tunme, pensointe , y/i/g.
compatriot , n.	Ikamfarat , g.
compensation , n.	Itunno , y/ef.
compete , vi.	Kambe , g.
competition , n.	Ikambe , g.
competence , n.	Ikamshe , g/i/y.
compile , vt.	Nojo , i/y.
complacent , adj.	Tewuyaya , y/h.
complain , vi.	Rahun, roka , y, g.v..
complainant , n.	O rahun, o roka , y, g.v..
complete , vt.	Duna, guton, zuton, , ed/i/y.
compliant 9adj.	Lefe , i/y/ed.
complex , n.	Isileka; idiga, ilega, kample, ifambu , i/y/g.
compliment , vt.	Kiene , y/I.
comply , vi.	Tekei, teisi, t'isi , y/h.
, comply with.	Tekei si, teisi kpe , y/h._
compose , vti.	Mejo
composer , n.	O mejo, imejo , i/y.
composition , n.	Imejo , i/y.
compound , vt.	Kpar , mixed up.

compound , n.	Hada, gauraya, yadi, dunso , h/y/I.
comprehend , vt.	Meze, diye , i/y.
comprehensible , adj.	Di meze, di diye , i/y.
comprehension, comprehensive , n.	Imeze, idiye, komprihensa
compress , vt.	Nnokpo , ef/y.
compressor , n.	Innokpo, kampresah , ef/y.
comprise , vt.	Kama , y/I.
compromise	Ikweba, ilagha, , i/y.
compulsion , n.	Idukwa , g.
compulsory , adj.	Dukwa , g.
compute , vti.	Kaba , y/ef.
computer , n.	Fekaba, o kaba , y/ed.
, computer machine.	Injin kaba
comrade , n.	Ifide, o finde , g , kamarada.
comradeship , n.	Ikamarada , g.
concave , adj.	Ganta , h, g.v..
con , vt.	Maro , i/y.
conceal , vt.	Zumo , i/y.
concede , vt.	Jeyen , y/I.
conceit , n.	Siem , g.
conceive , vti.	Dichi , i/h.
concentrate , vti.	Fiobi, fibisi , y/I.
concept , n.	Ichero , i/y.
conception , n.	Idichi , i/y.
concern , vt.	Konle , y/I.
concerning, prep.	Mani, konle , y/I.
concert , n.	Semba , g.
concession , n.	Ijaka , y/I.
conciliate , vt.	Tuido , y/h.
concise , adj.	Keru , i/y.
conclude , vti.	Mketon, cheton , i/y.
conclusion	Icheton, imeton , i/y.
concoct , vt.	Dite , y.
concoction , n.	Idite , y.
concord , n.	Konkad, isonda, , y/h/g.

concordance , n.	Lisonda , h/y.
concrete , adj.	Dindi , y/h.
concubine , n.	Sadaka, kwarkwara , h.
conclusion , n.	Imesheton, igwuton , i/y.
concur , vi.	Kweba, johan , i/y/h.
condemn , vt.	Juku, mebi , g/i/y.
condemnation , n.	Ijuku, imebi , g/i/y.
condense , vt.	Bete , g.
condescend , vi, n.	Reki , y/h.
condition , n.	Iwahe, ikpongba, meshe, , y/I.
	condole, condolence , vi, n.
, letter of condolence.	Wasia kondula, wasika itunime
conduct , vt.	Mekoso, bugbe , i/y.
, be of good conduct.	Di 'muwa rama
conduct , vt.	Mekoso, bugbe , i/y.
conductor , n.	O mekoso, koidotto, o muwa
confederacy , n.	Itarayya , h.
confection , n.	Ididin, didin , y, g.v..
connubial , adj.	Fure , i/h.
conquer , vt.	Bokei , y/h.
conqueror , n.	O bokei , y/h.
conquest , n.	Iibokei , y/h.
conscience , n.	Iribite , y/i.
conscious , adj.	Ribite, mima , y/I.
consecrate , vtn.	Simo , i/y.
conscription , vt.	Siri , g.
consecutive , adj.	Ke jisi , y, g.v..
consecutively , adv.	Keke jisi , y, g.v..
consent , vi.	Jeka , y/i.
consequence , n.	Ngbazu, izuba , y/i.
conservation , n.	Iyewa , h.
conservative , adj.	Yewa, itugbe , h, g..
, conservative party.	Itugbe 'riya
consider , vt, n.	Tunche, itunche, , iloro. , y/i.
considerable , adj.	Tunche, chenedi , y/i.

consideration , adj.	Itunchero, ichenedi , y/i.
consign , vt, n.	Filehan, kaya, ifilehan, ikaya , y/h.
consist , i.	Weni, wendi, jukun , i/y.
console , n.	Tiunmenu, itiunmenu , y/I.
consolation , n.	Itiunmenu , y/i.
consign , vt, n.	Filehan, kaya, ifilehan, ikaya , y/h.
consist , vi.	Weni, wendi, jukun , i/y.
console , n.	Tiunmenu, itiunmenu , y/i.
consolation , n.	Itiunmenu , y/i.
consolator , n.	O tiunmenu , y/i.
consolidate , vti.	Sokeh , y/h.
consonant , n.	Kansunat, baki , g/h.
conspicuous , adj.	Yokei , y/h.
conspiracy, conspire	Joneri, jomeshe , y/h.
conspiration , n.	Ijoneri, ijomeshe , y/i.
conspirator , n.	O jeneri, o jomeshe , y/i.
constable , n.	Kanstebu, mondokasi , g/y/ed./ur/iso/h.
conspire , vt.	Jome, joneri , y/i.
constant , adj, adv.	Kamu, kamu-kamu, shim, , h, g.v..
constipate , vt.	Wuru , g.
constipation , n.	Iwuru , g.
constituency , n.	Gurbi, igurbi , h0
constitute , vt.	Daki , y/h.
constitution , n.	Idaki , y/h.
construct , vt.	Kome, konstrokte , y/i/g, fe..
construction , n.	Ikome , y/i/g, fe..
construvtive , n, vt.	Ikome, kome
construe , vbi.	Landi , y/h.
consul , n.	Wakili , h.
consult , vti.	Bache, jube , y/i.
consultant , n.	Ibache, ijube, o jube , y/i.
consultation , n.	Ibache, ijube , y/i.
consume , vti.	Wuaton; chokulet , g/y.
consumption , n.	Iwuamton , iwuaton.
consumer , n.	O wuam, o wuamton , o wuam, o wuaton.

contact , n.	Ijikon, jikon
, please c. me.	Biko, jikon mi
contagious , adj.	Junso , h/y.
contain, content , vt.	Wesi , i/y.
contaminate , vt, n.	Meru, imeru , i/y.
contemplate , vt.	Meba, sharo , i/y.
contemplation , n.	Imeba, isharo , i/y.
contemporary , adj.	Tulegbe , h/y/ed.
contempt , n.	Igotin, ifindo , y/ed.
, c. of the court.	Igotin kotu, ifindo kotu
contemptuous , adj.	Kika , y/I.
contend , vti.	Jagha, tewuya , y/h/i.
contended , adv.	Tetewuya , y/h.
content, contain , n.	Iwesi, konteh , i/y.
, liquid content.	Likua konteh
contest , vti.	Jaghu, jaghuru , y/g.
contestant , n.	O jaghu, o jaghuru , y/g.
context , n.	Ipuesi , g/i/y.
continent , n.	Ikpornina, akpornina, kantinent , g/i/y.
, there are 5 c.	Ikpornina isen wa
continual , adj, adv.	Shim, shim-shim, shiene , g/y.
continuation , n.	Ishim, ishim-shim, isheiene , g/y.
continue, continuously	Rinshien, shim, shiene; kontinua , g/y/i/g/lat.
, continue going.	Shiene shienga
, go on.	Shienega
contraband	Kagbi , g/h.
, contraband goods.	Kaya kagbi
contraceptive , n.	Iduza , ed, g.v..
contract , vti.	Kentrat, kwede, agrimento , g/i/ed/y.
contractor , n0	Kentrato, o kwede, ikwede , g/i/ed/y.
contradict , vt.	Jika, choto , y/h.
contrary , adj.	Choto , i/y.
, c. to my expectation.	Choto si 'rekon mi
contrast , vti0	Cheya
contraven , vt.	Soize , g/y/ed.

contribute , vti.	Dayen, danno , y/i/ef.
contribution , n.	Idayen, idanno , y/i/ef.
contributor , n.	O dayen, o danno , y/i/ef.
contrition , n.	Ilila , g/ed.
contrivance , n.	Iero , y, g.v..
contrive , vti.	Mesheero , i/y, g.v..
controversy , n.	Inka, iroka , ag.
controversial , adj.	Nka, roka , ag.
control , n.	Ikoso, kentrol , y, g.v..
control , vti.	Koso , y, g.v..
controller , n.	O koso, ikoso, o kentrola , y, g.v..
convalescence , n, adj.	Ibarun, barun , y.
conversation , n.	Ikaso , ik/y/I.
conundrum	Alo , h.
convert , vt.	Tuasi , i/y.
conversion , n.	Ituasi , i/y.
convene , vt.	Meko, , i/y.
convenient , adj.	Rowuya, rowu , y/h.
convex , adj.	Fashe
convenient , n, adj.	Nfa, infa , y/h/g.v.
convey , vt.	Bushien , i/y.
conveyer , n.	O bushien, o bugbe
conventional , adj.	Sha , y.
conveyance , n.	Ibushien, ibugbe , i/y.
converge , vti.	Konokei , g/h.
convict , n.	Iloka , y/ik.
conviction , n.	Iloka, inikon , y/ik/ef.
convince , vti.	Nikon, soken, sokene , y/ef/ed.
convocation , n.	Ikonojo , g/y.
convolvulus , n.	Yaryadi , h.
convoy , n.	Isoletu, o soletu , i/y/h.
convulsion , n.	Selele , gu.
cook , vti.	Sie , y/I.
cook , n.	O sie , h/y/I.
cooker , n.	Kuka , gu.

cookery , n.	Isie , y/i.
cool, , adj.	Kule, tutu , gen/y.
, cool down, my friend.	Kuloe kasa, aboki
coop , n.	Akurki, karaga , h.
cooper , n.	Kangba , y/i.
co-operate , n.	Ikonomem , g/y/I.
co-operative , adj.	Konomeshe , g/y/I.
, co-operative bank.	Banki 'Konomeshi
, co-operative society.	Jam'iyya/tuegbe ikonome
co-partner , n.	Tumji , h/y.
cope , vi.	Bome , y/I.
copious , adj.	Kpo , y, g.v..
copper , n.	Kobo, tagulla, jan karfe , gen./h.
coppersmith , n.	O kobo, o tagulla , gen./h.
coppice , n.	Toho, dahuwa, kurmi , h.
copulate , vi	Sida , y/h.
copy , n.	Ineko, neko, kapi , i/y/g, fe..
, photo-copy.	Ineko hoto, , hoto-kapi.
copy-cat , n.	O neko-iwin , i/y.
copyright , n.	Aasheneko , y/i/ed.
coral , n.	Mujani , h.
coral beeds , n.	Juvuh mujani , g/h.
cord , n.	Igiya, kirtanio, mazagi, zarigya, yadi , h.
cordial , adj.	Zioka, rama , i/ik.
, cordial relations.	Iyore rama, iyore zioka
, be cordial.	Di rama, di zioka
core , n.	Kututu, tsakiya , h.
cork , n.	Mtikpo,l rufe , y/i/h.
corn , n.	Gero, hatsi, dawa, masara, alkama , h.
corkscrew , n.	Mtikpo , i/y.
, corn-stalk. , n.	Kara , h.
corner , n.	Kwana, kusurwa, lungu , h.
, corner-rest hotel.	Huta isimini kwana
, corner-stone.	Dutse kwana
coronation , n.	Imebaeze , i/y.

coronet , n.	Mokambi, monkambi , y/ed/ur/is/so/h.
corporal , n.	Kopul, inuti , g/i/y.
, corporal punishment.	Iriya nuti, iriya , y/I.
corporation , n.	Jalisar, hukuma, kamfani , h, g.v./h.
corps , n.	Eso ja , g/gen.
corpse , n.	Gawa , h.
corpulent , adj.	Isonji , h, g.v..
corral , n.	Shinge , h.
correct , adj.	Keree, saun, kamkpe, sam , ij/gen.
correctly , adv.	Kekeree, saun-saun , ij/gen.
correction , n.	Ikeree, isaun, ikamkpe , ij/gen.
correspond , vi.	Kode, feza, waika , i/y/h.
correspondence , n.	Iwakili, ikode, ifeza ikode , h/y/i.
correspondent , n.	Iwakili, wakili
corrigibe , adj.	Wanya , i/y.
corridor , n.	Swesi, iswesi , g.
, corridor of power.	Iswesi agba , g/y, g.v..
corroborate , vt.	Kamufa , g/y, h.t..
corrode , vti.	Dogun , y.
corrugate , vt.	Ka,
corrugagted iron, , n.	Ayan ka, kwano rufi , h/gw/nup.
corrugation , n.	Ika, gargada , y/h.
corrupt , vt.	Meje bele , i/y.
corruption , n.	Jibiti, imeje, ibele; biri-biri , i/y.
cosmetic , n.	Sosorobia , gen.
cosmopolitan , adj.	Laitan, mepolitan, sailobonga , y/g.
cost , vi.	Pia, pia, loi , ag/y, g.v..
, how much.	Eloi? Pi'elo?, Pie nua?
, at all costs.	Na rianya ncha
costly , adv.	Pipia, pipia , ag, g.v..
costume , n.	Tufani, kasium , h/g.
cosy , adj.	Gbanyar , y/h/I.
cot , n.	Garirir , h, g.v..
cottage , n.	Ella , g.
cotton , n.	Zaree, auduga , h.

, c. – seed.	Angurya , h.
, c – wool.	Zare wulu, auduga wulu
couch , vt, vi.	Gboga , y/h.
cough , vit.	Koho , uvw.
, whooping cough.	Kpuhu-kpuhu , g.
could, , anon fin.	Le , y.
council , n.	Jalisa , h, g.v..
councillor , n.	O jalisa, mukarabi, kansila; , h, g.v..
counsel , n.	Lula , h/i.
, crown counsel.	Lula baeze
count , vt.	Go , ag.
counter , n.	O go, igo, kanta , ag.
, count your blessings.	Go ikunzi e
countenance , n.	Ikwonu , ed/i/y.
counter sign , vt.	Ba sen, ju sen , y/ef/I.
counteract , vt.	Dihan, meje , y/h/i.
counterfeit , n, adj.	Adigboloja , gen.
, c. coins./money	Kudi adigboloja
counterfoil , n.	Dungu
counterpart , n.	Nkeji , i/y.
countless , adj.	Lai go , y/ag.
country , n.	Kasa, kauye, karkara, kara, , obodo. , h/i.
country man , n.	Bakauye, miji kauye, miji obodo, miji kasa
, fellow c. men.	Emutum kasa, jam'ar
county , n.	Kanti, lardi, ingila , g/h.
coup d'etat	Zaikpokpo
couple , n.	Gudeji, , h/y.
, married couple.	Mata'ti miji
courage , n.	Gudeji; , h/y.
courageous , adj.	Gboaya, di gboaya , y/I.
courier , n.	Ijozi, kuya , y/i.
course , vti, n.	Sambe, isambe, imuko , g/i/y.
, in due course.	N'ai faogolo sambe, n'isambe baya
, of course.	Na sambe, sambe
court , n.	Fada, kotu, gishari'a , h/h, g.v..

114

courteous , adj.	Mere , y/i.
couretesy , n.	Imere , y/i.
, courtesy call.	Ikono mere, ikeki sambe, ikono-kene
courtier , n.	Bafrade , h.
covenant , n.	Ikwade , i/y.
cousin , n.	Muwane , y/ed/ur/is/so/is/i.
cover , vt.	Bodo, tikpo, fala , y/I.
cover , n.	Ibodo, monkei, o tikpo, , y/i.
, cover cloth.	Esa bodo , og/y/I.
, cover note.	Aashe bodo, lasin
covet , vt.	Doro , y/h.
cow , n.	Malu , gen.
, bush-cow.	Bauna , h.
, cowboy.	Kaoboi , g.
coward , n.	Matsorachi, mumu , h/gen.
cowardice , n.	Imumu, imatsorachi, iraki
cowpeas	Kanana-kanana, saniya , h.
cowry, cowrie , n.	Wuri , h.
cowherd , n.	Olusho malu , y/gen.
crab , n.	Kaguwa , h.
crack , n.	Fashe, tsaga, tsage , h.
crack , vt.	Yajeh , y/i.
cradle , n.	Ijarido, ibredo , h/i/y.
, cradle of civilization.	Ijarido imuko
craftr , n.	Iyawa, wayo-wayo, fasaha, aiki
, handicraft. , n.	Aiki han , h, g.v..
crafty , adj.	Wayo-wayo , gen.
craftman , n.	Mijiyawa , h._
cram , vti.	Jenki , y, g.v..
cramp , n.	Fanji , y/h.
crane , n.	Gara, baba injin, kren , h, g.v./g.
crankshaft , n.	Kranshaf , g/h.
crape , n.	Tufele , g.
crash , vti.	Hari, gbam , y, g.v..
, plain crash.	Ihari flen/ugbofeh

crate , n.	Kalaba 9h, g.v..
crave , vt.	Chekpo , i/y.
, i crave your attention.	Mo chekpo feza e
craw-craw , n.	Karambau, kazuwa , h.
crawl , vi.	Ringakene, ringatufien, rintufien
crayon , n.	Fensa launi, fensa, kriyon
crazy , adj.	Feweh, imejekei, imejeisi , g/i/y/h.
cream , n.	Farari , h.
creamy , adj.	Farari , h.
crease , n.	Kari, karbu , h.
create , vt.	Meda, dasikasa, , y/i/h.
creation , n.	Imeda, idame, idasikasa , y/i/h.
creator , n.	O meda, o dasikasa , y/i/h.
creature , n.	Imeda , y/i/h.
credentials , n.	Tashida, satifiket, esatifiket
credible , adj.	Mekon , i/ef.
credit , n.	Ilewin, mere, imere , kredita. , also: kreda.
creditable , adj.	Lewin, nkeale kredita , y, g.v..
creditor , n.	Ilewin, o lewin, o mere, o kredita
creed , n.	Ijenini , y/ef.
creek , n.	Monkoh , y/ed/iso/ur/is/h.
creep , n.	Kosole , y/i.
creeper , n.	O kosole , y/i.
creeping , n.	Ikosole , y/i.
crescent , n.	Krisant, krisante , gfe.
cress , n.	Lafsur , h.
crest , n.	Tukku, tuntu, kantudu , h.
crevice , n.	Lila
crew , crow.	Kukuuh , g.
crew , n.	Itutum, kriu , i/h/g.
crib , n.	Yake , h.
cricket , n.	Gyare, tsanya, kurket, krikat , h.
crier , n.	Ikebe , y/i.
, town crier.	O kebe gari
crime , n.	Imika, imeshika , y/I.

criminate , vt.	Dambi , y, g.v..
criminal , adj.	Mugu, omika
crimination , n.	Idambi
criminology , n.	Imukodambi , i/y/g.
crimson , adj.	Jabeki , h, g.v..
cringe , vi.	Tisiba , y/I.
cripple , n.	Kimosa, kimo, ikimo , y/h.
crisis , n.	Nsohala, ijagbali, , y/I, g.v..
criterion , n.	Ifinaashe
critic , n.	Imoma, o moma , y/i.
critical , adj.	Gbuga , y/i.
criticize , n, vti.	Ichegbe, chegbe, imoma , i/y.
croackery , n.	Tasa, tangaram , h.
crocodile , n.	Kada , h0
, crocodile tears.	Ikebe kada, ikebe siro
crook , n.	Barawo , h.
crooked , adj.	Di barawo, barawo, mekoro , h/i/y.
cross , vt.	Soga, jafe , y/i/h.
crop , n.	Baroro e'nenen, birds , h.
cross , n.	Ketare , h.
cross , n.	Giciya, isoga , h/i/h/y.
, level crossing.	Gilma, igilma, isoga-kwa , h/i/y/enu.
, cross-country.	Ketare kasa , iroso kasa.
, cross-rods.	Mararraba , h.
, cross-examine.	Neri rama
cross word , n.	Ibionu, okahala, kahala , y/i/ik/gen.
crouch , vi.	Teba , y/h.
croup , n.	Efu , y.
crow , vi.	Kokorooko , g.
crowbar , n.	Kwalba, dagi, dugurusu8 , h.
crowd , n.	Taromuta, taromu , h, g.v..
crowing , n.	Ikokorooko , g. crown , n.
crown , vi.	Me kende , h/i/y.
crownbird , n.	Gauraka , h.
crude , adj.	Danye, likpon , h/y/g.

, crude oil. , n.	Ilikpon man
crucify , vt, n.	Kama, ikama , g.
cruel , adj.	Jika , i/y.
cruelty , n.	Ijika , i/y.
cruise , vt.	Lofeh , g.
cruiser , n.	Ilofeh, o lofeh , g., g.
crumble , vti.	Meru, meje, fosintintin , i/y.
crumbs , n.	Marmashi, barbashi, itintin , h/y/i/ed.
crumple , vti.	Chude, yamutsa , h, g.v..
crusade , n.	Krusada, krusad, ikrusad, ikempko , g/y/I.
cruse , n.	Kolobo
crush , vti.	Tegbu
crust , n.	Bawon, buredi tintin , h/gen./y/ed.
crusty , adj.	Buredi tintin, di tintin
crutch , n.	Sanda, hantsa , h.
cry , vit.	Kebe, libo; kemkpo , y/I, agbo..
crystal , n.	Farifa , h, g.v..
cub , n.	Muan , y/ed/ur/it/is/au/I.
cubit , n.	Firi , g.
culture.	Ifekasa wa, imisawa
culvert , n.	Kwalbati , h.
cumbersome , n.	Iyolionu, idihanyar , y/e/ed./h.
cummerbund , n.	Damara , h. cumulate , vt, n.
cunning , adj.	Meke, wayo, siro , i/y/gen.
cup , n.	Kwaf, finjali, kwafu , h. ,
cup of water.	Kwaf, ruwa , please give me a cup of water.
cupbearer , n. Biko nno mi kwafu ruwa	Zaba, chira , g.
cupboard , n.	Ikabad, kabit , h.
cupidity , n.	Idokoro , h/y.
cur , n.	Kare, kare buru , h/y.
curb , n.	Linzami , h.
curdle , vit.	Di , y.
cure , n, adj.	Meson, imeson , i/y
curative , adj.	Le meson , i/y.

curiosity , n.	Iyalicha , y/I. curiously , adj. Yalicha
curiously , adv.	, di yalicha. curl, curled
curled.	Mesa ti rodo curly , n.
currant , n.	Busasshen inabi,ula , h/g.
currency , n.	Kabodais, kudi, agba, karent; , g.
current , adj.	Ngba, ngba nsyi , i/y. currier , n.
curtain , n.	Labule, zane , h. , curtain raiser.
curve , n.	Kuru, baude, yin , y/h/g.
cushion , n.	Kushin, fukufuku , g.
custard , n.	Kastad , g., custard apple. Bizame kastad , h/g.
custody , n.	Ibibo , y/h.
custome , n0	Iwakasa, imiwakasa, iwaka , i/y/h.
customes officer customer , n. customary , adj.	, iwaka, hafsa. O rata, o gora Bietu , y/i.
customarily , adv.	Bibietu, bietutu , y/i.
cut , vti.	Gecha , y/i.
, cut it off.	Gecha pu
, cut the tree.	Be n'itache, be itache Be nama
, cut the meat.	Hanyar kuru, ibekuru
, short cut. cute , adj.	O wayo, wayo , gen.
cutlass , n.	Adda, ada , h/y.
cutter , n.	O gbede , y, g.v..
cycle , n. ,	Basiko, iyintua, kiri , h/g.
cycle round.	Yintua
cyclist , n.	O yanwa basiko , i/y/h.
cymbal , n.	Simba, kerohamba , g.
cycloneb cylinder , n.	Eziza , ishan/ed.
cynic , n.	Selinda, tukunjin , g/h, g.v..
	Ijikane, o nerijika, nerijika , i/y. Mon
	birni London, kakni h/y/ed/ur

D

d	di	Gen.
dab, n.	taba kpanshakpa	H
dabble, vt.i daft, adj. dagger, n.	tababbe, taba gwada	G(Y.t)
daily, adj., adv. dainty, adj.	rana-rana, rana'na	H
dairy, n,vti dale, n. dais, n.	daji	H/Y
	mansha, imansha afo	H(G.) Y/H
	monkali, tukuba	H(G)
		Y
		Y/Ed/Ur/Iso/It/H
dally, vti dam, n. damage,	mire datsiya, dem bamba, ibamba	H
n, vti. damask, n.	damas, kukumadi datsiya, dem	H Y/I
dam dame, n. damn, vt	mache, monde ntoo, huku,	H
damnation, n. damsel, n.	hukunba ihuku, into wundia ikuku	H
damp, adj., vti dance, vti	lekwa, lekwa-lekwa, lekwa-kwa	H/Y I/H
		H/I
		H/Y
		Y
		G
dancer, n.	ilekwa, ilekwa-lekwa, ilekwakwa, nye lekwa-kwa	G/I
dandle, vt. dandruff, n.	emoh, wimi yamosaka	G
.danger, n. dangerous,	idanja, danja di danja imiho,	H(G.t)
adj. .dandy, n dangle, vito	miho gbagan-gbagan meyiki,	H
dapper, adj. dare, pt.	meafinj dasha, gboaya	Bi/G
(you dare not do it)	e ma dasha mee (ma dasha)	G
		I/H/Y Y
		Y
daring, n.	igboaya, idasha iduji, duji	
dark, n., adj.,	bia swen duji iduji yi ntua	
(come before d.)		H/Y/I
darkness dam, vtl.		I/H/Y/I
		H/Y/I Y/H
dart, vti dash, vti (i d.	kasi	Y(G.t)
you) dastard, n.	fole (jump) yenno mo	Y/I/Efik
	yenno e imojo	I/Y

120

dark	Kputu
date , n.	Irana , h, g.v..
date , vti.	Rana , h.
, date of birth.	Rana ibi
daub , vti.	Fe , y.
daughter , n.	Monche , y/ed/sob/is/ur/is/au/h.
, daughter-in-law.	Monche-kuwa, , matada. , y/ed/sob/is/ur/is/au/h.
daunt , vti.	Foya, ruba , y, g.v..
dauntless , adj.	Ai foya, lai ruba , y, g.v
dawle , vit.	Sake , h.
day , n.	Rana , h.
, day time.	Ngba lana , i/y/h.
, day break .	Imon rana
, the day has break.	Rana ti mon
, day light.	Imon kasa//imon rana
daystar , n.	Tauro rana , h.
dazed , vt.	Lamu , g.
, completely dazed.	Lamu gbam-gbam
dazzle , vt.	Kashido , h, g.v..
d-day , n.	Baba-rana, Ne rana
dead , n.	Kutu, kuowun, ikuowun , h/y/i.
, dead body.	O kutu,
deadly , adj.	Kutu kha, le kuowun , h/y/i.
deacon , n.	Daikon , g.
deaconess , n.	Daikin , g.
deaf , n.	Ikitikoi, kitikoi , y/ed/h.
deal , n.	Renka, irenka , g.
, deal with.	Irenka kpelu , irenka kpe.
dealer , n.	O renka, omaye , g/ig/id.
dealings , n.	Irenka
dean , n.	Makambo , g.
dear , adj.	Ninda , ed.
, my dear.	Ninda mi

dear , costly.	Wonga, wonu , y/I.
dearth , n.	Oda , y.
death , n.	Imutuwa, ikuowun
death-bed , n.	Gado ikuowun , h/y/i.
debase , vt.	Medibu, dibu , i/y.
death-rate , adj.	Idiye-ikuowun
death-like , adj.	Bika-ikuowun , i/y.
death warrant , n.	Inindo-ikuowun , h/i/y.
debate , n.	Isharoka , i/y/ik.
debentrue , n.	Taigwo , h/ag/i.
debit , n.	Shali , g.
debility , n.	Imukumuje , y/g.
debt , n.	Igwese , ag/i.
debris , n.	Ikpanti , y/ag/i.
debtor , n.	O gwese , y/ag/I.
debunk , vt.	Bonke , g.
decade , n.	Adungo , y/i/h.
decamp , vi, n.	Mebudo, imebudo, , mebu. , i/h.
decapitate , vt.	Dumbulu , h/g.
decay , vi.	Dije , i/y.
decease , n.	Iwukutu, wuku , i/y/h.
deceit , n.	Iwayo, ikoje , gen/i/y.
deceive , vt.	Wayo, koje , gen/i/y.
deceiver , n.	O koje , y/I.
decency , n.	Ifindo, ifinde , y/i/h.
december , n.	Disemba, uki goma , g/ed/h.
decent , adj.	Findo, finde , y/i/hy.
deception , n.	Ijimu, ikoje , h/y/I.
decern , vti.	Yondo , y/h.
decide , vti.	Cheri , y/I.
deciduous , adj.	Chululu , g.
decimal , adj.	Dasima, dasi. , g.
decipher , vt.	Michoto , i/y.
decision , n.	Icheri , y/i.
deck , n.	Kpede kede , g.

decisive , adj.	Cheri , y/I.
declare , vti.	ikede
declaration , n.	Ikede , g.
decline , vti	Fazu, minku , i/y.
declutch , vi.	Me ku kulochi, gbukulochi
decompose , vti.	Dijewe , i/y.
decorate , vt.	Mosho , i/y.
decoration , n.	Imosho , i/y.
decrease , vti.	Minkuru, dikuru , i/y.
decree , n.	Imeasashe, dikiri , i/y/g.
decrepit , adj.	Gbola , y/i.
dedicate , vt.	Juba; dimor, , i/y.
dedication , n.	Ijuba; idimoh , i/y.
deduce , vt.	Faja , y, g.v..
deed , n.	Didi, also , aashe. , i/y.
deem , vt.	Loka , i/y.
deep , adj.	Jinka , y/h.
deepen , vti.	Jinkala , y/h.
deer , n.	Ogolo , g.
defame , vt.	Mekuloka; mekuloki , i/y/g.
default , n.	Mekuku , i/y.
defaulter , n.	O mekuku , y/i/y.
defeat , vt.	Megien , y/i/y.
defect , n.	Imekumeje , imekume. , y/i/y.
defective , adj.	Mekume, meje , y/i/y.
defence , adj.	Chebo, mekusa , i/y.
, ministry of defence.	Mini
defend , vt.	Kusa; difens , i/y.
defendant , n.	O mekusa , i/y.
defer , vi.	Buswido , buswi. i/y/h.
deference , n.	Ibuswido
defiance , n.	Ifoleh , y, g.v. deficiency/deficient, adj.
defile , vt.	Medigbi mekugbi, megbi , i/y.
define , adj.	Tuma , y/g/I.
definite , adj.	Dido , y/h.

deflate vt.	Mekufeh y/i/h.
deform , vt|.	Mukulele, kulele , y/i/y.
deformity , n.	Imekulele , y/i/y.
defraud , vt.	Mekuwuam, mekuleton , y/i/y.
defray , vt.	Songwo , y/ag/I.
defy , vt|.	Doka , y/I.
defunct , adj.	Kuchen, kuchene , y/I.
degenerate , vt.	Mekuzu , y/I.
degrade , vt.	Mekuka , Y/i/h.
degree , n.	Mekuye, digiri , i/y/g.
, by degree.	N'imekuye
, low degree.	Mekuye fiene
deign , vit.	Mereka , i/y.
deity , n.	Imiwachi, imiwa'basi , i/y/ef.
deject , vt.	Mekumenu , i/y/ef.
dejection , n.	Imekumenu , i/y/ef.
delay , vti.	Dachiu, mukuba, kuba , i/y/ed.//h.
deleb-palm	Gingiya , h.
delectable , adj.	Mekayo, dirama , i/y.
delegate , vt.	Mekauko , mekuko. , i/y/ed.
delegate , n.	O mekuko , i/y/ed.
delegation , n.	Imekuko , i/y/ed.
government delegate	O mekuko gomnanti
deliberate , adj.	Mekachero, mekache, mechero , i/y.
deliberation , n.	Imekachero, imekache, imecher, i/y.
delete , vt.	Mekareh , i/y.
deletion , n.	Imekareh , i/y.
delicate , n, adj.	Kanka, ikanka , i/y/h.
delicious , adj.	Mekadun, kadun. , i/y.
delight , n.	Mekayoli, mekadun , i/y.
delinquency , n.	Imekalika, imelika , i/y.
delight , n.	Mekayoli, mekadun , i/y.
delinquency , n.	Imekalika, imelika , i/y.
delirious , adj.	Mekasi , i/y/g.
delirium , n.	Imekasi , i//g.

124

deliver, delivered , vt.	Mekajo, ronhan, kajo , yopu.
delivery , n.	Imekajo, iron han , y/I.
deliverer , n.	O mekajo, o ronhan
delta , n.	Songi , g/hg.
delude , vt.	Kagu , i/y.
deluge , n.	Mekaza , i/y.
delusioni , n.	Imekaje , i/y.
demand , vt.	Jubi , i/y.
decocracy , n.	Demokrasi
democrat , adj.	Demokrata , i/y.
democratic , asdj.	Demokrata, democrat , i/y.
demeanour , n.	Ikoda , i/y/g.
demolish , vt.	Korun , i/y/g.
demon , n.	Ibilis , h.
demonstrate , vti.	Koneri , i/y/g.
demonstration , n.	Ikoneri , i/y/g.
demoralize , vt.	Kobibi, kobi , i/y/g.
demolition , n.	Ikokpo , i/y/g.
demure , vi.	Mekoro , i/y/g.
den , n.	Ikoho , iy/g.
, den of lions.	Ikohozaki , i/y/g.
denial , n.	Ikonu , i/y/g.
, self denial .	Ikonu wenji
denomiate , vt.	Koke , i/y/g.
denomination , n.	Ikoke , i/y/g.
denounce , vt.	Kolo, kposo , i/y/g.
denotation , t, n.	Mekoaashe , i/y/g.
dense , adj.	Kokpon , i/y/g.
density , n.	Dansiti, ikodi , i/y/g.
dent , n.	Imekote, kote. , i/y/g.
dental , adj.	Kokori, kori. , i/y/g.
dentist , n.	O mekokori , o kori. , i/y/g.
deny , vt.	Konu,
dfepart , vit.	Kopu, kota, meta, ropu , i/y/g.

department , n.	Dipatmint, Iyaka, iyahan, kopu, kota, imeta , i/y/g.
departure , n.	Imekoshyien, kota, imeta , i/y/g. ikota
depend , n.	Kogbe, kole , i/yg.
, i depend on you.	Mo kole yin /e
dependable , adj.	Le kole , i/y/g.
dependant , s, n.	Machiya, iyali, yara, yaba , h.
dependence , n.	Koleji , y/i/g.
deplete , vtr.	Kofo , y/i/g.
depict , vt.	Meko , y/ig.
deplore , vt.	Koyo , y/;i/g.
deplorable , adj.	Di koyo , y/i/g.
deport , vt.	Kopu, kikopu, kota , y/i/g.
depopulate , vtn.	Kotuka , y/ig.
depose , vti.	Koleze , y/i/g.
deposit , vt.	Kofre , y/i/g.
depot , n.	Daffo, bariki , y/ig.
depreciate , n.	Kodi y/i/g.
depress , vt.	Kore , kore. , y/i/g.
depression , n.	Kore , ikore. , y/i/g.
depreive , vt.	Kola , y/i/g.
depth , n.	Koji , ikoji., ijinka
depute , vt.	Koli Y/G
deputy , n.	Ashida, ishida; o shida Y/H
deputize , vt.	Shhida Y/H
derange , vt, n.	Yisi, iyisi , y/I.
deride , vt.	Muerin , i/y.
derision , n.	Imuerin , i/y.
derisive , adj.	Le muerin , i/y.
derive , vti.	Yibia , y/I.
derogate , vi.	Kuka , y/I.
derogatory , adj.	Ikuka , y/I.
descend , vit.	Fosi, zurchiya, yibiwa , zu/h/y/I.
descendant , n.	Ikologua, o zurchiya, o yibiawo
descendants , pl. n.	E kologua, e zurchiya

descent , n.	Iramiwa , y/I.
describe , vt.	Kpere; gowe , i/y.
description , n.	Ikpere; igowe , i/y.
desecrate , vtn.	Lavi , h.
desert , n.	Hamada , h.
desert , n.	Hamada , h.
desert-date	Duwa , h.
deserved , vti.	Diye; winye , i/y.
deserving , adj.	Winye, dinye , i/y.
desiccation , n.	Kekashewa, , h.
design , n.	Kokpe , i/y.
designate , vtn.	Mashe , i/y.
desirable , adj.	Wugfu , i/y.
desire , vtn.	Iwugu, iwugu , i/y.
desist , vi.	Dachiu , ed/i/y.
desk , n.	Tenur , hg.
desolate , vt.	Mero , i/y.
desolation , n.	Imero , i/y
despaire , vi.	Foyobi , y/I.
despatch , n, v.	Ronshien, ironshien, ironzi
, despatrch clerk.	Akawu ironzi, aekawu ironshien
, despatch rider.	O ronshien mutum, o ronzi mutum
desperate , adj.	Sokia , i/y.
despise , vt.	Meta , i/y.
despite , prep.	Sipu , y/I.
, despite the fact.	Saipu ezioka
despiser , n.	O meta , y/I.
despondent , adj.	Chewentin , y/I.
despot , n.	Iwenagba, o wenagba , y/I.
despotism , n.	Imiwagba , y/I.
dessert , n.	Denyoma, wessa , g.
, dessert spoon. , n.	Chokali wessa , h/g.
destination , n.	Ibisheien, ikadara , y/I.
destine , vt.	Kadara, bishien , y/h/I.
destiny , n.	Igukpin, iguton, ikadara , y/h/I.

destitute , adj.	Hoho , y, g.v..
destitutes , pl, n.	Ehoho , y, g.v..
destroy , n.	Runbi, runje, runme , y/i.
destroyer , n.	O rubi, o runje, o runme
destruction , n.	Irunbi, irunje, crunme , y/I.
detach , vt.	Yapu, yata y.
detain , vt.	Dachiou , y/I.
detect , vt.	Hundi , i/y.
detective , n.	Ihundi , i/h.
detention , n.	Idachiu , y/I.
deter , vt.	Gbuhan , i/h.
deteriorate , vti.	Kelerunbi , y/I.
determine , vti.	Chenu, ichenu , i/y.
detest , vtn.	Koji , y/h.
dethrone , vt.	Yoeze , y/I.
dewtonator , vti.	Harsashi , h.
detour , n.	kurdawa, zagawa , h.
detriment , n, adj.	Igbuji, gbuji , i/ed/h.
detract , vi.	Kpeta , y/i/ed.
devastate , vt.	Mofo , i/y.
devastation , n.	Imofe , i/y.
develop , vti, adj.	Hugbo , i/y.
development , n.	Ihugbo , i/y.
developer , n.	O hugbo , i/y.
deviate , vi.	Yapu, yata
deviation , n.	Iyapu, iyata , i/y.
device , n.	Dibais, , nke ife irushe., igbiche
devil , n.	Iblis
devious , adj.	Fe iblis, bibles , i/h.
devise , vt.	Chowa, chonja , i/y.
devoid , adj.	Kowen , y/I.
devolve , vti.	Kon , y, gf.v..
devote , vt.	Kpisi , y/I.
devotion , n.	Ikpisi , y/I.
devour , vt.	Wuaje , g/y.

128

devout , adj.	Lau , g.
dew , n.	Raba , h.
dewlap , n.	Bambakwali , h.
dexterity , n.	Imawa , g/i/y.
diabetes , n.	Iyabitis , g.
diabolic , adj.	Ilishushu, bilisi , h/y.
diabolic , adj.	Bilisi , h, g./v..
diadem , n.	Ideze , y/I.
diagnbose , vt.	Mafata , y/I.
diagonal , adj, n.	Godogodo , g.
diagram , n.	Ijuhan , y/h.
dial , n.	Ishoka, shoka , g.
dialect , n.	Iboda, boda y/I.
dialogue , n.	Isoka, soka, sokala , y/i/ik.
diameter , n.	Iyamita, yamita , g.
diamond , n.	Elila g.
diaphragm , n.	Tantani, murfi , h.
diarrhoea , n.	Ipioro-pioro , g.
diary , n.	Ilittarana, dayare , h.
diary , n.	Fegona , i/h.
dibble , n.	Changami , h.
dice , n.	Hambama ludo, dais , h/g.
dickens , n.	Kidini , g.
dictate , vti.	Konoso , g/y.
dictation , n.	Ikonoso , g/y.
dictionary , n.	Kamus , h.
did	Meshe, mshe , i/y.
die, , vt, pt.	Kuowun, mutu, megien , i/y/h.
diesel , n.	Gasa, dizu , h/g.
diesel oil , n.	Man gasa, man dizu , h/g.
diet , n.	Ifiene , g.
differ , vi.	Choto, fambu, cheto, kata , y/I.
difference , n.	Ifambu, ichoto
, the difference is clear.	Ichoto o shaka , ichoto shaka.
	differentiate , vti.

difficult , adj.	Lesiri , y/I.
difficulty , n.	Ileshiri , y/I.
diffidence , n.	Iberu , y/I.
diffuse , adj.	Tonka , y/h.
diffusion , n.	Itonka , y/h.
dig , vt.	Woka , y/h.
dig , find.	Chondi, gundi , i/y/h.
digest , vti.	Dachin , i/h.
digestion , n.	Idachin , i/h.
digger , n.	O woka, o chondi , y/h
digit , n.	Adadi, yatsa , h.
fignify , vit.	Buga , i/y.
dignitary , n.	O buga, ibuga , i/y.
dignity , n.	Ibuga , i/y.
dress , vt, n.	Sigle , ishan/kalabari
dilapidate , vt, adj.	Mewoka , i/y/h.
dilate , vti.	Obe , y/I.
dilatory , adj.	Irobe , y/I.
dilemma , n.	Ihoka , y/i/ik.
diligence , n.	Ijeje, ishienjeje , gen/y/I.
diligent , adj.	Jeje, shienjeje
dilute , vt.	Bula , y/I.
dim , adj.	Wini, meba , g/i/y.
dimension , n.	Ifangolo, ibuto , y/I.
, different dimension.	Ibuto, icheto
diminish , vti.	Dinta , y/I.
diminutive , adj.	Idinta , y/I.
diminutive , adj.	Idinta , y/I.
dine , vit.	Jechin, wuamchin , y/h/g.
ding-dong , adv, n.	Yali-yala, iyali-yala , g/y.
dinghy , n.	Dudu, kwale –kwale, gwaji-gwaji , h.
dinner , n.	Chinma , h, g.v..
diocesan , n.	Idayoses dayoses , g.
diocese , n.	Dayoses Gida baba limami kristia
dip , vti.	Boyen , y/I.

diptheria , n.	Igbefun , y, g.v..
diphtho9ng , n.	Ditong , g.
dsiploma , n.	Taashe, h/y/i/ed/g.
diplomacy , n.	sarabi, isarabi, ichegbon , h/y/i/ed/g.
diplotmat , n.	O sarabi, o chegbon , h/y/i/ed/g.
dire , adj.	zumkpa , y/I.
, dire need.	Ichiche bumkpa
direct , adj.	Juma, gon, whido , y/I.
, please direct me.	Biko juma mi
direction , n.	Ijuma , y/I.
directly , adv.	Whiwhido, gon-gon
director , n.	O juma, , direkta. , y/I.
, director-general.	Direkta-janar
directress , n.	Mache o juma , , h/y/I.
directory , n.	Ijumalita , y/i/h.
, telephone directory.	Jumalita telifon
dirt , n.,	Dauda, kazanta, datti , h.
dirty , adj.	Di datti , i/h.
disable , vt.	Foagba , y, g.v..
disabused , vt.	mekuihi , mek'ihi. , i/y.
disadvantage, n.	igbuanfa
disfaffection, n.	igbusinkwa
disagree, vi.	dicheto, difambu, gbukweba
disagreement, n.	idicheto, idifambu, igbukweba
disallow, vt.	Gbukweba, aiche
disappear, vt	Kilido, kili
disappearance, n.	Ikili
disappoint, vt.	diki, dianfa
disappointment, n.	idiki, idianfa
disapprove, vit.	Gbuaashe
disapproval, n.	igbuaashe
disarm, vt	gbuagba , gbugha.
disarmament, n.	Igbugha
disarrange, vt.	Zighi, aitole
disaster, n.	Ijambe

disavow, vt.	mekuko
disband, vt.	mediofo, megbi, aikweba
discard, vti	kosikasa
disbelieve, vti	di ainikan, ainikah, aikpani – I/Y/Ef.
disbeliever, n.	O ainikan, o aikpani
discern, vti	moncie
discernment, n.	Imonche
discharge, vt.	nira muku, mu'ta Y, G.v./I/Y
disciple, n.	almajiri
discipline, n.	ikozi, ijafun , disika.
discipline, n.	Almajiri
disclaim, vt	Jugba, juwen I/Y
disclose, vt.	Shihe I/Y
disclosure, n.	Ishihe I/Y
discolour, vti.	Gbulauni I/Y
discomfort, n.	Gbuisoleji I/Ed/Y/H
discompose, vtn.	Damu, idamu Y
disconcert, vt.	Dilihanya I/Y/H
disconnect, vt.	Yopu, yonojo, ainojo, winrin Y/I/H/G
disconnection, n.	Iyopu, iyonojo Y/I/H/G
disconsolate, adj.	Yinmenu, yotiunmenu Y/I/H/G
discontent (n)	Iyotewuya, aitewuya Y/I/H/G
discountinue, vti, n.	Dachen, idachen Y/I/H/G
discord, n.	Darudo, zigbi Y/I/Ed
discount, vt.	weku, iweku, diskante I/Y
discountenance, n.	idiot, dakwonu I/Y
discourage, vt.	mej'iyobi, ruguyobi I/Y
discourse, n.	katakata Gen
discourteous, adj.	mekumere, damere I/Y
discover, vt – chode	chowa, I/Y
discoverer, n – o chode	o chowa, I/Y/H
discovery, n – ichode	o chowa
dscredit, vt.	daiwon, mekuiwin Y/(G.v)I
discreet, adj.	shonji Y/H

discrepancy, n.	icheto, aikweba I/Y	
discretion, n.	ishonji Y/I	
discriminate, vit.	chet' ido (chetido), chewhido I/Y	
discrimination, n.	icheti 'do, ichewhido " Y/I	
discus, n.	diskos G	
discuss, vt.	Soli oka Y/I/Ik.	
discussion, n.	Ibasoka	
disdain, vt.	Meata Y/I	
disease, n.	Irun	
disengage , vt.	Yobale, mekubale, yorinta	
disengagement, n.	Iyobale, imekubale, iyorinta	
disentagngle, vti	Yosowu	
	Y/H	
disentaglement, n	Iyosowu	
disenthrone, vt.	Yobaleze Y/I	
disfavour, n.	Iyodore Y/I	
disfigure, vt.	Yofeli	Y/I/G
disgrace, n.	Ilinshasha, linshasha	Y/H/Ar.
disguise, n.	Ibido	Y/H
disgust, vt.	Nenji, shit, ooh!	I/H/G/Gen.
dish, n.	Tasa, akushi	H
disch-cover, n.	Monkei tasa	Y/Ed/Is/Au/Ur/Iso/H
dishearten, vt.	Gbuyobi	I/Ed/Y
dishonest, adj., n.	Aizioka, yozioka, iyozioka	Y/I/Ik.
dishonour, n.	Igbulaeze	I/Ed/Y
dishxonourable, adj.	Gbulaeze	"
disinclination, n.	Aichesi, yoichesi	"
disinfect, v.	Gbujamon	I/Ed/Y
disinfectant, n.	O gbujamon	"

133

disintegrate, vti	Yokoso, gbukoso, zighi koso	Y(G.v)/E
disinterested, adj.	Gbuichefe, gbuchefe	
disjoin, vt.	Yosogba	
disk, n.	Kudu	G
dislike, vt.	Iache, gbuche, aicho	Y/Ed/I
dislocate, v Alhun	Aihun, aineri, gbuhin, gbuneri, gbuhun,	
dislodge, vt.	Yozuga	Y/G
disloyal, adj.	Aifikeba	Y/Ed/I/H
dismal, adj.	Liki mejonu aniocha	I/Y
dismay, n.	Ilili imejonu	
dismiss, vt.	Leshien, ronshien imejonu	
dismount, vti.	Bkasa	Y/H
disbodience, n.	Igbisi aigbonti,	Y/I/H
disobey, vt.	Aigbonti, gbukeiba	
disorder, n.	Izighi-zagha, irugu-rugu	Ed/Y(Gen)
disorganize, vt.	Rugu-rugu	Y(Gen)
disown, vt.	Mekuwen, gbuwen, yowen	I/Y
dispatch, n.	Ronshien, ronzi	Y/I
dispel, vt.	Tuku	Y(G.v)
dispensable, adj.	Kikje	Y/I
dispensary, n.	Ikike, idisfensa	
dispenser, n.	O kike	Y/I
disperse, vti.	Gbaka	Y/G.
dispirited, vt.	Gbuyobi	I/Ed.Y
displace, vt.	Fili	Y/I
display, vt.	Fineri	Y/I
displease, vt.	Gbusolele, gbusondu, gbumenu I/Ed/Y	
displeasure, n.	Igbumenu, igbusolele, igbusondu	
disposal, n	Imede ijuta, dipoza	I/Y/G(fE)

dispose, vti.	Mede, juta, choto kizi, I/Y/G	
disposition	Ikisi, ichoto, mede	
dispossess, vt.	Gbuweni, gbuwen	I/Ed/Y
dispossession, n.	Igbuweni, igbuwen	I/Ed/I
disprove, vt.	Gbunundi, gbuhundi "	
disputable, adj.	Disaroka, m'aroka	Y/G./I
dispute, vti	Roka	Y/G./I
disqualify, vt.	gbu ikwashe, gbudoashe	I/Ed/Y
disquiet, vt.	Sisolioka, gbudankiti, aidankiti	
disregard, vt.	Gbukaya, abukasi	
disrepair, n.	Meje, airama, gbutunmeshe, imeje	
disrepute, n, adj.	Miw ika, imiwika	Y/I
disrespect, n.	Gbumbe, igbumbe	Y/I
dissatisfy, vt.	Gbusoken, mekusoken, gbusokene	
dissect, vt.	Raba	H
dissemble, vti	Gbebe	Y(G.v)
disseminate, vt.	Tughali, tukiri	Y/I
dissemination, n.	Itughali, itukiri	"
dissension, n.	Ibionu	Y/I
dissent, vi.	Yaiche	Y/I
dissimilar, adj.	Gbufene, gbujo	"
dissipate, vti.	Diofo	"
dissipation, n.	Idiofo	"
dissociate, vt.	Yahann, yaiche	Y/I/H
dissolution, n.	Igukpinfefe	I/Y/Ed.
dissolute, adj.	Chokuko	I/Y
dissolve, vti	Tusika, yiwah	Y/H/G
dissuade, v.	Gbuiche, yintua	I/Ed/Y
distance, n.	Ijinhann	Y/H
distant, adj.	Jinhann	Y/H
distate, n.	Igbudunso	I/Ed/Y

distemper, n.	Igbubionu gbuimuye	"
distend, vti.	Diwu, mewu	Y/I
distil, vti.	Tere	H(G.v)
(d. water)	Ruwa tere	
distinct, adj.	Honeri, hone shaka	
distinction, n.	Ihoneri, ihone	"
distinguish, vti.	Yasioto, mesioto	"
disort, vt.	Dirugu, merugu	"
distortion, n.	Idirugu, imerugu	"
distract, vt.	Fapu	Y/I
distraction, n.	Ifapu	"
distraught, adj.	Zata	G
distress, n.	Igbuyobi, ifoyobi	I/ed/Y
distribute, vt.	Kpeyen, kpenno, kabandu	
distribution, n.	O kpeyen, o kpenno, o kabandu	
distributor, n.	O kekpin	
district, n.	Lardi	H
distrust, n.	Gbutolye	I/Ed/Y
disturb, vt.	Yolionu	Y/I
disturbance, n.	Nsohala, katakata, iyolionu	
ditch, n.	Lambatu, tsanya, hanruwa	H/H(G.v)
disunite, v.	Gbudo, fre-udo (gbuudo) = gbu'do freudo	
ditto, n.	Daito, baate	G/Y/I
disuse, n.	Imekuluwe, ailuwe mo I/Y	
dive, vi.	Dompe	G
diver, n.	O dompe, o dupele	G
diverge, vi.	Yahann, yapu, yata	Y/H/I
divergence	Iyahann, iyapu, iyata	"
diverse, adj.	Yini	G
diversion, n.	Iyiri	G
divert, vt.	Yisi; tuasi	G/Y
diversity, n.	Iyisi ituasi	"
divest, vt.	Yopu	Y/I

divide, vti.	Kekpin	I/Y
dividers, n.	E kekpin	"
divination, n.	Isoliba	I/Y/Ef
dividend, n.	Ikekpini	I/Y
divine, adj.	Soliba	I/Y/Ef.
division, n.	Ikekpin, iyahann	I/Y
diviner, n.	O soliba	Y/I/Ef
divinity, n.	Isoliba	"
divorce, n.vt.	Ilepuma lepuma, frema	Y/I/H
divorcee, n.	O lepuma, o frema	"
divulge, vt.	Checkiri	I/Y
dizzy, adj., n.	Yikiri, iyikiri	"
(i 'am feeling dizzy)	Mo ng y ikiri	
do, (present t.)	Mena, meshe, sue (me-she) shekwa	
(do it quickly)	Meshe sokia mend sokia	
(do not)	Ma su, ma meshe, ma mena	
(do you)	She kwa	
docile, adj.	Mimiwa	I/Y
docity, n.	Imimiwa	"
dock, n.	Dak	G
(d. yard), n.	Yadi dak	G
dock, vt.	Tikpo	Y/I
dock, n.	Izinrawa	G/H
(dock worker)	O rushe dak	
docker, n.	O rushe dak, o dak	Y/I/G
doctor, n.	Likita, dokita, malamin mageni Gen./H	
doctrine, n.	Ikoashe, ikpasshe	Y/I/Ed.
document, n.	Dokiumen, iwasika, itakadar H(G.v)	
dodge, n., v.	Fuke, ifuke	G
doe, n.	Mezomo	H(G.v)
does, do	Meshe, medi;	I/Y

does not	Ko meshe	
dog, n.	Kare	
(wild dog), n.	Kyarkechi	H
dogged, adj.	Kaiti, kakar	Y/I
doleful, vt.	Kime	
doll, n.	'yartsana, dol	
dollar, n.	Liyari, idola, dola	H/G
domain, n.	Kawada	H(G.v)
dome, n.	Kubba	H
domestic, adj.	Zigida;	I/Y/H
(domestic servant)	O zida	
(domestic animal)	Nama zioda	
domesticate, vt.	Nama zioda	
domicile, n	mazauni, ibigbe	H/I/Y
dominant, adj., vti.	Juka	Y/I
dominion, n.	Ijuka, wenagba juka	
domino, n.	Iwilo	G
don, n.	Dan	G
donate, vt.	Rebun	Y/I
donation, n.	Irekun	Y/I
donation, n.	Irebun	"
done, (do); (cooked)	Shelv medi, di, meshe, wuula, jowu	
donkey, n.	Jamki	H
donor, n.	O bunre, o bunbe	Y/I
do not (don't)	Ma meshe (ma meh), naa	"
doom, n.	Imongulu, mongulu, gulu, gulu-gulu G	
doomsday, n.	Rana'mongulu, rana, igulu, rana gulugulu	
doob, grass, n.	Kirkiri	H
door, n.	Kofa, kyaure	H
doorkeeper, n.	O cheto kofa	I/Y/H
doormat, n.	Shimfa kofa	H(G.v)
(next door)	Kofa nkeji	H/I/Y

(next door neighbour)	Makusanchi nkeji	"
dope, n.	O kawad	G/H
dormant, adj.	Kitikoi	G/Ed.
dormitory, n.	Deki kolej, damitri	H/G
dose, n.	Imula	Y/I
dot, n.,	Digo, dat H/G	
dote, (vi)	Golo Y(G.v)	
double, adj.	Jieva Y/Ed/Ish.	
double-dealing	Irenka jieva	
(i don't want a double dealer)	Mii che o renka jieva	
doubt, vt.	Yopulu, aidido, puele Y/I/H	
doubtless, adv.	Laiyopulu, didido, puele, puelele	
doubtful, adj, n.	Diyopulu, yopulu	
dough, n.	Kuluredi H(G.v)	
dove, n.	Kurchya H	
down, n. adv.	Isala, fefefe, kale Y/I	
(down below)	Naka isala	
downcast, adj.	Jusisala Y/I	
down fall, n.	Faduwa, idashu isala H/I/Y	
down pour, n.	Izoruwa I/H	
down right, adj.	Ezioka fefefe I/Ik/Ed.	
downstairs, n.	Kasa, isala H/Y/I	
down town, n.	Isala kasa, isala gari H/Y/I	
dowry, n.	Kudima H(G.v)	
down ward, adj.	Sisala Y/I	
doxology, n.	Dusoloji, isolelo G	
doze, vi.	Kunyen G	
dozen, n.	Goteji H/Y	
drab, adj.	Wiziri, draf (of bank) G/fe	
draft, n.	Tsarawa, keneken, ikeneken H/G	
drag, vti.	Fa Y	
dragon, n.	Uyaya G	
drain, n.	Kpogbe, lambatu, hanruwa H(G.v)	

draingage, n.	Ihanruwa H(G.v
drama, n.	Igwuekwa, (guekwa), denmma I/H
dramatic, adj.	Guekwa, denma I/H
dramatize, vt.	Guekwa ya, guekwakwa, denna ya I/H
(dramatic society), n.	Ijumome guekwa I/H
dramatist, n.	O guekwa I/H
dramastic, adj.	Sigban Ed(G.v)
(draction action)	Ishemu sigban, iyaji sigban
draught, n.	Inese I/Y
draught, n. (of air)	Iyajifeh
draught (of game)	Draft G
draghtsman, n.	Dandara, o nese, fa, H/I/Y
draw, drew, vit.	Fa, nese Y/I
(don't draw me back)	Ma fa mi si zuba
(draw a line)	Nese lanyi
(the games was a draw)	Ifa guere
drawer, n.	Al jihu teebur, ifa H/Y
drawing, n.	Inese, ineko, inekode I/Y
(drawn, pp of draw)	Nekode Y/I
dread, n.	Iwugwu Y/I
dreadful, dreadfully, adj.	Wugwu Y/I
dream, vit., n.	Roza Y(Gv)
dreamer, n.	O roza
dreary, adj.	Wugwu, ambu, G/Y/I
dredge, n.	Gbedo Y(G.v)
dregs, n.	Gedegede Y(G.v)
drench, vt.	Funye G
dress, n.	Esa, tufafi, daure, iyiwo; munji H/I/Y/oa
dress (shift)	Sigie (pron. Sikie) Ish/Ka.
(dress up)	Yiwo tufa, yiwo esa Y/I/Og.
dress-maker, n.	O meshe tufa, o meshe esa I/Y/H/Og.
dresser, n.	O yiwo, o tufa I/Y/H
dressing, n.	Iyiwo, tufa, esa I/Y/H/Og.
dried, pt.	Kpogbe, kpako I/Y/Gen.
drier, n.	O kpogbe, o kpako I/Y/Gen.

drift, vti.	Yikie Y/Ish/Ka.
drill, n.	Iwuiho G
drill, vt.	Wuiho, masikei G/I/Y/H
drilling, n.	Iwuiho, imasikei G/I/Y/H
driller, n.	O wuiho, o masikei G/I/Y/H
drink, vt, n, adv.	Wonmu
(drinking stool)	Kujera imula
drip, vit.	Tue Ed.
dripping, n. adj.	Itue Ed.
drive, vti.	Leche, leta, yanwa Y/I
drive, n.	Iyanwa
driver, n.	O yanwa, o leche, o leta, direba
(driver-ants) n.	Kwarkwasa H
drivel, vi.	Maganzar H(G.v)
drizzle, vi.	Wini Y(G.v)
dromedary, n.	Rakuyan H(G.v)
droll, n.	O fa murin, ifa murin, ikhakha
drone, n.	Rago, namiji kuda H
droop, vit.	Renka
drop, vit.	Kpoi, bonka, bonkasa G/Y/I/H
(drop-out)	O bota; kpoi, ta.
dropping, n.	Ikpoi, ibonka, o bonkasa; ikpoikpoi
dropsy, n.	Ibe, be I
dross, n.	Idaro
drought, n.	Ikpogbe kasa, ikpogbe I/Y/H
drove, drive,	Leta, yanwa, leche Y/I
drown, vti.	Risi Y/G
drowning, n.	Irisi Y/G
drowsy, adj.	Buze-buze G
drudgery, n.	Isiwe G
drug, n.	Ogun, magani I/Y/H
druggist, n.	O magani I/Y/H
drum, n.	Ganga H
drummer, n.	O ganga
drunk, drunken, adj.	O lamusha, o gbaga I/Y/H/G

drunkard, n.	O wonmu – won
dry, dried, vti.	Kpoka; ikpako I/Y
(driver river)	Kogi kpoka H/I/Y
(dried morsel)	Kpako ife, kpako
(dry land)	Kasa kpoka
(dry season)	Ngba ikpoka
(dry up)	Kpikpoka
dual, adj.	Jieva Y/Ed
(dual purpose0	Ichedi jieva
dubious, adj.	Wuru-wuru Gen
(dubious person)	O wuru-wuru
duchenss, n.	Mataduk H(G.v)
duck, n.	rage, agwagwa H
dud, n.	Adigbolo I(G.v)
dudgeon, n.	Iron Y(G.v)
due, adj.	Rude ngba, tongba, ngba, rama, yerria Y/I
(in due course)	N'itongba, na ngba, na ngba rama
(pay him his due)	Son irama ya fun
duel, n.	Iyinba, yinba I
dug, pt. dig	Woka, ichondi H/I/Y
duker, n.	Gada, makwarna H
duke, n.	Duk G
dull, adj.	Kumbe, kunu; yeye G
duly, adv.	Torama, ngba-ngba, rarama
dum-palm, n.	Goriba, kaba H
dumb, adj.	Gbuka I/Ed/Ikw.
(deaf and dumb)	Idinkun gbuoka
dumbfound, vt.	Yalionu, gbu onu Y/I
dummy, n.	Kara H
dump, n., vt.	Datti, ju Y
dumpy, and.	Kuru
dun, n.	Idudigba, o kudigba H/Y
dunce, n.	Mumu Gen.
dune, n.	Iniva G
dung, n.	Taki, kashi

(dung hill), n.	Tudun kashin H
dungeon, n.	Kogoka H(G)
dupe, vt.	Rawo, tihan H/I
duplicate, adj.	Keji I/Y
duplicator, n.	Injin keji, o keji G/H/I/Y
durable, adj.	Kpangba Gen
duration, n.	Ikpongba; ikpangba, ingba Gen/I/Y
durbar, n.	Doba G
(durbar hotel)	Huta doba
during, prep.	Na ngba, ngba I/Y
dusk, n.	Swhido-safe Y/H/(G.v)
dust, n.	Kura H
(dubt-bin)	Kwano idatti
duster, n.	O funu, o shafi I/Y/H
dutiable, adj.	Rushe, tisiba I/Y
dutiful, adj.	Tisiba, rushe I/Y
duty, n.	Irushe, ishobe I/Y
(duty officer)	Hafsa rushe
dwarf, n.	Wada H
dwell, vi.	Bigbe Y/I
dwelling, n.	Ibigbe I/Y
(dwelling house)	Gida 'bigbe H/I/Y
dwindle, vi.	Renzu, renba Y/I/H
dye, n.	Rina, tura, shuda H
(dye-pit)	Karofi, baba tukunyar H
dying (die)	Kui-kuowun, ikuowun, kuowun, mutu
dyke, (dike)	Kogo, huda H
dynamite, adj.	Nakiya, dainamuait H/G
dynamo, n.	Janarato, ibalabala G
dynasty, n.	Imingala G
dysentery, n.	Jadi-jadi. Imenusah Gen/I/Y
dyspepsia, n.	Dispesia G

(each of them)	Tukon, ha
(each other)	Tukon mozo
eager, adj.	Winfee, winche I/Kwale/Y
eagle, n.	Juhurma H
eaglet, n.	Monjuhurma Y/Ed/Sob/Au/Ish/Ur/Iso/H
ear, n.	Kunne, zangarniya (eti) synonym)
(he turned a deaf ear)	Ko gbonti, o kitiko I
earache, n.	Ifota kunne I/Y/H
eardrum, n.	Dodo kunne H
eardrop, n.	Magani kunne, itue kunne H/G
earl, n.	Kutu sarangila H(G.v)
early, adj.	Kutu; (kutu)
(come early)	Bia 'kutu, bia sokia
(early in the morning)	Kutu, isafe, isokia safe
(it's too early)	O kutu kha (o kia kha)
earn, vt.	Gbali Y/I
earnest, adj.	Zioka I/Ikw.
(in earnest)	N'izioka I//Ikw
earnings, n.	Egbali Y/I
ear-rings, n.	Oruka-kunne Y/Ed/H
earth, n.	Kasa, kasala H/I
earthenware, n .	Tukwane yumbu, iyumbu H
earthquake, n.	Wiwo kasa, Y/H
earthwornm, n.	Tana H
earwig, n.	Tsatso H
ease, n.	Flesi, simini I(G/Y(G.v)
(do it with ease)	Meshe n'iflesi
easily, adv.	Fleflesi, sisimini, fli-flesi
east, n.	Gabas, igab as (ist) H/G
easter, n.	Irande, Kristi, Ista G
eastern, adj.	Gabas, fe gabas I/H
easy, adj.	Flesi, mini G
eat, vti.	Je, wuam Y/G
eatable, n.	Ije, iwuam Y/G
eau de cologne, n	Iu du kolone G

eaves, n.	Sashenka H(G.v)
eavesdrop, vi.	Gb'oka kele, mebo Y/Ik/Ed/Ur/Gen
eavesdropper, n.	O gb'oka kele, o mebo, amebo Y/Ik/Ed/Ur/Gen
eater, n.	O wuam G
ebb (vi)	Fasha
ebony, n.	Kanya, itache kanya, bekrin, ebona H/G
eccentric, adj.	Tashe Y/I
ecclesiastic, n.	Ilufa, eklishasti Y/I/G
echo, n.	Gboun, igbouna Y/(G/v)
eclipse, n.	Husufi H
economics, n.	Ekonoma G
economy, n.	Ikonoma, ireba, itawun G/Y/H/Sob./I
economical, adj.	Fe ikonoma, fe ireba
ecstasy, n.	Babayo, I/Y
exzema, n.	Inenu I(G.v)
edge, n. vit	Inenu I(G.v)
edible, adj.	Fewuam, wiwuam I/G
edict, n.	Ishikpe I/Y
edification, n.	Imuko I/Y
edit, vi.	Tungu, edit Y/I
edition, n.	Itungu, edishan Y/I
editor, n.	O tungu; edita Y/G
editorial, adj.	Tungugu, fe tungu, editeria,
edo, n.	Edo, benin
educate, vt.	Kozi Y/I
education, n.	Ikozi Y/I
eel, n.	Gwando, bano H
efface, vt	Kezi G
effect, n.	Iyokei, ibre, bre Y/H/G
effective, adj.	Yokei, bre Y/H/G
effeminate, adj.	Di mache, bika mache I/Y/H
efficacy, n.	Ituen G
efficient, adj.	Yokeisi, wenshe
effigy, n.	Neron ineron I/Y

145

effort, n.	Igbake Y/I
e.g.	n.i. (na ifineri)
egg, n.	Kwai H
(egg-shell), n.	Kwafsa H
(garden, egg)	Gauta H
(bad egg)	Kwai meje H/I/Y
egoism, egotism, n.	Sonkei H(G.v)
egress, n.	Ijita, ihanta Y(G.v)
egret, n.	Balbela H
eiderdown, n.	Ifidi H(G.v)
eight, n.	Asato I
eighteen, adj, n.	Goma ati asato H/Y/I
eighty, adj, n.	Sat I(G.v)
either, adj, prep	Biso G
ejaculate, vt. n.	Lopuepue, lopue G
eject, vt, n.	Japu, jata Y/I
ijection, n.	Ijapu,ijata Y/I
eke, eked, vt.	Fikun Y
elaborate, vt,	Diye I/Y
elastic, adj.	Ilastik, ififa G
elate, adj.	Gali, lido I/H
elbow, n.	Gwiwar, gwiwar hannu
elder, adj.	Lagbadi, ladi Y/I
eldest, adj.	Kobi, ladi kha Y/I
elect, vt, adj.	Yeya, yah G
election, n.	Iyeya, iyah G
elector, n.	O yeya, o yah G
electorate, electoral, n.	Eyeya, eyah G
elegance, n, adj.	Yoyo,iyoyo, oyoyo Gen/Y
eleganza, n.	Alugenza, oyoyo G/Gen/Y
electric, adj.	Lantiriki H
electricity, n.	Ilantiriki H
electrify, vt.	Lantiriki H
electrocute, vt.	Ikuowun lantiriki, fi lantiriki gbu
element, n.	Isali, rabi, kashi, alimint, ibibre H/G/I/Y

elementary, adj.	Bibre
(elementary school)	Makaranta bibre
elephant, n.	Giwa H
elephantiasis, n.	Alufantiasis, okotoko G
elevate, vt.	Fosie Y/I
elevation, n.	Ifosie Y/I
elevator, n.	O fosie Y/I
eleven, n, adj.	Goma na/ati dayo H/I/Y
eleventh, n, adj.	Nke goma na daya
elecit, vt, n.	Choja I/Y
eligible adj.	Zumkpa I/Y
eligibility, n.	Izumkpa I/Y
eliminate, vt.	Leta Y/I
elimination, n.	Ileta Y/I
elixire, n.	Aligza G
ellipse, n.	Molo H
elocution, n.	Okasoli, kasoli, ikasoli Ik/Y
elongate, vti	Faogo Y/I
elongation, n.	Ifaogo Y/I
eloquence, n.	Izumkpoka I/Ik
else, adv.	Mozo Y/I
elsewhere, adv.	Mimiozo, mbozo Y/I
elude, vt.	Boaka Y/I
elusive, adj, n.	Boaka, iboaka Y/I
emaciate, vt.	Jinrin G
emaciation, n.	Ijinrin G
emancipate, vt.	Mininta Y/G
emancipation, n.	Imininta Y/G
embargo, n.	Idihan, idigbu Y/H/I/Ed embark, vit, (embark upon)
embalmment, n.	Irono G
embarrass, vt.	Kuafere Y/I
embarrassment, n.	Ikuafere
embassy, n.	Jakadawa, embasiye
embellish, vt.	Mosho

embers, n.	Garwashi
embezzle, vt.	Jarawo
embezzlement, n.	Ijarawo
embitter, vt.	Roonu Y/I
emblem, n.	Ilemba; tambari G/H
(emblem of socrates)	Ilemba sokratis
embody, vt.	Ko jokin
embodiment, n.	Ikojokin
embrace, vti.	Fanji Y/H
embracement, n.	Ifanji Y/H
emboss, vt.	Tgeja, teta Y/I
embroider, vti.	Kibere I/H/Y
embroidery, n.	Ikibere I/H/Y
embryo, n.	Tayi H
emerald, n.	Mionomiono, zumurrudu, zubarjadu G/H
emerge, vi.	Jata, japu Y/I
emergency, n.	Isokiakia, sokia I/Y
(emergency exit)	Hanyar isokia
(emergency relief), n.	Ironhan sokia
emery, n.	Basamfefa H
emetic, n.	Ifuba H/I/Y/G
emigrate, vi.	Bobia Y/I
emigration, n.	Ibobia Y/I
eminent, and.	Gabu, gabu-gabu, zumkpa I/Y/Ed
(eminent personality)	Mutum gabu-gabu, mutum ezumkpa, iyonyen ezumkpa
emir, n.	Baba sarki, emir Gen/H
emissary, n.	Isinkwa, o sinkwa G
emolument, n.	Albashi H
emotion, n.	Ituki Y/H
emmanuel, n.	Imanueli afa Abasi G/H/Y/Ef.
emperor, n.	O keshan; sarkashe G/H/Y/Ed/I
(emperor haile selasi)	Sarkashe haile Selasi
emphasis, n.	Emfasiye iteonusi, teonusi, iteonu Y/I/Y
emphasize, v.	Emfabiye, teonusi, iteonu Y/I/Y

empire, n.	Ikeshan G/H/Y/Ed/I
employ, vt.	Yirushe, gbarushe, rushe Y/I
employee, n.	O rushe, o gbarushe, Y/I
employer, n.	O yirushe Y/I
employment, n.	Iyirushe
empower, vt.	Nnoagba Ef/Y
empty, adj.	Mkpiti; fege, n'oho; kpiti
(empty vessel)	Ihanbu o fege, ihanbu fege
enable, vt.	Muni Y/I
enamel, n.	Farnti H
enamelware, n.	Kaya faranti, H
encampment, n.	Zango, izango, H/Y/H
enchain, vt.	Daprusu Y/Ti
enchant, vt.	Meyoyo I/Y/Gen.
enclose, vt.	Fitikpo, tikpo Y/I
enclosure, n.	Ifitikpo, itikpo Y/I
encounter, vt.	Huba I/Y
encourage, vt.	Ronyobi nnoyobi, nnoyo Y/I/Ef.
encroach, vti.	Balesi I/Y
encroachment, n.	Ibalesi I/Y
encumber, vt.	Rubu Y/I
encumbrance, n.	Irubu Y/I
encyclopedia, n.	Balamitanda G
end, n.	Iguton, gukpin, I/Y
(end result) endeavour	Iyisi
ended	Igutonla, itongo, itonla (la)
endless adj.	Kpokpo,
endurance, n.	Ifamindu Y/I
endure, vti.	Famindu, faominu Y/I
enemy, n.	Itiwe, it'ilo Y/I
energetic, adj.	Kagba
energy, n.	Ikagba, Y/I
enfold, vt.	Dikpo Y/I
enforce, vt.	Figbake, nnogbake Y/I/Ef.

enforcement, n.	Ifigbake, innogbake Y/I/Ef.
enfranchise, vt., n.	Nnominera, fiminera Y/I/Ef.
engage, vti.	Fibale, file Y/I
engagement, n.	Ifile, ifibale Y/I
engender, adj.	Fata, fapu Y/I
engine, n.	Injin, H/Y/I
(railway engine)	Injin reliwe
engineer, n.	Ejiniya, injiniya H/Y/I
english, n.	Bature, obocha, oyibo H/Y/Ed/I
(english language)	Ede bature,
engrave, vt.	Jura, fikabari, fikushewa Y/H/G
engraver, n.	O fikabarfi, o fikushewa Y/H
enhance, vt.	Jesi I/Y
enhancement, n.	Ijesi I/Y
engulf, vt.	Fibukpo Y/I
enjoin, vt.	Fisogba Y/I
enigma, n.	Ficholo Y/G
enjoy, vt.	Gbandu; iriya Y/I
enjoyment, n.	Igbandu; miliki; iriya Y/I/ob
enlarge, vti.	Faibuto Y/I
enlargement, n.n	Ifaibuto Y/I
enlighten, vt.	Meliye I/Y
enlightenment, n.	Imeliye I/Y
enlist, vt.	Risi, wensi Y/I
enlistment, n.	Irisi, iwensi Y/I
enmity, n.	Ighata I/Y
enormous, adj.	Tobibu I/Y
enough, adj, n, adv.	Zuto, izuto, zuzuto I/Y
(enough is enough)	Izuto wu izuto
enquire, n.	Ijubi I/Y
enquiry, n.	Ijubi I/Y
enquirer, n.	O jubi I/Y
enrag, vt.	Fibionu Y/I
enrich, vt.	di riba, barika, riba I/H/Sob/Ed./Y
enrichment, n.	Idiriba, ibarika I/H/sob/Ed./Y

enrol, vti.	Fasi Y(G.)
enroute, adv.	Fahanyar, ronhanyar Y/H
ensample,	Meshakpere, meakpere I/Y
ensign, n.	Tuta injin H
enslave, vt.	Meshe bawa, fibaiwa I/Y/H
ensue, v.	Fasole, fisole, sole, disole
ensure, vt.	Fadido I/Y/H
entail, vt.	Diwesi, wesi I/Y
entangle, vt.	Sowu, sowuya Y/H
entanglement, n.	Isowu, isowuya Y/H
enter, vt.	Bale, woba wonyen
(enter quickly)	Woyen sokia
enterprise, n.	Dawongi Y/H
enterprises, n.	Edawongi Y/H
entertain, vt.	Miri G/Gen
entertainment, n.	Miri-miri, imuri G/Gen
enthrone, vtn.	Baleze, fibaleze, woyeneze
enthusiasm, n.	Igbowu, itonji Y/H
enthusiastic, adj.	Di gbowu, di tonji I/Y/H
entice, vt.	Fasiji Y/H
enticement, n.	Ifasiji Y/H
entire, adj.	Gbohan, kprakpata, kpafefe I/Y/Ed.
entirely, adv.	Gbogbohan, kpakpafefe I/Y/Ed.
entitled, vt.	Yeli Y/I
entitlement, n.	Iyeli Y/I
entomology, n.	Etom, etomoloji, ento G
entomologist, n.	O tomoloji, o tom G
entomb, vt.	Sinbari Y/H
entrance, n.	Hanyar H
entreat, vt.	Biyo It/I
(i entreate you)	Mo biyo yin
entrust, vt.	Fileyobi Y/I
entry, n.	Antri, ihanyar, ibale, G/H/I/Y
enugun, n.	Enugu, baba kasa Anambra
enumerate, vt.	Konoka G/Y

enunciate, vt.	Kwuso I/Y
envelope, n.	Evilop, chibolo, chibo I/Y/G
enviable, adj.	Fafeche, difeche
environment, n.	Ezinta, iyikazi I/Y/H (environmental sanitation)
envious, adj.	Feche, fechefeche, igbowuche
envoy, n.	Wakili, omaye H/Id/Ig
envy, vt.	Cheche I/Y
(envy no one)	Ma cheche eni mutum
ephemeral, adj.	Sibanzi G
epidemic, n. adj.	Igharun, epidema Y/I/Y
epilepsy, n.	Warakpa Y
epileptic, adj.	Warakpa, o warakpa Y
epilogue, n.	Ipilog G
epiphany, n.	Ifinene
episcopal, adj.	Episkopa G
episode, n.	Iwasiton H/Y
epistle, n.	Wasika H
epitaph, n.	Iyowo Ed.
epithet, n.	Iliwe H/Y
epitome, n.	Ilittiton, ibekuru H/Y
epoch, n.	Ibringba I/Y
equable, adj.	Bietu, ngbancha I/Y En.
equal, adj.	Diogba I/Y
equally, adv.	Didiogba I/Y
equalize, vt.	Mediogba I/Y
equality, n.	Idi8ogba
equator, n.	Ikweta G
equilibrium, n.	Ikulele, kulele, idiogba Gen/I/Y
equinox, n.	Ekuina G/Y/H/G
equip, vt.	Nnofun Ef/Y
equipment, n.	Innofun, ekwirushe
equity, n.	Imeshede I/Y
equitable, adj.	Meshede I/y
equivalent, adj.	Udiogba; shaka I/Y

equivocate, n.	Isiro; ai shaka Y/I
era, n.	Ingbiton, gbiton I/Y
(the christian era)	Ingbiton Krista, gbiton Krista
(the muslim era)	Ingbiton musulmi, gbiton musulmi
eradicate, vt.	Chare I/Y
eradication, n.	Ichare I/Y
erase, vt.	Kpafu Y/I
erect, adj. vt.	Koka, kondi, kundu Y/I
erection, n.	Ikundu, ikonka, ikondi Y/I
erode, vt.	Raje, jeta, jepu H/Y/I
erosion, n.n	Ijeta, ijepu, iraje H/y/I
err, vi.	Shihan Y/H
errand, n.	Maran, izinso G/I(G.v)
(errand boy)	Yaro zinso
erratic, adj.	Rede
error, n.	Ishihan; isipien
eruption, n.	Idompe G
erratum, n.	Ishinhante Y/H
erudite, adj.	Masokia I/Y
escape, vit.	Boaka, bohann Y/I
escort, n.	Isolele, o solele H/G
eskimo n.	Aprinini G
especial, ly (adj, adv.)	Katazi, ezumpka Y/Ed/I
esperanto, n.	Esferanto G
esperantist, n.	O sferanti, o sferanto G
essay, vti.	Yondo
(essay competition)	Ikambe yondo
esquire, n.	Askuaya G
essence, n.	Izumkpa I/Y
essential, adj.	Zumkpa I/Y
estacode, n.	Istakod G
establish, vt.,	Dakasa, dakundu Y/H/I
establishment, n.	Idakasa, idakundu Y/H/I
estate, n.	Estiti, eriba G/Sob/H/Y
(estate surveyor)	O mewon estiti

esteem, vt.	Buni I/Y
(high esteem)	Ibuni ga
estimate, vti, n.	Istimat, ikamanta, ikaddara, nofi G/H(G.v)
estuary, n.	Biki G(Zaire)
etc (et-cet-era) n.	Ei-se-ta (ei-se-ta) Ed
eternal, adj.	Akporlailai, akporlai, lailai Ur/Y
(eternal life)	Mindu lailai
(eternal rest)	Isimini lailai Y(G.v)
eternity, n.	Ikprlailai, ilailai Ur/Y
etiquette, n.	Imiwa I/Y
etymology, n.	Etimoloji, etim. G(Ef.)
etymologist, n.	O etimoloji, o timoloji G(Ef.)
eucalyptus, n.	Itagom H(G.v)
(eucalyptus oil), n.	Man itagom H(G.v)
eucharist, n.	Yiukaris, o kuile G
eunock, n.	O kubura, kubura Y/I/H
euphorbia, n.	Ufobia G
europe, n.	Turai, Yurop, kasa bature H/G/H
european, n.	Bature, o Yurop H/G
evade, vt.	Yeka, beka Y/H
evader, n.	O yeka, o beka Y/H
evangelist, n.	Ovanjela, o nesi (o vanjela) G/I
evangelise, vt. n.	Vanje nesi, inesi
evaporate, vti.	Gbepu, gbeta, gbefo, kpopu Y/I
evasion, n.	Iyesinka, iyinsika Y/H
eve, n.	Iyamma H(G.v)
eve, n.	Yamma H
even, n, adj.	Pkawu, idiogba, kpasi Y/I
evening, n.	Yamma
(good evening)	Eku yamma
(evening time)	Ngba yamma Y/I/H
event, n.	Isoka I/Ik
eventually, adv.	Isosoka I/Ik
ever, adv.	Biso; siti, kiken, keni; eni Y/G
(ever since)	Biso ngba; siti ngba/ngba siti

(ever after)	Biso izuba, ngb'izuein, siti ngba evergreen, n, adj, adv.
(evergreen tree)	Itatuwa, itache algasiti H/Y/G
everlasting, adj.	Kanzusiit, sitii I/Y/H
every, adj.	Ncha En.
(every time)	Ncha ngba En/I/Y
(every day)	Ncha rana H/I/Y
(every where)	Ebe-ki-ebe, ncha mbobe, n cha nso En/Y/I
(every body)	Ncha mutum En/H
everything)	Ife richa, nc'ife/nch'ihe En/I
(everyman)	Ncha miji
(every woman)	Ncha mache
evict, vt.	Jante Y/H
evictly, adv.	Jajante Y/h
evidence, n.	Ifineri, ishaida Y/I/H
(circumstantial evidence)	Ishaida ngba
evolve, vti.	Tupu, ituja, ituta Y/I
evolvement, n.	Itupu, ituja, Y/I
evolution, n.	Itupu, ituja, ituta Y/I
evoke, vt.	Hule I/Y
evil, adj.	Bujo, jika, njika I/Y
(evil doer)	O buijo, o mesh 'ibujo, o jika,
(evil doears)	E njika, e bujo
ewe, n.	Tunkiya H
exact, adj, vt.	Sam Gen
exactly, adv.	Dan-dan; sasam Owo/Gen
exactness, n.	Isam
exaggerate, vti.,	Mebimbu I/Y
exaggeration, n.	Imebimbu I/Y
exalt, vt.	Buga I/Y
exaltation, n.	Ibuga I/Y
examine, vt.	Chondi I/Y/H
examination, exam, n.	Ichondi I/Y/H
examiner, n.	O chondi I/Y/H
example, n.	Ifineri, ifineri Y/I

(example giving, e.g.)	Ri a/nno ifineri, (Ef/Y/I
exasperate, vt.	Rusonma Y/H
excate, vt.	Chohoh I/Y
excavation, n.	Ichohoh
exceed, vt.	Koga Y/I
exceeding, n.	Ikoga Y/I
exceedingly, adj.	Koga Y/I
excel, vit.	Kayo I/Y
excellency, n.	Kabiyesi, ikayo Y/I/Y
excellent, adj.	Kamkpe, kayo Gen.
except, vt.	Weku I/Y
exception, n.	Iweku I/Y
exceptional, adj.	Weku I//Y
(exceptional case)	N'weku oka
excess, n.	Ijukha, ijuka Y/I
excess luggage, n.	Kaya juka Y/I
exchange, n.	Echenj, isengi, ichoto H/I/Y
exchequer, n.	Echeka G (councillor of the exchequer)
excite, vt.	Rumbimbu, rumbi Y/I
exclaim, vt. i.	Kem,kpo Y/I
exclamation, n.	Ikemkpo Y/I
exclude, vt.	Mupu Y/I
exclusive, adj.	Mupu Y/I
exclusion, n.	Imupu Y/I
excrement, n.	Kashi, najasa H
exreta, n.	Kashi, najasa H
excrete, vt.	Ya kashi Y/H
excommunicate, vt, n.	Yopu, yota, yoja, iyopu Y/I
excursion, n.	Iringa fiene, irinrele
excuse, vt, n.	Wizii, iwizii, isigie G/Ish/Kal
excusable, adj.	Le wizii, le sigie G/Ish/Kal
execute, vt.	Gbukuo, meshe, kekpin I/Ed/Y
execution, n.	Igbukuo, ikekpin, imeshe I/Ed/Y
executor, n.	O gbukuo, o kekpin
executive, n.	O kekpin, o meshe I/Y

(executive officer)	Hafsa ikekpin, hafsta o meshe, o meshe hafsa
exempt, vt.	Fresiki, tusika Y/I/H
exemption, n.	Ifresiki, itusika, asasais Y/I/H
exercise, n.	Igwuerenji I/Y/H
(exercise book	Littafi 'gwuerenji
exert, vt.	Mekia I/Y
exertion, n.	Imekia I/Y
exhale, vti.	Meso I/Y
exhaust, n.	Imego I/Y
exhaustion, n.	Imego I/Y
exhibit, n.	Fine I/Y
exhibition	Ifine I/Y
exhort, vt.	Buyon I/Y/H
exhortation, n.	Ibuyon I/Y/H
exile, vt, n.	Pruta, ipruta Ti/Y
exigence, n.	Isokiakia I/Y
exist, vi.	Diwa I/Y
existence, n.	Idiwa I/Y
exit, n.	Hanyarta, azit; agzit H/|Y/G (fE)
exodus , n.	Esodu G
exonerate, vt.	Melare I/Y
exoneration, n.	Imelare I/Y
exofficio, adv.	Makeze, mamakeze, hafsa ikpoeze
expand, vt.	Fembu Y/I
exorbitant, adj.	Wonga Y/I
expatriate, n.	Kazim G
expect, vtn.	Rekon, irekon Y/H
expectant, adj.	Di rekon I/Y/H
(expectant mother)	Mamorekon (mama o rekon) Gen/Y/H
expectorate, vti	Kelebe
expedient, adj.	Yeli Y(G.v)
expedite, vt.	Ronkia, nnokia Y/Ef
(please expedite action)	Biko nnokia iyaji
expedition, n.	Ishienlajo Y/I

expel, vt.	Lepu, leta Y/I	
expeller, n.	O lepu, o leta Y/I	
expend, vt.	Nonkudi, nonku Y/H	
expenditure, n.	Inonkudi, inonku Y/H	
expense, n.	Inonku Y/H	
expenses, (pl.n)	Enonku Y/H	
expensive, adj.	Di nonku, wonga Y/H/I	
experiment, n.	Ifineri, imefine Y/I	
experience n	Ichegbon, iguko, ima	
expert, n.	Gwani, kwararre, iwin, win H/Y/Gen	
expire, vt.	Biako I/Y	
explain, vt.	Tuma moye, mediye I/Y	
explanation, n.	Ituma, imoye, imediye I/Y	
explicit, adj.	Dido Y/i/H	
explode, vti.	Wondi, gbuum Y/H/G	
exploit, n. vt.	Sokoh, isokoh G	
explore, vt.	Chokiri I/Y	
exploration, n.	Ichokiri	I/Y
explosion, n.	Igbuum, iwondi	G/Y/H
explosive, n. adj.	O wondi, rewondi, ifewondi, ifegbuum	
export, vtn.	Bueshien, ronga, ironga	Y/I
(export market)	Ironga kasuwa	
exports, n.	Eronga	
exporter	O bueshien	
expose vt.	Boesa, n'oho	
exposure, n.	Iboesa, in'oho igboloh	
exposition, n.	Ifineri, in'oho, iboesa	
express, expressed, vtn.	Soliye, isolifye, sogho	Y/I express, adj., adv.
expressly, adv.,	Disoliye, mesolifye, ifye	I/Y
expulsion, n.	Lefeh	I/Y
extend, vti.	Fago	I/Y
(extended family)	Baba yali	
extension, n.	Ifago, ekstensha;sese	

extensive, adj.	Fago	
extent, n.	Ifato	I/Y
exterior, adj.	Detifi	Y/I
exterminate, vtn.	Gbupu, gbuta, igbupu, igbuta	I/Y
external adj.,	Zunde, zunta	Y/I
(external affairs)	Ministri nke 'mani zunde	
extinguish, vt.	Gbuwuta	I/H
extinguisher, n.	O gbuwuta	
(fire extinguisher)	O gbuwuta	
extol, vt.	Yinga	Y/I
extort, vt.	Kokiene	G/Ur.
extra, adj.	Kufo	Y/I
extract, vt.	Yopu , yota	Y/I
(extract of the speech)	Iyopu n'oka	
extraction, n.	Iyopu, iyota	Y/I
extraordinary, adj.	Iyalionu	Y/H
(extraordinary meeting)	Mitin 'yalionu (extraordinary expenditure)	Inonku, yalionu extravagant, adj.
extreme, adj.	Xha-xha zita, fagolo, tain-tain	
extremity, n.	Ikha-kha; izita, ifagolo, itain-tain	Y/H
extricate, vt.	Dakasa	Y/H
extrication, n.	Idakasa	
exult, vi.	Mera, yoli tombi	I/Y
eye, n.	Ido, neri	H/I/Y
(eyeglass), n.	Ijongo ido	Ib/H
eyeball, n.	Kwayar ido	H
(every woman|)	Ncha mache	
evict, vt.	Jante	Y/H
evictly, adj.	Jajante	Y/H
evidence, n.	Ifineri, ishaida	Y/I/H
(circumstantial evidence)	Ishaida ngba	
evolve, vti.	Tupu, tuja, tuta	Y/I
evolvement, n.	Itupu, ituja, ituta	"

evolution, n.	Itupu, ituja, ituta	"
evoke, vt.	Hule	I/Y
evil, adj.	Bujo, jika ojika	"
(evil doer)	O bujo, o mesh'ibujo, oi jika	
ewe, n.	Tunkiya	H
exact, adj. vt.	Sam,	Gen.
exactly, adv.	Dan-dan; sasam, owo/Gen.	
exactness, n.	Isam	
exaggerate, vti.	Mebimbu	I/Y
exaggeration, n.	Imebimbu	"
exalt, vt.	Buga	I/Y
exaltation, n.	Ibuga	"
examine, vt.	Chondi	I/Y/H
examination, exam. n.	Ichondi	"
examiner, n.	O chondi	"
example, n.	Ifineri, ifineri	Y/I
(example giving, e.g.)	Na/nno ifineri, (n.f)	EF/Y/I
exasperate, vt.	Rusonma	Y/H
excate, vt.	Chohoh	I/Y
excavation, n.	Ichohoh	
exceed, vt.	Koga	Y/I
exceeding, n.	Ikoga	"
exceedingly, adj.	Koga	"
excel, vit	Kayo	I/Y
excellency, n.	Kabi yesi, ikayo	Y/I/Y
excellent, adj.	Kamkpe, kayo	Gen.
except, vt.	Weku	I/Y
exception, n.	Iweku	"
exceptional, adj.	Weku	"
(exceptional case)	N'weku oka	
excess, n.	Ijukha, ijuka	Y/I
excess luggage, n.	Kaya juka	"
exchange, n.	Echenji, isengi, ichoto	H/I/Y

excheguer, n.	Echeka	G (councillor of the exchequer)
excite, vt.	Rumbimbu, rumbi	Y/I
exclaim, v.i	Kemkpo	Y/I
exclamation, n.	Ikemkpo	"
exclude, vt.	Mupu	"
exclusive, adj.	Mupu	"
exclussion, n.	Imupu	Y/I
excrement, n.	Kashi, najasa	H
excreta, n.	Kashi, najasa	"
excrete, vt.	Ya kashi	Y/H
excommunice, vt. n.	Yopu, yota, yoja, iyopu	Y/I
excursion, n.	Iringa fiene, irinrele	
excuse, vt., n.	Wazu, iwizii, isigie	G/Ish/Kal.
excusable, adj.	Le wiziii, le sigie	"
execute, vt.	Gbukuo, meshe, kekpin	I/Ed/Y
execution, n.	Igbukuo, ikekpin, imeshe	"
executor, n.	O gbukuo, o kekpin	
executive, n.	O kekpin, o meshe	I/Y
(excutive officer)	Kafsa ikekpin, hafsa o meshe, o meshe hafsa	
exempt, v.	Fresiki, tusika	Y/I/H
exemption, n.	Ifresiki, itusika, asasais	"
exercise, n.	Igwuerenji	I/Y/H
(exercise book)	Littafi 'gwuerenji	
exert, vt.	Mekia	I/Y
exertion, n.	Imekia	"
exhale, vti.	Meso	"
exhaust, n.	Imego	"
exhaustion, n.	Imego	I/Y
exhibit, n.	Fine I/Y	
exhibition	Ifine I/Y	
exhort, vt.	Buyon I/Y/H	
exhortation, n.	Ibuyon I/Y/H	

exile, vt. n.	Pruta, ipruta Ti/Y	
exigence, n.	Iusokiakia I/Y	
exist, vi	Diwa "	
existence, n.	Idiwa "	
exit, n.	Hanyarta, azit; agzit	H/Y/G(fE)
exodus, n.	Esodu G	
exonerate, vt.	Melare I/Y	
exoneration, n.	Imelare "	
exofficicio, adv.	Makeze, mamakeze, hafsa ikpoeze	
expand, vt.	Fembu	Y/I
exorbitant, adj. expatriate, n.	Wonga	Y/I
expect, vtn. expectant, adj.	Kazim	G
	Rekon, irekon	Y/H
	Di rekon	I/Y/H
(expectant mother)	Memorekon (mama o rekon) Gen/Y/H	
expectorate, vti.	Kelebe	
expedient, adj. expedite, vt.	Yeli	Y(G.v)
	Ronkia, mokia	Y/Ef
(please expedite action)	Biko nnokia iyaji	
expedition, n.,	Ishienlajo	Y/I
expel, vt. expeller, n.	Lepu, leta	Y/I "
	O lepu, o leta	
expend, vt.	Nonkudi, nonku	Y/H
expenditure, n.	Inonkudi, inonku	"
expense, n.	Inonku	"
expenses, (pl.n)	Enonku	"
expensive, adj.	Di noinku, wonga	Y/H/I
experiment, n.	Ifineri, imefine	Y/I
expert, n.	Gwani, kwararre, iwin, win H/Y/Gen	
expire, vt.	Biako	I/Y
explain vt.	Tuma, maye, mediye, I/Y	
explanation, n.	Ituma, imoye, imediye I/Y	
explicit, adj.	Dido Y/I/H	

explode, vti.	Wondi, gbuum Y/H/I
exploit, n. vt.	Sokoh, isokoh G
explore, vt.	Chokiri I/Y
exploraton, n.	Ichokiri I/Y
explosion, n.	Igbuum, iwondi G/Y/H
explosive, n. adj.	O wondi, fewondi, ifewondi, ifegbuum, o gbuum
export, vtn	Bueshien, ronga ironga Y/I
(exprt market)	Ironga kasuwa
exports, n.	Eronga
exporter	O bueshien
expose, vt.	Gboloh, Y/Og.
exposure, n.	Iboesa, inooho, igboloh
exposition, n.	Ifineri, in'oho, iboesa express, expressed, vtn.
	Soliye, isoliye, sogho Y/I
express, adj. adv. fiam-fiam G	Esfres, lofeh, samsam,
expressly, adv.	Disoliye, mesoliye, liye I/Y
expulsion, n.	Lefeh Y/G
extendf, vti.	Fago I/Y
(extended family)	Baba yali
extension, n.	Ifago, ekstensha; esese I/Y
extensive, adj.	Fago I/Y
extent, n.	Ifato Y/I
exterior, adj.	Detiti Y/I
exterminate, vtn.	Gbupu, gbuta, igbupu, igbuta I/Y
external, adj.	Zunde, zunta I/Y
(external affairs)	(mininstri nke'mani zunde
extinguish, vt.	Gbuwuta I/H
extinguisher, n.	O ghuwuta
(fire extinguisher)	O guwuta
extol, vt.	Yinga Y/I
extort, vt.	Kokiene G/Ur
extra, adj.	Kufo Y/I
etract, vt.	Yopu, yota Y/I

(extract of the speech)	Iyopu n'oka
extraction, n.	Iyopu, iyota Y/I
extraordinary, adj.	Iyalionu, Y/H
(extraordinary meeting)	Mitinyalionu (extraordinary expenditure)
extreme, adj.	Kha-kha, zita, fagolo, tain-tair I/Y
extremity, n.	Ikah-kha, izita, ifagolo, itain-tain Y/I
extricate, vt.	Dakasa Y/H
extrication, n.	Idakasa Y/H
exult, vi.	Mera, yoli tombi I/Y
eye, n.	Ido, neri H/I/Y
(eyeglass), n.	Ijongo ido Ib/H
eyeball, n.	Kwayar ido H
eyesight, n.	Inerido I/Y/H
eyebrow, n.	Gira H
eyeservice, n.	Isini'do Y/G/H
eyelid, n.	Fatar ido H
eyesore, n.	Imejetombi I/Y
eyelash, n.,	Gashin ido I/Y
eyewitness, n.	O shaida G/H

F

fable, n.	Alo Y
fabric, n.	Fabriki G
fabricate, vt.	Meke I/Y
fabrication, n.	Imeke I/Y
fabulous, adj.	Tombibu Y/I
face, n.	Fuska, ido, kido H
faceless, adj.	Ai wen fuska Y/I/H
(long face)	Igungo fuska
(pull a long face)	Fa igungo fuska
(face to face)	Fuska-fuska, kido si kido
(bold face)	(ogboju)
faceache, n.	Ifota fuska, fifofuska
facial, adj.	Fe fuska, o fuska I/H
facile. adj.	Tinte I/H
facilitate, vt.	Meron I/H
facility, n.	Imeron I/H
fact, n.	Ezioka, izioka I/Ik
(fact of the case)	Ezioka nsohala
(as a matter of fact)	Ezioka nke magana (ezioka magana)
faction, n.	Iyahann, iyaga Y/H/I
factor, n.	Ifata, ezioka, fator – (Arith.)
factory, n.	Bajinka, fatiri, bejinka H/G
(factory worker)	O rushe fatiri/bajinka
(factory labourer)	Lebura fatiri/bajinka
factual, adj.	Zioka, ezioka, di 'zioka I/Ik.
faculty, n.	Iyawa, iminduyo, agba iyobi H/Y/I
fade, vti.	Chare H
faeces, feces, n.	Kashi H
fahrenheit, n.	Farinhait, semesinga G
fag, vt.	Sugu G
fail, n. vti, prep.	Shigo idiofoh, diofoh, ifoh, foh I/Y
faint, adj.	Nojo G
(fait-hearted)	Nojo-'yobi
fair, fairly, n. adj. adv.	Sera

(fair hearing)	Igbonti 'sera
(fair share)	Ikekpin sei
fairy, n.	Iwin Y
faith, n.	Izigbo I/Ef./Y
faithfully, adj.	Di zigbo, izigbo, ezioka I/Y
(yours faithfully)	Nke yin n'ezioka
faithfulness, n.	Izigbo, izimgbo I/Y
fake, n.	Igboloja, wayo I(G.v)/Gen
(fake drug)	Mageni gboloja H/I(G.v)
falcon, n.	Shaho H
fall, vi	Shuda, beka, zoro Y/I/H
fallacy, n.	Iroton I/Y
fallible, adj.	Le roton, roton I/Y
fallow, n.	Saura, hbura H
false, adj.	Siro, ai zioka, Y/I/Ik
(false teeth) n.	Hakori gboloja
(false witness), n.	(wayo shaida)
falsehood, n.	Isiromiwa I/Y
falsify, vt.	Mesiro, magomago I/Y
falter, vti.	Yipu Y/I/G
fame, n.	Inoki Y(G.v)
familiar, adj.	Mani Y/I
familiarity, n.	Imani Y/I
family, n.	Iyali, yali, dangi H
famine, n.	Iyunwa H
famish, vti.	Fini G
famous, adj.	Inoki Y(G.v)
fan, n.	Fanka, figini, mahuchi, mafifichi H
(fan belt)	Hambel, fifita, hanzuga H
(table fan)	Fanka tebur, faifa tebur H
fancy, adj.	Febi I/Y
(fancy shop/store)	Kisuwa 'rebi
fanatic, n.	O cheroka I/Y
fanatical, adj.	Cheroka I/
fang, n.	Fika H

far, adv, adj.	Jingolo, jijihan, jihan, jite, ijite, ishiene Y/H/I
fare, n.	Kudan, iyawa, yawa H/G
farewell, int.	Baiyo, k'odi ngba, abai, shiensike
fantastic, adj.	Opotopo,- izon/kalabari I\/I/Y/Eg
fantasy, n.	Icheriri
farina, n.	Gari, elubo Gen/Y/Ed.
farm, n.	Sule Ti
(farm house)	Gida sule H/Ti
(farm land)	Kasa sule H/Ti
farmer, n.	O sule G/Ti
farming, n.	Isule G/Ti
farrier, n.	Fariya G
farther, adv.,	Swiswido Y/I
farthest, adj.	Swido Y/H
fascinate, vt.	Fajiki Y/H
fascination, n.	Ifajiki Y/H
farthing, n.	Idanang, anini Y/Ef./Ed.
fashion, n.	Imaron, (fashon) I/Y/G
(fashion house)	Gida fazhon H/G
fast, adj.	Sokia, yaji
fast, vi.	Awe Y/Ed./Gen
fast, fasten, adj. vti.	Sodi Y(G.v)
fastener, n.	Isodi, o sodi Y(G.v)
fastidious, adj.	Moro
fat, n.	Ilabu, isonbu, isonji, sonbibu G/Y/I/H
(a fat man)	Milabu,
(a fat woman)	Malabu
fatal, adj.	Kugbu Y//I/Ed.
(fatal accident)	Ijambe ikugbu
fate, n.	Okeba, ikafu, kafu I/Y
father, n.	Uba, baba, mahaifi H/Y/Ed/Gen.
(father-in-law), n.	Suruki H
fatherhood, n.	Imiwa baba I/Y/H
fatherless, adj.	Ai wen baba, lai wen baba

fatherly, adj.	Bika baba, bibaba Y/I/Gen
fathom, n.	Gaba, inofi'sili; jinkaka H/Guob/I/Y
fatigue, n.	Irengu Y/I
fatten, vti.	Dilabu, melabu, mesonbu I/G/Y/H
fault, n.	Ishebi Y/G.v
faulty, adj.	Shebi, di shebi Y/G.v
favour, n. vt.	Inuere, nuere I/Y
favourable, adj.	Nuere, di nuere I/Y
favourite, n. adj.	O nuere, nuere, inuere I/Y
fear, n.	Irugu, igueru Y/I
(i am afraid)	Mo ng rugu
(it is fearful)	Odi rugu
feasible, adj.	Mime I/Y
feast, n.	Ikonje, ikowuam I/Y/G
(feast of tabernacle)	Ikonje tabanako
(feast divine)	Ikonje soliba, ikowuam soliba
feather, n.	Gashintsu H(G.v)
feat, n.	Irushagba Y/I
feature, n.	Inetu I/Y
february, n.	Fenbuari, uki meji na ardun
fed/feed	Jyuyo I/Y
federal, adj.	Fedrea, feriyya G(H.tone)
(federal government)	Gonmenti fedra (pederal gonment)
(federal character)	Imiwa fedra
federation, n.	Iferiyya I/H
fee, n.	Ikudi, ikugwo H/I
feeble, adj.	Kuagba, ai wen agba Y/I/Gen
feed, vti.	Wuam, jeri G/Y/I
(feeding allowance)	A lawas ijeri
feel, vti.	Wuche; dife, Mao, chofe, e, di I/Y
feeling(s), n.	Imao, ichofe H/G
feign, feint, n.	Bikuo, bikuowun I/Ed./Y
(i feinted)	Mo kuo, mo bikuo
fell, pt.	Shuda Y/I
felicitate, vtn.	Goyo, igoyo

fellow, n.	Imuke, imutum, ikama, isole H/Y/H/I
fellowship, n.	Isole, isolele I/Y
(fellow country men)	Emutum kasa, emonuwansa
felony, n.	Isegbu, ikuon Y/I
felt, feel	Mao, chofe I/Y
female, adj.	Ta, mache H
feminine, adj.	Mimache nke mache I/Y/H
fen, n.	Fadama H
fence, n.	Danga, shinge H
(don't sit on the fence)	Ma jondu na shinge,
fencing, adj.	Shinge, meshinge
fenced, pt.	Di shinge, di danga, shinge/danga
fender, n.	Ifinda G
fennec, n.	Feneryin-kayando H
fennec, n.	Yanyawa H
ferment, vti. n.	Rukan, irukan Y/Ed.
ferocious, adj.	Konlido Y/H
ferry, n.	Ugboko fito, fari H/G
ferry-man, n.	Miji fari, miji ugboko fito
fertile, adj.	Lido
fertilizer, n.	Taki, taki zamani H/G
fervency, n, adj.	Igbowu, gbowu Y/H
fester, n.	Igbinni Y(G.v)
festival, n.	Ikonodun, anivase
(festival of arts)	Ikonodun Cheko
fetch, vti.	Muta, mubia Y/I
(go and fetch me water)	Shien muta mi ruwa
fetish, n.	Eshugu Y/Ed/I/H
fetter, n.	Gigar, malwa H
feud., n.	Woga
fever, n.	Iba, igbowuji I/Y
feverish, adj.	Di'ba, gbowuji I/Y
few, adj.	Kele I/Y
(few people)	Emutum kele
fez, n.	Hula rama H/Y/I

fiancé, n.	Saurayi, fians H/G
fiancée, n.	Budurwa, fiansi H/G
fibre, n.	Faiba, uri G
fickle, adj.	Zi G
fiction, n.	Malasin, imalasin H/Y
fiddle, n.	Fido, tukono
fidget, vti,	Jikiri H/Y/I
fidelity, n.	Ifisiba, fisiba Y/I
field, n.	Filin H
(field work)	Irushe filin
(football field)	Fili kwallo, fili hubol
fierce, adj.	Giri, gbowu G/Y/H
fifteen, n. adj.	Goisen H/Ed.
fifteenth, adj.	Nke goisen I/H/Ed.
fifth, n. adj.	Nke isen (nk'isen)
fifty, n. adj.	Sen (noun & adj) Ed.
figs, n.	'ya'ya. H
fight, vti.	Jagha, ghagun I/Y
(free fight/free for all fight)	Ijagha kiri, ijagha nnonfe fighter, n.
figure, n.	Siffa, ifeli, ilamba H/Gen
figureative)	N'isiffa, n'ifeli
(figure head)	Ifeli 'si
file, n.	Fgail, zarto, goge, fike G/H
filial, adj.	Miwamo I/Y
fill, vti.	Jukmun I/Y
film n.	Flim, yana, garkwa, sinima ' H/Gen.
(film house)	Gida sinima, gida flim
filter, n.	Filita, filita, matachi G/H
filth, n.	Kazanta H
fin, n.	Kege, filafili kifi H
final, finally, adj. adv.	Iguton, meton, mesheton, giguton, gukpin finance, n.
financial, adj.	Kudi, noku, fekudi H/Y/I
(financial problem)	Nsohala kudi
financier, n.	O noku

finch, n.	Ivoseh G
find, vt.	chowa, hun, neri i/y
fine, n.	rama Y/I
fine, n.	gwole I/Y
finger, n.	Yatsa H
(finger nail)	Farche H(G.v)
(fore finger)	Monali H(G.v)
(little finger)	Yatsa kele, yatsa fiene
(finger printg)	Ami farche
finish, vti.	Gwuton, guton, finishe I/Y/G
(it is finished)	O gwuton/ o guton, finishe
finite, adj.	Di guton; finite I/Y/G(fE0
fir, n.	Vile G
fire, n.	Wuta, gobara H
(fire-arms)	Bindiga H
fire man, n.	Fayaman, miji o wuta G/H
fireworks, n.	Irushe wuta I/Y/H
(firing squad)	Mbi igbata wuta
fire fly, n.	Tashi wuta, tonwu-tonwu H/Y
firm, n.	Kamfani, isoleji G/IY
firm, adj.	Chile, sile, kamkpe, kpamgba, kpoi, shim
first, adj.	Konon whidokha Y/H/I
(first of all) n.	Ikonda I/Y/H
(first aid)	Fiadat mageni konan
(first aid box)	Akwati mageni?
(first time)	Ngba konda
(first and the last)	Konmda konzu
(first class)	Nu-nuke konda
first bank	Banki Konda
fiscal, adj.	Fiska G
fish, n.	Kifi, sunta H
fishmonger, n.	O kifi G/H
fisher, n.	O kifi, ikifi G/H
fisherman, n.	Masunchi, miji kifi H(G.v)
fist, n.	Dunkuhann H(G.v)

fit, adj.	Yedi I/Y
fitness, n.	Iyedi I/Y
fitter, n.	Makaniki, makaeson, ifinyen H/G/Y/I
fitting, adj.	Finyen, ifinyen Y/I
five, n, adj.	Isen Ed
fives, n, adj.	Isisen Ed
fix, vti.	Firi, dachiu, mechiu, dichiu, fie Y/I
flabby, adj.	Yigha Y/I
flag, n.	Tuta H
(flag bearer), n.	O bugbe tuta I/Y/H
(flag ship)	Ugboruwa tuta I/H
(flag staff), n.	Sanda tuta H
(flag house), n.	Gida tuta H
flagrant, n. adj.	Ihika, hika I/Y
(flagrant violation)	Igbaje hika
flake, n.	Flek, fulefule
flame, n.	Filem, iyaya, yayaya G
flamingo, n.	Imingo, mingo G
flammable, adj, adv.	Jowuta, jowujowu, jojowuta Y/H
flank, n.	Ibochie Y/I
flannel, n.	Yadulu H(G.v)
flap, n.	Ikpala, kpala G
flare, vi.	Jowufiene Y/H/Ed.
flash, vi, n. (flash of light)	Shanwuta, ichaun (flash light)
flask, n.	Gora
(water flask)	Gora ruwa H
flat, n. (of house)	Gida filat
flat, adj.	Lebe, filat Y/G
flatter vt.	Tonro Y/I
flatterer, n.	O tonro Y/I
flatulence, n.	Chikisu H/I
flavour, n.	Iveve G
flaw, n.	Ila, labuku Y
flay, vt.	Yola Y(G.v)

flea, n.	Ikuma H
fled, flee	Sapu, foleh, sata Y/I
fleece, n.	Gatun H(G.v)
fleet, n.	Jaru Y/H
fleet, n.	Jaru Y/H
flesh, n.	Inamaki, namaji, tsoka H(G.v)
fleshly, adj.	Namaki, namaji, di namaki, tsoka
flew, pt. fly	Lofeh, feh G
flexible, adj.	Yigbha, yiki Y/I
(flexible wire)	Waya yigha
(flick, n.	Itonshan Y/Gen.
flicker, vi.	Tonshan Y/Gen.
flight, n.	Ilofeh, ifeh G
(flight ticket)	Tikiti 'lofeh H/G
flimsy, adj.	Fale H/Y
(flimsy copy)	Kapitale, ineko fale I/Y
fling, flung, vti.	Sotu Y/I
flint, n.	Kanakara H
flippant, adj.	Gbuzioka, yayaya I/Ed/Ik/Gen.
flirt, vti.	Fiki, fikifiki G
flirter/ a flirt, n.	O fiki, o fikifiki G
float, vti.	Lele G
float, n.	Ilele G
flippant, adj.	Yeye, yayaya, iazioka Gen/I/Ik.
flippancy, n.	Iyeye, iyayaya Gen.
flick, n.	Garke H
flog, vt.	Luti Y/I
flood, n.	Ambaliya H
floor, n.	Dabe, bene, kasa, gindi H
flop. vit.	Nugurugu, shuda G/Y/I
flora, n.	Joli G
florin, n.	Fataka, dala H/G
flounce, vtn.	Yetu, iyetu Y/(G.v)
flour, n.	Gari, fulawa H
flourish, vit.	Yanfun Gen

flow, vi.	Sonru Y/H
flower, n.	Fulawa, fure, huda G/H
flown, vi.	Feh, lofeh G
fluid, adj.	Ruwa-ruwa H(G.v)
fluctuate, vi.	Fidoton Eg(G.v)
flung, fling	Sotu Y/I
flush vti.	Wopu, wota Y/I
fluster, vt.	Giche, gidima H
fluent, adj, n.	Rama, irama, saun Y/I
flute, n.	Fulut G/H/I
flux, n.	Ishion
fly, vt.	Feh, foga, foieh; fifeh; folefoleh G/Y/I
(fly out)	Fota, foga, fehta; H
fire-fly, n.	Tshi-wuta
fly, n.	Tashi H
flyover, n.	Obapase
foal, n.	Dukushi H
foam, n.	Kumfa, fuku H/G
(soap foam)	Fuku, fuku-fuku G
(mattress foam)	Kumfa H
focus, n.	Jule G
fodder, n.	Ingirichi H
foe, n.	Itiwe, ighata Y/I
foetus, n.	Tayi H
fog, n.	Gazo H
foil, vt.	Gbuhanya, dihanyar I/Y/H
foil, n. (of paper)	Felefe G
fold, n.	Itugbo I/Gen/Y
(a sheep fold)	Itugbo tunkiya I/Gen/Y/H
fold, vti.	Dikpo; dichi,
foliage, n.	Ganye, ganyaye H
folio, n.	Folo G
folk, n.	Mutane, jama'a, tughe H/I/Gen/Y
(folk songs)	Esonga itugbe
follow, vti.	Sole I/Y

(follow me)	Sole mi
(follower) n.	O sole
folly, n.	Igbumo I/Gen/Y
foment, vti.	Gboru Y/H
formentation, n.	Igboru Y/H
fond, fondly, adj/adv	Vule, vuvule, vuvulele
fondle, vt.	Vuvu G
food, n.	Abinchi, abinci
fool, n.	Mumu; oze Gen/Y/Ed/I
foolish, adj.	Mumu; H
foot, n.	Taki, kafa, futu H/G
football, n.	Kwallo, kwallo kafa, fuboi H/G
foot-bridge, n.	Gado-kafa, katako-kafa H
footpath, n.	Turba, hankafa H(g.v)
foot print, n.	Itite taki, itite kafa Y/H
foot-step, n.	Igafa kafa, igafa taki I/Y/H
for, prep.	Fun, funli, mani Y/Y(G.v)
forasmuch, conj.	Na funli I/Y(g.v)
forbearance, n, vti.	Ifajanda, fajanda
forbid, vt.	Lewo Y(G.v)
(god forbid)	Abasi o lewo
(god forbid bad thing)	Abasi o lewo ihe ika, Abasi o kwe ihe ika
forbidden, pp	Lewo
forcast, vt.	Woshido Y/H/I
force, n. vt.	Kagba, agba, ikagba
(by force)	N'ikagba, I/H
(police force)	Ikagba mondoka
(nigerian police force)	Ikagba Mondoka Naijeriya forcemajeure, n.
forceps, n.	Hantsaki H
ford, n.	Mashigi, maketari H
fore, n.	Nako, whido I/Y
forearm, n.	Hannu whido H/Y/I
forcast, vti.	Sowhido
forefather, n.	Kaka H

forefinger, n.	Manuni, mon ali H/Y/Ed/ ish/Ur/Is/It/Au/et
forgone, pp	Johannu Y/H
forehead, adj.	Whidokei, whidoshi, goishi Y/H/I
foreign, adj.	Kasimu H/Y
foreigner, n.	O kasimu H/Y
foreman, n.	Homan, heluma H
forename, n.	Afawhido I/Y/H
foremost, adj.	Whido jukha
forenoon, n.	Swenerana,iwhido rana ''
foresee, vt.	Nerai whido, neri na whido, hun whido
fore judge, vt.	Dakpe na whido Y/I/H
foreisgt, n.	Ineri whdo, ineri na whido, ihun whido
foreskin, n.	Loba, silli H
forest, n.	Daji, kurmi, duhuwa H
(forest tree) n.	Itache daji, H
(forest reserve)	Ichemo daji I/Y/H
forestall, vt.	Shane Y/H
foretell, vt.	Sole na whido Y/I/H
forethought, n.	Ichiro whido I/Y/H/Ed
forever, adv.	N'isiti, n'ilililai I/Y/G
forword, n.	Oka whido Ik/Y/H
forewarn, vt.	Gbulo whido I/Y/H
forefeit, vt.	Sofu I/Y
forefeiture, n.	Isofu I/Y
forge, vt.	Weja I/Y
forgery, n.	Iweja I/Y
forger, n.	O weja
forget, vti.	Chegba (chegba) I/Y
forgetful, adv.	Chechegbo I/Y
forgive vti.	Gbariji, i.e. gba-riji (gbari) I/Y
forgot, pt.	Chegba chega, gbafu I/Y
fork, vti.	Funku G
fork, n.	Fok H/G
(for-lift)	Injin obugbe kaya, faklif H/I/Y/G

for, n.	Kujera, ihanyar H
form vti.	Mundu, I/Y
formal, adj.	Bikmahan Y/I/H
formality, n.	Ibikahan Y/I/H
former, formerly, adj.	Lembu /I
fornicate, vt.	Magbe Y/I
fornicator, n.	O magbe I/Y
formidable, adj.	Sile Y/I
(formidable society)	Ijumome sile
formular, adj.	Mesheke, hanyar I/Y/H
forsake, vt.	Kosikasa, koka, fre, fisik
fort, n.	Ribadi, ribatsi H
forswear, vt.	Bubili na whido I/Y/H
forth, adv.	Japu, beeya, JG I/Y (and so on and so forth)
forth coming, adj. adv.	Biawa, bibiawa, japu biawa forthright, adj.
forthwith, adv.	Japukpe, jajapukpe Y/I
fortification, n.	Innon agba, innon agba si Ef/Y/I
fortify, vt.	Nnon agba, nnon agba si Ef/Y/I
fortitude, n.	Iwanya I/Y
fortnight, n.	Uzola meji, rana goinang Ed/Y/H/Ef.
fortold,	Sole whido
fortress, n.	Jula, igbarike G/Y/I
fortunate, adj.	Ishienda, also (fotiuna)
fortunately, adv.	Shishiende
(good fortune)	Ishiende rama
(bad fortune)	Isheien' ika
(ill fortune)	Ishiend'ijikele
(fortune teller)	O sole ishiende
forty, adj. n.	Na, (nan) Ef(G.v)
forward, adj, vt.	Whido Y/H
(fo forward)	Shien whido Y/I/H
forster, vt.	Cheto I/Y
(forster mother)	O cheto mama/mama cheto

fought, fight,	Jagha, ghagun Y/I
foul, vti.	Wayo Gen
(foul play)	Iwayo
found, vt.	Daka; choja; hun Y/I
founder, n.	O daka, o choja Y/I
foundation, n.	Idaka, ichoja, ikongi, gindi (foundation stone)
fountain, n.	Kagaggen marmaro, fantin H/G
(fountain-pen)	Alkalami fantin H/G
four, fours, n. adj.	Inang, ininan, enang (pl.) Efik
fourteen, adj. n.	Goinang, igoinang Ef.
fourtly, adv.	Nanang Ef.
four-footed, adj.	O kafa inang H/Ef.
fowl, n.	Kaza H
fowler, n.	Kpekpeiye, o gbuje onene Ed/Y/I/Og.
fox, n.	Faks G
foyer, n.	Bandeki H(G.v)
fraction, n.	Ida, frakshan Y/G(fE)
fracture, n.	Ikashi, imedi kashi H
fragile, adj.	Fifoji Y/I
fragment, n.	Guntu, gutsure H
fragrance, n.	Shanshan Y/G
frail, adj.,	Gbula I/Ed/Y
frame, n.	Fram, ilahan, weja H/Y
(frame up)	Weja
(frame work)	Irushe ilahan
franc, n.	Tamma H
franchise, n.	Iminera Y(G.v)
francolin, n.	Fakara, makwarwa H
frank, vt.	Tiko G
frank, n.	Franki G
frank, adj.	Ezioka, oka sam, oka sam-sam I/Ik/G
(franking machine)	Injin itiko H/G
fraternal, adj.	Kiji I/H
fraud, n.	Irawo Y(G.v)/H

fraudulent, adj.	Rawo Y(G.v)/H
free, adj.	Yonfe; nnonfe Ef/Y
(free-kiok)	Firi-kik
(free-size)	Otondo
(free gift)	Igaye nnonfe
(god's gift)	Igaye Abasi
freedom, n.	Iminira, minira, alafia, isimini Y
freewill, n.	Innonche Ef/I/Y
freeze, vti.	Gbuzeze I/Ed
freezer, n.	O gbuzeze I/Ed
freight, n.	Isukaya H(G.v)
freighter, n.	O sukaya, ugboko kaya H(G.V)/I/Y
french, adj.	Faransi H
frequent, adj.	Ngbani, ngbancha, gbangba, firi-firi
(frequent visitor)	Bako ngbani I/Y
fresh, adj.	Huntun I/Y
(fresh water)	Ruwa huntun
fret, vti.	Konji Y/H
friction, n.,	Awoso Y/I/Ed
friday, n.	Fraide G
fridge, refrigerator, n.	Firiji, akwatuji G/H/Gen/I friend, n.
(friend, please fry me egg)	Aboki, biko so mi kwai H/I/ Eg/Y/Ef/Itr/H
friendship n.	Iboki H(G.v)
frigate, n.	Ughoruwa o jagha, frigat I/H/G
fright, frightful, n.	Irugu Y/I
frighten, vt.	Tirugu Y/I
fringe, n.	Geza H
(fringe benefit)	Gezamfa, irire geza H/Y/G/Sobe
frivolous, adj.	Woloh G
fro, adv.	Sisa, bibia, bibniawa G/I/Y
(to and fro)	Isi sa Y/G
frock, n.	Rigar mata H
frog, n.	Kwado H
from, (prep)	Sa, mbo, lati, late, lati, also: ke G/Y

(from where)?	Sa'lee? Mbolee? G/I/Y
front, n.	Iwhido Y/H
(frontier), n.	Iwhido, kha, o whido
(frontier force)	Karfi whido, o jagha whido
frost, n.	Ituyi Y/I
froth, n.	Kumfa H
frown, vi.	Mejeido I/Y/H
frozen, freeze,	Igbuze I/Ed.
frugal, adj.	Toido, konoma Y/I/G
fruit, n.	'ya'ya H
(be fruitful)	Di 'ya'ya, wen 'ya'ya
fruition, n.	Infani, infa H/Y/G
frustrate, vt.	Gbuyobi I/Ed/Y
fry, vti.	So Egun
(frying pan)	Kwan so
fuel, n.	Man kasa, man wuta, fueli H/G
fugitive, n.	Maguji H
(fugitive of fender)	O jika maguji I/Y/H
fulfil your promise)	Mule ikwade e
full, adj.	Jukun, kamkpe, rama, fefe I/Y/Gen
fumble, vit.	Merun I/Y
fume, n.	Hamani, tunzu, itunzu H(G.v)
fumigate, vt.	Yaki I/H
fumigation, n.	Iyaki I/H
fun, n.	Wada, iwada Y(G.v)
(let us have fun)	Ka 'wa wada
(have fun)	Wen wada
function, n.	Irushe I/Y
fund, n.	Babawuta kudi, ikudi, susu, isusu H/Y/Ed.
furnance	Babawuta
fundamental, adj.	Zimkpa I/Y
funeral, n.	Isinkuo, isinmutu Y/I
fungus, n.	Fangus G
funnel, n.	Boto, kakaki, mazurari H

funny, adj.	Wada, di wada Y/I
fur, n.	Foh G
furious, adj.	Wuta, bionu, ruonu, gbowu I/Y
furlong, n.	Isuminda H(G.v)
furnace, n.	Babawuta G
(furnace of fire)	Babawuta
furnish, vt.	Mosho I/Y
furniture, n.	Ekayande, imosho H/G
furrow, n.	Rumaniya H
further, adj, adv.	Si, sisi Y
furthermore, adv.	Jukha I/Y
furthest, adj, adv.	Ju kha
fury, n.	Ibionu, iruonu I/Y
fuse, n.	Fiuz, zare G/H
fuss, n.	Roke Y/G
futile, adj.	Lofoh Y/G
future, adj. n.	Ngbawhido, iwhido I/Y/H G.

g.		Gi
Gabble, vti.		Yonunso
Gadfly, n		Bobuwa
gadget, n.		fon dabara, igaji
gag, n.		tianga, itianga
(press gag)		tianga fres, itianga, jaridu
(gaiety, n.)		imesondu
gain, n, vti.		iriba, riba, hunba
gain say, vt.		sonba
gait, n.		ihanta, (hanyar tafiya)
galazy, n		galaze
gala, n.		iriya
gale, n.		ifefe, iji
gall, n.		kumallo
(g. bladder), n.		matsarmama, ikpa, kumallo o
(g. stone)		dutse kumallo
gallant, adj.		gburu
galley, n.		gale, kinchi
gallery, n.		galeri
gallon, n.		galan, jala
gallop, n.		togi
gallows, n.		igalos
galvanize, vt.		gafanais
gamble, vti.		tete, kalo-kalo, chacha
gambling, n.		itete,k ikalo-kalo
gambler, n.		nye tete, nye kalo-kalo
gambol, n.		gembul
game, n		iregu, regu
(a game of luck)		irgu anfa
gander, n.		ganda
gang, n.		ikungiya, ingya, ingi
gangstar, n		taringi
gangrene, n.	ifonya, gangiri	G
gangway, n.	ganwa, zokungi	G
gaol, n.	kurkuku	H

182

gaoler, n.	yari, nye kurkuku	H/I
gap, n.	ela, holo	Y/Y(G.v)
(a big gap)	bab'ela, elalau	
gape, vi	yangboro	H/Y/I
garage, n.	garej	G
garbage, n.	datti	H
garden, n.	lambu	H
(g. egg), n.	gauta, yalo, data	H
gardener, n.	gadina, nye aiki lambu	H/I/H
gargle, vti.	mageniu	H/Y
garland, n.	galend, igulend	G
garlic, n.	itafarnuwa	H
garment, n.	itufa, gamint	H/G
gabble, vti.	Blabla G	
gadfly, n.	Bobuwa H	
gadget, n.	Irinkaya, rinkaya, gajit Y/H/G	
gag, n.	Itikpo Y/I/Ik.	
(press gag)	Itikpo presa Y/I/Ik/G	
gaiety, n.	Imedun, medunso I/Y	
gain, vti, n.	Rire, irire Y/Ed/Ikale/Sobe	
(gain saying)	Isoli choto	
gait, n.	Ihanshien H/Y/I	
gaiter, n.	Gaita G	
galaxy, n.	Igalazi, isunzar G	
gale, n.	Ifefe Y	
gala, n.	Iriya Y(G.v)	
gall, n.	Kumallo H	
(gall bladder), n.	Matsarmama H	
(gall stoner)	Dutse kumallo H	
gallant, adj.	Gburu, galante, chegbon G/I/Y	
galley, n.	Kiruwa, gali H(G.v)/G	
gallery, n.	Ifinzi Y/G	
gallon, n.	Galion, jala G/H	
gallop, n.	Galu-galu, dogi, idogi Y/G	

183

gallows, n.	Izingbu G/I/Ed
(gallows man)	Miji zingbu, o zingbu miji
galvanze, vt. gafanais	Gafanais G
gamble, vti.	Chacha; kalo-kalo, tete, gambul Gen./G(fE)
gambler, n.	O kalo-kalo, o tete Gen./G(fE)
(gambling man)	Miji tete, miji kalo-kalo
(roving gambler)	Baba tete, baba kalo-kalo
gambol, n.	Guerenji I/Y/H
game, n.	Igwuere I/Y
(game of luck)	Igwuere anfa
gander, n.	Ganda G
gang, n.	Kungiya, ikonojo H/G/Y
(gang up)	Konojo
gangstar, n.	Baba kungiya, jaguda Gen/H/Y
gangrene, n.	Gangirini G
gangway, n.	Hanyar ugboruwa, kankwe H/I/Y/G
gaol, n.	Kurkuru G
gaoler, n.	Yari, o kurkuku H
gap, n.	Ihoefe Y/I
(big gap)	Ihoefe bibu Y/I
gape, vi.	Gboro, ya Y(G.v)
garage, n.	Gareji, deki mota H
garbage, n.	Datti H
garden, n.	Lambu, gadin h
(garden egg), n.	Gauta, yalo, data H
gardener, n.	Gadina, o nushe lambu H/I/Y
gargle, vti.	Gbrugbruh G
garland, n.	Galand, igalandi G
garlic, n.	Tafarnuwa H
garment, n.	Riga, irudi baba, esa H/Og.
(garment factory)	Bejinka esa H/Og.
garrison, n.	Kungi soja, garisin H/G
(garrison commander)	O meashe igungi soja, kwamanda garisin

184

garrulous, adj.	O surutu, o chakwali H(G.v)
gas, n.	Gaz, gais, fekuku wuta G/I/Y/H
gasket, n.	Gaskit H/G
(cylinder gasket)	Gaskit selinda H/G
gasoline, n.	Fetur, gaisoline H/G
gasp, vit,	Yonu I/Y
gastric, adj.	Yonu-yonu, di yonu, yonu
gate, n.	Kofa H
gateman, n.	O chebo kafao, o chebo kofa Y/I/H
gateway, n.	Hanyar kofa H
gather, vti.	Konojo Y/Ed./H
gathering, n	Ikonojo, toro Y/Ed./H
gauge, n.	Geji, kwarma H
(gauge, vt.)	Nofi, nonwon
(gauge the tyre)	Nonwon taya
gaunt, adj.	Ru Y
gauntlet, n.	Ganlit G
gave, give,	Fun, nnon, gaye Y/Ef/I
gauze, n.	Koduga H(G.v)
gay, adj.	Daji Y/H
gaze, n.	Ihunri I/Y
gazelle, n.	Gaizol G
gazette, n.	Gazit G
gear, n.	Giya H
(gear box)	Akwati giya H
(gear oil)	Man giya H
geese, n.	Gizi G
gecko, n.	Tsaka H
geisha, n.	Gesha, omote imele nke jakpar
gelding, n.	Itenda Y(G.v)
gelignite, n.	Nakiya h
gem, n.	Lu'ulu'u H
gender, n.	Ijanda, G/H(G.V)
(masculine gender)	Ijannda miji,
(faminie gender)	Ijanda mache

general, generallyuy, adj.	Janar,kegogbo H/I/Y
generalise, vt	Di kegblgbl, mehe kegbogbo
generation, n. janarashon	Itugbe ardun goma,
(our generation)	Itugbe adun goma ' wa, ijanarzhion 'wa
(major –generatio n)	Mandajar - janar, manja kegbobo
(lieutenant-general)	Laftana-jaar, manja kegbobo
vt	Wuja, mubia, muta I/Y
generator , n.	Owuja o mubia, omuta, janaareeto
generosity, n.	Imere I/Y
generous, adj.	Meare "
genesis, n.	Jenisisi (je na isi ' si)I
(book of genesis)	Littafi jenisisi
genet	JanitG
geneticistm n.	Janitisi G
genial, asj.	Naya I/Y
genius, n.	Iwin o maon Y/I/G
gentilem n.	Jantail, kaferi G/Y
gentity,n.	Irayo I/Y
gedtle , adj	Rayo"L
(do it getly)	Mesherarayo
gentleman, n	Miji rayo; sah e sah
genuine, adj gentlemen	zioka I/IK
geograhy, n.	Ijiografi, ifakpor I/IK (geography master)
geometry, n..	Jiomiatri ikolain G/y/H
germ,, n.	Jam G
german, adj.	Zamani , jamus , bajamushe G/H/H
germinate, vti	Hugbo, lhu G/Y/G
gesticulate,	Jeka I/Y
gesture, n.	Imesi I/Y
(good getue)	Imesi rama
get, vti,	Rde Y/O
get (receive) / meet/met,	Hunri, hunba, rude, weni (get-out)
geyser, n.	Jisa,sifirini kasa /H

ghastly, adj.	Rugujiji
(hastly accident)	Ijamkbe rugujiji
ghost, n.	Ihindu
(ghost story)	Ilida hindu
giant, n.	Kato H
gibe, vi.	Solikah Y/I/Ik
giddy, adj.	Yikiri Y/I/G
gift, n.	Innon, ifun iganye I/Y/Ef. (gift of god) gigantic, adj.
gimlet, n.	Kayan ainta,jilmat H/G gin, n.
ginger, n.	Zamnjabir, cittar ho H giraffe, n.
(girl-fried),	Nindarinya Ed/H
girth, n	Bauji gist, n.
gizzard, n.	Kundu, bundukuli H glacier, n.
glad, adj.	Yoli, dunso Y/I (i am glad)
(glance through)	Neri firi /Y
gland, n.	Kaluluwa
glare, vit.	Donmna
glass, glasses, n.	Maidubi, gilas H
gleam, n.	Walkiya
glean, vit.	Shai Y/G
gleaner, n.	O hai ishai Y/G
glide, vi.	Melani I/H
glimmer,vt.	Monbai Y/G
glimpse, n.	Inewini I/Y
(catch a glimse)	Neri wini glitter,glittering, adj, vi.
gloat over,	Tula ukha
globe, n.	Kwallo,duniya, akpor H/Ur.
gloom, n.	Jonu (sad)
glorify, vt.	Mesh'go, m'ogo, bogo I/Y
glorious adj.	M'ogo, bogo I/Y
glory, n.	Ibogo /Y
gloss .	Walkiya H
glossy, adj.	Di wsalkiya, walkiya I/H
glove, n.	Safar annu, gulovu H/G

glow, vi.	Yowu /H
glucose n.	Sukar, glukos H
glum, adj.	Samaku, makukun H/Y
glut, vt.	Nnonju nnonjukha, nnonkha Ef/Y/I
glutton, n.	Machiya, o jekha Y/I
gluttony, n.	Ijekha Y/I
gnat, n.	Ginati G
gnaw, vti.	Jewuam Y/G
go, vi.	Loga, shienga, iringa, shien, shtene
(go-slow), n.	Ishienkele Y/I
(let us go)	Ka 'wa shienga, ka'wa lofeh
goad, n.	Tsinke h
goal, n.	Gida, gol, igwukpin, maksudi H/G/I/Y
goat, n.	Akuya, H
(he-goat)	Bunsuru H
(goat head)	Isi akuya I/H
(goat head pepper soup)	Ngwongwo isi akuya
goblin, n.	Gobilini G
god, n.	Abasi Efik
godly, adj.	Bika Abasi, imiwa abasi Y/I/Ef
god, n.	Ekwenshu I/Y
godfather, n.	Baba bika Abasi Gen/Y/I/Ef
godmothwer, n.	Mama bika Abasi Gen/Y/I/Ef
godsend, n.	Ishinende Abasi Gen/Y/I/Ef
god-speed, n.	Isokia Abasi, iyalionu I/Y/Ef
(god-speed recovery)	Isokia alafia Abasi
(i wish you god-speed recovery)	Mo shien e isokia alafia Abasi
god-fearing, adj.	Irugu Abasi Y/i/Ef.
goggles, n.	Madubi 'do, gagols H(G.v)/G
goitre, n.	Makoko h
gold, n.	Zinariya, zina ; goldi H/h(G.v)/G(fE)
(golden gate), n.	Kofa zina
goldsmith, n.	Gursuminti, (golsumit
golden, adj.	Fe zina, di zina, zina I/Y
golf, n.	Galf G

goliath, n.	Golayat, golozah G
gomorah	Gamorah G
gone, go.	Shien; ringa, ti shien
gondola, n.	Gendula G
gong, n.	Kuge, gwarjen shela H
gonorrhoea, n.	Gono, gonoyaya G
good,	Rama, irama, e rama (goods) Y/I
goodness, n.	Irama
9very good)	Rama kha
(good for nothing)	Of oh rama
(good-morning)	Eku safe y/H
(good-afternoon)	Eku rana Y/H
(good-evening)	Eku-yamma Y/H
(good-night)	Eku-tuu Y/Tiv
(good news)	Ikwiro rama
(good things to come)	Ishiende bibiawa, irama bibiawa
(good-bye)	Baiyo izon
(good-turn)	Iyintua rama
goods, n.	Ekaya, erama H/Y/I
goodwill, n.	Ishieni rama
goose, n.	Guz, tolotolo G/Gen.
gore, vt.	Jeni H/H
gorge, vit.	Tagbu I(G.v)
gorgeous, adj, adv.	Hone Y/I gorilla, n.
gospel, n.	Oka baibul Ik/G
(gospel message)	Iziron baibul
gossip, n.	Imebo, mebo Ur/Y/Ed/Gen
(gossiper, n.)	O mebo, amebo Ur/Y/Ed/Gen
got, get.	Weni, wenri, rude I/Y
gouge, n.	Kwakula, raraka H
gourd, n.	Duma, gora H
govern, vti.	Baeze, gonmenti, je baeze Y/Ed/I/h
government, n.	Gonmenti, ibaeze H/I/Y (government house)

governor, n.	Gofano, o obaeze, o gonmenti, (otogan)
(governor-general)	Gofano-janar, ibaeze kegbogbo
gown, n.	Riga H
(long gown)	Igungo riga
grab, vti.	Jau G
grace, n.	Ilinsha, idore H/Y/Ar
(by the grace of god)	N'ilinsha Abasi I/h/Y/ Ef/Ar graceful, adj.
(good gracious)	Ilinsha rama
(gracious me)	Idore mi, ilinsha mi
grade, n.	Ikpobe Y/I
gradient, n.	Iganga H(G.v)
gradual, adj.	Dieyo Y/I
graduate, n.	O digiri, gradwet H(G.v)/G
graduate, vt.	Digiri gradwet H(G.v)/G
graft, n.	Rikichi H
grain, n.	Hatsi, tsaba, kwaya daya, kadan H
(grains board)	Kwaminti nke tsaba H/I/H
grammar, n.	Ituranchi, girama H/G
(grammar school)	Makaranta turanchi, makaranta girama
grammarian, n.	O soli turanchi
gramme, gram, n.	Gram G(fE)
gramophone, n.	Garmaho H
granary, n.	Rumbu H
grand, adj.	Tonbi H
(grand finale0	Igwuton kpata
grand child, n.	Jika, omon tonbi H/Y/Ed/Ur/ Is/ Sob/Au/I grand daughter, n.
grandfather, n.	Kaka, baba tonbi H/i/y/gen.
grad parent, n.	Iyaye tonbi H/i/y
grandson, n.	Jika namiji, mongida tonbi
grandstand, n.	Ilega I/Y
grant, vt.	Gaye, ninnon Y/I/Ef
grape, n.	Inabi H

grapefruit, n.	Tonis, grehul H
grasp, vti.	Kagba
graph, n. adj.	Itisi, tisi G
grass, n.	Haki, chiyawa h
(green grass)	Ikore haki, algashi H
small grass	Wawa H
grasshopper, n.	Fara H
grassroot, n.	Gindi haki, igigindi H/Y/G.v
grate, n.	Goge H
grateful, adj.	Diokpe I/Y
(i am grateful)	Mo diokpe
gratis, adv, adj.	Ninnon Ef/Y
gratitude, n.	Idiokpe I/Y
(with gratitude to god)	N'idiokpe fun Abasi gratuity, n.
grave, n.	Kabari, kushewa, kushe H
grave-divver, n.	O woka kabari, o woka kushe
gravel, n.	Burji, tsakuwa H
gravity, n.	Gravite; iwegba G/Y
gravy, n.	Muya H
gray, grey, n.	Iwofa
graze, vti.	Jeko
grease, n.	Maiko, girisi, man H
great, adj.	Tombi, tombili (gidi) (for person) Y/I
(great man)	O gidi miji
(great woman)	O gidi mache
(great day)	Itombi ranae; rana tombi
(great patience)	Babaisundi, isundi tombi, isund tombili
(alexander the great)	O gidi Alegzanda
(great britain0	O gidi Briten
greatness, n.	Itombi, itombili
greed, n.	Wonji, iwonji Y/H
(you are very greedy)	O ng wonji kha
green, adj.	Kore, algashi H
(green grass)	Algashi H

greet, vt.

(greetings)

(i greet you)
(i greet you in the name of god)
Mo kine e n'afa Abasi

Nine I/Y

Ekine I/y

Mo ng kine e

grief, n.	Ikanbe
grew, grow	Tula, diagba
grey, gray	Launi toka-toka, wofa H
grey hair, n.	Furfura, gashi wofa H/Y
greyhound, n.	Grehon, idundi G
grief, n.	Ikanbe
grievance, n.	Ikanbe
grieve, vti.	Kanbe
griffon, n.	Girifon G
grill, n.	Gasa H
(a grill)	Gasa daya H
grim, adj.	Fagbu H/I
grimace, n.	Gwalo H
grin, vit.	Difagbu
grind, vti.	Lo y/i/ed
(grind the pepper)	Lo akoko Y/I/Ed/Id
grinder, n.	O lo (olo) Y/I/Ed
(grindstone), n.	Dutse lo, olo H/y/Ed.
grip, vti.	Gbamu, jimu I/Y
gripe, n.	Imerun I/y
grit, n.	Gari dutse H
groan, vit.	Befuta, kebefuta I/y
grocer, n.	O kantinchi H(G.v)
grocery, n.	Ileta kantinchi Y/I/H(G.v)
groin, n.	Koton y(G.v)
groom, n.	Ango, mon barga H/Gen
(bridegroom)	Gogi H
grope, vti.	Grop G
groove, n.	Gruvu g
gross,	Gogo ati nainang H/Y/Ef.

ground, n.	Kasa H
(ground floor, n)	Gindi kasa Y/H(G.v)
groundnuts, n.	Gyada, gujiya H
(groundnut oil)	Man gujiya, man gyada H
group, n.	Itugbe Gen/Gen
(group of people)	Itugbe emutum
(group of companies)	Itugbe kamfani
grouse, n.	Mita H
grovel, vi.	Resika Y/H/Ed
grow, vit.	Hugbo diagba G/I/Y
growth, n.	Ihugbo Idiagba G/I/Y
grower, n.	O diagba, o hugbo
(rice grows everywhere)	Shinkafa ng na nso ncha growl, vit.
grub, n.	Tsutsa H
grudge, vt.	Meji I/H
(don't harbour grudge)	Ma bute imeji, ma meji grudgingly, adv.
gruel, n.	Ikunu H
gruelsome, adj.	Kunu, di kunu H/I
grumble, vit.	Kunme Y/I
grunt, vit.	Gaun G
guano, n.	Tufo G
guarantee, n.	Iyobe, iyobele
guarantor, n.	O yobe, o yobele
guard, n.	Ikare, itsare, igadi, ichebo, be
(guard-room)	Deki 'chebo, deki gadi
(be on your guard)	Di chebo
(security guard)	O diwen gadi
guardian, n.	Wakili, waliyi, o chebo H/I/Y
guava, n.	Gwaba, goba, gofa H/y?Gen.
guerilla, n.	Guarila, ijaghuru G/Y/G
guess, vti.	Cheso I/Y
(you guessed right)	
Cheso I/Y	
(guess-work)	Irushe cheso I/Y

guest, n.	Bako, gesa
(be my guest)	Wu bako mi, wu gesa mi
guidance, n.	Imahan, ichebo Y/I
guide, n.	Imahan, ichebo Y/H
(guide me)	Mohan mi, ichebo mi
guile, n.	Meiro I/Y
guild, n.	Ituegbe Gen/Gen
guilt, n.	Idebi I/Y/(G.v)
guilty, adj.	Debi I/Y
guinea, n.	Zaza G
(guinea, corn), n.	Gero zaza
(guinea fowl), n.	Kaza zaza
(guinea pig), n.	Alade zaza
(guinea worm), n.	Tana zaza
guitar, n.	Molo H
(guitar box)	Akwati molo
(guitar boy)	Yaro molo
gulf, n.	Tukpo G

(gulf oil)	Man tukpo H/G
gullet, n.	Makogwaro H
gull, vti.	Gbo Y(G.v)
gully, n.	Kwazazzabo, kwaza H/G(G.v)
gulp, vti.	Kapu G
gum, n, vt.	Danko, karo, gam, lemu H/Y(G.v)
gun, n.	Bindiga H
(machine gun)	Bindiga nke injin H/I/G
(field gun), n.	Igwa, bingida fili H/G(H)
gunner, n.	Soja igwa H
(gun-powder), n.	Barudu, albarushi H
guosalogy, n.	Iguosaloji, sayesn nke ede
gush, vi.	Yobia Y/I
gust, n.	Tuwe G
gut, guts, n.	Hanji H
gutter, n.	Gata, tafai G
gymnasium, n.	Ijimnazhion G
gymnastics, adj.	Ejimnazhion G
gynecology,	Ganakoloji

H

ha, inter,	Haba H/Gen
habit, n.	Ibamu, ibigbe, iyisi Y/I
habitant, n.	O bigbe I/Y
habitual, adj.	Bamu, di 'bamu Y/I
habitable, adj. adv.	Bigbe, bibigbe I/Y
hack, vt. i.	Khai, gain G
had, have	Ti, ze Y/G
hades, n.	Ihuwu Agbo/H
haemorroids, n.	Yondidi Y/H/G
haggard, adj.	Hagba Ed
haft, n.	Kota, bota H
haggle, vi.	Yohann Y/H
hail, vti.	Eeh, kpenoh Y/I/G
hair, n.	Gashi H
hairdresser, n.	O gashi
hairy, adj.	Buzurwa h
hair-pin, n.	Ikoti Y/Ed
hake, n.	Haik G
hale, adj.	Dira, I/Y
half, n, adj, adv.	Afu I
(half-brother, n)	M'ubafu Y/H/Ed/Ur/Is/It/Au/Sob/I
(half-dozen)	Afu goteji I/h/Y
(half-sister)	M'uwafu Y/H/Ed/Ur/Is/It/Sob/Au/I
(half-hearted)	Afu 'yobi Y/I
(half-penny)	Afu kobo I/Gen.
hall, n.	Bandeki Gen/h
halleluyah, n.	Aleluyah Gen.
hallo, int, n.	Alo, aluao, alarek Ed/Kwale/Ber.
halo, n. hallowed	Kekasu kuru H
halt, vt.	Chiu I/Y
(railway halt)	Ichiu reluwe
(halting place)	Mbi 'chiu
halter, n.	Ragama, o chiu H/I/Y

halve, vt.	Afu I
ham, n.	Nalade H(G.v)
hamburger, n.	Ambuga, sefinchi G
hamlet, n.	Karakauye H(G.v)
hammer, n.	Masaba, gunduma, hama H
hammock, n.	Amuku, raga H
hamper, vt.	Dili hann Y/I/h
hand, n.	Hannu H
(hands up)	Ehannu si nuke
(hands down)	Ehannu si sala
(hands shake)	Gbawen hannu, nno hannu
(clap your hands)	Kwa e hannu e
handball, n.	Bolu hannu
handbell, n.	Agogo hannu
handcuff, n.	Ankwa H
handful, adj.	Jukun hann I/Y/H
handcap, n.	Idihann Y/H
handicraft, n.	Irushe hannu I/Y/H
handkerchief, n.	Adiko, mayani, akafifi H/G
handle, n.	Makama, mariki, bota, kota H
handle, vti.	Demu, toido I/Y/H
(handle with care)	June, demu n'irayo (dmu rayo0
handler, n.	O toido
handmaid, n.	Mongi mache Y/Ed/Ur/Is/It/Au/Sob/Ed
handrail, n.	Hannu gada H
handsome, adj.	Kare I/Y
handwriting, n.	Ikode hannu
(beautiful handwritin)	Ikode hannu rama
handy, adj.	Hannu, di hannu I/H
hang, vt.	Yopu, yota, sogbu, sha, kagbu, yoisi, Y/I/Ed/G/Y/I
hangar, n.	Hanga, o sogbu, o kogbu H/Y/I/Ed
hank, n.	Kurshe H
hanker, vi.	Meri I/Y
hanky-panky, n.	Isiro, iyikiri, aizioka Y/I/Ikw

hansard, n.

Ansad, siemha G

haphazard, adv, adj.

Zighi Ed happen, vi.

(what happened?)

Meni soka

(what happened then/three
– after?) Meni bia soka?

(it may happen)

O le soka, o le wu (let it happen/be)

happiness, n.

Idunso, igbandu, idunso happy, adj.

harass, vt.

Ha, yo li onu, rugu Y/I
(don't harass me)

harassment, n.

Iha, irugu, iyo li onu

harbour, n.

Bienruwa G/H

harbour, vt.

Bute Y/G

hard, adj.

Sile I/Y (very hard)

harden, vti.

Di sile, sile I/Y hardly, adv.

hardy, adj.

Silele

hare, n.

Zomo H

(hare brain)

O wauta

harlot, n.

O fiki-fiki, ashewo, fiki-fiki harm, n.

harmattan, n.

Hunturu, buda, sarara, kuyari – H

harmful, adj.

Meba jiba Y/I/H harmless, adj.

harmony, n.

Irundo Y/I harpoon, n.

harness, n.

Kandoli H (G.v) harp, n.

harsh, adj.

Rugu, diambu Y/I/G hartebeest, n.

harvest, n.

Igbore, ikote I/Y

has, have

Wen, ti, la I/Y

hasn't

Ko wen, ko la, ai wen; aila

has been

Ti

hasp, n.

Alharga, harga H

(hasp and staple)

Harga ati liqua

haste, n.

Isokia I/Y

(in haste)

N'sokia

hastily, adv.

Sosokia I/Y

(hasten up)

Meshe sokia I/Y

hasty, adj.

Sokia I/Y

hat, n.

Malafa, hana salla H

hatch, vti.	Gbuki I/Ed/H
hatchet, n.	Omo gatari Y/Ed/Ur/It/Is/Au/Ish/H
hate, vt.	Juhu G
hatred, n.	Ijuhu, aiche, igbuche G
(i hate gossip)	Mo juhu imebo, mii che amebo
haughty, adj	Jikiga H/Y
haughtiness, n.	Ijikiga H/Y
haul, vt.	Fako Y(G.v)
haulm, n.	Harawa H
hausa, n.	Hausa, emutum nke Nairjeriya eso
have, vt, pt.	Te, wen, also: shekw
(i have)	Mo wen, mo te
(i have known)	Mo te ma
(i have finished)	Mo te meshe ton/mo teemeton
(i have arrived)	Not te bia wa
haversack, n.	Amasaye h
havock, n.	Imeru I/y
hawk, n.	Shaho H
hawk, vt. n.	Letakiri, iletakiri I/Y/G
hawker, n.	O letakiri
hawking, n.	Iletakiri
(hawking is prohibited)	Ao gbakwe iletakiri, ao kweba iletakiri hay, n.
hazard, n.	Imewu, ifewu I/Y
haze, n.	Ikuafe, ikukiri, Y/G
hazy, adj.	Kuafe, kukiri Y/G
he (masculine pron.)	Ya, o, o, e. I/Y
(he is coming)	O ng biawa Y/I
(he said that)	O gbaameh kpe Y/Iz/Y
(for him/her)	Fun ya Y/I
head, n.	Isi, shugaba, keisi H/I
(the head)	O keisi
(the head of state)	O kaisi kasa
(many heads)	Ekaisi
(subject head)	Isi-oka

headache, n.	Ifota, ifotisi, nsohala Y/I/H
head-dress, n.	Gele Y
head-rest, n.	Isimini kaisi
head-gear, n.	Ibo kaisi
head-phone, n.	Fon kaisi G/H/I
head-lamp, n.	Wuta kaisi H/I
headlong, n.	Igburu, gburu G
headman, n.	Heluma, miji kaisi H/I
head-land, n.	Kasa kaisi
headmaster, n.	Megida o kaisi H/I
headmistress, n.	Uwargida o kaisi
headpan, n.	Kwano kaisi H/Nu/I
headpad, n.	Gammo H
head-quarters, n.	Hedkwata, mbikeibi H/I
headstrong, n.	Isilekaisi mbikeibi I/Y/H
headwalls, n.	Makari, bangokaisi H/I
headway, n.	Kaisi hanyar, ishienswhido
headword	Isi oka
heal, vti.	Kule (igbandu) – synonym
health, n.	Iki, ilafia Gen/Gu
good-health	Jikindu H/I
(ill-health), n.	Jiki-rubi
heap, n.	Tari, tuli, tsibi, dimbi, jibji
hear, vti.	Gbonti, nugbo Y/I
(hear me)	Gbonti mi
(do you hear?)	Igbola?, igbogo>
(i have heard)	Mo gbola, (agbola m'), mo te nugbo
hearsay, n.	Isoli-gbo I/Y (don't want a hearsay)
heart, n.	Zuchiya, rai, hali, (iyobi) H/Y/I
(be of good heart)	Wen iyobi, di 'yobi
heartbreak, n.	Imeje iyobi, igbuyobi
heartbreaker, n.	O gbuyobi
heart beat, n.	Iluti 'yobi (ilutiyo)
heart ache	Ifota 'yobi, igbuyobi
heart attack, n.	Itako yobi

heart-felt, adj.	Lendo-iyobi,
heart-failure, n.	Iyobi-foh
hearten, vt.	Meiyobi, di 'yobi I/Y
hearth, n.	Hait, soveh G
heartily, adv.	Yoyobi Y/I
heartless, adj.	Ai wen yobi, lai wen yobi, idi 'ka
hearty, adj.	Di 'yobi
heat, n.	Igbowu Y/H
heathen, n.	Kafiri, abokesha H/Y
heave, vti.	Sienu, hunri Y/I
(heave a sigh of relief)	Wen ironhann, hunri 'ronhann heaven, n.
heavenly, adj.	Di gworun
(heavenly body)	O gworun
(heavenly father)	Baba nke igworun (baba igwori)
heavy, adj.	Gbih G/I/G
hebrew, n.	Heberu, hibriu Y/G
(the book of hebrew)	Littafi heberu H/Y
hectare, n.	Heta G
hectic, adj.	Nsohala IIY/Gen.
heddles, n.	Allera, andira H
hedge, n.	Shinge, H
hedgehog, n.	Bushiya H
heed, vt.	Songbo, gbonti I/Y
heedless, adj.	Ai gbonti, lai gbonti, ai songbo
heel, vit.	Gika Y/H
heifer, n.	Karsana H
height, n.	Haiti G
(what is your height?)	Meni wu Haiti e?
heighten, vti.	Di heiti, Haiti
heir, heirs, n.	Magaji, ajoun H/Y/I
(heir apparent), n.	Honka magaji
held, pt. hold.	Jimu
(get hold of)	Jimu, jiwen
helicopter, n.	Halikota, folefole, ofelele G
heliograph, n.	Haliograf G

hell, n.	Biwuta Y/H
hello, int.	Ridao, alo; alua-o, alarek kwale/Ed/Kwa/ber.
(hello dear)	Alo ninda; ndao ninda
(hello my dear)	Alo ninda mi; ndao ninda mi
(hello my sweet)	Alo o dunso mi; ndao o dunso
(hello my sugar)	Alo suka mi; nda o suka mi
(hello my honey)	Alo zuma mi; ndaio zuma mi
helmet, n.	Kwalkwali, buke, halimet H/G
help, vti.	Nno hann, ron hann Y/Ef/H
(please help me)	Biko nno mi hann
(help him/her)	Nno ya hann
helpless, adj.	Ai wen inno hann
helter-skelter, adj.	Fiam-fiam, reso-kaza G/Y/I/H
(run helter-skelter)	Ireso-kaza
hem, n.	Kamasa, taushe, kalmashe H
hemisphere, n.	Duniya, akpor, hamisfe H/Ur/G
hemorrhoids	Kpokpokpo
hemp, n.	Rama, wi-wi, hempu H/G
hen, n.	Kaza, tsuntsuwa H
(hen-pecked), adj.	Aurarre H
hencoop, n.	Ago kaza Gen/h henceforth, henceforward
her, pron.	Ta (definite) ya (indef & neutral) H/I
(for her)	Fun ya
(ask her)	Jubi ya
(she did it herself)	Ta meshe ya ta
herbaccous, n.	Habekos – irudi fulawa –gadi
herb, n.	Hebu G
herd, n.	Garke, kora H
(herds of the swine)	Garke nke alade H/I
(herd of cattle)	Garke nke shanu H/I
herdsman, n.	Makiyayi H
here, adv.	Mbia, mbi, ebi, or ebibi, mbibi
(here and there)	Mbi ati ebe, ebi ati ebe
(here are you)	Neri e
hereabouts, adv.	Mbi nso, ebi nso

hereafter, adv.	Ebi zuein
hereditary, adj.	Tohann Y/H
heredity, n.	Itohann Y/H
heresy, n.	Inikinche Ef/I
heretic, n.	D'inikinche Ef/I
herein,	Mbibia Y/I
herewith, adj.	Mbiati, mbi kpelu Y/I
heritage, n.	Igayekaka Y/i/H
(african heritage)	Igayekka Afrika
hermaphrodite, n.	Sungulu, o sungulu, mamiji G/H(G.v)
hermit, n.	Sufi H
hernia, n.	Dadali H
hero, n.	Kaka baba H/Gen.
heron, n.	Balbela, zarbe H
heroin	Hiron G
hers,	ta, nke ta
hesitate, vi.	Meyeji I/y
(don't hesistate)	Ma meyeji
hesitation, n.	Imeyeji
hessian, n.	Algarara H
hew, hack, vti.	Gain G
hexagon, n.	Hegzagon G
hey, int.	Eeh, kai G/H
(hey, come here)	Eeh, biawa mbi
hey, vt.	Suwe G
hiccup, vtn.	Suke-suke G
hid, hidden,	Cheto I/Y
hide, vti.	Cheto
(hide me, oh god)	Cheto mi, Abasi
(hiding place), n.	Ebi 'cheto
(hide-and-seek)	Ichet '-ichowa
hiding, n.	Icheto
hierogliph, n.	Hiroglifi G
high, adj, adv.	Ganu, ga, ganu Y/I
(high tone)	Tiuma ga

high minded, adj.	Iyobi ga Y/I
(high-life)	Akpor-ganu
(high priest)	Baba fada Gen/G
(high reputation)	Inoki ga; inoki ganu
(high wall), n.	Tudu gia
(high speed)	Ireso ga, iyaji ga
(high official), n.	Baba hafsa
higher, adj.	Ga kha
(higher, executive officer)	Hafsa ga kha highlands, n.
highway, n.	Baba hanyar Gen/H
hill, n.	Tudu, tsauni, hawa H
(up hill)	Nuketudu
(hill-top)	Nuke tudu,
(up hill task)	Isile nuke
hillock, n.	Okiti Y
him, pers. pron.	Yanji I/H
hinder, vt.	Gbuhan, dihan I/H/Y
hind, n.	Izuba I/H
hindrance, n.	Ighuhan, idihan I/H/Y
hinge, n.	Hinji, almanani H
hint, n.	Gbofiene Y/G
hinterland, n.	Imenu kasa I/Y/H
hip, n.	Kwatan H(G.v)
hippopotamus, n.	Dorina H
hire, vt.	Haya H/G/Gen
(hire motor)	Haya mota
(hired motor)	Mota haya
(hire purchase)	Irata haya Y/I/Gen
his, pron.	Nke shi, nke ya I/H
(his money)	Kudi ya
(this is money)	Eyi wu kudi ya
hiss,	Shior, itsekiri
history, n.	Iliton; (itono) synonym
(history will tell)	Liton a soli
historian, n.	O liton

(history master)	Oga iliton
hit, vt.	Gam, gbah, luti O muko ilitor
(don't hit me)	Ma gbam mi; ma luti mi
(hit and run)	Luti reswo
hitch, n.	Ko
hitherto, adv.	Siti ngba
hive, n.	Maya H
(bee-hive), n	Amya H
hoard, n. vt.	Ikojo; kojo Y(G.v)
hoarder, n.	O kojo
hoarse, adj.	Le
hobble, vit	Woshen Y/G
hobby, n.	Iguere I/Y
hockey, n.	Haki G
hoe, n.	Hauya, fartanya, garma H
hog, n.	Alade, alhanzir
(war hog)	Gandu H
hold, held, vti.	Jimu, chendu I/Y
(hold on)	Chendu; chendu fo I/Y/Ish/Au
(hold him/her)	Jimu ya
hoist, n.	Ifale, fale, Y/G
hole, n.	Ihonu Y/I
(pot-hole)	Kotogbin, honu-honu, G/Y/I
holiday, holidays, n	Isimini H
hollow, adj.	Raka H
holy, adj	Somoh
(holy, holy, holy)	Isomon, isomon, isomon
(holy ghost), n.	Isomon Mindu
(holy water)	Isomon ruwa
(holy land)	Isomon kasa
(holy men of god)	Isomon emiji Abasi
homage, n.	Chaffa, igasin H/I/Y
(pay him/her homage)	Mesh' igasin fun ya; gasin ya home, n.
homeward, adj.	Ishiene gida, bibiawa gida
homicide, n.	Kisan omofon G(fe)

homophone, n.	Onohrara, homo.
homosexual, adj.	Kushili, omosezua H/G
hone, n.	Gwere I/Y
honest, adj.	Zioka I/Ik
honesty, n.	Izioka I/Ik
(honesty is the best policy)	Izioka wu ikoso rama kha honey, n.
honeycomb, n.	Ruwa zuma, sakar zuma H
honeymoon, n.	Ihutu mata 'ti miji, ibebi
honorary, adj.	Fanzi, ifanzi, onorara Y/I/G
honorary post	Ikpoze – fanzi, ikpoze norara
honour, n.	Ifanzi, onoh G/I
honourable, adj.	Fanzi, ifanzi, le fanzi, di fanzi
hood, n.	Kokuwa H
hoof, n.	Kofato H
hook, n.	Kugiya H
(hook worm), n	Kwarba, tsusta
(finishing hook)	Kugiya kifi H
hooligan	O katakata, o yoliionu Gen/Y/I
hoop, vi.	Jagba
(hoping cough), n.	Ikoho jagba, gbuhu-ghuhu
hoop, n.	Yaboto, yaboto H/Y/Gen.
hoopoe, n.	Alhudahuda H
hooray, hurray, int.	Hurrah! Gen
hop, vit.	Fokah G
hope, hopeful, n. vti.	Rekon, renti, irekon, irenti Y/I (i am hopeful), adj.
(hope in god)	Renti na Abasi
(i hope that)	Mo rekon kpe
hopeless, adj.	Lai rekon, ai renti, ai wen irekon
hopper, n.	Dango H
horizon, n.	Bago akpor H /Ur
horn, n.	Kaho H
hoover, n.	Huvah G
horizontal	Orizon G
hormone, n.	Homo G

horn, n. (motor horn)	Honu, pam-pam G
horology, n.	Ihoroloji, hor0oloji, imeshe agogo
horoscope, n.	Horosko, ineri kadara
hornbill, n.	Burtu, chilakowa H
hornet, n.	Hanit, kikon G
horrible, adj.	Rugu Y/I
horro, n.	Ighuru, ghuru, ghurubi G
horse, n.	Doki H
horseback, n.	Zuba doki H
horse dealer, n.	O doki H(G.v)
horseman, n.	O doki miji (hasman)
horse shoe, n.	Takalmi doki H
horsewhip, n.	Bulala doki
horticulture, n.	Shuke-shuke H
hosanna, n.	Hozana, ikebe ikelelo Abasi
hose, n. (pipe)	Tokun H/Y/Ed
hose, n. (socks)	Hos G
hospitable, adj.	Bika asibiti, ninnon Y/I/H/Ef
hospital, n.	Asibiti, H
hospitality, n.	Ininnon, inonku Ef/H
host, n.	Ikpone, elamba Y/I/G
host, n.	O mele Y/I
(my host/hostess0	O mele mi
(air hostess)	O mele aroplen, o dunso, ostes
hostage, n.	Ihostej, hostej, ijimugbam G/I/Y
hostess, n.	Ostes G
hostel, n.	Ostel G
hostile, adj.	Jagha, ghagun Y/I
hostility, n.	Ijagha, ighagun Y/I
hot, adj.	Ghowuta, muwuta Y/H
(hot cake) n.	Kek nke gbowuta
(hot eba)	Eba nke gbowuta
(hot tea)	Ti nke ghowuta
(the food is hot)	Abinchi gbowuta
(hot-headed)	Igbowuisi

hotel, n.	Huta, otel; otela G
hound, n.	Karod
hour, n.	Hawa, wakati H/Gen/Y
(faminu will be back in one- hour's time	
Faminu ga ha hawa daya nsiyii	
(at what hour?)	Ke wakati? Meni wakati?
house, n.	Gida, soro H
(the head of the house) (m)	Babangida H(G.v)
(the head of the house) (f)	Mamangida Gen/G(G.v) (the owner of the house)
(house breaker), n.	O foji gida, o rawo
household, n.	Iyali, emutum gida
house keeper, n.	O cheto gida I/Y/H
housewife, n.	Uwar gida, (lit) mata gida
housemaid, n.	Mongi mache Y/Ed/Ur/Is/Au/Sob/Ish/H
hovel, n.	Gida o siyen Y/I/H
hover, vi.	Fochiu Y/I
how, adv.	Bawo, keba, loi, loloi hanya Y/I/Y
(friend, how is it?)	Aboki, bawo k'odi?
(how are you?)	Bawo k' e di, bawo k'odi?
(how long)?	Keba ngba? Ke ngba?
how is work?	Bawo maka aiki/irushe?
(how many?)	Irisi-loi?
(how much)?	Elei-loi?
(how far?)	Bawo ishiene?
(howbeit)	Amo
however, adv.	Biotiche, biowu Y/I
howl, n.	Awuh Gen
hub, n.	Hobu, arin wili G/Y/G (hub-bearing)
hubbub, n.	Irimkpotu Y/I
huddle, vit.	Wunso Y/I
hue, n.	Irimkpo Y/I hug, vt.
huge, adj.	Luku Y/I
hum, vit.	Hom G

human, adj.	Mutum H
(human being)	Mutum, omo Adam Y/ Ed/Ish/Is/Au/Sob/H
humanity, n.	Mutunchi, imutum H/H(G.v)
humble, adj.	Lisi, relisi, Y/I (i humbly ask) Mo jubi n'ilisi
humid, adj.	Tuoyi Y/Ed/I
humiliate, vt.	Lisika Y/I/H
humiliation, vt.	Ilisika Y/I/H
humility, n.	Ilisika, igbumonji Y/I/H
humorous, adj.	Li muerin, fakua-mua Y/I/G
humour, n.	Imuerin, ikuakua
hump, n.	Tozo H
hundred, n. adj.	Igogo, gogo H(G.v)
(one hundred)	Ogo daya hung, hang
hunger, n.	O sogbu, hanga, isha
hungry, adj.	Guebi I/
(i am hungry)	E(mo ng guebi)
(a hungry man is an angry man)	
O guebi wu o bilionu	
hunt, vti.	Chowa I/Y
hunter, n.	Maharbi, mafarauchi, o chowa
hunting, n.	Ichowa
hurdle, n.	Nsohala, isilekha I/Y
hurl, vt.	Finuke, soki I/G
hurray, int.	Hurrah, hureh Gen/G
hurricane, n.	Harikan G
(hurricane lamp)	Fitila harikan G/H
hurry, n.	Isokia, iyaji, zai-zai I/Y/Ed/H
(hurry up!)	Soki-kia, zai-zai
(i am in a hurry)	Mi di sokia, mo ng zai-zai
hurt, vti.	Gbowu, gbuji I/Ed/H
(i will hurt you)	Maa gbuji e
(don't hurt me)	Ma gbuji mi
(it hurts me)	O gbuji mi

(it hurts so much)	O gbuji kha-kha
husband, n.	Miji, maigida H
husbandry, n.	Miji sule, o sule H/Tiv
hush, vti.	Sundi Y/I
husks, n.	Kaikayi, kofe, buntu, kono H
hustle, vt.	Chokia I/Y
(hustle and bustle)	Ichokia-kia; ichowa zai-zai
hut, n.	Daki, gida kele, gida fiene
hyacinth, n.	Yasint
(hydraulic brake), n.	Brek haidroliki
hyena, n.	Kura, siyaki H
hygiene, n.	Ileji Y/H
hydrophobia, n.	Haidrofobia, iswuelu G
hydro-electric, n.	Lantiriki aidro Gen/G
hydrocarbon, adj.	Wassid, aidrokolori
hydrofoil, n.	Aidrofo, ugboruwa G
hydrogen, n.	Aidrojin, igaiz, haidrojin, G
(hydrogen peroxide)	Aidrojin na agzaid G/I/G
hydropath, n.	Aidrofati G
hydroplane, n.	Aidroplen, aidroflen G
hydrophonics, n.	Aidrofoni G
hymen, n.	Haimen G(Geek)
hymn, n.	Isongimo G/Y
(hymn book)	Littafi 'songimo H/G/Y
hypertension, n.	Akpatensia Y/G
hyphen, n.	Haifin, afu G/I
hyphenated, adj.	Afu, meshe afu, di haifin
(hyphenated christian)	Kirista afu
hypnotic, adj.	Sikwale (abnormal sleeping condition)
hypocrisy, hypocrite, n.	Munafunchi H
hypodermic, adj.	Allurar huji H
hypo, n.	Aipo G
hypothesis, n.	Ibachero Y/I
hyssop, n.	Haisop G
hysteria, n.	Istera G

idea, n.	Ichenu I/Y
ideal, n.	Inera I/Y
identical, adj.	Yiba I/y
(the two are identical)	Fa/ha eji yiba
(they are identical)	Fa/ha eji yiba
identify	Me yiba, yiba
identity, n.	Iyiba I/Y
(funny-funny identity)	Iwad'iyiba
idiom, n.	Ikworo I/Y
idiomatic, adj.	Kworo I/Y
idiot, n.	Wawa, sakare H
idle, adj.	Gbushe, ia rushe, simini
(idle talk)	Oka igbushe
(idle hands)	Hannu isimini, hannu igbushe
idol, n.	Gumki, tsafi H
i.e.	Yien wu (y.w.) Y/I
if, conj.	Bi, bina Y/I
(if you)	Bi e
(if not)	Bi ko, bi bati,
(if i come)	Bi m'ba biawa
(if i,)	Bi m'
ignominious, adj.	Negon I/Y
ignition, vt. n.	Twini itwin-twin I/Y
ignorance, n.	Ijahilchi, ijahili H(G.v)
ignorant, adj.	Jahilchi, jahili H(G.v)
ignore, vt.	M'aikasi
(ignorance,)	Imaikasi
(i ignore you)	Mo maikasi e
iguana, n.	Damo h
ill, adj, n. adv.	Isono y/I
(i'm ill)	Mii gbandu, mong sono
(he/she is ill)	Ya o gbandu ya no so ni
(ill treatment)	Isono lo sie so ni
(ill will)	Isono ishieni
(ill wind)	Ifekuku sonro

(ill feeling)	Isono wuche
illegal, adj.	Gbufin, gbuiwufin I/Y
illegible, adj.	Ai hune, gbuhune, lai hune
illegitimate, adj.	Gbuiliwu, ai liwu, lai liwu
illicit, adj.	Yailiwu (y'iliwu), gbuiwufin
(illiticit gin)	Barosa y'iliwu, kain-kain, 404
(illicit love)	Ihunf' iy'iliwu
(illiterate, adj.)	Ai cheko, lai cheko, gbucheko
(an illiterate)	O gbucheko ai cheko
illiteracy, n.	igbuchoko (illiteracy could be a disease)
illuninate, adj.	Haska, haske H
illustrate, vt.	Meron, meneri I/Y
illustration, n.	Imeron, imeneri I/Y
illustrious, adj.	Bogo I/Y
(illustrious son)	Ibogo monmiji
(illustrious daughter)	Ibogo monmache
image, n.	Kama, gunki, kamanni H
imagination, n.	Icheri I/Y
imagine, vt.	Cheri I/Y
imam, n.	Limami H
(chief imam)	Baba Limami
imbalance, n.	Igelege, gelege (G)
imitate, vt.	Mera I/Y
imitation, n.	Imera I/Y
immaterial, adj.	Ai rubu, lai rubu Y/I
immature, adj.	Ai diagba, lai diagba ai nuke
immaculate, adj.	Farifat, fari kha-kha
immediate, adj.	Sam;
immediately, adv.	Sinta
immediately, adv.	Sam-sam
immemorial, adj.	ililoron
immense, adj.	Bibu Y/I
immensely, adv.	Bibibu Y/I
immerse, vt.	Boru Y/H
immersion, n.	Iboru Y/H

immigrant, n.	Makaurachi, o bale H/I/y
immigrate, vt.	Kaurato, bale H/I/Y
imminent, adj.	Sigkie whido, minento Kal/Ish/Y/H/G
immigration, n.	Ibale imakaurachi
(immigration department)	Iyahann Bale, (Depatmnt nke Imigrazhion) immobilize, vt.
immodest, adj.	Ai wara, lai wara, gbu wara
immoral, adj.	Ai iwa, lai miwa, gbu miwa
immortal, adj.	Lai kuowun, ai kuowun, mindulai Y/I
immortality, n.	Imindulai Y/I
immovable, adj.	Shimshim, chiu shim G/I
immune, adj.	Monji; miuna Y/H
imminity, n.	Imonji Y/H
impact, n.	Tegbi, ilegbi
impair, vt.	Meru I/Y
impale, vt.	Mika I/Y
impart, vt.	Kozi Y/I
(impart knowledge)	Kozi mi 'chigbon
impartial, ajd.	Ai megbe I/Y
impassable, adj.	Lai koga, gbukoga I/Y
impatience, n.	Ai sundi, gbuisundi, ai wen sundi
impact, n.	Tegbi, itegbi
impair, vt.	Meru I/Y
impale, vt.	Mika I/Y
impart, vt.	Kozi Y/I
(impart knowledge)	Kozi mi 'chigbon
impartial, adj.	Megbe I/Y
impassable, adj.	Lai koga, gbukoga I/Y
impatience, n.	Ai sundi, gbuisundi, ai wen sundi
impede, vt.	Fachiu, dachiu, gbuhanyar
imple, vt.	Whidofa H/Y
impediment, n.	Idachiu, ifachiu, igbuhanyar
impenetrable, adj.	Lai gunle, ai gunbale Y/I
imperative, adj.	Tameta G
impend, vi.	Bibia, whido I/Y/H

imperfect, adj.	Ai shaka, lai shaka, gbu shaka Y/I/G
imperishable, adj.	Lai megien, ai iru, lai rubisi
impersonation, n.	Lai kemu, ai kemu igbukemu
impersonation, n.	Igbukemu
impertinence, n.	Ai chenu, lai chenu, igbuchenu, iwayo
impetus, n.	Ikarfi, agba, impetusa, petusa H/Y
implements, n.	Ekayaki H(G.v)
implicate, vt.	Fanye Y/I
implication, n.	Ifanye Y/I
implicity, adj. n.	Fandi, ifandi Y/H
implore, vt.	biyo Y/It/I
(i implore you)	Mo biyo e
imply, vt.	(neri fandi)
impolite, adj.	Gbu wara, ai wara, lai wara
import, n.	Mu bia kasa G/Y/I/H
important, adj.	Gesi, izon, zumkpa, katazi It/I/Y
importunate, adj.	Biyosi It/I/H
impose, vt.	Gbelisi, gbesikei, meke Y/I/H
(self-imposed)	Imeke wenji, igbeisis wenji
impossible, adj.	Gbumeshe, ai meshe, lai meshe, lai di meshe
impostor, n.	Songona H(G.v)
(impostor god)	Ekwenshu, ibilis I/Y/H
impotent, adj.	Kubura Y/H
impound, vt.	Muwen, diwen Y/I
impoverish, vt.	Mela I/Y
impracticable, adj.	Gbu jilolo, ai jilolo, lai di jilolo
impregnate, vt.	Nnon menu, fun menu Ef/I/Y
impress, vt.	Temu Y/I(G.)
(impress on him/her)	Temu si ya
impression, n.	Item
impressive, adj.	Di temu
imprison, vt.	Ronshien prusu, ronga, prusu, fiye na prusu Y/I/Ti
improbable, adj.	Ai bowu, lai bowu

improper, adj.	Lia dita, ai ditto, gbu ditto Y/I
improve, vti.	Tunmeshe, masi, rama si I/Y
improvement, n.	Imasi, itumeshe, irama si (improvement scheme)
imprudence, n.	Ai zoye, lai zoye, igbuzoye I/Y
impulse,	Gbushaka, aishaka, lai shaka I/G
impure, adj.	Empos
imputation, n.	Ishungu, shungu Y/I
in, prep, adv.	Na, di, diwa (dia), fre, lai I/Y
in. prep.	Menu, si, na I/Y
inability, n.	Ifregbaran, ifregba, aigba Y/I/G
inadequate, adj.	Ifrezuto, ai zuto, lai zuto Y/I/G
inaudible, adj.	Fredigbo, fregbo, ai gbo, gboro
inaugurate, vt. n.	Dakasa, idakasa Y/H
incantation, n.	Ibubuyaya G
inborn, inbred, adj.	Mubi kpe I/Y
incapable, adj.	Freagba, ai gba, lai gba I/Y
incapacitate, vt. n.	Fremetisi, ifremetisi I/Y
incarcerate, vt.	Rongprusu Y/I/Tiv
incarnate, vt. n.	Jishaka, ibubu-yaya H/G
incautious, adj.	Fresoliki Y/I
incense, vt.	Fa ibionu, di bionu, bionu Y/I
incense, n.	Turare H
incentive, adj.	Imuisiya Y/I
(incentives)	Emuisiya
inch, n.	Inchi, insh G
inceptive, vt. n.	Fafe, ifafe Y/I
incessant, adj.	Ngba-ngba, aisimini, fresimini (incessant disturbance)
incise, vt.	Gebe Y/I
incite, vt.	Fata Y/I
incline, vt. n.	Chesi I/Y
include, vt.	Fiyen Y/I
incoherence, n. vt.	Ifremede, aijiemu Y/I
income, n.	Irire Sob/Y/Ed/H

215

(income tax)	Iharaji rire
incomparable, adj.	Fremuso, ai/lai muso
incompetent, adj.	Frekamshe, ai/lai kamshe I/Y incomprehensible, adj.
inconsideration, n.	Ifretunche
inconsistent, adj.	Fremeshiene, ai/lai meshiene I/Y
inconceivable, adj.	Ai/lai dichi, fredichi, gbudichi
inconvenient, adj.	Ai/lai rowuya, frerowu Y/H
inconsolable, adj.	Ai/lai shim, freshim Y/I/G
incorrect, adj.	Ai/lai saun, fresaun, gbukamkpe
increase, vt.	Kpoka, kpone
incorporate, adj.	Fibale, fiyensi, daka Y/I
incorporation, n.	Ifibale, ifiyensi, idaka
incredible, adj.	Frenikon, inkredula, lai le niko Y/I/G
increment, n.	Ikporinsi, ikpokasi Y/I
incorrupt, adj.	Ai bele, lai bele, frebele
incriminate, vt.	Firengwu Y/I
incubate, vt. n.	Gbukwai, igbukwai I/Ed/H
inculcate, vt.	Tenu /I
incumbent, adj.	Weni I/Y
incorrigible adj.	Ai wanya, lai wanya, frewanya
incur, vt.	Faqsi
(incur debt)	Fasi 'gwese
incurable, adj.	Ai meso, lai meson, fremeso
indebt, adj.	Di 'gwese, je igwese I/Y
indebtedness, n.	Idi 'gwese, ije gwese
indecency, n.	Ai finde, lai finde, frefinde
indecision, n.	Ai cherisi, lai cherisi
indeed, adj.	Na'meshe I/Y
indefinite, adj.	Ai dido, lai dido, fredido
indelible, adj.	Ai kapfu, lai kpafu, frekpafu
indemnify, vt.	Kudisi H/I
indemjity, n.	Ikudisi
independence, n.	Owenji, dipenda I/H/G
indent, vt.	Taku H(G.v)

index, n.	Ifineri, o fineri, fineri Y/I
india, n.	Idia Ed
indistructable, adj.	Ifrerunje, ai runje, lai runje
index finger, n.	Mon ali H/Y/Ed/Ur/Is/Uv/Sob/Ish
indicate, vt.	Tonika, fine, fineri Y/I
indicator, n.	O tonka, o fine, o fineri
indict, vt.	Kasin'wuya Y/I/H
indictment, n.	Ikasin'wuya
indigestion, n.	Ifredachin, ko dachin, ai dachin, lai dachin
indifferent, adj., adv.	Fregbonti Y/I
indigene,	Mokasa, nkekasa
indigenous, adj.	Ife/he kasa, nkekasa
indignant, adj.	Bilionu Y/I
indignation, n.	Ibilionu Y/I
indignity, n.	Ilisika
indigo, n.	Shuni, baba H
indirect, adj.	Lai fgon, ai gon, fregon
indiscernible, adj.	Ai monche, fremonche, lai monche
indiscipline, n.	Inidisika, ai kozi
indiscriminate, adj., adv.	Frechetid, ai chetido, lai chetido, ai chewidi indiscreet, adj.
indisputable, adj.	Freroka, lai roka, ai roka
indisposed, adj.	Ai kizi, lai kizi, frekizi
indistinct, adj.	Ai hone, lai hone, frehone
individual, adj.	Enina Y/I
indivisible, adj.	Ai kekpin, lai kekpin, frekekpin
indoors, adj.	Mengi I/H
indolence, n.	Menka I/H
induce, vt, n.	Yinyo, iyinyo Y/I
indulge, vt. i. n.	Yimesi, iyimesi Y/I
industrial, adj.	Letaleta, indusia I/Y/G
industrious, adj.	Rushe, ai simini I/Y
industry, n.	Indosia, gida injin, indostriala G/H
indwell, vti.	Gbime

(indwelling spirit)	Mindu igbime
inefficient, adj.	Frewenshe, freyokeisi
inestimable adj.	Ai nofi, lai nofi, frenofi
inevitable, adj.	Lai biekwe, freweku
inexcusable, adj.	Frewizii
infamous, adj.	Ai noki, frenoki, lai noki
inexhaustible, adj.	Ai mego, fremego, lai mego
infant, n.	Jariri, jinjiri, H/I/Y/Ed/Au/Ish
inexpedient. adj.	Freyeli, ai yeli, lai yeli
infantry, n.	Sojahann, ijariri etc
inexpensive, adj.	Frewonga, frenonku Y/I/Ef
infatuation, vt. n.	Jukunfe, ijukunfe I/Y
inexperience, n.	Ai chegbon, lai chegon, ifrechegbon
infect, vt.	Jamon
infection, n.	Ijamon
infer, vt.	Nefe
inferior, adj.	Zuein I/Y
inferiority, n.	Izuein
inexplicable, adj.	Frediye,
infernal, adj.	Keshu, biwuta I/Y
inexpressible, adj.	Freliye, ai liye, lai liye
infidel, n.	Keferi, frenikon (freni) Y/I/Ef.
infallible. adj.	Freroton, ai roton, lai roton
infinite, adj.	Aiguton, ai finite
infest, vt.	Yolonu Y/I
infection, n.	Iyolonu
infirm, adj.	Fresile
infirmity, n.	Ifresile
inflame, vt.	Fiyenna wuta, medi wuta, jowuta, jowu, diwu
inflammable, adj.	Jowuta, le jowuta
inflammation, n.	Ijowuta, idiwu
inflate, vt.	Feku
inflation, n.	Ifeku
inflexible, adj.	Ai yigha, freyigha, lai yiki

inflict, vt.	Jeafu, nnonafu Y/I/Ef
influence, n.	Fasi ifame Y/I
influenza, n.	Inflenza, irn tuoyi G/Y/I
influx, n.	Ifinju
inform, vti.	Koli; soli, (ipres) synonym
information, n.	Ikoli, shime Y/I
infra-structure, n.	Ikayanfa H/Y
infrequent, adj.	Ai gbangba, fregbangba, ko gbangba
infringe, vt.	Fregeza, ai geza, lai geza
infuriate, vt.	Fibionu Y/I
infusion, vti., n.	Wunsi, iwunsi I/Y
ingenious, adj.	Ai win, lai win
inglorious, adj.	Ai bogo
ingratitude, vt.	Ai diokpe, lai diokpe
ingratiate, vt.	Ai ninnon Y/Ef
ingredient, n.	Magani H
inhabit, vt.	Digbe, bigbe I/Y
inhabitant, n.	O bigbe, o zauni I/Y/H
inhale, vt.	Fanchi I/H
inherit, vt.	Jewen Y/I
inheritance, n.	Ijewen Y/I
inhospitable, adj.	Ai ninnon, lai asibiti, ai nure
inhuman, adj.	Ai mutum ai di mutum, miw'ika
iniquity, n.	Ijoshe I/Y
inimical, adj.	Taiwe (t'iwe) Y/I
initial, adj.	Bire I/Y
(initial capital)	Warkudi bire
initiate, vt.	Gbayen, bire I/Y
inject, vt.	Gunyen I/Y
injection, n.	Igunyen I/Y
injunction, n.	Iyondo Y/H
injure, vt.	Meru I/Y
injury, n.	Imeru, ijambe I/Y
injustice, n.	Ai zioka, lai zioka, ifrezioka
ink, n.	Tawada H

(ink bottle)	Ijongo tawada Ibira/H
inland, adj.	Isalande, menu kasa, isala I/H/Y
inkling,n.	Oka irayo Ik/I/Y
in-law, n.	Siriki, sirika H
in-mate, adj.	O tugbe gida, aboki I/Y/H
inmemoriam (lat)	N'iloron I/Y
inn, n.	Huta, otela G
innards, n.	Echiki, etumbi H(G.v)
innate, adj.	Bikpe Y(G.v)
inner most,	Imenu kha
innerkeeper, n.	O cheto menu abi otela
innocent, adj., n.	Ai joshe, lai joshe, ifrejoshe (Ifreshe)
innovate, vt. n.	Meshe huntun, ihuntun I/Y
innuendo, n.	Ihabaichi, habaichi H(G.v)
innumerable, adj.	Frediye I/Y
inobservant, adj.	Ai wone, ai hun, lai hun, lai wone
inoculate, vt.	Lollu Y/H
inoculation, n.	Ilollu
inoffensive, adj.	Lai fabionu, frefabionu, ai joshe
inquest, n.	Ichondi ikuowun I/y
inopportune, adj.	Ai wen iyoge, adi di yefe
inordinate, adj.	Jukha, ai zioka Y/I
inorganic, adj.	Ai wen firam Y/I/H
input, n.	Ifiyensi I/Y
inquire, vt.	Jubi I/Y
inquisitive, adj.	Mebo, chondi Ed/Ur/Gen/I/Y
inroad, n.	Itako jiji
insane, adj.	Wela, feweh Y/I
inpatient, n.	Ai sundi, ifresundi, ai wen sundi, ai di sundi
insatiable, adj.	Fretewuya, ai sokene
inscribe, vtn.	Finde, ifinde Y/I
inscrutable, adj.	Jinka
insect, n.	Kwaro H
insecticide, n.	Ogun kwaro, insektisaid Y/H/G

insecure, adj.	Ai diwen, lai diwen
insensible, adj.	Ai diwen, lai diwen
insensible, adj.	Ai chero, lai chegbon I/Y
insert, vt, n.	Wensi, iwensi I/Y
inseparable, adj.	Lai kaya, ai kaya, ai choto
inside, n.	Imenu I/Y
insidious, adj.	Kpachiwe I/Y
insignificant, adj.	Insogini, ai zunki, lai zunki I/Y
insight, n.	Inerime I/Y
(insight communication)	Isole nerime
insipid, adj.	Ai dunso, fredunso Y/I
insincere, adj.	Ai solezi Y/I
insinuate, vt.	Fayen Y/I
insist, vi.	Teonu, ai chiu, lai chiu Y/I
insolence, n.	Ihijika
insobriety, n.	Ai jiba, frejiba Y/H
insolvent, adj.	Ai sowara Y/G
inspect, vt.	Insfekt, beneri, ibidori, fidosi
inspiration,	Innogbon
insomnia, n.	Isomini; ifresunla
insomuch, adv.	N'ibate kha, n'ibate shien
instability, n.	Ai kundushim, lai kundushim
inspire, vt.	Nnoghon Ef/I/Y
install, vt.	Fintin, bugbesi Y/I
instalment, n.	Isonkele Y(G.v)
instance, n.	Ifine Y/I
(for instance)	Nifine, fouifine
instant, adj.	Kpam, ensant G/G(fE)
instantly, adv.	Kpam-kpam, ensantly
instead, adv.	N'iyefe I/Y
instep, n.	Jegbin kafa Y/H
instigate, vt, n.	Fame, ifameshe Y/I
instil, vt.	Fisimenu Y/I
instinct, n.	Imanu, ichegbinu I/Owo
institute, n.	Baba makaranta, makarento H(G.v)

institution, n.	Imakarento, idasikasa, ibire
instruct, vt.	Kozi Y/I(G.v)
instruction, n.	Ikozi, iherushe, H/I/Y
instrument, n.	Ifaiki, Ihaiki, ife rushe
insubordinate, adj. n.	Fretisiba, ifretisiba
insufficient, adj.	Ai zuto I/Y
insulate, vt, n.	Tikpo, itikpo Y/I
insulin, n.	Insulini, insulain G
insuperable, n.	Isile kha
insult, vt.	Yihi Y/I
insurance, n.	Inshuwara, idido H/H/Y
insure, vt.	Dido, medido, shuwara Y/I/H
insurgent, adj.	Kundu si, mote I/Y
insurmountable, adj.	Lai bokeisi I/Y
integrate, vt. n.	Koso, ikoso Y(G.v)
intellect, n.	Iyeze Y/I
intelligence, n.	Idi 'yeze, talijensha I/Y/G
intact, adj.	Lai tukon, huntun Y/I
intemperance, n.	Ai surundi, adi diye I/Y
intend, vt.	Gbiche Y/I
intense, adj.	Kinkon, gbowu, ga Y/I/H
intention, n.	Igiche, ichero Y/I
inter -, vt.	Sinkwa Y(G.v)
interact, vi.	Konoshe
inter-alia (lat)	Ati-'fe mozo Y/I
intercede, vi, n.	Biyo, ibiyo It/Y
interdict, vt. n.	Dachiu, idachiu Y/I
interest, n.	Iche, enfa, irire Sob/I/Y/H/Ed/ etc.
interfere, vi. n.	Kwusi, fionu, fionu si, ifionu tafia I/Y
interim, n.	Na ngba nsiyii, na ngba
interior, adj. n.	Menu, imenu I/Y
interject, vt. n.	Keji, ikeji I/Y
interlocutor, n.	O basoli Y/I
interlude, n.	In'arin, n'arin I/Y
intermarriage, n.	Igbemata dintu Y/I/H

222

intermediary, adj. n.	Narinji, inarinji I/Y
intermediate, adj.	Kesmeji, narinji
intermingle, vt.	Ramkpo Y/I
intermission, n.	Isiminu, (isimini)
intermittent, adj.	Japujata Y/I
intermix, vti.	Konomeji
interment, n.	Isinkuo Y/I
internal, adj.	Menu; I/Y
(internal affairs)	Intana Afies; oka/menu
international, adj.	Akporncha; intanayo Ur/Enuani/G
interphone, n.	Intafon, fondekideki G/H
interpol, n.	Mondoka intanayo, mondoka akporncha
interpose, vt.	Busiwhido, busiwhi I/Y/H
interpret, vi.	Solidiye, gbeso, tafinta Y/I/H
interpreter, n.	O solidiye, o gbeso, tafinta
interrogate, vt. n.	Jubi jubi I/Y
interrupt, vt. n.	Dikpo, idikpo
intersect, vti.	Keniya I/Y
interstate, adj.	Narin yakin kasa, intastet I/Y/H/G
intertribal, adj.	Narin dintu I/Y/H
(intertribal war)	Ijagha narin dintu
intervene, vt.	Balerin yenrin I/Y
interview, n.	Ifidokido Y/H
interweave, vt.	Sarka H
intestine, n.	Ana afi-zere (jarawa)
intimate, adj.	Fima Y/Owo
intimidate, vt.	Me di rugu I/y
into, prep.	Si, simenu, sime Y/I
intolerable, adj.	Lai kweba, frekweba
intoxicate, n. vt.	Ishagbu, shagbu H/I/Ed
intransigent, adj.	Wara ai trasnsi I/Y
intransitive, adj.	Lai wen ife gon; etransitiv
intrepid, adj.	Transit lai rugu, gboaya
intricate, n.	Idisile I/Y
intrigue, vi.	Rkisi

223

introduce, vt.	Muswene, muta, muma, Y/Owo/I
introduction, n.	Imuwhido, ifineri
introspect, vi.	Chonwenji I/Y/G
introvert, vt.	Neriyobi wenji
intrude, vti.	Bule I/Y
intuition, n.	Imangba Ow/Y/I
invade, vt.	Jagha is, ghagun si Y/I
invalid, adj.	Ai yemkpa, lai yemkpa, freluwe
invariable, adj.	Ai choto, lai yintua
innumerable, adj.	Lai le go, ko she go, ai go
inundate, vt.	Bokperu Y/H
invasion, n.	Ijagha si, ighagun si
invaluable, adj.	Lai luwe, freluwe
invent, vt.	Mubia, muta, hume, weja, mubiawa
invention, n.	Imubia, imuta, ihume, iweja, imubiawa
inventor, n.	O mubia, o muta, o hume, o we ja, o mubiawa
inventory, n.	Infentri, ilitafi kaya, H(G.v)/G
invert, vt. n.	Wusi, iwusi I/Y
invest, vti.	Bunle, cheto Y(G.v)/I
investment, n.	Icheto, ibunle
investigate, vt. n.	Chondi, ichondi, chowandi I/Y/H
invigorate, vt.	Medunso, nnon agba I/Y/Ef.
invigorate, vt.	Medunso, nnon abg a
invincible, adj.	Baba'gba Gen
invisible, adj.	Di ai neri, lai neri
inviolable, adj.	Lai me je, lai foji
invite, vt.	Invite G
invitation, n.	Ikono ikonozo G
invocate, vt.	Lissaro ikasuwa, konode H/Y
involve, vt.	Fayen, fabale
involvement, n.	Ifayen, ifabale
invulnerable, adj.	Lai bokeisi, lai tagbu Y/H/I
invoice, n.	Takasuwa, G H(G.v)
inward, adj.	N'imenu, n'whido I/Y/H

224

iodine, n.	Ayodain G
iota, n.	Itufiene, itintin, chief Ed/Y/I
iragbiji, n.	Iragbiji, gari nke ogunwale na kasa Oyo
i.o.u	M.J.K. – (mo je kudi)
irate, adj.	Bionu Y/I
iris, n.	Airis G
irish, adj.	Airish G(Y.tone)
irksome, adj.	Sohala, rengu I/Gen/Y
iron, n.	Ayan, ogun H/G/Gen.
iron, vt.	Lo, agba Y/Ed
(iron the cloth)	Lo esa Y/Ed/Ogori
(iron-lady)	Mache agba
iron-ore, n.	Ayan-ore G/Y
ironmonger, n.	O meshe ayan I/Y/G
irradiate, vt.	Tontsi Y/H
irrational, adj.	Nimanima, ai chero nk'eni G/Y/I
(irrational behaviour)	Ihumi nimanima
irreconcilable, adj.	Frelagha, ai lagha, lai lagha
irrecoverable, adj.	Frejirama, ai jikirama, lai jikirama
irredeemable, adj.	Ai kwuda
irreducible, adj.	Fredinpu, ai dinpu, lai dinpu
irrefutable, adj.	Ai bishuda, lai bishuda, frebishuda
irregular, adj.	Ai shiende, ai meshiene, fremeshiene
irrelevant, adj.	Ai zumkpa, lai zumkpa, frezumkpa
(irrelevant topic)	Ai 'sioka, lai 'siokka, freisioka
irremedy, adj.	Frelandi, ai landi, lai landi
irremovable, adj.	Aiyota, ai muku, freyota, freyopu
irreparable, adj.	Fretunmeshe, ai tunmeshe, lai tunmeshe
irreplaceable, adj.	Fresonzu, ai sonzu, lai sonzu
irrepressible, adj.	Lai muzuba, aimuzuba
irreproachable, adj.	Ai solina, lai solina,
irresistible, adj.	Gbakha, lai di kido, ai di kido
irresolute, adj.	Frerisi, ai cherisi, lai cherisi, ifrerisi
irrespective, adj.	Ai diumbe, ai gbashi, frediumbe
irresponsible, adj.	Ai meko fremeko, ai buwa

225

irretrievable, adj.	Lai wenba lai wenzu
irreversible, adj.	Lai yintua, lai yizuba, lai yizuein, freyintua
irrevocable, adj.	Lai konozu, lai konotua, lai konozuba, lai konozuein, frekonozu irrigate, vt. n.
irritate, vt.	Mubi Y/I
irruption, n.	Beu Y/G
is (see be)	Wu, je, diwa, di, dia, iwa, o wa I/Y
islam, n.	Islam; isinle profet Muhammed (Plural els am)
island, n.	Gungu, tsibiri, alande H/G
isle, n.	Ail G
isn't (see be)	Ko wu, ko di, ko diwa, ko di, bati
isobar, n.	Isoba G
isolate, vt.	Meoto, yaiche I/y
isolation, n.	Imeoto, iyaiche, bioto
isotherm, n.	Iosotam G
isotope, n.	Isoto G
issue, vti., n.	Omon, mubia, kekpin, ronshien, nnon, ok, isu
isthmus, n.	Istimus G
it, pro.	O, ya Y/I
(it is there)	O wa n'ebe/o a n'eba
(it is not there)	Ko di n'ebe/ko si n'ea
italic, n.	Itale G/Ed
itch, n.	Ipia-pia, pia-pia G
itching,	Ipia-pia G
item, n.	Ifekon, fekon I/Y
itemize, vt.	Fekon ya
iterate, vt.	Soli mozo Y/I
itinerant, adj.	Bisibi Y/I/G
it'll	A wu, Y/I
it's (it is/has)	O wu, oti wu (o wu/ot'wu), weni
itself, its	O weni I/
i've (i have)	Mo te, mi te Y(G.v)

(i have known)   Mo/mi te ma Y/I/Owo/G.

ivory, n.   Haure H

(ivory coast)   Ngate haure, (Aiviri kos)

ivy, n.   Igunyan tushe

J

Ja	jah
jackal n.	Jaka G
jab, vti.	Gham G
jabber, n. vt.	O gbam, y'onuso G/Y/I
jabbing, n.	Igbam, iy'onuso G/Y/I
jabot, n.	Jabat G
jack, n.	Jak, afa mutum G
jack, (do/work)	meshe
(jack of all trades)	O meshe irushe ncha
jack, vt.	Ayangba G/Y/Gen
(motor jack)	Ayangba mota
(jack the car)	Yangba mota zoom-zoom
jackal, n.	Jaka, kera gboro G/H/Y
jackass, n.	Jaki miji G/H
jackdaw, n.	Jado G
jacket, n.	Jakit, kwat G/H
jack-knife, n.	Baba wuka Gen/H
jack-plane, n.	Jaflen G
jack-pot, n.	Baba ishiende (jakpot)
jade, n.	Iremba Gen.
jaguar, n.	Jagua
jail, n.	Prusu, kurkuku Tiv/H
jailer, n.	O prusu
jalopy, n.	Idugbo mota, jalopy, zalopi I/Y/G (Iz. Tone)
jam, n.	Jam, (abinchi suka)
jam, vti.	Gbosa, gbam Gen/G
jamboree, n.	Ihunde igbandu, jamborii I/Y/G
jhampack, vt.	Taromuta, konojo H/Y
janitor, n.	O cheto kofa, abi yadi
january, n.	Jenuari, uki daya na ardun G/Ed/H/I/Y
janus, n.	Zanus G
japan, n.	Jakpan, kasa japan
jar, n.	Tulu H
jargon, n.	Isilo, isilokpo Ed/Y

(don't speak jargon)	Ma soli 'silo, ma suso silo
jasmine, n.	Jasmin G
jasper, n.	Jespa G
jaundice, n.	Jandis, iruande G/Y/G
jaunt, n.	Irinje kuru, irinje kele
javelin, n.	Jafelin G
jaw, n.	Mukamuki H
jay, n.	Jeh G
jazz, n.	Jas G (f/E)
jealous, adj.	Yowu G/Y
jeaslousy, n.	Iyowu
jean, n.	Esamkpa Og/G
jeep, n.	Jiip G
jeer, vit.	Uhh-uhhh, medi yeye G/Gen
jehovah, n.	Jihovah, afa Abasi G/I/Ef.
jelly, n.	Jail G.
jemmy, n.	Jami G
jenny, n.	Jani G
jeopardize, vt.	Medi danja, I/Y/H
jeopardy, n.	Imedi danja
jerboa, n.	Jeboa G
jerk, n.	Fonu (fonu), isoki-soki Y/I/G
jersey, n.	Esa erenji, jasi Og/Y/H/G
jest, n.	Igbuerin, gbuerin I/Ed/Y
jester, n.	O gbuerin
jesuit, n.	Jesutu G
jesical, n.	Jasika G
jesus, n.	Jesu, Jisos
jesus christ, n.	Jesu Kristi; oc hoja isinle Krista
jet, n.	Jat, isokia, ihono kele G/I/Y
jetty, n.	Jati, katako ibonka G/H/Y
jew, n.	Jiu, mutum Heberu G/H/TY
jewel, n.	Jiuweli G
(jeweller)	O jiuweli, o meshe jiuweli
jezebel n.	Jeziba, ziba-ziba G/Ed

jib, n.	Jibi g
jiffy, n.	Ngba-kene, ngba tufien I/Y/Ed
(in a jiffy)	Na ngeba-tufien
jig, n.	Jigi G
jigger, n.	Jiga Y/Ed
jihad, n.	Jihadi,ijagha Moslem
jilt, vt.	Konu, ikonu mache si miji
jim-jams, n.	Idi jijiya, iyi jijiya
jimmy, n.	Jimi G(Y.tone)
jingo, n.	Jingo, jingo G
jingoism, n.	Imiwa iyobi
jinks, n.	Baba arimkpo igbandu
jinx, n.	Itoke rubi
jitters, n.	Iyi jijiya kha-kha
jive, n.	Jaif G
job, n.	Irushe, aiki, ishobe
job, n.	Afa Jobu na baibul: mutum baba sundi
jockey, n.	Joki G
jocular, adj.	Kuakua, kuakuakua, muerin
jocund adj.	Yoli Y/I
jodhpurs, n.	Jopex G jog, vti.
joggle, vti.	Yigha Y/I
john, n.	Salga, shadda, H
john bull, n.	Kasa bature, zon Bul H/G(izn. Tone)
join, vti. (enter)	Bale konojo
join/joint	Sogba Y/I
joiner, n.	Jon-jon
jointure, n.	Isooba
joke, n.	Imuerin, ikuakua, igbuerin
joker, n.	O muerin, o kuakua, o gbuerin
jolly boat, n.	Isimini kwalekwale, igbandu kwalekwale
(jolly friend)	Aboki 'gbandu, aboki flesi
jonah, n.	Jona, Zona G jostle, vti.
jot, n.	Itintin I(G.v)

jot, vt.	Kokene Y/I
jotter, n.	Littafi ' kokene H/Y/I
joule, n.	Jul, agba lantiriki G
journal, n.	Janah, ikwiro takada, jarida, mujalla
journalist, n.	Janalis, o jarida, o kwiro takada
journey, n.	Irinje Y/I
(long journey)	Irinje gungolo (iringolo) (short journey)
jowl, n.	Mukamuki H
joy, n.	Isayo s'ayo, is'ayo
jubilant, adj.	O s'ayo, s'ayo, ifagolo s'ayo
jubilation, n.	Is'ayo, ifagolo s'ayo jubilee, n.
judaism, n.	Judas; eni jisi Jesu
judge, n.	Bika abasi abi Chiolu, alkali, joji , dakpu
judge, vt.	Dakpe, cherisi
judgement, n.	Idakpe judge, n.
judicature, n.	Baba kotu
judicial, adj.	Dakpe, di 'zioka, zioka, ife kotu abi idakpe
judo, n.	Zudo, judo, ijamgba kasa Jakpan
jug, n.	Bajongo Gen/Ibira
juggernaut, n.	Ikatakpiti, agba G/Gen
juggle, vit.	Wayo, siro Gen/I/Y
juice, n.	Ruyaya H(G.v)
jujitsu, n.	Ijudo nke jakpan,
jujisun juju, n.	Yuyu, agba ijikele Gen/I/Y/G
juke-box, n.	Juku-bos; akwati songa nke kudi
julian, adj.	Julien; nke Julios Siza (Julius Caesar)
july, n.	Julai, Uki asaa na ardun
jumble, vit.	Di rugu, rugu, meru I/Y
jumbo, n.	Ifoleh, jembo Y/I/G
jumper, n.	Jampa, dros G/Y
junction, n.	Isogba, iyahnaya; jankcha
june, n.	Jiun, uki isii n'ardun G

jungle, k, n.	Kurmi, rukuki H
(jungle justice)	Ai zioka, rugurugu Y/I/Gen.
junior, n.	Karamin, ntakere H/I/Y
juniper,	Junipa G
junk, n.	Karubi H/I/Y
(junk store)	Sito karubi H/I/Y
junk, n. (ship)	Jank G
junket, n.	Jankit G
junkie, junky, n.	Hiron G
junta, n.	Janta, kaki-kaki G
(military junta)	Soja kaki-kaki, o jagha kaki-kaki
junto n.	Iyaga, iyahann Y/I/H
jurisdiction, n.	Nso izioka, agba I/Y/Ik.
jurist, n.	O chegon n'ifinwu, o zioka
juror, jn.	O zioka
jury, n.	E finwu, e zioka
just, adj.	Rama, zioka, ken
just, adj.	Siki, ngba nsinyii,
justice, n.	Idakpe Y/I
judiciary, n.	Aga idakpe, edakpe
justify, vt.	Me di rama, me di zioka, merama
jute, n.	Jiut G
juvenile, n.	Ifoji miwa I/Y
(juvenile delin.)	Imelika foje 'miwa
juxtaposer, vt.	Finye n'egbe-gbe

kaffir, n.	Rizga H
(kaffir potato)	Rizga, risiga H
kaiser, n.	Kaiza, sarkashe nke Zamani swene ardun 1911
kaleidoscope, n.	Kaladosko G
kangaroo, n.	Kangaruh G
kaolin, n.	Kaline G
kapok, n.	Audugar rimi H
kaput, adj.	Kiu (kiyu) G
(it has kaput)	Ya ti kiu, (or) O ti kiu
karat,	Karat
karate, n.	Ikarate, ijagha, jokpan
karma, n.	Ikama G
kayak, n .	Kayaki, abara kele nke aprinini
kedgeree, n.	Kegere G
keen, adj.	Tonji G
keep, vt.	Cheto, shiene, balu, babi I/Y
keeper, n.	O cheto
(keep going)	Shiene ga, rinshien
(keep (abide)	Balu, babi
keeping, n.	Icheto
keg, n.	Jonru Ibira/H
kelp, n.	Kelpi G
kennel, n.	Kanel, deki kare G/H
kepi, n.	Kapi G
kerb, n.	Keb g
kerchief, n.	Adiko, mayani, akafifi H/G
kerosene, n.	Kananzir, eklasin, ikozin H/Isk/Urh/Uvh
kestrel, n.	Chi fara H Uwano etc.
ketch, n.	Kechi G
kettle, n.	Kitali, shanteli, ijongo-karfe – H/Ibr.
key, n.	Omo-igede; mabudi, makuli H
keystone, n.	Kiston G
khaki, n.	Kaki, harba H
kick, n, vti	TagbaY/G

(don't kick me)	Ma tagba mi
kid, n.	Omontakele, akunya kele H/Y/Ed/Ish./Et
kidnap, vt.	Jizu I/Y
(kidnapper)	O jizu
((kidnap a child)	Jizu omon
kidney, n.	Koda H
kill, vti.	Gbu I/Ed/etc
killing, n.	Igbu
kiln, n.	Kilit G
kilo, n.	Ikilo Ed
kilogram, n.	Ikilogram Ed/G
kin, n.	Monga Y/Ed(etc)/H
kind, adj.	Renu I/Y
kindly, adv.	Rerenu I/Y
(be kind)	Di renu; wen renu
kind, n. (type)	Irudi Y/I
kindergaten, n.	Kenagate; makaranta emontakele
kindle, vti.	Mubionu, tonwu Y/I/H
kindred, n.	Monta Y/Ed(etc)/H
kinema, n. (cinema)	Ginima G baeze b'eze
king, n.	Mambeze, oba, sarki, raya, eze, b'eze Y/Ed(etc) I/G.
kingfisher, n.	Kinfisha, irudi onene o gbu kifi na ruwa
kingdom, n.	Ibeze, kasa nke Oba, Sarki, Eze; Kendon
kinsfolk, n.	Itughe monga I/Y/H
minship, n.	Iyali monga, imonga kendom
kiosk, n.	Kios, kante, giswa kele
kip, n.	Ikipi G
kismet, n.	Ikadara, iguini Y/H/I
kiss, vti.	Konu Y/I
(kiss me quick)	Konu mi sokia (konu mi' kia)
kiss, n.	Ikonu
kit, n.	Inninon Ef (Y.tone)
kitchen, n.	Kichini, madafi H/H(G.v)
(kitchen equipment)	Inninon kichini

kite, n.	Kait
kite, n. (bird)	Irudi onene, kyait I/Y/Og./G
(kith and kin)	Di ati monga
kiwi, n.	Onene new Zealand, kiwi Og/G
knapsack, n.	Kanfas, abi ikpa fata G/Y/Tiv/H
knave, n.	O soli siro, o siro
knead, vt.	Kpogha Y/Ed/I
knee, n.	Gwiwa H
(knee cap)	Koko gwiwu Y/H
kneel, vi.	Kunlu Y/I
knickers, n.	Afu shokoto, nika I/H/Y/Bete
knife, n.	Wuka, aska, barho, cheru H
knight, n.	Nait G
knit, vt.	Kawun I/Y
knob, n.	Koko H/Y
(turn the knob)	Yintua koko
knock, n.	Kwalu, kiu, tigba I/Y
(knock on the door)	Kwaluna kofa
(knocked down)	Kiu (abi) kiyu si 'sala (the engine has knocked)
(knock him/her)	Tigba ya
knoll, n.	Dutse kele H/Y/I
knot, n. vt.	Kulli, kulla, kondo, koso
(knot it up) (tie/screw)	Koso ya
(knot-hole)	Ihonu kulla
know, vti. (knew)	Ma I/Owo
(i don't know)	Mii ma Y/I
(i have known)	Mo te ma
(you don't know)	E/o ma
knowing, adj.	Di ma, ma mima,
knowledge, n.	Ichigbon, ima I/Y
(knowledge i smore than power)	
Ichighon kha agba (ichigbon k'agba)	
knuckle, n.	Nakul
koala, n.	Koala, nama danji nke ostrelia Australia

kodak, n.	Kodak, kodaki G
kohi, n.	Kol, irudi sosorobia nke ido
kohlrabi, n.	Laneko. Lprano G
kookaburra, n.	Kukabura, irudi onene na kasa Ostrelia Australia
kola, n.	Goro H
(kola-nut), n. (he who brings kola brings life) Eni mubia goro, mubia mindu	Goro H
kopje, koppie, n.	Dutse kele na South Africa, kopja
koran, n.	Alkur'ani, kuran
kraal, n.	Kral, kurmi na South Afrika
kremlin, n.	Kremlin, rokwesa nke gari na (Rosha) Russia
kris, n.	Krisi – irudi wuka na maleya abi – (Malaya or Indonesia) Indonesa
krona, n.	Krona – kudi na Swidin (Sweden)
krone, n.	Kron – kudi na Dinmak ati Noweh (Dinmak and Noweh
kudos, n.	Ehsa
kukri, n.	Kukiri, baba wuka na kasa Gukasi (Ghurkas)
kumis, n.	Kumisi, irudi ogogoro abi kainkain na kasa tata (tartars)
kurus, n.	Kurus – kabodais nke Toki (Turkey)
kvass, n.	Kevas – irudi biya na rosha
kwara, n.	Kwara, siteti na naijiriya

la	Lah G/Gen
leager, n.	Oziti, tanti-tanti nke soja
label	Monkwa, lamba, labela Y/Ed/Ur/Ish?Au/H
labial, adj.	Labia, nke lebe G/I/
laboratory, n.	Deki bachike, laburatiri H/G
labour, n.	Irushe, aiki I/Y/H
labourer, n.	O rushe (pl.) e rushe
(ministry of labour)	Irushe ministry
laburnum, n	Labunu, irudi itache G/Y/I/H
lace, n. vt.	Kwaya, kwa Y/Ed/H/I
lace (of cloth)	Lesi Gen.
lacerate, vt.	Doya I/Y
lack, vti.	Shifu, ai wen, frewen Y/I
lackadaisical, adj.	Ai chofe, frechofe Y/I
laconic, adj.	Solikele, Y/Gen.
lacrosse, n.	Lakros, irudi 'guere na North Amerika
lactic, adj.	Latiki – wassid nke nono G/I/H
lad, n.	Yaro, saurayi H
ladder, n.	Lada, kuranga H
laden, adj.	Rubu Y/I
lading, n.	Isukaya, ladin G/Y/H
(bill of lading)	Bili ladin
ladle, n.	Baba chokali, ludayi Gen/H
lady, n.	Mata, kanamang, H/Afi-zere (ladies and gentlemen)
lag, vi.	Fazu Y/I
lag, n.	Lag, akwatin ruwa, ikpa ruwa
lager, n.	Laga, irudi bie G/Y/I
lagoon, n.	Lagun G
lake, n.	Tabki H
lakh, n.	Lakh, kudi nke India abi kpakistan
lair, n.	Kurfi, makwanchi H
lama, n.	Lama, na budi abi Mongolia
lamb, n.	Tunkiya H
lambent, adj.	Jowuwini

lame, adj.	Aro, gurgu, Y/Ed/H
lamentation, n.	Ikunbe Y/I
laminate, vti.	Laminint G
lamp, n.	Fitila H
lamprey, n.	Lampri, nama tekun g/H
lance, vt.	Bege I/y
lancet, n.	Rariya H
land, n.	Kasa, isala H/Y/I
land, vti.	Bibia, biawa kasa I/Y/h
landau, n.	Landu, doki o bugbe kaya
landing, n.	Ibibia, ibibiawa kasa, ibiawa kasa
landscape, n.	Filin karkara H
landmark, n.	Iyaka (boundary) H
lane, n.	Rariya, len H/G
language, n.	Asusu Igbo
languish, vt.	Frelafia, rengulu Y/I/Gen
langur, n.	Lango, irudi biri G/Y/I/H
lanky, adj.	Kpamgba Gen
lanolin, n.	Lanini G
lantern, n.	Fitila, fitila nke hannu H/I
lanyard, n.	Layadi G
lap, n.	Kafa H
lap, vti. (to drink)	Lamu, Y/I
lapel, n (of jacket)	Lapela G
lapidary, adj.	Lapidi, ikode na dutse
lapislazuli, n.	Lapilazu, dutse bimkpa
lapse, n.	Fazu, shienga, loga Y/I
lapwing, n.	Lapueng, irudi onene G/Y/I/Og.
larboard, n.	Labor, nke ugboko ruwa G/I/Y/H
larch, n.	Lash, irudi itache G/I/Y/H
larceny, n.	Baranja H/Y
lard, n.	Ilabu alade Y/I/H
larder, n.	Leida,irudi sito nke n/ama wiwuam
large, adj.	Lau, buto G/I/Y
largeness, n.	Ibuto

largo, n.	Laigo, ishien kele ugboko ruwa
lariat, n.	Leriyat laso, waya doki, sarbe
lark, n.	Lak, irudi onene o songa
larkspur, n.	Laspor, irudi fulawa,
larva, n.	Lafa, kwaro kele
larynx, n.	Laniks, tukun feh n'onu lascivious, adj.
laser, n.	Leisa, injin amplifaya G
lash, n.	Bulala H
lash, vti.	Luti, bionu si, bionu Y/I lass, n.
lassitude, n.	Irengu Y/I
last, adj. vi.	Fagolo, zuba; zuein; zizibu (at long last)
latch, n.	Lach nke kofa, sakata G/I/H lats, (of arrival)
later	Ngboizu, ngba kele, baya
laterite, n.	Marmara, tsukuwa H latest
latex, n.	Lates, nke nono roba
lath, n.	Lat
lathe, n.	Lat, mashin kofinta
lather, n.	lata, nke sabulu
lathi, n.	Lati, itache nke mondoka na India
latin, n.	Latin, ede nke kera Rom
latitude, n.	Iwaniya, latitiud, lati H/G
latrine, n.	Salga, shadda H latter, adj.
lattice, n.	Latais, irushe firam laud, vt, adj.
laudanum, n.	Ladinom, iirudi mageni G
laugh, vti.	Kuakua G
launchi, vti.	Budo, tokesa Y/i/G
launch, n.	Launsh, nke abara fasinja
launder, vti.	Fosa Y/I
laureate, adj. n.	Ikenze, kenze Y/I
laurel, n.	Larel, irudi itakele lailai
lava, n.	Garwashi H
lavatory, n.	Bayan gida, shadda H

lavender, n.	Lafinda, fulawa o sosorobia
lavish, adj.	Nnonku Ef. H
law, n.	Iwufin I/Y
law court, n.	Kotu, gida iwufin
lawful, adj.	Wufin, di wufin
law-breaker, n.	O foji 'wufin
law-abiding, n.	Ibalu iwufin, ibabi 'wufin
lawn, n.	Laun G
(lawn tennis)	Lan tanis
lawyer, n.	Lauya, o wufin G/I /Y
lax, adj.	Flesi I/Y
laxity, n.	Iflesi I/y
laxative, n.	Makashi, ogun kashi G/I/Y/H
lay, vti.	Toka, leta, mundu I/I
lay, n. (of priest)	Leh G
lay-by, n.	Akue-hanya I/y/H
layer, n.	Leya, iki, o toka G/Y
lazar, n. (disease)	Irun mutum I/Y/H
lazy, adu.	Ai rushe, gburushe, jafa Y/I
lazarus, n.	O biyo, lazaros It/I
lea, n.	Lii G
lead, n.	Darma, kuza h
lead, vti.	Gosin I/y
(lead me o god)	Gosin mi, Abasi
leader, n.	O gosin, shugaba I/Y/H
leaf, n.	Ganye, warka H
(leaf of paper)	Warka guda
leaflet, n.	Takarda wadda , liflit
league, n.	Lig, inofi (of measurement)
league, n.	Ikweba, agrimento, ikwede
leadk, n.	Jora, ijora Y/I
lean, adj. vti.	Ta, fiyenji I/Y?H
(lean on me)	Fiyenji si mi (fiyenji mi)
leap, vit.	Foso
(leap year)	Ardun ifoso, ardun ininang

240

learn, vti.	Muko
learner, n.	O muko, o mogu
leash	Koboko
lease, n.	Lis, irudi haya
least, n. adj.	Kinin; tufien, tine, tintin Gen.
leather, n.	Fata H
leave, vti.	Pule fre, isimini, ihutu, shienga; hu I/Y/H
leaves, pl. leaf	Ewarka, e ganye
leaven, n.	Lebin G
leavings, n.	E fre I/Y
lectern, n.	Lektan, irudi fitila G
lecture. n.	Ileko, lacha Y(G.v)/H
lecturer, n.	O leko, o lacha, malamin jami's
ledge, n.	Laj, bika boga (like a cliff)
ledger, n.	Daftari H
leech, n.	Matsattsaku H
leek, n.	Liik, irudi fejitebul G
leeway, n.	Liwe, nke ugboko ruwa
left, pt. of leave	Shiengala, shienga Y/I
left, (opp of right)	Hago, leif H/G
(left-handed)	Bahago H
leg, n.	Kafa H
legacy, n.	Ifesia I/H
legal, adj.	Wufin I/Y
legalize, vt.	Meshe wufin, me di wufin
legat, n.	Legat – ambasiye nke pope
legatee, n.	O fesia, eni wengba fesia
legation, n.	Ligazhion, gida irudi ambasiye
legato, adv.	Leligato, nke songa
legend, n.	Iliton Agbo/Y
legendary, ad.	Noki – (i.e. famous), idi'liton
leghorn, n.	Leghon, irudi kaza
legible, adj.	Hune Y/I
legion, n.	Lijion G
(nigerian legion)	Lijion nke Naijeria

legislate, vi.	Mewufin, wufin I/Y
legislative, adj.	Majalisar iwufin
legislator, n.	O wufin
legitimate, adj, n.	Year, diofin, idiofin Y/I
leguminous, adj.	Legomina, irudi kwaya
leisure, n.	Feh, imini Y(G.v)
(leisure time)	Ngba mini, ngba feh
lemming, n.	Lemin, irudi nama G/Y/I/H
lemon, n.	Lemo, laimun H
(lemonade)	Lemoned
lemur, n.	Lemor, irudi nama na kasa madagaskar
lend, vt.	Bolo Nem/Okrika/Kal/Izor
(money lender)	O bolo kudi
length, n.	Igungo, igungolo Y/I
lengthy, adj.	Gungolo kha, gungologolo
lenient, adj. n.	Langa, ilanga G
lens, n.	Lins, irudi maidubi G/Y/I/H
lent, n.	Lenti, nke Krista, lent G/I/H
lentil, n.	Lanti, irudi wake G/Y/I/H
lento, adj., adv.	Lento, lelento, ijuma songa
leo, n.	Leo, abi (Lio), lamba nk'isen na zodiak
leopard, n.	Damisa H
leper, n.	Kuturu H
leprosy, n.	Irun jiki abi fata, ikuturu
lesbian, n.	Lisbian, ivudu nke mache
lesion, n.	Iyintua si danja, ihuene, huene Y/I/H/G
less, adj.	Kiene Y/I/Ur
lessee, n.	Lesii, eni haya gida abi kasa, bika lisa
lesson, n.	Ikozi Y/I
lessor, n.	Leso, eni gaye lis
lest, conj.	Hege G
let, vti.	Ka, kweba, haya, mundu diki I/Y/H
(don't let me down)	Ma diki mi
(let me go)	Kam shienga
(house to let)	Gida fun haya

242

(let/allow)	Kweba
let's	Ka'wa
letter, n.	Wasika, harafi, baki, harafi H/G
(letter of credit)	Wasika imere
(letter-box)	Akwati wasika
(letter-head)	Takarda wasika
(letter-press)	Tite wasika, wasika tite
(lettered)	Iwin abi o ma turnachi
capital – letter, n.	Baba-afabit
lettuce, n.	Letius, irudi fejitebul
leucocyte, n.	Liukosat, imonkpa fari jinni
levant, n.	Livant, na gabas nke meditarenia
levant, vi.	Gbate I/H
levee, n.	Levil, idihan dabe kogi
level, adj.	Kwa, laini; Enuani/G(fE)
(level crossing)	Isoga kwa
(o-level)	Ikwa O
lever, n.	Ayan, liba H/G
leveret, n.	Libret, omontakele zomo
leviathan, n.	Lebitan, na baibul, irudi nama tekun
levite, n.	Livait, na Baibul
levy, vt.	Kuson, kudi I/Y/H
lexical, adj.	Turnachi, nke fokabulai
lexicography, n.	Ituranchi ifokabulai
lexicographer, n.	O turnachi, o fokabulai
lexicon, n.	Legzikun, kamus G/H
liability, n.	Igwese I/Y
liaison, n.	Omaye Idoma/Igala
(liaison officer)	Hafsa omaye (omaye)
liana, n.	Liyana, irudi ganye
liar, n.	O soli siro
lib, liberation, n.	Imenira I/Y
liberate, vt.	Menira
libation, n.	Iredu I/Y
libel, n.	Ibatanchi, abi imenira Y(G.v)

(liberty stadium)	Stadiom Ininira
libido, n.	Iche kha ivudu, ifololo
libra, n.	Libra, lamba asaa na zodiak
librarian, n.	Malami laburare, o laburare
liberary, n.	Laburare, izin littafi
libretto, n.	Littafi oka na isonga opere, librito
lice, n.	Kwarkwata H
licence, n.	Lasin, aashe H/Y/I/Ed
licentiate, n.	O lasin, ki o aashe
licentious, adj.	Vudu-vudu G
lichen, n.	Lichin, irudi ganye
lichgate, n.	Lichgat, kofa gawa na chochi, ebi 'chiu gawa na chochi
licit, adj.	Diwufin I/Y
lick, vti.	Chamu, lamu bebuh G/I/y
lie, vi. (leid) ft.	Siro, duka bebuh bebuh; toka /I/Y/H
(lie down)	Duka na kasa
lien, n.	Iyefe, liyen, abi lien
lieu, n.	Nefe
(in lieu)	Na nefe
lieutenant, n.	Laftana, o zugumiza H/G
(lieutenant colonel)	Leftana kanar
life, n.	Mindu, lakporj – synonym Y/I/Ur
(life time)	Ngba mindu
(life-giver)	O gayen mindu, o nno mindu
(life-guard)	Ichebo mindu, gadi mindu (matter of life and death)
lift, vt.	Liti; to-to, ogoja
(weight lifter)	O to-to iwan
(express lift)	Liti esfres
ligament, n.	Jijiya H
light, n.	Wuta, fitila H
(very light)	Fele kha, fele-fele
(light-house)	Gida iwuta
(light-skin)	Bature, obocha

(light-hearted)	Iyobi –fele, igbandu
lightly, adv.	Fele-fele
lightning, n.	Iwain-wain, wain-wain G
light, vti.	Jowu Y/H
lighter, n.	Lata, o juwuta
ligneous, adj.	Lignos, abiskos, irudi fulawa
lignite, n.	Lignat, irudi kwal abi gawayi
like, adj.	Bika, che, kabi, wu, chefe
(like this)	Bika kyi
(ii like bread)	Mo che buredi
(like you)	Mo che e
(i like you very much)	Mo che e kha-khaa
(it is like that)	Baate, o kabi kyien, o9 di baate
likely, adj.	Le wu
likeness, n.	Iche, ibika
likewise, adv.	Bietu, bibietu Y/I
(likewise yourself)	Bietu
lilac, n.	Lilak, irudi itakele (shrub)
lilliputian, n.	Omo lilliput, o liliput na irinje Gulliver
lily, n.	Bado H
(lily pond)	Kandami lili, abi (kandami bado)
(lily of the valley)	Bado kwari
limb, n.	Gaba H
limber, n.	Lemba, nke doki G/I/H
limbo, n.	Limbo, (ichagba kpongba)
lime, n.	Lemo, laim H/G
lime-juice, n.	Iruyaya laim, ruwa lemo
(lime-stone)	Jefa laim
(lime-light)	Ikemkpo, ibiawita
limey, n.	O tekun na Britis siman
limit, limited, n.	Ikezin, I/y/Ed.
limit, n (of end)	Iguini, guini I/Y
limitation, n.	Iguini I/Y
limousine, n.	Lumozin, baba mota zoom-zoom G/Gen/H
limp, adj.	Ai wen agba, tuke Y/I/G

limp, vt.	Ringa, kele, ringa tuke
limpet, n.	Lempet, irudi kifi G/I/Y/H
limpid, adj.	Lempid, irudi ruwa G/I/Y/H
line, n. vt.	Lain; jeri, sahu, tole, waya
(line up)	Tole si lain, tole na lain
lineage, n.	Lain iyali, ikaka, laini G/H
linear, adj.	Lenia, nke nofi G/I
line-man, n.	Miji waya, miji lain, o cheto lain, o lain
linene, n.	Linin, irudi esa G/I/Y/Og.
liner, n.	Laina, ugboko goma G/I/Y/H
ling, n.	Leng, irudi kifi na kasa bature
linger, vi.	Faogo Y/I
lingo, n.	Lengo, irudi ede ai ma
lingua franca, n.	Franka, baba ede nke kasa
lingual, adj.	Linguo, nke harshe, zeka-zudo G/I/H/Ed
linguist, n.	O zeka-zudo, o lingua
linguistic, adj.	Sayens ede, imuko lingua abi ede, linguosa

(linguistics association of nigeria)
Asosie, linguosa nke naijeriya

liniment, n.	Lenimint, irudi ogun abi mageni G/I/Y/H
linoleum, n.	Lada, irudi kanfas nke kasa, lenoniam
linotype, n.	Linotap, irudi injin
linseed, n.	Lensid, irudi oyil
lintel, n.	Lentel, nke kofa abi windo na gida
lion, n.	Zaki H
lioness, n.	Zaki mache H
(lion-heart)	Iyobi zaki Y/I/H
lip, n.	Lebe, baki H
(lip-service)	Irushe labe, irushe wayo
(lip-stick)	Jambaki, likstik H/G
liquefy, vti.	Nedi ruwa-ruwa, likuifai I/Y/H
liqueur, n.	Baba wain, irudi ogogoro, kainkain, burukutu, (likua) Gen.
liquid, n.	Likua; ife bia ruwa abi oyil, likua, pioro
liquidate, vti.	Sonzu Y/I

liquidation, n.	Tusika, iguton, isonzu
liquor, n.	Sha, ife sha, likua
liquorice, n.	Likuaris, irudi shuke-shuke
lira, n.	Lira, guda kudi na itili
lisle, n.	Lisol, irudi fabriki
list, n.	Ilisa, H/Y
list, vi.	Chero, tole I/Y
listen, vi.	Gbonti y/I
(listen attentively)	Gbonti rarama, abi gbonti rama
(listen to me)	Gbonti mi
(are you listening?)	Shekwa e ng gbonti mi? ina gbonti
(you don't listen/hear)	mi? (please listen to me)
litany, n.	Letni, irudi 'kpredu na chochi
lieteracy, n.	Icheko, I/Y
(literacy campaign)	Ikemkpo
(literal, adj.	Bietu icheko
(literal meaning)	Itiunma bietu
literary, adj.	Litrecha, keko I/Y
literature, n.	Ikode, ituranchi, litrecha Y/I/H/G
lithography, n.	Ititeli Y/H
(lithographer)	O titeli
litigant, n.	Letigante, nke iwufin, o kono oka na kotu
litigate, vit.	Letigant, oka nke kotu
litmus, n.	Litmus, irudi wuta G/Y/I/H
litre, n.	Lita, guda metriki G/H
litter, n.	Tuka, tuko H/Y
litter, vti.	Datti H/Gen
(doon't litter this palce)	Ma datti ebi little, adj.
(little boy)	Yaro kele
(little people)	E mutum kele
(little house)	Gida kele
(very little)	Kele kha, tufien, tintin, kene
(little-by-little)	Kele-kele
(little drops of water)	E boda kele ruwa

(little later)	Ngba kene, ngba tufien
liturgy, n.	Litoji, irudi gbobe nke chochi
live, vti, adj. hu	Idiwa, mindu Agbo/Y/I (come and live with me)
(i live at…)	Mo ng hu na
live, vit.	Mindu
(live wire)	Waya mindu, way wuta
(be alive)	Diwa mindu
living, n.	Idiwa, imindu
(the living and the dead)	Imindu ati kutu livelihood, n.
live-long, adj.	Gungo mindu, gungolo mindu
lively, adj.	Solendu, isolendu, garaun
(lively man)	Miji solendu
liver, n.	Hanta h
liverwurst, n.	Libawos, irudi sosej G/Y/I
livery, n.	Libari, gbata esa na gida baeze
lives, n. (pl)	E mindu
live-stock, n.	Nama-nama H(G.v)
livid, adj.	Libid, icheto launi G/I/Y/H
lizard, n.	Kandangare H
(lizard's first born)	Ifineri, kandangare
ilama, n.	Lama, inama na kasa South Afrika
lloyd's, n.	Loid, ijumome na London
lo, int.	Neri I/Y
load, n. vti.	Kaya, ikaya H
(carry load)	Gbize kaya
(load carrier)	O gbize
(loader)	O kaya
loaf, n.	Lof, nke buredi
(a loaf of bread)	Lof buredi
loaf, vit/.	Gbu ngba , fagolo ngba ringa kiri
loam, n.	Lom, yumbura G/H/Y
loamy, adj.	Di yumbura, yumbura
loath, adj.	Kore Y(G.v)
loan, n.	Bolo Nem/Okrika/Izon/Ka labari

(loan agreement)	Ikweba bolo, agrimento ibolo, ikwade' bolo
lob, vit.	Lobu, tagbam G
lobby, n.	Labi swesi G
lobe, n.	Lob, gindi kunne G/Y/H
lobster, n.	Lobsta, lakasha, irudi kifi
local, adj.	Lika; kalika Gen.
localism, n.	Ilika
locality, n.	Lardi H
localize, vt.	Medi lika, di lika
locate, vt.	Hin, ebi I/Y
location, n.	Ihin
loch, n.	Lok, tekun kele si kasa
lock, n.	Lak, nke gashi G/I/H
lock, vti.	Tichie, tikpo Y/I
(lock the door)	Tikpo kofa
locker, n.	O tikpo, makulli, kulle, kabad kele
locket, n.	Lokit, ikpa kele G/Tiv/Y/I
loccomotion, n.	Tren, ugboko kasa G/I/Y/H
locust, n.	Fara H
locution, n.	Isoli oka rama H/I/Ikwere
lode, n.	Lod, ife ayan
lodge, n	Izuga, gida kele, igbi, ifiyen G/H/Y/I
lodging, n.	Igbi
lodger, n.	O gbi, o zuga
lodgement,	Ifiyen
loess, n.	Los, irudi kasa na shaina
loft, n.	Dezin, ebi izin, deki 'zin
loft, vt.	Gbafom, gbafom bol
lofty, adj.	Nuke I/Y
(lofty idea)	Ichenu nuke
log, n.	Gungume, gungu, ijukun H/I/Y
(log of wood)	Gungu itache H(G.v)
log, n.	Log, nke mita abi agogo
(log-book)	Littafi log.
lobby – corridor	(swesi)

loganberry, n.	Loganbi, irudi shuke-shuke
logarithm, n.	Logarit, irudi aritmetik
loggerheads, n.	Ai kweba, ikolikei I/Y/H
loggia, n.	Lojia, akue gida
logic, n.	Ichegbon, isayens I/Y/G
logical, adj.	Di chegbon, di sayesn
loin, n.	Zudi I/Y
loiter, vit.	Rinfoh, shienfoh Y(G.v)
(no loitering)	Ma rinfoh
loiter, n.	O rinfoh, o shienfoh
lolipop, n.	Lolipap, irudi switi G/Y/I/G
lone, lonely, adj.	Lai wen o sole, konso 'golo
(long), adj.	Gungolo, gungo, gungologolo, faogolo 'Golo Y/I
(long-distance)	Ijihan gungo, ijihan golo
(long-leg)	Kafa golo
(long-life)	Mindu golo
(long-long life)	Mindu gologolo, mindu gungolo
(long-hand)	(ikode hann), hannu golo
(long-time)	Ifaogolo ngba
(long time no see)	Ao hun ke ngba, a o hun ke ngbagolo
(long-standing)	Ti chiugolo, ichiu golo, fa ngbagolo
(long-suffering)	Isundi, isundi lai roka
longevity, n.	Imetu
longitude, n.	Langiiu, na jiografi G/I/G
loofah, n.	Kanda, irudi soso Gen/H
look, vit.	Neri, I/Y
(look up)	Neri, o I/
(look up to)	Neri si
(look good)	Bika rama, kabi rama, di rama
(look here)	Neri mbi, neri ebi
(look for)	Chowa fun; chowa (what are you looking for)?
(look forward)	Neri whido, neri si whido
(look at you)	Neri e

(look at me)	Neri mi
(come and look)	Bia neri
(look out for)	Neri ta fun, bo ta, neri ta
(look through)	Neri kufe
(let me look)	Kam' neri
loom, n.	Masaka, injin esa H/Og.
loom, vi.	Fine shaka Y/I/Gen
loon, n.	Ofoke, irudi baba onene Y/I/Ogori
loop-hole, n.	Ihonu-horo
loose, adj.,	Tuka, Y/H
loose (lost), vt.	Funu I/Y
lot, n.	Irawo, igburu
(lloter, n.)	O rawo, o gburu
lop, vt. (cut off)	Bege I/Y (G.v) lop, vi. (hang down loosely)
loquacious, adj.	Solika, soli-rama, solisaun
loquacity, n.	Isolika, isoli-rama, isolisaun
loquat, n.	Lokwat, irudi itache na chaina ati jakpan
lord, n.	Kadei, baba, baeze, om'agba, O-Agba
(my lord)	Kadei mi, baeze mi, omoagba mi (not baba mi)
lord, n.	Chiolu
lore, n. (of handed knowledge) Babichegbon, babiche Gen/I/Y	
lorgnette, n.	Lognit, irudi ijongo ido G/Ibara/H
lorry, n.	Baba mota, baba wagunu, lari
(lorry load)	Losen ijukun lari, ijukun baba mota
loss, lost, n.	Ifunu Y/I
lot, n.	Ncha Enuani
(lots of money)	Encha kudi
(lots of people)	Encha emutum
(lots of time)	Encha ngba lot, n. (object of decision)
(let us cast lots)	Ka'wa jutu eyawa
lot, n. (of space)	Iyefe
(parking lot)	Iyefe mota
lotion, n.	Loshan, irudi sosorobia

lotto, n.	Loto, irudi 'guere anfa
lotus, n.	Lotus, irudi fulawa ruwa
loud, adj.	Gaun, ga, arimkpo, nuke, kemkpo leiu
(loud and clear)	Ga diye, saun-saun
(loud-speaker)	O soli gaun-gaun (lau-spika)
lough, n.	Lof, irudi tabki (lake)
lounge, vi.	Lanj, detadi G/H(G.v)
louse, n.	Kwarkwata H
louver, n.	Luva, maidubi iwindo G/H/Uvwe/Ur/Isok
lovable, adj.	Di hufe I/Y
love, n.	Ihufe, baba iche, iche kha I/Y
(love feast)	Ikowuam/konje hufe
(brotherly love)	Ihufe m'uba
(sisterly love)	Ihufe m'uwa
(lost love)	Ihufe funu
(love story)	Ilida hufe, ilidafe
(love song)	Isonga hufe
(love potion)	Ogun ihufe
(love at sea)	Ihufe tekun
lovely, adj.	Hufe, di hufe
lowver, n.	O hufe, ninda, o dunso, o miho
(muy lover)	O hufe mi, ninda mi, o dunso mi, o miho oni
(i love eba)	Mo che kha eba
(i love you my darling)	Mo hufe e ninda mi/mo hufe e imiho mi low, adj.
lower, adj.	Fiene kha
(too low)	Fiene khaka
(low-lands)	Kasa ka
lowly, adj.	Lisi
lowliness, n. ilisi	Ilisi Y/I
loyal, adj.	Fisiba
(loyalist)	O fisiba
lozenge, n.	Losenji, irudi zelili (diamond)
l.s.d. n.	ElESDI< irudi wassid

esd. n.	Elesdi, afa kudi nke British lembu, yien wu (y.w) kpon, shilin ati kobo
l-plate, n.	Eli-kwano, kwano mota fun o muko direba – Nupe?Hausa/Y/I/Gwari
lubricate, vt. n.	Liura, medon, iliura, imedon I/G
lucent, translucent, adj.	Di waen-waen Y/I/Ed
lucerne, n.	Lusen, irudi shuke-shuke na Greart Britain
lucid, n.	Gara, diye G
lucifer, n.	Lusifa, ekwenshu G/I/Y
luck, n.	Anfa, iyoge, iyefe, ishiende
(by luck)	N'ishiende
(good luck)	Ishiende rama
(bad luck)	Ishiende
ludicrous, adj.	Fakuakua Y/I
lucre, n.	Irire rubi Y/Ed/Sobe/I
ludo, n.	Ludo irudi 'guere G/Y/I
luff, vti.	Lof, oka irushe ugboko ruwa
lug, n.	Ilag, nke ugboko ruwa
luge, n.	Liuj, irudi togani G/Y/I
luggage, n.	Ikaya H(G.v)
(luggage hall)	Bandeki kaya
(luggage van)	Monkaya kaya (monka kaya)
lugger, n.	Luga, ugboko ruwa kele
lugsail, n.	Logsel, irudi ugboko ruwa
lugubrious, adj.	Libo-libo
lukewarm, adj. n. ai	Wunrio
lull, vti.	Chankiti I/Y
lullaby, n.	Lubali, irudi songa, irayo, irinbushe
lumbago, n.	Lakulaku Y (G.v)
lumbar, adj.	Lumba, nke zudi G/Y/I
lumber, n.	Lumban nke itache G/I/H
luminary, n.	Irisindi, ishaka, iwaen-waen, bika tauraro
luminous, adj.	Shaka-shaka, tonwuta
lump, n.	Dunkule, churi H
(lump sum of money)	Ichuri kudi

lump, vt. (put up/on)	Bule I/Y
lunacy, n.	Ifewe, ilaw I/Y
lunar, adj.	Luna, nke/uki G/I/H
lunatic, n.	O fewe, o lawe, ifewe abi lawe
lunch, n.	Lanch, abinchi nke rana
lungsin	Huhu
lupin, n.	Lupine, irudi e gashintsu rama, tonwuam, iwayo
lure, n.	Liurid, irudi launi ga, baba launi, kpodu
lurid, adj.	Liurid, irudi launi ga, baba launi, kpodu
lurk, vi.	Lume Y
lust, n.	Iche gbhowu I/Y/H
lustre, n.	Ishaka Y(G.v)
lustry, adj.	Kamkpe Gen
luxurious, adj.	Melani, gbandu Y/H/I
luxury, n.	Imelani, igbandu Y/H/I
luxuriant, adj. adv.	Tula-tula G-faransi
lycee, n.	Lisii, irudi makaranta na feronsi (France)
lye, n.	Alikali, oka sayens G/Ikwere/G
lying, n.	Isiro, iduka I/Y/H
lymph, n.	Kagbu, sogbu Y/I/Ed
lynch, vt.	Kagbu, sogbu Y/I/Ed
lynx, n.	Links, irudi muzuru (cat)
lyric, adj.	Lirik, ikode ati imejo songa (compose)
lysol, n.	Lisol, ruwa gbujamon (disinfectant liqud)

m	M
ma, n.ma, n.	Mama, ma Gen
ma'am, n.	Wworingida gbutu H
macabre, adj.	Gbutu, kuowun, isamba I/Ed/H
macadam, n.	Macadam, irudi hanya G/Y/I/H
macaroni, n.	Makrona G
macroon, n.	Makrun, irudi kek
macaw, n.	Mako, bab aku (parrot) na amerika
mace, n.	Mes, nevah G
mach, n. o.	Kak – nkme fekuku na ugboko feh
machete, n.	Baba adda Gen/Y/H
machination, n.	Irekereke Y(G.v)
machine, n.	Mashin, injin, na'ura; mashen H
(machine-gun)	Bindiga-injin
machinery, n.	Imashin, injin-injin, kaya injin abi kaya irushe
mackerel, n.	Mankere, kifi dadi, (oku-eko) G/Y/H(Y)
mackintosh, n.	Makinto (from 'ma je kin to), irudi kwat-ruwa
macrobiotic, adj.	Makrobayotik, o fago mindu
macrocosm, n.	Makrodkosim, itombi akpor, akpor ncha G/Y/Urh/Ed
mad, adj.	Fewe H
madness, n.	Ifeweh
(mad-man) (mad woman)	Miji fewe, mache fewe (mad person)
madden, vti.	Medi fewe
madm, n.	Woringida H
madame, n.	Mondon G
madder, n.	Mada, irudi rina (dye)
made pt make	Shelu (se+lu+ru) Y/I/others
madeira, n.	Madera, alande na baba tekun atlante
mademoiselle, n.	Mundia, abi wundia H/Y
madonna, n.	Madona, hoto abi mutummutumi nke Mary-mama Jesu
madrigal, n.	Madirga, irudi songa

maelstrom, n.	Bab'irunbi (irunbi – destruction)
maestro, n.	Eminat, iwin G/Y
maffick, vi.	Bab'iriya, iseliba Gen/Y/Ed
mafia, n.	Owegbe, bika Ogboni Ed/Gen./I
magazine, n.	Magani, sito abi ikpa harsashi G/H/Tiv/H
magazine, n.	Magezin, mujalla, baba jarida
magenta, adj. n.	Majenta, imajenta, o tunwu ja (bright crimson)
maggot, n.	Tsutsa h
magi, n.	Magi, afa Ọchegbon meta t'o mubia eyere (gifts) fun Ọmontakele jesu Kristi
magic, n.	Ijikele, majikele, agba eso ao ma; bubu-yay
magistrate, n.	Majistrit, hafsa iwufin n'abe joji
magnanimous, adj. n.	Mere, imere I/Y/Sob
magnate, n.	Iyenken, o yenken Ed. (G.v)
magnesia, n.	Magnesia, irudi mageni G/Y/I/H
magnesium, n.	Magnesium, irudi simbola nke aluminium
magnet, n.	Maganadisu, iyangba H/Gen
magnetic, adj.	Yangba, di maganadisu, fagba, magneta
magnetism, n.	Isayens nke yangba abi maganadisu
magneto, n.	Magnito, ife lantiriki t'o ng tonwuta chaun-chat
magnificat, n. daya (Luke Ch. 1)	Isongimo nke Budurwa (Virgin) Mary na littafi Baibul, Luke daftari
magnificent, adj.	Magniisa, tombibu G/Y/I
magnify, vt. n.	Finebu, ifinebu Y/I
magnitude, n.	Ibabinbu Y/I
magnolia, n.	Magnola, irudi itache
magnum, n.	Magnom, irudi ijongo wain G/Y/I/Ibira/H
magpie, n.	Magpi, irudi onene nke baba arimkpo
magyar, n.	Magya, bab'ede na kasa Hungeri (hungary)
maharaja (h), n.	Maharajha, nke India
mahjong, n.	Majonge, irudi 'guere na chaina
mahogany, n.	Madachi, mahogane H/G

mahout, n.	O yanwa giwa
maid, n.	Mongi Y/Ed/Ish/Au?Sob/etc/H
maidan, n.	Medani, kasa toka (parade ground)
maiden, n.	Yanrinya, burdurwa, wundia, mundia, ihuntuntun
(maiden name)	Afa huntuntun
(maiden edition)	Itungu huntun
(maiden speech)	Oka huntun
mail, n.	Wasika; ironsika, ironzi Y/H/I
(mail-bag)	Ikpa 'ronzi, ikpa wasika
(mail-boat)	Abara 'ronzi, abaa wasika
(mail-box)	Akwati 'ronzi; akwati wasika
(mail-corner)	Ironzi kwana, kwana wasika
(mail-man)	Miji wasika,
(mail-order)	Ekaya n'ironzi, fosta-hoda
(milling-card)	foskad
maim, vt.	Tagbulu Y/I
main, adj.	Katazi Y/I
(main thing)	Ife katazi
(main thing)	Ife katazi
(main fact)	Iezikoka katazi
(main issue)	Oka katazi
(main problem)	Nsohala katazi
(main entrance)	Hanya katazi
maintain, vt. n.	Juzi, ijuzi Y/I
maize, n.	Masara H
majestic, adj.	Baeze, di baeze, bika Oba/Sarki/Eze
majolica, n.	Majolica, irudi tukunya na itli
major, adj. n.	Katazi, ikatazi, manja – (nke soja)
(major dealer)	Omaye katazi Id/Ig/Y/I
(major distributor)	O kekpin katazi, (omaye)
majority, n	Imukha, mukha H/I (majority of the people)
maker, n.	O meshe
malacca, n.	Sanda ringa H/Y/I

malachite, n.	Malachat, irudi dutse, abi jefa
maladjust/ed, adj.	Yi tunme y/I
malady, n.	Irun, irunkaun Y/G
(social malady)	Irun tuegbe
malaise, n.	Yi gbandu, ijikale malapropos, adj. adv.
malay, adj, n.	Male, emutum nke malay
malcontent, adj, m n.	Yi wesi Y/I
male, n.	Namiji, miji; (mil) H/G(fE)
(male-child)	Omo mi ji
malediction, n.	Ihili (curse/cursing)
malefactor, n.	O mesh'ika
malfeasance, n.	Imesh'ika
malformation, n.	Iyi diwa I/Y
malice, n.	Isojikele, ikakele
(don"t keep malic)	Ma wen ikakele, ma di 'kakele
malign, adj.	Jagbu Y/I
malignant, adj.	Jukun fun ijamgbu, di 'jamgbu
malinger, vi.	Maran, gbu ngba G/I/Y/Id
(malingerer), n.	O maran, o gbu ngba
mallard, n.	Malad, irudi agwagwa gboro (wild duch)
malleable, adj.	Malibo, irudi hama o wen katako
mallet, n.	Malit, irudi hama o wen katako
mallow, n.	Malo, irudi shuke-shuke gboro
malmsey, n.	Mamsi, irudi wain isolele na kasa giriki abi supen
malnutrition, n.	Iyi tula, iyi diagba
malpractice, n.	Iy'meshien, yi, jilolo Y/I
malt, n.	Mat, imagani wain
maltese, adj, n.	Maltizi, ede nke kasa molta (malta)
maltreat, vt, n.	Yi losie, iyi losie
malversation, n.	Malfesa, gomnanti 'rubi
mamba, n.	Mamba, njika machi ji na Afrika
mamma, n.	Mama, afa uwa Gen/I/H
mammal, n.	Mammal, talikei masu G/H
mammon, n.	Njika I/Y

mammoth, n.	Mamat, irudi baba giwa lembu,
mammy, n.	Mami, afa ti omontakele ng kono uwa (mamma)
man, n.	Mutum miji, namiji, miji, imiji; ikagba
(man-eater)	O wuam mutum
(man-handle)	Agba-mi ji
(man-hole)	Manho, irudi 'honu na kasa
(man-hour)	Irushe miji na wakati daya
(man-of wa-)	(man nke war) soja o jagha na ruwa
(man-power)	Agba nke miji (agba irushe miji)
(man-servant)	Imongi miji
(man-slaughter	O gbu mutum
manacle, n.	Manako, irudi chen hannu G/I/Y/H
manage, vti. n.	Manij, cheto, imanej, icheto, o cheto, manija k'osi
management, n.	Manijment, nke manij
manatee, n.	Manatii, nama tekun buto
mandarin, n.	Mandarini, afa hafsa gomnanti na chaina
mandate, n.	Inn'ashe Ef/YI
mandolin, n.	Mandolin8i, irudi 'haiki songa (musical instrument)
mandragora, n.	Mandagora, shuke-shuke puezin
mandrill, n.	Mandrel, irudi buto biri nke gboro rama
mane, n.	Geza, rero H
maneuver, n, vt.	Igbokei, gbokei Y/H
manganese, n.	Manganiz, irudi mital
manger, n.	Manji, irun rubimkha
mangle, n.	Beru I/Y
mango, n.	Mangwaro, mangol H/Gen
mangosteen, n.	Mangostin, irudi itache o wen 'ya 'ya na gabas India (East India) mangrove, n.
manhattan, n.	Menhatan G
man-hood, n.	Ngba imiji, ngba miji
mania, n.	Mahaukachi tuburan, meniak, ifewe
(sesx-maniac)	O fewe vudu

manicure, n.	Maniko G
manifest, adj, n.	Hone, ihone Y/I
manifesto, n.	Manifesa, ibietuu, ibetu gomnanti G(fe) I/Y/H
manifold, adj. (the manifold wisdom of god) Iluwe ichegbon Abasi	Luwe Y/I
manikin, n.	Tufien, tufiene, tintin
manilla, n.	Manela, irudi faiba an fi mese takarda, abi evilop
manipulate	Meyi, mesheli I/Y
mankind, n.	Bika mutum Y/I/H
man-like, adj.	Iminiwa (quality) nke miji
manna, n.	Mana, irudi abinchi ti Abasi Kpeyen (provided) emutum izreli na littafi Baibul
mannequin, n.	Manikwin, irudi 'buto "don-bebi"
manner, n.	Imiwa I/Y
mannerism, n.	Imiwa dioto (peculiar)
mannerly, adj.	Miwa rama
mannish, adj.	Abga mache bika miji
manor, n. `	Manon, irudi kasa na ingilande, bika manon fak
mansard, n.	Mensad, irudi rufi G/I/Y/H
manse, n.	Mans, minincha chochi na skotlande
mansion, n.	Manshen, ibuto gida
mantel, n.	Mantil, ikongi (structure) n'mbi wuta
mantis, n.	Koki-koki H
mantle, n.	Mantir H
manual, adj.	Kehann, o hann I/H
(manual labour)	Irushe kehann, irushe hann
manufacture, vt, n.	Meja, imeja I/Y
manufacturer, n.	O meja
manure, n.	Taki, takanta H
manuscript, n.	Ikodehann Y/I/H
many, adj.	Risi (ri-si) I/Y

(many people)	Irisi emutum
(how many)	Eleri risi?, risi lei?
maori	Maori, ede so na kasa nu-zilande (ew Zealand)
map, n.	Ikpo, taswira, kpo G/H
(map-reading)	Igua kpo igua taswira
maple, n.	Mapul, irudi itache
maquis, n.	Makuiz, afa eso na frans,
mar, vt.	Dihan, gbuhan, meje, merugu
marabou, n.	Marabo, irudi onene na yamma Afrika (West Africa)
maraschino, n.	Marashino, irudi wain o solele
marathon, n.	Isongolo I/y/Gen
(marathon race)	Iresongolo
maraud, vi.	Ringa, kiri fun njika, gakiri fun irubi
(marauder)	O gakiri fun irubi
marble, n.	Mabul, dusheda G/H
march, n.	Manch, uki nk'eta na ardun/(adun)
march, vti.	Gakele, garayo I/Y
ardigras, n.	Madigras, na frans
margarine, n.	Magarini, irudi bota t' an fi wuam buredi
margin, n.	Iyefe, hashiya, bayala Y/i/H
mrigold, n.	Marigold, irudi shuke-shuke o wen fulawa yaran (yellow flower) marijuana, (cannabis), n.
marimba, n.	Maremba, ikaya songa
marina, n.	Marena, marinos, kasa tekun G/H
marine, adj.	Nke tekun, fetekun, tekunu,
marionette, n.	Mayonet, don-bebi kele
marital, adj.	Nke igbemata
maritme, adj.	Irushe tekun, maritam I/Y/H/G
mark, n.	Lamba, lain, alama, ibre H/G/H/I/Y
mark, n.	Mak, kudi nke Zamani
(market woman)	Mache kasuwa
(market hall)	Bandeki kasuwa

(market police)	Mondoka kasuwa
(market place)	Mbi/ebi kasuwa
(market days)	Irana kasuwa
(market town)	Gari kasuwa
(market noise)	Arimkpo kasuwa
(market fight)	Ijagha kasuwa
(market trend)	Iteshien kasuwa
marks-man, n.	O gbata saun-saun, maksman I/Y/Gen/G
marl, n.	Mal, irudi kasa o wen yumbu, kasa taki (fertilize
marmalade, n.	Mamalade, irudi jam nke abinchi
marmoset, n.	Mamosat, irudi biri na Amerika
marmot, n.	Mamot, irudi nama kele bika kurege (squirrel)
marocain, n.	Maroken, irudi esa nke siliki
maroon, adj, n.	Marun, irudi launi
maroon, n.	Maroni, irudi roka, abi lugbum (rocket)
marque, n.	Zijiu, wasika nke aashe fun eni mutum k'o fi tako ugboko ruwa na ngba ijagha
marquee, n.	Makii, ibuto tanti (large tent)
marquis, n.	Igbemata makwiz, ibire miji na Briten (noble)
marriage, n.	Ichogebe, I/Y/H
(marriage certificate)	Satifiket nke ibugbemata, tashaida bigbemata
(give into marriage)	Gayen na igbemata Y/I/H
(marriage ceremony)	Anivaseh igbemata, igbandu igbemata (marriage rites)
(marriage activities)	Irushe igbemata
married, adj.	Chogbe, eni ti chogbe, o chogbe mutum
marrow, n.	Barbo, kabushi H
(bone-marrow)	Kashi barbo, kashi kabushi
mars, n.	Mars, ekwenshu o jagha na kasa Rome
marsala, n.	Masala, o solele wain
marseillaise, n.	Masheleshe, isongi songa kasa frans

marsh, n.	Fadama H
marshal, n.	Makezi, mashali G
(field marshal)	Fil makezi fil mashali, baba makezi
marshal, vt.	Tolele (muster) Y/I
marsupial, adj. n.	Masupa, irudi nama eso
marten, n.	Maten, irudi nama kele
martian, n, adj.	Mashian, emutum na mars
martin, n.	Matin, irudi onene
martinmas, n.	Martinma,rana nke st. Dafidi
martyre, n.	Ijerituwa, mataya, ikuowun mutum fun inikan – (belief)
marvel, n.	Iyalionu
marxist, n.	Magzist, na kasa zamani
marzipan, n.	Mazikwan, irudi keke suka
mascara, n.	Mascara, sosorobia ido
mascot, n.	Masikot, o mubia ishiende rama
masculine, adj.	Mimiji; nke miji G/H/I/H
maser, n.	Masa, ife sayesns, ihaiki sayens
mash, n.	Mansh, abinchi nke nama
mashie, n.	Manshi, irudi sanda gwalf
mask, n.	Dongunu H/Y
mason, n.	Masi, o rushe dutse G/I/Y/H
masquerade, n.	Maskured, bandeki e dogunu
mass, n.	Inchani, ibaba, Enu/I/Gen.
(mass celebration)	Iseliba nchani (iseli nchani)
(mass meeting)	Baba mitin
(mass campaign)	Ibab' ikemkpo
(mass communication)	Isole nchani
(mass media)	Ihanyar isole nchani, mas-midia
(mass production)	Imubia nchani
mass, n.	Iseliba nke chochi rom
massacre, n.	Igbu-ki-gbu, igbu baba lamba emutum,
(the benin massacre)	Igbu-ki-gbu nke Bini na ngba kea (ancient time) message, n.
massif, n.	Massif, irudi mantin (mountain)

massive, adj.	Nchakha, babakha
mast, n.	Shimfa, masti
master, n.	Maigida, malamin, oga, katazi, iwin
(mass, n.	Iseliba nke chochi Rom
massacre, n.	Igbu-ki-gbu, igbu baba lamba emutum
(the benin massacre)	Igbu-ki-gbu nke Bini na ngba kera (ancient time) massage, n.
massif, n.	Massif, irudi mantin (mountain)
massive, adj.	Nchakha, babakha
mast, n.	Shimfa, masti
master, n.	Maigida, malamin, oga, katazi, iwin
(master jesus christ)	Malamin Jesu Kristi
(master builder	Oga o kogi
(master plan)	Filan katazi
(master of science)	Malamin Sayens
(master-mind)	Iyobi 'win, bab 'ichegbon
(master of the house)	Maigida
(master of ceremonies)	Oga igbandu, baba igbandu (master-piece)
mastery, n.	Ikentrola, iwin kentrola, oga kentrola
masticate, vt.	Be je wuam I/Y/G
mastiff, n.	Wuuh-wuuh, baba kera t' gboro
mastodon, n.	Mastodin, ibuto nama bika giwa
mastoid, n.	Mastid , kashin kunne
masturbate, vi.	Masubet, ivudu wenji
mat, n.	Shimfada, tabarma H
match, n.	Ashana H/Y/Gen.
(match-box)	Akwati ashana
(match-stick)	Sanda ashana (a shana daya)
(match-wood)	Itache ashana
match, n.	Iguere, ikambe (competition)
(football match)	Iguere hubol, ikambe hubol
match, vti. (fit)	Yedi
matchet, n.	Adda H/Y
mate, n.	Ituegbe, aboki rushe abi makaranta
mate, vti.	Vudu nke nama, onene abi mutum

mate, n	Met, irudi tii
mater, n.	Meta, yaro makaranta
material, adj.	Rubu, kaya, kpanti I/Y/H
materialism, n.	Irubu, ikaya
materialize, vi.	Dije, wu ezioka, bia chiu,
maternal, adj.	Uwa H
(maternal care)	Ijune uwa
maternity, n.	Mataiti, irudi asibitin
(maternity clinic)	Asibitin mataiti, asibitin haihuwa
(maternity hospital)	Asibitin mataiti
(maternity ward)	Ebi mache ng mubi omo, nso mubi
matey, adj.	Agba, o gbandu kiri, bika aboki
(matey man)	Miji agba (agba man)
mathematics, n.	Matimatis, isayens nk'elamba, (mats)
matinee, n.	Matini, iguere rana na bandeki sinima
matins, n.	Metin, irudi 'kpredu safe na chochi
matricide, n.	Metrisaid, igb 'uwa o wenji G
matriculate, vti.	Metrikule, ibale makaranta yunifasiti
matrimony, n.	Matrimona, di chogbe
matrix, n.	Matrik, yumbu dutse wuta ti a ng fi shana ayar
matron, n.	Metran, mache o cheto asibitin abi makaranta
matter, n.	Oka, iforo, nsohala (magana) sn Ikw/I/Y/Gen
(what is the matter?)	Meni s 'oka? (in the matter between)
(no matter what happen)	Kosi 'chegbon, ka en'ife soka (printed matter)
(as a matter of fact)	N'oka n'arin
(as a matter of rule)	N'oka iwufin
(as a matter of course)	N'oka sambe
matting, n.	Mattin, irudi hama kasa, gamu
mattress, n.	Katifa H
(mattress and pillows)	Katifa ati efilo
mature, vti. n.	Diagba, nuke, idiagba, Y/I

maul, vt.	Gbu n'imeru (injury)
maulstick, n.	Sanda-fenti H
maundy thursady, n.	Rana Tasde swene ista na littafi
	Baibul mausoleum, n.
maverick, n.	Mafriki, oi nikan mutum
maw, n.	Wo, won-wom bika o gboro nama
mawkish, adj.	Mumu irochele (sentimentally foolish)
maxi, n.	Magzi, irudi esa mache G/Y/I/Og/H
maxim, n.	Maizim, irudi bindiga sam-sam
maximize, vt.	Mekah-kah, jukunu
maximum, n.	Ijukunkha, jukunukha I/Y/(G.v)
(maximum use)	Iluwe jukunukha
may, anom. fin.	Lewu
(i may come)	Mo lewu bia
(may god bless you, amen)	Ka Abasi lewu kunzi e, aashe (Abasi a kunzi e, aashe) (you may or ou may not)
(may be)	O lewu
may, n.	Mei, uklisen na ardun/adun G/Ed/I/Y
(may day)	Rana konda n'uki Mei, (mei 1) irana ti e rushe ng seliba
may-day, n.	Mei-dey, telifon danja na ugboko-feh abi ugboko ruwa G/H/Gen/Y/I
may-fair, n.	Meifeh, nso eso na gari London G/I/Ed/H
may-hem, n.	Imeru buto I/Y
mayonnaise, n.	Mayonis, irudi abinchi bature G/Y/I/H
mayor, n.	Magajin gari, muayo H/Y(G.v)
mayoress, n.	Muayo Y(G.v)
maze, n.	Iugu, iyaghuru Y/I/G
mazurka, n.	Masuka, irudi songa, isamba nk'emutum kpolish (Poli)
me, pron.	Mi Gen.
mead , n.	Mid baba kain-kain
meadow, n.	Midow, fili shuke-shuke ati fulawa
meagre, adj.	Gbefiene, kiene
(meagre salary)	Albashi gbefiene, albashi kiene

meal, n.	Abinchi
(meal time)	Ngbaabinchi
meal allowance)	Alawas abinchi, kudi abinchi
meal, n.	Irudi abinchi safe bika oti
(oat-meal)	Abinchi oti
mealie, n.	Melis, irudi masara na South Afrika
mean, adj.	Sonkiti
(mean person)	O sonkiti, mutum sonkiti
(very mean)	Ssonkiti kha
mean, adj.	Arin
(in the mean time)	N'arin ngba
(greenwich mean time	N'arin Agogo Grinwich
(NAG) mean, meant, vi.	
(which means that)	Yien wu ipe
(the meaning	Itiunma ya (i maen that)
(do you mean that mr. barawo is a thief? Jewu kpe mazi Barawo wu barawo?	
(yes, i mean that)	Baate, mo jewu kpe
meander, vi.	Yikpoto Y/Egun
means, n. - inozo	
(ways and means)	Hanyar at inozo
mean-while , adv.	Na ngbeti
measles, n.	Mi zol irun omontakele G/Y/Igen
measure, n, vt.	Inofi, nofi
(full measurement)	Inofi jukun, inofi kamkpe
(measurement tape)	Tef inofi
(beyond measure)	Kaju inofi
(gone beyond)	O ti shienga nofe
meat, n.	Nama wiwuam H
mecca, n.	Meka, birni Muhammad ati
isinle islam (Islamic religion)	
mechanic, n.	Makaliki, o kwashe (repair) injin ati mota
mechanical, adj.	Irushe makaliki, ife makaliki

ALEX EKHAGUOSA IGBINEWEKA

mechanism, n.	Ikaya abi ihaiki injinj, makalizim
machanize, vt.	Iluwe (the use) mashin abi injin, makalais
medal, n.	Menda, lamba G/H
medallion, n.	Baba menda, ibuto menda
meddle, vi.	Tune Y/I
(don't meddle with)	Ma tune kpe
meddler, n.	O tune
media, n.	Ikemkpo, isocha Y/Enuani/I
(mass media)	Isocha ncha
medial, adj.	Fuda I/H
median,	na ifuda
(mediate, vit.	Lagha, narin Y/I (mediator jesus christ)
medical, adj.	Ife magani, ilikita, bika magani
(medical doctor)	Ilikita magani, dokita
(medical student)	O dalibi magani, omo makaranta magani
(medcal school)	Makaranta likita bi magani
medicament, n.	Ihaiki magani abi ogun (ogun) I/Y/H
medicare, n.	Medikel, ikpeyen magani, abi ogun
medicate, vt.	Fi magani losie (treat)
medicine, n.	Magani H
meditate, vti. n.	Charo, icharo I/Y
mediterranean, adj.	Maditarena, bantekun G/Gen/H
(mediterranean sea)	Bantekun tekun
medium, n.	Izono I/Y (medium of expression)
medley, n.	Meli, irudi iwakpo (mixture) songa G
meek, adj, n.	Jeyo, ijeyo Y/I
meet, vti.	Mie, hunde, Ed/I/Y
meet, n. (gather)	Ihunde, ihunko, ihunba, mitin Y/I, etc.
(meet my darling)	Mie ninda mi
(see my darling)	Neri ninda mi, or, hunde ninda mi
(meeting of the club)	Ihunko tuegbe
megacycle, n.	Megasaikol, na sayens rediyo abi wayalis
megadeath, n.	Megadat, iluowun ibuto lamba emutum na ijagha ukleh (nuclear war) megalomania, n.
megaphone, n.	Megafon, megahon, solimega G/Y/H

megaton, n.	Magatin, agba ogbuum (explosive force)
megrim, n.	Maigri, irudi 'yobi kha iyobi kha (type of low spirits)
melancholy, n.	Iyobi kha, imej 'onu Y/I
melee, n.	Irugu Y/I
meliorate, vti. n.	Meda, imeda, mena, imena I/Y
mellow, adj.	Kulele
melody, n.	O solele songa, songa o dunso
melon, n.	Guna, kankana H (melon seed)
melt, vti.	Wushana H/Y/G
(melting pot)	Tukun shana igbowuta
member, n.	Tumbe, yumbe
(club member)	Tumbe/yumbe tuegbe
(member of the house)	Itumbe gida member of the house of pariliament) Itumbe majalisar wkili
membrane, n.	Membrin, na jiki nama abi mutum
memnto, n.	Ilorone
memo,n. mema,	Cheron icheron, noti, iloron G/I/Y
memoir, n.	Mema, irudi tontum (biography)
memorable, adj.	Cheron, le cheron. Di cheron
memorandum, n	Memoranda, noti, irudi mema
memorial, n,	Memora n'loron, icheron; Iloron (f.e)
memorize, vt.	Cherisi
memory, n	Icherisi
men, n.	Emiji, maza, mutane H(G.V)
menace, n.	Danja, iyolionu, imeru
ménage n.	Icheto yali mend vti.
mendicant, n., adj.	O biyo, mendikan IT/Y/I
menfolk, n.	O tuegbe miji
meningitis, n	Manijaiti irudi irun rubi
menopause, n.	Menopas, igukpin huene G/I/Y/G
menses, n.	Ihuene, ngba mache ng hun jinni G/I/Y/H
mensuration,n.	Mensura imensura na sayens aritmatiki(f.e.)
mental, adj.	Keke cheronsi yisi fewe I/H

(mental arithmetic)	Aritmatik icheronsi
(mental derangement)	Iyisi, ifewe
mental deficiency)	Iyisi ifewe, ai wen icheronsi
(mental hospital)	Aro, asibitin ifewe, asibitin e yisi; asibitin kok
(mental home)	Aro, gida o fewe;gida ikeke
(mental patient)	O bujen yisi eni ko gbandu n isi; o keke
(mental specialist)	Likita ameze n'ikeke ab
(mental test)	Idone yisi
mentality, n.	Icheronsi, ichengbon I/Y
menthol, n.	Mentol, bika fefemint G/Y/I
mentholatum	Mentoletom, irudi lenimint
mention, vt.	Koda
(don't mention my name)	Ma doka afa mi (don't mention it)
(above mentioned)	Ikoda n'abe
mentor n.	Minto, o ronhan kele
menu, n.	Manu, ilisa abinchi (list) mephistophelian, adj
mervcantile, adj	Makintal, itasuwa abi ikasuwa (trade or commerce) mercator's projection, n.
(war mercenary)	O jagha naisi
mercer, n.	Mensa, o rushe fabriki
mercerize, vt.	Mensara, irushe fabrik
merchandise, n.	Hajja, ileta kasuwa, ikaya kasuwa
merchant, n.	Attajiri, o leta kasuwa
(merchant ship)	Ugboko attajiri, (kueru-keuru)
(wine merchant)	O leta wain abi kasuwa wain
merciful, adj.	Nube, jukun fun inube
merciless, adj.	Ai wen nube, ai di nube, lai nube, njika
mercury, n.	Makiuri, irudi ruwa azurfa (silva)
mercury, n.	Menkiuri, flanit
mercy, n.	Irere, inube, inubele
(have mercy on me)	Wen inube si mi
(i pray for mercy)	Mo kpredu fun inube
mere, adj.	Shala

mere, n.	Kandami – (pond)
merge, vti. n.	Boyen, iboyen Y/I
(merger)	O boyen
meridian, n.	Marindi G
(greenwich meridian time)	Agogo marindi nke grinwich (AMG) meringue, n.
merino, n.	Merino, irudi meeh
merit, n.	Marit, iyeze G(fe)/Y/I
meritocracy, n.	Marito, irudi gonmenti ichegbon
meritorious, adj.	Yeze, di yeze
mermaid, n.	Mamid, irudi hoto nke mache kifi
merry, adj.	Gbandu, yoli, dunso, solesole
(merry christmas)	Igbandu keresimesi
mescal, n.	Meskal, irudi sedi (cactus)
mesdemoiselles, n.	E mundia, e wundia
meson, n.	Mezin, irudi zarra (atom)
mess, n.	Mesoh, imesoh I/Y
mess, n.	Dekiwuam, kichini soja /iseza H/G/Gen.
(mess-pan)	Kwno dekiwuam Gwari/Berom/NU/H/G
message, n.	Iziron I/Y
(please message me)	Biko, ziron si mi
messenger, n.	O ziron
messiah, n.	Chiolu, Kristi, Okesi I/y/Gen
messrs, n.	E Mazi I(G.v)
mestizo, n.	Metizo , e mon Spen abi Kpotoki eso, nke spana
metablolism, n.	Imetabola, oka yotebala (biology)
metacarpal, adj. n.	Metakapa, kashi hannu G(fe)
metal, n.	Tsakurwa, mital, h/G(fe)
(metal box)	Akwati mital
(metal work)	Irushe mital
metallic, adj.	Mitali, bika mital G(fe)/Y/I
metallurgy, n.	Mitaloji, irushe mital ati tama (ore)
metamorphose, vt, n.	Yintu, iyinto G/Y
metaphor, n.	Okare, irudi oka na turanchi,

metaphorical, adj.	Na kare, bika okare
metaphysics, n.	Ichegbon mindu I/Y
(metaphysical phenomenon)	Isokali ichegbon mindu
metatarsal, adj, n. mete, vt.	Wono Y/Ef.
meteor, n.	Mashi H
meteorology, n.	Femashi, mitioroloji, sayens nke iska (meteorological dept.)
meter, n.	Minta, ihaiki a ng fi nofi G(fe) I/H/Y
meter, n.	Mita, bika metriki
methane, n.	Metan, irudi gaiz G(fe)/Y/I/G
method, n.	Inozo Y/I
(way and method)	Hanyar at' inozo
methodism, n.	Metodiziom, inozo
methuselah, n.	Metusalah, na baibul, miji nke ti diwa ardun 969
methyl, n.	Mentil, ogogoro G(fe)/Gen
meticulous, adj	Babijune Gen/I/Y
metier, n.	Irushehan I/Y/H
metric, adj.	Metriki, irud' inofi (metric ton)
metronome, n.	Mentronomi, ikaya agogo
metropolis, n.	Mentrokpoli, baba birni G(fe)/H
metropolitan, adj.	Nke mentrokpoli, o mentrokpoli
mettle, n.	Imeye (quality), isundi I/Y
mew, n.	Miaun, ilowe (sound) muzuru, ikebe muzuru, miaun
mezzanine, n. adj.	Mezzanine, irudi dabe (floor)
mezzo, adv.	Memezo, oka isonga, abi rinbu G
mezzotint, n.	Mezoti, ilanyar te (printin system)
mice, n.	E kusu H(G.v)
michaelmas, n.	Maikelmas, ikowuam Liyi Maikel, rana semtemba 29 feast of St. Michael)
mickey, n.	Mekua I/G
micle, n.	Tue-tue, ibuto lamba G
microbe, n.	Imekro (mekro) G(fe)/Y

microbiologist)	O mkrobala
(microbiological)	Mekrobala, ife mekrobala
microscosm, n.	Mekroka, mutum kera (ancient person)
microelectronics, n.	Mekrolantiriki G(fe)
microfilm, n.	Mekrofilim, (mekrofil) G(fe)
micrometer, n.	Mekrominta, irudi minta a ng fi nofi 'fohe kele (small object) micron, n.
micro-organism, n.	Mekrogane, imekrogane G(fe)
microphone, n.	Mekrofofo, mekro 'fo, mek G/Gen.
microscope, n.	Mekrosoh G(fe)
microwave, n.	Mekrobilu G/H/Y
mid, adj.	Rin, arin Y(G.v)
mid-day, n.	Rin-rana, arin rana Y/H
(mid-day news)	Ikwiro rin-rana
midden, n.	Dushin, tari datti abi kashin (heap) (drugs)
middle,	Rin, arin
middling, adj.	Arini (rini) (the middle of grading)
middy, n.	Ringbo Y/I
midge, n.	Minj, irudi kwaro (insect) G(fe)
midget, n.	Minjat, mutum tintin G/H/Gen
midinette, n.	Mindinat, o nonhan giswa na kasa kpeshan
midland, n.	Arinkasa, arin lande Y/H/G(fe)
midnight, n.	Arin tuu, agogo goeji (tuukputu) Y/Tiv/Gen/H/Y
(midnight hour)	Hawa 'rin tuu
midriff, n.	Minri, n'imenu (belly) G(fe)
midshipman, n.	Mijiko, aringbo H/Y/I
midships, adv.	Arin ugboko ruwa Y/I/H
midsummer, n.	Arin sunma, rinsunma Y/G(fe)
midway, adj.	Arin/rin hanyar Y/H
midwife, n.	Ungozoma (gozoma) H/G.v
(midwifery)	Irushe ungozoma, igozoma
mighty, adj.	Agba, rake gadu-gadu Gen/Y/I
(mighty man)	Miji agba, miji rake
(almighty)	o wen agba, o Rake

mignonette, n.	Minonit, irudi fulawa gadin G(fe)
migraine, n.	Igbam-gbam, baba ifota isi n'akue daya
migrant, n.	O gbiri
migrate, vi, n.	Gbiri, igbiri
migrate	Gbiri, igbiri
mike, n.	Ibekuru afa maikel
milage, n.	Inofi mail
milch, adj	Mich, irudi mamal, nso gida (mammal)
mild, adj.	DO, RAYO, LAI SILE
(mild fever)	iba do
(mild head ache)	ifot'isi oo, ifot 'isi rayo
mildwe, n.	madiu, irun shuke-shuke G(fe)
mile, n.	Maili, mail, yadi 1760
(mileometer)	Mailominta
(how many miles?)	Ma'loi?, maili loi? mai'loloi?
mile-sone, n.	Dutse mail, jefa mail h/G(fe)
mileage, n.	Inofi mail
miler, n.	O roso mail
militant, adj.	O jagha sam-sam, jagha sam, ogburu
(military police)	Mondoka iseza, mondoka milinti, mondoka soja militate, vi.
militia, n.	Agba farula, civilian force, igbokwenu
milk, n.	Madara, nono, miliki H/Gen(fe)
milk, vti. (draw out)	Fapu, fata Y/I
milky, adj.	Bika miliki, bika madara bai nono
(milky way)	Baba tara na sama, ukiwe
mill, n.	Injin ilo, mila H(fe) Y/I/
(mill-stone)	Dutse ilo
(mill-house)	Gida ilo
millboard, n.	Milbad, ikaya littafi
millennium, n.	Milenia, ngba ardun 1000
millepede, n.	Ekekere og
miller, n.	O lo, o wen mila, o mila
millet, n.	gero, milat H/G(fe)
milli,	Milin, igiram kele (gram)

274

million,	Milian, inofi 1,000,000 H(fe)
milometer, n.	Mailominta, injin o nofi maili
milt, n.	Milti, irudi kifi mache G(fe)
mimeograph, n.	Maimogra, ogboloja, ikayanki o meshe kapi (apparatus)
mimosa, n.	Gabaruwa H
minaret, n.	Hasumiya H
mince, vti.	Wuara G/Y
(mince meat)	Wuara nama
mind, n.	Iyobi, ikonbi
mind, vti.	Shokpala, shokpa, konbi, nsohala
(mind yourself)	Shokpala yin, shokpa e, shokpala y inwan, konbi e (mind your business)
(never mind)	Ma shokpa
minless, adj.	Lai shokpa, ai konbi
mine, pron.	Nkemi, 'kemi I/Y
(mine only)	Nkemi sosho
mine, n.	Baramu, ma'adini, idini H
miner, n.	O dini
(coal miner)	O dini gawayi, o dini kwal
mine, n. (of war)	Dum-dum G
(lay mine)	Toka dum-dum
mineral, n.	Miriala I(G.v)
(mineral water)	Ruwa miriala
(mineral salt)	Gishiri, gishiri miriala
mineralogy, n.	Isayens nke miriala, imirialoji
mingle, vti.	Wakpo I/Y
mini, prep.	Tuin, tini G(f/Ed/Y/I)
miniature, n.	Icheri tini (mini image)
minim, n.	Mini, oka isonga
minimal, adj.	Tinkele
minimize, vt.	Meshe tinkele, betini
(minimize it)	Betini ya
minion, n.	Meboso, monrushe o soli ofofoh

minister, n.	Mininsta, o ronzi, ironzi, a ronzi H(fe)/Y/I tony, momoh is a monister:
minister of information	Wu mininsta
minister, vt.	O ronhan, o kpeyen (provider)
ministry, n.	Mininstri, iyaka o rozi, iyaka mininsta
minnow, n.	Yinon, irudi kifi kele kha
minor, adj.	Kewe, kerekha I/Y
(minor languages)	E 'de kewe
(inor issue)	Oka kewe
(minor fault)	Ishebi kewe
(minor problem)	Nsohala kewe
minority, n.	Ikewe
(minorities)	E kewe
minotaur, n.	Mubi jimi H(G.v)
minstrel, n.	Minstra, o mejo songi (composer)
mint, n.	Minte, irudi shuke-shuke
mint, n.	Minti, mbi a ng meshe kudi
(printing and minting)	Ite ati minti
minuet, n.	Miluet, irudi 'songa irayo
minue, adj.	Mupu Y/I
(plus and minus)	Fie ati mupu
minuscule, adj.	Minukul, tini kha-kha
minute, n. (of hour)	Ishido, minti Y/H
minute, n. (of meeting)	Tazkira, kwimitin (kwamitin) H/Y(fe) (minute, book)
minx, n.	Ruzoye, meje izoye, omote o ruzoye
miracle, n.	Iyalionu, iyalibam-bam Y/I/G
mirage, n.	Isuka, irekon-ofoh (hope)
mire, n.	Maya, koto kasa G/Y/H
mirror, n.	Madubi H
(mirror image)	Icheri madubi
misadvantage, vt, n.	Shienfa y(G.v)/Gen.
misadventure, n.	Ijambele Y(G.v)
misadvise, vt.	Shisheniye, tonwuam Y(G.v)/G
misapply, vt.	Shiyensi Y/I

(misapplication)	Ishiyensi
misapprehend, vt.	Shiyela, ishiyela, shijimu Y/I
misappropriate, vt.	Shikeliye, ishikeliye Y/I
misbehave, vti.	Shihumi, ishihumi, frehumi, (yakulukebe) (stop misbehaviour)
(misbeliever), n.	O shinikan
miscalculate, vti, n.	Shikao, ishikao Y/I
miscall, vt.	Shikono Y/I
miscarriage, n.	Ishikokwa Y/I
miscarry, vt.	Shikokwa, shibugbe Y/I
miscellaneous, adj.	Wuru, wukpo I/Y
mischance, n.	Ish'anfa, ekwenshu, ishiende rubi
mischief, n.	Imeru, ijika rubi
mischievous, adj.	Fata imeru, faijika, meru, jika rubi
misconceive, vti.	Shighoye (misunderstand) Y/I
misconduct, n.	Ishimuwa, ishimekoso I/Y
miscount, vti.	Shikao Y/I
miscreant, n.	Ijika mutum I/Y/H
miscreated, ajd.	Shidakasa Y/H
misdated, adj.	Shirana, shi kode rana Y/H
misdeed, n.	Shimeshe Y/I
misdemeanour, n.	Ishikoda, imew'ika Y/I/G
misdirect, vt. n.	Shijuma, ishijuma Y/I
misdoubt, vt.	Aidido, yopulu (doubt) Y/I/H
miser, n.	O tawun, o reba I/Y/H/Sobe
miserable, adj.	Gbula, aiyoli, ai gbandu, fre gbandu
misery, n.	Ishigbandu, ishiyoli, italaunchi
misfire, vi.	Shitwini-twini, shitonwu, shiwuta
misfit, n.	Shidiye, shidito Y/I
misfortune, n.	Ishishiende Y/I
misgive, vt.	Shigayen, shinnon, aid dido
misgovern, vt.	Shigomna, shibaeze Y/H/I
misguide, vt.	Shiboche, shimohan Y/H/I
mishandle, vt.	Shit'ido (shitoido)
mishap, n.	Ijambe, ishiende rubi, irubisi

misinform, vt, n.	Shikoli, shisoli, ishisoli, ishikoli
misinterpret, vt.	Shigbeso, shitafinta I/Y/H
misjudge, vti.	Shidakpe, shicherisi
mislay, vt.	Shihin, shiebi I/Y
mislead, vt.	Shigosin, shijuma I/Y
mismanage, vt.	Shicheto, shiluwe I/Y
misname, vt.	Shikono, shikono afa Y/I
misname, vt.	Shikono, shikono afa Y/I
misplace, vt.	Shiebi, shimbi' funu Y/I
misprint,	Shite, ai te rama Y/I
mispronounce, vt.	Shisota, shisoli, shikono Y/I
misquote, vt.	Shinoso Y/G/I
misread, vt.	Shikua
misrpresent, vt, n.	Shichenduli, ishichenduli Y/I
misrule, n.	Ishi 'wufin, ishigonmenti, gonmenti 'rubi
miss, n. (failure)	Shi, goshi I/Y
miss, n.	Yarin, yrn. Yarinya H(G.v)
missal, n.	Minsal, littafi ikpredu na chochi katoliki
missile, n.	Gbam G
mission, n.	Ironzimo Y/I/G
missionary, n.	O ronzimo, or onzimo isinle (religion)
missive, n.	Wasika gesi (important) H/Izon
misspell, vt.	Shi-kugu Y/I
miss-spend, vt.	Shi-noli Y/I/H/Ef
missy, n.	Iriya, mote, budi H/Urh
mist, n.	Hazo H
mistake, n.	Ishi-chero; igoshi Y/I
mister, n.	Mazi (mz.)
(mister man)	Mzi I
mistime, vt.	Shi ngba, shi 'yefe Y/I
mistletoe, n.	Mistotu, irudi shuku-shuke G
mistral, n.	Minstra, irudi feh tuoyi sa Frans (from)
mistranslate, vt. n.	Shi-giotun, ishi-giotun Y/I
mistress, (mrs.) n.	Mamangida; mma Hef
mistrial, n.	Mintril, irudi oka iwufin G

mistrust, vt.	Shi-toye Y/I
misunderstand, vt.	Shi-goye shigoye) (shighoye) I/Y
misuse, vt.	Shi-luwe I/Y
mite, vt.	Mait, irudi kudi kera bika anini
mite, n.	Maiti, irudi kwirun abinchi (parasite)
mitigate, vt.	Bekuru, betain I/y/G
mitre, n.	Mintia, esa bishobu G
mitt, n.	Miti, gulovu bolu tushe (base ball glove)
mitten, n.	Miten, irudi gulovu g
mix, vt.	Wakpo I/Y
mixer, n.	O wakpo I/Y
mixture, n.	iwakpo, (ikparu) i/y/h
mizzen, n.	Mizin, irudi shimfa abi masti (mast)
moan, n.	Keberugu, keberubi Y/I
(the benin moat)	Gwalalo benin
mob, n.	Konta Y/I/G
(don't mob me)	Ma konta mi
(the mob)	E konta, e konogbu, e konosoli
mobcap, n.	Hulache, irudi dula nke mache H(G)
mobile, adj.	Yikpo, gakir, yikporkiri Y/I/Egun
(mobile bank)	Banki 'yikpo H/Gen/Egun
(mobile food)	Abinchi 'yikpokiri, abinchi 'yikpo
mobility, n.	Iyikpo, iyikpokiri, igakiri
(i am not mobile)	Mii yikpo, yien wu mii wen ugboko
mobilize, vti, n.	Konoru, ikonoru, Y/I
(mobilize forces)	Konoru agba
moccasion, n.	Makasen, irudi fata do (soft leather)
mocha, n.	Moncha, irudi kafi G
mock, vti, n.	Mekua, imekua I/G
modal, adj.	Muda, na turanchi G/I/H
mode, n.	Bietu Y/I
model, n.	Samfuri, imeneri, idiwa H/I/Y
(new model)	Imeneri huntun
moderate, adj.	Ba
(moderately low)	Iba ka

moderation, n.	Iba
moderator, n.	O ba
modern, adj.	Kengba, ikengba I/Y
(modern bus)	Bos kengba
(modern man)	Miji kengba
modest, adj.	Wara I/Y
modify, vt.	Metun I/Y
modister, n.	Melina, ronkwa, o meshe esa G/Y/I/Og.
modulate, vti., n.	Metuni, imetuni, molete I/Y/Y
module, n.	Ilahan, iwufe, inofile Y/H/HG
modus operande, n. (lat)	Iwuyi metuni, inozo ife
modus vivendi, n. (lat)	Hanyar idiwa, ikweba kensi (temporary) mogul, n.
mohammedan, n.	Mutum o sole Muhammed
moiety, n.	Irinda (i.e. one of two parts)
moist, n.	Tuyi Y/I
moisture, n.	Tuyiyi Y/I
molar, n.	Matauni H
molasses, n.	Molase, irudi suka G
mole, n.	Bedu (small dark or white sport on human skin), H/Y
mole, n.	Mole, irudi nama tini G
mole, n.	Ibuto dutse tekun, mola
molecule, n.	Molecule G(fe)
molest, vt.	Fagburu Y/G
moll, n.	Mache jaguda H/Y
mollify, vt.	Medi kule
mollusc, n.	Molus, irudi nama kifi G(fe)
moloch, n.	Moloki, na littafi baibul, irudi ekwenshu
molten, pp.	Shanana G/Gen.
molo, adv.	Multo, ijuma songi, oka songa
molybdenumm, n.	Molinom, irudi alimint azurfa (silvery element) moment, n.
(in a moment)	N'ngba tini
momentary, adj.	Lai fa ngba, ife ngba kele, ngba tini

momentum, n.	Mumenta, oka sayens G(fe)
monarch, n.	Shgabar, o keisi, baeze H/I/Y
monarchism, n.	Monakizi, irudi gonmenti baeze abi shugabar, ishugaba monastery, n.
monastic, adj.	Sinmiwa (obedience)
monday, n.l	Mande, rana nke miji (ramiji), rana bika agba miji
monetary, adj.	Kudi-kudi, ife kudi H/I
money, n.	Kudi, naira H
(money chnager)	O sengi kudi, o wayo, o rawo
(money doubler)	O wayo mutum o jieva kudi
(money market)	Kasuwa kudi, banki
(money monger)	O renka abi o rushe kudi, o kudi, (delaer)
monger, n.	O renka, o rushe
(iron monger)	O rushe ayan
(fish monger)	O rushe kifi
mongolism, n.	Mongo, omontakele a mubi rubi
mongoose, n.	Mangus, irudi nama kele o gbu machiji na kasa India
mongrel, n.	Mangrel, eni a mubi si iwakpo yali
monitor, n.	Manita, o cheto G(fe) (monitor the progress)
(class monitor)	Manita aji, manita, o cheto jiya
monk, n.	Mank, ijama 'a isinle eso
monkey, n.	Biri
(monkey game)	iguere biri, iwayo-wayo
(monkey business)	Irushe WAYO
monochrome, n.	Monukram, irudi 'nese (drawing/painting)
monocle, n.	Monuko, ijongo nke ido daya
monogamy, n.	Immmonge, ibugbemata daya
monogram, n.	Monugram, iode na takarda abi akafifi (handerchief)
monograph, n.	Monugra, irudi isolioka katazi
monolith, n.	Monuli, irudi dutse iloronsi abi ilililai
monologue, n.	Monula, oka iguekwa (drama)

monomania, n.	Monumana, iyobi fewe
monoplane, n.	Monuflen, uonuflen, ugboko-feh o wen folefole daya (wing) monopolize, vt. n,
monopoly, n.	Monupoli, irudi 'guere G(fe)
monorall, n.	Monura, irudi 'rushe reluwe
monosyllable, n.	Okada daya, manusilaba, okada da
monotheism, n.	Imonotete inikan si Abasi daya
monotone, n.	Itunmada Ed/H
monotonous, adj, n.	Tunme, itunme, iremba y/I
monotype, n.	Teda Y/H
(monotype machine)	Mashin iteda, injin iteda
monoxide, n.	Monuzaid G
monsieur, n.	Mazi, o rayo, mz
monsignor, n.	Mansigna G(from French)
monsoon, n.	Monsun, irudi feh Arabic
monster, n.	Bola-bola, o meshe ijika G
montage, n.	Mantej, irushe hoto G
month, n.	Uki, na kalanda – earana ta (30 days)
monument, n.	Iloronsi I/Y
moo, n.	Muuh, ikebe malu Gen.
mood, n.	Iwahe 'yobi, iwahe G/Y/I
mood, n.	Mudu, oka uranchi, inunu G/Y/I/Gen.
moon, n.	Wata H
moor, n.	Kasofo (open/empty land)
moor, n.	Fachiu, ifachiu (oka ugboko ruwa)
moor, n.	Muo, irudi e mutum Arab
moose, n.	Diya, irudi baba nama daji G(Hv.)
moot, adj.	Mufien, soi si 'ta fiene
(moot out an idea)	Mufien ichenu is 'ta
mop, n.	Mobu, esa a ng fi shaka dabe abi kasa
m(mop stick)	Iteche m0obu
mope, vi.	Me jonu (sad)
moped, n.	Mokwed, irudi keke injin G(fe)
moquette, n.	Mokwet, irudi fabriki a ng fi meshe kafit

moraine, n.	Mureni, irudi yumbu na mantin (mountain)
moral, adj, n.	Miwa, imiwa I/Y
(moral virtue)	Miwa imirun
morale, n.	Ikomu Y/I
moralist, n.	O miwa, o komu
moralize, vti.	Medi miwa, di miwa
morass, n.	Mora, irudi kasa ruwa, bika fadama
moratorium, n.	Moratera, aashe lati buswi ikweba (defer)
morbid, adj.	Runu, ai wen mindu Y(G.v)
more, adj.	Risi, yensi I/Y
(more food)	Abinchi risi, abinchi si
(more people)	E mutum si, e mutum risi
(kmore and more)	Risi risi, risi si
(more or less)	Risi kiene, yensi kene, risi abi kiene (oliver asked for more)
more-over, adv.	Jukha si, kha si, yensi kha, risi jukha
mores, n.	Isinmu (social customs) Y/I
morganatic, adj.	Moganatge, irudi igbemata n'arin mache kpelu miji
morgue, n.	Euh, izin kutu jiki, izin gawa G/H
moribund, adj.	Gbakuo, fienekuo (about dying) n.
mormon, n.	Momoh, isinle 'so na ardun 1830 na kasa Amerika
morning, n.	Safe H
(morning prayer)	Ikpredu safe I/Y/H
(early in the morning)	Na ukutu safe
(early glory)	Ibogo safe ((morning and evening)
morocco, n.	Moroko, irudi fata (leather)
moron, n.	Morun, eni 'yobi kele G
morose, adj.	Mofim konji (ill tempered)
moripheme, n.	Irudi oka turnachi
morphia, n.	Mafia, irudi magani abi ogun
morphology, n.	Mafoloji, oka ibalabala (biology)
morse, n.	Mas, irudi oka waya

morsel, n.	Itini
mortal, adj, n.	Kuowun, ife le kuowun, ikuowun
mortar, n.	Irudi biriki abi sunmunti
mortar, n.	Laimota, turmi H
(mortar and pestle)	Laimota ati tabarya
mortagage, vt.	Mofa I/Y
(mortgagee)	O wenri mofa (receive), mofari
(mortgagor)	O nnon mofa, mofanon
mortician, n.	Matisha, o juma isinkuo (director)
mortuary, n.	Gida kutu
mosaic, n.	Ife mozisi, bika mozisi
mosaic, adj.	Nke mozisi, na littafi baibul
moselle, n.	Mozeli, irudi kain-kain
moslem, n.	Musulmi H
mosque, n.	Masallachi, abi masallaci
mosquito, n.	Sauro, yanmu-yanmu H/Gen.
(mosquito bite)	Ijeta sauro, ijeta yanmu -yanmu
(mosquito net)	Koma sauro, koma yanmu-yanmu
moss, n.	Mas, irudi shuke-shuke
most, adj, n.	Risi kha Y/I
(most of them)	Risi kha fa risi kha fa/ha
(most of all)	Risi kha ncha
mote, n.	Ekufe Y/I
(eye mote)	Ekufe ido
motel, n.	Motela G(fe)
moth, n.	Asu, hasu, fada-wuta H
(mother, n.	Uwa, mahaifiya, mma, mami
(mother-in-law)	Suruka H
(mother love)	Ihufe uwa, ihufe mama
(motherless)	Lai wen uwa, ai wen mama abi uwa
(mother care)	Ijune mama, ijune uwa
(mother tongue)	Ede uwa
motif, n.	Imotife, ijuma isongi
motion, n.	Iyime Y/I
motivate, vt.	Nnon agba Efik/Y/I

motivator, n.	O nnon agba
motive, adj.	Rondi; fache Y/I
motley, adj.	Rondo, icheto launi Y(G.v)
motor, n.	Mota H(fe)/Gen
(motor-cade)	E mota
(motor-car)	Mota zoom-zoom
(motorist)	O mota, o yanwa abi direba mota
(motor-cycle)	Keke-mota
(motor-hearse)	Mota ukpadidi H/G
(motor-way)	Hanya mota
mottle, vt.	Kenekene Ed
motto, n.	Isioka okagbon Ik/I/Y
mould, n.	Iruka, ruka, ikpebu Y/H
(mould-boards)	Fukafuka Y/H
(moulder)	O ruka, ife ruka, okpebu
moult, vti.	Fehon Y/I
mound, n.	Kakiti H/Y
mount, vti.	Getele Ed(G.v)
(mount up)	Getele nuke
mountain, n.	Basani, ikpekpe H(G.v)/G (mountain kilimanjaro)
mountebank, n.	O leta magani na oka wayo (bambam)
mourn, vti, n.	Konu, ikonu y/I
mouse, n.	Kusu H
moustache, n.	Gashionu H/I
mouth, n.	Baki, (onu) – sysnonym
moveable, adj.	Le yikpo, yikpo Y/Egun
move, vti, n.	Yikpo, iyikpo Y/Egun
mover, n.	O yikpo
movie, n.	Sinima Gen(fe)
now, vt.	Bere Y/I/H
(mower)	O bere
(lawn-mower)	Injin bere
mr. mister	Mz, mazi I
(mister man)	Mazi

285

mrs.	Mt., Mata H
much, adj, n.	Loi, kha, I/Y
(how much?)	Elei-loi?
(how much is this?)	Elei-loi?
(how much more)	Eloi kha?
mucilage, n.	Musle, itache gam G(fe)
muck, vt, n.	Meje, imeje
(make a much of)	Meshe imeje, medi meje
mocous, adj.	Makus, nke jadi-jadi
mud, n.	Laka, tabo H
(muddy), adj, adv.	Laka-laka
(muddy ground)	Kasa laka
muddle, vti.	Meru, merugu I/Y
muezzin, n.	Ladan H
muffin, n.	Mafin, irudi keke G(fe)
muffle, vt.	Fandu (wrap for wamth) G
muffler, n.	Boya Y/H
multi, n.	Mallam, o ma iwufin
mug, n.	Age Y/H
muggy, adj.	Di kuku, kku
muhammad, n.	Muhamadua, Baba woli sinle musulmi abi islam; (o choja isinle Islam)
mulatto, n.	Mulati, mutum igbetu iwakpo (mixed races)
mulberry, n.	Mulbri, irudi itache
mulct, vt.	Kuson, guole (fine/punishment) I/Y
mule, n.	Alfadari, mol, irudi nama shigidi (stubborn)
mule, n.	Mole, irudi silifa (slipper)
mullah, n.	Molah, muko musulmi (learned)
mullein, n.	Mulin, irudi shuke-shuke
mullet, n.	Mulat, irudi kifi tekun
mulligatawny, n.	Mulikatani, irudi miya a ng fi wuamm
multi, n.	Ogidi, ogegetelege Ish/Ed/Gen.
(multi-million)	Ogidi-milian

multiform, adj.	Idiwa risi (many shapes), maltiforo (fe)
multilateral, adj.	Okarisi (of many dicussants/talks)
muniments, n.	Munimnt, oka iwufin G(fe)
mural, adj.	Che I(Gv)
(extra-mural aactivities)	Ikufo che rushe murder, n.
(murderer)	O begbu, o gbujiji
murmur, n. – kunbe	Y/I
(don't murmur)	Ma kunbe
murphy, n.	Mafi, irudi dankali (potato)
murrain, n.	Mureni, irudi irn o junso 9ju-nso)
muscatel, n.	Muskata, irudi baba wain
musole, n.	Tsoke H
muse, vi.	Che-ro-kha rokha (think deeply)
museum, n.	Muzium, izira G(fe)Ed/H/I
mushroom, n.	Nankaza G(f.H)
music, n.	Isongi, G/Y/I
(music box)	Akwati 'songi abi irinbu
musical, adj.	Di songi,di rinbu,ife songi/rinbu
musician, n.	O songi, o rinbu
musket, n.	bonge,
muslim, n.	Musulmi, o sole Muhamadu
muslin, n.	Musili, irudi auduga a ng fi meshe esa
musquash, n.	Musikwashi, irudi bera kele (small
mussel, n.	Musel, irudi mous (mollusc)
mussulman, n.	Musulmi H/G
(you m ust make it)	E kodo meshe ya
(you must go)	E kodo shien
mustachic, n.	Mustache, baba gashionu
mustang, n.	Monstag, nama gboro abi shigidi
mustard, n.	Shuwe H/Y
(mustard seed)	Kwaya shuwe
muster, n. vt.	Itole, tole (tol-le) Y/I
musty, adj.	Huene G
mutation, n.	Iwunyi (change/alter) (wun-yi) I/Y

mutatis mutandis, adv.	Yiokpo dofin yiokpo doton - Y/ Egun (f. latin) mute, adj.
mutilate, vt.	Gerubi, gerubisi, (ge-rubi)
mutiny, n.	Ighate (igha-te) I/Y
mutter, vti.	Kwuse I/Y
mutterer, n.	O kwuso
motton, n.	Nama rage H
mutual, adj.	Wukpo, (wu-kpo) I/Y
(mutual agreement) (don't muzzle the ox's mouth0 Ma muchiu onu takarkari	Ikweba-iwukpo, ikwede-iwukpo muzzle, n.
my, poss. adj.	Nkami, ikemi, 'mi I/Y
(my wife)	Mata 'mi
(my husband)	Megida 'mi
(my child)	Momo nke ni (monke mi)
(my mother)	Muwa 'mi
(my father)	Baba 'mi
(my house)	Gida 'nmi, gida nke mi
mycology, n.	Makoroji, isayens nke fangus, mak-oro-ji
myelitis, n.	Maletis, idiwu (inflammation) laka (spinal cord)
myopia, n.	Ihunkuru, neri kuru, ineri kuru
(myopic person0	O hunkuru, o neri kuru, mutum kuro
myriad, n.	Miyad, baba lamba, ibuto lamba, o gidi lam
myrmidon, n.	Izonbi G(fe)
myrtle, n.	Matol, irudi shuke-shuke
myself, pron.	Miwan Y/It/Gen/I
mysterious, adj.	Jinke (ji + kasa) Y/H
(mysterious person)	Mutum jinka
mystery, n.	Ijinka
mystic, adj.	Jinka, jinka kha, izin
(mystic power)	Agba izin, agba ijinka

288

mysticism, n.	Inikan n'izin, inikan n'ijinka, ife jinka
myth, n.	Ilidaka, ilida-ka Agbo/H
mythology, n.	Imuke lidaka, maitoroji
mythologist, n.	O maitoroji, o muko ilidaka
myxomatosis, n.	Maizomatosi, maizoma, baba irun bera

nab, vt.	Demu I/Y
nacelle, n.	Nasol, akwati injin G(fe)
nacare, n.	Naka, uwa nke inang G(fe)/H/I/Efik
nadir, n.	Kakha (lowest) I/G(fI)
nag, n.	Mondoki, doki kele (small horse)
nag, vti.	Chowa ishebi, bilionu, soli-so (find faul)
nagger, n.	O chowa ishebi, o bilonu, o soli-so
nail, n.	Kumba, kusa, farche H
(nail on the head)	Kumba n'isi, (gbu na kei), ifuta
naïve, adj.	Ai ma, ai debi, okpe
naked, adj.	Hoda Y/I/H
namby-pamby, adj.	Ya-ya-ya (yayaya) (a nambypamby, person)
(what is your name?)	Meni wu afa yin?/e?
(my name is)	Chie anofi guobadi a: mgaji afa mi wu G
nameless, adj.	Ai wen afa, lai wen afa
(name-killer)	O gbu afa
nameless, adj.	Lai le kono, lai kono, ai kono
namely, adv.	Kono kono-kono, afa'fa, ikono
nancy, n.	Nansi, irudi afa
nankeen, n.	Nankin, irudi esa
nanny, n	Nani, mongi mache
nanny-goat, n.	Akwiya H
nap, n.	Isunkele
nap, n.	Ido esa, fuska esa, rintsa, kailula – H?Og
nap, n.	Nap, irudi 'guere kad
napalm, n.	Napam, irudi fetrol bika jeli
nape, n.	Zuba wuya I/H
napery, n.	Napri, irudi linin
naphtha, n.	Nafta, irudi oyele
napkin, n.	Esa kele, nafkin G(fe)
nappy, n.	Napi, nafkin omontakele
narcissism, n.	Nasisizi, irudi 'fewe
narcissus, n.	Nasiso, irudi fulawa
narcotic, n. adj.	Nakpoti, irudi magani 'sunla abi isimini

nark, n.	Nak, mondoka ingilande
narrate, vt. n.	Jumaso, ijumaso
narrow, adj.	Hale, kwintin Y/I
(narrow-minded)	Iyobi kwintin, iyobi hale
narwhal, n.	Nahua, irudi wel (whale)
nasal, adj.	Hanyar hanchi, nasa
nasturtium, n.	Nastotom, irudi shuke-shuke gadin
nasty, adj.	Yakulu G
natal, adj.	Natale, G(fe)
(anti-natal)	Swene natale, swen natale, soko natale
(anti-natal clinic)	Klinike swene natale
nation, n.	Neshon, kasa, (obodo)syn
national, adj.	Nashona, nke neshon
nationalism, n.	Imiwa neson, ineson, imeshe nejhion
nationalist, n.	O neson, o nejhionel, o kwashe neson (repair)
nationality, n.	Nke mutum kasa, nejhionalite, omo kasa.
nationalize, vt.	Medi neson, wukpo si neson,nesoni (nasoni)
(nationalize it)	Medi nke neson, nasonaya
nationalization, n.	Inasona, iwukpo si neson
native, n.	Kakaza, omo kasa, monkasa
(naative of where)?	Omo kasa lee? Monkasa lee? Omo kasa mbo nativity, n.
natter, vt.	Kunme – (grimble) Y/I
(don't natter here)	Ma, junme ebi (mbi)
natty, adj.	Kamkpe i.e. (strong, smart, neat & tidy)
natural, adj.	Fe hali, hali, halitta, duniyar
(natural law of justice)	Iwufin 'dakpe nke hali, iwufin 'dakpe ha (natural forces)
(natural phenomena)	Isokali hali
naturalism, n.	Iwufin hali, ihali, nke hali
naturalist, n. o hali	O hali
naturalistic, adj.	Na hali, n'oka hali, di hali
naturalize, vti. n.	Medi hali, di hali, ihali

naturally, adv.	Na hahali, (na hali, hali-hali)
nature, n.	Hali, halitta, jiki H
(by nature)	Na hali, n'ihali
(nature study)	Inuko hali (morepheme: imu-ko hali)
(human nature)	Ihali mutum, hali mutum
maturism, n.	Imudis, o mudis, ihali
naught, n.	Nason I/Y
naughty, adj.	Yakulu kebe – (misbehaviour)
(don't be naughty)	Du yakulu kebe, ma yakulu kebe (don't be a naughty boy)
nautch, n.	Nach, irudi 'nofi G (from India)
nautical, adj.	Nateke, maili ugboko ruwa
nautilus, n.	Natelus, irudi nama kele na tekun naval, adj.
nave, n.	Nfe, na chochi – ebi buto kha
navel, n.	Chibiya H
navigable, adj.	Di jajunu, jakunu
navigate, vti, n.	Jakun, ijakun Y/Gen/H
navvy, n.	Nafi, o woka kasa (naval base)
nazi, n. adj.	Nazi, itugbe Mazi Hitler na kasa Zamani
neap, n.	Nere, firi, nke sonbi (tide) Auchi/H
near, adj.	Kusa
nearness, n.	Inure, inure
nearly, adv.	Nunure, tunfien, tunfiene Ed/ Ish (nearly cannot kill a bird)
neat, adj.	Fini, shaka, - (neat and slendu) – kenti
neatly, adv.	Shaka-shaka, fini-ni
nebula, n.	Nebule, nebuli G(fe)
nebulous, adj.	Dimare I/Y
necessarily, adv.	Katazi, zumkpa Y/I
necessary, adj.	Katazi, zumkpa
necessitate, vt.	Medi katazi, medi zumkpa The advert and adjective are the same The advert and adjective are the same

292

necessity, n.	Ikatazi, izumkpa Y/I
(necessities of life)	Ezumkpa nke mindu abi duniya
neck, n.	Wuya H
(bottle-neck)	Nsohala – (no plural form)
(neck-cloth)	èsá wuya
(neck-lace)	dutsen wuya
(neck-tie)	daure wuya, julla wuya, (tai)
necromancy, n.	ò solikutu, so-li-si kutu, isolikutu
(necromancer)	ò solikutu
nectar, n.	nakata, na kasa Grik, irudi wain nke ekwensh nee, adj. (of female)
need, anom fin.	Niwen Y/I (needs) plural
(needful/needed)	Di niwen
(needless), adj.	Ai niwen, ko niwen (needless you do it)
need, vt.	Che I/Y
(needs), pl.	E che, chiche, e chiche
needle, n.	Allura H
(eye of a needle)	Ido allura (thatching needle)
nefarious, adj.	Ijika, ifaru I/Y
negate, vt. Koke (to deby/ denial), (rafi) leave nullify)	
negation, n.	Ikoke, irafi; babas
negative, adj.	Zuba, Juti, I/Y (negative copy) negligence, n. Igbafu, lai fi-ye-bi-si (negligence of duty) Igbafu irushe negligible adj. Nke a kanbo gbafu; gale gbei
negotiable, adj.	Ju-bi, jubi negotiate, vt.
negotiation, n.	Ijubi
negress, n.	Mache Nigro, sa
negro, n.	Miji Nigro, emon Amerika eso sa Afrika
negus, n.	Negusi, irudi wain abi ruwa kasa
negus, n.	Negus, o wufin kasa Itiopia
neigh, vi. n.	Gheghe, ikebe doki Ed.
(the horse is neighing)	Doki ng gheghe
neighbour, n.	Ikusa inure (my neighbour)

(your neighbour)	O kusa e
(neighbouring country)	Kasa kusa
(neighbourliness)	Imakusa sam
neoglogism, n.	Ilaje Gen.
nemcon, adv. (lati.)	Nemkon, ikweba ikweba fefefe nemesis, n.
neo, n.	Kensi, nio, nke-ngba G I/Y/G
neo-colonialism, n.	Nio-kolo, nio-kolone G
neophyte, n.	Niofa, enikon eso na chochi Roma Katolik
nephew, n.	Monwa Gen/H
nephritis, n.	Nafiti, irun koda: G/I/Y/H
neoplasm, n.	Nioplasi, irun jiki G/I/Y/H
nepotism, n.	Nekpoti, irudi inuere G (favouritism)
neptune, n.	Naftiun, abasi nke tekun (god)
nereid, n.	Nere, irudi nama tekun
nerve, n.	Jijiya H
nervous, adj.	Ife jijiya, di jijiya I/H
nescience, n.	Neshin, ai wen ichegbon
nest, n.	Sheka H
nestel, vti.	Megion, megien (settle) G
(nestle down)	Megien si kasa, megien
nestling, n.	Nesli, onene kele kha-kha
nestor, n.	Nesto, na kasa Grik, baba ichegon miji
net, n.	Taru, koma H
(net-ball)	Nati-bol G(fe)
net-work, nat	Isile rushe, irushe nso ncha
(net-work news)	Ikwiro nso ncha, ikwiro natwok (ikwiro natwo net, nett. adj.
nether, adj.	Neda, ka-kha (lowest)
netherlander, n.	Nedalande, omo nedalande
netting, n.	Iluwe taru abi koma
nettle, n.	Nitol, irudi gboro shuke-shuke
neural, adj.	Nura, nke jijiya
neurasthenia, n.	Nurasenia, erengu abi iguton jijiya

294

neuritis, n.	Nurititi, irun jijiya G(fe)
neurology, n.	Nuruoloji, isayens mageni ijijiya
(neurologist)	O nuruoloji
neurosis, n.	Nuruosi, irun bika ifewe, ifewe G
neuter, adj.	Nuta, oka turanchi G
(neuter gender)	Janda nuta, lai wu miji abi mache
neutral, adj.	Yemeji, ai chiu na akue Y(Gv) (side)
neutron, n.	Nutron, oka isayens lantiriki
never, adv.	Dako ma, keh Y/I
(never you say that)	Ma soli yien
(never you depart)	Dako ropu, ma ropu
(never mind)	Ma shokpa, ma shokpala, ma nsohala
(never again)	Ma keji
nevertheless, adv.	Biotiwu, biotiche, cherosi Y/I
new, adj.	Kowele, (huntun) Agbo/I/Y
(a new look)	Ineri kowele, ineri (huntun) – synonym
(new dress)	Esa kowele
(happy new year)	Eku ardun kowele, eku a (r)dun huntun
(new book)	Littafi kowele, littafi huntun
(new testament)	Testamint Huntun.
(new year's eve)	Yamma Izugba rana na adun:P Disemba 31 (last) (newly weds)
(new wife)	Mata huntun
(new office)	Ofis huntun/kowele
(new arrangement)	Itole huntun
(newness)	Ikowele, ihuntun
(next day)	Rana keji
(nexzt tomorrow)	Lachi keji
nib, n.	Nibi, onu alkalami G/I/Y/Ed/H
nib-lick, n.	Bibli, irudi galf (gulf)
nice, adj.	Sei H(G.v) special preference
nicety, n.	Isam-sam – (accuracy)
nick, n.	Iniwu, sam
(nick of time)	Sam ngba
nick, n.	Ikpongba – (also condition)

nicki, n.	Nik, ibekuru afa Nikolas, Idugbo Nikolas – ekwenshu
nickel, n.	Nike, irudi kudi na Amerika
nick-name, n.	Ijelafe G
nicotine, n.	Nikotin, irudi puezin
niece, n.	Isi Ed(G.v)
(my niece)	Isi mi
nigeria, n.	Naijeriya
nigerian, n.	Omo kasa Naijeriya
nigerianphile, n.	Naijeriyafile; o hufe kasa Naijeriya ati ife ncha na Naijeriya: (person who loves Nigeria and everythig Nigerian).
niggard, n.	Ifiene (isonkiti) – meanness
nigger, n.	Niga, irudi afa Nigro
niggle, vi.	Roka Y/I/Ikw
nigh, adv. prep.	Sinso Y/Kal/I
night, n.	Tuu Tiv
(day and night)	Rana ati tuu H/Y/Tiv
(night after night)	Rana si na rana
(night allowance)	Alawas nke tuu
(night bird)	Onene tuu, bika Mujiya (owl)
(night club)	Otel tuu
(night dress)	Esa tuu, bika pinjamas
(night gown)	Riga tuu
(night fly)	Tashi tuu
(ight life)	Igbandu tuu, akpor tuu
(night light)	Wuta tuu
(night long)	Ifaogo tuu, igungolo tuu
(night-mare)	Ila rugu
(night safe)	Akwati ti a ng fi sefi kudi na tuu
(night swchool)	Makaranta tuu
(night shift)	Ngba irushe na tuu
night soil)	O bukpoh o bue kpoh,
(night stop)	Ebi 'chiu na tuu, (nke aroplen)
(night time)	Ngba tuu

(night watchman)	Megadi, o gadi
(night work)	Irushe tuu
(night worker)	O rushe tuu
(nightly)	Na tuu-tuu
nightingale, n.	Natingel, irudi onene o songi songa na tuu
nimbus, n.	Nembus, irudi oruka na isi malaika
nimrod, n.	Nimrodi, baba maharbi na Gen. 10:
nincompoop, n.	Shashasha, yayaya H/G
nine, n.	Esse Iz/kal
nineteen, n.	Goesse H/Iz/Kal.
nineteenth, adj.	Nke goesee
(nineteenth centruy)	Adungogo goessa
ninety, adj. n.	Sse Iz/Kal/G
ninth, adj, n.	Nk'esse, esse
nine-pins, n.	Nanpins, irudi 'guere
niobe, n.	Mache o kunbe kha-khaa (wee), o kunbe Lai simini
nipper, n.	Nipa, irudi 'haiki (instrument)
nipple, n.	Onu nono, nipo I/Y/Ed/H/G
nipponese, adj.	Niponis, nke Nipon na Jakpan
nirvana, n.	Nivana, nke Buddhism
nisi, conj. (lat.)	Fibi – (unless) I/Y
nissenhut, n.	Gida kwano H/Gwa/Nu/Kan.
nit, n.	Kwai kwaro H
nitrate, n.	Natre, shiri G/H(G.v)
nitre, n.	Nita G(fe)
nitric, adj.	Nitriki G(fe)
nitronchalk, n.	Nitrocha G(fe)
nitrogen, n.	Natroin, irudi gaz G(fe)
nitroglycerine, n.	Natroglisirin G(fe)
nitrous, adj.	Nita, bika nita G(fe)
nitwit, n.	Iwinsam, mutum o chegbon sam-sam
no. adj.	Kosi, ah-ah, un-un, beat baati Gen/I/Y
(no problem)	Kosi nso-hala, kosi nsogbu

(no need)	Kosi niwen ko niwen
(no one)	Kosi
(no body)	Kosi mutum
(not/no any)	Kosi eni
(no more, no less)	Ko risi, ko kiene
(it is of no use)	Ko wen iluwe, kko di'luwe
(no good use)	Ko di ' luwe
(noah, n.	Noah, na littafi Baibul
(noah's ark)	Abara Noah , Jenisisi 5: 9 nob, n. (of upper classes)
nobel	Nobela, na Swidish, o hume dainamai
(nobel prize)	Irajan irajan Nobeld
noble, adj, n.	Nobela bire, ibire Y/Ed
(noble birth)	Imubi bire
(noble man)	Ibire miji, mutum ibire
nobody, pron.	Kosi mutum; kosieni
noctambulist, n.	Fenabolis, o ringasunla (rin.ga.sun.la)
nocturne, n.	Naktun, isongi rayo na tuu
nod, vit,	Misi (mi.kisi) Y/I
(nod your head)	Misi kei, misi 'si, kweba
node, n.	Nod, ireshe itache (branch)
noel, n.	Noe, keresimesi
noggin, n.	Nojini, inofi kele G(fe)
no-how, adv.	Kosi 'ichegbon, kosi baate
noise, n.	Arimkpo Y/I
(noise maker)	O meshe arimkpo
(noisless)	Dankiti, ma meshe arimkpo
(noisless zone)	Isogbo dankiti (isogbo nkiti) nso kule
noisy, adj.	Baba arimkpo, arimkpo, di arimkpo
nomad, n.	Fulani, o yawo H(G.v)
nomenclature, n.	Nominklacha, lanya afa (system)
nominal, adj.	Lilamba Y/H
(nominal roll)	Itole lilamba
nominate, vt. n.	Kuko, konosi, ikonosi Y/Ed
nominee, n.	O konosi

non, pref.	Diosi, lai dio I/Y
(non-alignment)	Diosi-jera
(non-combatant)	Diosi – kakppu soja 'lafia
(non-commissioned)	Diosi-kwamishan, lai kwamishan (dio-kwam shan) (non-compliance)
(non-conductor)	Lai mekoso, lai bue, dio-mekose
(non-conformist)	O diosi tesiba, ai tesiba, o dio te' siba
(non-delivery)	Lai kajo, ai kajo, dio-kajo
(non-essential)	Lai zumkpa, ai zumkpa, dio-zumkipa
(non-event)	Ko soka, ifre,
(non-interference/vention)	Lai balerin, lai yenrin, dio-balerin
(non-member)	Dio-tumbe diosi tumbe, lai tumbe, ai tumbe, ko wu tumbe (non-payment)
(non-resident)	Lai resido, dio-resido
(non-smoker)	Lai mukoko, ai mukoko, dio-mukoko
(non-starter)	Dio-rebi, oi rebi, lai rebi, ai rebi
(non-stop)	Lai chiu, lai kudu, dio-chiu
(noon-violence)	Dio-rugu, ko miru, kosi miru, lai miru, ai mirugu (non-age)
nonagenarian, n.	Nonajine, (fe) mutum igboye n'arin ardun 89 si 100 nonchallant, adj.
non compos mentis (lat)	Non compo menta, oka iwufin, eni ko gbandu abi alafia nondescript, n.
none, pron.	Disi I/Y
(none-the-les)	Biocherisi, biotiwu
nonentity, n.	Ai zumkpa mutum, ai zumpka, ikienekha
none-such, n.	Ai diogba,
nonsense, n.	Boro-boro, shashasha
nonsequitur, n. (lat)	Nonsikita, oka iwufin
noodle, n.	Mudol, irudi abinchi
nook, n.	Ebi-ki-ebi
(nook and corner)	Ebi-ki-ebi, ebi ncha
noon, n.	Nun, arin rana G(fe)
(noon day)	Rana-dan-dan

no one	Kosi eni mutum, kosi mutum daya (dio-mutu)
(no one at all0	Kosi eni rada, kosi mutum rada
noose, n.	Azar (from azargiya) H(G.v)
nor, conj.	Abi Y
nordic, n. adj.	Nodik, nodiki
norfolk, n.	Noufok, na kasa ingilande
norm, n.	Nofile – (standard/yardstick)
normal adj.	Gentu I/Y
(it is normal)	O di gentu (it is not normal /abnormal)
(below normal)	Naka gentu
(normalize) (normalization)	Me di gentu, gentu ya, igentu
norman, n.	Noman, e mon skandinivian ati Franki
normative, adj.	Nomati, inofili na oka turanchi
norse, n.	Nosi, (Nors), baba ede kasa Norway (Nowe
north, n.	Not, kasa sonma G/H
(north-east)	Not-1st
(nort-west)	Not-ist
(north-west)	Not-uest
(orth and south)	Not ati saot
northern, adj.	Nke not, di not, omon not
norwagian, n. adj.	E mon kasa Nowe, ati ede ha
nose, n.	Hanchi (hanci) H(G.v)/H
(nose about)	Chowa kiri
(poke-nose)	Fionu-kiri, mebo-kiri
(nosey, nosy)	Mebo-kiri
nosh, n.	Nash, abinchi rama (fe)
nostalgia, n.	Benegeda, ai gbandu H(G.v)
nostril, n.	Ihonu hanchi I/Y/H
nostrum, n.	Nostrom, irudi magani abi ogun
not, adv.	Nat, kowu, baati, ma G(fe)/Y/I
(not as all)_	Kowu rada
(not as you think)	Kowu bietu e chero, (kowu bi e chero)
(not me)	Kowu mi, kowu miwan

(ndo not come)	Ma biawa
notable, adj.	Le kiesi, kikiesi
(notable among them)	Kikiesi na ha
notary, n.	Notri, o wufin abi lauya gonmenti
notation, n.	Simbola, Ilamba kiesi, oka isonga
notch, n.	Nach, simbola nke irama
note, n.	Ikiesi, mon, ikode
(note-book)	Littafi 'kode
(note-paper)	Takarda ikode, (ikode fefa)
(note of warning)	Ikiesi danjua, ishokpala kiesi
nothing, n.	Kodi 'fe, kosi 'fe, (kodi) (ko) (nothing good comes easy)
notice, n.	Ikiesi, atansha, notez aashe, note, wasika Y(G.v)/G(fe)
(notice-board)	Katako notez
(long notice)	Igungolo kiesi, ikiesi-golo
(short notice)	Ikuru kiesi
(bring to notice)	Mubia si kiesi
notify, vt.	Kiesi, soli, koli
notion, n.	Ichero I/Y
notorious, adj.	N'okili I/Y
notwithstanding, prep.	Sieba-sieba (si.eba-si.eba) (morephene), amo nougat, n.
nought, n.	Ifoh, ifoh Y(G.v)
noun, n.	Nao, oka turanchi; afa enimutum, ife abi ebi-ki-ebi
nourish, vtk, n.	Keche, ikeche Y/I
nous, n.	Nus, ichegbon lea (common)
nova, n.	Nuvah, irudi tauraro
novel, adj. (strange)	Fiten Y/I
novel, n. (of book)	Novela G(fe)
(novelist)	O novela
novelty, n.	Ifiten, ifitenten
(novelty match)	Iguere fitenten, iguere tenten
november, n.	Lovemba, uki godaya na ardun

now, adv.	Ngba nsiyii, ngba nsiyi, geyi (geyi) I/Y
(now-now)	Geyi nsi, ngba nsisiyi, ngba geyi
(just now)	Ngba geyi
(now and then)	Geyi ati geyien
now-adays, adv.	Ngba rana yi, rana-geyi, erana-geyi (pl.)
nowhere, adv.	Kosi ebi (nowhere in the world)
nowise, adv.	Ko niwen, ko luwe
noxious, adj.	Kpanji, gbunji
nozzle, n.	Nutokun I/Y
nub, n.	Dunkule kele kha, nobu
nubile, adj.	Wundia H/Y
nuclear, adj.	Gbuniya, o gbuniya I/Ed/H
(nuclear bomb)	Bom o gbuniya, abi (o gbuniya bom)
nucleus, n.	Arin. Gin, aringin Y/H
nude, adj. n.	Noho, inoho I/Y
nudge, vt.	Tukon rayo (touch gently)
neggert, n.	Nogiti, irudi ayan na kasa
nuisance, n.	Ibili.onu, o bilionu, shio Y/I/It.
null, adj.	Foh, rafi Y/Gen
(null and void)	Di of oh
numb, adj. n.	Ruge, iruge G
number, n.	Ilamba, lamba H(fe)
(times without number)	Ngba lai wen lamba, ngbangba (house number)
(my car number is 1635)	Lamba mota mi wu 1635
(i live at no. 9 bukuru street)	Mo ng gbi na lamba, Titi Bukuru numerable, adj.
numeral, n. adj.	Lilamba bika ilamba 1,2,3 est.
numerate, adj.	Numaret, mutum baba ichegbon sayesn
numerator, n.	Numareto, oka sayens aritmatik
numerical;	Umenra, nke lamba G(fe)
numerous, adj.	Tombili lamba, ibuto lamba
numinous, adj.	Solibaba
numismatics, n.	Numismat, imuko bietu an meshe kudi
numskull, n.	Izugo, o zugo (stupid/foolish person)

nun, n.	Non, mache krista G(fe)
nuncio, n.	Nonsho, ambasiye nke pop
nuptial, adj.	Nushal, nke igbemata G(fe)
nurse, n.	Ness o cheto feshent na asibiti
nursery, n.	O rushe aiki nes, nesri
nurture, n.	Cheto diagba, kombe
nut, n.	Kwaya
nutmeg, n.	Nomeg, irudi 'sile kwaya
nutrient, adj.	Kechele Y/I
nutriment, n.	Abinchi kechele
nutrition, n.	Ikechele
nuts, adj.	Lawere I/Y
(don't be nutty)	Ma lawere
nutshell, n.	Kwasfar kwaya
nuzzle, vti. hanchi si,	Hanchi si 9point nose at) nymph, n.
numphet, n.	(o fiki-fiki, yarinya abi omote o fikifiki)
nymphonmania, n.	Nifomenia, mache o vudu kha-kha

oh, int.	Kebe, irugu, idunta n'iyobi	
o'	Oka ibekuru	
oak, n.	Ok, irudi ibuto itache	
oakum, n.	Okun, irudi faiba	Y/Ed
oar, n.	Mutuki	H
oasis, n.	Yoesi	G(fe)
oat, n.	Ot, irudi kwaya abinchi	
(oat-meal)	Abinchi ot	
oath, n.	Ibulinji (ibu.li.n.ji) synonym	
obigato, n.	Obligato, oka isonga	
obdurate, adj.	Shigidi, ai gbonti	
obedient, adj., n.	Igbonti, sinmiwa, miwa rama	
obeisance, n.	Biyesi, baba ikumbe (respect)	
obelisk, n.	Obele, irudi "loronsi (monument)	
obesity, n.	Isonghuru, isonbibu – fatness	
obey, vti.	Gbonti, teisiba (t'isiba), fieza	
(obey me, please)	Gbonti mi, biko	
(obey the last command)	T'isiba imeashe zuba, gbonti oka	
izuma obiter dictum, n. (lat.)	Obika ditom – oka, abi isoli ngba	
obituary, n.	Obito, obichari, iyakutu	
		G (fE) /
object, n.	Abjekti; ifohe	I/Y
object, vit.	Juko	I/Y
(i object/ted)	Mo juko	
objection, n.	Ijuko	
objective, adj., n.	Cherondi, icherondi	I/Y
objectivity, n.	Icherondi, ai megbe	
objurgate, vit.	Sombala	Y/I
oblation, n.	Isebo fun ekwenshu (sacrifice)	
oblate, adj.	Lebe – (to flatten at ends)	

obligate, vt.,	Ikaya, kaya	H(G.v)
n. oblige, vt.	Buji, jubi, nno	I/Y
(i oblige you)	Mo jubi e	
oblique, adj.	Oblik, gangara – slope)	G(fe)/H
obliterate, vt., n.	Chare, ichare	I/Y
oblivion, n.	Gbavion, igbavion, gbafu	Y/Ed
oblivious, adj.	Ai kiesi, ai ma, lai ma, lai kiesi. Lai shokpala	
oblong, n., adj.	Oboro, boro, iboro	G
obscene, adj.	Mej'iwa (meje miwa)	
(obscene photo)	Hoto o mej'iwa	
obscure, adj., n.	Toche, itoche	Y/I
obsequies, n.	OSIkwi, isinmutu (funeral ceremonies)	
obsequious, adj.	Demu – (great respect)	H/I/Y
observe, vt, n.	Kiesi, cheto, neri, ikiesi, icheto, ineri	
observer, n.	O kiesi, o cheto, o neri	
(nigerian observer)	O Neri Naijeriya	
observation, n.	Ikiesi, icheto, ineri, ihun	
obsess, vt.	Jimu	
obsess the mind)	Jimu iyobi	
obsidian, n.	Osidian, irudi dutse ijongo	
obsolescent, adj.	Gagulu jalopy	G/Gen
obsolete, adj.	Jalopi	Gen
obstacle, n.	Idi hanya, o di hanyar, irubisi	
obstetric, adj.	Osetrik, na asibiti	G(fe)
obstinate, adj.	Ai kweba n'iflesi, gburu	
obstruct, vt, n.	Dihan, idihan, Y/H gbuhanya	
(don't obstruct me)	Ma dihan mei	
obtain, vti.	Weni, yi I/Y/Egun	
obtrude, vt.	Kpu nuke ichero – (push up opinion)	
obtuse, adj.	Gbiin, ai wen onu bika wuka, lai munko	
obverse, n.	Ovas, nke keredi (coin)	
obviate, vt.	Mupu, bokei Y/I/H	

obvious, adj.	Honekha, hunekha, hune Y/I
ocarina, n.	Okina, irudi 'kayanki 'songa
occasion, n.	Okashon, iyefe, G(fe)/Y/I
occasional, adj.	Na okashon, n'iyefe, na ngba
ooccupy, vt.	Bie jimu, kunu I/Y/G
occur, vt.	Soka H/I/Y/Ikwere
(it has cocured)	o soka la
(it has happened)	o soka laoccurrence, n.	Isoka
ocean, n.	Bantekun G/Gen/H
(ocean view)	Ineri oshan
(ocean liner)	Baba ugboko ruwa o yibo kaya
(pacific ocean)	Bantekun kpasifike
atlantic ocena)	Bantekun atlatnte
ochre, n.	Okara, irudi yashi (sands)
o'clock, n, adj.	Sam, isam, duna G??ed
(it is four o'clock0	Agogo inang sam, agogo inang duna octagon, n.	Oktagon, oka jiometri
octane, n.	Ukuten, irudi kparafine
octave, n.	Oktef, oka isonga Gfe)
october, n.	Oktoba, uki goma n'ardun
octogenarian, n.	Oktajinera, (ankoljin) Gfe) (onkoljin)
octopus, n.	Oktopuh, irudi nama tekun, o wen hannu asato
occular, adj.	Okula, nke ineri G(fe)
occulist, n.	O okula
odd, adj.	Aisi, kpasi (kpafu kpasi)
(odd and even)	Kpafu ati kpasi (kpafu kpasi)
(odd number)	Lamba kpafu
oddity, n.	Ikpafu
(odd man)	Miji kpafu
(odd person)	Mutum kpafu
occident, n.	Osidento, na Amerika at' Ingilande
occult, adj. n.	Buu, ibubu, agba ekwenshu, majikele

(occultism), n.	Ibu-yaya, imajikele	
(occultist), n.	O bubu-yaya	
occupant, n.	O kunu, o bigbe Y/I	
occupation, n.	Ibigbe, irushe, imuko I/Y	Meni wu
	(what is your occupation?)	irushe e
oddment, n.	Ikufo, ikufo, adimant Y/I/G	
odds, n.	Nsoflesi	I/Y
(in all odds)	Na ncha nsoflesi, na nsoflesi ncha	
ode, n.	Irenbu G	
odious, adj.	Dika – (hateful) I/Y	
odoriferous, adj.	Sosoleh G/Gen	
odour, n.	Isiki I/Y	
(bad odour)	Isiki rubi	
(sweet odour)	Isiki solele (isiki lele)	
odyssey, n.	Ishiengala, irinje gungolo, irinje golo	
of, prep.	Nke, 'ke (ke)	
(the house of god)	Gida nke Abasi; 9gida Abasi)	
off, adj.	Pu, fregbu, ai si, (af – (fe), peh, fiang also; shien; jaita	
(get off here)	Fre ebi	
(put off the light)	Gbu wuta, af wuta	
(on and off)	Non fre (non ati fre), non 'ti fre	
(off duty)	Ai si n'irushe, ifre rushe	
(i am off duty)	Mii si n'rushe,	
(off day)	Rana af, rana ifre rushe, rana isimini	
offence, n.	Ijika I/Y	
(what offence have i committed)?	Meni 'jika mo meshe?	
(offender)	O jika	
offend, vti.	Jika, mu bi onu, mu bilionu, meje, joshe	
(don't offend me)	Ma bili mi onu	
ofensive, adj.	Fa ijika, fa ibili onu	
offer, vti.	Yere I/y	
offerer, n.	O yere	
offering, n.	Iyere	

offertory, n.   Kabode, kudi ti a meko na hawa chochi

off-hand, adj.   Fre-hannu, mupu hann Y/I/H
office, n.   Ofis, ebi a ng rushe, gida irushe
(office boy)   Yaro ofis
(office girl)   Yarinya abi omote ofis
(office attendant) O dazi ofis
(office manager)   Majija ofis, megida ofis
officer, n.   Hafsa, o ofis
(chief legal officer)   Chief Lega Hafsa, baba hafsa iwufin official, adj.
officiate, vi.   Rushe ofis
officious, adj.   Winche kha
offing, n.   Isarah, ibibiawa, ibiawa nsiyi, ibiawa lai faogo
off-licence, n.   Af-lasin, irudi aashe lati leta wain abi ogogoro
off-print, n.   Af-prent tite fambu
off-set, vt.   Af-set, nke ite littafi; itunno – compensa kpa zuba – (pay back)
off-shore, adj.   Af-sho, kupu na gaba (sho)
off-side, adj. adv. Af-said, kupu n'akue (side)
off-spring, n.   Mon, e mon
off-street, adj.   Ai si na titi
off-white, adj.   Faren
often, adv.   Ngba kene-kene, ngba, ngba kene
(how often?)   Ngba kene loi?
(very often)   Ngba kene kha
(not very often))   Ko wu ngba kene kha, ko ngba kene kha (as often as possible)
(more often)   Ngba kene risi
(too often)   Ngba kene kha-kha
ogre, n.   Oga, irudi kato o wuam mutum (giant)
oh, int.   Oh Gen
ohm, n.   Om, (ohm) isimbola lantiriki
oho, int.   Ohh, iyalionu
oil, n.   Oyele, man G(fe)/H
(oil-field)   Fili oyele
(oil-palm)   Itache-oyele H/G(fe)

(oil-tanker)	Tenka-oyele
(oil-stick)	Sanda-oyele
oiler, n.	Oyela, ugboko ruwa o bue oyele
oily, adj.	Bika oyele, di oyele
ointment, n.	Ontmint, irudi magani abi ogun
okapi, n.	Okapi, irudi nama daji na kasa kongo
okay, adj, adv.	Oh-keh, (O.K.) Gen.
okra, n.	Kubewe H
old, adj.	Digbo
(how old are you?)	I wu gagbo elni?
(old man)	Mijigagbo
(old woman)	Irnache gagbi
(hold house)	Gida gagbi, irnache gagbi
(old sense)	Ichegbon gagbi
(old boy)	Yaro gagbo
(old person)	Mutum gagbo
(old-timer)	Agaracha,
oldage, n.	Igagbo, ngba idigbo, idigbo
oldster, n.	Olsta, o gagbo
oliander, n.	Olinda, irudi shuke-shuke ilililai
oleograph, n.	Oliogr (oliogra); G(fe)
oleomargarine, n.	Olomajarin, irudi oyele a ng fi meshe bota abi majarin; G(fe) olfactory, adj.
oligarchy, n.	Oligaki, irudi gari (pronounced "geri")
olive, n.	Zaitun; H
(olive tree)	Itache zaitun
(olive oil)	Oyele zaitun
(olive colour)	Launi zaitun
olympiad, n.	Olimpiad; (GfE)
olympian, adj.	Limpian, imiwa bika nke abasi
olympic, adj.	Olimpik G(fE) – olimpik
(olypic games)	Iguere Olimpik
ombudsman, n.	Oboman, hafsa majalisar na Briten
omega, n.	Omiga, afabit izuba na turanchi Grik
(alpha and omega)	Alfa ati omiga, irebi ati 'guton

omelet, n.	Omlet, irudi abinchi safe
omen, n.	Izi-zi-zi, (zizizi0, ihun-hun-hun
(good omen)	Izizizi rama
(bad omen)	Izizizi rubi
omission, n.	Ifoja, ifre, imupu (commission and ommission)
omnibus, n.	Tuke-tuke; Gen.
omnipotence, n.	Ai guton, lai guton, agba ti ko wen iguton abi gindi
omniscience, n.	Ominisayesns, baba ichegbon nke Abasi
onrjush, n.	Roso si, n'iroso
onset, n.	Itakose, irebi tako
onshore, adj.	Ansha, ita gaba G/Y/H
onslaught, n.	Itako-rugu, ijagha rugu, ijaghuru
onto, prep.	Sisi, sikei, fna
ontology, n.	Antoloji, iyaka fisis (physics)
onus, n.	Ikaru (ka.ru) H/Y
onward, adj, adev.	Whiwhido, iwhido y/H (from now onward) Geyi shien whido lati geyi shiene whido
oodles, n. oof, n.	Awuf Gen.
oomph, n.	Ivudi, ifioko G
ooze, n.	Ikpru, kpru G
opal, n.	Opa, irudi dutse bimkpa (precious)
opague, adj.	Gbuneri, gbuineri I/Y
opart, n.	Opati, ife jiomitri
open, adj.	Shie, ai tikpo Y/I
(open your eyes)	Shien ido e/yin
(open your mouth) Shie onu e/yin	
(open the door)	Shie kofa (declare open)
opening, n.	Ishie
opera, n.	Okpera G
operation,	Imeyi, imeyini ya ola imera, (onumatopia) operate,
operatta, n.	Ofreta, oka isonga
ophthalmia, n.	Oftamiya, irun ido oopthalmoscope, n. Oftamosko, ihaiki ido (eye instrument) ophthalmologist, n.

opinion, n.	Isiche, ofiom, irudi magani abi ogun
opossum, n.	Okposun, irudi nama kele na amerika
opponent, n.	O tawe, itawe Y/I
opportune, adj. n.	Yefe, yengba, yoge, iyefe, iyengba, iyoge
oppose, vt, n.	Tagb, kido, itagbu, Y/I/H
(opposition leader)	Shugaba ruju
opposite, adj.	Ruju, kido, ikido, whido
oppress, vt, n.	Temisi, itemisi, o temis Y/I
oppressors,	O temisi, e temisi n. (plural)
opt, vi.	Mayen Y/I (i opt for a
ophthalmologist,	n. Oftamolojis
optical, adj.	Nke oftik, ihe oftik
optician, n.	Oftishani o oftik, o rushe ihaiki oftik
optimism, n.	Mirima, inikonzi I/Y/Owo
optimum, n.	Rama kha ramakha-ka, ikpata
(optimum objective)	Icherondi kpata
option, n.	Imolo G
(i have no option)	Mii wen imolo
(my option is)	Imolo mi wu…
opulence, n.	Ibuto leze – (big wealth)
or, conj.	Abi
(or else)	Bi 'mozo, imozo, mozo
(this or that)	Keyi abi keyien (keyi keyien)
oracle, n.	Kabilisi Ikw/H
(speak as the oracle of god0	Osu bika kabilisi Abasi oral, adj.
(oral statement)	Isoli oka niso
(i don't want oral instruction)	Mii che ikozi niso (oral evidence)
(oral medication)	Megani okanu, ogun jiki
orange, n.	Monza H(G.v)
(orange tree)	Itache monza

(orange fruit)	'ya'ya monza
(orange, drink)	Imula monza
orator, n.	Osokamkpe, o sokamkpe
orate, vi.	Sokamkpe, soli-bam-bam
oratorio, n.	Oretoro, oka isonga
oratory, n.	Oritri, chple kele na chochi
orb, n.	Abi, iduniya, akpor G(fe)
orbit, n.	Abit, hanya obi
orchard, n.	Okia G(fe)
orchestra, n.	Okesa, e tugbe isonga G(fe)
ordain, vt.	Kono si beze, kononu G/I/Y
ordeal, n.	Ighali, ijali I(G.v)/Y
order, n, vt.	Maashe, imashe, jubele, ijubele, hoda kozili
(i order you)	Mo kozili e/yin
(on my order/ask)	N'ijubele mi
(order/approval)	Imaashe
(obey the last order)	T'isiba imaashe/ikozili zuba (order for more drinks)
(put it in alphabetical order)	Fiyen na itole afabit/transpose (put it in order)
order, vt.	Atanshan, dankiti
orderliness, n.	Iole-tole, itolele
ordinance, n.	Iwufini I/Y
ordinances, pl. n.	E wufini
(ordinances of god)	E wufini Abasi (government ordinance)
ordinary, adj.	Sonki, kpako Y/I/Gen
(ordinary person)	Sonki mutum
(ordinary bread)	Buredi kpako, kpafun
(ordinary seaman)	O tekun sonki, sonki siman
(ordinary share)	Ishee sonki
(ordinary floor)	Dabe kpako, kasa kpako, kasa n'oho
(ordinarily)	N'ikpako, n'isonki
ordinarily)	N'ikpako, n'isonki
ordination, n.	Ikononu
ordinance	Gindiga G/H

(army ordinance)	Gindiga Soja
(ordnance depot)	Daffo Gindiga, Bariki Gindiga
ore, n.	Ore, or, miriala G/(e)/Y/I (iron ore)
organ, n.	Ogan, en'ife G(fe)/Y/I
organ, n. (musical)	Ogene, ihaiki 'songa
(organist)	O gene
organic, adj.	Oganiki
organism, n.	Gane-gane G(fe)
organization, n.	Oganaize, kamfani, itugbe (united nations
organize, vt.	Organize, ganize
orgasm, n.	Iyeh, igbowu kha, igbowuta
orgy, n.	Miliki, imiliki, milichi, igbandu kha-ka
oriel, n.	Oria, irudi gida eso
orient, n.	Orien, afa kasa na Maditarena
oriental, adj.	Nke orien, ife orien, orienta
(orientate, vt.	Maliye – (bring to clear understanding)
orientation, n.	Imaliye
(orientation course)	Imuko maliye
origin, n.	Isikei, isi-si, irebili I/H
original, adj.	O wu zioka, sikei, si-si, rebili, ife rebili (it is original)
(it is not original)	Ko di 'sikei, ko rebili – ko wu isi-si
originate, vit.,	merebi, mubia, murebi I/Y
originator, n.	O merebi, o mubia, o mubiawa
oriole, n.	Orio, irudi onene G (fe)
orlop, n.	Olap, katako na ugboko ruwa ornament, n. ado. Onamint
ornery, adj., n.	Iyobi ekwenshu, mutum o wen iyobi kwensh
ornithology, n.	onitoroji, sayens imuko onene
ornithologist, n.	Mutum onitoroji
Orphan, n.	Maraya
(orphan child)	omo maraya
(child of an orphan)	omo nke maraya

ALEX EKHAGUOSA IGBINEWEKA

(orphanage), n.   gida abi ebi 'cheto maraya

orrisroot, n.   – orisu, orthodox, adj.

orthography, n..   orthopaedic, adj

ortolan, n.   oryx, n. Oscar , n. oscillate, vti.., n. (oscillator), n.

oscillograph, n.   Irudi itache sosorobia onsed, inikon aashe,
                      yemuko atografe, hanyar ikonoso (system of spell)
                      atokpadik imenson irun kashi (curing) atolan,
                      irudi igboro onene mariri, irudi igboro onene

Oska, irudi   H (antelope)
gwaki

yighali, iyighali   Eg/Y/I

oscilloscope, n. osier,   asiloko, oka sayens Osia, irudi 'gboro itache
n. osprey, n.   Aspri, baba shaho

                          o wuam kifi Osos, ijukun fun
osseous, adj.

                          kashi abi skaletin
                          Osifa, medi ko sile G (fe)
ossify, vti. ostensible,   Irondizi   I/Y
adj. ostenstation, n.   Honriba, horiba,

                          ihonriba, ihonriba
                          (imindu) abi idiwa honriba astiopati, irudi ' meson kashi
(ostentatious living)   JiminaH
osteopathy, n. ostrich,   Onenne jimina
n. (ostrich, bird) other, mizo, kufo, efe/ehe honrire
adj. (other persons)   e mutum mizo

(other places)   ebi mizo

(every other day)   Rana eji-jo, rana na   mizo
                          rana, rana si rana (other
                          items) – e fekon

otherwise, adv.   Bikowu, bintama, ntama Y/I
o yighali asilograf, ihaiki a ng fi nofi o yighali
kare ruwa, ota   H/G (fe)

Ijeze pem, ijeze nke   lembu/zuba out, adv.
a ti pem, ijeze

O ti jaita, abi ja 'ta,   O ti maran shlen,

314

(otherwise I'II slap you bikowu, ma tula e / yin

otter, n. jalolo, dumpe

(he/ she has played out)

(outside)

(outside the country)

outbalance, vt.

out blown, adj.

outbreak, n.

outcast, adj.

outclass, vt.

(a good outcome)

outcrop, n.

outcry, n.

(outcry demand)

Outdate, vt.

(outdated fashion)
Outdo, vt.
Outdoor, adj. (outdoor game) Outer, adj. (outer space) outermost, adj. outface, vt. (outfacing) Outfall, n. Outfit, n. Outfitter, n.

Outflow, n. Outgo, vt. (outgoing)

(outgoings) outgrow, vt.

(custed regime) (he/ she is gone out)

o ti guere shien 'ta (go out now)

ezinta

ezinta kasa

Wan si kasa, y.w. weight down)

feku-kpoli, fekpoi

Gbabe n' ita, gbanso

Jut 'ita

Shape, shap' ita

ija'ta rama

akro, irudi dutse na kasa

Ikemkp' ita, bab 'ikebe,

ikemkpo gbam-gbam
Ijubi 'kemkp' ita,

ijubi gbam-gbam Ai
luwe mozo, nke

kera, jaluwe
Imaron kera, imaron
jaluwe me she jukha
na fili, n' ita (na ita)
Iguere' ita
Ezinta, itakha, netita
Iyafe 'ta
Ezinta kha-ka doka – to defy,
iwhido n'iwhido, iwhio,
nineri kongi – (of river
fall) Riga, irudi riga a ng fi
jaita O leta riga, o <u>nofun</u>

riga (supply)
Sonruta
Jukha, bi fe'ja, shienga
o fe'ja, ifeja, o

shienga, ishienga ishienoita
diagba fe'ja, (diagba

ai wan out bid, vt.

I/Y

Y/I

G Outcome, n.

Y/I

315

ALEX EKHAGUOSA IGBINEWEKA

jukha), diafeja dunki
gida ezinta

H/I/Y

outgrowth, n (dunki)
Outhouse, n.
(outing service) outlandish,
n. outlat,vt. outlaw, n.

Ijaita,
atlandi, nke kasimu (foreign)
Jakpor – (survive)
Doka iwurin, imeje

outlay, n. (capital
outlay) outlet, n.
Outlie, vt.

iwufi, ifoji 'wufin
inokuno – (of expenditure) Baba/jari
inokuno hanyar ita, hanyar si ezinta
bokei (succeed)   Y/H

(outlier,) n.

outline, n.

outline, n.

(outliner) outlive, vt.

Outlook, n.

outlying , adj. outmanoeuvre, vt.

outmarch, vt.

(outmatching), n. outmatch, vt.

outmoded, adj.

outmost, adj.

Outnumber, vt.

out-of -date, adj.

out-of-the-way, adj.

Outpatient, n. Outplay, vt. outpoint, vt.

outport, n.

outpouring, n. output, n.

outrage, n..

(it is outrageous) outrange, vt

outrank, vt.

outride, vt. outrider, n.

outrigger, n.

outright, adj. outrum, vt.

outrunner, n.

outsail, vt. outset, n.

outshine, n vt.
(outside the office
hour) outside, n.
finekuru, finefiene

outside, n. (outside the house)

outside, n. (outside the house)

Y/I

o finekuru,
o finefienren
biejukha, diwa

316

tombili khan a lamba,
tombili kha fe ja
rana, nke kera,
idugbo, jalopi Aisi
na hanya, ai ma
feshent' ta guere
bokei, guere

kha, guere jukha
jukha na noba,

bokei na noba	G (fe) / Y
kpot ita	Ed/Y
i turu 'ta, ituru,	Ed/Y/I
itunja Iwanye si, if-	Y/(G.v)I

iyen ikabika o kabi-
ka khalamba, jukha,

n' ibafi (range) jukha   G (fe)/M/I G (fe)
n'ikpetu wayan jukha,
temonka atraida, o
yanwakiri ariga, nke
ugboko ruwa sh-
am-sham, duna-

duna, duna,

gbere sokia kha, gbere

jukha, gbere ya-
jiki arona oghere

whidi shikota   G (fe) Y/I

khaka, gbi khaka
ineri 'ta, ineri rama
diwa n' ezinta bokeisi
Gakele kha, gakele
jukha, igakele kha,
igakele jukha, koga,
diye jukha, diye kha
idigbo fasha Ita khaka

n' irebi, ibibre

waen jukha, waen-
waen kha

ilode, izuba

I/Y ilode, gida ilode hawa ofis

outsider, n. outsize, adj.
outskirts, n. outsmart, vt.
outspoken, adj. outspread,
adj. outstanding, adj.
outstation, n. outvie,
vt. outvie, vt.
(outward journey) outwear,
vt. outweigh, vt. outwit, vt.

o lode tondo jukha iyakita
(of borders) tuke kha
soli si 'ta, soli gbamgbam
gbinso kiri
kundu shaka tashan 'ta
kambe kha
shien lode, ishien lode
shi-shien lode, irinje lode
esa ita, e yiwo si, ra
wan. mon. ka (wanmonka)
cheye jukha

Gen/I/Ed
Y/I
H/Y
Og/Y
I/Y

(over-burden)
(over-cook)
(over-eat)
(over-empha-
size) (over-sea)
overact, vti.
overall, adj.
overarm, n., adj.
overawe, vt,. overbal-
ance, vit.

Oberbear, vt. Over-
bid, vti.

ikaya jukha
ise   jukha
i w u a m
jukha
iteonusi   kha,   iteo-
nu jukha ifeja-tekun
imeshe jukha
ijukha   ncha,   ijukha
mini ofaram, oka ig-
uere krikat rugu jukha
fre, wan, gbu wan,

wan jukha Ibue
jukha Gbanjo
abi kule khaz
Gen /Y/I/H

I/Y/H

outwork, n. (military
outwork)

ouzel, n. ouzol,
n. oval, adj,. n.

ovary, n. ovation,
n. (loud ovation)

oven, n. (oven
ware) over, adv.
(over and gain)

(over and against)

(over my dead body)

(over the face)

(over the road)

irush' ita, igbagun ' ta	Y/I tighagun 'ta iseza uze, irudi onene kele uzo, irudi kain-kain nke grik ofal, isiffa bika	
nkekwai, kpopio		
ofri, oka balabala		
ibori	Y/G	
iborimkpo		
zinwuta	G/H	
e tukunya ati kwano fèjá, sikei, 'ti mozo, feja keji		
feja'; hanyar, ifeja hanyar feja ìkútù mi		
dikel, jukha disi	I/Y/G	
gbumeshe, kparikpa gbiwo		

(he/she is over sixty)

overcricket, n.
(over-active)

(over-anbitiuos)

(over-anxious)

o ti feja ardun sii

jukha krikat iyaji
jukha ichowu juka
ichereji jukha

Overblown, adj.	Feh jukhaOverboard, adv.	N' akue ugboko ruwa, n; imeku kogi

Overburden, n. (don't over burden me)	Sohala jukha ma sohala mi jukha, ma sohala mi kha	
Overcapitalized, vt.	Ijukha istimat	
Over-cast, adj. (shadows over-cast)	Jonu kha, bodo jukha Iwanu bodo jukha, iwanu jonu kha Pia jukha Mare jukha	Y/I/H Ag/Y/I H/Y/I
Overcharge, vti,	Nusa mare jukha	
Overcloud, vti. (overclouded sky) (overclouded day) Overcoat, n. overcome, vt. overcrop, vt. Overcrowd, vt. overdo, vt, overdraft, n. overdraw, vti.	Rana mare jukha Jakit, obakwat bokeisi jukha, bokei jukha Obakrap taromu jukha meshe jukha obadraf fa kha – (not, not fa jukha), obadoro yiwo esa jukha, yiwo jukha	G(fe) G(fe) H/Y/I
overdress, vti. overdrive, n. Overdue, adj.	obadraif, nke mota tongba, abi rude ngba jukha	G(fe)
Overjoyed, adj.	Sayo jukha, sayo kha, yoli jukha	
Overkill, n.	Igbu rau-rau I/Y	
Overland, adj., adv.	Jaisi kasa (across the Fala jukha, (cover) land) Overlap, vti.	
Overlay, vt.	Toka jukha, toka – lay cloth, toka esa	
Overleaf, adv.	Aku eji – (side two)	
Overleap, vt.	Foso jukha, joso sisi	
Overload, vt.	Bue kaya jukha, bue kayak Mota o bue kaya jukha ha (overloaded motor) (overloaded vehicle)	
Overlord, n.	Kadei n isi, kadei si kadei jukha	
Overly, adv.	Jukha-ka	
Overmantal, n.	Obamante, irudi kongi (structure) Overmaster, vt.	Oga kwata-kwata
Overmuch, adj, adv.	Kha-kha, abi kha-ka	
Overnight,	n'isi tuu, hoya, yaji	I/Tiv (get ready overnight)
Overpass, n.	Obapase	G(fe)
Overpay, vt.	Kpa jukha	Agbo/Y/I Overpay, vt.

overplus , n.	Ifole kudi – (surplus amount)
overpower, vt.	bokei kha, bokei n' agba
Overprint, vt.	Prenti, l' isi
Overrate , vt.	diye jukha
Overreach, vt.	meje, meru, wayo jukha
Override, vt.	Konda kha, bue l'isi, bue n'isi (overriding interest) Iche konda kha, iche buele, iche bue l'is
Overrule, vt.	cheri disi – (to decide against)
Overrum, vt.	gbere, jukha, gbere kha, gbere l;isi
Oversea (s), adj	Isitekun, zuba tekun, kasa bature, obasii
Oversee, vt.	neri, abi hun jukha, cheto neneri
(overseer), n.	O cheto, o neneri
Oversexed, adj.	Vudu kha, vudu jukha
Overshadow, vt.	Wanu l'isi
Overshoe, n.	Obashu, irudi takalmi nke roba
Overshoot, vt.	Takpu jukha, gbata jukha
Overside, adv.	N' akue, n' akue ugboko ruwa
(go overside)	Shien n; akue
Oversight, n.	Ai neri rama, ai kiesi, ai tanshantt
Overskirt, n.	ai neri rama, ai kiesi, ai tanshan
Oversleep, vt.	Obasiketi
Oversleep, vi.	Sula l' si
Overspill, n.	benso kha, benso jukha
Overtstate, vt.	Soliye jukha, soliye kha, sogo kha

Overstay, vt.	du kha	
Overstep, vt.	Shien kaju	(beyond)
Overstock, vt.	Obasok	
Overstuffed, adj.	Zizi jukha, zizi kha	
Oversubscribed, adj.	Obasokrab	
Overt, adj.	6 vat, meshe na pobili	
Overtake, vt. - gba ba'	gbere jukha	(gbere fe)
Overtax, vt.	taks jukha	
Overthrow, vt.	ifeja ngba, kiu, yunto, bikwa	Y/I/G (ED
Overtime, n.	Izuba ngba, ifaogolo ngba, ngba jukha	
Overtone, n.	Tungba, oka songi	
Overtop, n, vt,	Kenu jukha, nu jukha	
Overture, n.	Igbamo – (approach)	
Overweight, n.	Iwan jukha, iwan kha	
Overwhelm, vt.	Temonka, te. Monka	
Overwork, vti.	Rushe jukha	
Overwrought, adj.	Rengu kha – ka	
Oviduct, n.	Ofido, oka ibalabala	
Oviparous, adj.	Ofiparosi, oka ibalabala	
ovum, n.	Ofum, na jiki mache	
Owe, vti.	jie	
Owing, n.	Ijie	I/Y
Owl, n.	Mujiya	H
Own, adj., pro.	Weni	I/Y
(who owns this car?)	Wha l'o weni mota zoom-zoom yii?	
Owner, n.	O weni	
(owner – driver)	O yanwa mota wenji	
(owner occupier)	O weni bie Iweni, wiweni	
(ownership) Ox, n.	takarkari Agzaid, irudi er Agzasetilini	H
(ox-tail),		G(fe)
Oxyacetylene, n.	Agzijin, aksijin, gais	G(fe)
Oxygen, n, Oyez, int.	Oda!, ikebe fun	G(fe)
	igbonti, idankiti Kawa, kunda, irudi kifi	H
Oyster, n. Ozone, n.	Ozo, irudi aksijin abi gais	

Pa, papa	Pa, papa. Baba, uba	Gen/H
Pace, n.	Iyafe 'ringa, (iyeringa)	Y/It
(go at a faster pace)	ringa sokia, yeringa sokia	
(set the pace)	mundu iyeringa, yeringa	
(pace-setter)	O mundu 'yeringa	
Pachyderm, n.	Kpekida, irudi nama bika giwa	G(fe)
Pacific, adj.	Kpasifik, kolela, kulele, alandu, ilandu	
Pacification, n.	Medi kulele, ilandi, ikolela	(not ikulele)
Pack, n.	Ikaya, iyokete, idikaya	H/Y
Pack, vti.	Kopu, koshien, yaji	Y/I/H
Package, n.	Kunshi, kaya, ikaya	H
Packer, n.	O kopu, o koshien, o yaji	
Packet, n.	Fakit, ifakit	
(a packet of Omo soap)	Fakit sabulu omo	
Packing, n.	Ikopu, ikoshien, iyaji, hoyah; ikuta	
Pact, n.	Ikweba, ikwade, ikwade ilandu	
Pad, n.	ganmo, chinkisa, fad	H/G(fe)
Paddle, n.	Wanya, filafi, ifilafi, iwayan,	Y/I/G
Paddock, n.	Fadok, irudi fili kele fun doki, makiyaya	
paddy, n.	Padi, Baba	t
(paddy man)	Padiman, Baba	
Padlock, n.	feda, shaflen nke iseza ati nefi	
Paen, pean, n.	fin, irudi songi a ng fi kine Abasi	
Paediatrics,	Fediatriki, fedia	
Pagan, adj.	Kafiri, keferi, oi Nikon	H/Y
Page, n.	Shafi, warka	H
(page two)	Shaf' eji	

sinle na kasa bature

(Please turn to page two) Pageant, n.		
(pageantry), n.		
Pagination, n.		
Pah, int.	aah, ikebe n'irengu	
Pail, n.	bokiti	H/Gen.
Paillasse, n.	Felasi, irudi katifa nke stra (mattress)	
Pagoda, n. Biko wara si shaf' eji Fejan, imiri pobili (public entertainment) Fejan		
feji, feji, ishafi, shafi-shafi	G(fe) / H fagoda, irudi gida	
Pair, n. (a pair of shoe) (pairs) (pair off)		
Paisley, n. Pal, n.		
Palace, n. Palaeo, Palatable, adj.		
Jieva	Y/Ed takalmi jieva e jieva	
fiyen n'ejieva, meshe 'jieva Faisli, irudi fabriki Kama, kamara, o	Iriya;, izono Ikweba, zono, o sundi,	
finde – (comrade)	o june (careful) fenti akwati fenti Burosh fenti Fenta, o fenti waya a ng fi zikpor abara abi ugbokoruwa	H
Palatal, adj., n.	falata, nke ilowe,	
Palaver, n.	ifalata, fail, ifali	H(G.v)
Pale, adj.	Nsohala, oka abi ikonokojo	(fence)
Pale, n.	Fuju	
Paleontology, n.	Fel, irudi itache a ng luwe fun shinge Feliontoroji, imu-ko oloda mutum	

324

ginb' e ze H/Y/
Gen/I falio, oka
sayens Di wiwuam,
wiwuam, kwi-kweba

Palette, n.
palimpsest, n.

Palindrome, n.

Paling, n.

Palisade, n.

Pall, n.

Pallet, n.

Falit, irudi katako
G(fe) Falimset,
irudi ife (writing)
a ng fi kode

Falindro, irudi oka
turanchi falin, irudi
shinge – (fence)
Falished, irudi
ginshiki pillar

file

H/Y falit, irudi
katifa – mattress

Palliate, vt. palm-oil

faliet, medi nsohala

kiene (less/lessen) ngo ginginya shihe woka Woka Sirande
Tombo, soguro famis o neri whido,

palm tree open your
palm palm Sunday palm-
wine Palmist, n.

Palmetto, n. Pampas, n.

o soli 'shiende
falmito, irudi bab' irn rubi Famfas, kasa
ai wen itache na Saot Amerika

Pamper, vt.

Kwenke

(over pampered)
Pamphlet, n.
Pan, n.
(pan-flat dish)
(frying pan) Panacea, n.
Panacea, n.

Kwenke kha-kha, kwen rubi
Kasida, likele, famflit   H/HGen/G(fe) kwano
Nupe/Gwarri tasa, lebe, akushi
fai-kwan   G(fe)/Nupe/Gwarri
Kwan-kek, irudi kek bota. Nupe/Gwarri/H
Fensia, ilandi nsohala –
(solution to problems)

Panama, n.

fenama, irudi malafa (a

Panatela, n.	type of hat) na Saot Amen	G(fe)
Panchromatic, adj.	fenatela, irudi siga abi	
Pancreas, n.	taba Fencromate, irudi	
	foto fenkris, fankris, irudi	
	kaluluwa na chiki (gland)	
kwenke, dan kwenke		
Pandemic, adj., n.	fendemi, irun na kasa	
	nche bika epidema	Zighizagh
	Ifendimonia, fendimonia,	
Pandemonium, n.	baba arimkpo ati fen,	
Pane, n.	gilasi abi madobi	
	bika 'pen windo'	
Panegyric, n.	Kpanajiri, (kpanaji) irudi	
Panel, n.	oaka a fi gogo mutum	
	Kwanel, nke kwamiti	
	abi kwano, (n.f.):	
'panel of experts':	kwmiti 'win; 'motor panel' Kwnel	
	mota, firem abi kiasisi mota Piam; irudi 'fudum soki	
Pang, n.		
Panga, n. Panhandle	– a type of sharp pain	
Panic, n.	Fenga, baba wuka	
(don't panic) (panicking)	Fenhando, oka jiografi	G(fe)
Panjandrum, n.	Igbuaya (gbu'ya), itugu	I/Y
	Ma gbu'ya, ma rugu Igbu'ya, irugu	
	ajakuntum, irudi afa (Y/H) fun baba mutum	
Pannier, n.	Fenia, irudi kwando	
	ikaya na doki fenkini,	
pannikin, n.	irudi kwaf kele	
	abi tufien kha-ka	
panoply, n.	fenofli, subu nke	
	ijagha abi seza	
panoptic, adj.	fenotik, imeneri saun-saun,	
	(complete illustration)	
panorama, n.	fenorama, ineri saun-	
	saun, ineri fefefe	
panpipes, n.	fenfa, ihaiki abi	
pansy, n.	iherushe songo kpansi, irudi fulawa bika biskos	

apantechnicon, n.	kpantilizm, irudi 'sinle	Ncha (everything)
	kpe abasi o wa ni ' ife	pantheon, n.
panties, n.	durosi; kpanti, shokoto kele	Gen (fe) pantile, n.
pantograph, n.	kpantograf, iherushe	kpanti,irudi deki
	hoto-kapi pantry, n.	n' ibotu gida
pants, n.	kpanti shokoto kele	
panzer, n.	kpenzi, irudi kungiyar	
	soja abi iseza	
pap, n.	abinchi ruwa, abinchi	
	emontakele	
papa, n.	papa, ibekuru afa baba	Gen
papacy, n.	kpapesi, ikpoze abi	
	aashe nke pop	
pawpaw, n.	f/o	
paper, n.	tarkarda, jarida, peipa	
(paper bag)	ikpa peipa (paper qualification)	
(paper back)	izuba takarda / peipa	
(paper-clip)	klif fefa, kilifi peipa	
(paper-hanger)	okpete fefa, o kpete	
	takarda (paste)	
(paper-knife)	wuka takarda, wuka	itugbe, abi emutum_
	fefa, wuka a ng fi shie	jafa (lazy group)
	wasika (paper-tiger)	
(paper-mill)	mila fefa, ebi a ng meshe takarda	
(paper-weight)	iwan fefa abi takarda	
(paper-work)	irushe fefa abi takarda	
(paper-up)	tikpo abi cheto ihe, zumo –	fefiamanche, irudi fefa
	conceal papier-mâché, n.	roba papistical, adj.
paprika, n.	paprika, irudi akoko	
papyrus, n.	fafiros, irudi takarda na kera ijipt	

par, n.	ifuda (of average/ normal level)
(par of exchange)	ifuda sengi
parable, n.	iwiton Y(G.v)
(parabolical), adj. parabola, n. parachute, n.	witon, n'iwiton farabola, oka jiomitri farashu, kayanki a ng fi
parachutist, n. parade, vti. (parade commander)	foma lati sonmafleh o farashu toshien, toleshien Y/I kwananda itoleshien, o
(parade ground) paradigm, n. paradise, n.	meaashe itoleshien kasa itoleshien, filli 'toleshien kparadigin, oka turanchi izinlafia, izindu, izin.
(paradise of God) paradox, n.	mindu (izinmindu) izinmindu nke Abasi oka iruju (statement
paraffin, n. paragon, n. paragraph, n. parakeet, n.	of opposite) kparafine, irudi oyele G imiwasaun, (complete virtue) igbolo, igboloka kparakiti, irudi aku
parallel, adj. (two parallel lines) paralysis, n. paramilitary, adj.	kele (parrot) handogo H/Y/I handogo eji igbutantan I/Gen kparasoja, kpara iseza, osja kele
paramount, adj.	jukwata, jukha-ka,
(paramount importance)	suprim, suprima igesi jukwata, igesi juka-ka, igesi H/ Tiv/G(fe) (sheet of paper) oga na peipa (on)
paramour, n.	kwarto, kwartuwa
parapet, n.	kparafit,kaya a ng fi
paraphernalia, n.	kogi gida, rawan e herushe, e faiki, e
paraphrase, vt. paraplegia, n. parasite, n. parasol, n.	kpankiti, jagbanjaitis tungbolo kparagbulu, igbutanji kwirun Y(G.v) Y/I kparazuh, irudi

laima (umbrella)
kutubam, kutube, ekutube

paratroops, n. paratyphoid, n. parboil, vt. parcel, n. (parcel post) parch, vt.	kparataifod, irudi iba gwolo, yeho kele kwuchi, dite ikwuchi fost kpo (dry)	G G I/Y I
pardon, n.	igbari	I/Y
(please pardon me)	biko gbari mi	
paregoric, n.	kparigori, irudi magani abi ogun	
parent, n.	iyaye, mahaifa	H
parenthesis, n.	kparintesi, irudi oka na turanchi	( )
paripassu, adv. lat.	kparikpasu, didiogba	G(fL) parish, n.
parisian, n.	omo paris, omo kasa paris	
park, n.	fak, ajiya, gadin, ijiya, chiu	H/G(fE)
(motor park)	ajiya mota, faki mota, ichiu mota	
(recreation park)	gadin ijiya (park your motor here) (parking space)	chiu mota e mbi
parkinson's disease, n.	irun kpakinsin, irun idugbo I/Y/G(f(E) parley, n.	
parliament, n. akawu majalisar wakili	kajalisar, H/G(fE) (stet)	
(parliamentarian)	o majalisar	
parlour, n.	basa – (substitute later with any other north)	
parmesan, n.	kpamesan, irudi bota abi chiz (chuku)	
parochial, adj.	kparokia, nke parisi, mutum iyobi kwintin (narrow	
parole, n.	kparo, irudi 'kwade nke o prusu (promise) paroxysm,	
n.	baba bili abi bab' ikuakua (anger) (laughter)	
parquet, n.	kpakueti, irudi daki (type of flloring)	

parr, n.	kpar, salmon kele (a young salmon) parricide, n.	
n.	gbusadi, eni gbu baba abi iyore ya (relation)	
parrot, n.	aku	H/TV
parry, vt.	dokpo, ta - (turn away) fuke – (dodge)	
parse, vt.	kpas, ikpere oka turanchi (description)	
parsley, n.	kpasli, irudi shukeshuke gadin	
parship, n.	kpasni, irudi fejitebul	
parson, n.	alufa, abi fada kparisi	
part, n. vt.	ikpaka, kpaka., iyahann	Y/I
(part-time)	ngba kpakpa/kpaka ngba	
(part-time worker)	o rushe kpaka ngba	
(part-time teacher)	o muko, kpaka ngba,	
	malami kpaka ngba yi	Egun/YI
(take part) part, vti. (separate) (don't let us part)	kpaka, di kpaka choto, kezin ma kweba k' awa	
(part differently)	kezin, ma kezin choto cheto, (also): choto	
partake, vit. yiaka; parterre, n.	fambu, choto kata yi kpaka, wen kpapa. pkatere, nke gadin o wen lebe shuke-shuke,	
	ati irudi bandeki	G(fe)
	kpatinojeisisi, oka baoloji	I/Y
	abi imo omotakele lai	Ikpaka
parthenogenesis, n. partial, adj. (partial judgment) participate, vi., n. participant, n.	vudu megbe, mekpaka, di kpaka idakpe kpaka ye kpaka, di kpaka, wen kpaka, o kpaka, patsipo	
participle, n. particoloured, adj.	patsipo, oka turanchi laun fambu, launi	G(fe)

particular, adj. (you in particular) partisan, n. (partisan politics) partition, n. (wall of partition)	kezin, laun cheto katazi yinwan katazi, gin katazi o tugbe, itugbe politi tugbe babbaka, akanga, shamaki bango babbaka, bango shamaki, bango kanga	Gen/Gen H
partitive, n. , adj. partner, n. (my life partner)	kpatitif, oka turanchi mboke mboke mindu mi, mboke akpor mi	H(G.V)

partridge, n. onene dutse og/H itugbe emutum, igbokwe,
party, n.

(let us go to a party) ikonogbandu; iriya kawa shienga ikonogbandu;

(soldier party/group) kawa shienga iriga Itugbe soja, itugbe

iseza, itugbe ejagha
(party men) emutum itugbe
(political party) paschal, adj. itugbe politike, miji politike kpaskal, ise liba

emutum jiu (jews)
pass, n. (pass quickly) pase, feja, fejala, bue G(fE)/I/Y feja
(i passed the examination) sokia, (fe sokia) mo pase ichondi
(he/she passed away) o ti fejala

(pass it on) bue shiene
passage, n. ifeja, wuchewa, ipase
(passage way) hanya ifeja
pass-book, (fas-buk), littafi pase, abi litaffi feja

n. passé, adj. shiengala   Y/I
passenger, n. fasinja, mutum gboko, erinje

(passenger bus) baba mota fasinja
passepartout, kpasekpato, fasefato, irudi gam foto

n. passer-by, n.
partnership, n.

passing, adj. , adv. o I/Y tarayyafèjá, fífèjá
fe ja, o feja n akue

(pass it on)	bue shiene	
passage, n.	ifeja, wuchewa, ipase	
(passage way)	hanya ifeja	
pass-book,	(fas-buk), littafi pase, abi litaffi feja	
n. passé, adj.	shiengala	Y/I
passenger, n.	fasinja, mutum gboko, erinje	
(passenger bus)	baba mota fasinja	
passepartout,	kpasekpato, fasefato, irudi gam foto	
n. passer-by, n.	o fe ja, o feja n akue	I/Y
partnership, n.	tarayya	
passing, adj. , adv.	fèjá, fífèjá	
passion, n. passionate,	imanu manu, di manu	I/Y
adj. passover, n.	ìfèjá, kpasofa, iseliba	I/Y
	nke mutum jiu	
passport, n.	fasfot, litafi aashe	
(passport photo) past, adj.-	nke gonmenti	Y/I
(past government) pasta,	foto fasfot	G/H
n. paste, n. (of mixture)	fèjá, shiengálá, zùbá	H/G(fE)
(past-board) (pasting), n.	gonmenti fífèjá	
pastel, n. pastern, n.	kpasta, irudi abinchi	
pasteurize, vt. pastille, n.	fulawa kpete, tuwo-tuwo	
	katako ikpete ikpete	
	kpestel, irudi foto a fi alli nese-(a type of photo drawn in chalk) kpesta, taki	
	doki makiyaya, faschoraiz,	
	me di fasho kpasti, irudi	
	magani bika switi	
pastime, n. pastor, n.	ife ja ngba, ifi gbu ngba	
pastoral, adj. pastorate, n.	alufa, pastor kasa maki yaya	H/Y
pasture, n. (green pasture)	ofis nke pastor, ikpoze	H
	pastor abi alufa kaki (kasa	G(H.v)/H
	haki) algashi, kasa algashij	G(H.v)/H
		H
pat, vti.	pem	G
(a pat on the back)	pem na zuba	
patch, n.	sokwa	Y/I

(patch work)	irushe sokwa	
(patch the trouser for	sokwa shokoto fun mi, sokwa wando fun mi	
patchouli, n.	kpacholi, irudi sosorobia na kasa esia	
patella, n.	kpatela, koko gwiwa – (knee cap)	
patent, adj.	feshant, aashe gonmenti	
(patent number)	lamba feshant	
pater, n.	kpeta, uba omo makaranta	G
pater familias, n.	kpetamila, o kei yali	
paternal, adj.	bika uba, diuba Y/I/H (paternal father)	baba
(paternity,)	idiuba	
paternoster,	kpetanosa, uba 'wa – (our father)	
path, n.	turba, turbobi H (path-finder)	o
(foot-path)	turba kafa	
(path of life)	turba mindu	
pathetic, adj.	jonu	Y/Gen
(pathetic story)	ilida jonu	
pathology, n.	ikpatoloji, oka sayens	G(fE)
(pathological), adj.	kpatoloji, nke kpatoloji	
pathos, n.	kpato, iminiwa isoli oka (quality of speech)	
patience, n.	isundi	Y/I
(a patient dog)	kare sundi	H/Y/I
(be patient)	di sundi, wen sundi	
patient, n.	feshent, ai gbandu, o bujen	
(patient's ward)	unguwa feshent, nsebi feshent	
(store)	gisuwa magani feshent	
patina, n.	kpatena, irushe itache (wood-work)	

patio, n.	kpasho, yadi gari abi yadi kasa	
patois, n.	kpatosi, ede idile kasa (common language)	
patrial, n.	kpatria, mutum o wen aashe bie kasa bature	
patriarch, n.	kpatia, idugbo mutum, bishobu, kaka bishobu	
patricide, n.	kpatrisaid, igbu uba abi baba	G(fE)
patrimony, n.	ijewen dukiya - (inherited property)	
patriot, n.	peitro, o hufe kasa ya (lover of his/her country)	
patrol, vti.	choki, boke	I/Y
(patrol van)	motaka ichoki (kpatrol fan)	
(patrol wagon)	wagunu kpatrol	
(patrol man)	mi ji kpatrol, o choki, o boki	
patrol, n.	albarkachi , innoyo, o nnoyo	H
(the patron shinkafi)	albarkachi klobu wa wu alha ju umaru	
patronage, n.	innoyo, (pronounced): innonyo, albarkache	nnoyo
patronize, vt.	nnyot	
patronymic, n.	kpatronimi, afa ti a yibia lati kaka (derived)	
pattem, n.	kpatin, irudi takalmi kpako	
patter, n.	kpeta, irudi soli oka ma jikele, obubuyaya	
patter, n.	kwaka, ilowe takalmi na kasa (sound)	
pattern, n.	ifineri	Y/I

(pattern of dress)	ifineri esa	
paul, n.	paul, abi pol, aposteli nke jesu kristi	
paunch, n.	panch,	G(fE)
pauper, n.	matsiyachi	H
pause, n.	chendu, chendu fo, chendu kele, (chenkele)	
pave, vt. , n.	dunte , idunte	I/Y (pave way)
pavement, n.	iduntete	
pavilion, n.	kpavilian, ago	G(fE)/Y/Ed.
paw, n.	dagi, dungu	H
pawl, n.	pol , ihaiki hakori	
pawn, n.	kpon, n iguere chez (chess)	
pawn, n.	o senofa, eni biotiche (any how)	
pawn, (pledge)	kweye, kwogo	I/Y
pawpaw, n.	gwada	H
pax, n.	alafia, ikule	H/Gen
pay, n.	ikpa, kpa	Agbo
(pay -off)	kpa peh	
(pay –day)	rana ikpa	
(pay -load)	ikpa, kpa	
(pay –master)	maigida/oga ikpa	
(pay –master general)	oga ikpa janar	
(pay packet)	ikpa fakit; fakit ikpa, (pe-fakit)	
(pay-phone)	kalukalu-fon	Gen
(quick paying job)	irushe ikpa sokia	
(pay-slip)	littafi kpa	
payable, adj. , adv.	nke a le kpa, kpikpa	
payee, n.	eni a kpa	
payer, n.	o kpa	
(pay back)	kpa zu, kpa dazu	
(payment), n. paid pt	kpikpa	
pea, n.	kpokpondo	Y

peace, n. (peace maker)	alafia, ilandu, igbandu	H/Y/I
(blessed makers)	ikunzi fun emeshe lafia	
(peace of mind)	igbandu iyobi, alafia, isimini	
(justice of the peace)	majistrit, alkali nke isimini	(AI)
(peaceable,)adj.	dina lafia, di gbandu, simini	
(live peaceable)	bie na lafia	
(peaceful), adj.,	alafia; simini; landu; kule , rayo	
peach, n.	pich, irude itache	
peacock, n.	okin	
(it is peaceful)	(Kwara)	
pea-jacket, n.	pi jakit, irude kwat nke o shikolo – (sailor)	
peak, n.	biki, ibiki	G/H
peal, n.	baba rimkpo	Gen/Y/I
peanut, n.	gyada	H
(peanut oil)	oyele gyada	
pear, n.	ube – (f/o from rivers/ cross rovers/ak ibom)	
pearl, n.	lu ulu u	H
peasant, n.	talaka, bakauye	H
(peasant farmer)	o gona talaka	Tiv/H
peat, n.	koriko	Y
pebble, n.	kankara	H
beachpebbes	e kankara kate	
pecan, n.	kpekan, irudi itache na kasa Amerika siro	
peaceable,	irudi aladi na kasa amerika	I/Y
peccary, n.	kpeki, inofie e rama kpo (measurement of dry goods
peck, n.	kpoi, fi onu tukon kele	

peck, vti.	kpekitin, nke kamisri kpetora,	
pectin, n.	dioto, choto, idioto, ichoto eyi	
pectoral,	dioto; eyi choto	
adj. peculiar,	maigida makaranta, fada feda,	
adj. , n. (this	mataki, gunyangunyan feda basiko,	I/Y
is peculiar)	feda keke	
pedagogue,	leta kiri o leta	
n. pedel, n.	kiri ileta kiri	G/H/Y
peddle, vti.	lètá kasuwa	/I
(peddler)	òlètá kasuwa, orinshien kírí	
(peddling)	ìlètá kírí, ebi o rinshien ng fe ja hanya kpediatri,	
pedesrasty, n.	iyahann magani nke amontakele kpedika, irudi	
pedestrian, n.	ìkèkáfà, o wen kafa meta kpedikoro, ilosie kafu	
pediatrics,	kpedime, irudi keteh na kasa grik (architecture)	
n. pedicab,	motar motsa jiki	
n. pedicure,	nkwantu	Akan
n. pedigree,	cosaan	Wolof
n. pediment,	hèlá, hèláfò	I/Y
n. pedometer, n.	kpedominta, irudi minta a ng fi nofi maili kafa ssii,	
pee, vt, n.	tòrúwá, ìtòrúwá, ìyùntò	
let me pee	ka m' ìyùntò	
peek, vi.	fiam, ineri fiene, inere sokia fiene	H/I/Y
peekaboo,	kpikabu, irudi guere omontakele fo	G
n. peel,	fò	

(peel the yam)	fò dóyà	
peep, n.	fini, ifini	
(peeper)	o fini	
peepul, papal,	kpikpukpikpa, irudi itache na india	
n. peer, n.	ituegbe – (mate)	
peer, vi.	neri nure –(look closely)	
peeve, vt.	mu bionu, bili	
peg, n.	peh, maratayi, kili	
(peg, pegged)	kili	
, vti. (pegged	kili si kasa	
down) pekinese,	kpekinis, irudi kara chaina	
n. pekoe, n.	kpekos, irudi beki tii	
pelican, n.	kwasa-kwasa, irudi onene	H
pellet, n.	kpelit, buredi abi littafi t o loru (wet)	
pell-mell,	so-sokia, na isosokia, irudi wuru-wuru, wayo	
adv. pelucid,	shakata, shaka kha-ka	
ad. pelmet, n.	kpelmit, kaya windo	G(fE)
pelota, n.	kpelota, irudi guere bolu na spein abi amerika	
pelt, n.	kept, irudi fata nama (skin)	
pelt, vti.	tagbu –(attack)	
pelvis, n.	kugu, kashin	H
pen, n.	alkalami, "ukeke" – (synonym)	H/Ed
(pen and ink)	alkalami ati tawada, ukeke ati tawada	
(pen and paper)	alakalami ati fefa/littafi	
(pen-friend)	aboki na kasa mozo	
(pen-knife)	wuka kele	
(pen-pusher),	akawu, o kode wasika	
n. penal, adj.	kpinail, oka iwufin, i jeafun	
penalize, vt.	riya, jeafun	I/Y

(you will be penalized)	e a riya, e ma riya, e a jeafun, a je yin afun	
penalty, n.	penaliti; i jeafun, iriya	
pennance, n.	kenas, i jeafun o wenji lati fineri irogha (repent)	
pence, n.	kwabo, kobo	H/Gen(fPortugese)
pencil, n.	fensa	H(fE)
pendant, n.	pendat, irudi ado (ornament)	
pendant, adj.	yoisi – (hanging)	
pending adj.	cheti	I/Y
pendulous, adj.	pendulo, yoisi kiri, yikpo kiri, yikiri	
pendulum, n.	pendula, ayan agogo nke o ng fi yikiri	
penetrate, vti	gunfeja, gunle, gunyen	Y/I
(penetrate), n.	igunfeja, igunle, igunyen	
penguin, n.	pengui, kpengui, irudi onene tekun	
(fountain-pen)	alkalami fantin	
penicillin, n.	kpenisilin, irudi magani o gbu bataria	
peninsula, n.	kasula, kasa t o ku fiene ka ruwa yiri ya (surror)	
penis, n. penitence, n.	bura, azakari irodazu	H
penitentiary, n. pennant, n.	zinprusu kpinat, irudi tuta	G/Tiv
penniless, adj. penny, n. ponolgy,n.	ugboko ruwa (flag) ai wen kobo, lai wen kobo, kwabo kpenoloji, imuko afun na	Gen (fPortuguese)
	iwufin ati 'cheto prusu isimishe, kudi simishe, fensho o simishe, o fensho ichenu, di loro, loro jinka,	Y(G.v)/H
pension, n. , (pensioner) pensive, adj.	loro kha-ka "deep thought" inunuloro, inunu chenu	
(pensive mood)		

339

pentagon, n.	kpentagun, oka jiomitri,	
	o wen akue isen	
pentateuch, n.	kpentatio, ikonon littafi	
pentathlon, n. pentecost, n.	isen na baibul (first)	
	kpentaton, iguere olimpik	
	kpentikos, ikonodun	
	igbore nke e mutum Jiu	

(pentecostal), adj. pent-	kpentikosta, nke	G(fE)
ouse, n. penumbra,	kpentikos gida-	Y/I/H
n. penurious, adj.	kpenti, irudi rufi gida	
(penuriousness), n. peony, n.	kpenubra, launi wata	
	siyen, talaka isiyen	
	kponi, irudi	
	shukeshuke gadin	

people, n.	e mutum, jama'a	H(G.v)
(people's republic)	ripoblika 'mutum,	
	(iminira e mutum) ikegba tisi	I/Y
	'kegba akoko, fefe fefemint	Idoma/Gen.
	Kpezin, irudi ruwa na chiki	I/Y
	Tu, tukon, na Tu mutum	Y/I Y/I Y/I
pep, n.	Tu ardun Tu senti	Y/I
(add pep to it) pepper, n.	Biowu, yana	
(peppermint) Pepsin, n.	Shiene kiri, ringa kiri	
Per, prep.	o shienen kiri, o ringa kiri	
(per person) (per year)	kiehun	
(per cent)	itu senti, inofi senti kpach,	
Peradventure, adv.	irudi kifi na ruwa bona, bi o	
Perambulate, vit.	wu , yeyefe kpekole, nke ifeja	
(perambulator) perceive,	ruwa ikpekoshan, nke ilowe	
vt. per-centage, n.		
perch, n. perchance, adv.		
percolate, vit. percussion, n.		
	abi isonga, koya songa	
(rapid percussion)	ikpekoshan sokiaka	
perdition, n.	ibida fefefe, ibida	
	Y/I/Ed	
perennial, adj.	shiene shim, lai simini	
(perennial problem)	nsohala shiene shim,	
	nsohala lai wen simini	
perfect, adj. (perfection), n.	shaka	G
	ishaka, shaka-shaka	
(near to perfection)	nure si shaka	
honu o honu, ihonu	Y/I	

(no one is perfect	in the world). perforate, vti. (perforator)	
perform, vti. n.	kosi eni shaka n'akpor	
mume, imume	Y/I	
perfunctory, adj.	irushe lai fi yobi si, lai june (care)	
pergola, n.	kpegola, ikpezi, irudi itache fulawa	
perhaps, adv.	biowu, yana	
perigee, n.	kperigi, oka sayens ati obiti	
peril, n.	lu, heu-heu, idanja rubi	G(Ed.v)
periolous, adj.	danja, iu, heu-heu	
(perilous time)	ngba danja, ngba iu, ngba heu-heu	
perimeter, n.	kperiminta	G(fE)
period, n.	ikongba, ikoge	Y/I
(periodic), adj.	n'ikongba, n'ikoge	
peripatetic, adj.	gakiri, shien kiri	I/Y
(peripatetic preacher)	o wasu o shien kiri, o wasu o gakiri	
periphery, n.	matuka izunde (external boundary)	
perphrasis, n.	kperifresi, boto kiri, bokiri (round about)	
periscope, n.	kperisko, irudi ifaiki foto, o neri whido	
perish, vit.	diru	I/Y
(perishable), adj.	le diru	
pristyle, n.	kperistail, irudi yadi abi nso	
peritonitis, n.	kperitonisi, irudi irun chiki	
periwinkle, n.	kperiwinko, irudi shuke-shuke algashi	
periwinkle, n.	kperewinko, irudi kodi tekun (snail)	

perjure, vt.	masoli siro, isoli siro n'ibuji (oath)
perk, vti.	garan, bia di shaka
	abi garaun (lively)
perm, n.	kpere 'to perm hair" G
permafrost, n.	ituyi gan-gan (to frost permanently)
permanent, adj.	paminint, gan-gan
(permanent address)	adresi gan-gan
(permanent secretary)	akawu gan-gan, paminint sekitri
permanganate, n.	kpamangana, nke sayens G
permeate, vti, n.	banso, ibanso I(G.v)
permission, n. adj.	ikweye, ikweyefe, kweye, ikweba
(you are permitted)	a kweye yin
(you are not permitted)	ao kwye yin, ao kweba fun yin
permutation, n.	kpamutesyhan, oka
permute, vt.	yitole "to change the order of"
pernicious, adj.	danja, meje, meru
peroration, n.	kperora, oka turanchi
peroxide, n.	kperogza, irudi ruwa ai wen launi (colourless liquid)
(hydrogen peroxide)	aidrojin kperogza
perpendicular, adj.	kpapkendikula, oka jiomitri
perpetrate, vt.	meda, fame I/Y
perpetual, adj.	ai wen iguton, lailai, ngba lai-lai
perpetuate, vt.	bue si whido, ibue si whido
perplex vt.	gbu iyobi
(i am perplexed)	o gbu mi 'yobi
perry, n.	kperi, irudi wain

persecute, vt, n.	jafun rubi, ijafun rubi	
(persecutor), n.	o jafun rubi	
persevere, vi.	fikiti, ifikiti Y/I	
persian, n.	omo kpesia	
persimmon, n.	kpesimo, itudi itache	
persist, vi, n.	tisimon, itisimon Y/I	
(persistent insistence)	itisimon lai chiu	
person, n.	mutum, o kanbo wu mi ji abi mache, iyonma eni mutum abi e mutum	
personable, adj.	ineri rama, mutum di 'neri rama, ineri rama mutum	
personage, n.	ihoneri mutum	
personal, adj.	keni, mutum, nke mutum, (kpesina)	
(personal character)	imiwa keni	
(personal assistant)	o nohann keni, (kpesina asistan)	
personality, n.	imutum, iminiwa keni (personal quality)	
personalize, vt.	meshi de keni	
personality, n.	kpesinati, oka iwufin, estit keni	
personate, vt.	meshe iyaka mutum	
personnel, n.	pesineli, e mutum irushe	
perspective, n.	icherondi	
(right perspective)	icherondi year, icherondi rama	
perspex, n.	irudi roba plastic ti a ng fi meshe madubi mota	
perspicuous, adj.	soli di shaka, soli shaka	
perspire, vi.	gumi (sweat)	H/Y
	(perspiration)	
persuade, vt. n.	Yobi, iyobi	I/Y/
	Its part, adj.	

pertain, vi, n.	kati, ikati	I/Y
pertinacious, adj.	shikolo (not giving up easily)	
pertinent, adj.	dogon	H/Y
(pertinent to mention)	idogon ka koda	
peso, n.	kpeso, irudi kudi na	
	kasa latin amerika kpesri, irudi magani o	
pessary, n.		
	yiwah na botu (dissolve) kpesimizi, irudi inikon	
pessimism, n.		
	kpe ife rubi kha le s'oka	
	mo ng kpesimizi	
(i am perssimistic) pest, n.	korkorun, kwaro	Y(G.v)/H magani kwaro abi
(pesticide), n.		
	kokorun, kpestisaid	
	whini, mu bi onu G ma whini mi mindu	
pester, vt.	ijakasa, ighakasa, baba yirun Y/H	
(don't pester my life)	tabarya	H turmi ati tabarya
pestilence, n. pestle, n.	don-bebi	Gen gisuwa don-bebi
(mortar and pestle)	hufe I/Y inukan, nukan I/G	
pet, n. (pet shop)	hotaka	H kpp-kpoh, irudi bom
pet, vt. (of affection)		
pet, n. (of ill temper)		
petal, n. petard, n.		
	kele na ngba kera	
Peter, n.	Pita, afa almajiri Peter	
(rob Peter to pay Paul)	na Baibul (disciple) Rawo Pita fi kpa Pol,	
	(rawo Pita kpa Pol)	
petite, adj.	Mache kenteh_(neat	
Petition, n.	an slender) Ikprebi	I/Y/Itsek.
(petitioner)	O kperebi O kode ikprebi	G
(petition writer) (petrel),	kpetere, irudi onene tekun	G(fE)
n. petrify, vt.	meleu_(terrorize) kemia-	G(fE)
Petrol-chemical, adj.	fetro fetro fetrolia	
petrol, n. petroleum,	fetrolia jeli	
n. (petroleum jelly)	fetroloji, imuko dutse	
petrology, n. (petroleum	prodat fetrolia peti kwat	
product) petticoat, n.	hala-hala, eni ng meshe	
pettifogging, adj.	nsohala fun eni 'fe	
petty, adj.	yekele, kpeti	Y/I/Gen

perturb, ti, n.	rusen, irusen	Y/I peruke, n.
peruse, vt, n.	nerisei, inerisel I/Y/H	
pervade, vt.	gbinsoso idakpe	I/Y
(perverse judgement)	igbin rubi seleke	Gen/Ed.
pervert, vt. peseta, n.	peseta, irudi kudi	
	na kasa Spen	

(petty cash)   kpeti kas, kpeti kabodais

(petty officer)   kpeti hafsa, nke soja

                           tekun abi nefi kpetua, ai wen sundi
petulant, adj.

pew, n. pewit, n. peyote, n.   kene, ibionu sokia
                           kujera-golo   H/Gen kpiwit, na basani (mountain)
                           kpiota, irudi sedi na Megziko (cactus)

pfening, n.   kpenin, irudi kudi

phaeton, n.   na Zamani
                           fetin, irudi mota doki na ngba kera

phagocyte, n.   fegosat, irudi monsu
                           na jiki (body cell) fabuh, ife ti ko wen ezioka,

phantom, n.
                           ife ti ko di ezioka Fero, afa baez nga

Pharaoh, n.
                           kera na Ijipt Farisii, omo Jiu famasis, o kono kojo

Pharisee, n. pharmacis, n.

                           magani, o rushe magani
pharmaceutical, adj.   Nke famasis, ife famasis,

                           maganagana
pharmacology, n.   isayens nke famasis,

                           famakoloji, famakoko famakpoya, littafi abi
pharmacopoeia, n.

                           kamus nke magani famasi, nke imeshe
pharmacy, n.

                           magani abi ogun feros, gida wuta fun
pharos, n.

                           e shikolo (sailors) rinse, kaya onu, farins ìbèchú_(of stages),

Pharynx, n. Phase, n.

(phase one)	nine (of side) inine daya Ibechú daya Inine
(stage one)	wata fisante, irudi onene a ng fi guere
(phase of the moon)	
pheasant, n.	
penobarbitone, n.	fenobaba, irudi magani
phenol, n.	abi ogun ti an fi simin: feno, na sayens, irudi wassid
phenomenon,	isokali, ife duniya abi hali (natural)
phew,	piu (like hissing sound), shio
phial, n.	jolo, ijongo kele fun magani
philander, n.	filanda, imeshe ivud lai fie yobi si
philanthropy, n. (philanthropist)	ichef 'akpor o chef 'akpor I/Y/Urh.
philately, n.	faleti, fostej samp, ihufe fostej sam, imeko fostej sai
(philatist)	faletis, o meko fostej samp
philharmonic,	filamoni, ikpisi si 'songa (devote/ted/ion)
adj. philistine,	filisin, na baibul, o jagha mutum
n. philology,	filoloji, filolozi, imuko igbadi ede (development)
n. (philology)	o filoloji, o filolozi
philosopher, n.	filosofa, imukezi, imuko ichegbon
(philosopher)	o filosofa, o mumeze, o muko ichegbon
(philosopher)	imukezi, ifilosofa, imoko ichegbon
philter,	magani abi ogun G ihufe, gaun-gaun
phlebitis,	kpilibiti, irudi baba irun G(FE)

346

n. phlegm,	kpiligeme, majini	G(FE)
n. phlox, n.	flos, irudi shukeshuke gadom	/H
phobia, n.	ikpoba, irudi 'rugu (a type of fear	
phoenix, n.	kponis, onene ilidaka (mythological bird)	G(fED.)
phone, n, vt.	tèlìwáya	
(phone-booth)	kíos- tèlìwáya	
phoneme, n	fonim, oka imuko ede, oka linguosa	
phonetic, adj.	fonet foneti	
phonic, ajd.	fifon; nke fon, nke ilowe (of sound)	
phonograph, n.	fonogra, o songi songa na rekod	
phonology, n.	fonoloji, oka sayens ede, oka linguosa	
phooey, int.	ummh, irudi ikemkpo na ngba idiki	
phosgene, n.	(disappointment)	
phosphate, n.	fosijin, irudi gaz, coc12	
phosphorescence, n.	fosfat, irdi gishiri (salt)	
phosphorus, n. photo, n.	fosi-fosi, oka sayens	
phosphorus, n. photo, n.	fosforas (p), ife a ng fi meshe wuta	
n.	foto, hoto	
(photo-copy)	hoto kapi	
(photo-copier)	o hoto kapi	Gen/H
(photo-electric)	hoto-lantiriki	
(photo-genic)	hoto-jena, ife di rama fun foto	
(photo-sensitize)	ai che foto, ia chefe foto abi hoto	

photograph, n.	foto, hoto, hotografa, fotografa
(photographer)	o foto, o hoto, hotografa, fotografa
(photography)	hotografi, fotografi
Phrase, n.	Igboka, nke turanchi,
Phenology, n.	ibekuru o ki Frenoloji, o muko kashi keisi (study of human
(photographic)	koso foto abi hoto,
photogravure, n.	nke hoto (related) hotografio, irushe
Photolithography, n.	hoto foto/hotolatografi, irushe
Photometer, n.	foto si na kwano abi dutse hotominta, injin o
Photostat, n.	nofi 'nure wuta Hoto/fotosat, injin o meshe hoto-capi skull
(phrenologist) phthisis, n.	o frenoloji kpitisis, tobakulosi
physic, n. Physical, adj.	nke huhu_(lungs) fisik, magani, fisik Kaya, nke duniyar abi akpor, fisika
(physical fitness) (physically), adv.	Idiot fisika, igbandu jiki fifisika, kakaya, n'fisika, n'kaya 'kpor, n'akpor likita magani, fisishan
physician, n. physicist, n. physics, n. physiognomy, n. physiology, n. physiotherapy, n.	iwin fisiks fisiks, na sayens fisiogonoma, irudi imuko fisioloji, irudi sayens G(fE) fisiokparapi irudi ilosie irun
(physiotherapist) physique, n. piano (pianist) piaster, n.	kpelu lekin_(massage) o fisiokparapi jihura, unke jiki I/I/Y 'kpátá Ed/Yr ò 'kpátá piasta, irudi kudi
piazza, n.	na kasa bature piazah, ebi pobli
pica, n.	na kasa jakpan kpaika, irudi ibuto

afabit nke tafreta kpikaleli, irudi abinchi fulutu kele
iyowe, yoji, yota   Y/I

piccalilli, n. piccolo,
n. pick, n. pick, n.
(pocket picker)

irudi kaya aiki abi kozo (tool) o yoji 'kpa, o yoji

(picker) picking, n.
pickle, n. picnic, n.

aijihu, barawo o yowe, o yoji, o yota irawo
fikol, ruwa gishirin G(fE) fiknik, irinje 'flesi fun igbandu

(picnicker) picric,
adj. pictorial, adj.

o fiknik
fikiri, ifena ng fi meshe launi hoto-hoto, na hoto,

picture, n. (picture
book) (picture card)
(picture gallery) piddle,
vtn. pidgin, n. pie, n.

ife hoto abi foto
hoto, foto   H/Gen littafi hoto kadi hoto
ifinzi hoto
yunto (to pass urine) I/Y brokin, turanchi brokin
pai, irudi buredi ati nama kpel fulawa

(meat pie)Piece, n.

(break into pieces)
(divide it in pieces)
(pieces of work)

piece-meal, adv. pied,
adj. námà pai, irudi
abinchi buredi ati
nama a guntu, gutsure

H foji si guntu
kekpin ya na guntu,

pier, n.

paya, irudi katako na ruwa

abi tekun fun ugbokoruwa
guma

pierce, vti. pieta, n.

piea, foto nke o budurwa   Y/I

piety, n.

mary (meri), na ngba
bue gawa jesu kristi kafa
ta iyati, ikpisi si abasi

(devotion to god (urhobo)
alade, alhanzir kulu-kulu,   H

pig, n. pigeon, n piglet,
n. pigment, n pigmy, n.
(pigmies of congo)

irudi onene omontakele alade G
ibora, nke launi ati fenti   Y/Ed
mukuru e mukuru kongo   H/Gen

pike, n.

kpaiki, igboro kifi ruw

pilau, n.

kpilau, irudi abinchi bature

pilchard,

kpicha, irudi kifi ruwa   G(fE)

n. pile,	kpoko, irudi ginshiki gida (pillar)
n. pile, n.	kole (to pile up)
pile, vti,	ikole bindiga – "where arms and rifles are kept"
n. pile, n.	kpaile, irudi kafet
piles, n.	kpokpokpoh, irudi jadi-jadi G
pilfer, vti,	jara, ijara Y/H
kekpin guntu irushe guntu abi gutsure na guguntu iwakpo launi nke onene (mixture of birds' colours	
n. (pilferer)	o jara
pilgrim, n.	alhaji, irinje H/Y/I
pill, n.	pili, magani abi ogunkele G
pillar, n.	ginshiki H
(pillar-box)	akwati ginshiki, irudi akwati ti a ng fos wasik;
pillion, n.	kpilian, irudi kujera doki abi keke-mota
pillory, n.	kpelori, irudi 'riya na ngba kera
pillow, n.	fuku-isi G/I
(pillow-case)	ikpa fuku-isi
pilot, n.	pailota, o yanwa sonmafeh, abi ugboko ruwa
(pilot officer)	hafsa pailota, hafsa kele khan a
(pilot-fish)	erh fos o yanwa kifi, irudi kifi na
pilot, vit.	ruwa yanwa, chowa hanya fun,
(pilot programme)	chowa iyanwa lit'eto, ifineri lit'eto

pimpernel, n.	kpinkpane, irudi shuke-shuke	G
pimple, n.	kurji	H
pin, n.	fin, fin	
(pin-head)	isi abi kai fin	
pin, n.	koso (to tie something)	
(pinned down)	koso si kasa	
(pincenez),	finez, irudi tabarau (spectacles)	
n. pincers, n.	kaguwa, hantsaki	H
pinch, vti.	takin	G
(don't pinch me)	ma takin mi	
(pinching)	itakin	
(pinch) to gather	takonojo, takono	G/Y/I
up pinch-beck, n.	kpin-bek, irudi ruwa tagulla (copper)	
pine, n.	kpain, irudi itache algashi	
pine, vi.	holo – (waste)	G
pineal, ajd.	kpini, irudi kaluluwa na jiki (gland)	
pineapple,	abarba, fainafo	H/H(G.v)
n. ping, n.	kpim, irudi ilowe "a type of sound"	
pinion, n.	kpinon, gashi onene "bird's feather"	
pink, n.	penk, irudi launi	G(fE)
pinnace, n.	kpines, abara kele	G(fE)
pinnacle, n.	shonsho	Y
pint, n.	painti, inofi	G(fE)
(pint of water)	painti ruwa	
pioneer, n.	o rebili, o rebile	Y/I
pious, adj.	kyobi, ikpisi si isinle (devotion to religion)	
pip, n.	iri (seed), kwaya	H
pip, n.	kpikpi, irun kaza	G(fE)

pip, n.	iri, kwaya, nke soja	
pip, vt.	kakpu, igbata bindiga	
pipe, n.	tukun-tuku tukunyar taba, tukun-tuku, tukun; kakaki	
(drain pipe)	tukun-kpogbe	
(gas pipe)	tukun-gaz	
pipe, vti.	fa ruwa	
(pipe-line)	faif-lain, tukun-gaz	
piper, n.	o tukun-tuku, o yakiti (bagpiper)	
pipette,	pifet, boto abi kakaki magani – "medical funnel"	
n. pippin,	kpifin, irudi apul	
n. pique,	kpiki, irudi faiba auduga	
n. piquet,	kpikwet, iguere kadi fun e mutum	
n. piranha,	meji kpiraha, irudi kifi ruwa na	
n. pirate, n.	amerika barawo tekun, kpairet, o rawo	H/G(fE)
(piracy), n.	irawoloh	
pirouette, n.	kpairut, irudi samba	
pisces, n.	feisis, nke lamba zodia	
piss, vti.	sssih, yunto	G/I/Y
pistachio, jn.	kpistacho, irudi kwaya	
pistil, n.	matuchi, fistili, nke fulawa	H/G(fE)
pistol, n.	libarbar	H
piston, n.	kpistin, ayan injin	
(pistion and rings)	kpistin ati oruka	
pit, n.	rami, hako	H
(pitman)	o rushe gawayi, fitman	

(pit-fall) pit, n.	fit, irudi kwaya abi boto	
pitapat, adv. pitch, n. pitch,	fit, irudi kwaya abi boto	
n. pitch, n. pitch, n.	kwakakwa, iluti sokia inofi –	G(fI)
	"measurement" ebi kasuwa	I/Y/H
	pich, nke iguere krikat	
	kpich, irudi kaya	
	kwalta (coal-tar) meshe	
pitch, vti.	kundu, kundi – "to	
	erect/set up), mu	H
	chiu kundu ijagha	F(fE) Y/I
	tulu	
	o pich, nke krikat fit,	
(pitched battle) pitcher,	nke shuke-shuke nube,	
n. pitcher, n. pith, n.	rere di rere, rere si ai	
pitiable, adj. pitiful, adj.	wen rere, ai nube kpitin,	
pitiless, adj. piton, n.	irudi ayan ti a ng	
	fu basani (mountain)	
pitter-patter, n.	ikpo-kpo, ikpo-kpo	
	ruwa – "rai drops"	
	pichu, irudi kaluluwa (gland)	
pituitary, adj. (pituitary	kaluluwa pichu irere, inube	
gland) pity, n. (have pity)	wen irere, wen inube	
pivot, n.	iringon, ibarin gesi	
	(important centre) kpiza,	
	irudi abinchi tomati	
pizza, n.	kpizikato, irudi 'songa	
pizzicato, adj, adv. placard, n.	flakad, irudi 'kemkpo	
	ti a ng kode na kadi ebi,	
	mbi, iyefe, ikpoze, (fie)	
place, n. (pace it here)	fie yam bi, fie mbi	
(pace it there)	fie ya ebe	
(go to places)	shienga ebi-ki-ebi, shien mbi-ki	
placenta, n.	flasinta, irudi ogan na chiki mache	
placid, adj, n.	kulele, ai wen nsohala, ikulele	
plage, n.	flej, kasa nso tekun, kate- (beach)	
plagiarize, vt.	gbonrawo, iluwe ichenu somutum lai wen aashe	

353

plague, n.	aashe ijakaka	Y/H(G.v) plaice, n.
plain, adj. (my words are plain enough) oka mi diye zuto	diye	I/Y
plain, n.	kpele, kasa kpele	G
plain, n.	flen, nke ikawun – "knitting"	
plaintiff, n.	flentif, mutum iwufin	G
plait, vt.	jolo	G
plan, n. (let me know your plan)	filan, igbiche, ka mi ma igbiche e (ka 'ma igbiche e)	Y/I
(building plan)	flan gida, dabara gida	
plane, n.	filen, irudi itache	
plane, n. (plane land)	fleni, ihaiki kafinta lande lebe, kasa lebe	
planet, n.	flanit	G(fE)
plank, n.	katako, kpako	H/Y/Gen
plankton, n.	flantin, irudi mindu ogan na tekun	
plant, n.	shuke-shuke, igbinso-so	H/Y/I
plant, vt.	gbinso	
plantain, n.	ogede	G
(plaintain leaf)	ganye ogede	
plantation, n.	igbinsule	T/Tiv
(plantain plantation)	igbinsule ogede	
plague, n.	flek, ife iloron	
plash, n.	sah, ilowe ruwa	
plasm, n.	flazim, ife monsu (cell) c	
plasma, n.	flasma, nke jini	
plaster, n.	kpala-kpala, flasta	G/G(fE)
plastic, adj.	flastik, irudi roba bature	

(plastic surgery) plasticine, n.   isajan flastik flastisin,
                                     irudi yumbu

                                     bika roba tasevo, kwano,evo

                                                        Nupe/H
                                     kwano fifoji
plate, n.   kwano madubi, kwano gilas kori kwano
(breakabe plate) (plate-glass)   fletiu, irudi kasa lebe si nuke
(plate-dental) plateau, n.   fleleya, o rushe hanya reluwe
plate-layer, n. platform, n.   dakali, katako   H/Gen flatinon,
platinum, n. platonic, adj.   irudi metal na kasa flato, irudi aboki

                                     lai wen ivudu kunsu, itugbe
                                     soja flata, irudi ibuto
platoon, n. platter, n.

                                     kwano abi tasevo flatifos, irudi name
platypus, n.

plausible, adj.   nke kasa ostrelia birondi, ife bika irondi
                                     (reasonable) (plausible cause) ifata birondi

play, n.   , vti, gwuere, iguere, meshe, songi, sole
(play-box)   akwati guere, nke

                                     omontakele yaro igwuere aboki igwuere itugbe
(play-boy)   igwuere kasa igwuere deki- 'igwuere
(play-mate)
(play-group)
(play-ground) (play-room)

(play-school) (play-thing)   makaranta omontakene ife 'igwuere ngba igwuere iwufin
(play-time) (fair-play)   imeshe 'guere, iguere-
(play-acting)

(play-house)   guere, e gwuere
(play-wright)   e tugbe 'guere, tati o damma (dramatist)
(play your card well)   guere e rama, meshe

                                     irushe e rama
(play your part)   meshe kpaka e, guere kpaka e songi dazu
(play-back)
(player)   o guere, o songi
                                     songa, o songi

(guitar player)   o guere molo

(playful)   gwuereke; guere kha,
                                     gwuere-gwuere

(play-field)   fili 'gwuere gwuere

(rough-play)	igwuereke	
plaza, n.	aza, irudi baba kasuwa, ebi kasuwa	
plea, n.	ibiyo	Y/Its
(plead)	biyo, oka ibiyo	
(i am pleading)	mo ng biyo	
pleasance, n.	flisa, gadin igbandu	
pleasant, adj.	dunso; miri-miri	
pleasantry, n.	idunso, ikuakua (humour)	
please, vti. (please, give me water biko fun mi ruwa; biko, nno_mi ruwa (synonym)	biko, dunso, somenu, sochiki	
(it pleased me)	o dunso mi	
pleasure, n.	idunso, isolele, isoflesi, idunsoso	
(pleasure car)	mota zoom-zoom	
plebeian, n, adj.	kuala-kuala, (coarse and lower class person)	G.
plebiscite, n.	flebisa, irudi cherisi nke politi	
plectrum, n.	fletrom, mita a ng fi guere molo	
pledge, n.	ikweye, ikwede	I/Y
(i pledge to nigeria my country)	mo kwede fun naijeriya kasa mi	
planary, adj.	flenari, nke miting	
(plenary session)	flenari seshan, ijondu flenari	
plenipotentiary, n.	flenikpotensha, flenikpotenshari, ambasiye	
plenitude, n.	ijukuno, irisi kha, ikpori	
plenteous, adj.	kpori-kpo, risi	Y/I plentiful, adj.
plenty, n.	isusu	

(plenty people)	enmutum susu, e mutum, mutum-mutum	
pleonasm, n.	lio, iluwe oka risi fun ikpere ife (description)	
plethora, n.	flitora, irudi irun na jini	
pleurisy, n.	flirusi, irudi irun na kirji (chest)	
plexus, n.	flizos, e hanya jinni na jiki	
pliable, adj.	yikpoton (easy to	
bend)	Y/Egun	
pliers, n.	flayas, irudi kaguwa_(pincers)	
plight, n.	isilekpo – "difficult condition"	
plight, vt.	ikwede, ikwade – "promise"	
plimsoll, n.	flimso,	
plimsolls, n.	flimso, irudi kanfas roba (rubber canvas)	
plinth, n.	flint, gindi (statute's base) mutummutumim abi bukoki	
plonk, n .	kpulum, ikpoi, irudi ' ruwa lowe nke ife t' o kpo na	
plop, n.	kplo, irudi wain	
plop, n.	ikpoi, bika kpulum	
plosive, n. adj.	flosi, nke oka turanchi abi linguosa	
plot	kasa	H
plot, vt.	manjo	Y/Owo/I
(don't plot against me)	ma manjo mi	
(plotter of coup)	o manjo zàìkpókp	
plough, n.	garma, huda	H
(plough the land)	huda kasa, huda lande	
plover, n.	flova, irudi onene na ingilande	
pluck, vti.	puyo ya, puyo fiam	
plug, n.	fulog	H

plum, n.	flum, irudi itache	G(fe)
pluage, n.	flumej, irudi gashi onene	
plumb, n.	flumb, irudi bol	G(fe)
plumbago, n.	flumbego, irudi mita	
plumbago, n.	bika darma (lead) flumbaigo, irudi shukeshuke fulawa	
plumber, n.	galumba, o rushe famfo	H
plume, n.	ibuto gashi onene – "large feather"	
plummet, n.	flumit, iwan ti a ng fu rushe famfo	
plump, adj.	boto, sonji	Y/I
plunder, vt. i.	meko, rile	I/Y
(plunderer)	o rile, o meko	
plunge, vti, n.	jubo, ijubo	I/Y
(plunge into the river) poem	jubo si kogi poke, vti, n.	
		fioko, ifioko

G

ipole, pole;	poke-bonnet, n.	po-banit, nke (Salvation Army)
sungo	poker, n.	kpoka, irudi ayan kwalta
	polar, adj.	kpola, nke Not (North)
G	(polar staf)	tara kpola
poet, n.	(polar bear)	bie nke kpola, nama daji kpola
o pole; o	pole, n.	muchiya (muciya)
sungo (poetry)	(electric pole)	muchirya lantiriki
	(jumping pole) muchiya ifoma	H/Y
	(police man)	miji mondoka/ mondoka miji
ioba	(police woman)	mondoka mache

juhann,	(police constable)	kanstebu mondoka, mondokasi
iloba,k ebi,	(police court)	kotu mondoka
mbo, mbi	(police dog)	kare mondoka
(point	(police horse)	doki mondoka
road)	(police office)	ofis nke mondoka
(police station)	tashan mondoka	
(Nigerian Police)	Mondoka Naijeriya;	
(Nigerian Police Force)	Mondoka Naijeriya	
Ikarfi Mondoka nke		
Naijeriya; Agba Mondoka		

(Military Police)	Monkoda Soja	
(Nigerian Military Police)		
Mondoka Soja nke		
Naijeriya (M.S.N)		

policy, n.	Ikoso	
(policy statement)	oka ikoso	
polio, n.	kpolio, kpoliomelaiti, baba irun	
polish, vti, n.	shakata, kpolis	Y/G
(polish my shoe for me)		
shakata takalmi mi fun mi		
(buy me shoe polish)	gora mi kpolis takalmi	
(shoe polisher)	o shakata takalmi	
politburo, n.	politburo, kwamiti politi	
polite, adj.	wara, imiwa rama	Y/I
political, adj.	politike, nke gonmenti	
(political party)	itugbe politike	
(politicize)	meshe di politike	
(political crisis)	ijaghali politike; nsohala politike	
(politician)	o politike	
politics, n.	ipolitike, isayens politike, (politike sayens)	

(political department)	iyaka politke;	
polity, n.	politi, irudi gonmenti	
poll, n.	ishabe,	
(polling booth/station)	buka ishabe, tashan 'shabe	
poll, n.	kpola, irudi aku (parrot)	
pollard, vt.	ibe itache, dungu_(stub)	
pollen, n.	bununi, buniya	H pollinattte, vt.
pollute, vt, n.	meba, me di dati, imeba	I/Y
polo, n.	holo	H
(polo club)	kulobu holo	
polony, n.	kpoloni, irudi buredi fulawa	
poltroon, n.	mumu, kawad	
polyandry, n.	mata e mutum mache t'o chogbe mijinch	
polygamy, n.	ikojo mata polemofu, ifeja igbadi fambuo (different state of development)	Y/Ed/H polymorphous, adj.
polypus, n.	folifo, irudi kari na hanchi (tumour)	
polysyllable, n.	kpolisilabu, oka nke wen ifambu okada (syllable)	
polytechnic, n.	kpoliteknik, irudi makaranta G(fE)	
polytheism, n.	kpoliteizim, irudi inokon ati isinle	
polythene, n.	kpolitin, kpoletin, irudi roba	
pomade, n.	amian (amheye) Kat/Kaj/kag/Mar/ Jab	
pomegranate, n.	kpomegranit, irudi kwaya	
pomelo, n.	kpomelio, irudi inabe (grape)	
pommy, n.	komi, e mutum Briten na Ostrelia	
pomp, n, vt.	imiliki; miliki Gen (fE. Obey)	

360

(pomp and pageantry)	igbandu ati miliki
pompon, n.	kponkpon, irudi ado (ornament)
pompous, adj, n.	wengesi, gugugu, + i I/Izon/Ed
(don't be pompous)	ma di wengesi, ma gugugu
punce, n.	maigida mache fiki-fiki, maigida of fiki fiki
pond, n.	kotogbi, kandami, kududdu G/H
ponder, vti.	loro I/Y
(ponder over it)	loro si ya
pone, n.	kpon, irudi buredi masara (maize)
pontiff, n.	kpontif, pontif, popG(fE)
pontoon, n.	kpontu, irudi ugboko fasinja
pony, n.	kponi, doki kele G(fE)
poodle, n.	kpudol, irude kare
pooh, int.	uhh, izizi – "smelling"
pool, n.	kotogbin-arin, kpoh G/Y
(typing pool)	tapin kpoh
(transport pool)	kpogboko
poop; n.	pup, deki na ugboko ruwa
poor, adj.	siyen Y/I
(poor person)	mutum o siyen
(poor people)	e mutum o siyen; (o siyen jama'a)
(poorverty)	isiyen
(poorverty is not good)	isiyen ko rama
pop, n.	kpoi, ilowe eso (some soun)
pop, adj.	popu, ibekuru popula
pope, n.	pop, popu, bishobu nke rom
poplar, n.	popla, irudi gingolo itache
poplin, n.	poflin, irudi esa siliki ati wulu
poppet, n.	pofet, nke omontakele

poppy, n.	popi, pofi, irudi shuke-shuke	
populace, n.	popule; e mutum jama'a, e mutum kasa abi gari	
popular, adj, n. (population, n. mutane, mutane, imutum,ijama'a, emutum kasa abi gari	noki, popula, ipopula	I/Y/G(fE)
populisim, n.	populizim, popu-popu, irudi gonmenti	
populous, adj.	ju-kun fun e mutum	
porcelain, n.	posilin, kwano yumbu nke chaina	
porch, n.	baranda, shirayi	H
porcupine, n.	beguwa	H
pore, n.	honu-gasi (hair hole)	
pork, n.	nama alade	H(G.v) pornography, n.
porous, adj.	o wen ihonu	
porridge, n.	kuntu	H
(please buy me porridge)	biko yámá mi kunu	
port, n.	nute, kpot	I/H/G(fE)
(sea-port)	nute tekun, si-kpot	
(air-port)	nute fekuku, nute erh, erh-kpot	
(port-hole)	iwindo na ugboko ruwa abi ugboko soma	
(port-hole)	galu-galu, koto kasa, koto hanya	
(port)	nke bindiga, pkoh	
portable, adj.	fifere, nke a le bue kiri	G/Gene
portal, n.	kpotali, irudi hanya gida	
porte-cochere, n.	kpote-kpocha, irudi hanya kofa na gida	
porter, n.	monkoh, o bue kaya na kpot abi tashan	

porter, n.	monko, o cheto kofa – "door keeper"	
porter, n.	kpota, irudi wain	
porterhouse, n.	kpotahaus, irudi abinchi	
portfolio, n.	kpofolio, kpofo, irudi abinchi	
portico, n.	kpotiko, irudi rufu gida	
portiere, n.	kpocheh, labule bibu (big curtain)	
portion, n. (play well your portion) meshe ebi yin/re di rama	rabi, rabo, ikpaka, ebi, mbi, iyahannu (this is your portion)	eyi wu iyahannu e
Portland, n.	Potlande, irudi dutse lain (lime-stone)	
(portland cement)	suminti potlande	
portmanteau, n.	kpotomanto, irudi akwati makarant	
portrait, n.	fotrit, foto a nese	
portray, vt.	nese, fineri, fihun	I/Y
portugal	kpotoki	Ed.
pose, vti. (pose for a photograph) chenedu fun foto	chenedu, hoyah, yaji	
posh, adj.	iwin, baba, kwata-kwata	Y/H/Gen
position, n.	ikpoze, ijuma	Y/I (which position)
positive, adj.	dido	
(are you positive?)	e dido?	
(yes i am positive)	baate, mo dido	
positivism, n.	kpoisitifizim, irudi inikon na ardun kera	
posse, n.	posi, itugbe kanstebu abi e mondoka	
possess, vt, n.	weni, iweni, e weni	I/Y

(possessive), adj.	winweni, di weni, weni
possible, adj, n.	dishe, dimeshe, idishe, idimeshe
possum, n.	kposun, iwayo simini
post, n.	ikpoze, itansfa, ibue shien, ironshien (what is his post?)
posse, n.	meni wu ikpoze ya?
(he/she has been posted) a ti roshien ya, a ti tansfa ya	
post, n.	muchiya (pole), pos
(goal-post)	(gol fos)
post, pref.	fost, izuba, zuein
(post production)	izuein 'mubia; fos prodashan
post, (of letters)	fost
(postage)	fostej, ifost, kudi fost,kudi ironshien wasika
(post office)	fostofis, ofis ironshien, ofis iron ga
(postal service)	irushe fost
(post bag) (post	ikpa fos
box) (postal	fost-bos; akwati fost
code) (post	ikodi fos
man) (post-	miji fost; fosman
mark) (post-	(fostmak)
paid) (postage	wasika a ti kpa ya; iflesifost – "free post"
stamp) (postal)	fostej samp; sampu fost
(postal order)	fosta, fost, nke fost
(post-date)	fosta hoda, fosta hoda
poster, n.	irana fost, iraya iron shien
poste restante, n.	fosta, irudi baba hoto abi flakad (placard)
posterity, n.	foste resante, iyaka fos ofis fun wasika

post exchange, n.	ngba izuba, ngba izuein, ngba baya	
post-graudate, adj.	fos echen, irudi kasuwa soja ati yali fa	
poste-humous, adj.	fos-graduit, imuko si n'izuba digiri	Ya
post-master, n.	fos-humon, omo ti a mubi n'izuba ikuowun baba/	
(post-master-general)	fos-masta, megida abi oga fos-ofis	
post meridiem, n.	fos-masta janar, oka kwata-kwata fos-ofis	
(p.m.)	fos-meridem (f.m) izuba abi 'zuein arin rana	
post-mortem, n,	fos-motim, ichowa ife fata ikuowun mutum	
adj. postpone,	fosfun, buswhido, ibuswhido, musohido	G/I/Y/H
vt, n. postscript,	foskri, irudi oka n'izuba kwiro abi wasika	
n. postulant,	fostulante, irudi omo chochi, okpoko (novice)	
n. postulate, vt.	jubi, jubilee (demand, ask/	
posture, n.	foscha, bietu a ng neri 'fe, ichiu ife/	
posy, n.	mutum kpozi, kurshe fulawa a be (bunch)	
pot, n.	tukunya, tukun, koto, boto	H/G
(pot-belly)	chiki boto	
potable, adj, n.	rama funlamu, lamu, ilamu	
(potable water)	ruwa ilamu	
potash, n.	kanwa	H
potassium, n.	kpotashom, kanwa abi gishiri	

(potassium permanganate)	kpotashom kpamangala, ungurni	G/I/H
potato, n.	dankali, monkali	H/Gen/H
(sweet potato)	o dunso dankali, o dunso monkali	
poteen, n.	kpotini, irudi wiski airish (irish)	
potent, adj.	gbaron	Y(G.v)
(potential), n.	igbaron	G
potion, n.	ivamu	
(love potion)	ivamu hufe, ivamu 'hufe	
pot-pourri, n.	iwakpode, iwakpocha	
(music pot-pourri)	iwakpode 'songa potsherd, n.	
potter, n.	o meshe tukunya, o tukun, o koto, o boto	
(potter's wheel)	wili tukunya, wili tukun, wili koto pouch, n.	
poulterer, n.	o renka tukunya, o tukunya	
(poultry farm)	sule kaji	
pounce, vi.	foleh, foleh si, ifoleh	Y(G.v)
(he/she pounced on it)	o foleh si, o foleh si ya	
pound, vti, n.	pando, kpaun, ipando, pan	G/G(fE)
pounder, n.	kpanda, o nofi, iwan injin (weighing engine)	
(oundage)	inofi kpaun, kpaundej	
(pounded yam)	pan doya	
pour, vti.	shuru, ishuru-shuru	Y/Ed
(pour water)	shuru ruwa	
(the water pouring away)	ruwa ng shuru 'ta	
poverty, n.	isiyen, o laka	
powder, n.	hoda, toka bature	
(gun powder)	hoda bindiga	
power, n.	agba, ikagba, wuta	Y/I

(power house)	gida 'gba, gida wuta
(powerful)	di agba, wen agba, o kagba; di 'kagba.
powerless, adj	lai wen agba, ai wen agba, ai kagba pow-wow, n.
india nke not amerika practcable, adj.	jilo, jilolo, di meshe, shedi
practical, adj.	jilo, jilolo, di meshe, nke a le meshe
(practical result)	iyisi jilo, iyisi di meshe, igwisi, igwuton
practice, n.	ijilo, ishedi
(practician)	o shedi,
(practitioner),	o shedi, o jilo, o jilolo
(general practitioner)	o shedi janar,
(legal practitioner)	o shedi 'wufin
(medical practitioner)	o shedi magani, likita
pragmatic, adj.	gwukpini I/Y
(pragmatist)	o gwukpini
(pragmatism)	igwukpini
prairie, n.	prari, irudi kasa-kasa na not amerika
praise, vt, n.	yinbo, iyinboh
(deserving praise)	di 'dinye iyinboh
(praise god, haleluyah)	yinboh abasi, aleluyah
pram, n.	mbrama, o ringa kiri, wili I
prance, vi.	prans, ifonu-fonu doki jerking of horse
prank, n.	o guere n'iwayo, o wayo, iguere wayo
prate, vi.	mebobo (gossiping and foolish talk)
prawn, n.	jatan lande H
pray, vti, n.	kpredu, ikpredu, biyo, ibiyo I/Y
(pray to god)	kpredu si abasi

(pray for something)	kpredu fun ife	
(pray for mercy)	kpredu fun inube	
(prayer house)	gida ikpredu	
(prayer group)	itugbe o kpredu	
(prayer book)	littafi 'kpredu	
pre-	swen, sene, whido	G/Y/I/H
preach, vti.	wazi, iwazi	Y/I
(preacher)	o wazi	
preamble, n.	imuswene, imuswido (to bring forward)	
pre-arrange, vt.	swene tole, sent ole, itole swene	
prebend, n.	friben, irudi dudi o wazi na chochi	
precarious, adj.	frelafia, danja, wugu	
pre-cast, adj.	swene nese	
precaution, n.	ishokpa	
precede, vti.	swene-whido, na whido, ilahanya, ifinere	
(bad precedence)	ilahanya rubi	
(good precedence)	ilahanya rama	
precentor,	prisento, e tugbe isongi na chochi	
n. precept, n.	ikozi 'miwa (of moral instruction)	
preceptor, n.	o kozi – "teacher"	
precession, n.	prise, nke ekwina	
precint, n.	ezinta I/Y	
precious, adj.	bimkpa, iramani	Y/I
precipice, n.	kele-kele (steep)	G
precipitate, vt, n.	fadu, ifadu, fata, fabia	Y/I
preci, n.	fresi, oka turanchi	G
precise, adj.	kuru-oka, kamkpe	
(to be precise)	n'ikuru-oka	
precision, n.	ikamkpe	

preclude, vt, n.	gbuhanya, gbuhan, dihan, dihanya, imupu
precocious, adj	prikoko – idigbo n'isokia, ichegbon n'isokia
precognition, n.	ima ife swene ngba, ima na whido
preconceive, vt.	isiche – whido – "advance opinion", rombu, rowhi
preconcerted,	ikweba na whido
adj. precondition,	iche na whido, iche-whi
n. precursor, n.	prikusa, ife bibiawa na whido
predecease, vt.	pridisi, ikuowun na whido, kuowun swene ngba
predecessor, n.	lembu Y/I
(my predecessor)	ilembu mi
predestinate, adj.	kadara, kadara whido, ebi 'shiene
(it has been predestined)	a ti kadara ya
predetermine, vt.	chenu na'whido
predicament, n.	isile, nsohala Y/I
predicate, n.	predikat, irudi oka turanchi – "predicate" ichoto abi ikezin ife – "part of something"
predict, vt.	soli na whido, gbameh na whido
(predictable)	nke a le soli na whido
predigest, vt.	dachin na whido (digest)
predispose, vt.	ikizi na whido, fawhido
predominant, adj. n	jukha na lamba, jukha 'gba pre-eminent, adj, n.
pre-empt, vt.	yi na whido – "to take in advance)

pre-exist, vi.	diwa na whido, ngba kera, mindu e mutum kera	
pre-fab, n.	kata, gida katako, kpako abi gida kpako	
preface, n.	<u>imediye na whido</u> (advance explanation)	
prefect, n.	prifet, o unguwa	G(fE)/H(G.v) (school prefect)

prefit

prefer, vtn	feka, ifeka	Y/I
(preferential)	ifeka jukha	
(preferential treatment)	ilosie feka	
prefix, n.	ifinyi na; prefis	
pregnant, adj.	biki, menu	Y/H/I
(pregnancy test)	ichondi biki abi imenu, idone biki (idon-biki)	
pre-histroic, adj.	swen' itono	
(pre-historic time)	ngba swen' itono	
prejudge, vt.	dakpe na whido, mesh' iyobi swene abi nawhido	
prejudice, n.	ngba zuba, isiche whido (opinion), prejudah	
prelim, n.	irebi, preli Y/I/G(fE)	
(preliminary examination)	ichondi preli	
prelude, n.	imubia si whido, imuma, ifineri	
pre-marital, adj.	swene igbemata, swene ichogbe	
pre-mature, adj.	swene idiagba, ketu	
premeditate, vt.	igbiche na whido	
premier, adj, n.	firimiya, ifirimiya	H(fE)
premiere, n.	o konda guere, o guere na whido	
premise, n.	fremis, irudi oka n'arin ife meji	

premises, n.	yadi, fremisi	H(fE)/G(fE) premium, n.
pre-natal, adj.	swene natale	Y/I pre-occupation, n.
pre-package, adj.	swene boma, boma na whido	
preparation, n, adj, vti.	munji, imunji; kemu; ikemu	Y/I/H
prepay, vti.	kpa na whido, kpa-swene	
preponderant, adj.	priponda, ibuto iwan abi lamba	G(fE)
preposition, n.	iprepo; oka turanchi	G(fE)
preposterous, adj.	(preposta) ichoto fefefe	
pre-record, vt.	swene-rekoda	
pre-requisite, n.	e jubi abi e che ketu, prerikuisa, preri	
prerogative, n.	prerogeta, anfa katazi, anfa kpata	
presbyter, n.	presbite	
prescient, adj.	mila, ichegbon lati ma ife na whido	
prescribe, vti, n.	prisika, ijuma	G(fE)/Y/R

presence, n.

(present sir)	wa sa – (i am here/present) or. (mo wa n'eba). these are prerogative phrases in guosa	
present, n.	itenda, ngba nsiyii,	
(at the present time)	na ngba nia	
presentable, adj.	rama inyenfun nyenfu	
preservation, n, vt.	icheto, di cheto, cheto	I/Y
(preservative)	nke a le cheto, ife icheto, icheto	
preside, vi.	keisi	H/I
presidency, n.	ofis nke presido, ofis presidente	
(presidential)	nke shugaba abi presidente, nke (presido)	

371

press, n.	ipres; presa; itite, ipresa
(letter press)	ipresa wasika, ipesa – "the press", ipres
(press agent/agency)	omaye presa, wakili presa, ofis nke presa
(press box)	akwati presa
(press conference)	ikonokojo presa
(press committee)	kwamiti presa
(press centre)	ofis nke presa ncha, arin presa
(press photographer)	o foto presa
(press briefing)	isoli kuru presa, isoli kuru na presa
(press release)	ituka presa, ituja presa
(press media)	ikemkpo presa
(concord press) press, vt. (to press something)	ipresa konkad, (konkad presa)
tite, itite	I/Y
(press the bell)	tite agogo
(press button)	pim, pim-pim
pretzel, n.	preze, irudi bisikiti
prevail, vi.	bokei, gbinso, benso, dile
prevalent, adj.	dile, di dile_– (common)
prevent, vt. n.	bogha, ibogha
(prevention is better than cure)	l'o rama jukha imeson
preview, n.	privion, ineri flim na whido
previous, adj.	lembu
itole	lembu
prevision, n.	proviso, ineri na whido
prey, n.	binchina, ibinchina
price, n.	iyenu, iloi
(price it)	yenu ya

(priceless)	lai le yenu, lai wen iyenu,
prick, n.	igbowu, gbuji – (hurt)
(prick oneself)	gbowu ji, gbuji
prickle, n.	frikol, itula noba na sitem (pointed growth
pride, n.	yanga, iyanga
goes before a fall0	iyanga na whido ishuda; yanga na whido
prie-dieu, n.	pridu, irudi katako ikpredu, kujera ikpredu
priest, n.	fada, alufa H(fE)/H (priest-hood)
prima, adj.	prama, gosin mache (leading woman)
primacy, n.	pramesi, ikayoka –
"pre-eminence" prima facie, adv, adj.	prama-fashe, shaida rama n'oka iwufin
primal, adj.	prama, igesi konon – "first of important matter"
primary, adj.	rebi, zumkpa, yokei, framari I/Y/H
(primary objective)	icherondi zumkpa
(primary school)	makaranta framari
(primary stage)	ikpobi framari, ikpobi rebi
(primarily)	n' icherondi, n'izumkpa
primate, n.	pramet,m nke bishobu
prime, adj.	praim, nke gesi kha-ka (mostlyimportant
(prime minister)	praim mininsta
(prime number)	ilamba praim
(prime time)	ngba praim, ngba igesi
primer, n.	igbum abi baum kele, ikpiti
primeval, adj.	pramiva, nke ngba kera-kera (earliest)

priming, n.	pini-pini, hoda bindiga – "gun powder" pini, irudi iwakpo fenti	
primitive, adj.	digue, kera	Ed
(primitive man)	miji digue, miji kera	
(primitive person)	mutum digue, mondigue, monkera, o digue	
primrose, n.	priors, irudi fulawa	
prince, n.	yarima, omo baize miji	H/Y/Gen/I
princess, n.	gimbiya, omo baize mache	
principal, adj.	prensipa, nke makaranta, baba, katazi	
(principal market)	baba kasuwa	
(principal business)	irushe katazi	
(school principal)	prensipa makaranta	
principle, n.	ibietu	
(you are a principled person)e wu mutum ibietu		
print, n, vti. itite, tite,		I/Y
(print me some copies) tite kapi e so fun mi		
(printing press) presa itite, ipresa		
(printer) o tite, prenta		
(printing machine) mashin itite		
prior, adj. swene		Y/I
(prior to the time) swene ngba		
priority, n. iwhido jukha, kiari		Y/H/I
(give it your priority fun ya atansha attention) iwhido jukha e		
prism, n.	pris, irudi isiffa jiomitri (geometrical figure)	
prison, n.	prusu, kurkuku	Tiv/H
(prison yard)	yardi prusu	
(prisoner)	o prusu	
privacy, n.	imbizu, ibizu	Y/I
private, adj.	mbizu: bizu	

(private room)	deki mbizu	
(private car)	mota zoom-zoom 'bizu	
(private doctor)	likita mbizu	
(private wife)	mata mbizu	
(private husband)	magida (megida) mbizu	
(private property)	dukiya mbizu	
privet, n.	praifet, irudi shukeshuke e so	
privilege, n.	danfa, enfa	Y/Y(G.v)
(privilege is not a right)	enfa ko wu yera	
privy, adj.n.	tiki, itiki	
prize, n.	irire	Y/Sob/Ed/Ish/etc
pro-chancellor	pro-kansilo	
pro and con, adv.	fun ati doko	
probability, n.	ibowu	Y/I
probable, adj.	bowu, le fata, fata	
probate, n.	probit, nke iwufin	G(fE)
t(probate registry)	rejistri probit	
probation, n.	iwone, iwoun	
probe, n.	iwoun,iwone	
probity, n.	imiwa year (right character)	
problem, n.	nshohala, wahela, nsogbu	I/Gen
proboscis, n.	probosi, nke giwa	Y/H/I
procedure, n.	ilashe	Y/H/I
proceed, vt, n.	ifre, ikufo, shienga si, shiene si	
(proceeds) n.	ifre, ikufo, e fre, e kufo	
(proceed to)	ringa si, shienga si, shiene si	
proceeding, n.	hanya ishiene, irushe	
(meeting proceeding)	irushe mitin	
proceess, n.	ilahan, hanya a ng meshe ife	
process, vi.	tole, ringa; meshe	
(rapid procession)	isole sokia	

procession, n.	isole	
proclaim, vt, n.	kemkpo, ikemkpo	Y/I
proconsul, n.	prokansol, gomina kasa rom	G(fE)
procrastinate, vt, n.	gbu ngba, igbu ngba	I/Gen/Y
(procrastination is the thief of time)	igbu ngba ngba wu irawo ngba	
procreate, vt.	wolo, imubi (born)	G
proctor, n. G(fE)	prota, na yunifasiti aksfod abi kembrij, irudi hafsa o wen ifambu irushe	
procurator, n.	wakili 'wufin	H/T/Gwa/Id/I/Y
procure, vt, n.	weri, iweri	I/Y
prodigal, adj.	gra-gra	Gen
(prodigal child)	mongra-gra (prodigal	
daughter)	omon mache gra-gra	
(prodigal son)	omon miji gra-gra	
prodigious, adj.	butolo	I/Y
prodigy, n.	iya-li-onu (iyalionu)	
produce, vti, n.	gbebia, igbebia	Y/I (farm produce)
(producer)	o gbebia	
(products)	e gbebia, igbebia	
(productive), adj.	di gbebia, gbebibia	
(productivity), n.	igbebibia	
profane, adj.	fago	G/Y
profess, vti, n.	kemkpokpo ikemkpokpo, kwede	Y/I
profession, n	irushiwin, irushe hannu	
(professional football)	irushiwin fubol, irushiwin bolu kafa	
professor, n.	profeso, o rushiwin, profeso, irudi digiri na yunifasiti	

proffer, vt.	yere – "offer", choche – "prefer"	
proficient, adj.	miwin, nke ichegbon kwata-kwata	
profile, n.	profile, ineri n'akue	G(fE)
profit, n.	irire	Y(Sob/Ed/Ish/etc.
(profit margin)	iyefe irire	
profitable, adj.	nke le mubia irire, di 'rire, ririre	
(profitable venture)	iyengi 'rire	
profiteer, vt.	meshe ibuto irire	
proforma, n.	profoma	G(fLat)
(proforma invoice)	envois, profoma	
profound, adj.	jindi, kondi	Y/H
(profound gratitude0	idiokpe kondi	
profuse, adj.	ribo, kproi jukha (very plentiful)	I/Y
(profuse gratitude)	idiokpe ribo	
prog, n.	kasi – "to place on charge" progenitive,	
adj.	rinbia, bibiawa lati ngba kera abi kaka	
progenitor, n.	o kaka	
progeny, n.	nke ikologua (descendant)	
prognosis, n.	isoli na whido, hun na whido, isoli swene	
programme, n.	iliteto	H/Y
(direkta iliteto(programme(s) officer)	hafsa iliteto	
progress, n.	ishiene whido, ishien si whido, iringa whido	
prohibit, vt.	gbuiche a gbuche irinfoh	
project, n.	proja, nke filan, irushe	

project, vt.	mubia, nno hann, chowa hanya fun	
projectile, n.	projeta, nke flim	
(projection)	ifilan, iproja, irushe	
(building project)	iproja ikogi gida, irushe ikogi gida	
(projector)	ife irushe flim, projeta, o filan	
proliferate, vit, n.	mubirisi, imubirisi	I/Y
prolix, adj.	prole igungolo oka abi 'soli	
prologue, n.	entrodt, imuswene	G(fE)/Y/I
prolong, vt.	faogo, faoglo, gungo, gungolo, golo	
(do't prolong matters)	ma faogo oka	
promenade, n.	prominad, ebi bika pak abi ajiya	
prominent, adj.	risikha	I/Y
(prominence) n.	irisikha	
promiscuous, adj.	ruambu	Y/I
promise, n, vti.	ikwade, ikweba, kwade, kweba	
promontory, n.	promonte, irudi kasa, isi kasa	
promote, vti, n.	buleke, ibuleke, isigkie whido	
(congratulation on your promotin)	e kuibukun na ibuleke, e ku ibuleke	
prompt, adj.	yaji, fata	
(prompt action)	Imeshe yaji, akshon yaji	
(prompt box)	prom-bos, kujera bosah	
promulgate, vti, n.	tonka, itonka, kemkpo, ikemkpo	
prone, adj.	fayen	
pronominal, adj.	pronao, oka turanchi	
pronoun	poronao	

pronounce, vti, n.	ikwoka
pronunciamento, n.	pronasimento,
proof, n.	manifesa gonment ishaida, ichebo,
(water-proof) (as a proof)	ezioka, ifineri ichebo ruwa n'ishaida
(proof read) prop, n.	kua ya fun ezioka, kua ezioka <u>itizu</u> (support)
propaganda, n, vti.	ipropagandus, propagandus G(fE)
propane, n.	profen, irudi gaz
propel, vt.	tikpu, (kpuswhido kpuswhido)
(propeller)	profela, o tigbu, o tiswhido
(propelling)	iprofela, itiswhido
(propelation)	titiswhido, itisigkie
propensity, n.	itenda, o fasi, o fayen, propenseta
proper, adj.	ditto, katazi
(do it properly)	meshe ya katazi
(it is proper)	o ditto
property, n.	dukiya
prophecy, n.	imumaso; isoli na whido, isoli swene
(prophesy), vti.	mumaso; soli na whido, soli swene
(prophet), n.	o mumaso; annabi, woli H/Y
prophylactic, n, adj.	profilate, irudi magani o dinhanya
propitiate, vt.	menso, meshe ife k'o dunso, mera
proportion, n, adj.	kekpini, isigkiekie, di sigkiekie Kal/Ishan
proposal, n.	iyesi, igbiche (propozu) Y(G.v)/fE
(propose)	yesi
(man proposes, god disposes)	mutum ng yesi, abasi ng mede
(proposal and disposal)	iyesi, abi igbiche ati imede

(proposition)	iloro (suggestion), iyesi, igbiche	
profound, vt.	faswido – "push forward"	
proprietor, n.	o weni	I/Y
propulsion, n.	propusi, agba injin	G(fE)
pro-rata, adv,	pro-rita, n'ikekpini – "sharing"	
(lat) (pro-rata	ihutu pro-rita, ismini pro-rita	
leave) prorogue,	proro, isimini majalisa lai rude ikweba	
vt. proscenium,	proscenia, ikpaka iguere denma (drama)	
n. proscribe,	kposo, ikposo	G
vt, n. prose,	prosi, irudi ede 'so	
n. prosecute,	lebutu, ilebutu	G
vt. proselyte,	prosilat, irudi o nikon	
n. prosody, n.	proshodi, irudi sayens nke mita (metre)	
prospect, n.	irekoni, irentini	Y/H
(rospective)	rekoni, rentini	
(prospective candidate)	kandide o rekoni, kandide o rentini	
(prospective applicant)	plikante o rekoni, plikante o renti	
prospectus, n.	proskechi	G
prosper, vit, n.	mire, imire	I/Y/Sob
(prosperous)	di mire, mimire	
(prosperous new year)	ardun huntun imire	
(i wish you happy christmas and a prosperous new year)	mo shien e igbandu keresimesi ati ardun huntun imire	
prostate, n.	postit, irudi kaluluwa na nama miji	
prostitute, n.	karuwa, (ashawo), o fikifiki	H/Y/G

(prostitution)	ikaruwa, ifikifiki; o rinjele	
prostrate, adj, n.	doba na kasa, (do kasa) idoba na kasa	
protagonist, n.	protagona, mutum katazi na oka	
protean, proteus	protine, o yintua kiri bika protius – baba ekwenshu tekun na kasa grik	
protect, vt, n.	chebo, ichebo	
(protector)	o chebo	
(protect me)	chebo mi	
protectorate, n.	ichebo, ichebo kasa, irudi gonmenti	
(north and south prot.)	ichebo kasa not ati saot	
protein, n.	pruten; irudi miriala na jiki	G(fE)
(protein food)	abinchi protin	
protempore, adv. (lat)	protim, protimpo, ki o	G(fL)
protest, n.	teonu, ikemkporo, ikido	Y/I
(protestant)	o kido, o kemkporo	
(protestant church)	chochi 'kemkporo – chochi protestan	
protocol, n.	prutokol, ilahanya bietu a ng meshe ife	
proton, n.	purupuru, jinejine igbum – bomb particle	
protoplasm, n.	prutoflazim, irudi ruwa bika jali8 o bue mindu	
prototype, n.	prutotapu, nke ifineri – "of example"	
protozoa, n.	prutozah, nke balabala	
protract, vt.	gungo, fago, golo, gungolo	Y/I
(protracted debate)	isharoka gungolo, isharoka golo	
(protracted illness)	isono golo	
protrude, vit, n.	gbugu, igbugu	G

protuberant, adj.	gbugu-gbugu, kuku – "swell"	G
proud, adj.	yanga, gabu, igabugabu, gabu-gbau	Gen
(a proud man)	miji yanga, miji gabu-gabu	
(proud person)	o yanga, o gabu, o gabu-gabu, mutum gabu-gabu	
prove, vti.	rindi, hundi, chonci, chowa	

(prove me right or wrong)
chowa mi zioka abi zioshi

provender, n.	prufenda, abinchi doki	G(fE)
proverb, n.	okatun	I/Ik/Ed
provide, vit.	kpenyen, kpenno,	Y/I/Ef./H
(provide me, please)	kpenyen mi, biko,	
(provide him/her)	kpennon ya, biko	
(provider)	o kpenno; o kpenyen	
(provided, conj.)		
(provided you agree)		
sokwele	sokwele, e kweba	
(providence)	ikpeyen si whido	
(the providence of god)	ikpeyen abasi, ikpenno abasi, ikabandu abasi	
province, n.	lardi	
(provincial)	nke lardi, gonmenti lardi	
provision, n.	ikpeyen, ikpeyen fun, kabandu	
psychich, n.	o bubu, mutum o wen agba ibilis	
psychic, adj.	fisiki, nke mindu abi iyobi	
(good psychic)	fisiki rama	
(psychich), adj.	fisiki, nke isokali akpor (of natural phenomena)	
psychoanalysis, n.	saikonana, irudi 'kule ifewe	

psychology, n.   saikolo, saiko, sayens imuko iyobi mutum

(psychological)   nke saikolo, saiko, di saikolo, ife saiko psychopath, n.
saikofa, irudi irun nke iyisi tuki (emotional off-set)

psychosis, n.   saikoko, irun ifewe abi iyisi
psychotherapy, n.   saikotera, imeson ifewe
ptarmigan, n.   tamingan, irudi onene o wen ifambu launi

pterodactyl   terodati, o foleh nama reftai
ptomaine, n.   tomani, irudi puezin
puberty, n.   puba, idiagba mutum
pubic, adj.   ubi, nke puba
public, adj.   pobli, gbobe, gbonso   G(fE)/Y/I
(public address system)   mekrofofo pobli, mekrofofo ikemkpo

(public corporation)   kamfani pobli
(public relations officer)   hafsa o nojo pobli, hafsa pobli

(public facilities)   imeron pobli
(public spirited)   inube pobli, o nube pobli
(public spirited person)   mutum o nube pobli
(public transport)   ugboko pobli, ugboko mutum ncha

pulican, n.   poblike, o pobli, o cheto gida pobli

publication, n.   ikemkpotu, itemkpo
(i want to publish a   temkp littafi
book) mo che i

(publisher)   o temkpo
publicist, n.   o kodemkpo   Y/I
publicity, n.   ikemkpotu
(publize it)   kemkpotu ya

(publicity agent)	wakili 'kekpotu (wakili 'kemkpo)	
(publish)	temkpo, kemkpo	
pucker, vti.	kwajo – "to gather together	I/Y
puddle, n.	<u>koto kele</u> (small pond)	Y/I
pudding, n.	podin, irudi abinchi e so	
pudenda, n.	kpobo, nke botu	I/Y pudgy, adj.
pueblo, n.	pubolo, irudi gida na Amerika	
puerile, adj.	ijubi omontakele – childish question	
puerperal, adj.	purepura, irudi iba ke ngba imubi – "a type of fever from birth"	
puff, n.	uff, irudi lowe lati onu, ilowe irengu	
puffin, n.	kpufin, onene tekun nke not atlante	
pug, n.	pogi, irudi kare bature	
pukka, pucka,	kamkpe, katazi	
pull, n, vt.	fa, ifa; kpo; ikpo	Y/G
(puller)	o fa	
(pull out)	fa ta	
(pull in)	fa menu	
(puul over) (pull through)	feja	
(pull off)	fa pu	
pullet, n.	sagara, kaza kele	H
pulley, n.	kura, o fa ife	H
Pullman, n.	Pulimah, reluwe o wen kujera kule	
pull-over, n.	pulofa, irudi esa	
pululate, vi.	kpoka sokia (to multiply rapidly)	
pulmonary, adj.	pulmenari, nke huhu (lungs)	

pulp, n.	popu	G(fE)
pulpit, n.	pupit, katako ti o wazi ng kundu sin a chochi	
pulque, n.	pulku, irudi nono nke kasa megziko	
pulsar, n.	pusa, irudi tara (star)	
pulsate, vti.	pulsat, ikpala (vibration)	
pulse, vti.	polsi, iluti nke ibeya na zuchiya (beating of the artries in the heart)	
pulverize, vti.	lo si hoda – "grind into powder"	
puma, n.	kpuma irudi ibuto nama na kasa amerika	
pump, n.	famf, famfo H(fE) (pump it) famfo ya	
(pumping maching)	injin famfo	
pumper-nickel, n.	pumpanike, irudi buredi	
pumpkin, n.	kabewa, (ugwu) – synonym	H/I
(pumpkin leaves)	ganye kabewa, ugwu	
punch, n.	panch, mashin a ng fi meshe hone si takarda	
punch, n.	fanch, irudi wain	
punch, vti.	luti, tigba	Y/I
(puncher)	o luti, o tigba	
punctual, adj,	koge, ikoge	Y/I
n. punctuate,	mishe, imishe	
vt. puncture,	pancha, fule, fulele	G(fE)/G
n. pundit, n.	pandi, o muko rama hindu	
pungent, adj.	kanmu-kanmu – "smell and stinging, biting	
punish, vt.	riya, afun, jeafun; wuaya	Ed/J
(punishment), n	iriya, ijeafun, iwuiya	
(punishable)	nke a le riya si, di riya, di	
punka, punkah, n.	afun punkeke, irudi esa na	

punnet, n.	india point, irudi kwando kele	G(fE)
punt, n.	ponti, irudi abara	
punt, vt.	putu, nke fubol	
puny, adj.	huene, ai wen mindu, irengu	G
pupil, n.	almajiri, omo makaranta, pupile	
puppet, n.	'yar tsana	H
puppy, n.	popi, kare kele	G(fE)
purchase, n.	rata, irata	Y/I
(hire purchase)	irata na haya	
(purchasing officer)	hafsa irata	
purdah, n.	kpudah, pudah, irudi labule (curtain)	
pure, adj.	shaka, di shaka	
(pure in heart)	ishaka n'iyobi, shaka n'iyobi	
(blessed are the pure in heart)	ikunzi fun o shaka n'yobi	
puree, n.	piori, irudi miya	G(fE)
purgative, n, adj.	ikpokpon; kpokpohG	
purgatory, n.	pogatri, pogatiri	G(fE)
purge, vt.	kpokpo	G
purify, purity, vt, n.	me di shaka, meshed i shaka, ishaka-shaka, ishaka	
purist, n.	akawu-kawu, o feza si iluwe oka turanchi	
purple, n.	shunayya	H
purport, n.	ichero	I/Y
purpose, n.	ichendi	I/Y
(what is the purpose)?	meni wu ichendi ya?	
purse, n.	alabe	H
purser, n.	kposah, hafsa na ugboko ruwa	
pursuance, n, vt.	ileche, leche, irekon	Y/I

pus, n.	yum	G
push, n, vti.	ikpu, kpu	
(push out)	kpu 'ta	
(push in)	kpu si menu, kpu menu	
(push forward)	kpu si whido	
(push backward)	kpu si zuba, kpu zuba	
(push aside)	kpu si akue	
(push off)	kpu shuda, kpu fre, kpu peh	
(push along)	kpu nasi	
(push up)	kpu nuke	
(poush about)	kpu kiri	
puss, n.	pus, afa muzuru (pusi-kat)	
put, vit,	finyen, fie, ton, meshe, medi, yiwo	Y/I
(put on)	fie na, fiyen na	
(put it there)	fie ya si ebe	
(put on the light)	tonwu wuta	
(put things right)	medi 'fe rama, meshe ife k'odi rama	
(i put all my hopes on you)	mo fie irekon mi fefe si yin	
(put away)	fie ta	
(put it back)	fie ya zuba, fie zuba	
(put it down)	fie/fiyen risi fie/	
(put more)	fiyen risi	
(put it in the right place)	fie ya si ebi yera	
(put on)	fie na, yiwo	
(put on your dress)	yiwo esa e	

(don't put me in trouble)   ma fie mi sin a nsohala
(put together)   fie jutu, fie konojo
(what god has put together) ka eni mutum ma yobe
(let no one put asunder)   if abasi ti konojo

putrid, putrefy, vti, adj.	bambi	Y/I
puttee, n.	pute, irudi bandeji	G(fE)
putty, n.	anda, shafiya, rati	H

puzzle, n.	ikpozoh, isile ijubi (diffucult question); also	
(put off)	ikawu; fie zuba	
pigmy, n.	ikuru-kere, mutum t'o kuru kha	Y(g.v) (the pigmies of congo)
pygamas, n.	finjama	G(fE)
pyorhoea, n.	firora, irudi irun nke gindi hakori (teeth gum)	
pyorhoea, n.	firora, irudi irun nke gindi hakori (teeth gum)	
pyramid, n.	ogege, ogegetelege	Ed
(ground nut pyramid)	ogege gyada	Ed/H pyrites, n.
python, n.	mesa, (machiji)	
pyx, pix, n.	fuks, irudi ijongo nke buredi sonmo na chochi	

q

q	kiyu	Gen/G
(quack doctor)	adigboloja, wayo, yayaya	I/Gen/G
quadrangle, n.	kwadongo, isiffa o wen akue inang (figure)	
quadragesima, n.	ikonda surabde ba kebt, kwada jisima	G(fE)
quadrilateral, adj.	kwadrila, isiffa o wen akue inang na jiomitri	
quadrillion, n.	kwadrillian	G(fE)
quadruped, n.	kwai-kwai, nama o wen kafa inang bika doki, kare, akunya baate-baate	
quadrupie, adj.	kwaduinang, o wen kafa inanng bika doki, kare, akunya baate-baate	
quadruple, adj.	kwaduinarg, o wen ikpaka inang	G/Ef.
quadruplets, n.	kwadunang, imbi e mon inang	G/Ef
quadruplicate, adj.	kwaduninang, nke rgba inang	G(fE)/Ef.
quagga, n.	kwaga, irudi onene na saot afrika	
quagmire, n.	kagamya, irudi kasa ruwa-ruwa	
quail, n. quail, vi.	karaya, irudi onene ke le	G(fE/H
quanit, adj.	yedu, o fata ikuakua mani kpe o ti digbo	
quake, vi.	gbuduh	G
(earth quake)	igbuduh kasa	G/H
quaker, n.	kwueka, itugbe e so na kasa faransi	

qualification, n.	ikwashe, takaashe, kwalifikeshan, kwalifikeson	G(E)/Gen/H
qualify, vti., n.	kwashe, ikwashe	G(fE)/Y/I/Gen
(what qualified you)	meni kwashe e?	
(i am fully qualified)	mo kwashe rama	
(you ae not fully qualified)	e kwashe rama	
quality, n.	idiashe, imeye, iminiwa, miniwa	
(good quality)	miniwa rama, iminiwa rama	
qualm, n.	kwam, nsohala, nsogbu	G(fE)
quandary, n.	iyalionu (iya.li.onu)	
quantitative, adj.	yewan	Y/Ed.
quantity, n.	iyewan	
(quantity surveyor)	o fika iyewan	
quantum, n.	kwatu, iyole nke a che (amount)	
quarantine, n.	kwaratine, ngba ichoto (separation)	
quarantine, n.	kwaratine, ngba ichoto (separation)	
quarrel, n.	igoni	
quart, n.	kwat, inofi – "measurement"	
quarter, n. kwata,	kwinang, mbigbe, gida	G/Ef/i/y
(quarter past two)	kwata feja agogo meji	
(quarter to two)	agogo kwata si meji (kwata si meji make in quarter meshe na kwinang	
(government quarter)	meshe na kwinang	
(government quarters)	mbigbe nke gonmenti, gida gonmenti	
(quarter-master general)	kwata masta janar, baba hafsa soja, o cheto sito (store)	

queue, n. vt.	itolain, tolain	Y/G(fE)
quick, adj.	sokia, sam-sam, hoyah, kia-kia	
(quick business)	irushe sam-sam, irushe kia-kia	
(quick tempered)	ibilionu kia-kia, ibilionu sam-sam	
quicken, vti.	medi sokia, meshe sokia, sokia	
(quickner)	o sokia	
quicksand, n.	kwikwan, irudi kasa fadama (swamp)	
quicksilver, n.	kwisiliva, irudi makiuri	
quid, n.	kwidi, irudi taba wiwuam	
quid, n.	kpaun nke briten	
quiet, adj.	dankiti, chankiti	Y/I
(keep quiet my friend)	dankiti aboki aboki dankiti; tikpo 'nu	
(quietness),	idankiti, ichankiti	
quietist)	o sole isinle kwayetizim	
quill, n.	kaya, alkalami gashintsu, nke ngba kera, alkalami	
quince, n.	kwis, irudi itache	
qincentenary, n, adj.	kwisentiri, iseliba G(fE) adun gogo iben	
quinine	kwini, irudi magani nke iba	
quinquagesima, n.	kwindajisi, sirande swene Lent, kwinkwakwa	
quinsy, n.	kwisi, ijowu wuya (inflammation of the throat	
quintal, n.	kwita, irudi inofi – "type of measurement"	
quintessence, n.	kwinekwine, ifineri shaka – perfect pattern	

quintet, n.	kwinteti, nke songi abi isonga
quintuplet, n.	kwaduisen, kwaisen, kwisen
(a woman gave birth to) q.	mache mubi e mon kwisen
quire, n.	kwaya, takada lamba jinang (24)
quit, vti.	lofeh, kopu G/Y/I
(quit notice)	wasika ilofeh
quite, adv.	kwata-kwata, saun, fefefe, kamkpe
(it is quite nice)	o di sei saun, o di kamkpe
quiver, n.	kwifa G(fE)
quiver, vti.	rugu, kpala – "vibrate"
quivive, n, vt.	ibo, bo – a"alert"
quiz, vt.	jubi – ask
(quiz master)	magida ijubi, oga ijubi
(quizer)	o jubi
quioin, n.	kwon, nke iyego irushe biriki – "of angular brick work"
quondam, adj.	lembu, lembubu
quonset, n.	kwonsit, irudi gida bagiri (hut house)
quorum, n.	kwora, nke mitinabi kwaminti
quota, n.	kota, nke ikekpin G(fE)
(quota system)	ilanyar kota
quotation, n.	ikonosi, inosoli
quote	konosi, nosoli; kwot
quotidian, adj.	kwotiti, irudi iba t'o biawa rana ncha
quotient, n.	kwotin, nke ilamba

R

Rabbi, n.	Rabai, o muko nke mutum Jiu	
rabbit, n.	wata dabba, rabitele	H/G
Rabble, n.	E tugbe izighi-zagha	
Rabid, adj.	Ifeweh	G/Y
Rabies, n.	Irun nke t'o ng fata ifeweh, irunfewe	
Race, n.	Igbere, iroso	
(race course)	Kasa iroso, igbere kasa, (leskuash)	
Race, n.	Igbetu,	
(racial regime)	Rejima igbetu, gonmenti 'gbetu	
Raceme, n.		
Rack, n.		
Racket, n.	Gragra	Gen.
Racket, racquet, n.	Rasim, irudi fulawa	
Raga	Ladiko, nke sayens ibalabala Rediyo, wayalis, iziworo, Kilikili	
Baba arimkpo	Iziron rediyo, iziron 'ziworo	
Rakit, sandal an	H	
Radar, n.	Ichaun 'ziworo, chaunchaun iziworo	
Radial, n.	firi rediyo, ifiri-firi 'ziworo	
Radiant, adj.	Inojo rediyo, inojo iziworo, inojo wayalis	
Radiate, vti.		

Radiation, n.

Radiator, n.   tanis abi babintin
Zogolo, leda

Leida, nke wili

Tonshan, tonshaka

Shaun, shaika

Ronshaka

Lagireta, nke mota; o ronshaka	G/G(fE) G(fE)	Y/G
(radio link)	Hanya iziron, hanya rediyo, hanya iziworo	
(radio-active)	Rediyo nkiti, iziworo kiti	
(radiography)	Foto iziworo, rediyografe	
(radiographer)	O foto iziworo, o rediyografe	
(radioisotope)	Rediyosofo, ife magani	
(radiogram)	Rediyogram, gramaho	
radish, n.	ladish, ireudi shukeshuke abinchi saladi	
radium, n.	lediom, irudi magani irun kinekine (cancer)	
radius, n.	ledius, nke laini	
raffia, n.	lafia, irudi faiba G(fE)	
raffle, n.	rehul, rafol H(fE)/G(fE) (raffle ticket) tikiti irafol ftito (ferry), raft	
rafter, n.	rafta, nke rufi gida	
rag, n.	raga, tsumma H	

(rag-bag)	ikpa raga, ikpa tsumma Tiv/H (rag-day) rana tsumma, rana raga, nke e mon makarant
(rags) pl. n.	e tsumma, (e raga) H/ (G.v) rage, n. liwuta; ibionu wuta
raglan, n.	ragilani, irudi suwaita
ragtime, n.	rataim, irudi song ati 'samba n'ngba kera
raid, n.vt.	gbele, leche, igbele, ileche
raid, n.	reli, irudi ayan golo
(railroad, railway)	hanya reli, reluwe, hanya ugboko lokoj a
(hand rail)	hangoda H(G.v)
(railing)	golo ayan
(raise it up)	gbeson ya si nuke, gbeson nuke
(raise the voice)	gbeson iluvi ya
raisin, n.	resin, irudi lemon abi inabi
rajah, n.	raja, rajah, nke kasa india
rake, n.	manjagara, 'jagara H/H(G.v)
(rake it up)	jagara ya
rake, vit.	reki, nke ugboko ruwa
rallentando, n. adj.	ralintendo, nke ilowe isonga
rally, vti.	kokiri, konosi, nno agba
(rally round)	kokiri nso, kokirikiri, konosi
rally, n (of sports)	rale, nke erenji
ram, n.	rago H
ramadan, n.	ramadan, nke musulmi
(ramadan fasting)	awe ramadan
ramify, vit	mkpori, meshe k'o kpori na nso

(ramification)	imkpori	
ramp, n.	rampe, ramf	G(fE)
rampage, vi.	rosokiri, irosokiri	Y/I
(the students have gone on rampage)	e mon makaranta ng rosokiri	
rampart, n.	ganuwa	H
ramrod, n.	rago, sanda bindiga H	
ramshackle, adj.	wiwosika, wo si kasa	
ranch, n.	ransh G(fE)	
(cattle ranch)	ranshanu	G/H
rancid, adj.	zizi – "of smell"	I/G
rancour, n.	irokin I/H	
rand, n.	rando, kudi nke	
random, n.	kasa saot afrika ifreche, eni ngba, lai chero sweh	
(random talks)	oka eni ngba, oka ifreche,	
ranee, rani, n.	ranin, nke hindu, sarauniya nke hindu	
range, n.	ibafi, iyefe, ebi, mbi	
(shooting range)	iyefe igbata	
(within the range)	n'arin abi na nso iyefe	
ranger, n.	renja, irudi gadi daji	G(fE)
rank, n.	ikpetu	Y/I
ranker, n.	ranka, nke ikpetu soja	
rankle, vi. n.	ifuta shim-shim – "continuous pain"	
ransack, vt.	chowa kiri	
ransom, n.	ikpamini	Agbo/Y
rant, vit.	oka shakara, shakara	
rape, vt.	jimu na agba, jigba	I/Y
(sexual rape)	imika vudu, vudu imeshika, vudu imika	
rapid, adj.	yaji, sokia, kia-kia	
(rapid development)	igadi kia-kia	

rapier, n.	refia, irudi wuka, irudi takobi (sword)	
rapport, n.	rapote, irudi 'koso (type of relationship)	
rapproachement, n.	rapoche, itunrudo (re-union)	
rapt, adj.	chiro kha-ka, chiroka	
rapture, n.	isayo (joy)	I/Y
rare, adj.	kene-kene, shienpeh, ai kpori, frekpori, ai hun n'ngba	
(it is very rare)	ko kpori, o frekpori jukha	
(rare bird)	ishienpeh onene	
rascal, n.	nison, inison; iyakulu kembe	Y(G.v)
(rascal boy)	yaro inison	
stop rascality	du iyakulu kembe	
rash, n.	kro-kro, irun jiki (kro-kro)	Gen
rash, adj.	gra-gra, ai jiki ba kasa	
rasp, n.	zarto, irudi ayan	H
raspberry, n.	rasbiri, irudi kurmi kele	G
rat, n.	baba bera, be	H
ratchet, n.	rachit, nke wili	G
rate, n, vti.	idiye, diye, inofi	I/Y
rather, adv.	kuku	Y/Gen
ratify, vt. n.	tenu, itenu – "confirm"	Y/I
rating, n.	zogara, retin, nke nefi	G/G(fE)
ratio, n.	lesho, inure ife si nk'eji	
ration, n.	lashon, abinchi iseza	G(fE)
rational, adj.	cherondi	I/Y/H
rationale, n.	icherondi, irondi gesi (important)	
rationalize, vt.	bekuru, meshe ikonoma, konoma	

ratlin, ratline, n.	kuranga igiya, lada igiya, lada jekobu	
rattan, rattan, n.	ratanta, irudi kologua faiba – "a type of fibre stem" for making basket	
rattle, vti.	kpram-kpram, kpohkpoh, irudi ilowe kiakia, irudi arimkpo	
ravage, vti.	meje, runje "destroy or damage)	
(skin damage)	irunje fata, irunje jiki	
rave, vi.	fewe kiri, soli kiri	Y/I
raver, n.	o fewe kiri, o soli kiri,	
raven, n.	o soli kha-kha ololo, irudi baki onene – "black bird"	
ravening, adj.	giri, gbowu (fierce)	
ravenous, adj.	iguebi kha-ka	
ravine, n.	kwazazzabo, ijinka kwari_(a deep valley)	H
ravish, vt.	zeri, jukun fun igbandu	
raw, adj.	yolo, noho, ai se, lai se	G/I/H/Gen
(raw egg)	kwai yolo	
(raw-material)	kpanti yolo, kaya yolo	
ray, n.	ichaun, chaun	G
(ray of light)	ichaun wuta/wuta chaun	
(ray of hope)	irenti chaun	
(x-ray)	ichanwuta, estri	
ray, n.	lei, irudi baba kifi	
rayon, n.	reyon, irudi siliki	
raze, rase, vt.	merubisi, meru, runje	I/Y
razor, n.	resa	H(fE)
(razor blade)	resa biledi	
(razor blade)	resa biledi	
re – (prep)	na (in)	I

398

re – n.	rhi, na imuko isongi	
re -	tun	Y
(repeat)	tunrebi, tunbre, (repite)	
reach, vti.	rue	Y/ I
react, vi, n.	meshezu, shezu, ishezu	
reactor, n.	o shezu, o meshezu	
read, vti.	Gua	I/Y
(reader), n.	o gua	
readdress, vt.	tun kode adiresi, yintua adiresi	
reading, n.	igua	
(reading glasses)	tabarau	H
(reading lamp)	wuta tebur	
(reading room)	deki 'gua, igua daki	
readjust, vt. n.	tun metun, itun metun	Y/I
ready, adj.	yaji, hoya, nyah	H/I/Y/Gen.
reaffirm, vt.	tun kimo	
rafforest, vt.	tun gbinso	Y/I
reagent, n.	rijant, irudi kamika	G(fE)
real, adj.	katazi, zioka, kha-ka	I/Ikwere/Y
(real estate)	estiti katazi	
(i am really sorry)	mo kpendo kha-ka	
(so sorry)	kpendu jukha	
realism, n.	n'ezioka	
reality, n.	izioka, ikatazi	
realize, vt.	goye	I/Y
realm, n.	kindon, rijan (kingdom, region)	
realtor, n.	o katazi	
ream, n.	rim, nke inofi takarda	
reap, vti. n.	kire, ikire	
(reaper)	o kire	
reappear, vi. n.	tun puja, itun puja	I/Y
reappraisal, n.	tun diye, (tun di),	Y/I

rear, n.	izuein (behind)	I/Y
(rear light)	wuta izuein, wuta zuein	
rear, vti.	biki, yota	
(rear up urgly head)	biki isi joburu, yopu/ yota isi joburu	
rearm, vti.	tun kama, tun makami	
reason, n. vit.	irondi, ezioka, rondi	I/Y/Ed/Is/H
reasonable, adj.	di rondi, di rama, di sei (fair)	
reassure, vt, n.	tun yobe, itun yobe	
rebate, n.	iweku, diskante	I/Y/G
rebel, n, vi.	ribel; itawaye, tawaye, ribela	H/G(fE)
rebellious, adj.	o tawaye, o ribela	
rebind, vt.	tun kedi	Y/I
rebirth, n.	rebate, tun mubi	G(fE)/Y/I reborn, adj.
rebound, vi.	tun foga, yintua, dazu	
rebuff, n.	izuka; idazunjo	
rebuild, vt.	tun kogi	Y/H
(i'll rebuild it in 3 days)	ma tun kogi ya na rana eta	
rebuke, vt.	tun solisi, tunkasi	Y/Ikwere/I
rebus, n.	rebas, irudi oka turanchi	
recalcitrant, adj.	ai gbonti, gbisi	
recall, vt.	tun kono, (tun ko), tun kpeko	
recant, vt. i.	reikante, gbu inikon	
recapitulate, vti.	rikatula, tun meshe	
recapture, vt.	tun mugba	Y/I
recast, vt.	tun nese, tun kaste	Y/I/G
recede, vi.	fazu	Y/I
receipt, n.	lisit, lisit, iyi	G(fE)/Egun
receive, vti.	wenri, yini	I/Y/Egun (receivable)
receiver, n.	o wenri, o yini	
recent, adj.	gensin	I/Y
receptacle, n.	igile	H/Y

reception, n.	iyini, lisepshan	Y/Egun/G recess, n. vt.
recessional, n.	irisesa, irudi 'songimo (hymn)	
recipe, n.	iresi, ijuma (direction)	
recipient, n.	o yini	
reciprocal, adj, n.	shezu, shezuba, ishezu, ishezuba	
recital, n. vt.	konisi, ikonisi, konogua	
recite, vti.	konogua	I/Y
reckless, adj.	woroh, woroh-woroh	Y/Y
(recklessness)	iworoh, iworoh-woroh	
reckon, vti.	gbashi, kao	I/Y
(ready reckoner)	redi-rekona, irudi o gbashi littafi	
(reckoner)	o gbashi	
reclaim, vt.	tun yite	Y/Egun/I
reclime, vit.	simijiki	Y/H
recluse, n.	renkubu, irenkubu, o bie sonsho	G
recognistion, n.	iloron, ima	I/Y/Owo etc
(in recognition)	n'iloron	
(do you recognize this man?)	shekwa e ma miji yi?, e ma miji yi?	
(yes i recognize him)	baate, mo ma ya	
recoil, vt.	shienzu	
recollect, vti. n.	cheron, loron, icheron	I/Y
recommend, vt.	suere, shinre, shienerere	
(i recommend him to you)	mo shienerere ya fun e	
(recommendation)	ishienerere ya fun e	
recompense, vt.	kpazu, kpazuba, kpazuein	Agbo/I/Y/H
reconcile, vt, n.	lagha, ilagha, laghagun, ilaghagun	
recondition, vt.	tun kpongba, tun meshe	
reconnaissance, n.	itun agba, tun agba (of force with force)	

reconnoiter, vti.	nurenti; nure nso ijagha	Auchi/I
reconstruct, vti.	tun kome, tun konstrokte	
record, n.	ikode, rekod, rekodi	Y/I/G(fE)
(record of service)	ikode safis, rekod nke safis	
(record)	ilissa (account)	
(recorder)	rekoda, o lissa, o kode	
recount, vt.	tun go, tun lissa	Y/Agbo /H
recoup, vt.	reikupe, tun meshe jiki	G(fE)
recourse, n.	ichowa iron hann, rikosa	
recover, vti.	yilafia, tun yite, gbandu	Egun/Gen/I
recreant, adj.	mumu (coward) (kawad)	Gen/G(fE)
recreation, n.	ijiya, irudi 'guere	H/Y
recrudescence, n.	rikuru, irudi irun	G(fE)
recrimination, n.	iswezon zuba (accusation in return)	
recruit, n.	kurutu, o kurutu, ivase	G(fE)/G
rectangle, n.	retangu	G(fE)
rectify, vt.	ma, meshe rama, rama	
(rectify it)	rama ya, meshe ya di rama	
rectilinear, adj.	retilaina, nke laini golo, laini tara (straight line)	
rector, n.	rekta, nke chochi abi makaranta	
rectum, n.	mulu, nke gindi ana (bottom of intestine)	
recumbent, adj.	rikonbenti, duka na kasa (to lie down)	
recuperate, vti.	sokini, sokene	Y/Ed
recur, vti.	dazu, tun'bia, tun biawa, tunzo	
(recurrent expenditure)	inonku dazu	
recurve, vti.	kuru, tun kuru	Y(G.v)
recycle, vt.	tun kiri, tun yintua	
red, adj.	ja	H
(red-carpet)	ja-kafet	

(red-crescent)	red-krisant, nke musulmi, (ja-krisant)	
(red-cross)	red-kros	
(red flag)	tutaja	
(red-handed)	jimu nangba sam-sam	
(red-indian)	india jija (red india)	
(red-light)	ja redden-kwuda wuta	
redeem, vt, n.	yi dazu, wengbazu, iyi dazu, iwengbazu o wengbazu jesu kristi	
redeploy, vt, n.	tun yikpo, itun yikpo	Y/Egun
redifussion, n.	redifishan, irudi rediyo	G(fE)
re-do, vt.	tun meshe;	Y/I
re-double, vti.	tun jieva	Y/Ed
redolent, adj.	zizi kain-kain (strong smell)	
redoubt, n.	izitako, ebi katazi n'itako abi ijagha	
redoubtable, adj.	di yopulu, tun yopulu	
redound , vi.	bupeh , fa peh ife	I/G
redress, vt, n.	meshe rama, me di rama, tun meshe	
(reduction in size)	dinpu itondo, bekuru n'tiondo	
redundant, adj, n.	ai niwen, meguru, imeguru	
(duplication)	itun keji	
(duplicator)	o tunkeji, injinkeji	
re-echo, vti.	tun gboun	
reed, n.	ridi, irudi shukeshuke itache	
(reed)	mutum ya-ya-yah, ai zioka	
reef, n.	rifi, nke ugboko ruwa	G/fE
reef, n.	rinf, nke dutse abi okuta	

reefer, n.	rinfa, irudi jakit nke o shikolo (sailor)
reek, n.	izizi rubi (bad smell)
reel, n.	rili, nke selinda
reel, vti.	gaun-gaun, "to shake toughly"
re-entry, n.	itun-antri, itun bale
reeve, n.	rif, chif majistrit
reface, vt.	tun fuska, tun meshe
refectory, nn.	rifekti, irudi bandeki fun abinchi na makaranta
refer, vti.	rifere, buezu
(i refer you to)	mo rifere e si, mo buezu e si
referee, n.	irifere, o buezu G(fE)/H
reference, n.	irifere, o buezu
(with reference to) referendum, n.	n'irifere si referenda, nke politike, irudi ijubi
refill, vt.	tun jujun Y/I
refine, vti.	rifan, meshed i shaka G(fE)
(refinement)	rifanmint, irifan
refiner, n.	o rifan
refit, vti.	rifite, tunme, meshed i huntun, kowele, tunjuku
reflate	ridazu – "restore"
reflect, vti.	tonwuta si, tonwu si, itonwu, loro jinka
(reflector)	o tonwu si
refloat, vt.	tun lofoh
reform, vt. n.	tura, itura, tun mundu G/I/Y
(law reform commission) refract, vt.	kwamishan itun mundu idakpe rifra,
	dazu wuta, irifra G(fE)
refractory, n.	igboro, isigboro, lai yissi – "unyielding to"

refrain, n.	rifren, nke isongi	
refrain, vi. refresh, vt. (refresher) (refresher course)	fazuba, dachiu, du meshera, mera, imera o meshera, o mera imuko meshera	Y/I/H
refrigerate, vt.	lefrijaret, meddi kule, gbuzeze	
(refrigerator), n. (refrigeration)	lefrijareto, o gbuzeze igbuzeze	
refuel, vt.	tun fueli, tun nno fueli, fiyen fueli	
refuge, n.	mbibo, ivute	Y(I.tone)/G
(take refuge)	yi mbibo, yi vute	
refugee, n.	o mbibo, lefuji, o vute	
refund, vt. refurbish, vt.	kpa dazu, rifunde, lifunde meshe di kowele, me di kowele, meshe kowele	Agbo/Y/I/G(fE)
refuse, n.	duh, ah-ah, juko	G/Gen/I/Y
refute, vt.	lifiut, hundi isiro – "prove wrong"	
regain, vt.	tun rire Y/Sobe	
regal, adj.	nke baize abi o keisi – "of monarch or king"	
regalia, n.	rigelia, esa nke baize abi o keisi	
regard, n.	keya, bulele, ibulele, ifie I/Y/G	
(with regard to)	n'ibulele si	
(regardless)	lai keya, lai bulele, lai fie	
(high regard)	ibulele ga	
regatta, n.	rigeta, ilule, iguere ugboko abara	
Regency, n.	irijant, rijant, nke kasa gret briten	
regenerate, vti.	tun muta, tun mbuia	

reggae, n.	rege, irege (from Omoregie) Ed.	
regicide, n.	rejisi, igbu baize	G(fE)
regime, regime, n.	rejima, ijeeze, gonmenti	
regiment, n.	renini, jimjim	G/G(fE)
regimental	nke renini, ife jimjim, rejimante	
(regimental solder)	iseza jimjim	
regina, n.	rejina, sarauniya elizabit	
region, n.	waje, sashe, rijan, nsoka	
(regional)	nke waye, nke sashe, nke rija, nke nsoka	
register, n.	rajista, irudi littafi	H(fE)
register, vti.	ilisa, kode afa abi ife si takarda	
registration, n.	ilisa, lilisa	
registry, n.	rajistri G/H(fE)	
reguius, n.	rijios, nke unifasiti oksfod abi griki	
regret, n, vt.	inurubi, nurubi	I/Gen/Y
regroup, vti.	tun tugbe, tun kojo	
regular, adj.	reguli, ngba ncha	
regularize, vt.	meshe reguli, reguli	
regulate, vt. n.	regule, iregule	G(fE)
rehabilitate, vt.	tunbilite	Y/G(fE)
rehash, vt.	tunhash	Y/G(fE)
rehear, vt.	tun gbonti, gbonti mozo, gbonti keji	
rehearse, vti.	tun shedi, tunhas, tunhase, masaun	
(rehearsal)	imasaun	
rehouse, vt.	tun kabandu, kpeyen gida kowele, nno gida huntun	
reign, n.	itogan	Egun(G.v)

(rehearsal)	imasaun	
(he reigned for eight years)	o togan na ardun asato	
(reigning)	itogana, o togana	
reimburse, vt.	kpa zuein, kpazu	Agbo/I
(reimbursement)	ikpazu, ikpa zuein	
rein, n.	igiya doki (horse rope), kentrol	
reincarnate, vt. n.	vorera, ivorera, eni kuowun weh biawa akpor	
reindeer, n.	rendidi, irudi nama daji	G
reinforce, vt.	nno tun agba, (tun nno agba)	
(reinforcement)	itun nno agba	
reinstate, vt. n.	tun yensi, iitun yensi	Y/I
reinsure, vt.	tun shuwara, tun dido	
(reinsurance), n.	itun shuwara, itun dido	
reissue, vt.	tun isu	Y/G
reiterate, vt.	tun soli, tun meshe, ritaret	
reject, n. vti.	juko, ijuko	Y/I
rejoice, vti. n.	yonso, iyonso, dunso, idunso	
rejoin, vt.	tun jokono	
rejoin, vti.	soyen, nke ifeza	
(rejoinder)	isoyen	
rejuvenate, vti.	me shaka, me gbandu	I/Y/G
rekindle, vti.	tun tonwu	
relapse, vi.	keu-keu, biazu, tunzo – "repeat"	
relate, vti.	gbaso, soli oka, koso	Izon/Y/I
relate, vti, n.	nure, inure, inojo	Aughi/Y/I
(our relationship is so strong)	inure wa sile kha	
relative, adj.	nure, yiore, inure, iyiore	
(relative clause)	klaus iyiore	

relativity, n.	inunure, iyiyiore	
relax, vti.	dunke, kule, kulele, kunmale	
(relaxation)	idunke, ikule, ikulele, isimini	
relay, n.	relei, irudi erenji	
relay, vt	gbe soli, tun gbaameh	Y/Ikwere/Izon
(relay stastion)	o gbe soli tashan	
relay, vt.	tun tole, itun tole kafet	
release, vt	tuka, tuta, tuja, fre	
(release at once)	tuja kene	
relegate, vt.	fasika	Y/H
(relegation), n.	ifasika	
relent, vi.	kiene, mini	
(don't relent your effort)	ma kiene igbake e	
relevant, adj.	zumkpa	I/Y
reliable, adj.	mekole – "dependable",	
	fiyen iyobi si imekole, ifie	
reliance, n.	'yobi si iverah, verah	
relic, n.		G
(relics of war) relief, n.	e verah i jagha	
religion, n.	isinle	Y/I
religious, adj. person)	di 'sinle, ife isinle, sinlele	
reline, vt.	tun laini	
reliquary, n.	relinkuari, irudi akwati fun ec e verah	
relish, n.	izizi rama (good/ sweet smell)	
relive, vt.	tun-hu, tun diwa,	
relocate, vti.	tun ebi, tun hin, itun ebi	
reluctant, adj.,	shaiche, ishaiche	Y/I
rely, vi.	meko, fie iyobi si	
remain, vi.	kufo, kuduh,	Y/I

reminder, n	ikufo, ikudu	
remains, n (pl)	ekufo, edudu; (not e kufo, e kudu)	
remake, vt.	tun meshe, tun medi	Y/I
remand, vt.	rimande, ironshien o swezon dazu ibibo "to send an accused back to custody"	
remark, n.	remake, notezi, kiesi, ikiesi	
remarry, vti.	tun gbemata, tun chogbe	
remedy, n.	magani, imeson fun irun (cure)	
remember, vti.	cheron ioron	
(rememberance)	icheron, iloron	
remilitarize, vt.	tun jagha, tun nno agba, tun tako	
remind, vt.	loron, cheron	
(remind me)	loron mi, cheron mi	
reminisce, reminiscence, n.	tun loro, itun loro, tun sol	
reminiscent, adj.	remini, iremini, liloron, cheron oka abi ife	
remiss, adj.	lai june, ai junene "carelessness"	
remission, n.	iberiji, irere	Y/I
remit, vti.	rere, beriji	
remittent, adj.	remiten, irudi iba	
remnant, n.	barbashi, ikufo (crumb)	H/Y/I
remonstrance, n.	kemkporo – "protest", ikemkporo	
remorse, n.	nurube – (inurubi) – "regret"	
remote, adj.	rimota, jin hanya, aisi na nso	
(remote control)	rimota kentrola	
remount, vti.	tun getele	

remove, vti.	yopu, yota, muku	Y/I
(remover)	o yopu, o yota	
(removerable)	nke a le yopu abi yota	
remunerate, vt.	rimona, kpa fun irushe, ikpa fun safis	
renaissance, n.	rinaisans, irudi krusada	
renal, adj.	rina, nke koda (of the kidney)	
rename, vt.	tun nno afa, tun kono	
rend, vt.	doya – "to tear apart"	I/Y
render, vt.	nnonzu	Ef/I
rendezvous, n.	rendevuze, ebi ikojo – "gathering place	
renegade, n.	renegade, o fre inikon	
renew, vt.	tun meshe, tun shaka, tun meshe kowele	
(renewal)	itun kowele	
rennet, n.	renit, kaya nono	
renonunce, vt.	kolo, juta – "to denounce"	
renovate, vt.	rinovet, tun meshe bika gida	
(renovation)	irinovet	
Renown, n.	inoki – "of fame"	
(a renown man)	miji o noki	
rent, n.	haya kudi haya, renti	H/G(fE)
(house rent)	kudi renti	
(rent agent)	omaye renti	Idoma/G (fE)
(rent and debt collector)	o meko renti ati igwese	
rent, n.	idoya, nke tufa abi esa	
renunciate, vt, n.	konu wenji, ikonu wenji "self denial"	
re-open, vti.	tun shie	Y/I
re-organize, vti, n.	tun tole, tun ganize, itun tole	
re-orientate, vti	tun maliye	I/Owo/Y

rep, rep, n.	rep, nke fabriki abi faiba	
repair, vt.	kwashe	
(reparable)	nke a le kwashe	I/Y
(repairer)	o kwashe	
reparation, n.	ikpasa me kpasa, irudi 'tunme funibije – "damage"	
repatriate, vt.	ronzu, ironzu,	
repay, vti. n.	tun kpa. itun kpa	Y/Agbo
repeal, vt.	konozu, mupu	
repeat, vti, n.	tunzo, itunzo, keji	
repel, vt.	lepu – "to drive away"	
repent, vti. n.	rogha, chenu, irogha, ichenu	
repercussion, n.	izuein, izuba ife	
(the repercussion will be bad)	izuba ya a di rubi, (izuba y'a di rubi)	
repertory, n.	iripeti, kamfani tiyeta	
replace, vt. n.	sonzu, isonzu, nnonzu	Y/I/Efik
replay, vt.	tun guere	
replenish, vt. n.	fijukun, ifijukun	Y/I
replica, n.	misali, raflika	H/G(fE)
reply, vti.	dazi, feza	Y/I
(in reply to your letter)	n'dazi si wasike e; n'feza si wasike e	
report, n.	ripot soli, gbaameh, loga	G(fE)/Y/I/Izon
(reporting)	iripo, isoli, igbaameh	
(reporter)	o ripot ripota, o soli, o gbaameh, o solile	
(report)	iripo, isolile – of account/happening	isolile mitin, iripot
(the report of the meeting)	nke mitin	
(i'll report you)	ma solile e	
(report to me)	biawa si mi	
(radio reporter)	o ripota rediyo, o solile tun gbinso rediyo repose, vt.	

repot, vt.   tun gbinso

reprehend, vt.   tun solisi, tunkasi

represent, vt.   simbola

(this represents)   eyi wu isimbola

represent, vt.   ripresento, finere, nikpoze,
                                    tun fiji (re-submission) mubia
                                    si whido, tun mubia

representative, adj.   wakili, omaye   H/
                                    Idoma repress, vt.

reprieve, vt.   repriveh fosfun, muswhido

reprimand, vt.   primande, tun solisi

reprint, vt.   tun tite

reproach, vt.   gon, solina, chowa riprobeta, eni
                                    shebi, ishebi – "fault finding"
                                    o shebi mutum ichowa ishebi
                                    na ikonu   reproduce, vti.
                                    – "finding fault with
                                    worrow" reprobate, vt.

(reproductive organ)   ogan igbebia

(reproductive)   gbebia, gbigbebia

reproof, n.   soko (blame)

reprove, vt.   bionunu, solisi na
ibilionu fun ishebi

reptile, n.   akuna-kuna, irudi e nama
eso bika kunkuru,
kada, abi kandangare
– "tortoise, crocodile
or lizard"

republic, n.   ripobli, irudi gonmenti
                                    (synonym: ripoblika)

republican, n.   o ripobli, o sole gonmenti iripobli
(federal republic of
nigeria) ripoblika
feriyya nke naijeriya

repudiate, vt.   gbuiweni – "disown"   I/Gen/Y

repugnant, adj.   shabada, iaiche   Y(G.v)

repulse, vt, n.   ripela, lepu, ilepu

(repulsive), adj.   fata ripela, lepu, ilepu

(repulsive agent)	ife abi omaye ilepu	
repute, vt, n.	noki, nke a ma, inoki, katazi	
(reputable dealer)	o renka katazi, o renka noki	
(high repute)	inoki giga	G(fE)/Y/I
request, n.	ijubi	
requiem, n.	rekwim, irudi 'songi	
fun eni to kuowun	I/Y	
require, vt, n.	che, iche	
(requirements)	e chiche, e che	
(what are the requirement)	meni wu echiche	
requisition, n.	ichiche, (rekwizishan)	
requite, vt	rikwite, kpa zuba ife, kpa zu (pay back)	
reredos, n.	ridos, nke chochi	
rescind, vt.	risinde, gbure	
(cancel), contract	I/Y	
rescue, vt.	yopu, yota	Y/I
research, n.	ichondi,	I/Y/G(fE)
(researcher)	o chondi, o risache	
resemblance, n, vt.	iyijo	Y/I
resent, vt.	risante, di konu – "to feel bitter"	
reservaition, n, vt.	ichemo, chemo	
(games reserve)	ichemo fun iguere	
(government reserved area)	nso ichemo gonmenti	
(reserved forces)	ichemo soja, ichemo agba	
reserve, vt, n.	chemo, sito	
reservoir, n.	o chemo, rizavoa	
reset, vt.	tun fie n'ikpoze tun yaji	
resettle, vti.	tun simini, tun kule	
(resettlement)	risato, irisatonment, mbi 'simini, mbi kule	
(resettlement camp)	sansani 'simini	
reshuffle, vt, n.	tun shaful, meru, imeru	G/I/Y

413

reside, vt.	risaide; gida, mbi inusi	G(fE)/H/Y/I
residence, n.	irisaide; gida, ihusi	
resident, adj.	ibie, risaide	
(resident doctor)	likita o risaide (resido likito)	
residual, adj, n.	di kufo, ikufo	
resign, vti, n.	freru, ifreru Y/I	
resilience, n.	resilia, iyilafia sokia (quick recovery)	
resin, n.	resin, ruwa itache abi ruwa shuke-shuke	
resist, vti, n.	kido, ikido I/Y	
resistor, n.	rezisto, ifie sol n'keji	
resolute, adj.	shim, shim-shim G	
(resolution), n.	ishim, ishim-shim	
resolve, vti.	chenunu – "determined, to determine"	
(i am resolved)	mo ti chenunu	
resonant, adj.	resonante, nke ilowe abi saund	
resonator, n.	resonanto, o resonante, ife irushe saund	
resort, vi.	liluwe, risote, mbi 'simini	
(pleasure resort)	mbi 'simini, nso isimini	
resound, vit.	tun saund, tun soli, soli gaun-gaun	
resource, n.	risose	
(resourceful)	di risose	G(fE)
respect, n.	ikumbe, kumbe	
(respectfully), adv.	kukumbe, ikukumbe	
(yours respectfully)	nke yin n'ikkumbe,	
(nke yin n'ikumbe)	G	
(respected)	kumbe	
(respectable), adj.	di kumbe, o kumbe	
respective, adj, adv.	diumbe, I/Y tukon, tutukon – "each"	
respire, vi, n.	hinmi, ihinmi	

respirator, n.	respirato, ife irushe ihinmi
respite,	irespato, respato, ngba iflesi abi isimini
respirator, n.	respirato, ife irushe ihinmi
respite, n.	irespato, respato, ngba
iflesi abi isimini	G/Y
resplendent, adj.	risplenda, shaka-shaka G(fE)/G
respond, n.	dazi, daza
respondent, n.	responda, o dazi; o daza, o mekusa –"defenda"
response, n.	idazi, idaza, ifeza
responsibility, n, adj.	ibuwa, imeko, ibuwa
(responsible person)	mutum ibuwa
(responsible government)	gonmenti 'buwa Y/I
responsions, n.	responshans, nke digiri aksfod
rest, n.	isimini, isundo
(rest a while)	simini kene, sundo kene
(resting place)	mbi abi ebi 'simini, ebi sundo
(laid to rest)	duka si 'sundo, duka 'simini
(rest house)	gida isimini
(rest room)	deki isimni abi sundo
(rest in peace)	sundo na'lafia, k'odi ngba
(restless/ly)	ai simini, ai sundo
(restlessness)	lai simini abi sundo
rest, n.	ikufo, kudu, ikudu
(the rest of you)	ikudu yin
rest, vti.	dankiti – "quiet"
rest, vi.	fi yobi si, wen 'yobi
restate, vt.	tun soli, tun kode
restaurant, n.	resorant, gida abi deki fun abinchi
restive, adj.	gboro – "stubborn"
restoration, n.	ikpa zuba, ikpein, kpein Agbo/I/Y

restore, vt.	kpein, fie zuba – "to put back	
restrain, vt.	du, fazu, jimuzu, fapu	
restrict, vt.	limite, guini (to limit)	I/Y
result, vi, n.	gwisi, yisi, igwisi, iyisi	
resume, vt.	tunrebi, tun rebi, tun bre	I/Gen.
(resume duty)	Tun rebi 'rushe	
resume, n.	rishumeh, ibekuru, abi astrakt	
resumption, n.	itun rebi, itun bre	
resurface, vti.	tun fuska	Y/H
resurgent, adj.	risajent, dazu shaka	G/Y/I/Gen
resurrect, vti. n.	jinde, ijinde	
(resurrection of jesus christ)	ijinde jesu kristif	
resuscitate, vti.	risositate, mubia shaka	G/Y/I/Gen
retail, n.	reitela, ileta kele-kele, ileta ife n'iyewan kele	
(retail shop)	Giswa ritela	
retain, vt.	toshimi	I/Y/G
(retainer)	o toshimi	
retake, vt.	tun yi, tun meshe	Y/Egun
retaliate, vi. n.	ritale, iritale, funzu, ifunzu	
retard, vt.	ritada, dihan G/Y/H	
retell, vi.	tun soli, tun gbaameh	Y/I/Ikw/Izor
retention, n.	itoshimi	
retentive, adj.	riten, reitenda, itoshem	G(fE)/I/Y
retexture, vt.	tun tekscha	
rethink, vti.	tun loro	Y/I
reticent, adj.	soli kele, ai soli ncha	
retina, n.	retine, nke ido	G(Urhobo)
retinue, n.	retinu, ilamba nke e mutum t'o rinje sole hafsa giga	

retire, vti.	ritaya, simini n'irushe, shihannu
retirement, n.	iritaya, ishihannu, isimini n'irushe
retool, vt.	tun tulu, tun kozo Y/G
retort, n.	rito, irudi ugboko ruwa ti a ng fi meshe kain-kain
retort, vti.	bram-bram, ifeza abi isoli oka bram-bram
retouch, vti.	masi, tun masi – (to improve upon)
retrace, vt.	tun chowa, tun chole Y/I
retract, vti.	yi dazu – "take back/ withdraw" fapu
retread, vt.	ritre, iritre idigbo taya, nke taya
retreat, vt.	kirizu G/Y/I
retrench, vti. n.	gbuduke, igbudukke I/Ed
retrial, n.	tun dunie, tun chondi Y/I
retribution, n.	retributa, nke iwuiya n'izuba
(law of retribution)	iwufin 'wuiya (w.w) (wuwu)
retrieve, vti.	wenriba I/Y/H
(i have retrieved my lost fountain-pen)	fantin mi to funu mo ti wenriba alkalami fantim mi t'o funu
retroactive, adj.	wunana, nke iwufin n'zuein
retrograde, adj.	ritogreda, fazu zuba, (fazu-zu)
retrogress, vi.	ritrogresa, ringa zuba abi zuein
retro-rocket, n.	kpam-kpam, irudi injin jat o jagha

retrospect, n.	ineri zuba, (nerizu)	I/Y/H
(retrospectively) adv.	inenerizu, nenerizu	
retrousse, adj.	peweh, (to turn u nose at the end)	
retsina, n.	ratsina, irudi wain kasa griki	
return, n. vti.	ibozu, yintua, iyintua, idazu	Y/I
re-union, n.	itun rundo, itu kpondo	
(happy re-union)	iyoli fun itun rundo, iyoli n'itun rundo	
revalue, vt.	tun yemkpa	
revamp, vt.	tunti; wenriba (tunti o)	
(revamp economy)	wenriba ikonoma; tunti ikonoma	
reveal, vt.	shineri; yaboto Y/I/G (it is revealed) o te shenire	
(revealing)	ishineri, shishineri	
reveille, n.	hebo, ihebo, nke iseza o jagha, irudi 'sigi-sigi fun e soja (signal)	
revel, vti.	revela, meshe igbandu – "make merry"	
(reveler), n.	o revela	
revelation, n.	reveleshan, ishineri	
(the book of revelation)	littafi reveleshan, (littafi ishineri)	
revelry, n.	idunso, igbandu	
revenge, vt.	kpasa, rivenja,	Agbo/G
revengeance, n.	ikpasa, irevenja	
revenue, n.	reveniu, kudi kasa dipatmin nke reveniu isalande	
reverberate, vt, n.	kplah, ikplah, kplah-kplah	G

reverse, vt, n.	yintua, yizuba, yizu, yizuein, ribas, iyintua	
(auto reverse)	ato ribas	
reverence, n.	ibube	Y/I
reverend, adj.	bube, di 'bube	
(reverend father)	baba ibube	
(reverend mother)	uwa ibube	
(reverend sister)	muwa ibube	
reverie, n.	ipera, irudi ila rama, ila dunso (sweet dream)	
reverse, vt, n.	yintua, iyintua, iyizu, ribas, yizuein, daxu	
revert, vi.	bozu si – "to return to", yintua si	
review, vti.	ribiu, tun neri	
revile, vti.	kala – (angry and abusive)	Gen
revise, vt.	ribas, tun loro, tunche	G(fE)/Y/I
revision, n.	iribas, itun loro, itunche (ilibase) – synonym	
(revision exercise)	asasais itunche, iribas asasais, asasais ilibase	
revitalize, vt.	tun faita, tun nno agba	
revival, n, vti.	ishoshaka, isonta, ijinde, sonta, jinde	Y/I
revocable adj.	konozu, konotua	Gen/I/G
revolt, vit.	tegha, tegun	Y/I
(the revolt of islam)	itegha musulmi	
revolution, n.	itegha, itegunu	
revolve, vti.	gakiri, konotua, konozu, ringa kiri	
(the world is revlving)	akpor ng ringa kiri	
revolver, n.	libarba, irudi bindiga	H
revue, n.	iduduke, duduke, igbandu flesi	G/Ed
reward, n.	ikpari, ikunzi, izuein	Agbo/I/Y

419

(good reward from god)	ikpari rama lati abasi	
rewire, vt.	tun waya, riwaya, nke lantiriki	
reword, vt.	tun soli, tun kode	Y/I
rhea, n.	ria, onene	
rheostat, n.	rostat, nke agba lantiriki	
rhesus, n.	risosi, irudi biri na kasa	
rhetoric, n.	india (monkey) isolila, iluwe oka jukha – "use of much words"	
rheumatism, n.	amosani, amosanka	H/G
reheumatoid, adj.	nke amosani abi amosanka, H/G atitis, kumburi	
rhinal, adj.	rina, nke ihono hanchi – nostrils	
rhinoceros, n.	karkanda	H
rhizome, n.	rizom, irudi shuke-shuke	G
rhododendron, n.	rondonrondo, irudi shuke-shuke ilililai – "a type of evergreen plant"	
rhomb, n.	rombu irudi isiffa o wn akue inang – "a type of figure having four sides"	
rhubarb, n.	rubabu, irudi shukeshuke gadin	
rhyme, n. vt.	isabe, sabe – "sameness"	G
(nursery rhyme)	isabe nesiri	
(rhythm of the rain)	ikpoi –kpoi ruwa	
(rhythm of the heart)	ikpum/ikpum – kpum zurbhiya	
rib, n.	hakarkari	H
ribbon, n.	kintinkiri, riban	H/G
riboflavin, n.	ribovn, irudi faitamin	G(fE)

rice, n.	shikafa	
(staple rice)	tuwo shikafa	
rich, adj, n.	ibarika, barika, riba, iriba	H/Gen
(rich man)	miji 'barika	
(good name is better than riches)	afa rama lo jukha e riba	
rick, n.	riki, nke shuke-shuke	G
rickets, n.	riketa, irudi irun omontakeleG(fE)	
rickety, adj.	rikita, ai sile, ai wen agba	
rickshaw, n.	rishor, irudi keke o wen wili eji	
rid, vt.	gbisi, lepu, leta	I/Y
(get rid of)	gbisi ya, lepu ya, leta ya	
riddance, n.	igbisi, ilepu, ileta	
ridden, pp.	temisi – "to oppress"	
riddle, n.	ikpozoh –ife sile, (puzzle)	
ride, n.	yanwa, gunyan	I/Y
(ride a donkey)	yanwa jamki	
rider, n.	o yanwa, o gunyan	
ridge, n.	ilaini, irudi laini tolo-tolo	
ridicule, n.	kuh-khuu, ikuakua G	
(don't ridicule me, please)	ma kuh-khu mi, biko	
ridding, n.	radin kujera na 'zuba doki	
riffle, vti. n.	raful, meru, shaful, I/Y/G ruvo, iruvo	
(riffle draw)	kalo-kalo raful	
riff-raff, n.	ya-ya-ya, mutum yah-yahyah, ai wen miwa rama	
rifle, n.	rukpoi, irudi bindiga	G/Y/I/H
rift, n.	iyajeh – "crack", ai kweba, iyahann, iyaru	

rig, vti. rig, (fraud)	yati, nke ugboko ruwa, tiyo G (he rigged the election)	
rigging, n.	iyati, nke waya ugboko ruwa	
right, adv.	gere; yasah, gon, whido, sam-sam, sam'; shim- shim	
(you are down right)	e gere sam-sam	
(right hand side)	akue rait, akue gere	
(right or wrong)	gere-goshi	
(which is theright way?)	meni wu iyasah hanyar?	
righteous, adj.	di yasah, di rati, di saun, di sam-sam, di whido	
(righteousness exalts a nation)	iyasah ng buga neshan, iyasah ng buga kasa	
rigid, adj.	kpiti, koi	
(your lawa are too rigid)	iwufin e kpiti jukha	
rigmarole, n.	eeh-eeh, irudi oka ai wen ezioka katazi	G
rigoromotis, n.	rigoma, ikagba gawa (stiffness)	
rigorous, adj.	gboro, tain, rugu	Gen/G/Y/I
rigour, n.	irugu, igboro, itain	
rill, n.	rivula, rafi kele – "ssmall streem"	
rim, n.	rim, rimi, ife wili, baki	G(fE)/H
rind, n.	bawo, fata	H
rinderpest, n.	bushiya, zagau	H
ring, n.	oruka; kawanya, zobe,	Gen/H
ring, vt. (of telephone)	waya, agogo	Gen(fE)/Gen
(rise against)	kunde doko	
risk, n.	iwugu, wugu	Y/I
(it is too risky)	o wugu jukha	
risotto, n.	risotto, irude abinchi shikafa	G(fE)
rissole, n.	risol, abinchi nama	G(fE)

ritual, n.	isuoro	I/Y
(ritual killing)	igbu n' isuoro	
rival, n.	hamayya	H
rive, vti.	doya n'isokia (tear quickly)	
river, n.	kogi	
(river side)	akue kogi	
(river-basin)	(riva-besin), nso kogi	
(river-bed)	gindi kogi, isala kongi	
(river-rine)	nso kogi	
rivet, n.	ribet, irudi ayan irushe na ugboko ruwa	
roach, n.	orchid, irudi kifi	G(fE)
road, n.	hanya, ilahan, ihanya	H
(road junction)	isogba hanya	
(road map)	taswira hanya, mapu hanya	
(road safety)	ikali hanyar,	
(road safety corps)	kamfani nke ikai hanyar	
(road works)	irushe na hanya	
(road-bed)	dutse, abi jefa hanya	
(road bend)	imeko hanya	
(road book)	littafi hanya	
(road mender)	o tunme hanya, lebura nke hanya	
roadster, n.	rodsta, irudi mota fun mutum eji sonsho (only)	
roam, vti.	gakiri, gburu, gburu-gburu	
(roam the streets)	gakiri n'e titi	
roan, n.	ron, irudi fata (a type of leather)	
roar, n.	gbruuh, ikebe bika zaki	
roast, vti.	dinse	
roasted	idinse	
rob, vt. n.	rawo, irawo	H(G.v)
(daylight robbery)	irawo n'ari rana	

robe, n.	riga	H
robin, n.	robin, irudi onene	
robot, n.	rabot, irudi injn bika mutum	G(f/E)
robust, adj.	boto	Y(G.v)
rock, n.	dutse, okuta	H/Gen
(rock stone)	jefa dutse	
rock, vti.	kpokiri – "swinging to and fro"	
rock, n.	rack, irudi isonga	
rocket, n.	roka, o tugbum, lugbum	G(fE)/G
rod, n.	sanda,	
(iron rod)	sanda ayan	
rodent, n.	rabitele, dabba	G(fE)/H
rodeo, n.	rodio, na kasa amerika	
rodomontade, n.	ishakara, shakara	Y/Gen.
roe, n.	roh, kwai kifi	
roe, n.	yoh, irudi nama daji bika ogolo_(deer)	
rogation, n.	rogashion, nke malaika na chochi	
roger, int.	roja, nke wayalis abi rediyo, iyezu	
rogue, n.	mugu, irawo, o rawo	
(you are a rogue)	i wu o rawo: e wu o rawo	
roisterer, n.	rostora, eni ng gbandu n' ihanya rubi	
role, n.	lovi, ilovi, nke ikpaka (part)	
(what role did you follow?	(meni 'lovi e sole?)	
roll, n.	kondo, itole; itolo	G/I/Y
(call the roll)	kono itole	
(roll it)	kondo ya	

(rolling stone)	jefa tolo
roller, n.	rola, o kodo, o tole G(fE)/I/Y
roman, n.	roma, nke kasa rom
romance, n.	ilida Agbo
romance, n.	miri, imiri – nke ivudu
romance, adj.	romanse, nk'ede faransi, itli, spana kpotoki, rumena ati e mozo bibiawa lati latin
romantic, adj.	nke ichenu, ihufe abi imiri-miri (idea)
romp, vi.	rompeh, iguere kiri n'nso
rondeau, n.	rondi, irudi 'pole (poem)
Roneo, n.	Ronio, irudi mashin abi injin o keji takarda (duplicator)
rood, n.	ugangan, irudi ketare fa kusa jesu kristi – (tye type of cross which jesus christ was nailed)
roof, n.	rufi, rufu, jinka H(fE)
(roofing sheet)	fale rufu, rufi shit
roof frame	tsaiko rufu
rook, n.	rukuku, irudi baba onene beki
rook, n.	o bebeye (trickster), o wayo
rookie, n.	o kurutu huntun – new recruit
room, n.	daki (H)
roost, n.	iyaga abi muchiya fun onene ati kaza katako onene abi kaza
root, n.	tushe, gindi, saiwa, rutu H/G(fE)
(root crop)	mabunkusa kasa
rope, n.	igiya, waya G/Gen(fE)

rosary, n.	roszri, luzi G(fE)/G	
rose, n.	roz, irudi fulawa abi shuke-shuke	
(rose flower)	fulawa roz	
roseate, adj.		
rosite, irudi launiG(fE)		
rosemary, n.	rosmeri, irudi fulawa ilililai	
rosin, n.	rosine	G(fE)
roster, n.	ikono tole, rosta	
rostrum, n.	rostra, katako wazi (preacher's pulpit)	
rosy, adj.	di roz, rozi, bika roz, nke roz	
rot, vit.	bije	I/Y
(rotten egg)	kwai bije	H/I/Y
rotary, adj.	rotri, iringa-kiri, iboto	G(fE)/ I/Y/ Gen
(rotary club)	klob rotri, ituegbe rotri, (klob nke rotri)	
rotate, vit.	foci, gaki, gaboto, ringa-kiri Y/I/Gen	
rotation, n.	ifoki, igaki, igakiri, igaboto, iringa-kiri	
rote, n.	iliom, imuko ife si 'yobi n'iflesi	
rotisserie, n.	rotisri, dibais t' a ng fi sie abinchi (device)	
rotogravure, n.	otogravu, nke ititie (of printing)	
rotor, n.	rota, nke injin abi mashin	
rotter, n.	kpafun, mutum rubisi – "worthless person"	
rotund, adj.	fuska boto – "round face"	
rotunda, n.	rotunda, irudi gida boto – "a type of round building"	
roiuble, n.	rudin rasho, robol, irudi kudi na kasa soviet abi sofiet	

rounge, n.   ronj. irudi hoda rama – (a type of fine powder)

rough, n.   ileke, ikpako, isile, igra-gra, idatti

(it is rough)   o di leke, o di kpako, o di sile, o gra-gra

(rough paper)   takarda kpako
(rough work)   irushe kpako
(rough-rider)   o yanwa gra-gra
(rough play)   iguere gra-gra
(rough state/condition)   ikpongba gra-gra, iwahe gra-gra

roughage, n.   rofej, irudi abinch   G(fE)
roulette, n.   rulet, irudi 'guere gambol abi kalo-kalo

round, adj.   boto: rondo
(round cheeks)   e kunchi boto

(round game)   igwuere boto

(round dance)   isamba boto

round figure)   ilamba boto

round eye)   ido boto

(round head)   keisi boto
round, adv.   kampke, boto-boto, nsebi (also): boboto

(come around/come   (we are working round the
round) (round the clock)

round figure)   ilamba boto
round eye)   ido boto
(round head)   keisi boto
round, adv.   kampke, boto-boto,
                                    nsebi (also): boboto

(come around/come   (we are working
round) (round the clock)   round the clock)

round-about, adj.	boto-kiri, randi-baut, hanyar rondo	
roundelay, n.	randile, irudi songi kuru ati flesi	
rounders, n.	randas, irudi 'gwuere fun itugbe eji: (a type of	
rouse, vti.	kuniede	I/Y
(roused to anger)	kuniede si 'bilionu	
rout, n.	imegion sam-sam – "complete defeat"	
rout, n.	fatattaka – "subdivided country"	
route, n.	hanya, (uzo) – synonym	H/I
routine, n.	rutine	G(Urhobo tone)
rove, vit.	logburu, loga gburu, loga gburu-gburu, gburu, loga kiri	
(roving round)	gburu kiri, gburu boto	
row, n.	jera, nke lamba e mutum n'ijondu na kujera	
(next row)	igboncha nkeji, igbongba keji	
row, vti.	tikpu – "to propel"	
(row-boat)	abara tikpu, abara titikpu	
row, n.	baba 'rimkpo, ichaghuru Gen/Y/I/G	
(row-boat)	abara tikpu, abara titikpu	
row, n. rowan, n.	baba 'rimkpo, ichaghuru Gen/Y/I/G rowan, irudi itache kele nke iyali roz	
rowdy, adj.	gra-gra, chaghuru, arimkpo	
rowel, n.	rawili, nke wili G	
row-lock, n.	rolo, nke abara – "boat"	
royal, adj.	bub-eze	

428

(his royal highness)	bub'eze, o mambeze	Y/H/I/Gen
royalty, n.	ibub'eze	Egun
rub, n.	sisa	
rub-a-dub , n.	rubaduba, ilowe ganga (sound of drum)	
rubber, n.	danko, roba H/G(fE)	
(rubber-stamp)	roba-samp	
(rubber-neck)	wuya-roba, o neri jukha	
rubbing, n.	roben, nke itite si farin karfe (brass)	
rubbish, n.	datti, ijuta, e juta Gen (fE)	
rubble, n.	dutse, robul	
rubic, n.	rubriki, ikeisi wasika	
ruby, n.	rubi, jiuweli ja (red jewel)	
ructions, n.	oka ibilionu, ikido (protest)	
rudder, n.	ruda, fowu, nke ugboko ruwa	
rude, adj.	gbiwa	Gen/Y
(very rude)	gbiwa kha	
rudeness, n.	igbiwa	
rudiment, n.	irudimant, rudiment	G(fE)
(rudimentary)	nke rudimint	
rue, n.	ruh, irudi shuke-shuke ilililai ti o konu (bitter)	
ruffian, n.	o leke, o kpako, o sile, mutum gra-gra	
ruffianis, n.	i leke, ikpako, isile, igra-gra	
ruffle, vti.	kpati, yolionu, nnon nsoha; ai kule	
rug, n.	kilishi	H
(rug-carpet)	kafit kilishi	
rugby, n.	rugbi, irudi fubol na kasa briten	

rugged, adj.	di sile, gburu, di dutse, dudutse, ai gbonti
(the old rugged cross)	idigbo ketare o gburu, idigbo ketare t' o gbun
ruin, n.	ibida, irunje – "destruction"
rule, n.	ij'eze, iwufin Y/I
(ruler)	o j'eze; (rula) – of paper
(ruling government)	gonmenti o j'eze, gonmenti nke ngba
(the rules of the game)	e wufin nke igwuere
(rules of the road)	e wufin hanya
(according to rules)	bietu iwufin, bietu e wufin
rum, n.	rom, irudi kain-kain bature
rumba, n.	rumba, nke songa, irudi samba n'ngba kera
ruminant, n.	ruminante, irudi nama bika malu abi ogolo (deer)
ruminate, vi.	chesaro, charo (meditate)
rummage, vit.	gindiso, ichowa kiri, ichowa siti gindi
rummy, n.	romin, irudi 'gwuere kadi
rumour, n.	hun-hun-hun, ihun-hunhun, imebo (rumour monger) o rushe hunhun-hun, amebo, o bemo, o soli hun-hun-hun
rump, n.	romp, gindi nama fun abinchi, kuturi
rumple, vt.	medi 'datti, meshed i datti (don't rumple your dresses) ma meshe e esa e di datti
rumpus, n.	igbaga, arimkpo, nsohala Gen
run, n, vti.	gbere, roso, gbapeh, lofeh
(runner), n.	o gbere, o roso,

(he/she has ran away)	o ti lofeh, o ghapeh	
(run quickly)	roso sokia	
(running/race)	iroso	
(run-way)	hanya ilofeh, raniweh	
(run/ran into)	gbere si, roso si	
(run back)	gbere dazu, roso dazu, gbere zuba	
(run back home)	gbere zuba gida	
(run on) / (go on)	ringa shien, rin shien	
(run through)	roso feja	
(run up)	roso, gbere sokia	
rung, n.	kala, irudi ketare na lada (crossbar on ladder) runnel, n.baba gata na 'kue hanya (big gutter on the road side)	
runny, adj.	folo, roso	G
(runny nose)	folo hanchi/hanchi golo, o folo hanchi	
runt, n.	kunte, mutum kuru jukha	G/Y
run-way, n.	ron-wey, hanya iroso na erh-kpot abi fili ugboko sama	
rupee, n.	rupii, kudi kasa india, kpakistan, nepali, murishios ati siri lanka	
rupiah, n.	afa kudi nke kasa indoneisha	
rupture, n.	ijunbe	Y/G
(ruptured appendi)	ikube akpendisiasia; akpendisiasia to kunbe	
rural, adj.	lula, akue kasa abi gari	G
(rural area)	nso lula	
(rural areas)	nso e bi lula	
ruse, n.	hanya iwayo	H/Gen

rush, n.	sokia, kia-kia, yaji, japu	I/Y
rush, n.	rosh, irudi itache	G(fE)
rusk, n.	roski, buredi kele	
Russian, adj.	Nake Kasa Rosha	
rust, n.	diogun, idiogun	
Rusticate, vit.	Lepupu	Y/I/G
Rut, n.	Imuwa abi imiwa irushe, hanya irushe – (character or way of doing something/job)	
Ruthless, adj.	Njika rugu, ai wen inube kaka S	

Sabbatarian, n.	Sabatera, o sabate, o cheto sabate abi o cheto sirande	
Sabbath, n.	Sabate, rana isimini, sabati	
Sabbatical, adj.	Sabatele, irudi 'simini abi huntun	
(sabbatical leave)	ihuntun sabatele, isimini sabatele	
sable, n.	sebol, irudi nama rama kele	
sabotage, n	samboka, isamboka, (sambo) (isambo)	
(economic sabotage)	samboka ikonoma	
(saboteur)	o samboka, o sambo	
saber, n.	seba, baba takobi (big or heavy sword)	
sac, n.	kpoki	Ed
saccharin, n.	sakarine, irudi suka	G(fE)
sacerdotal, adj.	shakadota, nke fada abi alufa	
sachet, n.	sachet, ikpa kele	G(fE)
sack, n. sack,	tungu, ibuto ikpa	G
vt. sackbut,	jape – "to sack from work"	
n. sacrament,	saboti, irudi 'faiki likita fun isongi	
n.	isakramint	G(fE)
sacramental, adj.	sakraminta, nke isakramint,	
sacred, adj.	hemo, bika abasi abi ife chiolu	
sacrifice, n. vt.	isebo, sebo	I/Y
sacrificial, adj.	sebo	
(sacrificial lamb)	tunkiya isebo, eni a gbu abi luwe fun ife rubi	
sacrilege, n.	isebola, isebo	

sacring bell, n.	sakrin-bel, irudi agogo kele na chochi	
sacristy, n.	sakistri, daki/deki kele na chochi	
sad, adj.	jonu	Y/I
sadhu, n.	sadu, nke hindu	
sadism, n.	sadizim, irudi 'vudu rubi – bad sexual intercourse	
safari, n.	safari, nke ist abi sentra afrika	
safe, adj.	kali, lafia	H/Gen
safe, n.	(sef) ikpa, akwati, banki, ebi 'cheto, sito, ibo	
(safe-keeping)	icheto kali	
(safe-deposit)	ikale-kofre	
safety, n.	sefti, ibibo, icheto, sito, banki	
(road safety)	ikali hanyar	
(road safety corps)	kanfani ikali hanyar	
(safety first)	ikali konda	
(safety belt)	belit ikali	
(safety valve)	bawul ikali	
(safety-pin)	fin ikali, sefti-fin	
saffron, n.	saffron, irudi launi bika launi monza – (orange)	
sag, vi.	wangu, wanka n'arin (sink/ weigh down in the middle)	
saga, n.	iyebu	Y/I
sagacious, adj.	maye, ichegbon	
sagacity, n.	idakpe rama, ichegbon	I/Owo/Y
sage, n.	miji o gbegbon, o sam-sam	
sage, n.	sej, irudi shukeshuke algashi	
sagitarious, n.	sajitarious, nke lamba zodiak	

sahib, n.	sahib, sah (sir) na kasa india	
said, pt. pp of say	soli, gbaameh	
sail, n.	horo, ife ugboko ruwa bika kwalekwale	
sail, vit.	shiko, o shikolo	
(sailor)	o shiko, o shikolo	
saint, n.	wali, waliyi, (Liyi)	H/Y/G
(Saint David)	Waliyi Dafidi	
sake, n.	irima, rima	
(for your sake)	n'irima e, kani e (because of you)	
salaam, n.	salaam, ikine Musulmi; Alafia, igbandu	
Salacious, adj.	Salashos, irudi foto abi ife rubi	
Salad, n.	Salad, saladi, abinchi bature	
Salamander, n.	Salamenda, irudi nama goro t' o ng bie na wuta n'ngba kera (a type of stubborn animal living in fire in ancient times)	
salary, n.	albashi, kudi uki	H
Sale, n.	Ileta	Y/I
(sale or return)	Ileta abi dazu	
(sales department)	dipatmint ileta, iyaka ileta	
(sales clerk)	akawu ileta	
(salesmanship)	ileleta, ichegbon n'ileta	
salient, adj.	katazi, risikha (prominent), ezumkpa	
(salient point)	mbi katazi, mbi ezumkpa	
saliferous, adj.	salishiri, nke gishiri	H/E
saline, adj.	sashiri	H/E
salinity, n.	isashiri	

salinometer, n.	salinominta, ife a ng fi nofi gishiri	
saliva, n.	yau, miyau	H
sallow, adj.	salo, nke fata mutum rubi – "bad human skin"	
sally, n.	kpgri, nke so ja e jagha – of fighting soldiers in sudden revenge)	
salmon, n.	salimon, irudi baba kifi	
salon, n.	saloni, ebi 'rushe abi majalisar	
saloon, n.	salune, irudi daki na ugboko ruwa	
(saloon car)	mota salune, mota zoom-zoom salune	
salt, n.	gishiri	H
salpetre, n.	solpita, kpotashom, irudi gishiri	
salutation, n.	ikine, ishendo	Y/I
(salutation is not love)	ikine ko wu ihufe	
salute, n.	kine, ikine, e ku a bia, e ku bibiawa	
salvage, n.	dezi – "to save, keep"	
salvation, n.	idezi	
(Salvation Army)	Soja Idezi, Soja Krista	
salve, n.	salf, irudi magani oyele	
salver, n.	salfa, irudi tre (tray)	
salvia, n.	salfia, irudi shukeshuke gadin	
salvo, n.	salfo, ilowe kakpu-kakpu nke bindiga fun ikine	
salvolatile, n.	salfolate, irudi magani gishiri	
Samaritan, n.	Samaritan, Samaritin, mutum inube	

(Good Samaritan)	Samaritin Rama, Samaritan Rama	
Samba, n.	Samba, igwuere emon Afrika na ngba kera, nke bia wu igwuere kasa Brazil, n'ngba yii	
Same, n.	Sem, baate,	G/I/Y/G
(same time)	Ngba sem	
(same place)	Mbi sem, ebi sam	
(sameness)	Isem	
(all the same)	Sem ncha	
Samovar, n.	Samofa, irudi tukunya tii na kasa Rosha	
Sampan, n.	Sampa, irudi kwalekwale t'o lebe na gindi	
Sample, n.	Misali, ifineri, samfo	H/Y/I/G(fE)
Sampler, n.	Samfla, irudi esa ti a fi allura meshe (needle)	
Sanatorium, n.	Sanitoriam, mbi igbandu abi irudi asbitin	
Sanctify, vt.	Meshe di somn, somon – make holy	
Sanction, n.	Ikweye – permission	
Sanctity, n.	Isomon	
Sanctuary, n.	Sanchuari, mbi 'somon na chochi	
Sanctum, n.	Santom, ebi somon	
Sand, n.	– "holy place" Yashi	H
(fine sand) /white sand)	Rairayi	"
(sand flies)	Kyashi	"
(sand insect)	Gelgema	Kanuri
(sand-paper)	Sam-fefa, takarda kafinta	
Sandal, n.	Fade	H
(sandals shoe)	Takalmi fade	

Sandalwood, n.	Sandahuu, irudi katako abi itache ti a ng fi Meshe ukpadidi coffin/casket	
Sandwich, n.	Sanwish, irudi huredi nke gunduwa eji (two slis)	
Sane, adj. Sanguine, adj.	Leji, lehu, gbandu Rekono, rentini	Y/H/I Y/G/I
Sanitary, adj.	Cheleji chelehu, lafia	I(G.v)Y
(sanitary inspector)	Insfekta ichelehu	
(sanitary officer)	Hafsa ichelehu, hafsa ilafia	
Sanitation, n.	Ichelehu, ilafia	
Sanity, n.	Ilafia, igbandu, irama	
Sanskrit, n..	Ede nke kasa India na ngba kera, sankriti	
Sap, vt.	Rengu, kpogbe	Y/I
Sap, n.	Zao, irudi kpulum soja (a type of soldier's tunnel)	
Sapient, adj.	Sagbon, chegbon – wisdom	
Sapphire, n.	Safirah G(fE)	
Sarcasm, n.	Ikegon, shakasizim, ikiesi	
ti o kopu	(bitter remarks)	
Sarcophagus, n.	Shakofagu, ukpadidi nke dutse "stone coffin"	
Sardine, n.	Sadine, abinchi kifi	
(sardine in oil)	Sadine na oyele	
Sardonic, adj.	Shado-shado, nke yeye	
Sari, n.	Sari, irudi esa nke mache Hindu	
Sarong, n.	Saron, esa e mutum kasa Malays	
Sarsaparilla, n.	Shashakparila, irudi ogogoro ti a tushe	
Satan, n.	Ekwenshu I/Y	

438

(satanic), adj.	Kwenshu, nke ekwenshu
Satchel, n.	Sachil, irudi ikpa kele G(fE)
Sateen, n.	Satine, ifili-fill, ihoneri
Satellite, n	Hogoh-hogoh, satilat, satilatG/G(fE)
Satiate, vt.	Sokene – fully satisfied Ed
Satiety, n.	Isokene
Satin, n.	Adalashi, telibeti H/Igala
Satinwood, n.	Satinwuun, irudi katako a ng fi meshe kujera
Satire, n.	Meshe yeye, iyeye
Satisfactory, adj.	Soken Ed
Satisfy, vti, n.	Soken, isoken
Saturate, vt.	Ibruku, jukhun fun ruwa I/Y
Saturday, n.	Satide, rana asea na uzola, rana nk'asaa
(Saturday Night)	Tuu Satide, tuu igbandu
Saturn, n.	Saten, irudi baba flanit; ibuto flanit
Saturnine, adj.	Satenelia, irudi anivase fun Ekwenshu Saten na kasa Rom
Saturnine, adj.	Jonu – "gloomy", ijonu
Satyr, n.	Sataya, na kasa Rom, ekwenshu daji – (in Rome, a forest god) a wen afu
	nutum atu afu nama daj.
Sauce, n.	Saus, irudi ruwa iyuwe
(Maggi Sauce)	Maggi Saus; ruwa iyuwe nke Magi
Saucy, n.	Igbiwa, ai feju – "rude"; "shameless"
Saucepan, n.	Kwano saus Kan/ Nupe/Gwarri

Saucer, n.	Sausa, irudi kwano lebe kele "a type of flat little plate"
Saunter, vi.	Yarah, iringa flesi, iringa mini – "leisure walk"
Saurian, n., adj.	E kuna-kuna – "reptiles
Sausage, n.	Sausej, abinchi buredi G(fE)
(sausage roll)	Ikondo sausej
Savage, adj.	Kurmi, baubawa, mutum t
kurmi Savanna, savannah, n.	Safana, safanah, kasa ti ko
wen itache (savannah Bank)	Banki Safanah
Save, vti.	Dezi, - "to keep" (also) seex "safe"
(same me)	Dezi mi
Save, preps, (except)	Weku I/Y Saviour, n.
Jesus Christ)	Sefio Jesu Kristi: Chiolu Jesu
Kristi:	O Dezi Jesu Kristi
Savoury, n, adj.	Itoka, nke idunso abi ikonu
Savoy, n.	Safoi, irudi kabeji whinta – "winter cabbage"
Saw, n.	Zato, goge, kaya irushe kafinta
(saw-dust)	Gari katako; kurazato, kura-goge
(saw-mill)	(so-mili) (so-mil), zato injin
(sawyer)	O zato, o goge, o so-mili
Sax, n.	Saks, isaks
Sax-horn, n.	Sakshon, instrumint, abi ife irushe songi

Saxon, n. adj.	Sakisa, saksin; emon kasa Briten to Biawa lati Zamani n'arin adungogo isen abi isii	
Sexophone, n.	Saksohon, saksofoh, instrmint isongi	
(Saxophonist), n.	O saksohon, o saksofoh	
Say, vti.	Soli, gbaameh	Y/I/Izon
(say something)	Soli fekon	
(say well)	Soli rama	
(what do you say?)	Meni o soli?	
(he said that)	O gbaameh kpe	
Saying, n.	Isoli, inotezi – "remark"	
(Sayings of the wise)	Isoli o chegbon	
Scab, n.	Konko, konko kinini – sore scrab	
Scabbard, n.	Ikpa takobi, akwati takobi	Tiv/Gen/H
Scabies, n.	Kazwa, irudi irun fata –	
A type of skin disease	H	
Scaffold, n.	Shikafod, irudi katako	G(fE)
Scale, n.	Kambori kwele, nke fata nama abi kifi	
Scale n.	Sikeli, nke inofi	
Scale, (n) (quantity)	Iyewan, idile (common)	
Scale, vt.	Gunyan – (to climb)	Y/I/Isok/U
Scallop, n.	Skalor, irudi fkifi kele	G(fE)
(scallop-shell)	Gida skalor, ikpa skalor, kwarya-skalo	
Scalp, n.	Kokuwar	H
Scalpel, n.	Skabe, irudi wuka kele	G(fE/Ed/Y)
Scamp, vt., n.	Mekia, imekia, lai kiesi, ai june (care less)	
Scamper, vt.	Tirugu – "fright", tiru	Y/I
Scan, vti.	Hem, neri rama	G
Scandal, n.	Skendal, isorubi	G(fE)/Y/I

Scandinavian, n.	Skandinivian, nke kasa Dinmak, Nowe, Swindin ati Ais-lande	
Scape-goat, n.	O kabandu, eni a jeafun fun E mozo – "someone punished for others	
(scape-gotism)	Ikabandu	G
Scape-grace, n.	Yeye mutum, o yeye, mutum yah-yah-yah	
Scapula, n.	Skakpola, allo kafada – (shoulder-blade)	
Scar, n. (the scar remains)	Tabo, kufai, adabali Tabo kufo, kufai kufo, ikufo kufai	H
Scarab, n.	Skara, irudi buzuzu – type of beetle	
Scarce, vt., n.	Chiri, ichiri, chinri	G/Gen
Scarcely, adv.	Chinechiri	
Scarce, vti.	Tiru – "fright"	
(don't scare me)	Ma tiru mi	
(scare crow)	Mutummutumin	H
Scarf, n.	Adiko, dankwali	H
Scarlet, n.	Skalit, ja wur	G(fE)/H
(scarlet-fever)	Iba skalit, irudi irun	
(scarlet runner)	Skali-runa, irudi shuke-shuke wake	
(scarlet woman)	Mache o fiki-fike, (prostitute)	
(scarlet ribbon)	Skalit riban, riban kintinkiri	
Scarp, n.	Skap, irudi tudu – "a type of hill"	
Scartter, vti.	Gbaka, gbakiri, yiwa	

(scartterer), n.	O gbaka nso, o gbakiri nso a yiwa nso	
(scarttering the seeds)	I yiwa kwaya	
Scavenger, n.	Skafinja, o koshien idatti	
Scenario, n.	Senario, ikodi igwuere okpera	
Scene, n.	Mbi isoka, shen, ishen	
Scenery, n.	Isheneri, sheneri	G/I/Y
Scenic, adj.	Sheniki	
Scent, n.	Sosorobia, lafinda, kanshi, turare nke izizi	Gen/H/G
Sceptic, n.	Ipuele, "doubting"	G
(Christian sceptic)	Ipuele, abi o puele Krista, o puele isinle Krista	
(sceptical) adj.	Di 'puele' puelex	
Sceptre, n.	Septa, sanda aashe, sanda ofis	G(fE)
Schedule, n.	Shedul, irudi ilisa abi itole irushe abi agogo irinje: "a type of list of duties or travelling time-table."	
Scheme, n.	Skim, itole,	G(fE)
Schist, n.	Skis, irude dutse	
Schizophrenia, n.	Skizofewenia, irudi ifewe	G(fE)
Schnapps, n.	Shnaps, kain-kain bature	
Scholar, n.	Monkaranta, H/Y/Ed/Ur/	
Scholarship, n.	Sob/Iso/ Ger Imuko abi ichegbon turanchi	
Scholarship, n.	Skolashep, ikpa kudi fun imuko monkaranta	
Scholarstic, adj.	Nke makaranta, imuko turanchi	

Scholasticism, n.   Skolastisizim, irudi muko na yunifasit

School, n.   Makaranta   H
(primary school)   Makaranta framari H
(secondary school)   Makaranta sekondiri   H/G(fE)
(post-secondary school)   Makaranta izuein sekondiri
(schools management board)   Kwaminti mani jment
                                     nke makaranta

(school-book)   Littafi makaranta
(school-boy)   Yaro makaranta
(school-days)   ngba makaranta, irana
                                     makaranta, e rana

(school-fellow)   O sole makaranta,
                                     mutum makaranta

(school-house)   Gida nke makaranta
(school-gate)   Kofa makaranta
(school-mistress)   Uwa makaranta, miss, mis
(school-man)   Baba makaranta, essah   H/G
(school-mate)   Aboki makaranta
(school-time)   Ngba makaranta
(first school leaving certificate   Satifiket frmari

(school lessons)   ikozi makaranta
(school of African and Oriental   makaranta nke imuko
                                     Afrika ati Orienta,

Studies – University of   Yunifasit: nke London

London)   London
(school of dentistry   makaranta kokori
School, n,.   Ibuto lamba kifi,
                                     kpulu-kpulu

Schooner, n.   Skuna, irudi ugboko ruwa

Schwa, n.   Shua, irudi simbola
                                     na turanchi

Sciatic, adj.	Shatiki, kwatan (hip), ji jiya kafa	
Science, n.	saiwin, iwin; ichezighi, irokata	G/(fE)/I/G
Scientific, adj.	Nke sayens, sayentifiki, nke irokata, rokata	
(scientific study) Scientist, n.	Imuko sayens, imuko rokata O sayens, o chezighi, o rokata	
Scimitar, n.	Shimita, irudi wuka bika takobi (sword)	
Scintilla, n.	Kram – "spark", tufiene (smallest)	
Scintillate, vi.	Kram, tufiene	
Scissors, n.	Almakashi	H
(surgical scissors)	Almakshi sajan	
Sclerosis, n.	Sklerosi, irudi irun zuchiya	
Scoff, vi.	Kegon	Y(G.V)
Scoff, vt.	Wuam abinchi sokia, hawum	G
Scold, vti.	Somba, wimba	Y/I
Sconce, n.	Skons, kujera abela (candle stand)	
Scone, n.	Skon, irudi kek	
scorpio, n.	skopio, lamba asato na zodiak	
scorpion, n.	okpaganagana	Ogori
scotch, adj.	skoth, nke skotlande	
scottish, adj.	mutum skotlande	
scoundrel, n.	o banza, o jika (wicked and villain person	
scour, vti.	chowa kiri, chowa ife n'isokia	

scourge, n. vti	bulala – irudi koboko: a type of whip, jeafun, funta	
scout, n.	sikawut, sikaot	H/G(fE)
(boy scout)	yaro sikaot, omon skaot	
scout, vt.	lega, (to dismiss something)	
scow, n.	skau, irudi kwalekwale t'o lebe na gindi	
scrabble, n.	skrabol, irudi 'gwuere nke iluwe oka kago,	
scrap, n.	ita mutum abi nama: "lean person or animal"	
scram, vi.	japeh, dompeh: "to run off"	
Scoop, n.	Woja, irudi shebur – "a type of shovel	
Scoot, vi	Dompeh: "run away quickly"	G
scooter, n.	o dompeh, sukuta	
(motor – scooter)	(mota skuta)	
(rabbit-schooter)	sukuta rabitele	
scope, n.	anfa, enfa, iyefe	Y/Y(G.V)/I
scorch, vti.	jone, fi wuta jowu	
score, n. scorn, n., vti	siko, iloro, ji (20) iyagon, x yagon	G(fE) Enuani/Y

sramble, vit.	gunya (climb); choghuru. "to struggle for "	
scrap, n.	gagowa	H
scowl, n.	duburna	H
(scrap of paper)	takarda ragowa, peipa ragowa	
scrap, n.	Ijagha	Y/I
scrape, vti.	Chan	I/Y
(scraper), n.	o chan, ichan	
scratch, vti., n.	skai-skrepa, igungolo gida pia, pia-pia, ipia-pia	
scrawl, vit.	kode sokia, kode ife n'isokia	
scrawny, adj.	di kashi (bony) of bones	I/H
scream, vit.	kebe, yeeh	Y/I/G
screech, vit.	fiin, irudi ilowe bika nke breki mota: "a type of sound as of motor brake"	
screen, n.	kara, kanga, ife karawa	H/I/H
(motor-screen)	kara	
(screen printer)	o tite kara	
scribble, vti.	kikode, ikode ife n'isokia	
scribble, n.	akawu, o kode wasika	Gen
scrimmage, n.	idarugu – "confusion"	
script, n.	skrif, ikode hannu	G(fE)
(script writer)	okode skrif	
scripture, n.	skrifcha, littafi krista, Baibul Isomon	
scrivener, n.	koteh, akawu t'o ng kode wasika	
scrofula, n.	shkrofla, irudi ikoho bika tobakulosi	
scroll, n.	shkrol, ikondo takarda: "roll of paper"	

scrooge, n.		
	o tawun tain-tain: "extreme mean miser"	
scrotum, n.	shkroto, jakar kwalatai	G(fE)/H
scrounge, vti.	yi 'fe na hanya rubi, yi n'iwayo: "get	
Scrub, vti.	wecha	Y/I
(scrub the floor)	wecha dabe	
(scrubbing brush)	burosh iwecha	
scruff, n.	shkrof, zuba wuya – "back of the neck"	
scruffy, adj.	datti, zizi	
scruple, n.	shkropu, nke inofi: (20 grains)	
scrupulous, adj.	kiesitain; "paying attention to least details"	
scrutineer, n.	o chondi	I/Y/H
scrutinize, vt.	chondi	
scrutiny, n.	ichond	
scuff, vit.	kabu, ringa kelekele na kasa	
scuffle, vi.	gharu, gharudu	I/Y
scull, n.	kashi keisi	H/I
sculptor, n.	o fin	Y(G.v)
scum, n.	shku, idatti n'ikenu ruwa (dirts on top of water)	
scupper, n.	shkupa, ihonu na ugboko ruwa	
scurf, n.	bambaroki – (dandruff)	H
scurrilous, adj.	gbru-gbruh – (of violent words)	
scurry, vi.	gbere zai-zai, zai-zai: (run hurriedly, hurr)	
scurvy n.	ekuru, irudi irun jinni	Y
scut, n.	bindi kuru: short tail	H/Gen

scuttle,	slite, kwano gawayi, kwano kwalta	
sea, n.	tekun	H
(sea man)	o tekun, siman	
(sea scout)	sikawut tekun	
(seamanship)	irushe tekun, simanshef	
(sea bird)	onene tekun	
(over-sea)	ifeja-tekun, oba-si	
(sea-board)	kasa n'akue tekun	
(sea-boat)	ugboko tekun	
(sae-dog)	kare tekun	
(sea-fish)	kifi tekun	
(sea-food)	abinchi tekun, nama tekun	
(sea-god)	ekwenshu tekun	
(sea-going)	o ringa abi o loga tekun, ugboko tekun	
(sea-gull)	sigo, irudi onene tekun	
(sea-level)	laini tekun na ugboko ruwa, laini tekun	
(sea-lion)	zaki tekun	
(sea-lord)	chiolu tekun, na kasa london	
(sea-plane)	ugboko sonma o tekun, si-filen	
(sea-port)	nute tekun, sikpot	
(sea-rover)	o logburu na tekun	
(sea-shore)	isiki tekun	
(sea-side)	akue tekun	
(sea-snake)	machiji tekun	
(sea-urchin)	siyochen, irudi nama tekun	
(sea-wall)	bango tekun	
(sea-water)	ruwa tekun	
(sea-way)	hanyar ugboko ruwa	
(sea-wave)	isonbi tekun	

(sea-weed)	sako, abi shukeshuke tekun	
(sea-worthy)	rama fun tekun, weda fun tekun	
seal, n.	Hatimi, irudi nama ruwa	
seal, n.	sili, nke was (wax)	
seam, n.	sem, laini na ebi a kwa esa	
seamstress, nn	o kwaesa,	Y/I/ Ogori
search, vti.	guolo, chowa	Ed/I/Y
(search your heart/mind)	Chowa iyobi e	
(in search of)	n'ichowa	
(what are you searching for?)	meni o ng chowa?	
(search thoroughly)	guolo rama	
(searcher)	o guolo, ochowa	
(search warrant)	inindo guolo, iguolo nindo, aashe fun ichowa	
(search party)	itugbe chowa, itugbe chichowa, itugbe guolo-guolo	
Season, n.	ikongba, ngba	
(season's greeting)	ikine ngba	
(season's greetings)	ekine ngba	
seasonal, adj.	na ngba, ngbangba, n'ikongba	
seat, n.	kujera	H
secateurs, n.	sikatu, irudi almaksashi fulawaw: a type of flower scissors.	
Secede, vin.	Fapu, fata – "to withdraw from" o fapu, o fata	
(secessionist)		
seclude, vt.	Yahann	
Second, adj.	nkeji, neji	
(second-best)	nkeji rama kha, neji rama jukha	
(second-class)	itugbe nkeji, (sekon-klas)	

(second-floor)	dabe nkeji, (sekon-fla)	
(second-hand)	iluwe nkeji, itun leta, (sekon-han)	
(second-lieutenant)	leftana nkeji	
(second thoughts)	ichiro nkeji	
Second, n.	neji, ineji	
Second, n.	tain, nke hawa agogo	G
secondary, adj.	nkeji, na nkeji, n'eji	I/Y
(secondary grammar school)	Makaranta girama nkeji, kolej girama nkeji	
(secondarily)	n'eji	
secrecy, adj, n.	kpache, kele, ikpache, ikele	I/Y
(secret service)	irushe kpache	(safis ikpache)
(secret agent)	omaye/wakili ikpache	Id/H/I/Y
(keep our secret secret)	kpache ikpache 'wa	
(secret ballot)	tabo ikpache	
secretariat, n.	ofis akawu,	
(secretary to the Federal Military Government)	akawu gonmenti Soja	
(secretary-general)	ivenda-jana, Akawu-Janar	
(Secretary of State)	Akawu kasa, akawu gonmenti, ivenda kasa	
(parliamentary Secretary)	Akawu Majalisar Wakili	
(Permanent Secretary)	Akawu katazi, ivenda katazi	
secrete, vt.	kioron: "produce by secretion" dezi	
secrete, v.	kpache: secret	
sect, n.	ikwandoh G	
(religious sect)	Ikwando sinlele, ikwando sinle	
sectarian, n.	o kwando	
section, n.	iyaka G/I/Y	
(section by section)	iyaka-yaka; yaka-yaka	

sector, n.	ikwankpa G/Y	
secular, adj. Secure, adj.	nka akpor, akpor I/Urhobo Twi nka bambo	
security, n.	ibambo	
(Security Guard)	o bambo	
(security van)	motaka bambo	
(security patrol)	ichokiri bambo,	
(security police)	mondoka bambo	
(security council)	jalisa bambo	
(State Security Service)	irushe bambo kasa	
(security document)	dokiumen idiwen	
sedan, n.	sedani, irudi kujera o wen hannu	
	ati rufi na ngba kera	
sedative, n.	sedeti, irudi magani abi ogun	
sedge, n.	sej, irudi shuke-shuke	
sediment, n.	Gane-gani, dalaki	G/H
sedition, n.	imote, mote	I/Y
seduce, vt.	tonwuam, ton	Y/G
(seducer)	o ton, o tonwuam	
seduction, n.	itonwuam, iton	
see, vti.	Neri, hun; hunri	I/Y
(see you)	hun e lachi	
(we shall see)	a wa ga hun	
(seeing is believing)	Ineri wu inikon; (ineri wu inikon) kam'	
(let me see you off)		
	solele e (escort)	
(see you at Kafanchan)	Awa ga hun na Kafanchan; hun e na Kafanchan	
(see you later)	hun e baya, hun e n'ngbazu	
(sight-seeing)	ineri nason; ineri fun ido	
(see to it)	Neri si, neri si ya	
seedling, n.	Monkwaya Gen/H	
seedy, adj.	wen kwaya, winwen kwaya	

452

seek, vt.	chokiri, chowa	
(seek and you will find)	chowa e ga hun	
(seeker)	o chowa, o chokiri	
seem, vi.	kabi Y/I	
(it seems that)	o kabi kpe	
(it seems as if)	o kabi bi	
seep, vi.	piri	G
seer, n.	o neri whido, o hun whido	
seersucker, n.	siasoka, irudi fabriki tinrin	
see-saw, n.	siso, irudi igwuere: a type of game	
segment, n.	ikpoto	G
segregate, vt. n.	yaji, iyaji	Y/H
seine, n.	sien, baba koma kifi: "large or big fishing net"	
Seismic, adj.	seismi, nke wiwo kasa: "of earthquake"	
seismograph, n.	seismogra, irudi ife aiki, ife irushe jigba jiyi	
seize, vti.		I/Y/ Egun
(I seize this opportunity)	mo jiyi anfa yii	
Seizure, n.	ijigba, ijiyi	
Seldom, adv.	ngba kene-kene, ngba kene, gbakene	
(I seldom eat rice)	mo ng wuam shikafa n'ngba kene	
selector, vt. n.	kere, ikere	Izon
(selector)	o sele, o kere	
selenium, n.	selaniom, ihe irushe lantiriki, nke sayens	
self, n.	wenji	I/H
(self-addressed)	adresi o wenji, ikode adresi o wenji	
(self-addressed envelope)	evilop nke adresi o wenji	
(self-confidence)	igboaya o wenji	

(self-control)	ikoso o wenji
(self-defence)	imekusa o wenji; idifens o wenji
(self-denial)	ikonu o wenji
(self-employed)	irushe o wenji, iyi rushe 'wenj
(self-esteem)	ibuni o wenji
(self-evidence)	ishaida o wenji
(self-examination)	ichondi o wenji
(self-determination)	ichenu o wenji
(self-explanatory)	imediye o wenji
(self-help)	innon hann o wenji
(self-interest)	irire nke o wenji;
(self-possessed)	enfa o wenji igboaya o wenji; ikule o wenji
(self-reliance), n.	imeko o weni; imeko si o wenji
(self-made)	imedi fun o wenji
(self-righteousness)	iyasah o wenji
(self-sacrifice)	isebo o wenji
(self-seeker)	o chokiri fun o wenji; o chowa fun o wenj
(self-starter)	itwin-twin o wenji
(self-sufficient)	izuto fun o wenji; izutoo wenji
(self-supporting)	Itizu o wenji
Selfish, adj., n.	tin tin, itin-tin
Sell, vti.	leta; reta
(selling price)	iyenu leta;iyenu reta
(seller)	o leta; o reta
Selvedge, selvage, n.	Karbu
Selves, pl. n.	ewenji; e wenji
Semantic, adj.	Girima
semblance, n	Ijijo

Semen, n	Maniyi
Semester, n	Siminsta
semaphore, n	Senmakpor, irudi inji fun iziron
semi, prep. (semi-circle)	Sebe sebe kiri
(semi-colon)	sebe iyame
(semi-final)	(iguton-sebe)
(semi-finalist)	o guton-sebe
(semi-vowel)	baweli-sebe
seminar, n.	seminah
seminary, n.	semini, irudi kolej na
	chochi Roma katoliki semolina, semo
semolina, n.	G(fE)
senate, n.	senit
(senator)	O senit, senita
(senatorial)	nke senit, nso abi agba senit
(senate president)	Presido senit; o keisi senit; shugaba senit
Senate, n.	senit
(senatorial)	o senit, senita
(senate president)	presido senit; o keisi senit; shugaba senit
send, vti.	ronga, ronshien Y/I
(send packing)	le shien, le kuta, le'ta, le peh, ron peh
(send down)	ronshien si 'sala
(send down the rain)	ronshien ruwa si 'sala
(send off)	ronshien, ron peh
(send off party)	ikonogbandu fun ironshien, ikonogbandu fun ironpo o ronshien, o ron peh, o le 'ta, o
senescent, adj.	bujele; ife ti o ng digbo:
senile, adj.	buje: jiki abi icheronsi nke ti fresi: (mental)

senior, adj.	shato	
senna, n.	sena, irudi ikpogbe warka	Y/I
	nke itache kasia:	
	a type of kasia plant or tree dried leaves	
sensation, n.	iwuche – "feeling"; sensashon	
sense, n.	ichegbon	I/Y
senseless, adj.	lai wen ichegbono; ai wen ichegbon,	
	fre chegbon (mumuh)	
sensibility, n.	agba ichegbon	
sensitive, adj.	chichegbon	
sensual, adj.	di chegbon, wen ichegbon, keda	
sentence, n.	sintens, nke turanchi abi girama	
sentence, n, vt.	libi	Y(G.v)
Sentiment, n.	roche, rochele,	
sentimental, adj.	Roche, rochele	
(sentimental music)	isongi sentimental; (muzik sentimental)	
sentinel, n.	sentiri, soja mai gadi	
sentry, n. sepal, n.	sentiri, soja o gadi sepra, nke	
(epicalix of sepal)	fulawa epikali nke sepra	
		G(fE)
separate, adj., vti, n.	choto, ichoto	
Septic, adj.	nke sesis, ife sesis, sesi	
(septic tank)	tanki sesi	
septicemia, n.	setisemya, puezin jinni: (blood poison)	
septuagenarian, n.	setuajine-jine,	
	mutum ardun saa	
septuagesima, n.	setuajisima, sirande nke eta swene Lenti	

Sepulcher, n.	jufosile; irudi kambari: a type of tomb;	G
sequel, n.	sikuen, nke ngba 'zu; ngba izuba	
sequence, n.	itolezu, tolezu, itolele	Y/I
sequestrate, vt.	sikuestrit; oka iwufin: "legal word"	
sequin, n.	sikwin, irudi azurfa (silver)	
sequoia, n.	sikwoya, itache ilililai, itache algashi	
seraph, n.	serafin, irudi malaika	
serenade, n.	seined, irudi isongi irayo na ngba tuu	
serene, adj.	shaka-kule; (clear and calm)	
serge, n.	sej; irudi esa wulu	
sergeant, n.	sajan, vita	H(fE)/G
(seageant-major)	samanja, vita-manja	
sericulture, n.	serikalcha; o webi tana siliki: "breeding silk-	
series, n.	iseli; isele, nke isole lamba	
serious, adj, n.	chenu; ichenu	I/Y
(it is very serious)	,o di rugh, o chenu kha-ka	
sergeant, n.	sajiene, sajien, nke iseza	
(sergeant-at-arms)	sajien-na-am	
sermon, n.	iwasu, samon	Y/G(fE)
serpent, n.	machiji; wayo mutum	H
serpentine, adj.	bika machiji	
serrated, adj.	seret	G(fE)
serum, n.	sarum; irudi ruwa na jinni: "a type of water in the blood"	
servant, n.	monshe; mongi;	Gen/Y/H/G(fE)

(master and servant)	oga ati omo ise; maigida ati monshe	
(ready to serve)	yaji lati rushe; yaji fun irushe	
(public servant)	monshe domesa	
(civil servant)	monshe finja, (mon-finja)	
(your humble servant)	nke yin monshe lisi	
serve, vti.	rushe	I/Y
(serve one-another)	rushe tukonono	
(serve yourselves)	rushe e wenji	
(serve yourself)	Rushe wenji	
service, n.	irushe, safis, o rushe, isinle (worship)	
(go into service)	loga rushe; shiene rushe	
(on active service) (died on active service)	n'irushe ngba o kuowun n'irushe ngba; o kuowun n'irushe	
(service dress)	esa irushe	
(service station)	tashan safis	
(serviceable)	nke le rushe, di rushe, rushe	
(service boy)	yaro safis; o rushe yaro	
service girl)	omote safis	
serviette, n.	sevite, irudi nafkin tebur	
servitor, n.	safitoh: miji safis	
servitude, n.	irushe fala-fala	
servo,pref.	safo, nke injin breki	
sesame, n.	sesim, irudi shuke-shuke: "a type of plant"	
sesquipedalian, adj.	seskuipedah	G(fE)
session, n.	seshan	G(fE)
set, n.	mundu, yaji (ready); fiyen/fie; itumon;	
(set aside)	mundi si akue; cheto; fre	
set, vti.	levoh	G
(sun set)	ilevoh rana	

(set example)	mundu ifineri
(set it on fire)	jowu ya; fie, wuta si; fiyen wuta
(set in motion)	fiyen n'iyime
(set off)	yaji peh; dom-peh
(set free)	fre fefefe
(set-back)	fa si azu, iyintua
setee, n.	satii G(fE)
setter, n.	sata, irudi kare bature (dog)
setting, n.	firem, irushe firem: "frame work
settle, n.	kule, kulele, isimini, megien, ribose; lagha
(settle down)	kule kasa; wen sundi; simini; kulele
settle, vti.	kpa: "to pay/pay off"
(have you settled your debt?)	e ti kpa igwese yin?
settlement, n.	ibisim, ikpa;
(my father settled in lagos)	baba mi bisim na bia/ kuleh lagos; baba mi
settlement, n.	ikolo: (colony); bisim G/Y/G.v
(we have settled here)	awa ti bisim-bi; a ti bisim-bi
settler, n.	o bisim; o kolo
seven, n.	asaa; lamba asaa
seventh, adj, n.	n'asaa; nk'asaa
(seventh position)	ikpoze asaa; lamba asaa
(the Seventh Day)	Rana nk'asaa; rana asaa na uzola; igukpin uzola
(seventeen)	goasaa
(seventeenth)	nke goasaa; lamba goasaa
(seventy) sever, vti.	saa yapu, yata
	Y/I
(sever relationship)	yapu inure; yata inure

(several people)	mutum kposhin; e mutum; mutane
(several times)	ikposhin ngba
(several miles)	maili 'kposhin
severally, adv.	kpokposhin
severe, adj.	tankiti G
(severe punishment)	iriya tankiti
sew, vti.	kwa
(sew your clothes here)	kwa esa e mbi esa yin mbi
(sewing maching	kmashin-kwa; mashin ikwa
(sewer)	o kwa
sewage, n.	suwej: irudi datti
sewer, n.	shuwa; irudi hanya na gindikasa (underground)
sex, n.	e ya: nke miji abi mache
sex, vti., n.	vuduh; ivuduh; fioko;
sexagenarian, n.	zaza jineria; mutum ardun G sii jukha ele (person of sixty years or a little above)
sexagesima,n.	zaza jesima; sirande nk'eji swene lenti
sextant, n.	sektan, irudi ihe irushee a fi ng nofi rana
sextet, n	sekte, irudi songi kele
sexton, n.	sektin miji o cheto abi bo gida chochi
sexual, adj.	ivuduh; ifioko
shabby, adj., n.	kumehume
(shabbily dressed)	iyiwo esa kumekume esa
shack, n.	buka n',kumekume
shacle, n. mari, gigar;	ruka a ng fi koso o prusu: "a ring for tying a prisoner";malwa
shad, n.	shad, irudi kifi na amerika Gen

460

shaddock, n.	shaidok irudi itache inabi	
shade, n.	inuwa; launi	
shadow, n	inuwa	
shady, adj.	nke nuwa, ilauni; di nuwa, nuwa	
(shady business)	irusshe launi; irushe rugu; biznes irugu	H
shaft, n.	irudi sanda ayan nke mota	H
shaft, n.	bota, kota	
(shaft bearing)	shaf biyerin – nke injin	
shag, n.	shaga, irudi siga bika (tobako)	
shaggy, adj.	gargasa, buzubuzu: something roudgh, untidy	H
sheikh, n.	sheikh, nke musullmi abi arab	
shake vti.	rugha(ruga);	I/
shake, (of hands)	meyeji; rufe yi mi hann; nnon mi hann	Y/
(shaking)	irugha: (iruga): imeyeji; imeyeji; idrufe; iyi hann	
(shaky)	ruga, meyeji; rufe	
shakespeare, n.	shekspie	
shall,	gama abi gama; maa, ishekwa/shekwa	
(i shall be grateful)	madiokpe	
(you shall be grateful)	e maa diocpe	
(we shall be grateful)	awa moo dridcpe	
(i am grateful)	mo diokpe	
(you are grateful)	e diokpe	
(we are grateful)	awa diokpe; awa diokpe	
(i shall give you)	ma nno e; ma nno yin (i shall give you money)	ma nno yin kudi

shallop, n.	shailop, irudi kwalekwale abi abara, moru	
shallot, n.	shailot irude albasa	
shallow, adj.	lai jinka; ai jinka; ai jinka; fele	
(shallow-well)	rijiya fele	
shalom, int.	shalom; ikine nakasa Heberu (Hebrew)	
sham, vit. n.	bebeye (wayo)	Ed/Gen.
shamble, vi.	dongili: "walk in unsteady manner"	G
shambles, n, adj.	itagbu; tagbulu	Y/I
Shame, n.	feju	Y/H
(you are not ashamed of yourself)	ee feju o wenji e; ee 'wenyin	
(I'm ashamed)	mo ng feju	
(shameless)	ai feju, lai feju	
shampoo, n.	shamfo; shamfoh G/Gen	
shandy, n.	chandi; irudi wain; (shandi)	
shank, n.	chank; kashi kafa	
shanty, n.	isiyen bagiri: "poor hut"	
shape, n.	idiwa; ikpongba	
(in a bad shape)	n' idiwa rubi	
(in good shape)	n 'idiwa rama	
shape, vti.	homoh: (to shape something); ihomoh	
shard, n.	shaid, nke akioloji	G(fE)
share, n.	ikekpin; (sherh)	I/Y/G(fE)
(ordinary share)	sonki sherh; (kpako sherh)	
(share capital)	sherh afita; warkudi	G/H

(share certificate)	satifiket sherh; satifiket nke sherh	
(share holder)	o jimu sherh; o jimu warkudi, sherhoda	
shark, n.	shaki; irudi baba kifi na tekun	G(fE)
sharp, adj.	wogo; muko; soki;	I/Y/Ed(G.v)
(sharp knife) (sharp boy)	wuka wogo-wogo Yaro o muko; (o muko yaro)	
shatter, vti.	fowa Y/I	
(shatter hope)	fowa irekon	
shave, vti.	chochor G	
(shaving-stick)	sanda-chochor	
(shaving)	ichochor	
she, pron.	ta	H
sheaf/sheaves, n.	dami	H
shear, vt.	kpaso: "of strip bare"	G
shears, n.	shias, baba almakashi (big scissors)	
sheath, n.	kube	H
shed, n.	rumfa, buka	H/Gen.
sheen, n.	imoshaka, ishaka	Y(G.v)
(sateen sheen)	ishaka satin; satinshaka; (satin shin)	
sheep, n.	meeh; tunkiya, tumaki	G/H
(sheep-dog)	karen asako	H
(sheepish)	muzumuzu	H
sheer, adj.	duna, sam-sam; fefefe	
(sheer rubbish)	idatti sam-sam; idatti fefefe	

sheet, n.	fale (fale)	H/Y
(sheet of paper)	fale takarda (fale takarda)	
(roofing sheet)	fale-rufin	
sheet, n.	shiti, nke ugboko ruwa	
shekel, n.	shekele, irudi kudi abi kobo na kasa jiu	
sheikh, n.	shehu, sarki	H(fArab)
sheldrake, n.	sheldrek, irudi rage (duck)	
shelf, n.	kanta, saga	H
(book-shelf)	kanta littafi	
shell, n.	kwarya, korofo, gbaza: kakpuh	H/I/Y/G
(snail-shell)	kwarya kodi; kwarya katantanwa	
(shelling of soldiers)	igbaza iseza; ikakpuhkpuh soja	
shellac, n.	shelak, ife a ng fi meshe fenti ati rekod.	
shelter, n.	Tsari, mafaka, fake	H
(a shelter in the time of storm)	tsari/fake n'ngba dumdum; ifake n'ngba	
shelve, vt.	fiyen; fie, gbepu; buswhido	
(let us shelf the matter)	k'awa buswhido magana yien	
(put the book in the shelf)	fiyen littafi na tsari	
shepherd, n.	o tumaki;	
(the Good Shepherd)	o tumaki Rama; O Hufe Jesu Kristi	
Sheraton, n.	sheratin; sherata	G
(Sheraton Hotel)	huta Sheratin; Otel Sheratin	

sheriff, n.	sharif, nke Kotu Ganu	
sherry, n.	shari, irudi kain-kain bature	
(sherry brandy)	brande shari	
Shield, n. v.	garkuwa, kariya, ibo	H/Y/I
(shield me)	bo mi	
shift, n. vt.	isigkie; sigkie, yintua	Kalabari/Ishan
(please shift forward)	biko sigkie zuba	
(shift backwards)	sigkie zuba	
(shift position)	yintua ikpoze	
shilling, n.	sile, kudi kasa Briten ati Naijeriya lembu	
shilly-shally, vi.	ai cherisi; lai cherisi: "indecision"	
shimmer, vi.	wuta-wata: "moonlight"; kyalkyali	
shin, n.	kwauri, sangali	H
(shin-guard)	gadi-kwauri; gadi-sangali	
(shinbone)	kashi kwauri; kashi sangali	
shine, vit.	shana; wain-wain	Gen/ G(fEd)
(the moon is shining bright)	wata ng shana shaka	
(shoe-shiner4)	O shana bata o shana takalmi	
shingle, n.	bulaliya, tamaula	H
Shingles, n.	shengos, irudi irun jiki	
Ship, n.	konga; baba ugboko ruwa	Y/I/H
(ship-builder)	O kogi ugboko ruwa; (o kogi konga)	
(ship-wreck)	ijambe kongio; ijambe ugboko ruwa; (iwere kongi)	

(ship-yard)	Yadi ugboko-ruwa; yadi kongi;	
(shipment)	ironshien na ugboko ruwa	
shirk, vti.	Shiri: avoid	
shirt, n.	yèré, taguwa,	Wolof/H/I/Igala
(long-sleev)	taguwa; taguwa-golo	
(short-sleeve)	taguwa; taguwa-kuru; afe kuru-hannu	
(put on your shirt)	yiwo taguwa; yiwo taguwa	e/yin
shit, n.	kashi, izizi	H/I
(damn shit)	shior	It/Ur/is
shiver, vi.	riri; riri; (gri-gri)	Agbor/Aniocha/G
shoal, n.	ishole; ilau lamba kifi na ruwa	
shoal, n.	shoh; kasa fele na tekun: "shallow area in the sea"	
shock, n.	kpumu; igbu 'yobi ikumu	
(i was shocked)	mo gbu 'yobi	
(it shocked me)	O gbu mi 'yobi	
(shocking news)	kwiro igbu 'yobi	
(shocking news is not good)	kwiro igbu 'yobi ko rama; kwiro o gbu 'yobi ko rama	
(electrical shock)	ikumu lantiriki	
shoddy, adj.	Yeye; yah-yah-yah	Y/G
shoe, n.	takalmi; bata	
(shoe-black)	O shakata bata: "shoe polisher"	
(shoe-polish)	kpolish abi shakata bata	
(shoe-lace)	lesi nke bata; lesi	

(shoe-leather) (leather-shoe) (shoe-meaker)	bata abi takalmi fata bata; fata takalmi Bata nke fata; takalmi nke fata O meshe bata; o	
(horse-shoe)	meshe takalmi Bata doki	
shogun, n.	shogun; baba kwamanda	
	na soja jakpan; ihumon: "of new growth"	
shoot, n.		
shoot, vit.	gbata; sogbe; takpu;	
	akpu i/y/g gbata bindiga	
(shoot the gun)		
(shooting range)	iyefe igbata bindiga	
(shooting area)	nso igbata wuta	
(shooter)	o gbata; o sogbe; o takpu; o kakpu	
(trouble-shooter)	o lagha: "reconciliator"	
(shooting stars)	ihumon tara	
shop, n.	kisuwa; knati	H(G.v)/ Gen
(shopping center)	baba kasuwa;	
(shopping complex)	ilega kisuwa;	
	kampleks kisuwa o cheto kisuwa	
(shop-keeper)		
(shop-boy)	o feza kisuwa	
(shop-girl)	omote kisuwa	
(shop-lifter)	barawo kisuwa	
(shop-window)	iwindo kisuwa	Uvwe/H
(window-shopping)	ineri kisuwa; igora ife	
	kia-kia na kisuwa o rushe kisuwa	
(shop-worker)		
shore, n.	gaba, kasa na tekun	H
shore, n (of wooden support)	fun kongi itizu sanda; sanda itizu	

short, adj.	kuru	Y/Gen/I
shorthand	shothan	Y/Gen/I
(short-person)	mutum kuru	
(short-lived)	mindu-kele	
(short-time)	ngba kele	
(short-space)	iyefe kele	
(short-circuit)	sakut kuru (sakutu-kuru)	
(short-comings)	e goshi	
(our short-comings)	e goshi 'wa	
(short-sigh/sighted)	ineri kuru; o neri kuru	
(short-notice)	notezi kuru; ikiesi kuru	
(short-term)	ikponu kuru	
(short-term capital)	warkudi ikponu kuru	
(long and short)	gungolo ati kuru	
(short bread/cake)	buredi abi kek kele	
(short-wave)	Ibilu kuru; nke rediyo abi wayalis	
short, adv.	buku; funu	
(shortage)	ibuku; ifunu	
(I am short of money)	mo buku kudi; mii wen kudi	
(I had shortage in the market)	mo buku na kasuwa	
shorts, n.	wando abi shokoto kuru; nika	
shot; n.	igbata; ikappu; isogbe; itakpu	
shot, vt. (of photo)	kliki	G
should,	shekwa/shekwa	

(should i go?)	shekwa mi shienga?; shekwa mi loga?	
(i should be grateful)	ma shekwe diokpe: (better: ma diokpe)	
shoulder, n.	kafada, kartata	H
(shoulder-blade)	allon kafada	H
(rob-shoulder)	tugbe	
(shoulder-high)	yanga-tolotolo	Gen
(shoulder-arms)	shodah-am	
shout, n.	kemkpo; ikemkpo	
shove, vti.	kpuh: (to push)	G
shovel, n.	shebur	H
show, n. vti)	ifineri, fine; fihun;	
(show-boy)	hone; ikuaku yaro kuakua; (o kuakua yaro); sho-boli	
(show-man)	(o kua-kua miji); (sho-man)	
(show me)	fineri mi; fine mi	
(show-down)	Ifineri sam-sam; fineri sam	
(your yourself)	hone ownei e; hone owenyin; yopu; jait	
(show me the way)	fine mi hanya; fihun mi hanya	
(show him the way)	fine ya hanya; fihun ya hanya	
(show-up)	hone; fine	
shower, n.	yayyafi; iyayyafi; ruwa sama	
(showers of the rain)	yayyafi ruwa	
(showers of blessing)	iyayyafi 'kunzi	
shred, n.	kinrin G	

shrew, n.	mache njika: wicked woman
shrewd, adj.	gbonchi; gboncha: of sound judgment
shriek; vit.	shiri; shikiri; shiki G
shrike; n	shaik; irudi onene
shri ii, adj.	kwili G
shrimp, n.	shiremp ogege G
shrine, n.	kushewar wali; H/G
(African Shrine)	ogege Afrika ogege
shrivel, vti.	koloh: dried up or curled due to heat
shroud, n.	likkafani H
shrove – tuesday: n.	shovede; rana swene
shrub, n.	irebi lenti karamin itache; takele H/Gen
shrug, vt.	karuo "lift up shoulders showing unconcern or indifference
shudder, vti.	rugu; irugu
shuffle, vit.	meru; shaful; miri I/Y/ G(fE)/G
shun, vt.	shiri: "to avoid something"
shunt, vti.	ronshien: "send away" tikpo; gbure; wi
shut, vti (close/lock)	Y/I/G
(shut up your mouth)	tikpo 'nu
(shut up)	gbure
(close your eyes)	wi ido e/yin; wi 'do
shutter, n.	shota, ife iwindo
shuttle, n.	koshiya; shatol H/G
(shuttle service)	shatol safis; irushe shatol
shy, adj, n.	feju; ifeju

siamese, adj.	munji: isogba emon eji na imubi (birth)
(siamese twins)	emon ejimo; munji ejimo
sibilant, adj.	sibilante; irudi arimkpo bika fito
sick, adj, n.	ai gbandu; bujen; ibujen; bujen-bujen; (ibujene)
(took ill)	yi bujen
(sick-leave)	isimini bujen; isimini fun ibujen
sickle, n.	lauje H
(sickly-cell)	(siko-sel); ibujene rubi nke jinni
side, n.	akue, kwegbe
(your side)	kwegbe e; kwegbe yin
(watch your side)	bo ikwegbe e/yin; bo akue e/yin
(take side)	yi akue; megbe; yi kpaka; ya kpaka
(side attraction)	ifaneri akue; ifaneri na 'kue
(side-by-side)	na 'kue-kue
(side-walk)	irinshien na 'kue; iringa n'akue
(side-plates)	kwano akue
siding, n.	saide; irudi hanya reluwe
(side-board)	tebur akue
siege, n.	kpiri G/Y
sienna, n.	siena, irudi yumbu
sierra, n.	Sera; irudi basani – a type of mountain

siesta, n.	isimoh; (siyesta)	
(i am on siesta)	mo wa n'isimoh; mo ng simoh	
(siesta time)	ngba isimoh; ngba isiyesta	
sieve, n.	asien	Ed
sift, vti.	sien	Ed
(sifter)	asien, o sien	
sigh,	Mini	Y(G.v)
sight, n.	ineron, iyefe	I/Y
(second-sight)	ineron ngba eji; ineron na ngba nk'eji	
(sight-seeing)	ineron nso	
(sight-seer)	o neron nso	
sight, vt.	neri; hun	
(sigh somebody)	neri mutum, hun mutum; neri eni	
short-sighted)	ihun kuru; ineri kuru	
(long-sighted)	ineri golo; ineri ife H/Gen lau; ineri whido	
sightless, adj. sign, n.	fido; ai neri; lai neri lamba, alama, shaida, allo	
(sign-board)	sain-bod; allo-lamba; Efik katako lamba	
sign, n. (of writing)	sen	
(sign here, please)	sen si mbi, bika; sen mbi, biko	
(sign your signature)	sen itofa e/yin; sen hann	
(sign off)	sen-ta	
signal, n.	sigi-sigi; waya waya;	

(send me signal)	ronshien mi wayawaya; ronshien mi sigi sigi (sigi-sigi me)
(signal-box)	gida waya-waya; gida sigi-sigi
(signal-man)	miji waya-waya; miji sigi-sigiY/I
signal, adj. (of sign)	fine; hone
signatory, n.	isen-hann: eni sen hannu G/G(fE)/G si ikweba abi agrimento
signature, n.	itofa; signacha, sigi-sigi I/Y
significance, n; adj.	izunkaka; izunka; zunkaka
signification, n.	izunkaka; ifineri; iripresento; itiuma
(the significance of this is)	izunkaka eyi wu Y/I/G(fE)
signify, vti, n.	hone; sigini; isigini
signor, nn	signor: afa "mazi" na kasa itli
sikh, n.	sik; (sikh); nke hindu
silence, n.	da nkiti; (dankiti); idankit
(silence in court)	dankiti na kotu; ka gbonti
silencer, n.	sailinsa; o dankiti
silence, adj.	zùumkpó gbonti G(fE)
silhouette, n.	silihu, irudi foto
silica, n.	selika (si02); nke sayens
silicate, n.	selike, nke selika
silicon, n.	selikon; irudi iferushe fenti
silicosis, n.	selikosa; selikosi; irudi irun datti na huhu: (lungs)
silk; n.	siliki; itufi zare: (thread)
silken, adj.	siliken; ife dido ati muru: (soft and smooth)

silky, adj.	sili-sili; sili-siliken; bika siliken	
(silk-worm)	tana-siliki	
sily, adj.	wele	
(don't be silly)	ma di wele	
(you are silly)	o ng wele	
(silly boy)	yaro wele	
(silly girl)	omote wele; yarinya wele	
silo, n.	sailo, nke fekuku abi erh	H/G/Y
silver, n.	azurfa; siliva; silifa	
(born with silver spoon)	eni a mubi kpelu ileze gidi	
(silver-paper)	takarda siliva	
(silver-fish) (sliver-smith)	silifa-fish; irudi kifi bika silifa makeri-	
(sliver-light)	siliva; o meshe silifa; wuta-siliva	
(silver-jubilee)	jubrili-siliva: anivaseh	
(silver-wedding)	nke ardun jisen iwede siliva; anivaseh ardun jisen n'iwede	
simian, adj., n.	simien, irudi biri	G(fE)
similar, adj., n.	yijo; iyijo; bika; (kabi);	I/Y
(this is similar to that)	eyi rufe si yien; eyi kabi	
simile; n.	irufe; irufene	Y/I
similitude, n.	iyijo; semilitiu	I/Y/ G(fE)
simmer,	gboho; fiyen na wuta; (shiene wuta) (keep boiling); shiene gbowuta.	
simony, n.	simona; irudi jika abi imeje rubi	

simoon, n.	saimunu, irudi fekuku na kasa sahara	
simple, adj.	rowu; flesi; mini	Y/I/G
simpleton, n.	galallawa	H
simplicity, n.	irowu; iflesi; imini	
simplify, vt, n.	muneri, mune, semplifai; imune	
simulate, vt.	meshebi mebika; pritenda: (prentence)	
simultaneous, adj.	jumesoka; isolela; solela; ijumesoka	
(it happened simultaneously)	o soka n'solela	
sin, n.	ijoshe; joshe; jika; njika	
since, adv.	kengab; ririnbu; lateh	
(since yesterday)	kengba layen; lateh lateh	
sincere, adj, n.	zindo; izindu ezindu	
(are you sincere?)	e di zindu?; e zindu; shekwa zindu	
(yours sincerely)	nke yin n'izindu; nke yin n'ezindu	
sincere, adj, n.	zindo; izindu ezindu	
(are you sincere?)	e di zindu?; e zindu; shekwa zindu	
(yours sincerely)	nke yin n'izindu; nke yin n'ezindu	
sine die, adv. (Lat.)	Sindi; lai wen rana: wasika ti ko wen irana; ai dido: (indefinitely)	
sinequanon, n.	sinkwana:	"ai
sinew, n.	jijiya; isile (tough)	H/Y/I
sing, vit.	songi; rinbu	

(singer/musician)	o songi;	
(sing praises)	songi 'yinboh	
singe, vti.	joki; fi wuta jowu kashi na tipi (tip)	
single, adj.	konon, tukon; tukonon; sonsho	Ed/I/Y
(single-combat)	ijagha	
(single-handed)	hannu sigen; imeshe ife sonsho; imeshe sonsho	
(single person)	mutum sigen; mutum kono; ikono; itukono	
single – single	sigen-sigen	
singlet, n.	singileti; shinmi	H(fE)/ Gen
singleton, n. sing-song; n.	sengotin; irudi igwere kadi itugbe o songi songa	
singular; n. isigen;	isigola; nketuranchi, abi ife rama jukha-ka	
(singular and plural)	sengola ati flura	
(singular charater)	imiwa sengola	
singhalese, adj.	singalize; nke siri-lanka	
sinister, adj.	shiru; nke jika: of evi	
(sinister intention)	ichero shiru; ichero njika	
sink, n.	Senk; nke kichini	
sink, vit.	woka	
(sink/sank/sunk/down)	woka kasa; bale gindi	
sinker, n.	senka, ikaya t'o ng woka taru kifi (finishing net)	
sinology, n.	semology; imuko abi ichegbon na ede chaina	

sinus, n.	senos; irudi ihono n'arin kashi (a type of hole in the bone)	
sip, vti.	sinrin, lamu ruwa kele-kele	
siphon, n.	sekpolo, ife kuru abi koro: something bent	
sir, n.	sah (from anglo – indian)	
sire, n.	siren, n. bab; kaka	
siren,n	whio-dwhio, baba fito	
sirocco, n.	sairoko, irudi fekuku na kasa itli; isioko	
sisal, n.	sisah irudi shuke-shuke a ng fi meshe faiba	
(sisal nut)	kdwaya sisah	
sister, n	munwa; monwa; sista	Gen/H
(sister-in-law)	monwata; munwata	
(nursing sister)	sista ness	
sit, vti., n.	jondu; ijondu	Y/I
(sit down)	jondu na kasa	
sit on the floor	jondu n' isala	
(sitting arrangement)	itole jondu; itole na ijondu; itole fun inondu	
(sit for examination)	jondu fun ichondi	
sitar, n.	sita nke hindu	
site, n.	nok; wuri; noki	Jaba/kaje/kataf/
(building site)	inoki gida	Maro languages
sitter, n.	o jondu; o jondu fun ichondi	
situate/situated, adj.	sholo; kedo	Y(G.v)
(the parcel of land situated at)	ikwuchi kasa t'o sholo na	

situation, n.	ikponge, ikpongba	I/Y
six,	isii	I
(sixes)	n'isii-sii	
six-footer)	o futu isii	
(sixteen)	goisii	
(sixteenth)	nke goisii	
(sixth)	Nk 'isii;	
(sweet sixteen)	b;udurwa/wundia	H/Y
sixty, n, adj. size, n. , adj.	sii itobi,tobi; itondo, inofi	
(big size)	otondo	
(sizer)	o tondo	
(sizeable)	itondo; titobi	
size, n.	saiz, nke gam	
sizzle, vi	shihh, irudi ilowe	G
skate, n.	siketi	G(fE)
skate, n.	sketi, irudi kifi	G(fE)
skeleton, n.	skaletin; tsaiko jiki mutum	
sketch, n,	zana	H
(rough sketch)	ikpako zana	
skew, adj.	sikiu; ife t'o yikpo s'akue: something twisted to one side	
skewer, n.	dtsinke	H
ski , n.	sikii; irudi gwere na ais	
skid, n.	darje; sikidi; nke mota doki zame	G(fE)/H
skid, vt.	foke; nke iloga na kasa	

skiff, n.	skif; irudi ugboko ugboko ruwa kele	
skilful, adj.	riche; miche	Y/I
skill, n.	iriche; imiche	
skilet, n.	skilat;irudi kwan so: a atype of frying pan	
skim; vti.	sikim; nke bika nono	
skimp,vte.	skemp; iluwe ife kiene jukha iloi nke a che (to use something less than the amount required)	
skin, n.	fata, pata	H
(skin and bone) bonga;	kashi ati fata	
(thick skin)	fata ki	
(skin-diving)	sken-daifing; irudi gwuwere	
skin-head)	gorimakpa Y/Gen	
skin-disease)	i;run fata; irun pata	
skink (from hausa);	kulba H	
skint, adj.	ai wen kudi	
skip; vit.	fonu-fonu; "to jump lightly; feja; boaka	
skip, n.	sikip; irudi bokiti kaya na idini: a type of bucket carriage in the mine.	
skipper, n.	skepa; skipen; kaftin fubol	
skirmish, n.	ijagha kele	
skittish, adj.	chinkili; solendu: (lively) exciting	
skettle, n.	sikito, irudi igwere bolu	
skua, n.	sigo lau: "large seagull"	

skull, n.	konki	H(G.V)
(human skull)	konki mutum	
skullduggery, n.	skolidoja: o wayowayo; (trickster)	
skunk, n. sky; n. (skylight) skalat;	skukune; irudi nama daji kele na amerika nuson; enudson; (enu) iwindo na rufu: a roof window	H/I
(skypilot)	skapalo; chaflen na ugboko ruwa nke soja (chaplain)	
(sky-lark)	skalak; irudi onene kele to'o on songi songa	
(sky-rocket)	inonku-ka: very expensive	
(it is very expensive)	o nonku-ka; o di nonku-ka	
(sky-scraper)	igungolo gida	
blue-sky)	inuson bulu; nuson-bulu	
(as blue as the sky)	(ibulu bika nuson)	
slack, adj. slacken, vti.	due-dkue; ai kiesi; fre kiesi; rowu Ife nke 'ti duedue; idue-due; rowu	
(slacken your belt)	rowu beliti e	
slag, n.	kwa, filko	H
slake, vt.	silek; nke kemika	
slam, vti.	gbam itikpo kofa gbagah: "to shut the door violently"	
slander, n. vi	imeshata; ishata oka rubi si mutum	
(slanderous statement)	oka irubi	

slang, n.	Ila jeh; ede abi oka bika ede "keneri"	
slant, vit.	gere	Y
slap, vt, n.	kpala; ikpala (also:tula)	G/Y/I
(i'll slap you)	maa tula e: maa kpala e	
(what a dirty slap?)	meni itula arubi?	
(slap in the face)	Ife zuka: rubuff something; idazu	
slash, vti.	sha	Y
(slash down)	sha si kasa: sha si 'sala	
slat, n.	silat, irudi sanda iwindo	
slate, n.	wala	
slattern, n.	kmache datti	
slaughter,	kpagbu	Y/I
slave, n.	bawa, baiwa	H
(slave-trade)	itasuwa bawa	
(slave-trader)	o tasuwa bawa; o leta bawa	
(slavery)	ibawa; ibaiwa	
slavey, n.	slevi monshe makaranta: (school servant	
slay, vt.	gbulu	I/Gen/Y
sleazy, adj.	slezy; ai cheto; ai bo; datti	
sledge, n	slej ; irudi keke snoh; irudi baba ayan	
sleek, adj.	siliki; ido bika gashi nama; "soft as animal's fur or hairs	
sleep, n., vt.	isunla; sunla; isimini	

(sleeping-sickness)	ibujen isunla; (ibujen 'sunla); irudi irun tsando: (tsetse-fly); ibujehen-isimin
sleeve, n.	silivi, hanu golo taguwa: (shirt)
(slinder-size)	lenge-lenge Y/Gen
sleuth-hound, n.	itobi lenge sliuhond; irudi kare iwin
slice, n.	gunduwa H
(slice of bread)	gunduwa buredi
slick, ajd.	siliki: "boro-boro": (slippery)
slide, n.	iyopu; yopu; silaid:
(sliding-door)	kofa silaid
(sliding-seat)	kujera-silaid
slight, adj.	kinrin
slim; adj.	firin G
(slim-fit)	(slem-fit) (firin-fit)
sling, n.	hamila, majajjawa H
slip, n.	bou
slipper, n.	silifa H(fE)
(bath-room slippers)	kpankere G
slippery, adj.	ibou
slipshod, adj.	ai shokpa; ai june; ai kiesi
slit, n.	raba; keta H
slither, vi.	bibou
sliver, n.	sliva, irudi sanda-itache kele
slobber, vti.	gono-gono; nke yau lati onu: (of saliva from the mouth)

(sleeping and slobbering)	isunla gono-gono
sloe, n.	sloh; irudi ya'ya daji: type of bush/forest fruit
slog, vit.	shobeh G/Gen
(we shall slog it out)	awa ga shobeh ya
slogan, n.	kirari H
sloop, n.	sulupul; irudi ugboko ruwa kele
slop, vit.	toboh "to spill"
slope, n.	hook; ikpeyen nke kpanti fun o shikolo: (supply of materials to sailor)
slope, n.	gangare, gongara H
sloppy, adj.	di gangare; di gongara;
slot, n.	ihonu kele: "little hole"
sloth, n.	izomah: "laziness" G
sluch, vi.	meshe ife n'izomah; zomah
slough, n.	kunekun; fata ti nama daji ti fre, bika machija: abandoned skin of a wild animal, such as a snake.
sloven, n, vti.	izomata: zomata
slow, adj.	kele; rayo Y/Gen/I
(go-slow)	ishien-kele; iloga kele; iloga rayo
(slow-motion)	iyime rayo
(slow-coach)	mutum o kele
slow-worm; n.	slo-wom; irudi nama akuna-kuna: "a type of

sludge, n.	reptile" fadema: irudi fadama: "a type of swamp"
slug, n.	silogi: irudi nama bika kodi. " a type of animal such as snail"
sluggard, n.	digbe-digbe; rundenrunden; idigebe-digbe;
(sluggard (of person)	mutume digbe-digbe; mutum runden- runden; o digbe-digbe; o runden-runden
sluice, n.	babban lambatu, slos H/G
slum; n.	rami: hole in the ground or pit
slumber, vti.	sunpeh Y/G
(wake up, slumber)	jinde, o sunpeh
slump, vi.	tumku H(G.v)
(slumped down)	tumku si 'sala' tumku si kasa
slur, vti.	buku: "joining of letters and words badly
slurry, n.	slari; irudi iwakpo ruwa-ruwa: "type of liquid mixiture" yumbu-snoh
slush, n.	
sly, adj	guereke: iwayo ati ikpache I/Y(secrecry)
(a sly on me)	iguereke si mi G/Y/I
smack, n.	kpai; iluti G/Y/I
smack, n.	simaki; irudi abara abi moru kele
small, adj.	kele; tunfien; tinkin; tinkini

(smallness)	ikele; itunfien; itinkin; itinkini	
smart, adj.	yaji; tuke; kia; kia-kia	
(smart-bus)	tuke-tuke	
(smartness)	iyaji; ituke;	
(smart boy)	yaro o yaji	
(smart-girl)	omote/yarinya o yaji	
(you think you are smart)	e loro kpe e ng yaji	
(bad smartness)	mutum tuke-tuke	
(excess of smartness is	ijukha 'yaji wu ifeweh madness)	
smash, vti.	fowa	Y/I
smear, vti.	rikpo: to cover or mark something at the surface; spread over something	
smell, n., vti.	izizi; zizi	G(fI)
(your mouth is smelling)	onu e ng zizi	
smelt, vt.	wushana	H/Gen
smelt, n.	simet; irudi kifi eso: some types of fish	
smilax, n.	ilua-ke; ikua kele; ikuakua kele; kua-ke	
(smile my dear)	kua-ke ninda	
smite, vti.	kpah	G
smith, n.	makeri	H
(cooper-smith)	makeri-oko (blacksmith) (smithy)	
duba	H	
kuma	H	
smog, n.	sumoh; irudi hayaki mota	

smoke, n.	hayaki; kyafe; mukoko; taba H
(no smoke without fire)	kosi hayaki lai si wuta
smoke, vt.	o mukoko; mu taba abi siga
smoker, n.	o mkoko; o mu taba; o siga
(smoking joe)	o mu jukha taba;
smooth, adj.	o hayaki
(smooth skin)	muru; muru-muru; yoyooyoG
(smooth face)	fata muru; fuska muru-muru
(smooth face)	fuska muru; fata muru-muru
(smooth edge)	inukki muru
smother, vt.	wujo; gbu kpelu wuta; gbu mindu
smoulder, vi.	jowuta kele
smug, adj.	isokene o wenji: "self-satisfaction"
smuggle, vt.	yawa G
(smuggler)	o yawa
smut, n.	burtuntuna H
snack, n.	shnaki; abinchi kele-kele:
snaffle, vt.	hebezu; iyi 'fe lai wen aashe : to take something without permission"
snag, n.	tushe itache: (tree-root);
snag, n.	okuta, na gindi ruwa: kwandu G
snag, n.	ikwangi; ilesiri ti ai rekon: "unexpected difficulty"
snail, n.	kodi, katantawa H

snake, n.	machiji; maciji	H
(snake-charmer)	o piri machiji	
(snake-island)	alande machiji; irudi alnde na kasa eko abi Lagos	
snap, vti.	kili; bika iyi foto: "like taking fotograph"	
(snap-shot)	ikili foto	
(snappy)	kia-kili: iyaji	
snare, n.	tarko	H
snarl, vit.	kumbe: "to murmur"	
snatch, vti.	jayi, jawe	Y/Egun/I
(car snatcher)	o jawe mota	
(husband snatcher)	o jawe maigida	
sneak, vit.	minrin	Y
(sneak in)	minrin bale	
(sneak out)	minrin si 'ta; minrin 'ta	
sneer, vi.	toloh	G
sneeze, n., vt.	giri; fi hanchi fa fekuku to meshe ilowe bika arimkpo tuoyi: "draw air through the nose to make	
snigger, n.	sound like that of cold" ikua-kua kele: "small laughter"	
snippet, n.	ikoli fiene:"bit of information	
snivel, vi.	imuson; o muson" "one who gives much Respect	
snook, n.	To the wealthy and despices lower class" uwaka; nke	
	iloku abi i buihi: abusive	

snooker, n.	sunuka: irudi igwere eso
snoop, vi.	isimini kele: little rest or sleep
snore, vi.	isimini: 'to breathe noisly" G
snorkel, n.	halipe: ijongo roba nke u-tekunu: submarine air-tube"
snort, vit.	fim: kpu fekuku jaita lati hanchi: to force air out through the nose
snot, n.	maskus, abi jadi-jadi nke hanchi: "nose mucous/mucus
snout, n.	konto; onu nama; onu kifi
snow, n.	snoh; bika ais
(snow-white)	fari snoh
snub, vt.	sme-smen Gen
snuff, n.	sinof; irudi taba nke hanchi
snug, adj.	idunso
snuggle, vit.	sikuene; nure mutume: "to near or close to somebody
so, adv.	In order to get warmth" baate; bietu; bietutu; jukha; risirisi; jukun
(so and so)	baate-baate
(so much to do)	risirisilati meshe
(so much money)	jukun fun kudi
(there were so many)	o risi; o risi jukha
(so far, so good)	o ti rama baate
(so far from him)	o jingolo si ya

(not so much)	ko risi; ko risirisi
(so much that)	o risi kpe
(so called)	ti a kono baate; kono baate
(so that)	baate kpe; ka le
(so divine)	soliba jukha
(so as to)	ka bietu; ka bietutu
(and so on, and so forth)	baate-baate
(so to speak/say)	ka soli baate
(so therefore)	n' sisiri; sisiri
soak, vti.	dibo
(soak in water)	dibo na ruwa
(soak cloth in water)	dibo esa na ruwa
((soaking)	idibo
(rain-soaked)	idibo ruwa; idibo ruwa sorma sabulu
soap, n.	
soar, vit.	foga
sob, vit.	sukunie
(don't sob)	ma sukunie
(sobbing)	isukunie
sober, adj.	jiba, somba; kule; loro
(sober reflection) soccer n.soka	iloro jinka; itonwu si gbetu; mutum ncha; tuegbe; sosha
(social development)	ihugbo sosha
socialism, n.	isosha; isoshalizm; imuko sosha
(social justic)	idakpe sosha
(social welfare)	alafia abi igbandu sosha

socialite, n.	o sosha; o sia-sio; agba mutum; mutum Sosha	
society, n.	sasaiti, ijumomeshe	G(fe) /Y/I
sociology, n.	sosholoja; imuko abi sayens nke sosaeti	
society, n.	sasaiti, ijumomeshe	G(fe) /Y/I
sociology, n.	o sosholoja	
sock, n.	sokia nke bata, soks	G(fe)
socket, n.	sokat nke lantiriki;	
(electric socket)	sokat nke lantiriki	
socrates, n.	sokratis;,afa baba mutum n'ngba kaka	
soda, n.	isoda; soda; nke kamikal	
(soda water)	ruwa soda	
sodium, n.	sodium; nke gishirin	
sodomy.	sodami ; irudi ivudu n' arin e miji	
so-ever	eni ife: (eni 'fe)	
(who so ever)	eni mutum	
sofa, n.	doguwar kujera, shufa; irudi kuje	
soft, adj.	do; kpokokooko; kpoko	
(soft currency)	kudi dido	
(soft-hearted)	o simple; mutum o rere abi o nube	
(soft-palate)	sof-palit; nke ilowe oka n' onu	

(soft-pedal)	meshe abi soli oka na irayo: to do or say something gently.	
(soft-spoken)	o soli n'irayo: "spoken gently"	
(softiness)	izugolo: (stupidity)	
soften, vti.	dido	
soil, n.	kasa; imeje; idatti	
(soil erosion)	iraje kasa	
(don't soil your garment)	ma meje abi datti riga	
so journ, vi.	suguna; irinje	G/Y/I
(sojourner)	o suguna; o rinje	
solace, n.	isolendu	G/I/Y
(i solicit for your solace)	mo gbi fun isolendu e / yin	
solar, adj	sola; shola; nke rana	
(solar energy)	agba sola; abi agba shola	
solder, n.	molo; imolo	G(fEd)
(solder-lead)	fensa imolo; irudi ayan ti a ng fi molo ife (soda-ledi)	
soldier, n.	soja; iseza; o jagha Gen(fE) (monghara)	
sole, n.	sol; nke gindi bata G(fe)	
sole, adj	sonsho: "of single" I/Y	
(sole administrator)	o kpeyen sonsho	
(solely) ; adv.	so-sonsho	
solecism, n.	ishihan ede: "language error"	
solemn, adj.	roche;loro	Y/I
solemnity, n.	iroche; iloro; ichenu	
solemnize, vt. n.	cheronu; icheronu; ikonojo	

(marriage solemnization)	ikonojo gbemata;	
solfa, n.	sofah; nke isongi; itunmaisongi	
solicit, vti.	gbi; gbiyo (biyo)	Itsekiri/Y
solicitor, n.	o gbi; o gbiyo; (o biyo); soliseta	
solid, adj.	sile; siagba	Y/I
solidity, n.	isile; isiagba	
solidify, vti.	siagba; di sile; sile; sile-sile	
soliloquy, n.	solishosho: isoli si o wenji	
solitary, adj.	gbensho: "to leave alone"	
solitude, n.	igbensho; mbi konso: "lonely place"	
solo, n.	holo, nke isongi; irudi iyaji kia-kia	
solstice, n.	sostis; ngba eso na rana ikweta	
soluble, adj.	yiwah: dissolve; wara	Y/I/G
solution, n.	ilandi: "of answer"; iwara: "of dissolving	
solve, vt.	landi	Y/H
solvent, adj	sowara	G
(water is a solvent)	ruwa wu sowara	
sombre, adj.	jonu: "sad"	Ed
(some people)	e mutum eso; mutane eso	
(some men)	e miji eso (e miji eso)	
(some women)	e mache eso (e mache 'so	
(some times)	ngba eso	
(some days)	rana eso	

someboy, pron.	mutum eso; eso eni
somehow, adv.	hanya eso
someone, n.	mutum eso
some-place, adv.	mbi eso; ebi eso
somersault, n.	takiri
something, pron.	ife 'so
some times(s)	ngba eso
(some how, some way)	mbi at hanya eso
somewhat, adv.	kuku: "rather"
somewhere, adv.	mbi eso; ebi eso
somnambulism, n.	somnabolo: iringa sunla: "walking and sleeping
son, n.	monji; mongida;
(the son of god)	ne monji abasi
(son-in-law)	suruki; siriki
sonar, n.	alazi: irudi dibais ti a ng fi chowa ife na gindi tekun
sonata, n.	sonnet, irudi isongisongi: of musical composition
song, n.	songa; nke songi
(sing a song)	songi songa
sonic, adj.	sonek; sonek; nke saund
sonnet, n.	iremba; nke irinbu
sonny, n.	soni
sonorous, adj.	sonera; nke iluvi abi saund
soon, adv.	ngbansin; nke ngba nsiyii; ngba
(soon after)	ngba izuba

(sooner or later)	ngbansin abi ngba	
(as soon as possible)	izuba/baya ngba o dishe: ngba o di meshe	
sooth, n.	igboto I/Y	
(sooth-sayer)	o gboto; o soli gboto; o gbafoshe	
soothe, vt.	medi kule; kulele: (calm)	
sop, n.	sop; irudi buredi kele na ruwa	
sophism, n.	isiro saroka: "false argument"	
sophist, n.	o chegbon n'isaroka: "clever argumentator"	
sophisticated, adj., n.	sileka, isileka; roforofo	
sophomore, n.	sofomori; omo makaranta na ardun inang	
soporific, n.	sokporiki; irudi ogogoro o fata isunla: "type of drink causing sleep"	
soprano, n.	sopreno, nke iluvi songi ganu: "of high	
sorcerer, n.	singing voice" maye; hatsabibi; o majikele	
sordid, adj.	siyen; kume-kume: "poor; shabbily"	
sore, adj.	junian	Y/H
sorghum	soguro	G
sorority, n.	soro-riti; itugbe e mache eso na yunifasiti	
sorrel, n.	shorel; irudi shuke-shuke	
sorrow; n.	ikonu; ariri; iriri	I/Y/Agbor

(sorrowful)	di 'konu; di 'riri	
sorry, adj.	lendo; kpendo	Y/I/Gen
(i feel sorrty)	mo kpendo (not mo kpendo)	
sort, n.	irudi; itugbe	
sort, vit.	choja; chowa; tolele: "find out; arrange things" mashin o teolele (sorting machine)	
sortie, n.	zagri-gri; irudi itakko soja	
S.O.S	dezi mindu 'wa: (D.M.W.): irudi iziron na ngba danja	
so-so,	rama die: (just fair)	
adj.,	mutum ogogoro; o ogogoro; ogogoro	
adv. sot, n.	mutum	
sotto voce; adve. sou, n.	iluvi kele; iluvi fiene sou; kudi faransi	
soufle, n.	soufo; irudi abinchi kwai	
soul, n.	mindu; imindu	Y/I
sound, adj.	iandu; lafia; kamkpe; kpamgba; saun	
(sound-box)	akwati 'lowe; garmaho	
(sound-effects)	flim nke saund; (saund ifekts)	
(sound-wave)	saund-wef; gaun-gaun saund	
(sound-track)	hanya abi laini saund; (saund-trak)	
sound, vti.	san; nke tekun	
sound, n.	halulu; (a strait) G	
soup; n.	miya H	

(pepper-soup)	ngwon-gwo Gen	
sour, adj.	tanu; tain	G
source, n.	ifata; mafari, tushe, asali, masom; ifabia	
soutane, n.	Suten; na Chochi nke Rom	
south, n.	Kudu; saut;	
(South Africa)	sauti Afrika	
(South-East)	kudu-gabas: (sauti-ist)	
(South-West)	kudu-yama; (sauti-uest)	
(South-North)	kudu-sonma (sauti-not)	
southern, adj.	nke kudu; ife kudu; o kudu	
southwards, adv.	irinshien kudu: "towards the south"	
Southerly, adj.	Fekuku kudu: "of southern winds"	
(southerner)	monkudu; o kudu	
souvenir, n.	tsaraba: igayen iloron; ife iloron abi icheron *something given for rememberance*	
sovereign, adj.	kemezi; okemezi	Ed
(soverign nation)	kasa okemezi; kasa 'kemezi	
soviet, n.	sofiet; sofi; majalisar	G(fE)/H
(soviet union)	kasa sofiet; kasa sofi	
sow, n. sow, vti.	soh; alade mache:	
	(female pig) gbin gbin nso	Y
(sow around/about)		
(sower)	o gbin	
(parable of the sower)	iwiton nke o gbin	
soya, n.	soyah; irudi wake	

spa, n. spah; kasa miriala:
"mineral ground" iyefe; ikoge

space, n.

spacious, adj. di 'yefe; wen iyefe; di koge

spade; n. siped; shebur; sp G/H(fE)

(spare this) fre eyi; fre keyi

spaghetti, n. kpagati; irudi abhinchi na kasa Itli

span, n. sifan; inofi; iyefe

spangle, n. sifango; irudi ado: "a type of ornament"

spaniard, n. omo kasa Sufen

Spain, n. Spen; (Sfen)

spank; vti. spar, vt. kwanki; iluti omontakele

spar, n. na gindi: beating of a little child at the buttocks kpah; irudi ijagha

koneri: a type of demonstrative fight" spah, irudi miriala

spare; adj. spie; fi jukun; itisi:

aditional; yonfe: (free)

(spare-partss) (spie-pat) (e spie-pat:

"plural of spare-part") itisi-kpaka: spare-part

(please buy me car spare-part) biko gora mi itisi-kpaka mota zoom-zoom

spare, vti. fre: (to leave/ abandon); (spare his/her life) gbari: (to pardon

gbariji: (to forgive) gbari mindu ya

(spare time) ngba iyonfe

spark, n. ichaun; chan-chaun G

sparkle, vi. kyalkyal; kyalkyali H

(sparkling)	ikyalkyali	
sparrow, n.	gwarrow	H(fE)
Spartan, n.	talaka; bika o siyen	H
spasm, n.	giri; igiri	Y/Gen
spasmodic, adj.	sfamodi; giri-giri	G(fE)/Y/Gen
spat, vit.	kpata: igonu kele: little quarrel	
spatch-cock, n. (spatch-cock sacrifice)	okwekwe: kaza ti a gbu sie fun abinchi ngba sam: "fowl that was killed and cooked at the same time for eating" isebo okwekwe	
		G/Y/G
spate, n.	sipet; irudi karent nke ruwa tekun	
spatula, n.	spatule; irudi kozo: a type of tool	
spavin, n.	sfaven; irudi irun doki	
spawn, n.	lanya; lamya: kwa kifi abi kwado: "fish or for eggs"	
speak, pp. (he/she spoke) (he/she said)	soli; kwuso; gbaameh; zeh o soli; o gbaameh	
(i spoke/said)	mo soli;	
(you will say/speak)	k'e soli	
(he/she did not speak)	ko kwuso	
(speak your language)	zeh 'de e; zeh 'de yin	
(language speaker)	o zeh 'ede; (o zeh 'de)	
(who is speaking)	uani ng soli?	

(loud speaker)	lau-sfika; o solimkpotu; o kemkpo
(two loud-speakers)	o kemkpo eji; au-sfika eji
spear, n.	mashi H
(spear-head)	o keisi; keisi; gosin: "to lead", champion
spear-mint, n.	spie-mint; magani fefemint
Special, adj. –kataze,	Meze; zumkpa; gesi G/I/Y/Izon
(you are a special person)	E wu mutum katazi; I wu mutum katazi
(special invitee)	Ikonozo katazi
(special invitees)	E konozo katazi
(special/important)	Igesi; izumkpa; gesi; zumkpa
(specially important)	Gesi zumkpa
(specially important person)	mutum o gesi zumkpa; o gesi katazi; gesi mutum
(special) – syn	katazi
(specialist)	o gesi; o katazi; igesi; ikatazi; o chegbon
(specialist hospital)	asibiti katazi
(special licence)	lasin katazi; aashe katazi
(special right)	iyasah katazi; aashe katazi
Specialize, vit.	chegon; win
(I specialize on engineering)	mo chegbon si irushe injin
(eingineering specialaist)	iwin injiniya
speciality; n.	ichegbon; iwin
species, n.	skpeshi G/(fE)
(be specific)	di kwatazi; di choto
specification, n.	ikwatazi; ichoto

speicify, vt.	kwatazi; choto	
(specify the type you want)	kwatazi 'rudi e che	
specimen, n.	misali samfo; kpesimen	H/H(fE)/ G(fE)
speck, n.	ami; irudi launi jiki: "a type of skin spot or mark"	
(skin-speckle)	koi fata	
spectacle, n.	tabarau	H
spectacular, adj.	shaka-shaka	G
spectator, n.	o neron	I/Y
(spectators)	e neron	
spectre, n.	imendu; bika mindu: ghostly	
spectroscope, n.	spektosko; irudi instrumint ti a ng fi neri rana	
spectrum, n.	spektram; launi nke bakan gizo: colours of the rainbow	
speculative, adj.	di cheba; di loro	
speech, n.	oka; ikwuso	
(i don't wan long speech/es)	mii che igungolo	
(speechless)	lai kwuso; kitikoi	
speed, n.	iroso; iyaji; ikia-kia; igbere; sam-sam	
(speed-boat)	abara sam-samp; abara iroso	
(speed-cops)	Spikolo, mondoka iroso, irudi mondoka o gunya keke-mota: (a type of police motor- cyclist who monitors motor-speed)	
(speed-indicator)	o fine iroso; o fine igbere	
(speed-merchant)	o yanwa mota bi keke- mota n'igbere kha-ka; o gbere iwin	
(speed-way)	hanya fun igbere	
(speed-up)	yaji; roso	

(speed-ometer)   spidominta; minta o fine igbere abi iroso

(god-speed)   igbere abasi

(god-speed recovery)   igbandu abi alafia nke igbere-abasi

speed-well, n.   spi-wel: lrudi shukeshuke fulawa

spelaeology, ,n   spelaloji; sayens imuko kurfi: science of the study
                             of caves

(spelaeologist)   o spelaloji

spell, n.   bubu; ibubu; o bubu-yaya

spell, n.   ijaghuru

(spell-bound)   atanshan; ifeza

spell, vti.   konoso; konogu

(spell me "man")   konoso mi miji

spelt, n.   spelit; irudi alkama:
                             a type of wheat noku

spend, vti.
(spend money)   noku kudi; (no kudi)

sperm, n.   spam

spermatozoa, n.   spamatozo; nke spam

spermaceti, n.   spamasati; irudi spam nke baba-kifi "wel"

sphagnum, n.   sfagunu

sphere, n.   gaya

sphinx, n.   gulu-gulu: irudi doka dutse: "kind of stone stat-
                             ute"

spice, n.   yaji

spider, n.   gizo

(spider-cob)/(cob)   gida gizo; sakar gizo

(spider-man)	miji gizo
(spider-net)	irushe gizo
spigot, n.	sfigat
spike, n.	hekra: irudi ayan bata
spikenard, n.	fakinad; irudi ontmint pipia: "a type of costlyointment"
spill, vti.	toboh
(spilled all over)	tobo si nso
spin, vti.	fa okun; meshe sili: to make thread; sili
(spining-wheel)	injin sili; injin ti a ng fi meshe sili
spinach, n.	alayyafo
spinal, adj.	sfaina
(spinal cord)	jijiya sfaina; sfaina kod
spindle, n.	mazari, kwakwaro; spendol
spine, n.	sufain; kashin baya; kashin zuba
spinet, n.	sfinet; instrumint isongi
spinnaker, n.	sfineka; nke abara abi moru
spinner, n.	o sili; injin sili
Spinster, n.	Wundia; spensta; sfinsta
Spiral, adj.	Yika; o yika
Spire, n.	Hasumiya: "minaret"
Spirit, n.	Imindu, iyobi, oka, iwin, sha; ogogoro; kainka:
(human spirit)	Imindu mutum
(good spirit)	Iyobi rama

(public spirited)	o wen iyobi fun pobli abi o wen iyobi rama fun mutum ncha
spiritual, adj.	nke mindu; win; nke iyobi
(spiritualist)	o soliba – "diviner"
(spiritualogist)	o mini-mini; o mindu; sayens imuko mindu
(spiritualism)	inikon
spirituous, adj.	ogogoro; kain-kain; oguro, tombo
spit, vti.	tipi
spite, n.	iyobi rubi; njika; jika
spittle, n.	yau, miyau; tipi
spittoon, n.	tukunyau: "spitting nontainer"
spiv, n.	ogbologbo
splash, vti.	tombo
(splash water)	tombo ruwa
(money splash)	itombo kudi
spleen, n.	saifa, marabiya, bakin chikin
(i hope you had a splendid time)	mo nikon kpe e wen ngba rama/tomboh
(it was so splendid)	o miri-miri jukha
splendour, n.	ishakah; tombibu; magnifisa
splice, vt.	splays: sogba waya si waya: joining or weaving of rope into rope"; kino
splint, n.	karan dori (bonesetting instrument)
splinter, n.	o yala; instrument an fi yalu 'ife
splint, vti.	yala; iyanga tolo-tolo; itiri-teren

splutter, vit.	emn; soli oka gra-gra
spoil, vti.	meje; meru; rubi
spoke, n.	sufok: nke keke
spokesman, n.	o solile spoliation:
sfoliashon: meko:	(plunder)
spondee, n.	sfondii; nke pole: of poetry
sponge, n.	soso
spontaneous, n.	isfontenia; sfontenia;
spool, n.	tariya, matari
Spoon, n.	Chokali; (shin-shin)
spoon, vi.	woi: nke ihufe abi imiri:
(of love or romancing)	romancing at the park
spoor, n.	lawani; irudi turba shanu: a type of cattle path
sporadic, adj.	tale; tale-tale
(sporadic shooting)	igbata tale; ikakpu tale-tale
spore, n.	ikpor: nke imubi fulawa
bi shuke-shuke:	(of flower or plants reproduction)
sport, n.	erenji; igwuere
(football is a game)	fubol wu igwuere
(i love sports)	mo hufe erenji
(sports is good for your health)	erenji di rama fun jiki e/
yin (sports car) mota erenji (sports jacket)	jakit erenji
(sports commentator)	o soliye renji
(sports editor)	edita erenji
(sports officer)	hafsa erenji
(sportsman-like)	bika miji erenji
spot, n.	kurji: "pimples, boil, abscess"
spot, vt.	digo: to dot a place
spot: (of scar)	tabo

504

(spot on the skin)	ta bo na pata
spot, vt (to find)	chowa
spot: (of place/particular place)	mbi dandan; mbidaan ibidan; ebi daan (spot) : of tv/radio) siko
(spot announcement)	ikemko siko
(tv spot announcement)	ikemko siko telibijin (spotted fever) manijaiti;
spotlight, n.	irudi irun rubi sfotlait: irudi wuta ti a ng fi neri fe katazi: "a type of light for looking at something properly"
spouse, n.	maigida abi mata
spout, n.	sfaut; irudi boto: a type of funnel"
sprain, vt.	sfren
sprat, n.	sfrat, irudi kifi kasa bature
sprawl, vi.	shulu
(sprawling)	ishulu
spray, n.	fesa; fesara
(spray-gun)	bindiga fesa; irudi instrumint
(money spraying)	ifesara kudi
(spray me)	fesara mi
(spray-jet)	shonron
(sprayer)	o fesa; o fesara
spree, n.	isolendu; ishakah
(spree time)	ngba isolendu; ngba ishakah
(spending spree)	inoku shakah

spring, n.	mabubbuga; sfrin: "of water-spring)
spring, n.	foma: (of something jumping or springing out)
spring, n. (of round wire)	sfrin: "mattress spring" spring, n. fring; ikongba na kasa bature
sprinkle, vt.	tinkin
(sprinkling of water)	itinkin ruwa
sprint, vi.	sukuwa; gbere fiam; sprinter, n.
sprite, n.	sprait; iwin
sprocket, n.	froket; nke wili keke abi keke-mota
sprout, vit.	huwe; (to grow leaves)
spruce, adj.	paka; di shaka; yiwo esa abi munji shaka spruce appearance
spur, n.	kaimi; fanye; fanzi: (to urge) i hope this will spur you: agement of nigerian populace spurred me to write this book: mo rekon kpe eyi a fanzi e
ifaiyobi	popule (e fanye mi si ikode littafi yi)
spurious, adj.	gboloja: (not genuine, false)
spurious looking	ineri gboloja;
spurn, vt.	juani; jugon: (reject or refuse completely)
spurt, vi.	kpulu; kpulu-kpulu: "sudden burst out of liquid or fire"
sputnik, n.	hongenik: irudi satilat atifisa: "a type of artificial satellite"
sputum, n.	kpoto; miyau
spy, n. vt.	magewayi: "military spy"
spying is dangerous	ifiri di danja
spy, n.	o firi

spy-hole	ihono firi
spy-glass	talisko firi
squab, n.	hopo: omontakele onene
squabble, vt.	sugen-sugen; igonu kele: small quarrel internal squabble
squad, n.	kunjiya; kungiya
squadron, n.	skwadon; gidigbo
squadron leader	shugaba skwadon; shugaba gidigbo
squalid, adj.	siyen; ai bo; ai june: "poor, uncared for"
squall, n.	ikemkpo abi ikebe jiji: "sudden noise or cry"
squalor, n.	isiyen: "of poorverty situation"
squander, vt.	skwenda; jofa
squander money	jofa kudi; skwenda kudi
squander time	jofa ngba; gbu ngba
square, adj.	golina; sukwue
tafawa balew square	golina tafawa balewa
square hole	ihono golina
squash, vti.	tegbu: "to crush or press down completely" squash-rackets
squash, n.	huju; irudi guma: "a type of gourds"
squat, vi.	jekiri: "squat from place to place" quatter, n.
squatting, n.	ijekiri
squawk, vi.	piri-piri: irudi ikebe kemkpo

squeak, n.   onane: "loud cry of birds" kwiki: ikebe
                                kuru abi ikebe kele onene

squeamish, adj.   farani: eni ng bujen n'ngba ncha

sqeeze, vti.   tegbulu; kwagbulu squeeze the paper

squeeze to death   tegbulu kuowun tegbulu gbu

squeeze out   kwagbulu ta; kwagbulu jaita

cash squeez   ikwagbulu kabodais; itegbulu kudi squeeze out the
                                drops kwagbulu ikpoi ta; kwagbulu ikpoi si 'ta

squid, n.   skwid; irudi kifi

squiffy, adj.   soguro: "to be slightly or slightly durnk"

squint, vi: wini: "eyes which does not turn together but
                                sees different directions at the same time"

squirrel, n.   kurege

squirt, vti.   kpuja: "to push out"; kputa

stab, vti.   guma: vube

stable, adj.   dushim

stability, n.   idushim

stabilization, n.   idushim; ikundushim

stable, n.   sebol; gida doki

staccato, adj.   stakito

stack, n. (pile):   tari; bushiya; zogari

stadium   baba fili; stadiom

508

national stadium	stadiom nashona; (nashona stadiom)
staff, n.	sanda; kandiri
staff of office	kandiri nke ofis
staff, n.	sitaf; o rushe na ofis: "office worker"
stag, n.	namiji daji; sitag; ibechu
stage, n.	dakali;
theartre stage	dakali tiyeta stage, n.
stage an attach	mundu itako stage a peaceful protest mundu ikemkporo rayo
stager, n.	mutum o chegbon digbo: "person of old experience
stagger, vit.	yeji
stagnant, adj.	chendudu
stagnant water	ruwa ichendudu: kotogbin: "pool"
stagnancy, n.	ichendudu
stagy, adj.	dakali tiyeta; imiwa dakali tiyeta: "manner of style theatrical"
staid, adj.	gizi: imiwa
stain, vit.	zugon; datti; imiwa zugon; imiwa rubi
please don't stain my dress	biko ma datti esa mi
stained character	imiwa datti; imiwa zugon; imiwa rubi
stair, n.	matakala, mataki;
safarago stair-case	mataki; lada gida

stake, n.	tangolo: "hard pointed long wood or metal used for supporting plants; or post/pole"
stake, n.	tete; kalu-kalu; iwugu: "risking"
i'll stake my car for it	maa wugu mota mi si
stale, adj.	huenen
stale food	abinchi huenen
it has staled	o ti huenen stalemate, n.
stalk, n.	kard: " of leaf stalk"
stalk, vit.	kwai-kwai; ringa kwaikwai na kasa n'ngba iyana: "walking proudly on the floor so as to show off"
stall, n.	sitol; irudi daki fun nama abi kasuwa; kisuwa abi kanti
stall, n.	sitol; irudi daki fun nama abi kasuwa; kisuwa abi kanti
stall, n.	sitoli: nke ayoplen: "of aeroplane"
stallion, n.	ingarma; namiji doki
stalwart, adj.	kpamgba; kpoi; agba
stamen, n.	stamin; nke fulawa
stamina, n.	idugba; ikagba
stammer, vit; n.	giri, igiri
stammerer, n.	o giri
stamp, vti. n.	kpai; ikpai; samp, kpawai
	stamp your foot down fostej samp; sampu fostej
postage stamp	
stam collector	o kole samp
stamp duty	(samp diuti); kudi sampu
stampede, n.	sampid;ijapu jiji nke mutum: sudden rush of people
stance, n.	stens;
stand, n. vit.	kundu; chiu; sanda; shim-shim; ikpoze; tanda yaji; kiesi; a tansha

stand up	kundu
take your stand	yi 'kpoze e; cheri: (decide)
(wash-stand)	sanda-ruwa ti a ng fi wesa hannu
stand up for your right	kundu fun rait e
stand-by, tape is rolling:	atansha; tef ne tolo; atansha, tef n tolo
stand firm	kundu shim-shim
standing place	mbi 'chiu; mbi kundu
stand-point	mbi 'neri
stand-still	kundu siti
stand-by	kundu n'akue; kundu n'nso; ribose
standard, n.	inofili
above standard	kaju inofili; jukha inofili
below standard	naka inofi; n'abe inofili; ai siti inofili kudi
standard bank	banki 'nofili; sandad banki, ngba- nsiyii: banki
	konda: (fest banki) inofili kudi
monetary standard	
standarize, vtn.	medi 'nofili; meshe inofili standing, n.
standing order	hoda shim-shim; (sandin hoda) stanza, n.
staple, n.	stepol, irudi ayan kudu: "a type of u-shaped iron"
staple, n.	stepul, nkemashin takarda: stepula; stepul-mashin
staple, n.	ikpokpoh; kpokpoh; idile: (common) staple food

star, n.	tara; taura
star-fish	kifi taura; irudi kifi na ruwa
star-light	wuta taura; wuta tara
star-shine	ishaka-taura
as bright as a star	haske bika taura; shaka bika taura
starboard, n.	ayoplen
starch, n.	sitaachi
stare, vti.	nefiri; neri firi: look fixedly" don't stare at me
stark, adj.	kpiti; fefefe; sam-sam: "completely" stark, adj.
starling, n.	zara, irudi onene na kasa bature
start, n.	Rebi, renbi
starting time	ngba irenbi
start on time	renbi n'ngba
starter, n.	o renbi, nke igwuere startle, vt.
starve, vit.	guebi
starve to death	guebi kuowun
starving/starvation	iguebi
starver, n.	o guebi
state, n, (condition)	ikpongba; iwahe
state, n (of country)	sitet; sitetei; gandu h(fe)/g
(State House)	Gida Gandu; Gida Sitet
state, vt.	soli; kode; gbaameh
statement; n.	ikode; isoli
statement of fact(s)	ezioka; isoli ezioka: ikode 'zioka

statesman, n.	o gandu; o keisi kasa; miji-gandu, mutumsitet
statesmanship	ikeisi kasa; imiji gandu; irushe
static, adj.	kpam-kpam; ai shiene; ai loga; kudu (balance); ai rinshien si whido abi zuba.
station,n.	tashan
station-waggon	mota wagunu; tashan wagunu
stationary, adj.	kitikpi; ai ringa; lai yikpo-kiri; dunie
stationer, n.	kpankiti
stationery store	sito kpankiti
stationer, n.	o kpankiti
statistics, n.	satistiks;' ikodo
statuary, adj.	nke mutummutumi
statue, n.	mutummutumi
stature, n.	ihomoh, idiwa
status, n.	ibindu
status quo, lat.	statos kuo
statute, n.	doka
staunch, adj.	shim-shim
staunch supporter	o kpusiwhi shim-shim
stave, n.	huda: irudi jega
stave, n.	stef, nke stenza: (stanza)
stay, vit.	chendu: "stay, wait"; du; chiu stay a while/little
stay at home	chendu na gida

it has come to stay	o ti bia chiu
don't stay long	ma du golo; ma fa ngba
stay clear	du ropu
stay the course	chiu siti
stay execution	du hoda; chiu hoda; du imeshe
stay, n.	stei; irudi waya abi igiya ti a ng fi koso masti: "a type of wire or rope used for tying mast"
stead, n.	iyefe; ikpefe
in its stead	n'yefe ya; n'ikpefe ya steadfast, adj.
be steadfast	di dushim
steady, adj.	kundu; shim-shim
steak, n.	yakin nama
steal, vit.	jiri; rawo
don't steal	ma rawo
steam, n.	tururi; stim
steam ahead	loga stimi
steel, n.	karfe; ayan
steel cabinet	kebinet karfe
steel band	dauri karfe
steel works	irushe ayan; irushe karfe
steel-yard, n.	stilyad, irudi instrumint fun iwan: "type of instrument for balancing"
steep, adj.	tere
steer, vti.;	togene; shiri
steer the ship	togene ugboko ruwa
steer clear	shiri: "to avoid something"
steering wheel	wili togene

motor-steering	itogene mota
steerage, n.	stierij, nke ugboko ruwa
stele, n.	steli; irudi ginshiki: "type of pillar
stellar, adj.	stela; nke tara: of star
stem, n.	elogua
plant stem	elogua itache; elogua shuke-shuke
stem, vt.	jau: "of source"
stench, n.	izizi rubi; izizi rubisi
stencil, n.	stensil; irudi takarda tinrin: stensa
stencil sheet	shiti stensil; shiti stensa
stengun, n.	stingan; irudi bindiga
stenography, n.	senografi: of kode shothan
stenographer, n.	o senografa; senografa
stentorian, adj.	sentoria; nke iluvi lau: "of loud voice
step, vit.	gafa; isole
stepping-stone	irebi-si-si; dutse abi jefa gafa
step-ladder,	kuranga; lada
steps	lada; lada gida; sitep
step aside	kpu si akue: "push aside"
step out	ringa kia-kia; ja 'ta
step in	biawa; ringa bale; wonye
step-mother	isole-uwa; isole-mama; uwakinta
step-father	isole-baba; ubakinta
step-parent	isole-yaye
step-child	agola; isole-mon stereo, n.
stereogram, n.	stierogram

stereophone, n.	stierofon
stereophonic, adj.	stierofoni; nke stierofon
stereoscope, n.	stierosko; irudi instrumin hoto
stereoscopic, adj.	stieroskoko; nke stierosko
stereotype, n.	stierotaip; stieroglifik
sterile, adj.	hogofu; ai wen agba imubi
sterility, n.	ihogofu
sterling, adj.	stalin; irudi kudi na briten
pounds sterling	kpaun ati stalin
stern, adj.	kpam; siri: (strict)
sternness, n.	isiri; ikpam; kpam-kpam
stern, n.	siten: nke ugboko-ruwa
sternum, n.	stenonm, kashi kwintin na kirji: "a type of narrow bone in ithe chest
stertorous, adj.	gbririririh: gbirih lilau: "loud snoring"
stet, vi. (lat)	steti
stethoscope, n.	stetosko; instrumint nke likita
stetson, n.	stesin, irudi malafa nke miji: "a type of masculine hat
stevedore, n.	istifudo; stifudoh; lebura abi o rushe kaya na ugboko-ruwa; stifudoring
stew, vti.	stiyu; isie miya; sitiu; dafa
steward, n.	stiuwad; boyi
stewardess, n.	stiuwades; rinyan
stick, n.	sanda; itache; kirare
stick, vti.	shimkpa
stick to it	shimkpa si
sticker, n.	o shimkpa; stika
stick-out	shimkpa si

stickler, n.	o hipo; mutum o hufe ife katazi abi ife saun- saun: "person who loves something of importance or accuracy
sticky, adj.	di shimkpa; shishimkpa; shimkpa-shimkpa
stiff, adj	kagba
stiff penalty	iriya kagba; ijeafun kagba
stiffness,n.	iriya; ijeafun
stifle, vti.	funkan; imime agba: "breating powerfully difficult"
stigma, n.	ihine: ife ilinshasha: something of disgrace
stigma, n.	ilaini; laini; lamba
stigma, n.	stigma; nke fulawa
stigmatize, vt.	linshasha; medi yeye; yah-ya-yah
stiletto, n.	stilato, irudi gwada; "a type of dagger
still, adj, adv.	siti; sisiti; kpiti
still-born, adj.	omon-kpiti; mon-kpiti
stillness, n.	isiti; ikpiti
still, n.	stili; irudi akparatos ti a ng fi meshe wain
stilt, n.	dankwaro; kwarakwara
stimulate, vtn	simele; isimele
stimulant, n.	o simele; stimulante
sting, n, vt.	ikain; kain
sting like a bee	kain bika zuma
stingy, adj.	kinien
stingy penson	mutum kinien
stinginess, n.	ikinien
stink, vit, n.	yankan; runka; irunka; izizi-rubisi

stint, vti, n.	iguini: "restrict, restriction"
stipend, n.	stipenda: albashi klaji
stipulate, vti, n.	sokpini; isokpini; tenda;itenda
stir, vit.	kparu; yikpoto; bagu: of annoyance
stirring, n.	ikparu;
stirrup, n.	likkafa; sterop: kashi kunne¨(ear-bone)
stitch, n, vt.	ikwar; kwar
s stitch in time	ikwar n'ngba
stitiches, pl.	e kwar; kwar-kwar
stoat, n.	stot, nama bika bera
stock, n.	stok; nke sito; kaya; ikpenye; nama; ijapu
stock available	stok; nke sito; kaya;ikpenye; nama; ijapu
out of stock	ko vele
list of stock	ilisa abi itole stok
stock-taking	iyi stok; igo stok
stock-in-trade	baba irushe; irushe katazi
stocked with wisdom	kpenye fun ichegbon
live-stock	nama-mindu; nama abinchi: nama rama fun abinchi; nama sule
stock-yard	yadi nama; (agbomalu); yadi malu
stock-broker	sto-broka; o rushe stok
stock-exchange	stok-eschenj
stock-holder	o yi stock; o wen stock; sherhoda
Igbo-stock (of races)	o japu Igbo; o japu n'Igbo

laughing stock	o yeye; o yah-ya-yah; yah-ha-yah; yeye
stock-fish	kpanla; okporoko stock: (of garden plants) toke: nke
stockade, n.	stokid: irudi
stock-in-ette, n.	stokinat; irudi faiba lastik: (a type
stocking, n.	soks; nke bata
stoep, n.	stowe: irudi baranca na kasa Saot Afrika
stoke, vti.	dawuta: put up or spark off fire stoker, n.
stole, n.	stola; irudi boya: (a type of muffler)
stolid, adj.	gbidi: (not excited easily)
stomach, n.	chiki; tunbi H
stomach ache/pain	ifota abi ifuta chiki
stomach trouble	nsohala chiki; nso-tumbi
stomach bite	ijeta chiki; ijeta-tumbi
stomach-full	ijukun chiki
stone, n, vt.	dutse; dutse
rock-stone	okuta
gall-stone	okuta-kumallo
stone him/her tod eath	fi dutse gbu ya; gbu ya kpelu dutse;dutse ya he who lives in a glassp-house should not throw stone: eni ng hu na gida gilasko shekwa juma dutse /okuta gida dutse
stony, adj.	di dutse; jukun fun dutse abi okuta the rice is full of stones okuta risi na shikafa: (note not dutse)
stooge, n.	awada Y
stool, n.	sutulu; irudi kujera G(fE)
foot-stool	kujera kefa

stoop, vit.	kpana 'chiu bas (bas-stap) du
full-stop	ful-stap; ichiu-kpiki
stop-cock	stap-kak; irudi instrumint
stop-press	ipres gbigbowuta;
stop-watch	stap-wach; irudi agogo
Stoppage, n.	Ichiukiti; ikundu-kiti
stoppage of salary	ichiukiti albashi; ichiu albashi
stop pay	chiu ikpa
stop-over	chiu-feja
stop him/her	da
put a stop to	da chiu si; fanye igwukpin si
stop work	chiu irushe; chiukiti 'rushe
the workers	e rushe ti chiukiti n'irushe;
have stopped work the workers	e rushe ti chiukiti have stopped work at the factory: 'rushe na fatiri
store, n.	sito; taska; kanti; cheto H/I/Y store-house gida taska; gida sito
store-room	daki kaya; daki 'cheto
store-keeper	o cheto sito; o cheto taska; (sito- kipa)
storey, n.	sitori; nke gida-golo abi gida ganu: (of long or high house)

four-storey building	gida sitgori inang
stork, n.	shanuwa; irudi onene eso: (some types of bird)
storm, n.	duduh; iduduh; igbulum; irubi; nsohala heavy storm
the rain and the storm	ruwa ati 'duduh
storm-cloud	mare-duduh
storm-troups	taro-gulum; taroduduh; soja–duduh
story, n.	ilida; ichero; ilissafi Agbo/ I/Y long-story ilida-golo
i don't want long story	mii che ilida golo the story of guosa language the stories of ancient nigeria ilida ede guosa ilida nke naijeriya kera
gbost-story	ilida imindu
story-book	littafi 'lida
children'story	ilida e montakele
story time	ngba ilida
sotry-teller	o soli 'lida; o lida give a story of how it happened lisasafi bietu os oka; chero bietuo biasoka
story: (of account)	ilissafi; ichero stoup, n.
stout, adj.	kpangba; kamkpe Gen stout-looking idi
stove, n. stow, vt.	kpangba; idi kamkpe murhu; sitof kepu: "to pack up something carefully"
straddle, vti.	yakata: "to sit or either stand with one's legs widely apart"
straggle, vi.	strago: hugbo abi gbinso na imiwa rubi
straight line	laini tara
straight road	hanya tara

straight the records	meshe ilissafi di rama	
go straight	loga tara; ringa tara; shienga tara	
straight ahead	n'itara; na whido gon	
straight, n.	streti: igwuere trak	
straight-forward	iwhido-tara; iwhido gon-gon	
straight-away	gienren	Y/Ed
strain, n.	iyogbu; yogbu	Y/I
strait, adj.	streit; na jiografi	G(fE)
strand, n.	strande; kasa yashi: coarse sand	G(fE)
strand, n.	stran; nke faiba zare, abi gashi of thread fibre or the hair	
strange, adj.	shiriche; shariche	Y/I(G.v)
it is very strange	o shariche jukha	
it used to be strange	o shariche lembu	
strangeness	ishiriche; ishariche	
stranger, n.	bako; o shiriche	
strangle, vt.	kwanguli	G
strap, n.	kegi; irudi fata	G
strategy, n. adj.	icheton; cheton	I/Y
device a strategy	gbiche icheton	
straw, n.	karan alkalmi; sitro	H/G(fE)
strawberry, n.	sitrobri; irudi dhuke-shuke	G
straw, n.	karan alkalmi; sitro	H/G(fE)
stray-bullet	iyata harasashi	
streak, n.	layi; irudi laini na fuska	H

stream, n.	rafi	H
street, n.	titi, layi, hanya	
street number	lamba titi	
what is the number of your street?:	meni wu lamba titi yin?	
street-girl	o fiki-fiki: (prostitute)	G
strength, n.	ikagba	I/Y
strenuous, adj.	kagba; rengulu; gbu-agba	I/Y
streptococcus, n.	streptokoko; irudi bateria t'o ng fata irunrubisi: "a type of bacteria causing sevenillness"	
streptomycin, n.	streptomaisin: irudi magani antibotik	
stress, n.	ifanu: (stress of the mouth)	
stress, n. stress, n.	ifagba: (of strength) ifagbu: (of pressure)	
stress, n.	irengu;nsohala (tiredness; problem)	
stretch, n.	ifagolo; fago; fanyen	Y/I
stricken, adj.	nulu	
strict, adj.	siri; gangan	G
very strict	siri jukha	
very strict man	miji gan-gan	
structure, n.	ikuoka: of rebuke, sever criticism or blame gaga	
stride, vti.		
long stride	igaga golo	
foot stride	igaga kafa	
foot strides	e gaga kafa	

strife, n.	ijabele	G(fY(S.Ade)
strike, n, vt.	inulu; nulu: to hit with blow; kakpu	
strike, n.	ichiukiti; ikwudo; (of work)	
strikers, (pl. n.)	e chiukiti; e kwudo	
strikingly, adv.	kwudodo	
striking, n.	ikwudo; ijabele; ichiukiti; inulu; ikekpu	
striker, n.	igbam o kakpu; o nulu: (of football) etc	
string, n.	siriri; kirtani, tsirkiya; waya H	
guitar-string	siriri molo	
stringent, adj.	strinjant; siri: "strict"	
strip, vti.	webo	
he has been stripped	ha webola ya ikende his title	
stripe, n.	ratsi	
strive, vi.	zughu; kido H	
stroll, n, vt.	irin-rayo; rin-ra Ed/Y/H	
(we are strolling)	awa ng rin-ra; awa ng rin-rayo	
let's take a stroll	ka 'wa rin-rayo	
strong, adj.	Denden, kamkpe; kpamgba; sile; kagba	
strong-minded	Iyobi denden, iyobi sile; Twi/Y/I/Gen. iyobi kagba; kakarankan	
strong-drink	ruwa denden, ruwa alkwan, kain- kain; ogogoro;	
strong-smell	izizi rubi; izizi rubisi	
strong-language	oka irubi; oka isile	
strong-verb strontium, n. structure, n. structural adjustment	vabu kamkpe; stronshom, irudi azurfa ikongi; stracha stracha fun itunme Y/H/G(fE) koso; stracha	
policy:	itunme koso	

524

struggle, vi.	zigolo Ed	
i am struggling	mo ng zigolo; mo ng luta	
we are struggling	awa ng zigolo; awa ng luta	
they are struggling	fa ng zigolo; fa ng luta	
the struggle continue	izigolo ng shiene	
strum, vit.	strom; nke isonga; songi biotiche: (sing any how)	
strumpet, n.	ashawo; fiki-fiki	
strut, vi.	shuta; iringa-kiri fun isoken o wenji "walk about for self-satisfaction"	
strychnine, n.	strinain; irudi puezin kpamgba; baba puezin	
stubborn, adj.	shigile; gboro; aigbonti	I/Y
stucco, n.	stuko; irudi flasta abi sumunti	
student, n.	mon-makaranta; omo makaranta; (student)	
studio, n.	sutudio	G/(fE)
photo-studio	sutudio-foto; sutudio nke foto abi hoto	
studio-hand	iron-hann sutudio; o rushe sutudio	
studio-manager	manija-sutudio; imanija-sutudio	
nta studio	sutudio nta	
study, n, vti.	imuko; muko; sutodi	
study for knowledge	muko fun ichegbon	
study, n.	sutodi; daki abi deki 'muko	
stuff, n.	tarkache: (all sorts of things) (tarkace)	H
stuff, n.	kaya; ikpanti	
stuff, n.	irudi: (type; kind)	
stuff, n.	jukun: (to fill up)	

stuffy, adj.	rusi: (of smell); zizi	
the room is stuffy	daki ng rusi (not daki ng zizi; the word zizi: - smell is used for humand and animals	
the man is stuffy	miji yien ng zizi	
stumble, vi.	mebu	I/Y
stumbling-stone/block	o fata imebu; godo-godo	G
stumble, vi.	ringa izighi-zagha: (walk zigzagly)	
stump, n.	dungu; kututture	
stupid person		o zugo mutum; o zugo; o mugu
stupor, n.	igbiri	
don't be stupor	ma gbiri; ma di gbiri	
sturdy, adj.	gbeleu: (something strong and solid)	i
sturgeion, n.	stojion; irudi s onene wiwuam: (a o	
type fo edible fish)		
sty, n.	sitai; irun ido; hazbiya	
G(fE)/H	k	
style, n. sibe; sibele; sibela	isibe; isibela	a Y/I(G.v) stylish
stylist, n.	o	a
sibe; o sibele; o sibela hair stylist	i	
o	d	
sibela gashi	i	
sylus, n.	sitailus; nke allura: (of needle)	p
stymie, n.	sitaimi; nke igwuere galf	e

526

syptic, n, adj.	sitaiptik: nke jine: (of blood)n G(fE)
sub, n.	sob a G
subaltern, n.	sobatan; irudi 'kpoze na soja: sobotan
subatomic, adj.	sobatome l G(fE)
sub-committee, n.	chob-kwamiti; kwamiti-kele i
subconscious, adj.	mima-kele; makele; ma-kele
sub-continent, n.	sob-kantinent; kantinent kele; nso d kantinent
subcontract, n.	sob-kentrat; ikpa- p
kentrtat; ikpaka-	e
ikwede; ikpala-	n
agrimento; iyahann-	d
kentrat	a
sub-cutaneous, adj.	sob-kutano; irun fata (skin dise ase)
sub-divide, vti.	sob-kekpin; ;sob-kepini ;
subdue, vt.	bokei; bokei jukha; bokeisi b
sub-edit, vt.	sob-edita; ronhann edita a sub-editor, n.
edita; o ronhann edita sub-heading, n.	sob- u
isioka; isioka-kele	l
sub-human, adj.	mutum-kiene batulu u si iwahe iska; batulusi ikpongba iska
sub-way, n. succeed, vti.	hanya kele bokei; b isi; (mogaji)
	Y/H/I
success, n.	ib isi;
successfully, adv.	bib isi

succession, n.	isoleji isoleni
rapid succession	isoleji kia-kia
successive, adj.	soleni
successor, n.	magaji, o sole H/I/Y
successive government	gonmenti isoleni
muritala muhammed's	gonmenti nke muritala
government succeded	mohammed lo b isi ofis
yakubu gowon's adminstration:	yakubu gowon
my successor in guosa language	mogaji mi na ede guosa
subject, adj.	isioka; ai dipenda; lai
subject-heading	dipenda; batulu; isioka; keisioka (keisi-oka)
subject to weather	batulu si iwahe iska; batulu si
condition	ikpongba iska
the king and his	mambeze ati e dipenda ya; baeze
subjects	ati e dipenda ya.
subjective, adj.	batulu
subjoin, vt.	finye-si; nye-si; sogbakpaka; finye-kpaka
subjudice, (lat)	sobjudais; ife ti a ng dakpe si: (something under judicial consideration)
subjugate, vt.	bokei; bokeisi: (subdue); temonka
subjugation, n.	ibokei; ibokeisi; itemonka
subjunctive, adj.	sobjanktiv; irudi oka turanchi
sublease, vti.	lis-ikpaka; hayaikpaka; sob-lis

sublet, vti.	sob-lis; lis-ikpaka; haya-ikpaka
sub-lieutenant, n.	sob-leftana; leftanakele; omon-leftana
sublimate, vt.	soblimante: irudi oka sayens
sublime, adj.	ai rugu; gboro khaka; soblima; aima ife
subliminal, adj.	ai ma-fiene: (of the highest oblivion)
submarine, adj.	sobo-kunu; gob-marino; sob-marinos; tekunu-kele
sub-mariner	o sobo-kunu; mutum sob-marino; mutum o sob-marinos
submerge, vti, n.	nuse; inuse
submit, vti, n.	basa; ibasa; nno; gbonti Y/H/Ef
i submit/submitted	mo basa
he/she submit/tted	o basa; ya basa
i am submitting	mo ng basa
i am submitting herewith:	mo ng basa mbi kpelu
please submit the key:	biko, basa omo-igede; biko, nno omo-igede ai gbonti
sub-normal, adj.	ai gentu; na'be gentu; lai gentu
sub-orbital, adj.	kiene si abit: (less than
subordinate, adj, n.	orbit); sob-abit
	monabe; imonabe; G/
	dipenda; idipenda
my subordinates	e monabe mi Ed
subordinate clause	klaus imonabe; (monabe klaus)
subpoena, n.	sobkponia: (pronounced: sokponia) oka iwufin
sub-rosa, lat.	sobrosei: oka kominikashon; nke ife-izi of something confidential
subscribe, vit.	finye si; kweba si; finye; jubi; jube

subscriber, n.	o finye si; o kweba si; 'o finye;
subcription, n.	ifinye; ifinye si; ikweba si; ijubi si
newspaper subscriber	o finye kudi si nus-pepa G/Ed i subscribe to your idea mo kweba si ichenu e
subsequent, adj.	sobsiba; sole-baya g(fe) /h/i/y subsequently, adv.
sub-serve, vt.	sob-rushe; rushe kpaka; ron-hann
subservient, adj.	sob-safient; nke ikumbe jukha: (of too much respect, or giving to much respect)
subside, vt.	kiene
it has subsided	o ti kiene subsidiary, adj.
subsidy, n.	kudianta: irudi kudi H/G fun iron-hann
subsist, vi.	diwa; idiwa
sub-soil, adj.	sob-kasa
sub-sonic, adj.	sob-sonek; kiene si sonek
substance, n.	ikatazi; ifiwa; izumkpa; iyewan
substancial matter	ifiwa ife; ife katazi; oka zumkpa
substancial amount of money	iyewan yole kudi
sub-standard, adj.	nofili-kiene; nofili-kele (less or small in standard)
substantiate, vt.	solendi
substantival, adj.	sobstantifal; nke oka turanchi; nke katazi
substantive, adj.	katazi; zumkpa substantive lieutenant
sub-station, n.	sob-tashan; tashan-kele
substitute, n. substitute it	irikpoto; ife a finye n'ikpoze: something put in other's stead" (imikpo); mikpo rikpoto ya; mikpo ya

substratum, n.	sobstratom: nke ikwa kiene; ikwa ka of: - lower or less level
sub-structure, n.	o ron-hannu ikogi; sobstracha; ikongi-kele;
substend, vt.	sob-tandi: nke ijiomitri
subterranean, adj.	karkashin kasa; sobterenia H/G(fE)
subtitle, n.	izoya-kele
subtle, adj.	hueke Y/Ed
subsrtract, vt.	kiene; yopu; yota
substract two from six	yopu eji sa isii
sub-tropical, adj.	sob-tropike G(fE)
suburb, n.	igbenso; nso gari Y/I/H
subvention, n.	ikudinta
subversive, adj, n.	shuda; kpu shuda; ishuda; ikpu shuda
subversive element	mutum o kpu shuda
subvert, vt.	shuda; damkpu Y/I/G
sub-way, n.	hanya kele
succeed, vti.	bokei; b'isi; (mogaji) Y/H/I
success, n.	ib'isi
successfully, adv.	bib'isi
succession, n.	isoleji, isoleni
rapid succession	isoleji kia-kia
successive, adj.	soleni
successor, n.	magaji, o sole H/I/Y
muritala muhammed's	gonmenti nke muritala
government succeeded yakubu gowon's administration: my successor in language	mohammed lo b'isi ofis yakubu gowon mogaji mi na ede guosa

succinct, adj.	kpinrin; tufiene	G/Ed
succinct words	oka kpinrin; oka tufiene	
succour, n.	innon-hann; idunso; kule; ikule; tizu	
succulent, adj.	suku; suku-suku	G
succumb, vi.	da'kue; kiu; yili	
such, adj.	kayan; rudi; rude	G(fAu)
to such extent such-like	rude ifaogo rudi-bika	
suck, vti. sucker, n.	pio o pio	
		G
suckle, vt. suction, n, vt.	bòbí	General
	ijiyo; jiyo: to remove by stealing	
sudden, adj. suddenly, adv	gbaga	
	gbagara; lai chero abi loro swene	
suds, n. soap suds	fukumblo fukumblo sabulu	
sue, vti.	koma; konoka ma konoka e si kotu	
i'll sue you to court		
suede, n. suet, n.	swed, irudi fata swet	G(fE)
		G(f)
suffer, vti. sufferer, n.	jeafun o jeafun	
suffering, n. suffice, vit.	ijeafun n'ikua-kua furu:	
	izuto: (enough)	
		G
suffice it to say sufficient, adj.	furu ka soli zuto; sokene	
		I/Y/Ed
self-sufficient suffix, n.	isokene o wenji sofiks; nke turanchi	
		G(fE)
suffocate, vti, n.	fukun; ifukun sofrajine:	
suffragen, n.	nke bishobu	G(fE)
soffuse, vt. suffrage, n.	sokeh sofraj: aashe fun	G
	ivota: authority to vote	
sugar, n. sugar-cane	sukar; gishiri bature reke	H(fE) H/Y
sugar-coated sugar-coated lips	itikpo abi ibodo sukar	
	o soli oka sukar	

sugar-daddy, n. sugary, adj.	(agba-man) baba-sukar; dadi-sukar sukar-sukar; di sukar; o sukar
suggest, vt. suggestion, n.	cheba; loro I/Y icheba; iloro
suggestion box suicide, n.	akwati 'cheba; akwati 'loro igbu wenji; suisa I/H/G(fE)
commit suicide	fadon suisa
suit, n.	sutu; kwat G(fE)
suit, n.	ikonoka; ikoma
suit, n.	suwit ikpa-kele: (brief-case)
suit, vti.	yema I/Y
suitable, adj.	yema
it is suitable	o yema
suitably qualfified person	mutum o yema kwashe
suite, n.	sute; irudi daki na huta
suitor, n.	suta: eni ng chowa mata
sulfa, adj.	solfa: nke magani abi ogun G(fE)
sulfate, adj; n.	solfit; isolfit: nke magani G(fE)
sulfide	solfait: oka magani G(fE)
sulfonamides	solfanamaits: oka sayens magani
sulfur	salfor (solfor) G(fE)
sulk, vi.	dikpo; dankiti kani ibilionu: to keep sealed lips because of annoyance.
sullen, adj.	fumu: njika mutum; ai gbariji: wicked and
sulpha, n.	solfona: solfonamaits

sulphate, n	solfit: gishiri nke wassid salfor	
sulphide, n.	solfait: nke salfor ati alimint: yien wu aidrojin (S A): i.e. (H S)	
2	2	
sulphonamides, n.	solfonamaits: irudi	
sulphur, n.	baba-magani salfor: (solfor): irudi alimint – (simbola S) sulphuric acid	
2	4	
sultan, n.	sultan; sarki;	H sultana
sultana, n.	saltana; irudi resin: (raisin)	
sum, n.	iye	Y
total sum	iye tota; iye kpancha	
sub-total	sob-tota; iye kpancha kele	
sum up	kpancha	
sumach, n.	sumak, irudi shukeshuke abi itache	
summary, adj.	kuru; lai faogolo summarize it	
summer, n.	sonma: irudi iska na kasa bature summer-house, n.	
summer-holiday	holude sonma	
summer-school	makaranta sonma	
summer-time	ngba sonma	
summit, n.	kokwa; koli; kolokuwa	H
summon, vt.	folori; kono si kotu fun oka G	
summons, n.	oleri: irudi hoda nke kotu	
sump, n.	sompu: kwano gindi injin	

sumptuary, adj.	somchuari G(fE)
sun, n. sun-rise	rana H
	ishana rana
sun-set	ilevoh-rana
sun-burn	ijowuta rana; (son-bon)
sundial	sondia
sun-fish	sonfish
sun-flower	fulawa-rana (son-fulawa)
sunglasses, n.	ijongo-rana (son-gilas)
s sun-god	ekwenshu-rana
sun-helmet,	halimet rana
sun-lamp	wuta-rana; (sonlamp)
sun-light	wuta-rna; wuta iska
sun-shine	ishaka-rana
sun-shade	kparazoh; ife bika
	laima (umbrella) sonstrok; irudi irun rana
sun-stroke	
sunny	soni; haske rana; ishaka rana
sunny side of life	akue shaka mindu
sundae, n.	sondaiG(fE)
Sunday, n.	Sande;
Sunday-school	Makaranta e montakele na chochi
Sunday Service	Safis Sande; Sande Safis
sunder, vt.	yapu; yata; yakata Y/I/Gen
sundries, n.	ifambu; e cheto I/Y
sundry,	icheto; ifambu
sup, vt.	wuam G
super, n.	supa; (synonyms: sukpa; shukpa) kpamgba

superabundant, adj.	supa-risi
superannuate, vt, n.	supanuet; isupanuet G(fE)
superb, adj.	sukpab; kamkpe; paka G(fE)
supercargo, n.	supa-kaugbo G(fE)/Y/I
super-charger, n.	supa-chaja; nke injin G(fE)
supercilious, adj.	supacile G(fE)
supercortimajior, n.	supakotimanja G(fE)
superficial, adj.	supafeisha; gbanjo G(fE)/Gen
superficies, n.	supafeisi; gbanjo; adigboloja
superfine, adj.	suparamma G(fE)/Y/I
superfluous, adj.	risi jukha
superhuman, adj.	jukha-mutum; supa-mutum
superimpose, vt.	supa-gbele G(fE)/Y
superintend, vti.	suprintenda; supaboche
superintendent/ce, n.	suprintenda; o supaboche
police superintendent	suprintenda mondoka; osupaboche
superior, adj.	mondoka. supera; ramma jukhaG(fE)
superiority complex	ifambu supera; ijukha
superlative, adj.	supera supaletif; supaletitifG(fE)
super-superlative	supa-supaletif
superman, n.	supa-mutum; shukpa-man
super-market, n.	supa-kasuwa; babakasuwa; kasuwa –lat
supernal, adj.	wigwe: (divine, heavenly)
supernal love	ihufe wigwe
supernatural, adj.	supa-mindu; baba mindu; mindu-lau supa- halitta

supernormal, adj.	supa-gentu; gentu jukha	
superscrition, n.	supaskrishan	G(fE)
supersede, vt.	yi 'kpoze: (to take the place of somethinig)	
supersession, n.	iyi 'kpoze	
supersonic, adj.	supa-sonik; supa-sonek	
superstition, n.	ifokwe	Y/I
superstitious belief	inikon ifokwe	
superstructure, n.	supastracha; supa-kongi	
supertax, n.	taks jukha	
supervene, vi.	sheka	
supervise, vti.	nerin; supafais	I/Y/G(fE)
supervisor, n.	o nerin; supafaiso	
supine, adj.	supin	G(fE)
supper, n.	supe: abinchi yamma	G
supplant, vt.	yi 'kpoze	Egun/Y/I
supple, adj.	bukon; meko n'iflesi; yi-kiri (bend about)	
supplement, n.	soplimente; ifinye	
supplementary list	itole soplimente; ilisa soplimente	
suppliant, n.	o biyo; biyo n'irayo Y/It/I	
supplicate, vt.	biyo n'irayo: "to beg gently/humbly" biyo n'ilisi: "beg humbly"	
supply, vt.	kpenye (pronounced: kpeyen)	
supply and demand	ikpenye ati 'jubi	
short supply	kpenye-kele; kpenyekuru; lai zuto	
supply and transport	ikpenye ati ugboko;	
supplies officer	hafsa ikpenye	

supplier, n. support, vt.	o kpenye kpu-n' azu; kpuzu	
supporter, n.	o kpunazu;	
supporters' club	klob e kpunazu	
supporting staff	sitaf ikpunazu; ikpunazu sitaf; o rushe; e mon irushe	
suppose, vt.	biwu	Y/I
itotowa supposed to come	itotowa biwu biawa	
i supposed to ask you	mo biwu jubi yin	
supposing,	bi-biwu; ibiwu	
supposition, n.	ai dido: not sure	
suppository, n.	sopositri: irudi magani	G(fE)
suppress, vt.	teisi: (t'isi); temon	
suppression	itisi; (itemon)	
suppressor	o t'isi; o temon	
supernational, adj	shukpa-nashona	
supreme, adj.	suprim; suprima	G(fE)
sureme headquarters	suprim hedkwata; mbikeisi suprima	
supremacy, n.	isuprima	
surcharge, n.	ijubi jukha	
surd, n.	sond; ilau lamba (large number)	
sure, adj.	dido	Y/H
are you sure?	o dido? e dido?	
i am sure	biko, di dido	
please, be sure	biko, did dido	
surely, adv.	didido; n'idido; n'ezioka; baate	

538

surety, n.	iyobele: (guarantee)	
surf, n.	sorf; nke tekun abi sabulu	
surface, n.	ezi-fuska; nso-fuska; ifuska (sofes)	
surface-cable	sofes-kebol;	
surface-mail	wasika-sofes	
surfix	sofis	
surge, vi.	kparu "to roll on"	
surgeon, n.	sajan; likita fida	
surgery, n.	sajiri; isajiri; isayens nke sajan daki sajan	
surgical, adj.	nke sajan abi sajiri	
surgical instrument	instrumint sajiri	
surgical scissors	almakashi sajiri	
surly, adj.	kwinsi: ibili-onu rubi: "bad temper"	G
surmise, vti. surmount,vt.	chesoli (to say by guesing); soli n'isi jukaisi	Y/I
surname, n.	afa uba; afa baba	I/H/Y/Gen
surname first	afa uba konon	
surpass, vt.	sorpase; ramma juka	G(fE)
surplice, n.	riga alufa	H/Y
surplus, n, vt.	ikufo; kufo; huenen	Y/I/G
surprise, n.	iyalionu; yalionu	
surprise visit	kibia iyalionu	
i am surprised	o ya mi lionu; o ya mi l'onu	
don't be surprised	ma ya lionu; ma ya l'onu	

surrealism, n.	sorilizim; nke icheko adun gogo ji:" of 20th century arts)
surrender, vti.	tisiba
surrender yourself	tisiba o wenji e/yin
surrogate, n.	sorugate; nke ishida bishobu: of deputy bishop
surround, vt.	yiboito; inso; nsobi
surrounding, n.	nsobi
keep your surroundings	clean: cheto nsobi yin shaka
surtax, n.	sortaks G(fE)
surveillance, n.	iboche-ramma: "to watch very well); igadi
survey, vt.	fika; saveh G/H/G(fE)
surveyor, n.	o fika; o saveh
quantity surveyor	o saveh kwantiti; kwantiti saveh
survival, n.	idiakpor Y/I/Urh.
survite, vt.	diakpor
survival of the fittest:	ijaghuru-ghuru
susceptible, adj.	yaji-yisi; yaji ma ife; yamonji
suspect, vt, n.	kasi; ikasi
robbery suspect	ikasi rawo
suspend, vt.	soke; kpu si whido Y/I
suspender, n.	o soke; sospenda
suspense, n.	ichereji: (anxiety)
suspension, n.	ichereji; sospenda
don't keep me in suspense:	ma fre mi si 'chereji
let us suspend the job:	k'awa kpu irushe si whido

suspension file	fail sospenda	
suspicion, n.	ifuji	Y/H
sustain, vt.	gbebo	Y(G.v)
sustenance, n.	igbebo; abinchi rama	
sutler, n.	sotla: o leta kabandu fun soja na tanti	
suture, n.	sucha: (irudi sili): "a type of thread	
svelte, adj. swab, n.	suvelt: "graceful and slender woman" swabu; irudi mobu (esa-kele)	
swag, n.	suwag: (ijiri kaya) "stolen goods"	
swallow, n.	suwalo; irudi onene	
swallow; vit.	kpurum; kpuruh	G
swallow tablet	kpuruh tablit	
swami, n.	suwame; na hindu irudi o muko: "a type of teacher in hindu" fadama,	
swamp, n.	damba, bakuwa	
swampy area	nso fadama; nso bakuwa	H
swan, n.	suwan; irudi onene-ruwa	G(fE)
swank, vi.	blah-blah; soli oka shakara	G
swap, vt. (swoop)	woi: "to exchange something by barter"	
sward, n.	ledu: something hard and turf	G
swarm, n.	hozin: "large number of insects moving about together"	

swashbuckler, n.	arimkpo-shakara: "boastful noise-making"	
swath, n.	suwat; kaikayi: "chaff"	
sway, vit. n.	kin-kon; ikin-kon	
sway to and fro	yi-kpotoh	
swear, vti.	buhi; buhili	Y/I
sweat, n.	gumi; jubi; zuffa	H
sweater, n.	suwaita	H(fE)
sweep, n.	gbaza	
swept clean	gbaza shaka	
sweep away	gbaza ta	
sweeper, n.	o gbaza; igbaza	
sweep-stake	sanda-igbaza	
sweet, adj., n.	dunso; solele; idunso; suwiti Y/I/G	
sweet potato	dankali o dunso; isolele dankali	
sweet bread	buredi o dunso; isolele buredi	
my sweet heart	ninda mi o dunso; o dunso mi; o solele mi; imiho mi	
sweet sugar	suka o dunso	
sweet, n. (sweets)	switi	
swell, vit,	beu; kuku; diwu	G/Y/I
swollen hand	hannu beu	
swollen leg/feet	kafa kuku	
swollen stomach swollen	headed chiki diwu yanga; idiwu isi	
swelter, vi.	gbowu: "heat"	Y/H
swerve, vit.	dokpo Egun	
swerving	idokpo	

swift, adj.	fiam Gen	
swift, n.	sweft, irudi onene o	G(fE) wuam
	kwaro: "a type of insect eating bird"	
swim, vit, n.	foru; iforu Y/H	
swimmer, n.	o foru	
swimming-pool	kotogbin-foru; (swimin-kpoh)	
swimming-trunks	shokoto-iforu; (swimin-nika)	
i don't know how to swim:	mii ma iforu	
i know how to swim very well:	mo ma iforu rama	
I can swim	Mo kanbo foru	
I cannot swim	Mii kanbo foru	
let us go and swim	k'awa shienga foru	
swindle, vti.	tije: "cheat"	Y/I
swindler, n.	o tije	
swine, n.	alade, garke	H
swing, vit; n.	yiki; iyiki; janglo	Y(G.v)
swinging to and fro	iyiki-kpotoh; yiki-kpotoh	
dancing and	isamba ati iyikikpoto; iyiki-kpoto	
swinging- to and fro	ati 'samba.	
swirl, vit.	ziza: "of fast movement of air or flow of water"	Ed/Isham
swish, vti.	shiih" "of hissing sound"	G
switch, n.	tsumangiya; itonwu; (suwich)	H/Y/G
switch-board	katako-suwich; katako-itonwu	

543

switch-lever	ayan-suwich; ayanitonwu; suwich-liba	
switch-on the light	ton wuta: (not "tonwu-wuta")	
switch off the light	gbu wuta: (note the word "gbu")	
switch on	tonwu	
fly-switch	izga	H
swivel, n.	janglovah	Gen
swivel-chair	kujera-janglovah	
swizzle, n.	suwizoh, irudi ogogoro bature	
swoop, vi.	gbrum: "to rush down"	G
sword, n.	takobi	H
sword-fish swot, vit.	kifi-takobi hula: "to study seriously for an examination"	G
i am studying hard for	mo ng hula fun ichondi mi my examination	
sycamore, n.	sinkamor; irudi itache na kasa briten	
sycophant, n.	ibebeye; bebeye; bebeye	Ed
sycophancy, n.	ibebeye	
sycophantic, adj.	bebeye	
syllable, n.	okada;ikada; sila-sile	Ikwere/H
two-sylabied word	oka okada eji	
syllabus, n.	silabas G(fE)	
syllogism, n.	isilo-silo: "logical reasoning" G(fEd)	
sylph, n.	silf, irudi ekwenshu fekuku: G(fE) "a type of air goddess"	

sylvan, sylvan, adj.	daji-koi-koi" "thich forest"	
symbiosis, n.	isimba: "to associate and live with other groups/ races in harmony"	G(fE)
symbol, n.	simbola	G(fE)
this symbolizes His body	eyi wu isimbola nke jiki Ya; eyi simbola jiki ya	
this is the symbol	eyi wu isimbola; eyi wu ne simbola eyi simbola	
this symbolize		
symmetry, n.	simintari: nke ife rama: "something good and beautiful"	
sympathy, n; vi.	ibakolo; bakolo	Y/G
sympathizer, n.	o bakolo	
in sympathy	n'ibakolo	
thanks for sympathy	shendo fun ibakolo	
(don't mention)	ma soli	
symphony, n.	semfoni; nke isongi	G(fE)
symposium, n.	simkpozia; semkpozia	G(fE)
symptom, n.	ikpehun; isimbola	Y/I/G(fE)
what are the symptoms of fever	meni wu ikpehun iba?	
synagogue, n.	senagogu; gida ibinle	G(fE)
synchroflash	senkroflashe	G(fE)
synchromesh, n.	senkromash	G(fE)
synchronize, vti.	sinkoro; senkoro; isoka n'ngba sem "happening at the same time"	
synchrotron, n.	senkroten; irudi instrumint lantiriki	

syncopate, vt.	senkofit: ilowe songi: of musical sound	
syndicate, n.	ituge; kunjiya; sindika	I/Y/H/G(fE)
syndrome, n.	sindrom; itusimbola	
Acquired Immune Deficiency Sundrome:	(Akwai Imiuna defishensi Sindram)	
synod, n.	senad, irudi mitin nke hafsa chochi	
synonym, n.	isimona; n'ikpoze; oka bika	
synopsis, n.	senopsa; sinopsa	G(fE)
syntax, n.	sentaks; iwufin girama: "grammatical rule"	
synthesis, n.	sentesi; isentesi; sentesa	
synthetic, adj.	senteta; sentesa	
synthetic fabric	fabriki senteta; senteta fabriki	
syphilis, n.	uyahya; sifilia	G/G(fE)
syringa, n.	sairenga; irudi fulawa	G(fE)
syringe, n.	sirin; kotar allurar likita	
syrup, n.	ruwar suka; siropa	H/G(fE)
system, n.	ilayan; iwufin; (sestem)	Y/H/I/G(fE)

ta	T	
ta; bika omontakele	Gen	
tabard, n	tabat, irudiafe kuru-hannu: "a type of short- sleeve shirt"	
tabernacle, n.	ago-abasi; tabanako; gida isolile: "place of	Y/Ed/Ef/G(fE)
the tabernacle of god:	gida isolile abasi; ago-abasi	
table, n.	tebur, jadawali; bunye	H
dining-table	tebur-ijechin; tebur abinchi	
dressing-table	tebur-esa; tebur fun imunji	
tea-table	tebur-ti	
billiard-table	tebur-ti	
table-cloth	atamfa-tebur; esa-kele	
drinking-table	tebur-wain; tebur-ilamu	
table-knife	wuka-tebur; abe	Y/Igala/Ed
table-mat	shimfada-tebur	
table-spoon	chokali-tebur; shin-shin-tebur	
table-land	kasa-tebur; lande-tebur	
table-spoonful	ijukun chokali-tebur	
table-talk	oka-tebur; oka na tebur	
table-tennis	tanas-tebur; tbur-tanas	
table-ware	kwano-tebur	
table-time	ngba-abinchi	
table a motion/motion	nyensa bili	
table-d'hote	tabuta; irudi otela abi huta	
tablet, n.	tablit, kwayar magani; danfalle	H
tabloid, n.	felebe	Y/G.v
taboo, n.	ifoho; ifegbih	
tabor, n.	tagboi; irudi ganga-kele: "a type of small drum"	G/(fE)
tabulate, vt, n.	toleta; itoleta; (kala)	Y/I/G

tacit, adj.	nkiri; nke ichegbon lai soli oka: "of understanding without the use of words"; fini	
taciturn, adj.	tasitan; nkiri	
tack, n.	tki; kumba-kele (small-nail)	
tack, vt.	tuwe; ijuma ugbokoruwa: "ship's direction"	
tack, n.	takeh; irudi bisikiti nke ugboko-ruwa	
fishing-tackle	ikagba-kife; takol-kifi	
tackle, vt.	kagba	
tackle the job	kagba irushe	
tackling, n.	ikagba	
tacky, adj. tact	shimkpa-shimkpa: "wet and sticky" ichera	
fishing-tackle	ikagba-kifi; takol-kifi	
tact and discretion	ichera ati ishonji (ichera 'ti 'shonji)	
tactic, n, adj.	icherati; cherati	
tadpole, n.	talibambam; irudi kwado: "a type of frog"	
taffeta, n.	tafita: irudi siliki-shaka: "a type of shining silk"	
taff-rail, n.	taf-ril; nke ugboko-ruwa	G(fE)
tag, n.	tagi	H/Y/
question-tag	ijubi; oka ijubi;	
tag, n.	taig: irudi igwuere emontakele	G(fE)
tag,	isoma	
file-tag	isoma-fail	
tail, n.	bindi; wutsiya	H

tail-board,	tel-bod: nke ugboko	
catch your tail	jimu bindi e/yin: nke emontakele	
tail-coat	tel-kwat; irudi kwat abi rigar	
tail-end	igwukpin-bindi; igwukpin wutsiya	
tail-light	wuta-bindi	
tail-spin	tel-sfin: nke aroplen	
to tail something:	to follow something closely: solekinin	
tailor, n.	madinki; tela; o kwa esa	H/H(fE)
tailor-made	imedi tela; imeshe tela; nke	
taint, n.	madinki iziun: "trace of bad quality"	G
take, vit.	yi; jimu	Egun
take something	yi 'fe	
take up	yiyi; yi-peh	
take a town or fortress:	kinu gari	
take-home pay	albashi gida	
take advice	yi 'meniye	
he/she doesn't take advices:	ko meshe yi 'meniye; ko yi 'meniyi	
don't take chance	ma gbu ngba	
take the cow to the stream:	gbe malu shien rafi	
take position	ribose	
take-out	yi puta; yi 'ta; yi jata	
take away	yi 'ta; gbe shien	
take-home	yi shien gida	
take notice	yi kiesi; yi notez	

take opportunity it	yi 'yefe; yi ngba o ma yi
will take one hour	hawa daya; a yi hawa daya
it will take long time	a yi ngba golo
take it for granted take charge	yi ya ninnon di kasinwu; <u>boche:</u> (to watch)
take me down	gbe mi shien
take something down	jimu ife shien; yi 'fe shien
take off	rebi: "to begin/start"
take off	yi pu
don't take me back	ma yi mi dazu: (for discussions only)
don't take me back	ma gbe mi zuba (for persons)
take your change	yi sengi e; yi ringi e
take over	yi sikei
taker, n.	o yi
taking, adj.	irire: "of business profit"
talc, n.	talk; irudi miriala-muru "a type of smooth- mineral"
Talcum, n.	Talkom; irudi hodatalkom "talcum- powder"
tale, n.	ilida; ilissafi Agb/H(G.v)
tell-tales	mebobo; mebo;mebo-mebo Gen
tale-bearer	a mebo; o mebo; o mebobo; o lida
talent, n.	izimba; zimba
talent hunt	ichowa zima
taleng-gift	iganye-izimba; iganye-zimba
talented artist	o hunron o wen zimba; o zimba- huron
talisman, n.	talimani; talisima

talk, n, vti.	iroka; soli; isoli; oka talk of the town	
oka gari:	(pronounced:	
oka geri);	oka ngba: (talk of the day/time)	
small-talk	ikaso-kele; oka-kele;	
iroka-kele	(note: ikaso means "conversation")	
talkative, adj.	o soli kha; o soli kha-ka; o soli-soli	
talk-talk	piam-piam-piam	
round-talk	oka boto; oka-rondo	
talking-point	oka izumkpa;oka katazi; o keisi- oka	
talkie, n.	tolki: nke sinima	G(fE)
tall, adj.	gungolo; golo	Y/I/Gen tall-boy
tall-man it is too tall miji-golo	o gungolo jukha; o golo jukha	
tall-story	ilida-golo; ilida-golo-golo	
tallow, n.	kitse	H
tally, n.	tali; irudi baji: a type of berge tally-clerk	
talon	kambori	H
talus, n.	talus; irudi guntu:	F(f H
tamarind, n.	"a tpe of fragment" tsamiya; (tamarinde)	
tamarisk, n.	tamaris; irudi shukeshuke ilililai	
tambour, n.	tambor G(fE)	
tambourine, n.	tamborii; irudi gangakele: "a type of small-	
tame; adj.	drum tikpo; tichi	
tamer; n.	Y/I o tikpo; o tichi	

tammany, n.	tamane; irudi oganaize na niu-york
tam-o'-shanter, n.	tamoshenta: "a type of cap" G(fE)
tamper, vti.	chambo Y/H
don't tamper with it	ma chambo ya; ma chambo
tan, n.	jema; jeme ton; irudi launi H/G(fE)
tandem, n.	tandim; irudi keke fun mutum eji
tangent, n.	tanjint; irudi laini-tara; a type of straight-line
tangerine, n.	tanjariya; ruwa lemo H
tangible, adj.	nezi Y/I
tangle, adj.	idarugu: "confusion" Y/I
tango; n.	tengo; irudi 'songi fun isamba na saot-amerika
tank, n.	(tanki) – of water tank
tank, n. tanker, n.	ghum-ghum: koi-koi: G "armoured-tank" o gbum-ghum; o koikoi: irudi ugboko o
tankard, n.	tenkad; irudi kwaf lau fun bie
tanner, n.	tena; irudi kudi lembu na kasa briten; yien wu "sisi" : (a type of british money formerly, which was six-pence"
tannin, n.	tannin; irudi wassid
tannoy, n.	tinitin: irudi lau-spika bibuto: "a type of largely loud-speaker"
tansy, n.	tensi; irudi magani

552

	shuke-shuke danjiri	
tantalize, vt.		Y/G
tantalus, n.	tentalos; irudi instrumint	G(fE)
tantamount, adj.	tentamante; godozi	G(fE)/I
tantrum, n.	ikain-kain; ibilionu-rubi: "bad tember" kain-kain	
tap,n.	famfo (water-tap)	
tap; vtn.	kwarsa; kpam: "of quicklight hit or blow	(G)
tap on the door	kwarsa na kofa; kpam kofa; (kpam-kpam)	
tap-root, n.	uwar saiwa	H
tape, n.	tef; kintinkiri	H(fE)/H
measuring-tape	tef; kintinkiri	H(fE)/H
tape-recorder	tefrikoda	H(fE)
sello-tape	selo-tef	
magnetic-tape	iyangba-tef	
tappet, n.	tapit: nke injin ugboko	
magnetic tape	tef-magneta tape; vti (to join)/join with tape;	
tape, n.	tef	G(FE)
taper, n.	tefa; irudi abela-lengelaenge: "a type of slender-candle"	
tutef	H	
tapioca, n.	abinchi shimkpashimkpa: "starchy food"	
tapster, n.	tapbie: o safis bie: "beerserver or service"	
tar, n.	kwalta, kalo	H
tarmac, n.	hanya aroplen; tamak	H/G(fE)

tardiddle, n.	wayo-wayo: "untruth"	Gen
tarantula, n.	tarangizo: "a type of large and poisonous spider"	
tarboosh, n.	taboshe; irudi hula: "a type of cap"	
tare, n.	ter: irudi sako t'o ng hugbo n'arin gero: "type of weeds growing among grain- plants"	
target, n.	aweyen, igumala edo	
tariff, n.	kudi t' a ng fi gora ife na kasuwa; terif	
tarn, n.	tan; "small mountain lake"	
tarnish, n. vti.	bi je; datti	
taro, n.	tiro; irudi shuke-shuke o wen ishimkpa: "a type of plant with starch in it"	
rarpaulin, n.	tamfol; tapoline	H(fE)/G(f)
tarpon, n.	taujoib; irudi "buko kifi na oshan atlante	
tarragon, , shuke t' a ng luwe	taragone: irudie shuke- fun abinchi saladi	
tarry, vt.	chendu kpe	
tarry with me	chendu kpe mi	I/Y
tarsal, n.	tasak: kashi-anko: "ankle-bone"	G(fE)
tart, n,	mache sole-sole: "follow-follow woman"; o rinjele (prostitute)	
tartan, n.	tatan; irudi wulu nke skotish: "a type of stotish-wool"	

tartar, n.	taita; irudi wassid abi ogogoro	
tartar, n.	o gbologbo: "roughian and a violent all-purpose person"	
task, n. vt.	irushega; rushega; isile the task before you irushega na whido e/yin it is taskful	
tuntu, alakwayi	"bunch of threads"	
tastem vti (to taste something)	tohun	Y/I
tata, int.	tata; ede jariri abi omontakele	
tatter, n.	kisa; tsumma: (rags) tattered dress	
tattle, vit.	mebobo: mebolo: gossip	
here and there;	of idle talk	
tattler, n.	o mebobo: o mebolo tattoo, v jarfa; shasshawa	
taunt, n.	ikpegu: oka rubi: "bad words or remakrs:	
taurus, n.	tauros; nke zodiak	G(fE)
taut, adj.	guze; waya abi ijiya	G
tautology, n.	isololoji; eem-em; irudi oka ti ko wen ifambu si nke lembu	
tavern, n.	taven, irudi kanti n'gba lembu	
tawny, adj.	saara: irudi launi saayara: 'a type of brownishyellow colour"	

tawse, n.	tawis, irudi koboko fun omontakele: "a type of "koboko" (whip) for small children"
tax, n.	(direct tax taks); (haraji) GfE)/H taksi gon-gon
indirect tax	taksi 'fregon; (ifregon taksi)
tax-collector tax-payer taxi, n.	o kodo-taksi o kpa-taksi
tax due	haraji nke a le taksi; di taksi;
taxable adult	agagba nke a le taksi G(fE) takasi; tazi; (tazi)
taxi-cab taxi-meter	moto zoom-zoom tazi; (tazi-kab) minta-tazi
taxi, vt.	taisi – (nke ugbokofekuku) (aroplen)
illegal taxi	kabu-kabu
taxidermy, n. tea n.	taizidemi tii, shayi G(fE) H(fE)/H
tea-bag	ikpa-tii
tea-break tea-cake	isimini: fun tii; ifre irushe fun tii kek-tii
tea-cosy,	tii-ch
tea-chest	oka-kele n'ngba tii
tea-chat	kwaf-tii; finjali-tii
tea-cup	kwaf-tii; finjali-tii
tea-garden	gadin-tii
tea-gown,	riga-tii
tea-kettle	kitali-tii
(kettle-tea)	tii-kitali; tii nka kitali
tea-party	iriya-tii; ikonogbandu-tii
tea-pot	butu-tii
tea-room	daki-tii

tea-set	tii-set; e kwaf-tii	
tea-spoon	chokali-tii	
tea-spoonful	ijuku chokali-tii	
tea-table	tebur-tii	
tea-time	ngba-tii	
tea-tray	tire-tii	
tea-trolley	wagunu-tii	
teach, vti.	koli, muko;	I/Y
teaching, n.	ikoli imuko;	
teachings	e koli e muko	
teach us something	muko 'wa ife/ihe	
teachable	nke a le muko; di muko; di 'koli	
teak, n.	tiki; irudi itache ilililai t'o gungolo	
teal, n.	tile; irudi agwagwa o gboro: "a type of wild	
team, n.	duck" tim; itugbe	
football team	tim-fubol	
soccer-team	tim-soka	
team-work	irushe itugbe; irushe-tim	
team-spirit	imindu-'tugbe	
tear, vti.	doya	
tears, n.	ariri; arigo	
tear-drops	ikpo-arigo; ikpo' arigo	
tearful	jukun fun ariri; ariri abi arigo	
tear the paper	doya takarda	

tear-gas, n. tease, vt, n.	kakpum; tagas; harashi toka tokeh; itokeh: yeye	G/G/H G/Y/Gen
don't tease me	ma tokeh mi; ma meshe mi yeye	
teaser, n.	o tokeh; o yeye	
teasel, n.	kaya: (thorn)	
teat, n.	tet: "nipo" – (nipple)	
technical, adj.	teknike; nke ichegbon mashin abi injin	G/I
technician, n.	o teknike	
technicolor, n.	teknilauni; nke launi foto	G(fE)/H
technique, n.	itekini; (itekni); ichegbon eni 'fe: "knowledge or wisdom of anything"	
technocracy, n.	tekinokeresi: irudi gonmenti eso: "some form of government" teki-teki	
technology, n. college of technology	kolej nke teki-teki	
technoligist	o teki-teki	
technolotgical expert	iwin teki-teki	
teddy bear, n.	tedi-bie; irudi namiji-daji	
tedious, adj.	sileru	I/Y
the job is too tedious	ne irushe o sileru; irushe of sileru	
tee, n.	ti; nke igwuere gwalf	
teem, vi.	kpisi: (of large numbers)	I/Y
teem-up	kpisi; kpisi-jo	
teens, n.	yara; e yara	H
teenage, n.	'itakele	

teenager, n.	omontakele: mutum nke ti hugbo siti ardun ji eji: "person who has grown up to 22 years of age"
teeter, vi.	rugara: kundu abi ringa lai wen agba "to walk or stand powerlessly unsteady"
teeth, n.	hakori H
tee-to-tal, adj	goloza; eni ko lamu G ogogoro abi wain; ai lamu wain kinien
tee-to-taller,	o goloza
teetotum, n.	titotom G(fE)
tegument, n.	toguma; bika kwarya kunkuru: "like the tortoise' shell"
telecast, n.	telikase; telikase: nke isoliwaya na telebijin "of television broadcast"
telecommunications, n.	telikominikashon; ikwekwele; isoligolo
post and telecommunications	telikominikashon ati fos; (alternatively) fos an telikominikashon; ikwekwele ati fos
telegram, n. telegraph, n. telgrapher, n. telegraphese telegraphy, n.	iziron teligra; iziron wayawaya; teli-kia- G/Y/I kia telikiakia, waya-waya; isoli-waya o waya-waya; o soli- waya waya-kuru telive-ve teli-saun
telemetry, n.	solimitri G(fE)
teleology, n.	solioloji; irudi inikon eso: some types of beliefs"
telephathy, n.	isolipati; solipate G(fE)
telephone, n.	teliwaya; soliwaya; solifon; soligolo; G (note: you could choose any of above)
telephone-booth	buka-teliwaya
telephone-directory	littafi ijuma teliwaya; daretri teli idaya; daretri teliwaya
telephone-exchange	gida-waya-waya; gida teliwaya

telephone operator (male or female)	opareta teliwaya; o yini teliwaya
telephonist	o teliwaya
telephoto, n.	telihoto
telephotography, n.	ifoto-foto
teleprinter, n.	telipresa; teli'pres; solipresa
teleprompter, n.	telipota; solipromta – (either of the two)
telescope, n.	teliska; solisko G(fE)
telescopic, adj.	teliska; nke isolisko; teliskosa
television, n.	telibijin; telifoto; solifoto G(fE)
telex, n	- waya – waya
telex machine	mashin teli-saun-saun
tell, vti.	soli; sole; gbaameh Y/I/Izon
tell him	soli si ya
tell them	soli si ha
tell me	soli si mi
i said that	mo soli kpe
he/she said that	mo soli kpe
i will tell you	maa soli si/fun e/yin
do not say i told you	ma soli kpe mo sole si yin
what are you telling me?	meni o ng soli si mi?
go and tell him	shienga soli si ya
teller,	o soli; tela: (nke banki)
telpher, n.	o gbefoloh
telstar, n.	telsta; solsta: irudi hogohogo abi salilat nke
temper, n.	telibijin: "a type of television satellite" ikpobi Y/I

good-temper	ikpobi-rama	
bad-temper	ikpobi-rubi	
temper, vti.	tenwu: "to heat iron or steel with fire/heat"	
temper, vti.	wakpo: "to mix something with another" finye	
temper justice with mercy:	wakpo idakpe kpelu inube	
temperament, n.	ikpobi	I/Y
temperance, n.	ikoso o wenji: "selfcontrol"; ba: "moderate"	
temperate, adj.	biba: "of moderacy"	
temperate zone	isogbo biba	Y/H
tempest, n.	ifukugba; fukugba	G/Y
tempestuous, adj.	fukugba-gba	
raging tempest	iliwuta fukugba; fukugba-iliwuta	
template, n.	templat; irudi instrumin ayan	G(fE)
temple, n.	haikali	H
the temple of god	ne haikali abasi; haikali nke abasi	
tempo, n.	temkpo; nke isongi abi muzik	G(fE)
tempos in high-life	akpor-ganu na temkpos; akpor- ganu temkpos	
temporal, adj.	nkensin; kensin; nke ngba	I/Y
temporary, adj.	nke ngba kene; kengba	
temporize, vi.	kuba icherisi abi ifeza:"to delay decision or answer"	
tempt, vt.	duleu	Y/I/G

temptation, n.	iduleu, tenda – (synonym)
tempter	o duleu; o duleu-leu; o tenda
deliver us from temptation	yopu wa sa iduleu-leu; yopu wa n'iduleu-le
ten, n. adj.	goma H
tenth, n, adj.	nke goma; igoma
tenable, adj.	mekusa; nke a le kusa: "that which can be defended"
tenacious, adj.	numo Y(G.v)
tenacity, n.	inumo
tenant, n.	haya; eni haya gida; o haya
tenancy, n.	ihaya
tenancy agreement	ikweba haya; ikweba fun ihaya gida
tench, n.	tanch; irudi kifi G(fE)
tend, vi.	chesi-si: "inclined to" I/Y
tendency, n.	ichesi-si
tendentious, adj.	tandishos: irudi oka sisoli: "a type of speech-writing"
tender, adj.	kanka: "something delicate"
tender, vti.	tenda; irudi ikp fun kaya; itenda
tender-board	itugbe-tenda; kwamiti-tenda
tennis, , n.	tenin: itache abi omo turmi G(fE)
tenor, n.	ijushe: "one's daily routine"
tenor, n.	teno: "of musical highest voice" G(fE)
tense, adj.	kwaru;
the situation is tense: ikpongba di kwaru tense, n.	ikoge; nke girama
present tense	ikoge ngba
past tense	ikoge zuba
tension, n.	igbowuta; igbowu; ikwaru Y/H high tension wire waya igbowuta ganu tension-battery

tent, n.	tanti; laima; alfarwa H mosquito-tent tanti-sauro
oxygen-tent	tanti-agsijin
tentacle, n.	ifile-fila; irudi
jiki nama: " a	type of animal's body"
tentative, adj, n.	ichene; chene I/G tentative arrangement itolele chene
tentatively, adv.	chene-chene; n'ichene; fun ichene
tentrhooks, n.	tentahuh: (ichereji ganu) "high-suspension or high anxiety"
tenth, n, adj.	nke goma; ke goma I/H tenth position ikpoze goma; ikpoze 300 years anniversary" nke goma
tenure, n.	inuen; ngba Y/I tenure of office inuen ofis my tenure of office inuen ofis mi; ngba mi na ofis tercentennial; nn. tasetinina; nke anivase ardun gogo eta "of
tergiversate, vi.	dikpotun: "to make a complete change by one's opinion"
term, n.	ikponu; nke ngba
first-term	ikponu-konon
second-term	ikponu-nk'eji
third-term	ikponu-nk'eta
school-term	ikponu-makaranta
term, n, (of condition)	iwahe
terms of agreement	e wahe ikweba; e wahe agrimento
term, n, (of relation to)	inureli
termagant, n.	atabala; mache arimkpo ati 'bilionu "quarrelsome and noisy woman"
terminal, adj.	kpi-kponu: "of term"; gwukpin
terminal leave	isimini kpi-kponu

railway terminus	igwukpin reluwe; mbi 'simin reluwe; "taminos nke reluwe"	
terminate, vti, n.	legwu; ilegwu	Y/I
termination of appointment:	ilegwu irushe	
terminology, n.	itame-tame	G(fE)
termite, n.	gara, zago	H
tern, n.	tan; irudi onene-tekun: " a type of sea-bird"	G(fE)
terrace, n.	tireshi	H
terracotta, n.	terakote; irudi yumbu: "a type of clay" (terakoko) G(fE)	
terrafirma, n.	terakote; "kasa-kpako; kasa-kpogbe "dry- land or empty dry-land"	
terraincognita, n.	dajinso: "unknown territory; unexplored places"	
terrain, n.	vairin: ifagolo kasa:	
terrapin, n.	"stretch of land" terapine: irudi kunkururuwa: "a type of water-tortoise"	
terrestrial, adj.	veringo: nke ife akpor; ife duniya G(fE)	
terrible, adj.	lerugu; teisi Y/I	
terrific, adj.	lerugu;	
terrify, vt.	di lerugu; terisi; lerugu; leru	
territorial, adj.	nsoka	
territoril integrity	imenuza nsoka	
territory, n.	insoka; nsoka	I/H
terror, n, vt, adj.	igbuaya; gbuaya; leu-leu	

he is a terror	ya wu o gbuaya; ya wu o leu-leu
terrorist, n.	o leu-leu
terror-man terror-woman	miji o gbuaya; miji-leuleu mache og buaya; mache o leu-leu
terrorize	gbuaya; leu-leu
terse, adj. tertiary, adj.	kwintin; oka ichegbonkele teta; nke eta: thirdly
terylene, n.	tereline; irudi fabriki G(fE)
tessellated, adj.	tasilate; irudi mabul G(fE)
test, n.	iwone; iwoneri; inerifiene; ichondi ihunri;
let me test you	ihundon ka m' hundon e; ka m' hunri yin
test-drive	iyanwa hunri
test-transimssion	iwone-ronwya
testament, n.	testamint; irudi isheni: " a type of wil or will"
new testament	testamint kowele; testamint huntun
old testament	testaming digbo
testate, n.	o sheni: eni meshe testamint swene o kuowun
testicle, n.	lunsayi; gwaiwa H
testify, vti.	shaida H
testification	ishaida
testify to it	shaida si
testimony, n.	ishaida; ikende: (declaration)
testimonial, adj.	shi-shaida; testimona: irudi takarda shaida

testy, adj.	bilionu kia-kia; ai wen 'sundi: impatience"
tetanus, n.	titana; irun rubi: bad disease G(fE)
tete-a-tete, n.	itete mitin ibizu: "private meeting"; tete-tete
tether, n.	turke; talar H/H(fE)
text, n.	ikezi G/I
text-book	littafi 'kezi
textile, adj.	testal; imeshe esa abi tufa G(fE)
textile industry	indusia testal; fatiri testal
texture, n.	tescha; itole fabriki na testal
thalidomide, n.	talidoma; irudi maganne G(fE)
than, conj.	jukha; kha Y/I
more than	risi jukha
more than that	risi jukha yien
thank, vt.	shendo; kene; idiokpe
thank you	shendo
thank your very much	shendo kha
thank you so much	shendo kha-ka
thank god let's thank god	shendo abasi k'awa kene abasi
give thanks	nno ishendo
let's thank god	k'awa kene abasi
give thanks	nno ishendo
give thanks to god	kene abasi
thanks-giving	idiokpe
thanks-giving service	isine nke idiokpe (isinle-diokpe)
thanksfulness/lly	di-diokpe;
be thankful to god	diokpe si abasi
that, adj.	yien; kpe; kayien

this and that	kayi ati kayien
i said that	mo soli kpe
he said that	o gbaameh kpe
that man	miji yien
that place	mbi yien – (to be amended)
thatch, n.	ibogi
thatched-house	gida ibogi
thatcher, n.	o bogi
m. thatcher	(afa praim minista nke kasa briten, yien wu magret thatcher)
thaw, vit.	gbowu: (make hot)
thaw it	gbowu ya
the, def. art.	ne (please note that the Ed definite article "ne" (the) is infrequently used in guosa language. it may be used in such cases when referring to some higher names and titles; other cases are matters of interest and grammatical smoothness in guosa.
the house	ne gida; (or): gida
this is the house	eyi wu ne gida
let the man come	ka ne miji biawa; k'o biawa
the house of god	gida nke abasi (not "ne gida nke abasi) alhaji u. shinkafi – the
marafan sokoto:	alhaji umaru shinkafi – ne marafa nke sokoto
alexander the great	alaxander ne ogidi
the great god	abasi ne ogidi; (o gidi abasi) (contrarily to the english language, the word "ne" – (the) is not so frequently used in guosa language.
the wise man:	o chegbon miji (not "ne chegbon mini")
the more you look; the less you see:	bietu e ng neri risi; bietu e ng hunri kiene: (in other words; neri risi – hunri kiene)

567

theatre, n. theatre, n.   tiyeta; gida samba G/(fE)/H/G(fBr)
                                                 G goru: (nke asibitin)

theatre-room   daki/deki goru

theft, n.   car theft

their, adj.   theirs, pron.

theism, n.   them, pron.

theme, n.   themselves, pron.

then, adv.   now and then

thence, adv.   thence-forward

theocracy, n.   theocratic, adj. theocrat theodolite, n.

theology, n.   theory, n. theoretical theosophy, n.
                                               therapeutical, adj. theraphy, n.

ili; irawo   Y/I/H
ili mota; irawo mota

kesu nke kesu deizim; inikon si abasi   I/H

daya n'akpor; su; <u>ha; fa:</u> (synonyms)   H/I

isioka; topike wensu; o wensu (not wenha or wenfa)   I/Ikwere/G(fE)

geyen   I/Y

geyensi geyensi whido

itiokeresi; irudi isinle nke itiokeresi o tiokeresi tiodolat;   G(fE)

baba maidubi   G(fE)/H

itioloj a iroche   G(fE)

n'iroche   Y/I

itio-tio; irudi 'sinle abi inikon   G(fE)

terafi; nke imeson: of

curative iterafi; terafi: G(fE)
imeson: (cure)

there, adv. it is there i am there here and there over-there
there-about thereafter, adv. thereby, adv. geyi ati geyen
(geyi geyen) ebe: - synonym; o wa n'ebao mo wa n'ebo
mbi ati eba n'eba 'be nos; nso iba izuein; n'izuba si eba

therefore, adv. therein, adv.	n' irondi; sisiri sisili; rondi-si; eba si; ebe si; jujukun	
all things therein thereinafter, adv.	ife ncha jukun si; ife ncha sisili sisili zubaya; izubaya sisili: (either is o.k.)	
thereof, adv. thereto, adv.	sa eba: (from there; from that source) ebe si; eba si	
thereunder, adv.	n'abe; n'ebe-abe	
thereupon, adv.	ibe-si; eba-si;	
therm, n. thermal, adj.	temah – (from etemah); nke igbowuta: of heat temah; nke temah	
thermo, n.	temoh	G/E
thermo-dynamics	temoh-zagba	
thermo-nuclear,	temoh-ghuniya	
thermo-plastic	temoh-roba; temoh-flastik	
thermo-stat	temoh-kyaka; temoh-sat	
thermometer, n.	temohminta; giri-giri	G(fE)/G
thermos, .	temos	G(fE)
thesaurus, n.	tezaros: nke oka girama	G(fE)
these	e kayi	I/Y
t hese are the things	e kayi wu ne ife/ihe	
thesis, n.	igere; teas	G/G(fE)
thews, n.	tsoka: (muscles)	H
they, pron. plural	su; (synonym: ha/fa)	H/I
thick, adj.	diki; koi-koi; jukun	Y/I/G
thickly	dikili; koi-koi; diki	
thickly populated	jukun fun mutane	
thick-skin	fata koi-koi	
thickness	idiki; ikoi-koi	
thicket, n.	duhuwa, omon-kurmi H/Gen/H	

thief, n.	barawo, rawo; o rawo	H/H(G.v)
thigh, n.	chinya; katara	H
thimble, n.	shafi	H
thin; adj.	kintin G/Y	
thing n.	ife/ihe I	
things, pl.	ife/ihe; e kaya	
every thing will be all	ife ncha ma di rama; ife ncha a di	
right:	rama	
think; vti.	loro I/Y	
thinking, n.	iloro	
think twice	loro n'ngba eji; loro n' eji	
i am thinking of you	mo ng loro e; mo ng loro yin	
think about	loro kiri; loro mani	
think about it	loro mani ya; loro ya	
stop thinking my friend	du iloro aboki	
think-tank	kwamiti iloro	
thinker	o loro	
great thinker	io loro gidi	
thinkable third, adj. n.	nke a le loro si nke eta; 'k'eta I/Y	
the third month	uki nk' eta	
third-party	mutum nk' eta	
third-rail	tereil; nke karent: (current)	
third-world	akpor nk' eta	
thirst, n.	hahah; ihahah	G
i am thirsty	moong hahah	

i thirst for you	mo ng hahah fun e; mo ng chowa e	
thirsty;	ihahah	
thirteen, adj, n.	goeta:	H/Y
thierteenth	nke goeta;	
thirty, adj, n.	ta: <u>eo</u>	Y(G.v)
thiertieth, adj, n.	nke ta	
this, pl.	eyi; (kayi: synonym)	Y/I
this girl	omote yi; yanrinya yi	
this man	miji yi	
this woman	mache yi	
this or that	kayi abi kayien	
this and that	kayi ati kayien	
this is the news	eyi wu ikwiro	
this house	gida eyi	
this place	mbi 'yi; ebi 'yi	
thstle, n.	egun; (to be replaced with north)	
thole, n.	tol; nke abara abi kwalekwale	G(fE)
thong, n.	iluti nke koboko: "whip's lash"	
thorax, n.	gali; kirji : (chest)	
thorn, n.	kaya	H
thorn and thisle	egun ati kaya	
thorough, adj.	rau-rau; shaka-shaka; meshe ya ramaka	
do it thoroughly	meshe ya shakashaka; meshe ya	
completely	ramaka	
	bad: o ti meje rau-rau; o meje rau-rau (thoroughly)	

thorough-seraching	iguolo rau-rau; ichowa rau-rau	
thoroughness	ishaka-shaka; iramaka	
thoroughfare, n.	baba-hanya; hanya	
no thoroughfare	kosi hanya; kosi baba-hanya	
there is thoroughfare	baba-hanya di; babahanya o wa	
those, (pl. of that)	e kayien; e yien	
those people	e mutum yien	
those areas thou, pro. though, conj.	e gbonso yien; nso ebi yinwan amo	Y/I Y
though he went still	amo o shi shienga; amo o shienga-siti	
thought, n.	iloro; agba iloro: (power of thinking)	
second thought	iloro nk'eji	
take a second thought	loro si nk'eji	
i thought that	mo loro kpe	
thousand, adj, n.	gogo-goma <u>ioo-io</u>	H(G.v)
thousands	e gogo-goma	
thousands of people	mutum e gogo-	
goma thrail, n.	ibawa: (slavery)	
thrash, vti.	ghukah	I/Ed/G
thread, n.	zare; iringa	H
threat, n.	irungu	
three, adj, n.	eta	
three-cornered	kwana-eta: (of triangle)	
three-dimensional	ifangolo-eta	
three-figure	isiffa abi ilamba eta	

three-pence	kobo-eta	
three-lane	hanya fun mota;	
three-piece	hanya-eta; len-eta guntu-eta; irudi esa kwat	
three-ply	iyanwa-eta; (tiri-flai)	
three-quarter	kwata-eta	
three-storey	sitori-eta	
threnody, n.	iyuya: isongi 'kunbe; isongi isinmut "song of lamentation or funeral"	
thresh, vti.	bubo: to beat grains out	I/Y
thresher	o bubo	
threshing-machine	injin o bubo	
threshold, n.	baki-kofa; onu kofa	H(G.v)/I/H
thrice, adv.	ngba eta; nk'eta; na nk'eta	
i came to your house thrice:	mo biawa gida e n'ngba eta	
thrift, n.	irere; ikomamin	Y/Ed/ Sobe/G
nta co-thrift	ikonamin nke nta	
thrill, n.	miri-miri; miri; dunso; imiri; idunso	G/Y/I
sweet thrill	imiri rama;	
thrive, vi.	gburuh	I/Y
thriving	igburuh	
throat, n. throb, vi.	wuya; makogwaro luku	H Y(G.v)
throe, n.	garan ikebe omontakele G n'ngba imubi "the cry of a baby at birth"	
thrombosis, n.	trombosisi; irudi irun rubi nke jinni	
throne, n.	iyeze Y/I	
he has ascended the throne:	o ti gbake iyeze	
throng, n.	taron; ikonojojo	H/Y(G.v)

we are passing through	awa ng feja; awa ng feja kufe
go through	shiene feja; gua feja: (read through)
throughout, adv.	fefeja; fejata
throughout the time	fejata ngba yien; fejata ngba
throw, vti.	juma; gbagba Y/I/G
don't throw stone in a glass house:	ma juma dutse na gida maidubi
throwing	ijuma
throw away	ijuma ta
thrush, n.	tirosh; irudi onene ti o ng songi-songa: "a type of song-bird"
thrush, n.	chizar; alafa H
thrust, vti.	fugun: push violently G/Y
thug, n.	o gra-gra: o kpako: mugu: o mika
thumb, n.	baba yatsa hannu; (bhatsa)
thumb-high	ganu-bhatsa
thump, vti.	gbamu-gbamu; iluti ganga: "beating of the drum"
thunder, n.	shango; (shongo) Ed/Y
thunder-bolt	ishanwuta-shango; ichaun-chaun-shango
thunder-storm	iduduh-shango
thunder-strike	inulu-shango
thundery, adj.	shango; shongo
thursday, n.	tasde; rana nk'isen n'uzola
thus, adv.	bika 'yi; bietutu; baate; sieba
thwart, n.	tuwati; irudi kujera na ugboko-ruwa
thwart, vt.	kwaru G
thy, adj (thine)	gisi; nke yin

thine is ithe kingdom	nke yin wu ib'eze; gisi wu ib'eze
thyme, n.	gosoh; irudi shuke-shuke G
thyroid, n.	izonbaG
thyroid-gland tiara, n.	kaluluwa izonba; (kazonba) tiera; kende eta nke popu: "three crowns of the pope"
tibia, n.	tibi; kashi-kwauri; (shin-bone)
tic, n.	gbrih; iwinrin tsoka: (tightening of the muscles)
tick, n.	ikain; kain: ilowe agogo: "sound of a clock"
tick, n.	ewinwan: "small parasite like spider that fastens itself to the skin of cow, dogs and other animlas and sucks blood"
ticker, n.	greza "telegraphic machine which prints news automatically"
ticket, n.	tikiti: takarda ibale
tickle, vti.	rijin "to excite the nerves of skin by touching lightly"
tiddler, n.	tida; irudi kifi-kele G(fE)
tide, n.	sonbi; sonbe
tide-mark	ilaini-sonbi; lain-sonbi
tide-way	hanya-sonbi; hanya-sonbe
tidings, n.	ihinhin G(fEd.)
the good tidings	e hinhin-rama
glad-tidings	e hinhin idunso; ihinhin-' dunso
tidy, adj.	fini; shaka
tidiness, n.	ifini; ishaka
tidy up	fini-fini; fini; di shaka
tie, n.	o koso
tie, vti.	koso

head-tie	koso-isi; ikoso-isi; o kosoisi (also: ikoso-kei)	
tier, n.	taiya: "of shelf or number parallel rising one above the other"	
tiff, n.	ijaru: "a slight quarrel:	
tiger,	taga	
tight, adj.	wiring; wini; sile; <u>gbowu:</u> (of heat)	
the place si too tight	ne 'bi wiring jukha; o wiring jukha	
tight-rope	waya-gangan;	
walking on a tight rope	iringa na waya-gangan	
tight-face	iwinin-'do meshe ido wini; wini	
tight your belt	sile belit; koso belit e	
tights, n.	tats; irudi riga kafa	G(fE)
tile, n.	fale-fale	H
till, (until)	siti	Y(G.v)
till, vt. till the soil tiller, n. tiller, n.	guoka: (of tilling the soil) guoka kasa o guoka; tila; irudi instrumint nke kwalekwale	
tilt, vti.	faru; yiru: "to turn the table to a sloping position by lifting one end"	
tilth, n.	tili; ijinka nke kasa: "depth of the soil"	G(fE)
timber, n.	timba;nke ilowe abi saun: of sound	
time, n.	ngba; agogo; iyoge	
what is it by the time?	meni wu agogo?	

the time if sour o'clock:	agogo inang sam
God's time is the best	ngba abi iyoge abasi lo rama jukha
time waits for no one	ngba ko chendu eni mutum
from time to time	sa ngba si ngba
from time immemorial	ke ngba ililoron; sa ngba ililoro
the time is at hand	ngba ti sigkie; ngba ti sigkiele
time/up time is up	agogo ti sam
come on time, please	bia n'ngba, biko; biawa n'ngba
i will come on time	maa biawa n'ngba
don't waste time	ma gbu ngba
fools die before time	mumu ng kuowun swene ngba
have a good time	yi ngba rama; wen ngba rama
time-keeper	o cheto agogo
timothy, n.	timote: irudi shuke-shuke abinchi malu: "type of grass grown as cows food"
timely, adj.	n'ngba-ngba; n'ngba; n'agogo; na iyoge
timid, adj.	diambo G
time-table, n.	itole-ngba; takarda ngba
timpani n.	timgbagba; irudi gangan bika kital "a type of kettle-like drum"
tin, n.	kuza; kwano; kwango H/Gwa/Nupe
tin-can	ten-kan
tin-can island	alande ten-kan
tin-foil	tin-fo: (tin-wrapper)

577

tin-god	duduke
tin-hat	halimet-kwano; halimet-kwango
tin-smith	o rushe makeri; (tinsumit)
tin-tack, n.	tin-tak; kumbakuru: "short-nail"
tin-tack, n.	ten-tak: irudikwango fun abinchi
tiredness	irengu; irengulu; iremba
tiredless	lai rengulu; ai rengu; ai remba
i am tired	mo te rengu; mo rengulu;
tiresome	rengula;rengulu jukha
it is tiresome	o ng rengula
tiro, tyro, n.	tiyoto: "beginner or Ed knowledge" someone with letter
tissue, n.	teishu; fale-fale G(fE)/H
tissue-paper	peipa-teishu; (teishu-peipa);takarda-fele
tit, n.	titibiiti: irudi onene kele: (a type of small bird)
tit-for-tat	meshe-mi-meshe-e
titan, n.	agbagidi; irudi yali kato nakasa giriki
titanium, n.	titeniam; irudi miriala G(fE)
tit-bit, n.	titibiiti: "derived from the ('titibiiti); choice
tithe, n.	tait; ikpaka nke goma; ikpaka goma nke ife: "tenth part of something"
titillate, vt.	titillate; simele: "stimulate"
Don't titillate me to anger:	Ma simele mi si 'bilionu

titivate, vti.	tikio-kio: "to adorn and make smart" titivate yourself at the mirror: tikio-kio o wenji e na maidubi
title, n.	izuh; (afa: "of name") G
the title of the book is:	izuh nke ne littafi wu…
title belt:	ikende-belit
i'll strip you of your title-belt:	maa webo e ikende-belit
title-page	izuh-shafi
title-deed	takarda-shaida; assheikende; didi- kende
title-credita	izuh-kredita: "of names of people who produced radio/tv programme"
tittle, n.	tinkin: "of the least particle of bit" tinin
titular, adj.	tetula: "to hold or obtain G(fE) by virtue of title"
tizzy, adj.	di jijiya: "to feel nervous"
t.junctoin, n.	iyahanya-t; (t-jankcha)
near to quarter to	nure si kwata si
i'm off to wrok:	mo te ng shien irushe: (note the omission of "to" in this sentence)
give it to him/her	fun ya
he/she wants to go	o che is shenga. note: "the words" si/ fun" (to) are not strictly followed or applied as in the english language. the application depends on the mode and pattern of vernacular
from house-to-house	sa gida-si-gida
from time-to-time	sa ngba-si-ngba
not to me	kowu fun mi kowu si mi;
toast, n.	akara; kyafe Gen/G
toast, vt, n. (of wish & happiness: toast for peace,	sioko fun alafia, igbandu at idunso. healthand happiness:)

let us toast for peace, health, and happiness:	k'awa sioko fun alafia, igbandu ati idunso	
popose a toat	ghiche isioko	
toast for it	sioko si	
toaster: (someone who toasts):	o sioko	Gen(fE)
toaster, n.	tosta; injin ti a ng fi meshe akara: "bread-toaster"	
toaster, n.	tosta; injin ti a ng fi meshe akara: "bread-toaster"	
tobacco, n.	taba; tabako	Gen(fE)
toboggan, n.	tobogane	G(fE)
tobyjug, n.	tabijag; irudi bajongo: (a type of drinking jug)	
toccata, n.	tokata; nke isonga G(fE)	
tocsin, n.	tokosen; lada agogo G(fE)	
today, adv, n.	nita; nitata	
today, adv, n.	nita; nitata	
today is …	nita wu… Y/I/Ikale	
toddle, vi.	tete: (to walk short and Ed unbalance like a baby)	
toe, n.	yatsar kafa; H/G(fE)	
from top to toe	sa nuke yatsar kafa si; sa nuke si atsar kafa	
from head to toe	sa isi siti yatsar kafa; sa kai si toi	
toff, n.	munji rama: "well-dressed"	
toffee, toffy, n. toga, n.	tofi; irudi suwiti; wata alewa tonga; irudi baba-rigar n'ngba kera na kas rom: "a type of loos flowing gown or garment of men in ancieint rome"	
together, adv.	jujutu; jutu; nojo Y/I	
together we stand	konojo awa kundu	
togetherness	ikonojo; ijutu;	

together with	jutu kpe; jutu kpelu
they are living together:	su ng hu jutu; awa ng konojo hu jutu; su ng konojo hu; fa ng hu jutu
we are living together	awa ng hu jutu; awa ng konojo hu
together again	ikonojo mozo; ikonojo keji
what god has put togther	ife abasi ti konojo, ka eni mutum
let no man put asunder:	ma yobile. (alternatively): "ka eni mutum ma yobile ife ti abasi ti konojo"
toggle, n.	tagol, itache abi sanda keleG(fE)
toil, vi.	rushele; "to work long and hard on a task"
toil away	rushele ta
toiler, n.	o rushele
toilet, n.	salga; shadda H
i'm going to the toilet:	mo ng shienga shadda abi salga
someone is in the toilet:	mutum 'wa na shadda/salga
the toilet is engaged:	shadda file
toilet soap	sabulu-shadda
toilet paper/roll	peipa-shadda; takarda salga/shadda
toils, n.	ikoma; taru: "net or snares" (tarko)
tokay, n.	tokei; irudi suwiti: "type of sweet"
token, n.	halama; tokinien H/G(fE)
this is a token of my appreciation:	eyi wu itokinien imaye mi
token of things to come	halama nke ife bibiawa

told, pt, of tell	sole; gbaameh	Y/I/Izon
tolerate, vt, n.	kweye; ikweye	I/Y
j.i	don't tolerate nonsense:	
j.ii	kweye shashasha	
toll, n.	gele; kudi irinje	G
toll-gate	kofa-gele; kofa kudi irinje	
toll-bar	sanda-gele	
toll-house	gida-gele	
toll-call	tolkal; nke teliwaya G(fE) tomaha; irudi gatari-fele: G(fE)	
tomahawk, n.	"a type of light-axe	
tomato, n.	tumatir, tomti	H/Gen./fE
tomb, n.	kabari H	
tombola, n.	tembola; tambola; G(fE)/Gen gida-kalu-kalu	
tombola-boy	yaro-tembola; yaro tambola	
tomboy, n.	tomboi: omote o hufe G(fE) igwuereke: "girl who loves rough-play"	
tomcat, n.	muzuru; (muzurumiji): "male-cat"	
tome, n.	littafi lau: "large and heavey book"	
tomfool, n.	imugu; mugu; mutum muguGen.	
tommy-gun, n.	gbam-gbam; irudi bindiga sob-mashen	
tomorrow, adv, n.	lachi (from: "ola + echi") Y/I	

no credit today,
come tomorrow?
kosi kreda nita,
biawa lachi
tomorrow will
never end: lachi
ko dako gukpin
who knows
tomorrow? uani
ma lachi? nobody
knows tomorrow
kosieni ma lachi

god knows tomorrow	abasi ma lachi	
next-tomorrow	lachi nkeji	
tomtit, n.	tomati; irudi onene-kele: "type of small bird"	
tomtom, n.	tomtom; irudi ganga afrika abi esia: "type of african or asian drum"	
ton, n.	toni; taun	G(fE)
tone, n, adj.	itunma; tunma	Ed
high-tone	itun-ga	
moderate-tone	itun-ba	
low-tone	itun-ka	
tone-up	kagba; (to energize); kagba-nuke	
tone-down	kagba si 'sala	
toner	otunma	
tonga, n.	tonga; irudi keke doki	G(fE)
tongs, n.	hantsaki; irudi instrumint bika fok	H
tongue, n.	harshe; ede	H/Y
tongue-tied	gbuka; dinkun; kitikoi:	
tonic,	tonike	G(fE)

tonic-water	ruwa-tonike	
tonight, adv.	nituu	Y/Tiv
tonnage, n. tonsil, n.	itaun; itoni tonsili	G(fE) G(fE)
tonsillitis, n.	tonsilite; irudi irun tonsili	
tonsorial, adj.	tonsora: "hairdresser"	G(fE)
tonsure, n.	tonsure" "shaving of head in rediness for initiation"	G(fE)
tontine, n.	tontinien; irudi 'chocho: "a type of annity"	
too, adv.	riju; jukha; risi	I/Y
it's too much	o riju kha	
its too early	o kutu riju; o yaji jukha; o yaji riju	
too many	o risi riju; o risi jukha	
too many cooks	e sie risi	
tool, n.	kozo; kaya irushe	G
tools	e kozo	
toot, n.	pampunnh: "sharp short warning sound from trumpet or whistle like ship's toot"	G
tooth, n.	hakori	H
tooth-ache	ifota-hakori	
tooth-pick	tutu-frik; monsawaki	G(fE)/ Gen/H
tooth-brush	asawaki	H
tooth-paste	ikpete-hakori	G/H
tooth-less	ai wen hakori	
tooth-less bull-dog	o shakara	
top, n.	nuke; sonma (also "enu), kwatakwati	I/Y/H

top-speed	fiam; fiam-fiam
i am on top	mo wa n' enu; mo wa na nuke
i am on top of the world:	mo wa n' enu akpor
top-ranking	ikpetu-enu; ikpetu-nuke
top-mast	shamfa-nuke
top-sail	tosel: nke ugboko-ruwa G(fE)
top-secret	dikpache-nuke; ikpache kwatakwata
top-less	topiles: irudi esa nke mache
top-news	ikwiro-ngba; ikwiro nsiyi
top-man/woman	oga kwata-kwata
topaz, n.	zabar jadu; irudi miriala H
tope, vit	booz; buuz; "to drink and get drunk excessively
topi	tokpi; irudi halimet G(fE)
topic, n.	isioka; topike I/Ik/G(fE)
topography, n.	tokpografe; rivers, roads" G(fE)
topper, n. topping, adj.	topa; "malafa-nuke" – (top-hat) kwata-kwata; nuke kwata-kwata
topple, vit.	shuda; shuru Y/I
tops, adj, n.	sonma; isonma; rama jukha
topsy-turvy, adj, adv, n.	idarugu: "confusion"; ishuda; shuru; darugu
tor, n.	gaf: "a small hill or G rockp-peack"
torch, n.	tochilan; tocilan H(fE)
torch-light	wuta-tochi; tochilan H(G.v) (fE)
torment, n.	ibutala; iyolionu
tormentor	o butala; o yolionu
tornado, n.	hadari; hadiri H
torpede, n.	tafido G/H(fE)

torpid, adj.	kunu: "something dull"	G
torque, n.	gleja: "a type of necklace of twisted metal"	
torrent, n.	iturante	G(fE)
torrential-rain	iturante ruwa-enu	
torrid, adj.	gler: "of weather or country: G very hot- of tropical"	
torso, n.	toroso: "broken statute G(fE) of human body without head or limps"	
tort, n.	tote:oka iwufin: "lega word" G(fE)	
tortoise, n.	kunkuru	H
torture, vt.	riya; iriya rubi, ijeafun rubi	
torture him/her	riya ya; jeafun ya rubi	
toss, vti.	bishenba; ibishenba	Y/I
toss-about	bishenba-kiri	
let us toss (of coins)	k'awa bishenba	
tot, n.	gada: very small child	G
tot, vti.	fiko: "add; add up"	G
total, adj.	kpancha; sam-sam;	Y/I/Gen
total amount is	iyole kpancha wu	
total it	kpancha ya	
completely deaf	o kitikoi sam-sam	
totalitarian, adj.	totaliteria; irudi gonmenti	G(fE)
totalizator, n.	totalaizato: irudi mashin kalu-kalu	G(fE0
totter, vi.	tata: "to walk with weak and unsteady steps"	G
totter about	tata kiri	

toucan, n.	taukan; irudi onene na kasa Amerika	G(fE)
Touch, n, vti.	Tukon; itukon; rue; rama	I/Y
Don't touch me	Ma tukon mi	
Touch-line Don't touch	Lain itukon Ma tukon	
Touch and go	Tukon ko shien	
I want to touch Ibadan quickly	Mi che I rue Ibadan kia-kia	
Finishing touch	Iguton rama; ifinisherama; finish e rama	
The Master's touch	Itukon nke Maigida (Itukon Maigida)	
Touching, adj.	Tuekon: "of pathetic, pity or sympathy"	
Touchy, adj.	Garan; tukonie: "easily offended"	
Touchy mind	Iyobi garan	
My mind is touchy	Iyobi me di garan/tukonie	
Tough, adj.	Slegan	Y/I
A very tough man	Miji o silegan-gan; o sile kha-ka	
Toughness	Isilegan	
Toupee, n.	Taupii; irudi hula: "a type of cap"	G(fE)
Tour, n.	Irinje; rinje	Y/I
Tourist	O rinje	
Nigerian Tourist Board	Kwamiti Erinje nke Naijeriya	(K.EN)
Tournament, n.	Tonamint; itole na giwuere; igwuere-tole	
Tourniquet, n.	Tonikuti; irudi instrumint nke likita	G(fE)
Tousle, vt.	Yiwa: "to scatter, of hair"	Y/I

Tout, n.	O jati G	
Touting, n, vt.	Ijati; jati	
Tout about	Jati kiri	
Tow, vt.	Fashi Y/G	
Towing	Ifashi	
Towing-rope	Waya-ifashi	
Towards, prep.	Yasi; rinshien; iyasi; irinshien	
Towel, n.	Tawul, adiko	H(fE)/H
Towel-rail	Hanga-tawul; hanga-adiko	
Tower, n.	Hasumiya	
Tower-house	Gida-hasumiya	
Water-tower	Ginshiki-hasumiya; hasumiya-ruwa	
Town, n.	Gari	H
Twon-centre	Arin-gari	
Town-clerk	Akawu-gari	
Town-crier	O kemkpo-gari	
Town-councillor	O jalisa-gari; (kansila-gari)	
Town-hall	Bandeki-gari	
Down-town	Isala-gari	
Towns-man	Miji-gari; omogari; (mon-gari)	
Townee, n.	Taneh: eni ng husi na kamfos yunifasiti	
Township, n.	Karami nke gari; (karamin-gari)	H/I/H
Town-planning, n.	Tan-flanin; igbiche-gari	G(fE)
Town-planner	Ogbiche-gari	

Toxaemia,	Tuzameya; irudi puezin nke jinni: "a type of blood-poisoning"
Tue-tue	G
toxic-waste toxicology	idatti-tue-tue; (datti tue-tue) itue-tue-koloji; nke sayens imuko itue-tue
Toxicologist	o tue-tue-koloji
toxin, n.	togzen; ife puezin G(fE)
toy, n.	gala-gala; ife igwuere G nke omontakele
toy-shop	kisuwa gala-gala
toy-with	fi meshe gala-gala; fi gala-gala
trace, n.	Chowalf I/Y
Traceable	chi-chowali; nke a le chowali
not/untraceable	lai le chowali
trace-back	chowali-zuba
tracer, n	o chowali
tracer-element	Alimint-o chowali;
tracery, n.	trasari; irudi onamint na iwindo chochi: "a type of ornament in a church window"
trachea, n.	trache; tukun-tuku fekuku: "wind-pipe"
trachoma, n.	trachioma; irudi irudi irun rubi nke ido: "a type of serious eye disease"G(fE)
track, n.	laini;ibuya G(fE)/G
track, n.	ikpaka: "of parts" Y/I
track, n.	famflit: takarda-kele G(fe)
traction, n.	ibuya: "to draw something over surface"
tractor, n.	tarakta; tan-tan; injin-ikagbaH(fe) /G/I/Y

trade, n., vt. stock- intrade trade- mark	itasuwa; tasuwa; irushe-hannu irushe-hannu; baba-irushe; (tred-maki) irushe- katazi lambaitasuwa; ilamba-irushe;	Y/H
trade- union	Ikpondo-tasuwa; Ikpondo – suwa)	
trade- unionist	o kpondo-suwa	
Trade Union Congress	Taro Ikondo-Suwa	
trades-man	o cheto-kanti: "shopkeeper"; mutum irushe-harnu; o rushe-hannu	
trading, n.	itasuwa	
trading is prohibited	a che itasuwa; a gbuiche itasuwa	
trader, n	o tasuwa; (tireda)	
tradition, n.	asha	Y
tradition of the land	asha kasa	
tradition of our people	asha e mutum 'wa; asha jama'a	
traditionalist	utum ashe	
traduce, vt.	ishata: "slander"; mebobo: "tell tales about'	
traffic, n.	trafiki; trafike; trafis	
traffic-light	wuta-trafiki; wuta-trafis	
Trafficator	o tafili; trafike; o trafike	
traffic-warden	mondoka-trafiki; maja-maja; "yelo-fiva"; wadin-trafike	
traffic-controller	o koso trafiki; kentrola nke trafiki; (trafik-kentrola)	
tragedy, n.	ijambe	Y(G.v)
tragic, adj.	ijambe; jambe; nke ijambe	
tragic accident	asidento ijambe	
trail, n.	ilaini; hanyar; ifineri	G/H/Y/I
train, n.	* ugboko-lokoja, also ugbo-golo	I/Y/G

train, vti.	kozi; tiyoto	
Training	ikozi; itiyoto	Y/I/Ed
Trainee	omo ikozi; o tiyoto; o kozi	
Trainees	e mon ikozi	
Trainer	eni kozi	
trining college	kolej ikozi	
traint, n.	igiezi: imiqa-shaka; imiwa-kayo "excellentquality or charaqcter"	G
traitor, n.	O fiele: "someone who betrays"	G
trajectory, n.	tajektri	G(fE)
tram, n.	ugboko-titi; takasititi nke lantiriki	
tram-line	Hanya ugboko-titi	
trammel, vt.	dili-hannu: "to walk zigzagly and unsteady"	Y/I/H
tramp, vti	ringa gra gra: to walk zigzagly and unsteady	
trample, vit	temisi	
trample down	temisi na "sala; temisi "sala	
trample under feet trample, n.	temisi na abe kafu; (or: temisi na kafu) o temisi	
trance,n.	isikwale: "of sleeping condition or hypnotic"	
tranquil, adj.	sundo; o kulele; o simini: lafia	Y/I/Gen/H/Gen
tranquilizer n.	o sundo; o kulele; o simini "irudi magani" ti a ng kono: tranwileza"; (itrankwele)	
transact, vt, n.	sowu; sowu G	
buiness transaction	isowu irushe;	

transatlantic, adj	so – atlante; nke ifeja atlante: "beyond atlantic
transcend, vt	do-shend; ringa abi shienga G(fE) nawhi shien-feja: to go or be beyond rangee of human knowledge, belief, powers etc"; so-shenda
transcendental, adj.	so-shendint: nke ikeyo abi kamkpe: of excellent
transcendental, adj.	so-shende ta: "of G(fE) something beyond human wisdom; something that cannot be discovered or understood practically"
transcontinental, adj.	so-akpornina; so-kantinenta G/Urh/E
transcribe, vt. , n.	pulu; ipulu G
Transcript, n.	Ipululu
transept , n.	transeh; irudi gida chochi G(fE)

transfer, n.   tansfa; iyikpo   H(fE)/Gen/Y(G.
he/she has gone on transfer: o ti shien transfa; o ti yikpo

transfer certificate   satifiket iyikpo; satifiket nke tansfa

Transfigure, vt., n. iyikpoto; yikpoto   Y(G.v)
the transfiguration of Jesus ChristIyikopto nke Jesu Kristi

transfix, vt	sogun: "to pearce through, especially with a spear"	G/Y
transform, vt. , n.	sozuh; isozuh	G/I
transfuse, vt.	shuru: "poru"; transfa; yikpo: "to transfer"	
blood transfusion	iyikpo jinni; itansfa jinni; (not 'shuru-jini"	
transgree, vti. n.	sonjika; isonka	G/Y/I
transgression of law	sonjika iwufin	
transient, adj.	"of short period or time" ngba kele	
transistor, n.	kili-kili	G/G(FE)

transistor radio	rediyo; ikili kili	
transit, n.	zango; transit	H/G(FE)
transit camp	zanfo; tanti-tanti; sansani	H
transit bed	gado zango; gado transit	
transit village	zango; zango-kurmi	H/H(G.v)
transit house	gida zango; tantitanti; sansani	H(G.v)
transition, n.	inyintua: changing	
transitional period	ngba iyintua	
transitive, adj.	transetif: "a type of verb"	G(FE)
transitive verb translate, vt.	vabu-transetif translate;	
	giorotunm;	G(FE)/G
translation, n.	itranslate; o giorotun	
translator, n.	o translate; igiorotun	
transliterate, vt.	soicheko: "to write in characters of different language or system, e.g Arabic transliterate into Hausa"; sogiorotun	G/I/Y
translucent, adj.	yolo-dulu/translusa: "of ligh passing through"	G/G(FE)
transmigration, n. , vt.	ijoromi; joromi: "the	Ed.
migration of soul at death into another body"		
transmission, n.	ironwaya; ironshien	Y/Gen/I
transmit, vt.	ronwaya; ronshien	
transmitter, n	o ronwaya; o ronshein	
transmitting station	tashan ironwaya; tahsan ironshien	
transmitter equipment	ennonfun ironwaya	

transmogrify, vt	Somajikele: "to change something majically"	
transmogrification, n.	isomajikele	
tranmute, vt.	yintua: "of transition"	
transoceanic, adj.	soshan; ifeja oshan abi bantekun: "beyond the ocean crossing"	
transom, n	tanson; irudi sanda iwindo: "a type of	
transparent, adj. transpire, vt. transpire, vt transplant, vit. transpolar, adj transport, n	window horizontallybar" yolo-yolo kosa: "of event that took place" Gumi: "of perspiration" tun-gbinso " to replant (a palnt) in another place" feja kpola: "across polar regions" Ugboko	G H Y/I
transport, vt.	gboko, kokowa: (of goods)	
transport me to sokoto	gboko mo shein sokoto	
transporter, n.	o gboko	
transporters, n (pl)	e gboko; o rushe ugboko	
transporters association	asosie o gboko; asosie ugboko: "trasport association"	
transportation, n	gboko-gboko	
transpose, vt	yinkpo	
transposition	iyinkpo	
tranship, vt.	transfa na ugboko-ruwa	
transubstantiation, n	sosasieshan; (irudi ikoashe na choch sosasieshan)	
transverse, adj	transfas	
trap, n.	takolo almanjir; itakolo	G/H
don't fall into trap	ma shuda si "takolo"	

death trap trapper, n trapeze, n	itakolo-ikuowun o takolo trepis;; sanda orizon:	
trapezoid, n.	"horizontally bar" trezo, isiffa abi ilamba o wen akue inang: "of	
trappins, n	four sided figure" tira- tira: "ornamental decorations epecially	G(FE)
traps, n	e kpankiti, abi kpankete: "personal effects-of public buildings" bags and baggages etc.	
trash, n trauma, n	basn; ai year; rubisi "worthless" turuma, nke jiki	H G/(FE)
travail, n	ifudun; irudi fota: "a type of pain" ringe	
travel, vti.		Y/I
travel-agent	omaye abi wakili irinje	
travel-bureau	ofis irinje	
travelling	irinje	
traveller	o rinje	
travel-sickness	ibujen-rinje	
travel's cheque	cheki o rinje	
traverse, vt.	rinje-feja: "to travel across"	
travesty, n.	ikpoduh; kpoduh: description or imitation"	
trawl, n	igodo; baba-koma: "large or big net"	
fishing trawler	igodo-kifi; o godo-kifi	
trawler	O godo	
tray, n	tire; bab-kwano lege; "big-flat plate or pan"	
treacherous, adj, n	ikoje: "deceptive"; koje; miwareke o miwareke; o koje.	

treacherous friend	aboki koje; aboki o miwareke
treacle, n	tiriko; iridi ruwa suka G(FE)
tread, vti	takawa; taka H
tread upon	taka Sikei, taka n'isi
treadle, n.	feda, mataki (machine pedal)H(FE) /H
treason, n.	itiote; treasonable: "tiote": I/Y To betray treacherously.
treasure, n.	ishura Y(G.V)
treasure house	gida ishura
treasurer	o shura; O cheto ishura
treasury, n.	shura; ishura; Y(G.V)
treat, vti.	losie Y/I
don't treat me like this	ma losie mi baate`
treatment, n.	ilosie; ililosie; imeson:- (cure)
treaty, n.	imuka; ikweba; ikwede
let us make a treaty	k!awa meshe ikwade; ikweba abi imuka(note: the head word here is "imuka"; others are synonyms of the head word)
treble, adj., n.	teta: "of three times higher or much"
treble, n. tree, n.	tirebol; tiri-teren itache G(FE) /G H/H (itace); bishiya (G.V) /H
tree-top	enu itache
trefoil, n.	trefol: irudi shuke-shuke G(fE)
trek, vi.	ringa: "to walk on foot" Y/I
trek on	ringa; (rin-shien)
tremble, vi.	sogiri G
trembling	isogiri
tremendous, adj.	bungara G

it is tremendous	o bungara	
tremolo, n.	tremolo: irudi voisi !songi: "a type of musical voice"	
tremor, n.	igbuduh: "of trembling /shaking "	G
earth-tremor	igbuduh kasa	
trench, n.	ikpekpe; lambatu	G/H
trend, n.	iteshien	Y/G
trend of event	iteshien isoka	
trepan, vt.	trekwan: "to make a round hole in the skull by operation "	G (fE)
trepidation, n.	arimkpo; irumbi: "alarm / noise; excitement "	
trespass, vt. , n.	fashe; ifashe	Y/I
trespasser	o fashe	
trespasser will be penalized:	o fashe a riya o fashe	
treatle, n.	akunga: "a horizontal G wood-beam with two stand at ends used in pairs to support planks by builders"	
trials, n.	iduniye; ichondi	
triangle, n.	alwatika; H	
triangular	nke alwatika	
tribe, n. , adj.	iyatu; yatu Y/I/Gen	
tribalistic	di !yatu; yatu; yayatu	
tribulation, n.	nsohala; nsohela; nsoghuru	
in time of tribulation	n! ngba nsoghuru;	
tribunal, n.	n!ngba nsohala kwamkali; ikwamkali H(fE) /H	
tribunal of enquiry	Ijubi kwamkali	
tribune, n.	trebiun G(fE)	

597

tributary, adj.	karami nke kogi; (tribiuti)	H/I/H/G(fE)
tribute, n.	Igandu H(G.v)	
let's pay tribute to	k! awa gandu fun	
trice, n.	nke eta: "of three times"	
trick, n.	iwayo; tonka; (ton) ;	G(Ur.v) /Y/I/Ed
don't trick me	bebeye (note: "ton" is	
	old use in Guosa" ma wayo mi; ma tonka	
	mi (not "ma ton me") o wayo; o tonka; o bebeye;	
trickster		
tricky	wayo-wayo; bebeye; mutum	
	bebeye; o bebeye mutum	
trickle, vti.	terekele: "cause to flow in	
	drop" "thinly- drops"	
tricycle, n.	keke nke wili eta;	
trident, n.	keke-gbosah	
	trident;irudi mashi o wen	
	onu eta: "a type of spear	
	with three mouth"	
triennial, n, adj.	adunta; trayenia	I/Y/G(fE)
trifle, n.	fiene; yeye: "something	
	of the least value	
	or importance"	
trifler	mutum fiene; yeye	
	mutum; o fiene; o	
trigger, n.	yeye kunama	H
trigonometry, n.	tregonomatri; irudi	G(fE)
Trilateral, adj.	matimatis	
	Kwadeta; "of three	
	sided agreement be "	
trillion , adj., n.	tirila	G(fe)
trim, adj.	gere "trim to good shape"	G
trimaran, n.	tirimara, irudi moru	G(fE)
	abi kwalekwale: "a a	
	type of small boat"	
trinitrotoluene, n.	gigiligolo-gbum: "a very	G
	high explosive"	

trinity, n.	trinita, nke kerista	G(fe)
trinity-sunday	sirande-trinita	
trinket, n.	trinkat; fadaka	G(fE)/Y
trio, n.	treyolit; irudi ipole: "a type of poem"	
trip, vit.	jerin	
take a trip	yi 'jerin; jerin	
tripartite, adj.	kwadeta; ikwade abi ikweba n'arin mutum	
tripe, n.	tumbi	H
triple, adj.	keta: "made up of three parts" of three parts"	
triplet, n.	Ejieta	I/Y(G.V)
triplex, adj.	ngb'eta; nketa: "of three times"	
triplicate, adj.	trelikat; nke ngba e ta abi ife eta	
tripod, n.	tirifod; trifod; kafa kamera: "camera-stand"	
tripos, n.	na kyunifasiti nke kembrij: "successful candate in an examination for a degree of cambridge university	
triptych, n.	tripaya; irudi hoto abi ifin na gida chochi: "a type of photo or carving in a church building"	
trisect, vt.	traset: kekpin laini si mbi eta: "divide a line into three places"	
trite, adj.	or place that is no longer new" G(fE)	
triumph, n.	isayo; imegun I/Y/Ed(G.v) ibokei; isokene	
triumphant	o sayo; o sokene (not o megun, or o bokei)	
triune, adj.	trekun: nke eta na daya: "of three in one"; (treun keisi abasi): "three godhead, and the trinity"	

599

trival, adj.	tofien: "something of small G value or small importance"
trodden, trod,	taka: "see tread"
trojan, n., adj.	trojen G(fE)
trolley, n.	kura H
trollop, n.	akuna: mache imiwa rubi: "woman of bad
trombone, n.	trombon; instrumint isongi G(fE)
troop, n.	kungiyar; kamfani H
military troop	kungiya soja; kungiyar iseza
troop-carrier	ugboko-ruwa o gbe kungiyar soja
troop-ship	ugboko-ruwa nke kungiyar
trophy, n.	jelin; G
tropic, n.	tropike G(fE)
tropic of cancer	tropike kensa; ropike nke kensa
tropic of capricorn	tropike nke kaprikan
trouble, vit.	nsohala; nsogbu; kpalava; kata-kata;
trouble-maker	mutum kata-kata; o kata-kata
trouble-shooter	o lagha; "reconciliatory" Y/I
trough, n. – komi; akala	irudi kwano abinchi nke nama: "a type of animal'feeding plate" (H):
troupe, n.	kamfani; kungiya; kunjiya H
trouser, n.	wando; shokoto; H/Beteh/Gen
trousau, n.	kio-kio-kio: "a type of G outfit for the bride"
trout, n.	dtura; irudi kifi e so na ruwa: "some types of fish in the water"
trowel n.	turawa; "a flat-bladed tool for bricks and mortar"

troy, n.	trai; irudi inofi na kasa briten: "a type of british measurement"
truant, n.	kuru-kele; ikuru-kele
truce, n.	agirimento; ikweba; ikwade G(fE)/I/Y
truce-breaker	o meru ikweba; o meru ikwade (not o meru agirimento)
truck, n.	turoki; baba-mota wili; mota wili-wili
Truckle, vi.	Shudani: "to submit timidly or cowardly"
Truckle, n.	Trakol; irudi gado-wili;"a type of wheeled-bed"
Truculent, adj.	Gbolo-gbolo: "violent and looking for trouble and fight
Truculancy, n.	Igbolo-gbolo; o gbolo-gbolo
true, adj., n. : adv.	ezioka; izioka; toka; tezi
yours truly,	nke yin
truffle, n.	trefol: "a type of fungus growing under ground and used for flavouring"
trug, n..	adudu-gadina:" gardener's basket"
trump, n.	ikpokpoh; ikemkpo G/Y/I
trumpet,	kakaki; kaho; ikempo ikpokpoh
n. blow your trumpet	o kakaki; o kaho; feh kakaki e; kemkpotu; " to make noise"
trumpery adj.	jatutu "of little-valued ornament of something
truncate, vt. tronkete	"of something shorten by cutting off the tip or top
truncheon, n.	gajerar sanda H
trunk, n.	gorar H

trunk-call	ikono-gora	
trunk-line	liani-gora; waya-gora	
runk-road	hanya-gora	
truss, n.	bankara; bankare; "bundle of hay or straw)	F
trust, n.	itoye: "confidence and strong belief"	
i trust you	mo toye e	
trust-fund	kudi toye	
trust-worthy, adj.	yera - toye	
trustee,n	O toye; itoye	
truth n.	ezioro; ezioka: (synonym)	I/Y/Ikwere
truthfulness	izioka (not izioro) ; ezioka	
yours truthfully	nke yin n' ezioka	
be truthful	di ezioka	
to be truthful	ka di ezioka; ka soli ezioka	
in truth	n'ezioka	
try, vit	tiri; kpenren; dani	G
i am trying	mo ng tiri(not mo ng kpenren)	
he is trying	o ng tiri; o ng kpenren	
don't't ever try it	ma kiken kpenren; ma kpenren	
a trial will convince you	itiri a sokene e	
trial (of court)	idani	
trial – judge	o cherisi idani; o dakpe si idani	
try me	tiri mi	
try your hands on it	tiri hannu e si ya	
tsetse-fly, n.	tsando awuru	H

t-shirt, n.	afe-t	I/Igala
t-square	golina-t; sukwue	H/Ef/G(fE)
tub, n.	tab: irudi baba-kwano	G(fE)
tube, n.	butu-roba: butu	H(G.V)
tyre-tube	butu-taya	
tuber, n.	ligi	G/Y
yam-tuber	ligi-doya	
tuberculosis, n.	tobakulosi; irudi baba irun t'o rubis:bika ikoho: "a type of very bad disease such as caughing"	G(fE)
tuck, n.	toki; kafi; ikwar esa: "stitching of dress"	G(fE)
trucker, n.	toka; irudi esa	G(fE)
tuesday, n.	chusdei: rana nk'eta n'uzola: "the third day of the week"	
tuft, n.	zanko, tuntu: "buch of feathers, grass, hair etc; held together by the basement"	H
tug, vti., n.	shobe; ishobe	General
tug-boast	kwalekwale-ishobe: (ishobekwale-kwale); ishobe-abara	
tug-of-war	eeh-shobe	Gen.
tuition, n.	ikweke	I/Y
tuition-fee	kudi-kweko	
tulip,n	tuli;irudi shuke –shuke	G
tulle,n	tula; ''a type of fine, soft silk and net-like dress material	G (fE)
tumble, vit.	gazo; garu; shubele	
tumbled upside-down	o ti garu	

tumbled-weed	tombowidi; irudi G (fE) shuke-shuke
tumbler, n.	finjali; gilas; turkpula H/H (fE) /G
tumbrel, n.	tomrel; irudi mota o prusu "a type of prisoner's motor-cart"
tummy, n.	bele Gen (fE)
tumour, n.	kari H
tumult, n	igbagudu; igba-gudu-gudu G
tumulus, n.	tumula: (mound of Gf earth over a grave)
tundra, n.	tunda: "a white treeless plain in russia"
tune, n.	tiuna: i luvi "of succession G of notes forming song's melody, hymn etc."
he who plays the pipe dictates the tune:	eni ng songi tukun-tuku lo ng konoso i luvi ya
tuning-knob	koko-tiuna
tuner, n.	o tiuna; o luvi G (fE)
,tung-oil, n.	tonyele: "tree-oil used in G varnishing wood- work"
tungsten, n.	tangstan; (simbola "w"); '' G grey metal used in making steel and electrical lamp filamend,(symbol "w")
tunic,n	tiunek; irudi kwat abi jakit F nke soja abi mondoka
tunnel, n. tunny, n. tup, n. turban, n.	kpulu G tiunen; irudi kifi-tekun "a G(fE) type of large sea- fish" rangon: male sheep or ram" H(G.v) (note: of large sea-fish rawani: "man's headdress" G(fE) tobide: "thick, muddy and not clear liquids"
turbid, adj.	tobide: "thick, muddy G(fE) and not clear liquids"

turbine, n. turbo-jet	fogo-fogo	G
	jat-fogo-fogo; (tobo-jet)	
turboprop, n.	o tikpu fogo-fogo; (tobopro)	
turbet, n.	tobat: irudi kifi-lau "a type of lage fish	
turbulent, adj.	gbagudu	G
turbulent weather	iska igbagudu	
turd, n.	kashi H	
tureen, n.	baba-tasa: "large or big dish"	
turf, n.	Hwagga: "soil-surface with low-grass roots on it"	H
turgid, adj.	tojo: "of swollen or bloated and pomposity"	G
turkey, n.	Tatolato; tolotolo	Gen
turkey, n.	toikin mutum kasa turkey	G
turkish embassy	embasiye toikin	
tumeric, n.	gangamau; irudi shuke-shuke	H
turmoil, n.	iyirih; arimkpo abi nsohala	
turn, n., vit.	yizu; yintua; dazu; itole; itulele; ngba	
turn-by-turn	itolele	
turn about	yintua kiri; yizu kiri; yikiri	
one good turn deserves	irenutukon diye nkeji; (or) imiwa	
another	rama … diye nkeji	
wait for your turn	chendu fun ngba e/yin	
take your turn	yi ngba e; chendu fun ngba yin	

turn-table	iyikpo-kiri; iyikpoto; (tan-tebur)	
what is turning your head?	meni ng yikpoto e n'isi?	
it's head/brain is turning	o ng yikpoto isi; oyikpoto isi	
turn on the light turning point turn off	tonwu wuta mbi iyikpoto; mbi 'yizu; ebi 'yizu fre: "to leave"; kpawu: "to put off"	
turn to	yintua si;	
turn over	yizu l'isi; yizu feja	
turn out	yapu; yata; bia wu	
it turns out to be true	o bia wu ezioka	
good turn out of people	iyata abi iyapu rama nke 'mutum; e mutum ilamba lau: (large numbers of people)	
please turn round	biko yintua kiri; (yi'boto)	
turn up	biawa: (come); yizu nuke: (turn something up)	
turner, n.	afingi; tena	G/G(fE)
turning, n.	mararraba; (cross-roads, or place where a road turns)	H/Y/I/G
next turning	mararraba nkeji; iyintua nkeji	
turnip, n.	zanke; irudi shuke-shuke eso: "shom types of plants"	G
turpentine, n.	tupete; irudi oyele t' a ng weni na obtainable in certain trees and used as	G(fE)
	solvent in mixing paints, varnish as well as medicine"	
turpitude, n.	igbakwu: "wickedness G or depravity	
turquoise, n.	tukwa; irudi okuta abi jefa algashi:	
turret, n.	turati: "a small tower at the corner of the house"	

turret, n.	igegaun-gaun: "a steel structure that protects gunners, made so as to revolve with the gun"	G
as impenetrable as a turret:	ai le gunle bika igegaun-gaun	
turtle, n.	kififiya	H
green-turtle	kififiya-algashi	
turtle-wax	whuas-kififiya	
tush, int.	ha-ha; ai wen sundi: "expression of impatience	G
tusk, n.	haure	H
elephant tusk	haure giwa	
tussle, n, vi.	ijagba; jagba	Y(G.v)
tussore, n.	tusa; isile siliki: "strong silk" G(fE)	
tutelage, n.	tiutilaij G(fE)	
tutor, n.	tituta; malami G(fE)	
twaddle, n.	ikwaka; oka yeye; oka rubi: "foolish and idle talk"	
twain, n.	ifeji	I/Y
twang, n.	gwain: "sound of a tight string/wire when pulled and released"	G
tweed, n.	fudah; irudi esa wulu t' o do: "a type of soft woollen dress"	
tweeny, n.	subela: " a young servant girl who helps both in cooking and domestic work" (also: mongi)	G
tweetr, n.	tuweta; iruidi lau-sfika	G(fE)
twelfth, adj, n.	nke goeji	
twelve	goeji ( )	H/Y
twenty, adj, n.	ji ( )	

twice, adv.	ngba eji; n'eji; ngb'eji once or twice	
twig, n.	kirare	H
twilight, n.	iwiri; iduku: "of remote period about which little is known"	
the twilight of guosa language history twill, n.	iwiri nke iliton ede guosa tuwile; irudi esa auduga: "a type of cotton material G(fE)	
win, n.	ejimon	Y/I/Gen
twine, n.	kirtani; eliki; eliwaya	H/I/Y/Gen
twinge, n.	ikain: "of sudden sharp pain" kain	
twinkle, vi.	twenkol; winin	G(fE)/G/Y
twinkle-twinkle little star: -	ura kele winin-winin	
twirl, vit.	yikonkon: "turn something round and round quickly"	
twist, vit.	yikiti	
twitch, n, vt.	ijarau; jarau; "of sudden, quick and uncontrollable movement of the muscle; a sudden quick pull"	
twitter, vi.	tue-tue: "a succession of soft short sounds of birds or persons" the twitter of bird itue-tue onene	
two, adj, n.	eji (	
tycoon, n.	taikunuG(fE) buxsiness tycoon	
type, n.	irudi	
a type of plants	irudi shuke-shuke	
type, vit.	presa	
typist, n.	o presa; o tafreta	
type-script	skrif ipresa; (ipresa)	
typewriter	tafreta; irudi injin t' a ng fi presa takarda	

typing sheet	fale presa; (taipin-shet)	
type-setter,	taip-seta; irudi injin ipresa H(fE)	
type-cast, vt.	taikas	G(fE)
typhoid, n.	ifolo	G
typhoid-fever	iba-folo	
typhoon, n.	jafuun; (taifuun)	G(fE)
typical, adj.	rudi-sam	
typography	taikpografe; irudi presa: "a type of printing"	G(fE)
typographer	o taikpografe	
typographical error	isipien taikpogrfe	
tyranny, n.	ijamandu	Y/I
tyrannical	jijamandu	
tyrant,	ijamandu	
tyre, n.	tayaf; akpala-kpala	
motor-tyre	akpala-kpalaf-mota	
motor-car type	akpala-kpala nke mota zoom- zoom	

U

u	yuh
u-boat	bara-bote; irudi sobo-kunu zamani: "a type of german sub-marine"; "b.b." – that is: "bara-bote"
ubiquitous, adj.	risi-nso; (formerly: "wandoki") also: wanso:
udder, n.	nono, hantsa
ugly, adj.	joru (formerly: "buku"
ugly person	mutum joru
ugliness	ijoru
ukulele, n.	ulele; irudi molo
ulcer, n.	gyambo; muki
ulna, n.	uluna; kashi hannu: "the inner of two bones of the forearm"
ulterior, adj.	nahun; alteria
ultimate, adj.	gbazu; gukpini
ultimatum, n.	ikprenren (formerly: "kia-kia; saun-saun) ref. vol. i
ultra, pref.	altra
ultramarine, adj, n.	altramarine; irudi launi bulu: "a type of blue colour"
ultramontane, adj.	altramonte; nke aashe popu; "of pope's authority"
ultrasonic, adj.	altrasone; altrasoniki; nke saun, abi ilowe: "of sound system"
ultraviolet, adj.	altravola
ultravires, adj, adv. (lat)	altraveya: "of something beyond the powers of law or authority
ululate, vi.	kelule: "to wail oor cry loudly"
umber, adj, n.	emba; "of yellowish-green colour"
umbilical, adj.	chibiya; chibiyaki
umbrage, n.	iyeshe; "to feel unfairly treated"
umbrella, n.	laima
umlaut, n.	imulat, nke turanchi zamani
Umpire, n.	alkali (old use: yakali)
un, pref.	lai; ai
unbashed, adj.	ai deyah: "not embarrassed; un-embarrassed"; (old use: aidinku)
unabated; adj.	ai bukon; ai bukon; lai bukon

610

unable; adj.	lai hegbe; ai hegbe
i am unable to	mii hegbe; mii heghe si
you are unable to	ee heghe; ee hegbe si
I am unable to do what you want	mii hegbe meshe ife ti e che
unaccompanied, adj.	lai sole; ai sole; lai kafani; ai kamfan
he went unaccompanied	o shienga lai wen kamfani
unaccountable, adj.	lai di kante; ai di kante
unaccustomed, adj.	ali maji; ai maji
unadopted, adj.	ai gbali; lai gbali
unadvised, adj.	aimeniye; lai meniye
unaffected, adj.	ai ontu; li kontu
unalienable, adj.	ai kolejo; lai kolejo
unalloyed, adj.	ai ambi
unalterable, adj.	a tunme; lai tunme
un-nigerian, adj.	ai wu naijeiya; ai miwa niajeriya
unanimous, adj.	soliken
unannounced, ad.	ai solikputo; lai solimkpotu
unapproachable, adj.	ai gbamo; lai le gbamo
unarmed, ad.	ai munji; lai munji
unasked; adj.	ai jubi; lai jubi
unassuming, adj.	ai kpu; lai kpu: "not pushy"
unattached; adj.	ai fiba; lai fiba; ai nojo
unattended; adj.	ai dazi; ai feza; ai gbonti
unavailing, adj.	ai vele; lai vele
unavailable; adj.	ai vele; lai vele
unaware, adj.	ai kmiesi; lai kiesi
unbacked, adj.	ai fiba (not attached) (or not supported)
unbalanced, adj.	ai kudu; ai wan lai kudu; lai wan
unbearable, adj.	lai le sungbe; lai sungbe; ai sungbe
unbeaten, adj.	ai bokei si; lai bokei si;
unbeaten record	ikode shaka; "clean record"
unbecoming, adj.	ai kmeliye; lai keliye: "not appropriate"
unbelief, n.	ai nikon; lai nikon; o fre inikon

unbend, vi.	ai koro; lai meko; ai yisi; lai yisi
unbizassed, adj.	ai dari; lai dari
unbidden, adj.	ai kule; lai kuele ai gbanjo
unbind, vt.	ai kedi; lai kedi
unblushing, adj.	ai feju; lai feju: "shamesless"
unborn, adj.	ai mubi; lai mubi
unbosom; vt, shielu-le	"to reveal one's sorrows"
unbounded/bound-less; adj.	ai kedie; lai kedi
unbowed, adj.	ai bolo; lai bolo
unbridled; adj.	ai linzami; lai zami
unbroken; adj.	ai meje; lai fojie
unbroken record	ai fojie ikode abi imiwa
unbuckle; vt.	shishie bokul; shien bokul ai bokul
unburden; vt.	kweye; simini; ai nno nsohala
unbuttoned, adj;	ai anini; ai botin; shie botin
uncalled-for	ai niwen: "no need"; lai zumkpa: "unnecessary"
unceasing, adj.	lai dachen; ai dachen; ai simini
unceremonious, adj.	lai serimona; ai konogbadu; lai konogbandu
uncanny; adj.	lai wu ifeakpor
uncared-for	ai june si; lai bo fun; lai bo
uncertain; adj.	ai dido; lai dido
uncharitable, adj.	ai chiwa; lai chiwa
unchecked; adj.	ai wone; lai dache
unchrsitain; adj.	ai krista; lai krista
uncivil; adj.	ai sifoh; lai sifoh
unclad; adj.	ai suweh: "noth clothed; naked or nude"
unclaimed, adj.	ai yite; lai yite
uncle, n.	kawu; rafani; babani
my uncle	kawu mi
uncle-gin	unkul-veveh: "a male elderly sweetheart"
unclean, adj.	ai shaka; lai shaka
uncleaned spirit	ekwenshu
unclouded; adj.	ai haske; lai haske

uncoloured; adj.	ai launi; lai wen ilauni; shaka-shaka
uncommitted; adj.	ai fadon; lai fadon; ai wen nsohala
uncommon, adj.	ai dile; lai dile
uncompromising; adj.	ai kweba
unconcerned; adj.	ai konle;; lai konle
unconditional; adj.	ai wahe; lai wahe
unconditional love	ihufe ai whahe
unconscious; adj.	ai ribite; lai ribite
unconsidered; adj.	ai loro; ai tunche
uncork; vt.	ai tikpo; lai tikpo
uncouple; vt.	ai sodi; lai dodi: "unfasten"
ucover; vt.	ai bod; lai tikpo
uncrossed, adj.	ai soga
unction, n.	umpula: "to anoint with oil as a religious rite"
undated, adj.	ai kode rana; ai rana; lai rana
undaunted, adj.	ai foya; ai ruba; lai foya; lai ruba
undeceive, vt.	ai wayo; lai koje
undecided, adj.	ai cheri; lai cheri
undeclared, adj.	ai kede; lai kede
undefended; adj.	ai kusa; lai kusa
undemonstrative, adj.	ai koneri; lai koneri
undeniable; adj.	lai le konu; ai konu
undemominational; adj.	ai wu ikoke; lai koke
under; adv.	abe
under; prep;	kiene: "less" uroba
under-act; vit.	meshe-kiene
under-arm; adj.	ndaram: "of cricket or tennis game"
under-belly; n.	abe chiki
underbid, vt.	kule-kiene: gbanjo-kiene
undercarriage; n. (road)	krusa-'be (kurusa'be)
undercarriage; n.	(of aircraft's landing gear: ndakarij
undercharge; vt.	kasi-kiene: "to charge less"
underclothes; n	esa'be
undercover; adj.	bo'be: "of person(s) who associates with criminal suspect"

undercurrent; n.	ndakarent: "of current of water flowing under the surface"
underdeveloped; adj.	ai hugbo; lai hugh; hugbo-kiene
under-done; adj.	jowu-kiene: "not cooked thoroughly"
underestimate; vt.	nofi-kiene
under-expose; vt.	gboloh-kiene
under-fed; adj.	juyo-kiene
under-foot; adj.	abe-taki
under-garment; n.	riga nke abe; (riga'be)
under-go; vt.	fefeja; ima; ichegbono; ichegbono-kon: "of passing through; knowledge; experience"
undegraduate, n.	o kiene gradwet; omo gradwet
underground, n.	abe-kasa
under-growth, n.	kolo-kolo; kpoki-kpoki; shuke-shuke skin
under-growth	kolo-kolo; kpoki-kpoki; shuke-shuke
under-grwoth (of plants; shrubs etc)	kolo-kolo; kpoki-kpoki; shuke-shuke
under-hung; adj.	yoisi n'abe; yota n'abe
underlay, n.	itoka n'abe; itoka 'be
under-lie; vt.	toka si abe; toka n'abe
under-line, vt.	laini n'abe; laini abe;
under-line it	laini abe ya
under-lying issue	oka abe
under-manned; adj.	ai miji rama; miji-kiene
under-mentioned; adj.	koda n'abe
under-mine; vt.	kiene;kagba; kiene-agba: "to weaken"
under-neath; adv.	n'abe; be-ala
under-nourished; adj.	keche-kiene
under-pants; n.	durosi;
under-pass; n.	ifeja n'abe; irudi hanya n'abe hanya
under-pay; vt.	kpa-kiene; kpikpa-kiene
under-payment, n.	inkp/ikpikpa-kiene
under-pin	ndafin: "to pace a support of masonry under the wall
under-populate	populashon-kiene under-
under-privileged; adj.	danfa-kiiene; ai wen anfa rama

the under-privileged	e danfa-kiene
under-proof; adj.	ndapuruf: "of something containing less

alcohol than profit spirit

under-production, n.	igbebia-kiene
under-quote, vt.	konosi-kiene; konosi-kele
under-rate, vt.	diye-kiene; diye-kele
under-secretary, n.	akawu-kele; kele-sakitiri; nad-sakitiri
under-sell, vt.	leta-kiene
under-sexed; adj.	vuduh-kiene; fioko-kiene: "having less secual potency or desire than usual"
undersheriff; n.	o shida-sharif: "sheriff's deputy"
under-shoot; vt.	feja raniweh: "of aircraft – to land short or over the run-way"
under-shot; adj.	ndashat: "a mill wheel propelled by water"
under-sign, vt.	sen-n'abe: "to sign under"
under-sized; adj.	tobi-kiene; nofi-kiene
under-slung; adj.	ndaslan: "of vehicle having springs fixed at the axles from below"
under-staffed; adj.	sitaf-kiene
understand; vti.	yebi (synonym): goye
do you understand?	o yebi
i understand /understood	mo yebi
understandable; adj.	yiyebi: gigoye; nke a le yebi/goye
under-state; vt.	soli-kiene; kode-kiene
under-stock; vt.	sito-kiene; sito-kele: "to equip a stor with less stock"
understrapper; n.	o godo-godo; "contemptuous; official or employee of low rqnk or insignificant
under-study; n.	muko; mimuko
under-take; vt.	meshe ife; mesh'ife; rushe; kweba; kwade
undertaker; n.	o meshe; o mesh'ife; o rushe
under-tone; n.	itunma-kele: "of low-tone"
undertow; n.	ndato: "of current caused by backward flow of a wave breaking against the beach"
under-value; vt.	yekpa-kiene; yekpa-kele
undervest; n.	sigileti: "singlet"

under-water; adj.	abe-ruwa
under-wear; n.	esa'be
under-wear (plural)	esa'be
underword; n.	ngunu: "a place for the departed spirits of ead"
under-writer; vt.	ndarait: "a type of insurance"
undesirables (pl.)	ndiwugu
undeterred; adj.	ai gbuhan; lai gbuhan
undeveloped, adj.	ai digba; ai hugbo; lai digba; lai hugbo
undid; pt.	ai meshe; lai meshe; fre; ifre
undischarged; adj.	ai nira; lai nira
undock; vit.	lupo: "to uncouple a module, especially of a spacecraft"
undomesticated; adj.	ai zigida; lai zigida
undoubted; aj.	ai yopulu; lai yopulu
undreamed; adj.	ai roza; lai roza
undress; vti;	ai yiwo esa; noho: "nude"
undue; adj.	ai tongba; lai tongba; ai yema; lai yema
unduly critical	iguba lai yema; igbuga n' ai tongba
undulate; vi.	ndulate: "of a wave-like motion or look"
undying; adj.	lai kiu; ai mutu ai mutu
un-earned; aj.	ai gbali; lai gbali
un-earth; vt.	mubia 'ta: "to rbing out"; ai chode: "un- discovered"
unearthly; adj.	hihindu: "gbostly"
uneasy; adj.	ai flesi; lai flesi
uneasy lie sthe head that wears the crown:	ai flesi w isi kende
uneaten; adj.	ai wuam; ai je
uneducated; adj.	ai kozi; lai kozi
unemployed; adj.	ai yirushe; lai yirushe
unending; n.	ai guton; lai guton; dongaga
unenlightened; adj.	ai meliye; ai kozi; ai ma; ai chegbon
unequal; adj.	ai diogba; lai diogba
unequivocal; adj.	shakasa; ho-ha; ai siro: "very clear and without false or doubtfulness"
unerring; adj.	ai shihan; lai shihan; saun-saun: "accurate"
unexampled; adj.	lai fineri; ai fineri; ai wn ifineri

unexceptionable; adj.	n'ai weku; lai weku; ai weku
unfailing; adj.	ai shigo; lai ghigo; aid diofoh
unfair; adj.	ai sera; lai sera
unfaithful; adj.	ai zigbo; lai zigbo; ai ziok; lai zioka
unfaltering; adj.	ai yipu; lai yipu
unfamiliar; adj.	ai mani; lai mani
unfathomable; adj.	ai jinkaka; lai jinkaka
unfeeling, adj.	ai wuche; lai wuche
unfeigned; adj.	ai bikuo; zioka: "genuine"
unfit; adj.	ai yedi; lai yedi
unflagging; adj.	ai dikpo; lai le dikpo: "uninterrupted
unflappable; adj.	lai kpala: "undisturbed or never upset"
unflinching; adj.	ai rugu; lai rugu: "fearless"
unfold; vit.	shie; ai tikpo; lai tikpo
unforgettable; adj.	ai chegba; lai chegba; lai le chegba
unfortunate; adj.	ai shiendera lai shiendera fotiuna; lai fotiuna
unfounded; adj.	ai wen gindi; lai chode
unfrequented; adj.	lai ngbani; ai firi-firi – lai firi-firi
unfriendly; adj.	lai aboki; ai aboki; lai oyi; lai wu aboki
unfrock; vt.	ai tugbe: "of priest guilty of misconduct and consequently dismissed"
unfruitful; adj.	lai 'ya'ya; ai wen 'ya'ya; ai di 'ya'ya
unfurnished; adj.	ai mosho; lai mosho
ungainly; adj.	goru: "of something clumsy"
ungated; adj.	ai wen kofa; lai wen kofa
ungenerous; adj.	ai mere; lai mere
ungodly; adj.	lai miwa abasi; ai abasi
ungovernable; adj.	lai gomna; lai le gomna; ai gonmenti
ungrateful; adj.	ai diokpe; lai diokpe
unguarded; adj.	ai bo; lai bo; ai kiesi
unguent; n.	nguant: "soft substance used as an ointment"
unhallowed; adj.	ai somon: "unholy"
unhand; vt.	fre; fre hannu: "to let go"
unhappy; adj;	ai dunso
unheal thy; adj.	ai landu; meba; jiba

unheard; adj;	ai nugbo; lai nugbo; ai gbonti
unheard of	ai nugbo-kene; lai nugbo-kene
unhinge; vt.	ai hinji; lai hinji; "to take a door or gate out of its hinges"
unholy; adj.	ai somon; lai somon; njida: "wicked"
unhoped for, adj;	ai renti; ai rekon; lai renti abi redon
unicorn; n.	yunikon: "a horse-like animal with a long horn"
unidentified; adj;	ai yiba; lai yiba; ai ma unidentified flying objects
uniform; adj.	sarigar; yunefom
uniformity; n.	isarigar
unify; vt.	kpodo
unification; n.	ikpodo
unilateral; adj;	kuedaya: "of or done one-sidedly"
unimpeachable; adj	ai jubi; lai jubi; ai noka; lai noka
uninformed; adj.	ai soli si; lai soli abi sole si; ai ma; ai koli; ai muko; lai chegbon etc.
Uninhibited; adj.	ai dihan; lai dihan: "without hinderance"
Uninspired; adj.	ai nnogbon; lai nnogbon
uninterested; adj.	ai che; lai che
union; n.	irundo; ikpodo; itugbe
U.S.S.R.	irundo; nke sofiet sosha ripobli
trade union	irundo tasuwa
unionist, n.	o rundo; o kpodo; o tugbe
unique, adj;	kengbe; saun – saun
unique opportunity	iyefe kengbe; iyefe saun-saun
unisex; adj.	yunisaks: "of a style designed for both sexes"
unison; n.	Ikweba; ikwede; agirimento
unitarian, n.	yunitera; o unitera; irudi chochi eso
unite, vti.	kpodo; rundo; koso: (syn)
unity; n;	ikpodo; irundo; ikoso:- (synonyms)
universal; ad;	nke akpoabi duniya
universe; n.	duniya; (synonymn: akpor)
university; adj.	yunifasiti; yunefasiti
unkempt; adj.	ai fini; lai shaka "untidy"
unkind; ajd..	ai reni; lai renu; njika

Unknowing;,adj.	ai ma
unknown adj.	ai ma; ai yiba: "unknonwn or unidentified"
unleran: vt.	ai ma: ai ma
unleash; vt.	ai koboko: "to let go from leash"
unleavened; adj.	nlebin: :of bread without yeast"
unless; conj.	kowu
un lettered; adj.	ai kozi; lai kozi: "uneducated"
unlike; adj. prep.	ai bika: lai bikai: lai kabi; ai kabi
it is not like this	ko bika eyiti; kowu eyi; kowu baate
it is like this	o wu baate: baate
unlikely, adj.	ko le wu
unlisted, adj.	ai tole; lai tole
unload: vit.	ai kaya; lai gbize kaya
unlooked for, adj.	ai chowa fun; lai chowa fun
unloose, vt.	ai tuka; lai tuka
unman, vt.	ai kagba; lai kagba si
unmanned, adj.	ai wen kriu; ai kriu: "having no crew"
unmannred, adjj.	ai miwa; lai miwa; imiwa rubi
unmask; vti	ai dogunu; shie;- "open'
unmatch; adj.	ai yema; lai yema
unmeaning; adj.	ai tiunma; lai jewu; lai wen ituunma
unmeasured; adj.	ai wen inofi; lai nofi
unmentionable; adj.	lai le koda; ai koda; lai koda
unmindful; adj.	chichegba: chegba: "forgetful and ablivious"
unmistakable; adj.	lai goshi ; ai goshi; lai shi-chero
unmistigated; adj.	ai betain; lai betain abi bekuru; "complete and absolute"
unmoved; adj.	ai yikpo; lai yikpo; kpokp
unnatural; adj.	ai halitta lai halitta: lai duniya
unnecessary: adj.	ai katazi lai zumkpa
unnerve; vt.	fre jijiya; cause somthing or someone to lose selfcontrol and power of decision"; ai jijiya; lai jijiya
unnoticed; adj.	ai kieai; lai kiesi; ai ma; ai hun
unnumbered; adj.	ai lamba; lai lamba
unobtrusive; adj.	ai kpu si enu; ai kpu si 'nuke
unofficial; adj.	ai hafsa; lai wu nke ofis abi hafsa

unorthodox, adj.	ai yemukp
unpack; vit.	ai kaya; lai yokete
unparalleled; adj.	ai handogo; lai handogo
unparliamentary; adj.	lai wu nke majalisar; ai majalisar; lai wu ife majalisar
unpick; vt.	yopu; yota
unplaced; adj.	ai yefe; lai kpoze; ai fie
Unplayable; adj.	ai gwuere; lai le gwuere
Unpleasant; adj.	ai dunso; lai dunso; ai miri-miri
unpractised, adj.	ai shedi; lai shedi; lai jilo; ai jilo
unprecedented; adj.	ai swene-whido; lai swene-whido
unprejudiced; adj.	ai prejudah; lai prejudah
unpretentious; adj.	ai wara; lai wara; "of modesty"
unprincipled; adj.	ai bietu; lai bietu unprincipled and
uncultured:	sususu; o su-su-su; ai masa 'ti bietu; ai masa-bietu
Unprintable; adj.	ai tite; lai presa; ai presa; lai lo tite
unprivileged, adj.	ai danfa; lai danfa
unprofessional; adj.	ai rushiwin; lai di 'rushiwin
unprompted; adj.	sfontenia: "of something happening by itself"; ai yaji; lai yaji; ai fata; lai fabia
unprovided; adj.	ai kpenye; lai kpenye
unprovided for	ai kpenye fun; lai kpenye fun
unprovoked; adj.	ai kokunu; lai kokunu; ai bilionu
unqualified; adj.	ai kwashe; lai kwashe
unquestionable; adj.	ai jubi; lai jubi
unquiet; adj.	ai dankiti; lai dankiti
unquote; v.	ai nosoli; lai nosoli; ai kwot; lai kwot
unravel; vit.	medi 'choto; di choto: "make to become separate"
unreal; adj.	ai zioka; lai katazi; yebu-yebu
unreasonable; adj.	ai rondi; lai le rondi; lai rondi
unreasoning; adj.	ai rondi; lai rondi
Unrelenting; adj.	ai kiene; lai lai kiene; ai mini; lai mini
unreliable; adj.	ai mekole; lai le mekoli
unrelieved; adj.	ai kweye; lai kweye
Unrequited; adj.	ai rikwite; lai rikwite

unreservedly; adv.	ai guini: "without restriction or limitation" ai chemo; lai chemo
unrest; n.	ai simini; lai simini; ai sundo; ai kule nsohala; rugu-rugu
unrestrained, adj.	ai limite; lai guini
unrivalled; adj.	ai hamayya; lai hamayya
unruffled; adj.	kulele: "calm"; ai kpati; lai yolionu
unruly; adk.	sighi-zagha; rugu-rugu: "zigzagly; rough
unruly behaviour	Ihumi rugu-rugu: (not ihumizighizagha
unsaid; adj.	ai sole; lai sole; ai gbaameh; lai gbaameh
Unsavoury; adj.	ai toka; lai dunso; k[ako
unsavoury grammar	turanchi ai toka; kpako-turanchi
unscripted, adj.	ai kode; lai skrif; si skrif
unscrupulous; adj.	ai kiesitain; ai ribite; lai ribite "not paying attention at the least; also, unguided by conscience"
unseasoned; adj.	ai kongba; ai wen ngba; lai ngba
unseat; adj.	yopu na kujera
unseemly; adj.	imiwa rubi: "bad behaviour"; imiwa kpako
unseen; adj.	ai hun; ai neri; lai hun; lai neri
unsettled; vt.	ai simini; ai kulele; a kundu
unsex; vt.	ai vuduh; lai vuduh; ai wu mache abi miji: "neither male or female"
unsightly; adj.	ai dunso abi rama fun ineri "do: "unpleasing or good for the sight"
unskilled; adj.	ai riche; lai riche
unsophisticated; adj.	ai sileka; ai roforofo
unsound; adj.	ai landu; ai lafia; ai saun
unsparing; adj.	ai fre; nawo; "liberal"
unspeakable; adj.	nke ai le soil
unspotted; adj.	lai wen ikurji; shaka-shaka: "purely", "without spot"
unstop; vt.	ai fa chiu; ai du; lai kundu abi kwudu
unstrung; adj.	ai kagba: "powerless"
unstuck, adj.	ai shimkpa; lai shimkpa: "not sticky"
unstudied; adj.	ai muko; halitta: "natural"
unswerving; adj.	ai dikpo; lai dokpo
unsyllabic; adj.	ai kada; lai kada; ai sila-sile

unthinkable; adj.	nke ai le loro; lai le loro; ai loro
unthought of	nke ai loro si
untidy; adj.	ai fini; ai shaka; zighi-zagha
until; prep., conj.	Siti
until this time	siti ngba yii; siti ngba nsiyii
untimely adj.	ai yoge; lai yoge
Untimely death	ikuowun lai yoge; ikuowun ai yoge
untiring; adj.	ai rengu; lai rengulu
untimely death	ikuowun laid y oge; ikuowun ai yoge
untiring; adj.	ai rengu; lai rengulu
unto; prep.	Sisi
untold; adj.	ai soli; soli si; <u>ai le nofi</u>: without measure"; al nofi; (risi jukha) – too many; ai wen lamba: "number-less"
untouchable; adj., n.	lai le tukon; ai tukon; lai tukon
untoward; adj.	ai dunso; ai shiende; ai fotiuna; lai fortiuna
Untoward generation	ai shiendera; janarashon; (or) janarashon ai shiendera; janarashon lai fotiuna; e mutum t'o shiendera;
untruth; n.	lai zioka; ai zioka
untutored; adj.	ai koli; lai koli; "un-tautht"
unused; adj.	ai luwe; lai luwe
unveil; vit.	yopu ibolo; (yo ibolo); shie "bolo: "to open a secret"
unvoiced; adj.	ai voisi; lai voisi; ai luvi; lai luvi
unwieldy; adj.	lilau; lai voisi; ai luvi; lai luvi
unwind; vit.	ai kikpo; lai dikpo: "not winding or foldingup"
unwitting; adj.	ai ma; ai chegbon; lai gbiche abi chero:
unwritten; adj.	ai kode; lai kode
unzip, vt.	shie szipi; ai zipi; lai zipi
up; adv., prep.	nuke; ruo; sonma; (enu; - synonym) ganu-ke
up-and-coming	Biblia-whido; ishienga-rama; ibiawa-ram;
up-and-down	enu-ati-'sala; iyikpoto; iyikiri
turn up	Biawa; yizu nuke
up-to-date	siti rana yii; siti-rana
up-till-now	siti ngba vii

up-beat; n.	ititi: "unaccented beat of music, especially at the end of a bar when the music conductor's hand is raised)	G
up-bringing; n.	mubia enu; mubia enuke (mubia 'nuke); kozi: "educate"; tiyoto; "train"	
up-country; adj.; adv.	isala-kasa	Y/I/H
up-date; vt.vt.	mubia si rana; mubia-rana; mubia si ngba	
up-heaval, n.	kpobe nuke	
great up-heaval	baba 'rimkposa; arimkposah-gidi	
up-hill; adj.	igbake: "ascending"; sisile; igunyan-tudu: "hill-climbing"	
up-hold; vit.	jimu-nuke; kpuzu: "support"	
upholster, vt.	afulsta: "to cover seats etc. with padding, springs, and other materials for comfortability:	
up-keep, n.	kudi 'cheto	G(fE)
up-land, n.	isala-kasa; isala-lande	Y/I/H/G(fE)
up-lift	fanuke; fanye si enu	
up-most; adj.	enu-jukha; nuke-kha; nuke-jukha	
upon, pron.	sikei; sisi;	Y/H/I
upon all	sikei ncha; sisi ncha	
upper; adj.	jukha-ka; (opa:-synonym); isisi	
upper Sakpoba	Isisi Sakpoba; (synonym); Opa Sakpoba) Ititi na gari Benin: "a street in Benin City"	
up-right; adj.	shim-shim; tara; - "syn."	
up-rightness	ishim-shim	
up-right position	ikpoze shim-shim; ikpoze-tara	
uprising; n.	iyeeh!; yeeh!; itegun: - "revolt"	
uproar; n.	arimkpoh-kpoh; arimkpo-kpo (either of the two); also: nsoghuru	
up-root; vt.	bundi	I/Y/H
upset; vti	gbu-iyobi	
don't upset me	ma gbu mi 'yobi	
up-shot; n.	igwisi: - "result"	
up-side-down; adv.	enu-si-'sala; nuke-si-'sala; rugu-rugu; iramkpata	

everything up-side-down;	ife-noha ramkpata;' yikpo enu-si-sala	Y/I/G
up-stairs; adv.	enuke; nuke	I/Y/H
go up-stairs	logo enuke; shiene 'nuke	
up-standing; adj.	kundu-shim-shim; kundu tara; "standing erect"	Y/I/H
upstream; adv.	disi sonbe: "against the tide" kparu-nuke: "to	G(fE)
upsurge; n.	surge up"; arimkpotu konta; konta-ta; kon-tain-	Y/I
up-tight; adj.	tain: "extreme- tensive and nervious" Y(G.V)	
up-town; adj.	isala-gari	
up-turn; n. uranium,	iyikpo nuke: "upward change" yurenia;	
n. uranus; n.	irudi miriala: "a type of mineral or metal"	
urban; adj. urchin; n.	Juranius; flanit nke asaa: "the	
urdu; adj., n.	seventh planet" G(fE) aban	
urge; vt.	akpoka: "troublesome little boy" also;	
i urge you, please	G a mischievous small boy". odu; ede	
urgent; adj. urgently;	'so na kasa kpakistan: "a type or some	
adv. very urgent	types of language(s) in Pakistan"	
urgently; n uric; urine;	wusi; fanye; fanzi	
adj. don't urinate	mo wusi e; biko kiangwa; sokia; yaji kikiangwa;	
here pass urine	sisokia; yiyaji kiangwa jukha; kiangwa jukha-ka	
	ikiangwa; isokia; iyaji yunto; torimi	
	ma yunto si mbi; ma yunto si ebi (or)	
	Tomiri, yuntp	
urn; n.	Aun;"a type of ancient vase"	G(fE)
us; pron.	awa; 'wa	Y
usage; n.	iluwe	Y/G
use; n., vt.	iluwe; luwe	Y/Ed/G
don't use it	ma luwe ya	
i will use it	maa luwe ya	
user, n.	o luwe	
used; anom. fin., pt.	liluwe; ti luwe; luwela	
used to, adj.	mima; ma: (goma): "known; familiar or acquainted with"; shimi; i am used to the same i am not used to the man: (used to : i.e. accustomed) to the habit) mo ma igwuere yien; mo ma ne igwuere; mii ma miji yien used cars mota zoom-zoom nke a ti luwe; iluwela- mota-"used motor"	Y/I/G
useless; adj.	okpoko; ai luwe; ai che; rurubi	
usefule, adj.	di luwe; chiche; liluwe	
usher; n.	o yeh	G
usher, vt.	yeh	

ushers, n. pl.	e yeh	
useless; adj.	okpoko; ai luwe; ai che; rurubi	
Usual, adj.	bietutu; bietu	Y/I
usually; adv.	bietutu	
usurp, vt.	sape; "to take someone's authority or yi kpoze	
usurp authority	sape aashe; sape ikagba	
utensil; n.	kaya kichini; kaya madafi; yutensa	H/G
uterus; n.	mahaifa	H
utility; n.	iyefe; iluwe; ililuwe	
utility assistant	o nonhan	
utilize; vt.	luwe	
utmost; adj.	ziju	I/Y
utopia; n.	yutopi: "of imaginary perfect social and	
	political system"	G(fE)
utter; adj.	giguton: "completely"; guton; duna-duna	
utter; vt.	giguton: "completely"; guton; duna-dana	
utterance, n.	kwuso: "to make a sound or say something	
utterances, pl. n.	through the mouth" ikwuso e kwuso	
uttermost; n.	iziju beli; 'yar-wuya	G/H
uvula; a uxorious; adj.	vuiche: "excessively fond of one's wife"	G/I/Y

	v	
V	viih; vi	G/Gen
vacancy, n.	iyefe; ikpiti; igboloh; mkpiti	Y/I/G
vacant, adj.	yefe; kpiti; gboloh; mkpiti	
vacant post	ikpoze gboloh; iyefe; iyefe gboloh	
vacate, vt.	kopu; freye	Y/I
vacation; n.	ikpozu; ifreye; fifreye	
vacator, n.	o kopu; o freye	
vaccinate; vt.	gunji; fasinet	Y/H
vaccination; n.	igunji; ifasinet	
vaccinator, n.	o gunji; fasineto	
vaccine, n.	fasin; magani ' fasinet; fasin	
vacillate; vi.	ye'ji: "to waver"; meyeji: "to hesitate"	
vacuum, n.	igbolou; vakun	G
vagabond, adj.	ringa-kiri; o gakiri; eni ko wen ihusi: "i.e. someone without fixed dwelling place"	
a vagabond, n.	o ringa-kiri; o gakiri; eni ko wen ihusi: "i.e. someone without fixed dwelling place"	
vagina, n.	botu	Y/I
vagrant, adj.	ringara: "a wandering life"	Y/I
vagrancy, n.	iringara	
vague, adj.	duduh; ai shaka: "of something not clear or distinct"	
vain, adj. vain-glory	nofoh; nohoh; sonkiti ibogo nofoh; ifogoh	I/Y/I/G
valediction, n.	ibibaiyo: "words used in expressing a farewell	
valedictory, adj.	bibaiyo varicose, adj.	
valence, n.	falins; atam:- "atom"	G(fE)
valentine; n.	falentin; falentine; rana iseliba nke st. st. falentain: fenbuari 14 na ardun-ardun	

valerian, n. valerian,	faleriyan; irudi shukeshike	G(fE)
n. valet,, n.	fulawa faleriyan; irudi shuke-shuke fulawa falit; "a manservant	G(fE)
	who takes care of his mater's clothes"	G(fE)
valetudinarian; adj.	ai kabandu: "not being	
	healthy; not healthy" "falitude" delila; di yobi: "bravery" yemkpa oka iyemkpa	
valiant, adj. valid; adj. valid	"soldier's kit-bag"	G(fE)
statement/words valise,	kwari	G/Y/I Y/I
n. valley, n. valour, n.	gburuh: "bravery"	H G
valuable, adj.	year	Y/I
valuables, p.; n.	e year	
valuation, n.	iyera; iyiyera	
valuation officer	hafsa iyiyera	
valuation report	irepota yiyera	
value, n.	iyemezi; iyemkpa	Y/I
valuer, n.	o yemezi; o yemkpa	G(fE)/H(fE)
valve, n.	vaf, bawul	
radio-valve	vaf-rediyo	
vamoose, vi.	dompeh; jalolo	G
vamp,	tielo	G
vampire, .n.	vempaya; ekwenshu	G(fe)/I/Y
van, n.	monka; vani	H/G(fe)
vanguard, n.	vengad: "advance party of an army	G(fe)
vanadium, n.	vanadium: "a hard-grey metyallic element: irunbi	
vandal, n.	irunje; o runbi	
vandal, n.	o runje; o noba: "pointer"	
vane; n.	inoba; o noba: pointer"	
vanilla, vi.	vanela; ("of pods or beans plant with sweetsmelling flowers" G(fE)	
vanish, vi.	fium; foga	G/Y/I

vapid; adj.	shololo: "of something tasteless or uninteresting"	G
vanquish, vt.	megien: "defeat" (bokele)	G
vanity, n.	vanpid discussion iyofoh ibasoka shololo	Y(G.v)/I
vapour, n.	tururi	H
variance, n.	icheto; ifambu	I/Y/G
they are at variance	fa di n'icheto; fa/ ha di n'ifambu	
variation, n.	ifambu; icheto: (any of the two words)	
varicoloured, adj.	ifambu-launi: "of varied colours"	
varicose, adj.	verikoko: "permanently swollen or enlarged vein"	G
varicose vein	jijiyar jinni-verikoko	
variety, n.	ifambu-ifambu; ichicheto	G/I/Y
variety entertainment	imiri-cheto; imiri-fambu	
variorum, adj.	veriora: "of shakespeare edition of play"	G(fE)
various adj.	cheto; fambu	
varmint, n.	o yamint; iyamini: "mischievous person or animal"	G
you varmint	yaminwan o yamini; o yamini	
varnish, n.	fanish; irudi fenti	G(fE)
vary; vit.	icheto; yiche	
vascular, adj.	veskula: "made up of vessels or ducts through which blood lymph or sap	
vase, n. vasectomy, n. vaseline, n. vassal, n.	flows" kasko vasikoto: "a simple surgical operation to make a man sterile" basilin o kwase; kwase; "someone who held	G(fE) H G(fE) H(fE)

vault, n. Vaunt, vit.	ifoma: "of jumping:; ibem	
veer, vi. vegetable,	shakara; shishakara:	Gen
vegetarian, n. vegetation, n.	"of boasting"	
	yipeh: "to change direction" G	
	vejitele G(fE) o vejitele	
	ivejitele; nke shukeshuke abinchi land in return for	
	which he pledged to offer military service	
	to the owner of	
	the land; a feudal tenant" G	
vast, adj. Vast land	buto; bibu I/Y	
vat, n. vatican, n.	ibuto kasa; ibibu kasa vait; "a tank or big vessel for	
	holding liquids" G(fE)	
	vatiken; gida popu na kasa rom	
vehement, adj.	vehicle, n. veil; n.	
	vein; n. velocity, n.	
	velvet, n. venal, adj.	
kagbali; kagbalile	I/Y ugboko	I/Y
ibolo	G jijiyar jinni	H
felositi;	velosai-sai belibeti H/Igala	
	*(fE) agba-mutum: "someone	
vend, vt. vendor,	suwe: "to sell"	G/Y
n. vendetta, n.	o suwe	G
	ikpokiri: "a hereditary	
	feud between families in	
	which members of each ready	
	to get what he wants by all	
	means and dishonesty" family	
	revenge by commiting muders	
	for previous murders"	
veneer, n.	finien: G(	
venerable, adj.	kulumbe	G
venerable property	dukiya kulumbe; ife kulumbe	
venereal/veneral	selele	G
veneral disease	ifrun selele	
venetian, adj.	venishan	G(fE)
venetian-blind	zane venishan	

vengeance, n.	ikpasa; (synonym; irivenja)	Agbo/G
don't take vengeance;	ma kpasa	
vengeful; adj.	kpikpasa; jukun fun ikpasa; di kpasa	
venision; n. venom; n. vent, n. ventilate ventilation, n. ventilator, n. ventricle, n. venture, n. no venture no success	nama ogolo: "deer meat" guba fantili; fanti fantili ifantili o fantili fentrikol: "body cavity, especially that of the heart" fagu; faguru kosi b'isi abi ibokei	H/G H G G(fE) Y/G
venue, n. venus, n.	lai si 'faguru mbele venus: "the goddess of love and beauty; also: the second planet from the sun"	Y/I G(fE)
veracious, adj. veran- dah, veranda, n. verb, n. verbal, adj. verba- tim/verbatim, adv.	nzioka; izioka baranda, kafe, shirayi vab(u); oka turanchi oka onu vabatem; oka-fun-oka: "word-for-word"	G(I/Ikwere H(fE) G(fE) Ikwere/I
verbatim reporter verbena, n.	o ripota vabatem; o solile vabatem vaibena, irudi fulawa	
verbose, adj.	gadin bika habekos vaibosi: "using and containing of more words than needed" idakpe: "judgement" dinjali:	
verdict, n..	"green substance formed on metals	Y/I (H)

verdigris, n	such as copper, bronze or brass surfaces as rust is formed on
	iron surfaces" vaidor: "of fresh green G(fE) colour of growing vegetation"
verdure, n.	inonu: "edge"; I(G.v)
verge, n. verger, n.	vaija: "an official with
verify, vt. verification,	various duties in the
n. verisimilitude, n.	church of university"
	chisi; chondi I(G.v)Y/H ichisi; ichondi
	vairisimili: "appearance
	or resembalance of truth or something
veritable, adj. vermicelli, n.	somewhat truthful"
	katazi: "something real" G/Y/I vaimisili:
	"paste of white G(fE)
	flour made into long slender threads
vermiculite, n.	such as spaghetti"
	vaimikuli: "a form of G(fE)
	mica of which when heated, expands into
vermiform; adj.	threads and used for heat insulation in buildings"
	vaimifam; ife bika G(fE)
	tana "something of worm-like in shape; the
vermifuge, n.	illus at alimentary" ikpokpoh:
vermilion, adj, n.	"purgative" danja; jashaka: "of
vermin, n.	bright-red colour" vaimini: "wild animals such as rats, foxes, weasels etc. harmful toplants, man, bird and other animals"
vermouth, n.	vaimut: "a type of white G(fE) flavoured wine with herbs"
verna cular, adj.	ede nke kasa Y/I/H
vernal, adj.	vaina: "the seaso G(fE) n of spring "
veron al, n.	vairon a: "slee- causin G(fE) g or induci ng drug"
versatile,	G
versatility, n.	ngbe
verse, n.	vais; ivais G(fE)

version, n.	iyaka Y/I
verso, n.	biso; "the left hand side of a book; also the reverse side of a medal or coin"
versus, prep. (lat.)	fesos G(fLat.)
vertebra, n.	vaitibra: "any one of the backbone segments of a skeleton"
vertebrate, n, adj.	vaitibrat: "backboned animal" vertex, n.
vertical, adj.	faitika: "of a plane or line in up-right position to the earth surface"
very, adj.	kizi; Ed(G.v) very much kizi kha; kha
thank you very much	shendo kha: (note: not shendo kizi kha
very good	rama kha
not very good	ko kizi rama
very careful	shokpa rama
be very careful	shokpa rama; kiesi rama
the very person	mutum sem
Very/Verey, adj.	feiri: "a light cloured signal flare fired from a pistol as a signal of distress from a ship"
Vesicular disease:	Irun veisikul
Vespers, n.	Feispa/veispa: "an evening church service and songs"
Vessel, n.	Godogodo "hollow passage for liquid; also a ship or large boat"
Vest, n.	Singileti H(fE)
Vest, vit.	Kas: "to give or furnish someone with right/authority"
Vestal, n.	Veista: "a virgin; pure; chaste in
character"	G(fE)
Vestibule, n.	Feistibula/veistibula: "entrance or lobby hall to a building where hats and outergarments may be left"
Vestment, n.	Veistmint: "garment worn by priest in the church or a ceremonial robe"

Vestry, n.	Veistiri: "a place where vestments are kept in the church"	
vex, vt.	bionu; bilionu	Y/I
via, prep. (lat)	sai; fia	G/G(flat)
viable, adj.	faebo; winre	G(fE)/I/Y
viaduct, n.	fiadot: "a long bridge carrying rail or road across the valley"	
vial, n.	fial, irudi ijongo kele: "a type of small bottle"G(fE)	
vibrant, adj.	shakasah: "vibrating and thrilling"	
vibraphone, n.	faibrafon; irudi	
	instrumint isonga: "a type of musical instrument" G(fE)	
vibrate, vit. vibration, n.	kasah; shakasah G ikasah; ishakasah	
vibrato, n.	faibrato; "tremulous and G(fE) or throbbing effect in plaing stringed and wind instrument or singing with rapid variations in pitch"	
vicar, n.	veika: "a clergyman in charge of parish"	
vicarious, adj.	shiafun Y/I	
vice, n.	njika; ife ibilis; imiwika I/Y/H	
vice, n.	vias; era; n'ikpoze, "of second in command" etc	
vice-president	era-presido	
vice-admiral	era-hessa; era-admira	
vice-versa, adv. (lat.)	fais=fasa, i.e. "the GfL other way round"	
vicinity, n.	kusanchi H	
vicious, adj.	miwika; njika; ife rubi Y/I	
vicious-circle	ikiri-ka (ikiri-miwika)	
vicissitude, n.	iloyi, iyintua; ilozu	
victim, n.	igenren, fiktim G/G(fE)	
victim of circumstance	igienren ngba	
victor, n.	vikta; o bokei; ibokei; (vikto)	

victoria, n.	viktoria	
victorian, n. adj.	mutum nke ngba nke ngba mindu kwin	
victory, n.	iboki; ib'isi Y/H/I	
vicua, n.	vikuna; irudi nama eso	
vide, v.	irudi nama eso	
vide your letter	bietu wasika e; sa wasika	
vide-licet (viz.) adv.	vizi; na'fa'fa G(fE)/I(G.v)	
viz:	na'fa'fa; (or): vizi, i.e. namely	
video, n.adj.	fidio; "television broadcasting set"	
video-tape recorder	tef-rekoda fidio, trf.	
vie, vi.	hi	G
vie for it	hi si; hi fun ya	
view, n.	ineri, neri	
view-point	mbi-neri	
viewers, n.pl.	e neri	
Vigil, n.	n.ijinife; bibo	Y/I
Keep vigil	Di jinie, di bibo	
vigilance, n.	ibibo	
vigilante, adj.	o bibo; o jinie	
vignette, n.	viginet: "of ornamental design"	G(fE)
vigour, n.	ikagba	I/Y
vikking; viking	vikin	G(fE)
vile, adj.	runjo: "bad language"	Y/I
vilify, vt.	shata: "si anderous"	I/Y
villa, n.	bila: "semi-detached	h."G(fE)
village, n.	kurmi; kauye	H
villager, n. villain, n.	kurmi; o kauyeo njika; o miwika	I/Y/G(fE)
vim, n. vindicate, vt.,	ikagba; vim	Y/H
n. vindictitive, adj.	liji; iliji ai gbari; lai gbari:	I/Y
vine, n.	"uniforgiving" itache inabi	H
– vain; vinegar, n. vintage,	viniga; ruwa-vain vintaj: "time of	G(fE)
n. vintner, n. vinyl, n.	grape-harvesting" attajiri wain; o rushe abi	G(fE)
	leta wain: "wine-merchant"	H(G(fE)
	vinail, irudi flastik:	

viol, n. viola, n.	"a type of plasti" vaiyo; irudi kaya isonga	G(fE)
viola, n.	vaiyola; instrumint abi ikaya isonga faiyola;	G(fE)
	irudi shukeshuke: "types of plant of	
violate, vt., n.	one colour only"	
violent, adj., n.	gbaje; igbaje; soize I/Y gabagah; igbagain; miru	
violet, n.	G/I/Y faiyolat; (vaiyolat); irudi G(fE)	
violin, n.	fulawa abi launi	
	vaiyolini; irudi instrumint	
	isongi abi isonga: "a typeof musical	
	instrument"	
	vaiyololo; irudi vaiyolini lau	
	bida, kububuwa H	
	atabala: "violent and	G
	ill-tempered noisy	H
violoncello, n. viner,	woman" budurwa;	
n. virago, n.	budurwa-mari;	
virgin, n. virgin-mary		
	uwa jesu kristi faijina:	G(fE)
	"square spinet	
	without legs of the	
	16th and 17thcc"	
virginal, n. virginia, n.	vaijiniya; irudi taba	
	nke kasa amerika	
virgo, n.	vaigo; lamba nke	
	isii na zodiak vaigule:	
	"a diagonal	G(fE)
virgule, n.	mark (/)" kizi kasa kizi	Ed
virile, adj. virile nation		
virility, n.	ikizi	
virology, n.	vatroloji; layens imuko	
	keke; (ikek oloji)	
virtu, n.	imisam: "something of	
	attracting interest"	
virtual, adj.	kieke;	G(fEd)
virtually, adv.	kiekele	
virtue, n.	imirun: "of goodness	I/Y
	or excellent quality"	
virtuous, n.	nke imirun; mirun; o mirun	
a virtuous woman	mache imirun; o	
	mirun mache	

virtuoso, n.	imasam: "someone with special knowledge or gifted talent or skill"	I/Y (G.v)
virulent, adj.	virus, n. visa, n.	
vis-à-vis, adv.,	prep. they sat vis-à-vis: vis-à-vis: (synonym):	
viscera, n.	viscid,adjj.	
viscous, adjj.	viscount, n. visible, adj.	
visiion, n.	visionary, adj	
visit, vit. visit a	friend visit ibadan visiting card	
visitor, n.	visitors, n. pl. my visitor visitation, n. visor, n. vista, n.	
visual, adj.	audio-visual	
visualize, vt. vital, adj. vital point		
vitality, n. kokain: "strong deadly or	Y/G wicked and hatred feeling" ikeke: "poisonous elements G smaller than bacteria" fisa: "approval to show	G(fE) that a passport has been examined and fa jondu si-do
vis-à-vis: veisera; ana: "intestine" veisid: "sticky and semi-fluid" veiskosi; veiskosa veiskant: "nobleman	G(fE) G(fE)/Afi-zere	
higher than a baron" firi; nke a le hun: "that which can be seen" ifiri; ineri nke ifiri abi ineri; ai	I/Y I/Y	
katazi; ai-zumkpa kiele diele aboki kiele kadi kiela o kiesa e kiele o kiela mi ikela faiso: "in olden days, the movable part of a helmet. also, the peak of a cap " finrin: "of long and narrow view"	G(fE)	

certified by the officials of a foreign country" nure-si: "in relation to "; si-do: "to sit face-toface, or facing one- another"; "c"

nineri; hun; neri odyo-hun; (odio-hun) neri na whido; neri n iyobi kaizi   Y/I

inoba kaizi ikaizi; nke ikagba katazi: "of vital power or

vitalize, vt. vitamin, n.   kaizi; medi kaize faitamin; irudi magani

                                             to tama frn jiki kafaita: "to lower the

vitiate, vt.

                                             quality or weaken or destroy   G(fE)
                                             force" faitros: "of a glass-like   G(fE)
                                             rocks and brittle" fitiri: "to change into a   G(fE)
vitreous, adj. vitrify,   glass-like substance" fitrol: G
vt.i. vitriol, n.   "of sulphuric acid   G
;vivacious, adj., vivid,   or any of the salts of sulphuric acid. "
hoha; viviparous, adj.   garaun: "lively"; vive katah: "of bright
                                             and intense light" viveparos: "of
                                             offspring which develop

within themother's   vaiviset: "to operate or   G(fE)
body" vivisect, vt.

vodka, n.   voka; "a type of strong   G(fE)
vogue, n. voice, n. void, adj.   russian alchoholic distilled   G/Igbo
null and void   drink." voge: "order of   G/French/Eng
                                             the day" voisi; iluvi   G/Y/I
                                             folh; ikpiti; iyefe;
                                             gboloh folo-foh; ai
                                             wen agba; ai kagba

voile, n.   filih: "thin and light

volatile, adj.   dress material" volate: "of a liquid that   G(fE)
                                             can easily change into gas or
                                             vapour". also of a person, lively
                                             and changing quickly

and easily from one interest or mood to another"
ekpangidi; (synonym: G/G(fE)

volcano, n.	folkano)	
vole, n.	fol: "a rat-like animal	
volition, n. = volife:	like mouse"	G/Y
volley, n.	"something done at one's own will, power of choice etc." foli; "of hurling or shooting of a number of missiles, arros, bullets,	
	stones etc togetherat once. " bolu-foli folt: "unit of electrical current " foltej; ifoltej iyikpo-	G(fE)
volley-ball, n. volt, n.	ido (iyikp ido):	
voltage, n. volte-face, n.		
	"complete round-turn to the opposite direction" somkpo: "being able to talk rapidly and easily" folium; ifolium	Y/I
voluble, adj. volume, n.		G(fE)
voluminous, adj.	di folium; iyewan gidi: "great quartity foliumina"	
voluntary, adj.	kweyo	I/Y
volunteer, n.	o kweyo; ikweyo	
vomit,vt.	huo	G
voodoo, n.	vuu-duh: "a form of religion, sorcery and witchcraft and practised by some west indies negroes"	G(fE)
voracious, adj.	jerire: "very greedy or hungry and desiring much "	Y/I
vortex, n.	eziza: "of whirling mass fluid or wind such as whirlpool"; "to be engross and engulf in activity, hence: "ziza"	Ed/Ishan
votary, n.	ikwera; kwera: "person who G devote his time and energy to something or a course"	
vote, n.	vota G(fE)	
voter, n.	o vota	

voter's list	ilisa vota
vouch, vi.	nyoka "to be responsible" I/Ikwere
voucher, n.	o nyoka; enyoka; baucha I/Ikw./I/H
vow, n.	ikwe I/Y
vowel, n.	bawel; nke oka abi turanchi bika afabit a, e, e, i, ii eiseta
vox, n. (lat.)	voisi; iluvi
vox populi vox dei	voisi jama a wu voisi abasi; or, iluvi jama a wu iluvi abasi, i.e. "the voice of the people is the voice of god"
voyage, n.	irinje-teku abi irinje ruwa: "journey by sea, ocean or by water"
vulcanize, n.	falkanaiza: "to recondition G(fE) punctured tyretube"
vulcanizer, n.	falkanaiza; also: (folikanaiza)
vulgar, adj.	folga
vulga fraction	folga-frakshan
vulgate, n.	folugate: "the vulgate latin version of the bible in the 4th century"
vulnerable, adj.	kwezah: liable orexposed G to damage
vulture, n.	ungulu H
vulva, n.	ubotu: "the opening of female genitals

W

w	dobol-yuh	G(fE)
wad, n.	whad: "a lump of soft materials of keeping things apart or in place"	
waddle, vi.	dadu: "to walk with slow steps along sideways roll"	G
wade, vti.	don; janyen: "to move or wade in"	
wafer, n.	weifa; irudi bisikiti	
nasco wafer	weifa nasco, irudi biskiti rama	
waffle, n.	waifol, irudi keke kele	
waffle, vi.	oka ya-ya-ya: "careless, vague and unnecessary talk"	I/Ikaw/Gen.
waft, vt.	jansi "to carry lightly"	Y/H/I
wag, vit.	le: "to waive or move left and righ, up or down"	
the god is wagging its tail:	kare ng le wutsiya ya; (or kare ng le bindi ya.	
wag; n.	o ligo; k"someone full of merry and amusing talks and fond of joes" (old use: miri/date	
wage, n.	ikpa: "payment"	Agbo
wake-keeping, n.	ibo-gawa	Y/H
wake, n.	izuba: "after or following an event"	
walk, vti. walk-on/along walk-about walk-away walker, n. walk-over, n. walking, n. walkie-talkie, n. walkiing-stick, n.	ringa; (old use: shien, rinje ringa-shien ringa-kiri ringa-ta o ringa ringa-feja: "to defeat easily" iringa o ringa-soi-soli sanda-iringa (old use: sandinga)	Y/I
wall, n.	katanga, bango	H
wall-tonwall	bango-si-bango	
=wallet, n.	wall-eyed, n.	

wallop, vt.   wallow, vi.

wal-nut wal-rus, n.   wand, n.
                               wander, vti.

wanderer, n.   wander-land
                               wane, vi.

wangle, vt.   wangler, n. wangle
                               your way

through want, vti, n.   wants, pl. my wants
                               are before god

wanton, adj.   wanton destruction

wantonness, n. war,   H/H(fE)
n. wage-war

war-dance, n. world-   G/Gen
war war-office   G
                               G(fE)
                               H/Y

warble, vti. warble-   Y/I
fly, n. ward, vt,   G(fE) Gen.

ward-off ward, n.
                               Y/I

ghagun; jagha isamba-
ijagha ijagha-'kpor; ijagha
duniya ofis ijagha

woro (old use: kobu) bobuwaH warbler, n. o woro   G
bo: "to keep watch

over something or protect" sokeh; lepu   G/Y/I
unguwa; gari: "quartyer   H
or area of a town" (also, a division ofr separate room in a

warden, n. traffic-warden

warder, n. prison-warder

warderess, n. (fem)

ward-robe, n. ward-room, n.

ware, n. hard-ware ware-house warm, adj.

warm-hearted, adj. reception

warn, vt. i warned you warning, n.

warp, vti. building especially in hospital).

wadin; o bibo	G(fE) /Y(G.v)
wadin-trfike duroba; (synonym: wada) H/G(fE) duroba-prusu;	
wada-prusu duroba; (wadaris)	
kabad-esa;	H/Ogori
wadrum: "living and	G(fE) eating apartment for senior officers in a war-ship"
kawo: "manufactured	G
goods or items" kawo-kasuwa	
gida-kawo; (gikawo)	
wuno	H/Y
iyobi 'hufe: lovely and kind mind"	
iyini-wuno gbulo	I/Y

warrant, n. warrantor, n. warren, n.	from usual or natural shape" Iyamini (synonym: warante) Eg/G o warante	
	warin: "area of land in which there ar eots of burrows in which	G(fE)
warior, n. wart, n.	rabbits live and breed" o jagha, o ghagun; (epithet: jarumi) wait; "a small hard and	Y/I/H
wary, adj.	dry skin-growth" wori: "to be caustions and in the habit of watching for possible	
was, that was wash, n, vit.	danger or trouble" wu; di; wa; nee yien wu wesa: "this is us3ed for non-human, other matters and anumals; but wecha is used for person, e.g. wash the plate: 9wesa kwano); i am going to bath/	I/y/I

	wsh: (mo ng shienga wecha). kwano/ tasa iwesa washa; o wesa mo gbulo e igbulo kebe: "become or	
wash-basin washer, n.	make bent and twisted	G(fE)/Y/I
washer-man	washing-machine washy;	H
washing, n.	wishy-washy, adj.	Y/Ef/I/E
wasp, n. waste/	waste-basket don't waste	G
wastage, adj, n.	money wastrel, n.	Y(G.v)
watch, n.	watch-out watching, n. watchers, n. pl. god is watching yu watch, n.	G/H/H(fE)
watch-dog, n..	water-house water-man water-boy under-water water-bird	H
water, n	water-biscuit water-borne disease water-bottle water-closet, w. c. water-channel	H(G.v)
water-colour, n.	water-course water-jacket water-level	Ogori/H

water-mark washa-man; o wesa
iwesa; iwecha injin abi mashin
iwesa; o wesa – mashin ya-ya-ya
zanzaro; rina: "a type of flying
insect with a narrow waist, black
and yellow stripes and a powerful
sting in the tail" nowu; inowu;
datti; fagolo kwando-datti ma
nowu kudi iholo: "a good-for-
nothing fellow" bo; ibo bo; bo'ta
ibo; bibo e bo abasi ng bo e/
yin agogo: "small instrument
measuring time that cn be carried
in the pocket or worn on the
wrist" (agogo-wuhan or simply:
agogohannu) kare o bo ruwa gida-
ruwa o ruwa-miji o ruwa-yaro
n'abe-ruwa; abe-ruwa onene-
ruwa bisikiti-nke-ruwa kaya-
ruwa irun kaya-ruwa ijongo-ruwa
ekpuruke chana-ruwa; gudana-
ruwa wata-kolo hanya-ruwa jakit-
ruwa kwa-ruwa; laini-ruwa jukun
fun ruwa; jukun-ruwa lamba o
meja: "manufacturer or designer's   G(fE)
mark in some kinds of paper   G
which can be seen when Gen.   Ebira/h

water-logged, adj.

held against light;
also mark of high reputation,

	tide or river" guna-ruwa	
water-melon, n.	mafadar-ruwa; gangare kogi	
water-fall water-leaf water-lilly, n. water-mill water-power water-proof	gori H/Afi-Zere	
	bado H	
	mila-ruwa agba abi ikagba ruwa wata-purufu; o bo	
	ruwa; robaruwa akue-ruwa	
water-side water-snake	mesa-ruwa; machiji-ruwa iwirin-ruwa	
water-tight water-tower	hasumiya-ruwa; (wata-tawa) irushe-ruwa	
water-works water-spring water, vt, i.	ifoma-ruwa tinkin-ruwa: "to	
watering-can water-loo	sprinkle water" ijongo-gadina iyohoh: "to be finally and crushingly defeated in a contest,	Ebiura/H(fE) G
	especially after a seeming success" ruwa-ruwa; ai sile turanchi ruwa-	
watery, adj. watery english		H/Y/I
watt, n. wattle, n. wattle, n.	ruwa: ya-yaf-ya turanchi what; nke lantiriki; (whait) whaito: "sticks structure or twigs" layu, lebatu: "the red flesh hanging down from the head or throat	G(fE) G(fE) H
	of some birds, e.g. cock or turkey" yeji yeji si n'akue; (yeji	
wave, vti. wave-side		Y(G.v)
waving, n. wave your hand	akue); yeji s'akue iyeji yeji hannu e/yin;	
wave, n. wave of event the waves (poet) wave, n.	(yeji hannu) ikpodi: "of long ridge of water or sea falling upon another" (force) ikpodi 'soka ekpodi igbeleh: "of steady increase of spread"	G G

long-wave short-wave medium-wave waver, n. wax, n. wax-paper sealong-wax wax, adj waxing strong way, n. give way and let me pass:	igbeleh-golo igbeleh-kuru igbeleh-izono o yeji was takarda was isili-was kidi: "to get stronger" kagba kidi; idi-kpoi hanya (old use: uzo) kuro na hanya kam' feja; colloquial: kuro	G(fE) G H
the way of the cross go out of one's way make/ pave way for lead the way	n'uzo kam' koja) hanya kalfari nke jesu kristi zigolo hanya munji fun: "to prepare for" gosin hanya	
by way of/by the way	na hanya/n'kue hanya	
out of the way	ta hanya	
it is out of the way	o ta hanya; ko si na hanya	
on the way	na hanya	
ways and means	inozo ati hanya; (or: hanya 'ti 'nozo)	
way ahead	hanya na whido	
way in way out	hanya si ati hanya ta; (hanya si/ta)	
under way	wa na hanya; na hanya	
and way	bi o wu; (bi o ti wu); eni-hanya	
way-bill	ilisa-kaya hanya; (ilisa-kaya)	
wayfarer, n,	o ringalo: " a traveller – poet" (also: o rinkpoto)	
wayfaring	iringalo: "travelling (poet)"	
way-side	akue-hanya	
way-lay, vt.	kelebe	
way-ward, dj.	waru	Y/I
we, pron.	awa	Y
weak, adj.	mere	Twi
weal, n.	birdi	H
wealth, n.	ifanzi	G
he/she is wealthy a wealthy man	o fanzi miji fanzi	
wean, vt.	wen: "to teach and master a young baby or animal to feed other than from its mother's milk"	
weapon, n.	makami	H G(fE)
wear, n (cloth)	sa	Ogori

wear, vti.	yiwo
wear dress	yiwo esa
wear, (of wear & tear)	yolo
it has worn out	o ti yolo; o ti yolo
i'm worn out weary, adj. you wearied? i'm not wearied weariness weasel, n.	ta; o ti yololo mo ti yololo hebu; remba: "tiredness" G are e hebu? (or o hebu?) mii hebu; mii remba . ihebu; iremba G(fE) wisely: "a small fierce animal having redbrown fur and living
weather, n. good weather bad weather weather-map	on rats, rabbits, eggs, biers, etc iska H iska rama iska rubi o kpo-iska: "diagram showing the detail of the weather
weather-cock weather-man weather-forecast weather-station weather-vane weave, vit weaver, n. weaving, n. weaver-bird web, n. cob-web webbing, n.	over a wide area" akuko-iska; o fineri-'ska o sowhido-iska; o sowhi-'ska isowhi-'ska tashan-iska; ofis-iska buledi o fineri-'ska wuntu Y/I o wuntu iwuntu gado, jira H wuntu-gizo, yana H wuntu-gizo webin; irudi fabriki ti a ng fi meshe belit: "a strong or type of
wed, vit.	fabric used for the manufacture of belt" wede: "to marry or unite" Y/H?Ed
wedding, n.	iwede; (iseliba wede:
wedding-breakfast	marriage ceremony) abinchi-'wede: "meal for the bride and bride and bridegroom as well as their relatives, friends
wedding-cake wedding-ring wedding-bell silver-wedding	and well-wishers" kek-iwede; (kekwede) oruka-wed agogo-iwede iwede-siliva: (anivase ardun jisen nke iwede: 25th
anniversary of a wedding) golden-wedding	iwede-zinariya: iwede-goldi: 50th anniversary
diamond-wedding	of a wedding) iwede-elila; (iwedi-
wedge, n.	elila): "75th anniversary of a wedding" whuej: "used to

support or keep two things apart.

iweda: "condition of

wedlock, n.

wednesday, n.   being married" wenesde; raninang. 4th day of
the week (anivase ardun sen nke iwede: wee-
wee, n. days from saturday midnight to the
next saturday midnight Ed. weep, vit.

weeping, n. weevil,   ikube maya   welfare, n.
n. weft, n.   H   icheb o; 'laifa
    takwala: "cross-threads   ;
    taken over and H under the
    weving's i want to wee-wee

weed, n.   weeds, n (pl.)

week, n.   ssih; "a word used for   H
    kids to pee mi che
    i ssih sako, nome

sawun: "black clothes   Ogori/Y/I

worn by a widow   uzola: "a period
for mourning"   of seven

weigh-down weight, n.   Y/Ed weighing-machin
my weight is…
weight-lifting   mashin-iwan   I/Y/H welfa
something" weir-   wan si 'sala iwan   re office r
down weird, adj.   Y/Ed what is your weight?   hafsa o cheb
    meni wu iwan yin?   o well, n.
    iwan mi wu…   r
    itoto-iwan   i j i
    Ogoja/Y/Ed weir, n.
    kpo: "wall or barrer across
    kpo si–sala shubi: "something
    unnatural and unearthly.
    G strange and difficult to understand.
    someone eccentric in mode of

    dressing and behaviors"   y

welcome, adj. kweba; yi   eku a bia; (synonym: bibia); h
welcome address i don't   Y/I/Egun welcome sir   i eku a bia sah; (bibia   e n
welcome rubbish: sah) oka ibibia
`welcome my friend   mii kweba idatti; mii yi 'dattie

        w
    bibia   a

'boki; eku a bia, aboki   t
you are welcome

bibia	e	
weld, vit.	keke	r
G	-	
welder, n.	o keke	w
welding	ikeke	e
ll	rijiya	
i wish you well	mo wizi e rama; mo sciene e rama	
do it well	meshe ya rama stand up well/stand well as well as this ati ra' eyi	
well, n.	kundu rama 'lafia; igbandu	
i am not well	mii gbandu; mii lafia	
are you well?	jeu e gbandu? ju igbandu?	
well-being	lafia; igbandu	
well-to-do	fifanzi	

warp" igban weigh, vit. wan "of measure of balance" duwellington, n. welt, n.

went, pt. of go wept, pt. pp. of weep were, pt. of be we'are (we're) we are going wesleyan, n, adj.

west – huest, n. west-end

western, adj, n.

wet, adj. wet-bed wet-blanket bed-wetting

wetterk, n. we have (we've) whack, vt.

whale, n. whaler, n. whang, vt.

wharf, n. Apapa Wharf Sapele Wharf

Calabar Wharf Port-Harcourt Wharf what, adj. what is your name? what are you doing here? what is the matter? what is happening ere?

walentin: "high water-
proof boot"
walt: "a strip of leather
to which the sole and upper part of a
shoe are stitched." shiengala; logala
kube; kubele
wu
awa wu,awa ng awa ng shienga huesliyan; nke chochi
ti jon huesli choja:
"of the church founded

by john wesley" huest: "a point where
the sun-sets in the horizon"
igukpin-huest: "an area
in london with the largest and most
fashion shops" nke huest; ife huest:

hui-huest; ihuest loru

gado-loru gwado-loru iloru-gado; iynto

na gida, itomiri si na gida. o loru
awa ti gham: "to strike someone

or something with a hard blow" dova: "a
large sea animal" G mharbi dova: "a

whale-hunter" gbosah: "to strike

heavily and loudly"

kwate   H/Y

Kwate Apapa Kwate Sapele

Kwate Calabar

Kwate Port-Harcourt

meni; bawo   H/Y/I meni wu
                                                   iafa yin? meni o
                                                   ng meshe mbi?

meni soka? meni ne soka mbi? what has
brought about problems? what about you?

whatever, adj. whatsoever

wheal, n. wheat, n. wheedle, n.

wheel, n. wheel-barrow wheel-
chair, n. wheeze, vti.

whelk, n.

whelp, n.

when; adv. when? (what time?) whence, adv.

whence he came? whensoever, conj. mbi
whenever, adv. where, adv. where-abouts
wherever whether, conj. whether you'll whether
or not whew, (of hissing sound) whey, n.

which, interr. adj. which one? which
way? whichever, adj. whiff, n.

while, n. whim, n.

bawo maka yinwan?; yinwan nko?
eni 'fe: (any thing) ife-ki'fe; eni 'fe t'o wu

kpawu
alkama   H
huedol: "to flatter and

get what one wants" wili; gare; kafa jaki   H(fE)
kujera o wen wili;   H
(kujera-wili) migirih: "to breath
noisily and with a whistling sound in

the chest like when suffering from asthma" huelk; "a type of marine   G(fE)
mollusc like a snail)
popi\: "young dog,

lion, bear, tiger etc. ngba;   I/Y

whine, n. whip, n. meni fata nsohala?

or source?) sa mbo?: (from where)? sa eni mbi; sa mbi-
kieni ngba; ngba-k-ngba mbolee; lee; mbo nso-ebi eni
mbi woya; bi o wu; woya e le wu; bi e le wu
bi o wu abi ko wu whiu
hue: "of liquid part

                                                               Gen
of sour milk   Y/I
wodu wodu konon? wodu hanya? wodu eeni;
wodu keni hech: "sound of slight

puff or breath" gbeti; ngbe ichu: "of sudden   I/Y
desire or idea" irike bulala; koboko ke ngba?   G
(rarely ngba 'wo?) sa: (from what place   Ben. I/Y
                                                               H/Gen

horse-whip whip, vit.
don't whip me whipping-   bulala-doki   H(G.v)
stick whipping-post   bulala; koboo ma bulala mi
whippoor-will, n.   sanda-bulala; sanda koboko itache-bulala

                               huipohui: "a small

                               amerikan bird" kafe ikafe;   H/Y/I
                               huisk: "a small bursh
whirl, vit.
whir-pool, n. whisk, n.

whisk, vti. whisker, n.	for removing dust"	G
	piam: "to take or	H
	remove quickly	
	and suddenly"	
	saje: "shaving head except	
	narrow line over	
	top of the head	
whisky, n.	between templess" huiski;	Gen
whisper, vti. whispering	wisiki; "ogogoro bature"	G/I/Ikw/Y
hope whistle, n. whit,	jewan; solitin jewan	Y/H/G
n. not a whit white, adj.	renti ifito; fito; pioroh	G
white-hourse white-house	tin: "least particle"	H/Y/I
whirte-man white-wash	kosi tin fari; bocha	
	doki-fari gida-fari	
	bature; iyinboh; o bocha	
	huait-wash: "mixture	
	of powdered lime	
	or chalk and	
	water, used for	
	coating ceilings, walls, etc."	
whiting, n.	huit: "a type of small	
	sea-fish used as food"	
whitlow, n.	igenge: "small inflamed	
	spot on a finger or toe	
	usually near the nail"	
whitsun, n.	huitsan: "the 7th	
whizz-kid, n.	sunday after easter"	Ed.
	winzi-winzi: "bright,	
	inventive young	
	person having	
	progressive ideas and	
	achieves rapid success"	
who, interr.pron. who	uani uani eyi? uani e?;	
is this? who are you?	uani yin?; (simple form:)	
who, pron.	nketi; ti	
the man who knows all	miji to ma ncha nke maa; t'o maa; uani t'o	
who'll (who will) who'll	maa biawa; bibiawa uani meshe ya;	
come who-dun-it		
	(ua'lo meshe ya?	
whoever, pron.	eni-biso; eni-mutum; eni-so	

whole, adj.
the whole of them whole-
number my whole heart
wholesale, n. nchani;
ncha   I/Enuani fa/
ha ncha lamba-ncha
iyobi mi ncha

whole-some, n.	quanties"	Y/
whoop, n.	ilandu: "healthy and	G
whooping-cough	favourable to the body and	G
whoopee, n.	soul" ighuhuh; gbuhuh	
	ikoho-ghuhuh	
	igbelele: "to take part in	
	noisy entertainment or rejoicing"	

whop, vt. whore; n.	kpawai: "to beat or defeat"G ifiki: "to prostitute"
whore-monger fornicates"	G o fiki: "man or woman who

whorl, n.	huol: "of rings of leaves, petals, shells, etc. such as mollusc or fingerprint"

whose, pron.	nk' eni; nke ti; ti
whose house is this?	gida nke ti wu eyi? (or: ua'lo wengida' yi?)

whose shoes?	bata nke uani?; takalminke uani?

who-so, adv.	eni-wu; eni-so	
who-soever will	eni-so che; eni-so t'o che	
why, adv.	mani; (also: keza)	Y/I
why did you fail to come	keza t'o biawa?; mani o biawa?	

wick, n.	lagwani: "lenth of thread through a candle

wicked, adj.	njika; ijika	I/Y
wicked person	mutum njika; mutum ijika; njika mutum	

ileta-lau: "sellling of goods in large

wickedness, n.	ijik	
don't be wicked	ma jika; ma di jika	
wicket, n.	wuket: "small sliding window"	G(fE)

wicket, n.	wukat: "of criket game"	G(fE)

wide, adj.	kporo	Y/I
widgeon, n.	wenjion: "a type of wild fresh-water duck"	G(fE)
widow, n.	o kpoma	G/H
widower, n.	o kpomi: "man who lost his wife and has not re-married"	
widow-hood	ngba ikpoma	
widower-hood	ngba ikpomi width, n.	
what is the width?	meni wu ikporo ya?	
wield, vt.	boro: "have and use at one's disposal" wield a knife	
wield authority	boro aashe	
wield power	boro ikagba; boroagba G/H	
wife, n.	mata; aure	H illegal-wife
wives	e mata	
illegal-wives	e wube	
wig, n.	hula; tagiya	H
put on wig	yiwo hula	
wigging, n.	iwimba: "scolding"	Y/I
wild, adj.	gboro; gbi-gboro	Y/Y(G.v)
wild-animal	nama-gbigboro	
wild-person	mutum gbi-gboro; o gboro mutum	
very wild	gboro kha	
don't be wild	ma gboro; ma di gbigboro; ma gbigboro	
wild-fire	wuta jambele	
wild-rumour	jambele hun-hun-hun	
wilderness, n.	igenji	Y/H
wilful, adj.	gbiche: "intentional"	Y/I
wilfun act	imesh' igbiche	
will, anom fin. vti. n.	shekwa; 'aa (i.e. maa); ashei; che; sibo	
I will	m'aa (maa);	

I will not	mii
will you?	ua? e shekwa; o shekwa; (shekwa?)
i am willing	mo che; mo di che
will you get out	sibo jaita
the Will of God	Ashei Abasi
this is my will	e yi wu ashei mi
I will be going to school	I will like to go home now
when there's a will – there is way	maa shienga makaranta mi che I shienga gida nsiyii bi 'gbiche ba diwa; hanya a diwa
I will like to fly out	maa che I feh ta
will you come?	E a biawa?; o a biawa?
I will come	maa biawa
will he/she	O a?
last will	ashei zuein
willingly	iche; o wenji
willow, n.	weilo: "types of tree or shrubs with thin, easily bent branches" G(fE)
Wilton, n.	Wilitin; irudi kafet: "a type of carpet" G(fE)
win, vti.	bokei; (synonym: b'isi i.e. bokeisi); coklloqual: megion/megun Y/I/G/H
who won the game?	Ualo b' isi n'igwuere? (aulo blisi 'gwuere?
we won the game	awa b'isi 'gwuere
you either win or lose	e biso b' isi abi funu
winner, n.	o b' isi; o bokei; o bokeisi
winning, n.	ib' isi; ibokeisi
wince, vt.	kara
wince at	kara si
winch, n.	huinch: "a type of machin for hoisting or pulling down something" G(fE)

wind, n.	fekuku; ifeh; (synonym: geveve)	Y/I/Itigidi
wind of event	igeveve	
wind-gauge	geji- 'fekuku	
wind-instrument	instrumint-fekuku	
wind-jammer	jamawindi: "a merchant sailing- ship"	
wind-mill	famfo	H
wind-pipe	tukun-fekuku	
wind-screen	gilasi-fekuku na mota; gilasi- fekuku unguwafekuku: "in the direction in the wind"	
wind-ward	unguwa-fekuku:	
windy, adj.	"in the directionof the wind"	
wind, vti. (curve or twist)	fekuku; di fekuku; fifekuku	
wind-up	koi: "to move in a curving, G twisting or spiral manner"	
wind-up (to close down)	koi-nuke; koisonma koi-koi	
winder, n.	o koi; (waina); ikoi	
windfall, n.	ishienda rama; (fotiuna); Y/I/G(fE) of good fortune	
winding-sheet, n.	esa-fekuku: "wind-clothing"	
windlass, n.	ikpoh-injin"pulling engine"	
window, n.	iwindo Ha/Urh/uvwe	
window-envelope	chibolo o wendo; chibolo o win. gilasi abi maidubi	
windowpane	'windo nineri kaya na kasuwa; nineri kasuwa	
window-shopping		
wine, n.	wain; ruwa inabi; mate	
wine-glass	tukpula-wain; tukpu- la-mate	

wine and dine	gbigbandu: (gbi-gba:ndu): "to eat, drink and entertain"	
wing, n.	folefole; fiffike;	G/H
wings of a dove	e folefole kurchiya	
wing, n (of section/dept)	iyaka	Y/I
wing-commander	kwamanda-iyaka	
wink, vti.	shido: "to close and open one's eyes and get rid of something by not bothering oneself"	Y/I
winkle, n.	wenkol:"a type of sea-snail used as food"	G(fE)
winnow, vt.	fole: "stream of air separating the dried outer coverings from grain or to blow away (chaff) from grain"	
winsome, adj.	masam: "of a person, i.e. his out-look, attractive, pleasing and presentable personality"	

winter, n. winter-wind winter-garden wipe, vit. wipe your feet here wiper, n. wiper-blade wire; n.

bared-wire wireless, adj.

wisdom, n. wisdom-tooth wise, adj. wise decision wise counsel wise man wise men wise men bank with u.b.a wish, vit. i wish to go

i wish you well good wishe(s) wishy-washy, adj. wit, n.

witch, n.

witch-craft, n.
witch-doctor, n.

with, prep. come
with me withdraw,
vit. withdrawal i have
withdrawn withdrawal
from the service:

huinta: "season
between autumn and
springi.e. november. or
december to february
of each year. ifekuku-
huinta lambu-huinta;

(gadin-huinta)

chanu   I/Y chanu kafa o chanu; waipa; whai-
                              whai buledi waipa; buledi

whai-whai waya bab-waya teliveveh; telikia-kia: G(fE)
"communication without wire such

as telegraph" ichegbon; ima baba hakori chegon   I/Y
icheri chegbon ilula chegbon o chegbon miji e   I/Y
chegbon miji e chegbon miji ng bank na u.b.a

sioko; che mo che i shienga; (or: Ed/I/Y

mo che i loga) mo sioko e rama isioko
rama; isioka rama yeye; ya-h-yah-yah
(yah-yah-yah)
icheye: "of intelligence,   Y/G
                                                        I/I

quickness of the mind and understanding"
ijoso: "evil and magic-   Y/I

power woman" ijoso; jijoso o magani; miji abi

mache magani; (also: likita o joso) nasi kpe
                                                        I/Y/I

bia nasi mi yota; fapu; fre; du iyopu; ifapu
mo ti fapu; mo ti yota ifapu n'irushe

wither, vit. withhold, vt.   kpokpo: "to dry up" fachen   G

within, prep. without, prep.   merin (ime:irin) meta   Y/I/G I/Y

within and without   (ime:"ta) merin meta   I/Y

without, prep.   nifre lai wen (not

without money   having); singi lai wen kudi;

without problem   n'iflesi; lai wen nsohala;

nifre nsohala kegba   Yin/e withstand, vt.

God bears me witness   Abasi wu shaida mi   , don't ber false

witness   ma mubi shaida isiro; ma

wen shaida   isiro   n

wives; n.   e mata

wizard, n.   o sokelei; o majikele: "a magician or male with super-natural and amazing ability"

Wobble, vti.   Woro (move unstedily from side to side)   G

Wobbling, n.   Iworo; woro-woro

Wobbler, n.   O woro; o woroworo Woe, n.   Ifunya I/Y

Wolf, n.   Gbolu: "a wild, flesh=eating animal of the G dog family"

Woman, n.   Mache (from Hausa: mace)

H Woman-hood, n.

Imache; mimache;   imiwa mache

Woman-like   Bika mache; di mache

Women, pl. n.   E mache Womb, n.

Wonder, n.   Iyalionu; iyabu;   Y/I I wonder any

Mo yabu za: mo yabu: o   (morepheme; iya; li: onu) yamilionu

What a wonder   Iyabu 'za; meni 'yabu

Won't (will not)

Woo, vt.   Dudu G I/Y/Ed/ Eg

s n k e t u m a k i : Wufu:

W u l u; i r u d i g a s h i

Don't woo me into marriage

Ma dudu mi si 'gbemata;

ma dudu mi su 'chogbe

"of crossed threads

Wooer, n.	O dudu
Wooing	Idudu
Wood, n.	Itache; kurmi; kpako H/H/Y
	Wood-work Irushe-itache Ifin-itache
Wood-carving	
Wood-cutter	O gecha-itache
Woodchair	Kujera-itache
Wood-house	Gida-kpako in a
	woven Fabric" Iworoh: "radio lou-
Woofer, n.	
produce low notes"	G
Woodspeaker, n.	Makodiya; makwakkwafi H
wool, n.	wulu; irudi gashi nke
	tumaki: "hairs of sheep" esa-wulu G(fE)/H/H/H
woollen clothes	
word, n.	oka
word-for-word	oka-fun-oka; oka-si-oka
good words	oka rama bad words oka rubi
Word-processing	Itole abi meshe oka: "word
	arrangement or making" Irushe; (synonym: aoki) I/Y
Work, n.	
I am going to work	M ng shienga irushe;
	mo ng shienga aiki
Hard work	Irushe si-sile; irushe 'kagba
Work hard	Rushe kagba
Work and pray	Irushe ati 'kpredu; rushe ko kpredu Hard

work does not kill	Anyone; irushe 'kagba o gbu eni mutum Hours of work Public works department Dipatmint irushe nke pobli; (deeper:
	Iyaka iruhe nke gbonso)
Public works	Irushe pobil; irushe gbonso
Work-in-man-like	Bika o rushe-miji;
Workshop All work and no play)	Kisuwa irushe; kanti-'rushe (igwuere lai rushe ng
Makes Jack a dull boy:)	meshe yaro Jak (yeye)
Work out	Rushe 'ta; rushe
Work out	jaita; mubiawa Rushe 'ta; rushe
Work-book	jaita; mubiawa Littafi-'rushe
World, n.	Duniya; (synonym; akpor) H/Urh.
This world	Duniya 'yii; akpor'yi (colloquial Guosa: akpor nka self,
Worldly, adj.	i.e. this world self) Nke duniya; ife akpor abi duniya; Duniya-duniya
Worldly minded	Iyobi duniya
Worldliness	Iduniya-duniya
Worm, n.	Tana H
Earth-worm	Tana-kesa H(g.v)
Round-worm	Tana-machiji H(g.v)
Thread-worm	Ambuwa; kwarba H
Tape-worm	Tsila, daudar chiki H
Hook-worm, n.	Tsutsa; kwarba H
Ring-worm	Makero H
Worn/wear	Yiwo; moeje

Worn-out	Meje; mimeje	
It has worn-out	O ti meje	
Worry, vit.	Sohala; (abbreviation; soha)	
Don't worry	Ma soha; ma sohala	
I will worry	Maa soha; (ma soha; ma sohala)	
Don't worry me	Ma sohala mi; ma soha mi	
Worrier/troubler	O sohala; o soha	
Worriness, n.	Isohala; isoha	
Worse, adj.	Rubi kha	Y/I
Worship, n.	Isolile; "reverence to God"	I/Y
Your worship	Kabiyesi; isolile	
Worshiper, n.	O solile	
Worst, adj.	Rubi kha-ka; (synonym: rubisi)	
Worst offender	O jika rubisi	
Worsted, n.	Wasted: "twisted woollen material" Year; yema	
Worth, adj.		Y/I
Well-worth	Year-rama; year'ma	
Worth-while	Year ngba; year fun ngba	
Worthless, adj.	Rubisi	
Worthy, adj.	Weda	I/Y
Worthy example	Ifineri weda; ifine weda	
Worthinese, n.	Iweda	
Wound, n. (to hurt)	Isogbu	
Don't wound me Wow, n. (exclamation) Wraith, n.	Ma so gbu mi Wao Iwireti: "an apparition of someone or person immediately before or after his death"	G(fE)

G(fE) |
| Wranglie, vi. | Wogiri: "to take part | |

	in a noisy or Angry argument"	G
Wrap, vit.	Boma	Y/I
Wrapping, n.	Iboma	
Wrapper, n.	O boma; iboma	
Woman's wrapper	Iboma mache	
Wrath, n.	Ibili-gidi	Y/I
Wreak, vt.	Riki: "to express or give effect to something On one's feeling over	G(fE
Wreath, n.	an issue or matter" Igogo: "flowers or leaves twisted or woven together into circle (worn on the head as a garland, or placed over	
	a coffin, grve or a memorial to the dead"	G
Wreathe, vit.	Bolo: to cover or encircle with flowrs or other things, e.g. a Lake"	G
Wreck, n.	Irunje; (synonym:	
	iwere): "ruin or destruction"	I/Y
The wreck of NNS RiverGurara Ship in 1989..	Irunje nke baba ugbokoruwa NNS Guarara Na ardun 1989; (also: irunje Konga NNS Gurara	
	n'ardun 1989) Wren, n. Jamgba	Y/I
Wrestle, vi. Wrestling, n.		
Ijamgba W	Ichero;	
Write, vti.	Kode Y/I Write down Kokode Wr i t t e n d o w n or not to do something' akaunt: "written	

Writing-paper   account/statement Takarada
ikode Writingbook Littafi
"kode Writer O kode

Under-writer Abda-raita (professional term only) Writingpad Fad-kikode Hand-
writing Ikode-hannu

Writhe, vi.   Sagolo: "to twist oneself
and roll about In pain" G Writhing in pain i

K

k   Isagolo n'iriyao

Wrong, adj.	= ai gere; ai yasah; lai yasah; (rang); goshi; njika
Right or worng	Gere – goshi
Wrong step	Igala goshi
Wrong steps	E gafa goshi
Wrong doer	O njika
Wrong procedure	ilashe goshi
wrongful	gigoshi
Wrong doer	O njika
Wrong procedure	ilashe goshi
wrongful	gigoshi
You got me wrong	E/o goshi oka mi;
	e/o gigoshi mi E/o goshi me
You wrong me	
Don't get me wrong	Ma goshi oka mo;
	ma gigoshi mi
You are wrong	E/o goshi; ee gere; ee yasa
Wrought, pt. Pp of work	Medi; mimeshe; mimedi I/Y
Wrought iron	Ayan medi; ayan mimeshe
Wry, adj.	Dibi: "pulled or twisted G
Wry-face	out of shape" Fuska-dibi
Wry-mouth	Onu abi baki dibi

664

Yatch, n.	Kwale-kwale bature; kakanda (formerly "yas/yache ref. Vol. I dictionary)
Yatch-club	Klob-kakanda; klob-kwale-kwale
Yah, int.	Yah
Yam, n.	Doya; yaya
Cocoa-yam, n.	Koko-yaya
Yam-flour	Fulawa-doya; elubo
Water-yam	Doya-doya
Pounded-yam	Pando-yaya; pando-ya (abbreviation: pando)
Yam-beetle	Buzuzu-doya
Fried yam, n.	dundu
Yankari, n.	Yankari
Yankee, n.	Yanki, emo Nu Ingilande
Yap, vi.	Wuh: "of dog barks"
Yap, vi.	Yabisi: "to talk noisily and foolishly"
Yard, n.	Yadi
Yard-stick	Inofile – (of standard)
Back-yard	Izuba-gida (old use: "azu yadi")
Front-yard	Iwhido-yadi; iwhido-gida
One yard	Yadi-daya
A yard of cloth	Yadi esa Works-yard
Yarrow, n.	Yairo: (irudi shuke-shuke fun magani)
Yashmak, n.	Yasima: "veil worn in public by some Muslim women in some countries
Yawl, n.	Yoal: "a small sailing-boat having two masts"
Yawn, vi.	Miyan

Yawning, n.	Imiyan
Yaws, n.	Tunjere, kyambi
Yeah, adv.	Baate, "yes"; "it is so"
Year, n.	Ardun; a'dun
This year	Ardun yi
Last year	A'dun zuein; a'dun zizuba
Yearly, adv.	Ardun; a' dun
Yearling, n.	Ikege; kege: "of animal between one And two years of age"
Yearn, vi., n.	Yonu; iyonu
Yeast, n.	Yisti; irudi magani bika fulawa
Yell, vit.	Kebele
I will yell at you	Maa kebele si e/yin
Yellers	E kebele
Yelling, n.	Ikebele
Yellow, n., adj.	Year
Light-yellow	Yara-fele
Yellow-fever	Iba-yara
Yelp, vi.	Ooh; "to utter short, sharp cry of Pain, exitement or hunger" also; yeh
Yen, n.	Yen: "unit of currency in Japan"
Yes, particle,	Baate; en
Yesterday, adv.	Layen
Yet, adv.	Siba (old use: "simbe")
Yew, n.	Yiu; "an evergreen-dark leaves used For garden hedges"

Yiddish, n.	Yidishi: "international language of The Jews"
Yield, vit.	Yissi
Don't yield to temptation:	Ma yissi si tenda
Yobo; yobbo, n.	Iyobi-yobo: "an objectionable teenager"
Yoga; n.	Yuga; magani Hindu: "Hindu medication"
Yogurt, n.	Yugat: "fermented milk liquor"
Yoke, n.	Jula; taula
Yokel, n.	Yokilo" "a simple-minded country man"; (also: o kill)
Yolk, n.	Gwaiduwa
Yonder, adj., adv.	Bahun (old use: n'ohun") Go yonder
Yoruba, n.	Yoruba; emon eso nke kesa huest na Naijeriya
You, pron.	E, I, o, q, yinwan, u; (Note any of The six is suitable depending on The situation or circumstance), e.g.
You wil	Ea; oa
You (yourself)	Yinwan
Young, dj.	Takele; yaro; kele
Young child	Omon takele
Young boy	Yaro kele; (yaro)
Younggirl	Wundia; (synonym: omote)
This young girl	Wundia yi; omote 'yi Unmarried young girl of arriageab age;Budurwa
Youngter, n.	O takele; o kele
Your, aj	Nke yin; (nke)
Yourself	Yinwan; wenyin
Yourselves	O yinwan; o wenyin - o wenyin
Yours sincerely	Nke yin n'ezindu

Yours faithful,	Nke yin n'ezioka
Yours truly,	Nke yin tezi
Yours obediently	Nke yin n'igbonti
Yours ear one	Ninda nke yin; (ninda yin)
Your dear wife	Ninda mata e/yin
Your dear husband	Ninda maigida yin
Your sweet heart	Ninda suka yin
Yours in love	Nke yin n'ihufe
Your sweet	Suka e/yin
Your darling	Ninda e/yin
Yourse, pron.	Yinwan
Your lives, pl. pron.	E yinwan; e wenyin
Youth	Ibongo
Youthful	Di 'bongo; bibongo
You'v(you have)	E te; e ti
Yucca.	Yuka; irudi shuke-shuke ilililai bika fulawa bado; "a type of ever-green plant like the lily fowers" G(fE)

Z

Z, z	Zii	Gen
Zeal,	Itono; (synonym: itonji)	Y/H
Zeais, adj.	Tono; tonji	
Zealo n.	O kpadu: "someone who shows great and uncompromising interest and enthusiasm for a religion, party or	
	other cause; also a fanatic:	G
Zebra.	Zibra: "a wild hourse-like Afrikan	
	Animal" (old use: Zinbra	G(fE)
Zenit, n.	Iziga: ziga: "highest point of fame,	
	Fortune etc). (o.u.; zanet; aziga)	G
Zephy, n.	Ilule; irudi 'fekuku irayo: "a type of	
	Gentle wind"	G
Zeppen, n.	Dekpelini: "a rigid airship used by The Germans in the first World War"	
Zero	Kondo; guezet; ofo	G
Zest.	Ikin (o.u. "ibukin"	G
Zig-z, n.	Izighi-zagha; (zigi-zaga)	Ed.
Zinc, n.	Tutiya; "hard, bluish-white metal:	H
Zinc ointment	Ontmint tutiya	
Zion, n.	Zaiyon; (o.u., Zayon); kasa e mon Jiu	
Zip, n.	Zif	F(fE)
Zip code, n.	Kodi-fost: "postcode"	
Zither, n.	Sita: "a musical instrument with	
Zodiac n.	Zodiak	G(fE)
Zommbi; n.	Zombi	
Zone,	Iyaka; zon	Y/I/G(fE) Zona, adj.
Zoo, n.	Izuh; "zoological garden"	G(fE)
Zoology, n.	Izuholoji	
G(fE) Zoologist, n.	O zuholoji	

Zoological, dj.	Zuholoji	
Zoom, n	Zuum; (zum) "like the sound of a motor- car" G/Gen	
Zoophtye, n.	Zofita: "plant-like sea-animal"	G(fE)
Zounds, int.	Yeekpah; "cry of anger, indignation, Protest, discomfort etc."	Y

www.ingramcontent.com/pod-product-compliance
Lightning Source LLC
Chambersburg PA
CBHW081035050426

42335CB00052B/2440